2017

苏州统计年鉴

SUZHOU STATISTICAL YEARBOOK

苏州市统计局
SUZHOU STATISTICS BUREAU
国家统计局苏州调查队 编
STATE STATISTICS BUREAU SUZHOU
INVESTIGATION TEAM

总期29期 NO:29

中国统计出版社
China Statistics Press

图书在版编目（CIP）数据

苏州统计年鉴. 2017 / 苏州市统计局, 国家统计局苏州调查队编. -- 北京 : 中国统计出版社，2017.7
ISBN 978-7-5037-8152-0

Ⅰ. ①苏… Ⅱ. ①苏… ②国… Ⅲ. ①统计资料－苏州市－2017－年鉴 Ⅳ. ①C832.533-54

中国版本图书馆CIP数据核字(2017)第129110号

苏州统计年鉴-2017

作　　者 / 苏州市统计局 国家统计局苏州调查队
责任编辑 / 陈越月
装帧设计 / 苏州市新彩视广告印务有限公司
出版发行 / 中国统计出版社
地　　址 / 北京市丰台区西三环南路甲6号　邮政编码/100073
电　　话 / 邮购(010)63376909　书店(010)68783171
网　　址 / http://csp.stats.gov.cn
印　　刷 / 苏州印刷总厂有限公司
经　　销 / 新华书店
开　　本 / 890mm×1240mm 1/16
字　　数 / 1400千字
印　　张 / 48印张
版　　别 / 2017年7月第1版
版　　次 / 2017年7月第1次印刷
定　　价 / 350.00元

本书附同版本CD-ROM一张，光盘内容以书面文字为准。
如有印装差错，由本社发行部调换。

编　　辑：苏州市统计局　　国家统计局苏州调查队

出　　版：中国统计出版社

印　　刷：苏州印刷总厂有限公司

Edited By: Suzhou Statistics Bureau State Statistics Bureau Suzhou Investigation Team

Published By: China Statistics Press

Printed By: Suzhou General Printing House Co.,Ltd.

编 者 说 明

1.《苏州统计年鉴-2017》以大量统计数据，全面、系统地反映2016年苏州经济、社会各方面的发展情况。

2.本年鉴内容包括：发展成果图，综合，人口、劳动力，农业，工业，建筑业，运输、邮电业，贸易餐饮业，对外经济、国际旅游，服务业，能源消费，固定资产投资，企业调查，财政、金融、保险，物价指数，人民生活，科技，教育、文化，卫生、体育，民政、司法，城市建设、环境保护，城市比较等二十二个部分。

3.本年鉴辑入的统计数据以2016年为主，主要指标还列示了建国以来主要历史年份的统计数据。资料主要来自苏州市统计局、国家统计局苏州调查队的各项定期统计报表和抽样调查资料，部分资料来自苏州各主管部门。

4. 根据国家统计制度的变化，部分历史数据作相应的调整，读者在使用历史资料时，凡以往年鉴与本年鉴有出入的，均以本年鉴为准。

5.2012年9月吴江撤市设区，原沧浪区、平江区、金阊区合并设立姑苏区。本年鉴表内全市数据包括姑苏区，吴中区，相城区，虎丘区、高新区，工业园区，吴江区，常熟市，张家港市，昆山市，太仓市，市区中包含吴江区数据（气象、水文、物价指数除外）。

6. 本年鉴中的符号说明：

"…"　表示数据不足本表最小单位数；

"空格"　表示该项统计数据不详；

"－"　表示无该项统计数据；

"#"　表示其中数。

《苏州统计年鉴》公开出版以来，受到社会各界的关注和支持，不少读者对年鉴的内容和编辑工作提出了许多宝贵的意见，对此，我们深表感谢。欢迎读者一如既往地对年鉴的不足之处批评指正，帮助我们进一步提高编辑水平。

Complier's Note

Ⅰ.***Suzhou Statistical Yearbook 2017*** is a publication which provides comprehensive and systematic data covering the economic and social development in Suzhou Municipality in 2016.

Ⅱ.This yearbook is comprised of 22 parts including Achievement Graphs and Charts, General Survey, Population and Labor Force, Agriculture, Industry, Construction, Transportation, Post and Telecommunication, Wholesale, Retail Sales and Catering Business, Export-Oriented Economy and International Tourism, Services, Consumption of Energy, Investment in Fixed Assets, Enterprises Survey, Finance, Banking and Insurance, Price Indices, People's Livelihood, Science and Technology, Education and Culture, Public Health and Sports, Civil Administration, Judiciary and Other Items, Urban Construction and Environmental Protection, Cities Compare.

Ⅲ. The statistics in the yearbook are mainly the statistics in 2016, and the main indicators also list the statistical data in the key years since the founding of the People's Republic of China. The data mainly comes from the periodic statistical reports and sample survey data of Suzhou Municipal Bureau of Statistics and Suzhou Investigation Team of National Bureau of Statistics, and some of the information comes from administrative departments of Suzhou municipal government.

Ⅳ. According to the changes of the national statistical system, some historical data is adjusted accordingly, and in the use of historical data, when the data in previous yearbooks is different from that in this yearbook, the data in this yearbook is to be used.

Ⅴ. In September, 2012 Wujiang City was changed into Wujiang District, and the original Changlang District、Pingjiang Dictrict and Jinchang District were merged to become Gusu District. The whole city's data in the yearbook includes the data of Gusu District, Wuzhong District, Xiangcheng District, Huqiu District、 Suzhou New District, Suzhou Industrial Park, Wujiang District, Changshu City, Zhangjiagang City, Kunshan City and Taicang city, and the data of the central city includes that of Wujiang District (except the data of meteorology, hydrology and price).

Ⅵ. Explanations on symbols used in this yearbook:

"..." indicates that the data are not large enough to be rounded into the minimal unit,

"space" indicates that the data is unknown and indicates the data not available,

" – " indicates the data not available,

" # " indicates the component items.

Here we'd like to express our sincere thanks to the readers who have provided us so many invaluable suggestions on content selection and compilation of the yearbook. Our thanks also go to those friends in all circles of society who have shown their support and care to the publication of the yearbook. We welcome any suggestions and comments from readers at large so as to help us to further improve our work of compilation.

2016年的苏州

- **15475.09** 地区生产总值（亿元）Gross Domestic Product (100 million yuan)
- **7975.82** 服务业增加值（亿元）Added Value of Service Industry (100 million yuan)
- **25864.26** 年末金融机构人民币存款余额（亿元）Deposits Balance of Financial Institutions by Year End (100 million yuan)
- **21924.44** 年末金融机构人民币贷款余额（亿元）Loans Balance of Financial Institutions by Year End (100 million yuan)
- **102.7** 居民消费价格指数（以上年价格为100）General Consumer Price Index of Urban Residents (preceding year is taken as 100)
- **1064.74** 年末常住人口（万人）Year-end Total Population (10000 persons)
- **678.20** 年末户籍人口（万人）Year-end Population (10000 persons)
- **54341** 城镇居民人均可支配收入（元）Per Capita Disposable Income of Urban Households (yuan)
- **27691** 农村居民人均可支配收入（元）Per Capita Disposable Income of Rural Residents (yuan)

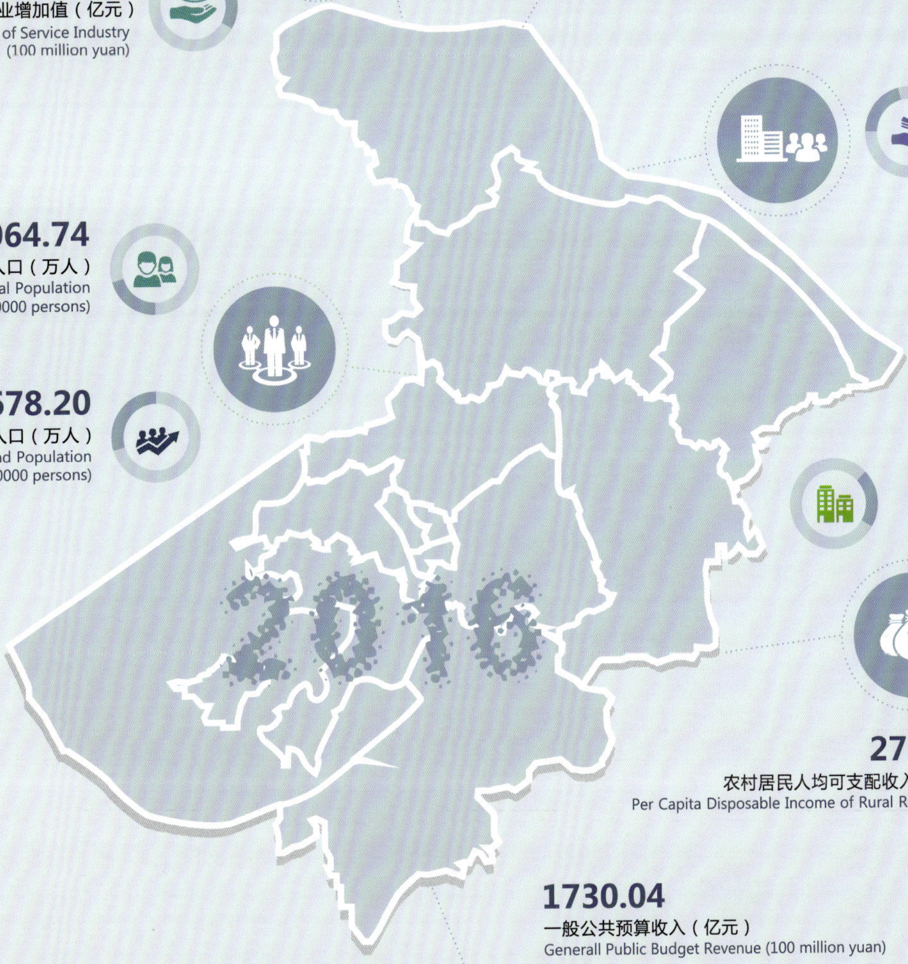

- **1730.04** 一般公共预算收入（亿元）Generall Public Budget Revenue (100 million yuan)
- **30713.99** 规模以上工业总产值（亿元）Gross Industrial Output Value Above Designated Size (100 million yuan)
- **5648.49** 全社会固定资产投资额（亿元）Total Value of Investment In Fixed Assets (100 million yuan)
- **4936.79** 社会消费品零售总额（亿元）Total Retail Sales of Consumer Goods (100 million yuan)
- **1639.41** 出口总额（亿美元）Exports (USD 100 million)
- **2737.58** 进出口总额（亿美元）Total Imports and Exports (USD 100 million)
- **60.03** 实际使用外资（亿美元）Amount of Foreign Capital Actually Used (USD 100 million)

创新驱动

全社会R&D经费支出占GDP的比重（%）
The Proportion of R&D Expenditure Ratio of The Whole Society in GDP (%)

2008年	2009年	2010年	2011年	2012年	2013年	2014年	2015年	**2016年**
1.94	2.20	2.34	2.42	2.50	2.57	2.62	2.66	**2.78**

规模以上工业企业研发经费投入（亿元）
Expenditures on Research and Development of Above-Scale Industrial Enterprises (100 million yuan)

年份	投入
2011年	223.23
2012年	260.30
2013年	297.38
2014年	318.02
2015年	336.83
2016年	**361.50**

年末万人有效发明专利拥有量（件）
Effective Invention Patent Ownership Per 10000 Persons by Year End (unit)

年份	拥有量
2011年	5.68
2012年	10.13
2013年	14.19
2014年	18.51
2015年	27.42
2016年	**38.25**

发明专利授权量（件） Applications Granted of Inventions (unit)	年份	发明专利申请量（件） Applications Examined of Inventions (unit)
13267	**2016年**	**47429**
10488	2015年	43241
5264	2014年	40842
4413	2013年	44477
4309	2012年	31984
2492	2011年	21765
1370	2010年	12935
148	2005年	988
32	2000年	224
41	1995年	47

年末高层次人才（人）
High-level Talents by Year End (person)

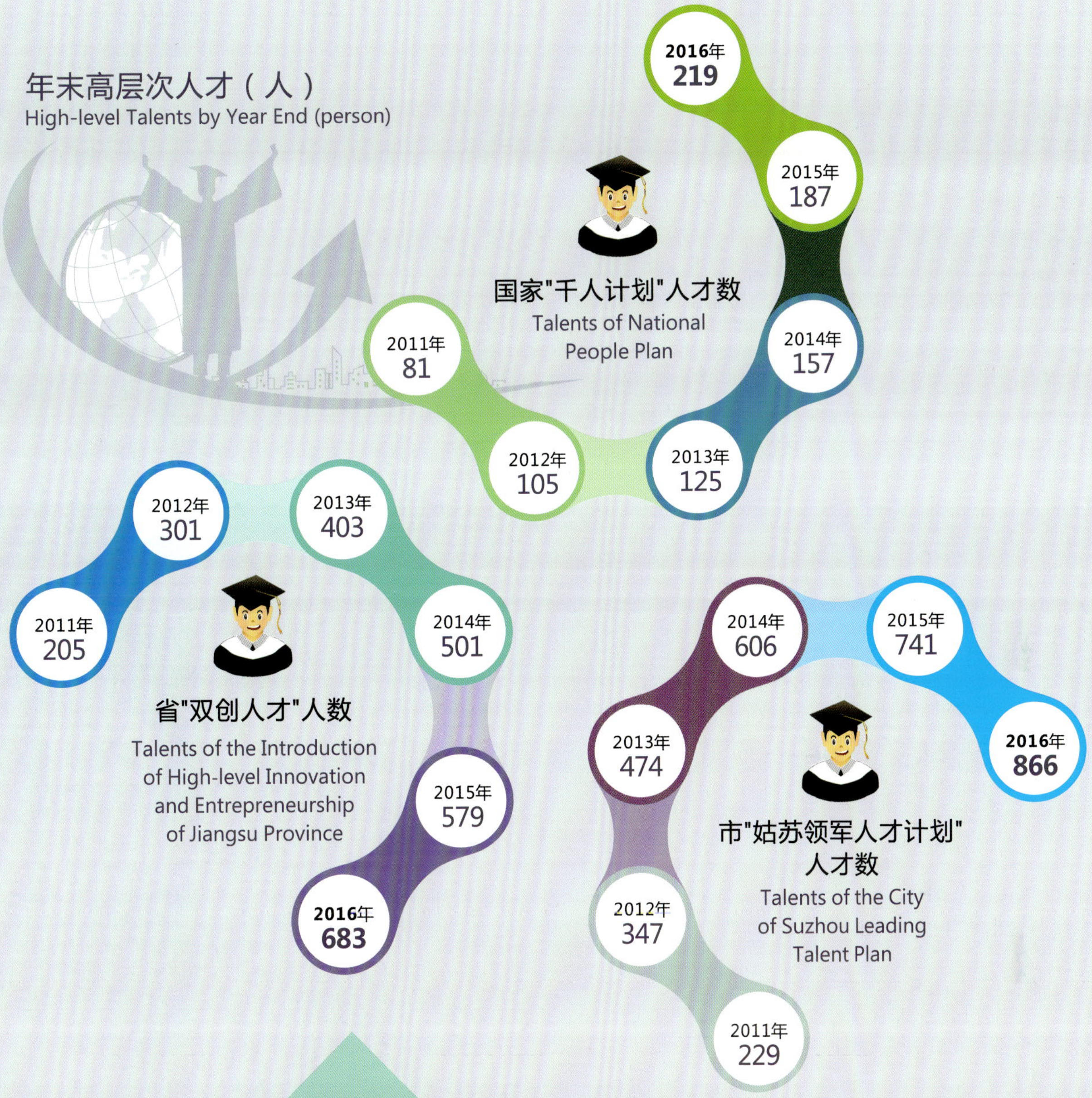

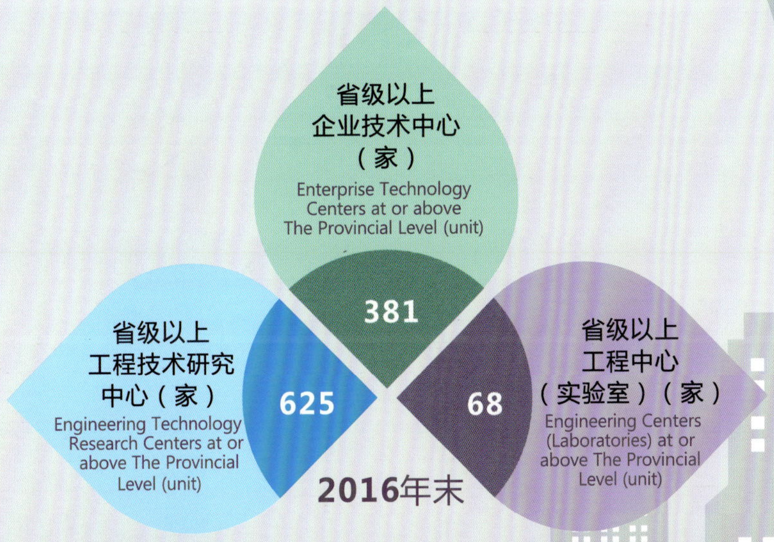

富民增收

	2011年	2012年	2013年	2014年	2015年	2016年
城镇居民人均可支配收入（元） Per Capita Disposable Income of Urban Households (yuan)	33243	37531	41143	46677	50390	**54341**
城乡收入比（农村=1） Income Ratio Between Urban and Rural Areas (rural=1)	1.93	1.93	1.91	1.98	1.97	**1.96**
农村居民人均可支配收入（元） Per Capita Disposable Income of Rural Residents (yuan)	17226	19396	21578	23560	25580	**27691**

2016年

	合计	食品烟酒 Food, Alcoholic Drinks and Tobacco	衣着 Clothing	居住 Residence	生活用品及服务 Daily Necessities and Services	交通通信 Transportation and Communication	教育文化娱乐 Education, Culture and Entertainment	医疗保健 Healthcare	其他用品及服务 Other Supplies and Services
城镇居民人均生活消费支出（元） Per Capita Living Expenditure of Urban Residents (yuan)	33305	8882	2084	7540	1796	5918	4728	1411	946
农村居民人均生活消费支出（元） Per Capita Living Expenditure of Rural Residents (yuan)	18820	4832	1058	4468	1084	3484	2171	1194	529

在岗职工平均工资（元）
Average Wages of Staff and Workers (yuan)

1985年	1106
1990年	2450
1995年	6944
2000年	11778
2005年	25016
2010年	45566
2011年	51660
2012年	57622
2013年	61416
2014年	66956
2015年	72291
2016年	**79870**

市区居民消费价格总指数（以上年价格为100）
General Consumer Price Index of Urban Residents (preceding year is taken as 100)

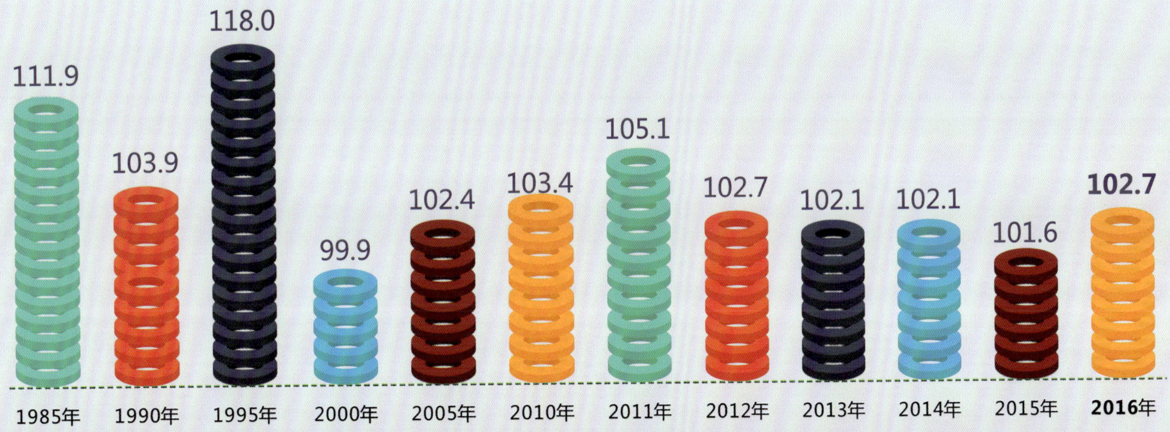

2016年
17.11 新增就业（万人）
The Number of Newly-employed People (10000 persons)

2016年
1.89 城镇登记失业率（%）
The Urban Registered Unemployment Rate (%)

2016年
98.52 苏州籍应届高校毕业生就业率（%）
The Employment Rate of The Fresh College Graduates of Suzhou Nationality (%)

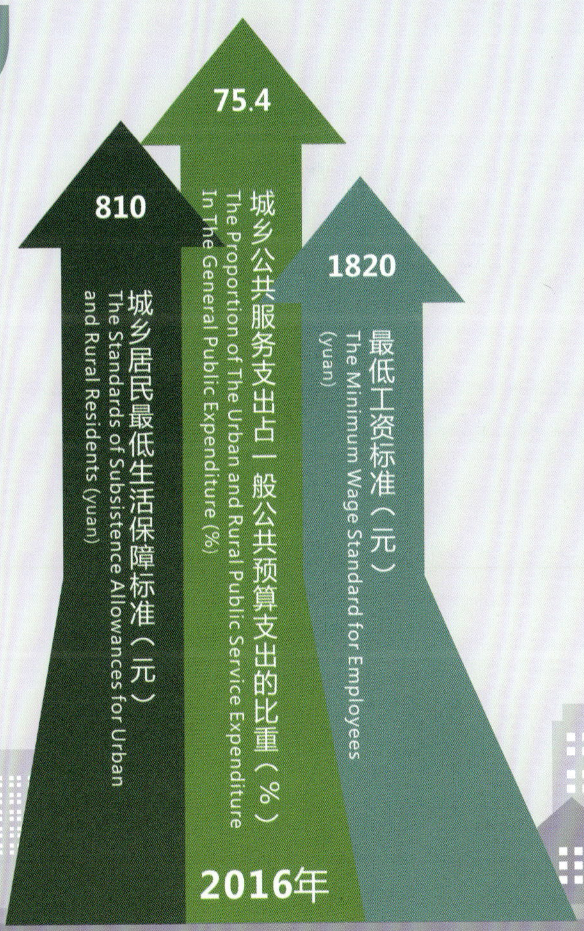

经济发展

地区生产总值（亿元）
Gross Domestic Product (100 millon yuan)

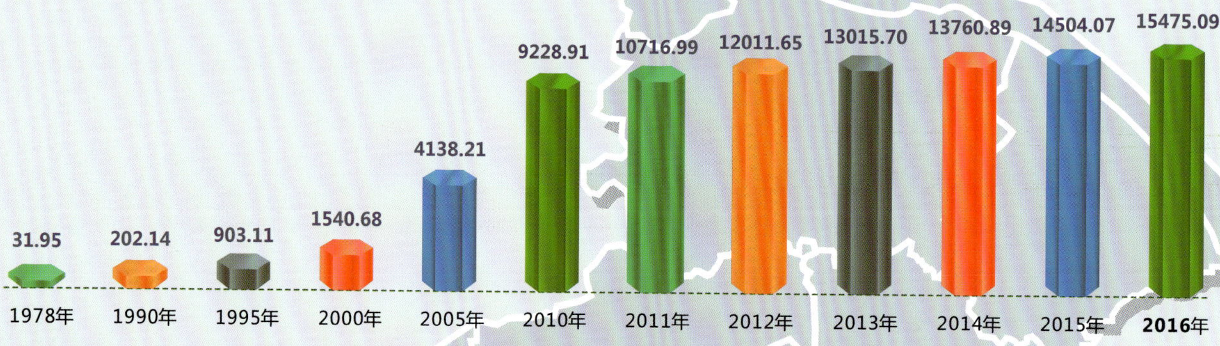

社会消费品零售总额（亿元）
Total Retail Sales of Consumer Goods
(100 million yuan)

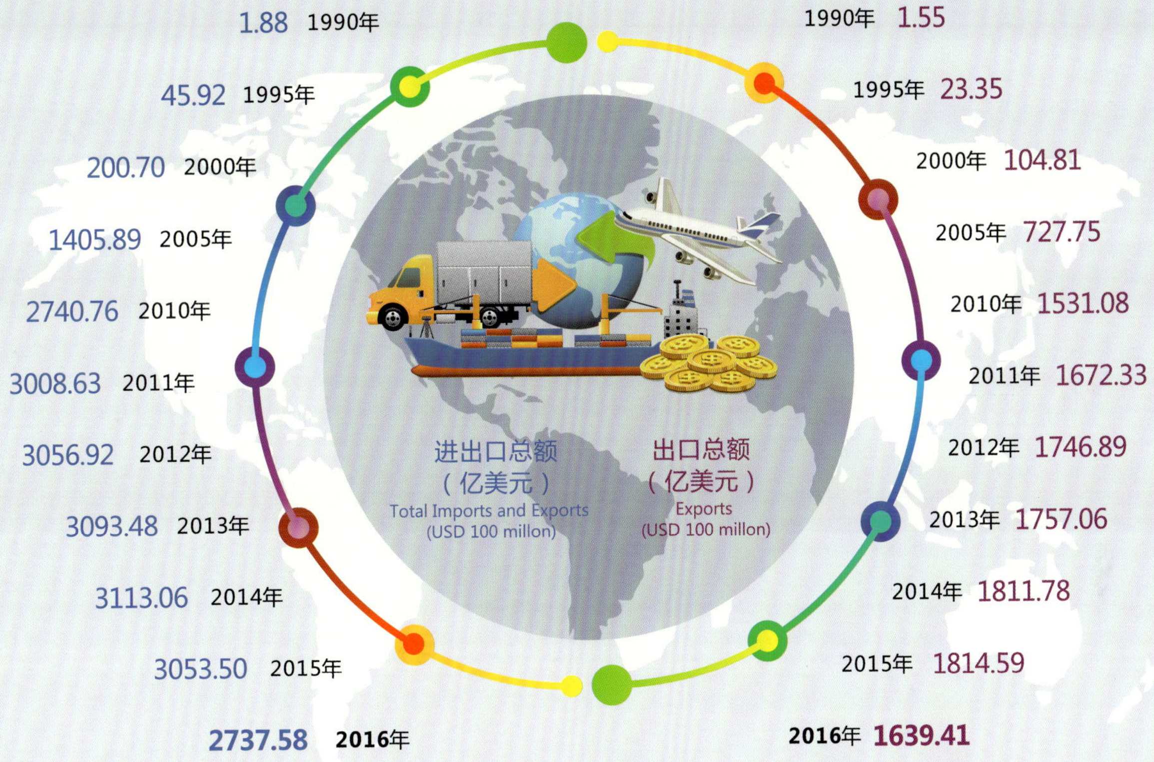

全社会固定资产投资完成额（亿元）

Total Fixed Assets Investment (100 million yuan)

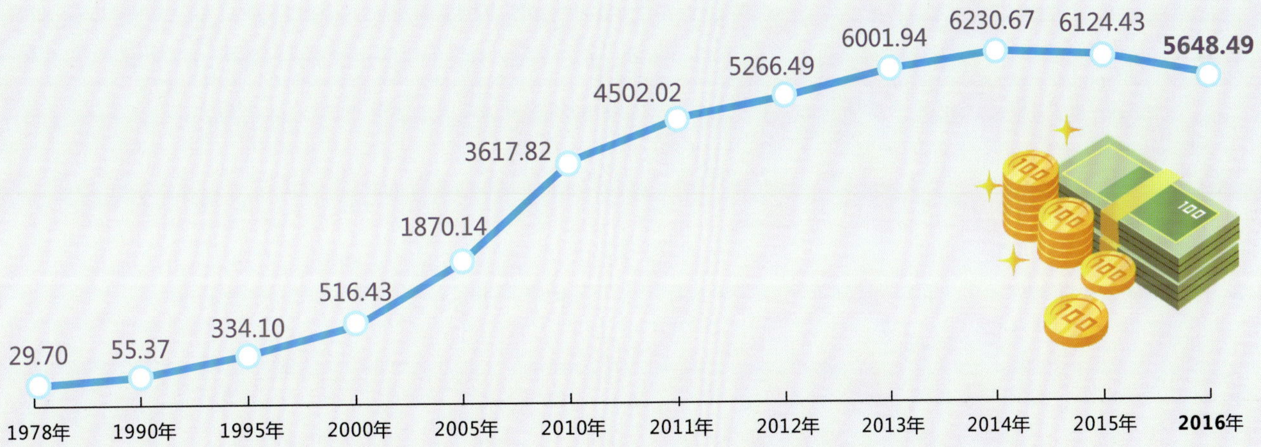

产业结构

地区生产总值构成（%）
Proportions in Gross Domestic Product (%)

100 地区生产总值 Gross Domestic Product

	2011年	2016年
第一产业 Primary Industry	1.5	1.5
第二产业 Secondary Industry	55.6	47.0
第三产业 Tertiary Industry	42.9	51.5

从业人员构成（%）
Proportions in Number of Employed Persons (%)

100 从业人员 Number of Employed Persons

	2011年	2016年
第一产业 Primary Industry	3.7	3.4
第二产业 Secondary Industry	61.8	59.6
第三产业 Tertiary Industry	34.5	37.0

金融机构人民币存贷款
Deposits and Loans Balance of Financial Institutions

	2011年	2012年	2013年	2014年	2015年	2016年
金融机构人民币存款余额（亿元）Deposits Balance of Financial Institutions (100 million yuan)	15180.78	17663.50	20037.58	21755.17	23659.10	25864.26
住户存款余额（亿元）RMB Savings Deposits of Urban Households (100 million yuan)	5078.59	5787.75	6408.32	7022.63	7358.04	7913.85
金融机构人民币贷款余额（亿元）Loans Balance of Financial Institutions (100 million yuan)	11873.89	13626.86	15495.24	17247.94	19200.10	21924.44

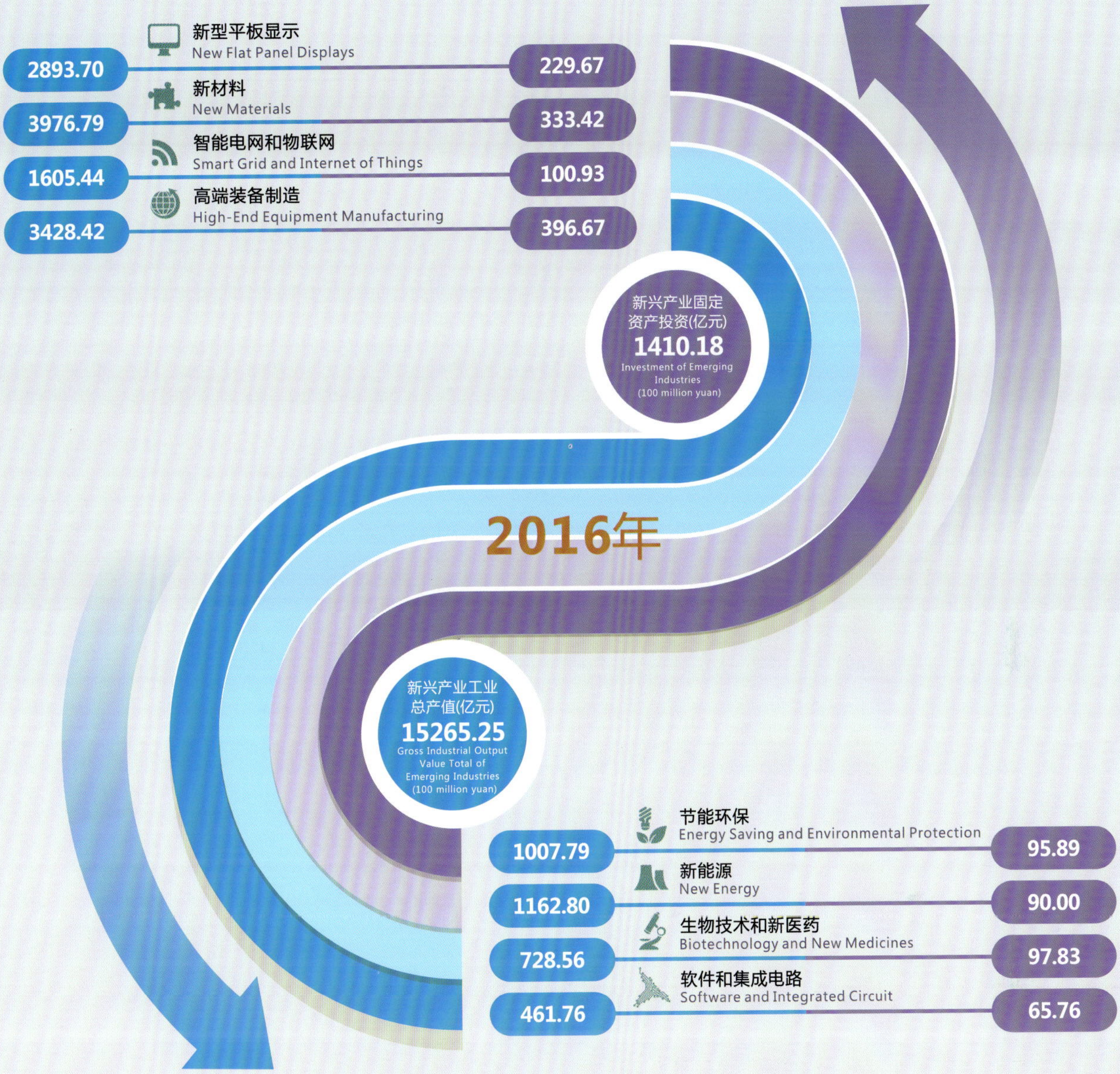

新兴产业产值占规模以上工业总产值比重（%）

The Proportion of Emerging Industries in Gross Industrial Output Value Above Designated Size (%)

民生保障

基本养老保险参保人数
Number of People Covered by Endowment Insurance

2012年 472.88
2013年 492.44
2014年 506.06
2015年 511.57
2016年 520.68

生育保险参保人数
Number of People Covered by Childbirth Insurance

2012年 403.97
2013年 421.27
2014年 431.99
2015年 437.26
2016年 450.76

基本医疗保险参保人数
Number of People Covered by Medical Insurance

2012年 541.56
2013年 570.48
2014年 593.94
2015年 611.72
2016年 635.09

工伤保险参保人数
Number of People Covered by Work Injury Insurance

2012年 404.07
2013年 408.36
2014年 418.88
2015年 426.25
2016年 439.30

失业保险参保人数
Number of People Covered by Unemployment Insurance

2012年 375.74
2013年 383.78
2014年 400.93
2015年 423.54
2016年 446.62

43.97
节能环保支出
Energy Saving and Environmental Protection Spending
95.20
科学技术支出
Science and Technology Spending
89.36
农林水支出
Agricultural, Forestry and Water Spending
142.39
社会保障和就业支出
Social Security and Employment
93.63
医疗卫生与计划生育支出
Expenditure for Medicine and Public Health
37.57
文化体育与传媒支出
Culture, Sports and the Media
61.68
交通运输支出
Transportation Spending
262.32
教育支出
Expenditure for Operating Expenses of Education
2016年一般公共预算支出
1617.11亿元
General Public Budgetary Expenditure
(100 million yuan)

教育卫生

普通高等学校在校生（人）
Student Enrollment of Institutions of Higher Education (person)

2010年	2011年	2012年	2013年	2014年	2015年	**2016年**
187829	188750	192206	201926	209479	214816	**219347**

2016年

	2016年
学校数（个）Number of Schools (unit)	754
毕业生数（万人）Number of Graduates (10000 persons)	26.86
高等教育毛入学率（%）The Gross Enrollment Rate of Higher Education (%)	68.5
专任教师数（万人）Number of Full-time Teachers (10000 persons)	8.20

专业技术人员（万人）
Scientific and Technical Personnel (10000 Persons)

1990年	1995年	2000年	2010年	2011年	2012年	2013年	2014年	2015年	**2016年**
13.18	15.23	29.12	84.66	96.45	109.99	123.48	136.61	149.64	**163.42**

年末卫生机构数（个）
Number of Institutions by Year End (unit)

2011年	2858
2012年	2992
2013年	3007
2014年	3063
2015年	3121
2016年	**3175**

每千人拥有卫生机构床位数（张）
Number of Beds in Health Institutions Per 1000 Persons (unit)

2011年	4.09
2012年	4.37
2013年	4.88
2014年	5.21
2015年	5.59
2016年	**5.94**

每千人拥有机构养老床位数（张）
Number of Beds in Old-age Care Institutions Per 1000 Persons (unit)

2011年	2.93
2012年	4.38
2013年	4.90
2014年	5.46
2015年	6.03
2016年	**6.13**

每千人拥有医院床位数（张）
Number of Hospital Beds Per 1000 Persons (unit)

2011年	3.38
2012年	3.69
2013年	4.28
2014年	4.61
2015年	4.97
2016年	**5.32**

每千人拥有注册护士数（人）
Number of Professional Nurses Per 1000 Persons (person)

2011年	1.86
2012年	2.08
2013年	2.28
2014年	2.39
2015年	2.66
2016年	**2.88**

每千人拥有医生数（人）
Number of Doctors Per 1000 Persons (person)

2011年	1.86
2012年	2.20
2013年	2.30
2014年	2.39
2015年	2.47
2016年	**2.60**

环境保护

	2011年	2012年	2013年	2014年	2015年	2016年
城镇污水处理率（%） Treatment Rate of Sewage in town (%)	90.22	91.87	94.54	95.03	95.26	**95.18**
建成区绿化覆盖率（%） Coverage Rate of Green Areas in Developed Areas (%)	42.46	42.58	42.79	42.93	43.08	**42.66**
人均公园绿地面积（平方米） Per Capita Park Green Areas (sq.m)	15.21	15.44	15.35	15.36	15.31	**15.01**
生活垃圾无害化处理量（万吨） Volume of No Harm Disposal of Garbage (10000 tons)	281.82	325.50	278.74	355.90	383.82	**427.41**

	2011年	2012年	2013年	2014年	2015年	2016年
单位GDP化学需氧量排放强度（千克/万元） Chemical Oxygen Demand Emission Intensity Per GDP (kg/10000 yuan)	0.95	0.83	0.69	0.57	0.47	**0.42**
单位GDP二氧化硫排放强度（千克/万元） Sulfur Dioxide Emission Intensity Per GDP (kg/10000 yuan)	1.87	1.62	1.33	1.25	1.04	**0.87**
单位GDP氨氮排放强度（千克/万元） Ammonia Nitrogen Emission Intensity Per GDP (kg/10000 yuan)	0.16	0.14	0.12	0.11	0.10	**0.09**
单位GDP氮氧化物排放强度（千克/万元） Nitrogen Oxide Emission Intensity Per GDP (kg/10000 yuan)	2.87	2.43	1.99	1.73	1.37	**1.21**

规模以上工业六大高能耗行业
Six High Energy Consumption Industry Above Designated Size

六大高能耗行业综合能耗占规模以上工业企业综合能耗比重（%）
The Proportion of Comprehensive Energy Consumption of Six High Energy Consumption Industry Accounted for Industry Above Designated Size（%）

行业 Industry	2011年	2012年	2013年	2014年	2015年	2016年
纺织业 Textile Industry	7.6	6.9	6.0	5.8	5.8	**5.8**
造纸和纸制品业 Papermaking and Paper Products	5.4	5.0	5.3	5.3	5.3	**5.3**
化学原料和化学制品制造业 Raw Chemical Materials and Chemical Products	6.0	6.3	6.5	6.7	6.9	**7.6**
非金属矿物制品业 Nonmetal Mineral Products	3.2	3.0	2.9	2.6	2.1	**1.5**
黑色金属冶炼和压延加工业 Smelting and Pressing of Ferrous Metals	30.2	32.1	32.3	33.2	34.1	**33.9**
电力、热力生产和供应业 Production and Supply of Electricity and Thermal Power	32.0	30.2	30.1	29.3	28.6	**28.7**

2011年	2012年	2013年	2014年	2015年	**2016年**
84.5	83.5	83.1	82.9	82.8	82.8

六大高能耗行业综合能耗占规模以上工业企业综合能耗总比重（%）
The Proportion of Comprehensive Energy Consumption of Six High Energy Consumption Industry Accounted for Industry Above Designated Size (%)

公共交通

公共汽车营运车辆（辆）
Operating Bus Routes (coach)

2011年	2012年	2013年	2014年	2015年	**2016年**
5656	6306	6573	6948	7355	**7710**

公共汽车营运线路总长度（公里）
Length of Bus Routes (km)

2011年	2012年	2013年	2014年	2015年	**2016年**
10345	11624	11847	12187	12561	**13002**

公共汽车客运总量（万人次）
Number of Passengers Carried By Bus(10000 person-times)

2011年	2012年	2013年	2014年	2015年	**2016年**
80205	91246	94061	95708	95717	**87698**

	2013年	2014年	2015年	**2016年**
公共自行车租赁点（个） Public Bicycle Rental Point (unit)	2359	2794	3227	**3691**
公共自行车累计投入车辆（辆） Total Number of Public Bicycle (coach)	56090	68525	75985	**89686**

年份	出租车运营车辆（辆） Operating Vehicles (coach)	出租车客运总量（万人次） Number of Passengers Carried by Taxi (10000 person-times)
2013年	8297	24793
2014年	8988	23992
2015年	9018	22814
2016年	9018	19256

	2015		2016	
	地铁 Metro	有轨电车 Tram	地铁 Metro	有轨电车 Tram
运营车辆（辆） The Number of Operating Vehicles(coach)	215	90	320	90
营运线路总长度（公里） Total Length of Light Rail Transit Operating Routes (km)	52.3	17.8	67.9	17.8
客运量（万人次） Number of Passengers Carried By Light Rail (10000 person-times)	13633	148	14851	206

公共事业

年份	供水总量（万立方米）Total Volume of Water Supply (10000 cu.m)	天然气供气总量（万立方米）Total Natural Gas Supply (10000 cu.m)
2011年	104458	201092
2012年	114213	229211
2013年	104092	266552
2014年	105978	284811
2015年	108649	273861
2016年	**112829**	**279408**

建成区面积（平方公里）Build Up Area (sq.km)	2011年	2012年	2013年	2014年	2015年	**2016年**
	698.90	719.94	727.16	735.15	747.84	**733.39**

城市实有道路长度（公里）Length of Roads of Urban Civil (km)	2011年	2012年	2013年	2014年	2015年	**2016年**
	5524	5672	5841	5977	6109	**9373**

目　录
CONTENTS

二、人口、劳动力

POPULATION AND LABOR FORCE

三、农　业
AGRICULTURE

四、工　业

INDUSTRY

五、建 筑 业

CONSTRUCTION

六、运输、邮电业

TRANSPORTATION , POST AND TELECOMMUNICATION

七、贸易餐饮业

TRADE AND CATERING BUSINESS

八、对外经济、国际旅游

FOREIGN TRADE ECONOMY AND INTERNATIONAL TOURISM

九、服务业

SERVICES

十、能源消费

CONSUMPTION OF ENERGY

十一、固定资产投资

INVESTMENT IN FIXED ASSETS

十二、企业调查

ENTERPRISES SURVEY

十三、财政、金融、保险

FINANCE, BANKING AND INSURANCE

十四、物价指数
PRICE INDICES

十五、人民生活

PEOPLE'S LIVELIHOOD

十六、科　　技

SCIENCE AND TECHNOLOGY

十七、教育、文化

EDUCATION AND CULTURE

十八、卫生、体育

PUBLIC HEALTH AND SPORTS

十九、民政、司法

CIVIL ADMINISTRATION, JUDICIARY

二十、城市建设、环境保护

URBAN CONSTRUCTION AND ENVIRONMENTAL PROTECTION

二十一、城市比较

CITIES COMPARE

2016年苏州市国民经济和社会发展概况

2016年，面对错综复杂的宏观经济环境，全市上下在苏州市委、市政府的正确领导下，深入贯彻党的十八大和十八届三中、四中、五中、六中全会精神，以习近平总书记系列重要讲话特别是视察江苏重要讲话精神为指引，自觉践行五大发展理念，坚持稳中求进工作总基调，坚定不移推进供给侧结构性改革，积极应对各种风险和挑战，统筹推进稳增长、促改革、调结构、惠民生、防风险等各项工作，全市经济运行总体平稳、稳中有进、稳中向好，经济结构加快调整，改革创新深入推进，生态环境持续改善，民生质量不断提高，社会发展和谐稳定。

一、综合

经济运行总体平稳。全市实现地区生产总值15475.1亿元，按可比价计算比上年增长7.5%。人均地区生产总值（按常住人口计算）14.56万元，按年平均汇率折算达到2.19万美元。

经济结构持续优化。服务经济发展提速，服务业占比首次超过50%。全年实现服务业增加值7975.8亿元，比上年增长9.7%，占地区生产总值的比重达51.5%，比上年提高1.6个百分点。

宏观效益稳定提高。财税收入平稳增长，全年实现一般公共预算收入1730.0亿元，比上年增长10.8%。其中税收收入1505.8亿元，增长12.5%，税收收入占一般公共预算收入的比重达87%，比上年提高1.2个百分点，财政收入总量、增量和税收占比保持全省首位。财政支出更多投向民生领域，全年一般公共预算支出1617.1亿元，比上年增长5.9%。其中城乡公共服务支出1219.9亿元，城乡公共服务支出占一般公共预算支出的比重达75.4%。

市场主体活力有效激发。年末全市市场主体总量达到112.8万户，总注册资本4.4万亿元，苏州成为省内首个市场主体总量超过100万户的城市。全年新增私营企业8.3万户，比上年增长27.7%；新增个体工商户10.9万户，比上年增长12.3%。新增私营企业和个体工商户注册资金分别比上年增长57.1%和19.1%。

“三去一降一补”年度任务全面完成。全年关停、淘汰落后低效产能企业977家；新增企业直接融资1399亿元；降低企业成本300亿元；基础设施、生态环境等111个“补短板”重点项目完成投资200亿元。

二、农业和农村建设

农业生产保持稳定。全市实现农林牧渔业总产值424.67亿元，按可比价计算比上年下降1.4%。全年粮食总产量97.68万吨，比上年下降9.7%，其中夏粮产量28.91万吨，下降20.6%；秋粮产量68.77万吨，比上年下降4.2%。全年猪牛羊禽肉产量9.74万吨，比上年下降10.0%；禽蛋产量3.8万吨，比上年下降12.4%；水产品产量25.49万吨，比上年下降2.7%。

现代农业生产方式加快转变。全年新建成高标准农田3.5千公顷，新增现代农业园区面积5.47千公顷，年末现代农业园区总面积75.5千公顷。农业适度规模经营比重达92%，农业综合机械化水平达88.5%。创新产销对接模式。搭建一批农产品产销对接平台，年末全市共有5家省级农产品电子商务示范单位，46个农产品电子商务“淘宝村”，全年农产品生产和经营单位年网上交易额超过26亿元。

农村改革稳步推进。年末全市农村各类合作组织4407家，持股农户比例超过96%。年末农村集体经济总资产1720亿元，村均年稳定性收入801万元，分别比上年增长6.8%和3.2%。全市618个村完成农村承包土地确权登记颁证工作。

三、工业和建筑业

工业生产保持平稳。全市实现工业总产值35767亿元，比上年增长0.1%，其中规模以上工业总产值30714亿元，增长1.1%。规模以上工业中，国有及国有控股工业产值783亿元，比上年增长1.8%；外商及港澳台资工业产值19868亿元，比上年增长1.3%；民营工业产值10217亿元，比上年增长0.6%。电子、电气、钢铁、通用设备、化工、汽车六大行业实现产值20552亿元，比上年增长1.7%，占规模以上工业总产值的比重达66.9%。

先进制造业加快发展。全市制造业新兴产业产值15265亿元，比上年增长2.2%，占规模以上工业总产值的比重达49.8%，比上年提高1.1个百分点。工业机器人、光伏、轨道交通、新能源汽车、生物技术和新医药五大新产业实现产值1915亿元，比上年增长5.2%。其中工业机器人产业产值161亿元，增长14.8%；光伏产业产值615亿元，增长10.3%。高端产品产量快速增长。工业机器人产量比上年增长171.3%；运动型多用途乘用车（SUV）产量增长110.7%；锂离子电池产量增长67.9%；光电子器件产量增长25%；医疗仪器设备及器械产量增长29.2%。

工业效益稳定改善。全市规模以上工业经济效益综合指数235.6%，比上年提高13.3个百分点。规模以上工业企业主营业务收入30380亿元，比上年增长1.7%；实现利润1773亿元，比上年增长14.1%。规模以上工业企业亏损面19.3%，比上年回落4.3个百分点；规模以上工业资产负债率52.3%，较上年下降0.8个百分点。工业生产效率提升。规模以上工业全员劳动生产率22.7万元/人，比上年提高8.3%；总资产贡献率9.0%，比上年提高0.4个百分点。

建筑业基本稳定。全市完成建筑业总产值1856亿元，比上年下降5.1%，其中建筑、安装工程产值1842亿元，下降

5.1%。竣工产值1702亿元，比上年增长3.6%，竣工率为91.7%。全市资质以上建筑业企业房屋施工面积9682万平方米，比上年下降11%，其中新开工面积2730万平方米，下降1.8%。年末拥有总承包和专业承包资质建筑企业1395家，实现利税146亿元，比上年下降2.7%。建筑业全员劳动生产率32.29万元/人，比上年下降1.1%。建筑业企业在外省完成建筑业产值513亿元，比上年增长19.4%。

四、固定资产投资和房地产开发

固定资产投资提质发展。全年完成全社会固定资产投资5648.49亿元，比上年下降7.8%。分产业看，第一产业完成投资0.91亿元，比上年下降76.4%；第二产业完成投资1987.31亿元，比上年下降9.8%，其中工业投资1982.29亿元，下降9.9%；第三产业完成投资3660.27亿元，比上年下降6.5%，占全社会固定资产投资的比重达64.8%。民间投资比重提升。全年完成民间投资3237.93亿元，比上年下降1.4%，民间投资占全社会固定资产投资的比重达57.3%，比上年提高3.7个百分点。

“两新一改”投资占比提高。全年新兴产业完成投资1410.18亿元，占全社会固定资产投资的比重达25.0%，比上年提高1.5个百分点；高新技术产业完成投资820.22亿元，占工业投资的比重达41.4%。工业技术改造投资1427.03亿元，占工业投资的比重达72.0%，比上年提高2.6个百分点。

房地产市场平稳发展。全年完成房地产开发投资2163.24亿元，比上年增长16.0%。商品房新开工面积2966.51万平方米，比上年增长37.8%；商品房施工面积12124.1万平方米，比上年增长7.4%；商品房竣工面积1882.07万平方米，比上年增长13.8%；商品房销售面积2494.05万平方米，比上年增长16.9%，其中住宅销售面积2258.6万平方米，比上年增长16.4%。

五、国内贸易和旅游

消费市场稳步提升。全年实现社会消费品零售总额4936.8亿元，比上年增长10.7%。其中，批发和零售业零售额4343.0亿元，比上年增长10.8%；住宿和餐饮业零售额593.8亿元，比上年增长9.6%。按经营单位所在地分，城镇消费品市场实现零售额4312.2亿元，比上年增长10.6%；农村消费品市场实现零售额624.6亿元，比上年增长10.8%。消费升级类商品增势较好。限额以上批发和零售业中，通讯器材类商品零售额比上年增长12.1%；家具类商品零售额比上年增长13.3%；汽车类零售额比上年增长10.6%。

年末全市拥有国家级特色商业街18条，拥有亿元以上市场82个，实现市场成交额6056.62亿元，比上年增长8.8%。新型商业模式迅猛发展。2016年电子商务交易额9000亿元，比上年增长30%。限额以上批发和零售业实现互联网零售额比上年增长29.1%。

旅游市场健康发展。全市实现旅游总收入2082.0亿元，比上年增长11.7%，其中旅游外汇收入21.67亿美元。全年接待入境过夜游客161.3万人次，接待国内游客11300.4万人次，分别比上年增长6.7%和6.6%。年末全市共有5A级景区6家（11个点）、4A级景区36家，五星级饭店28家。省级以上旅游度假区10家，其中国家级2家。苏州获评全国首批、全省唯一"国家全域旅游示范区"创建的地级市。游客满意度和旅游市场秩序指数保持全国前列。

六、开放型经济

对外贸易基本稳定。全市实现进出口总额18066.4亿元，其中出口10812.2亿元，进口7254.2亿元。按美元计价，全市实现进出口总额2737.6亿美元，其中出口1639.4亿美元，进口1098.2亿美元。全市一般贸易实现进出口额924.07亿美元，比上年增长3.1%，占进出口总额的比重达33.8%，比上年提高4.4个百分点。从出口市场看，全年对美国出口额439.27亿美元，比上年下降0.1%；对东盟出口额149.5亿美元，比上年下降1.5%；对欧盟出口额334.98亿美元，比上年下降3.1%；对日本出口额127.36亿美元，比上年下降13.2%，对"一带一路"沿线国家出口额占全市出口总额的比重达20.3%，比上年提高1.5个百分点。

服务贸易发展良好。全市服务贸易进出口总额141.16亿美元，比上年增长15.0%。服务外包平稳发展。全年服务外包接包合同额128.45亿美元，比上年增长7.8%；服务外包离岸执行额66.88亿美元，比上年增长6.7%。

使用外资层次提升。全年新设外商投资项目784个，实际使用外资60亿美元，其中服务业实际使用外资占比42.9%，比上年提高4.8个百分点；战略性新兴产业和高技术项目实际使用外资占比50.0%。区域性外资总部集聚区建设取得新成效，全市新设具有地区总部特征或共享功能的外资企业30家，年末累计超过260家。

"走出去"步伐加快。全年新批境外投资项目中方协议投资额32.09亿美元，比上年增长56.8%，其中第三产业项目中方协议投资额占比58.6%；民营企业境外中方协议投资额占比74.9%。全年完成对外工程承包营业额11.57亿美元，比上年增长11.2%。"一带一路"战略效应进一步显现，对"一带一路"沿线国家协议投资额5.99亿美元，占比达18.7%。

开放水平继续提升。苏州获批国家跨境电子商务综合试验区、服务贸易创新发展试点城市。51项自贸区改革试点经验在我市复制推广。年末全市拥有国家级开发区14家、省级开发区3家、综合保税区7家、保税港区1家。"苏满欧"国际铁路货运班列运能不断提升，全年累计发运出口班列120次，运载货物10706标箱，货值9.77亿美元。

七、交通运输、邮政电信

交通运输发展平稳。年末全市公路总里程13207.5公里，其中高速公路598.3公里。全市完成公路、水路客运量3.21亿人次，比上年下降7.3%，旅客周转量122.23亿人公里，比上年下降7.7%。公路、水路完成货运量1.35亿吨，货物周转量224.55亿吨公里，分别比上年增长3.9%和5.2%。全年铁路旅客发送量4059.05万人次，比上年增长8.5%。铁路货物发送量82.32万吨，货物到达量103.65万吨。苏州港港口货物吞吐量5.79亿吨，比上年增长7.3%，其中外贸货物吞吐量1.51亿吨，比上年增长7.5%。苏州港集装箱运量547.92万标箱，比上年增长7.4%。

汽车保有量稳步增长。年末拥有汽车313.3万辆，其中私家汽车268.4万辆，分别比上年增长16.6%和17.1%。

邮电业务快速发展。全年邮政业务收入134.14亿元，比上年增长23.6%。全年发送快递8.5亿件，比上年增长50.9%；实现快递业务收入114.15亿元，比上年增长28.9%。电信业务收入192.64亿元，比上年增长4.0%。年末固定电话用户252万户；移动电话用户1690.6万户，其中4G用户1079.7万户。年末互联网宽带用户数达473.52万户，比上年末净增64.13万户。

八、金 融

金融运行保持稳定。年末全市金融机构总数774家，金融从业人员7.5万人，金融总资产4.4万亿元。年末全市金融机构人民币存款余额25864.26亿元，比年初增加2205.16亿元，增长9.3%。年末金融机构人民币贷款余额21924.44亿元，比年初增加2724.34亿元，增长14.2%。

保险业务稳步增长。全年新增保险机构6家，年末保险机构81家，各类分支机构921家。全年保费收入525.19亿元，比上年增长42.6%；保险赔款和给付支出156.38亿元，比上年增长14.5%。保险深度、保险密度分别达到3.39%和4933元/人。

证券业务平稳发展。年末全市证券交易开户总数227万户。证券机构托管市值总额6123亿元。全年各类证券交易额5.32万亿元，期货市场交易额3.10万亿元。

资本市场作用凸显。全年新增上市公司13家，年末上市公司总数达113家，累计募集资金1582亿元。新增“新三板”挂牌企业203家，累计达432家。全年新增债券融资1373.8亿元，比上年多增688.1亿元。

九、科技和教育

科技创新加快推进。全市财政性科技投入95.2亿元，占一般公共预算支出的5.9%。研究与试验发展经费支出占地区生产总值的比重达到2.78%。全市新增高新技术企业920家，累计4133家。高新技术产业产值14382亿元，占规模以上工业总产值的比重达46.9%，比上年提高1.0个百分点。全年新增省级以上民营科技企业1472家，全市民营科技企业累计达11840家。

创新载体加快培育。全年新增24家国家级众创空间，41家省级众创空间，年末共有国家级众创空间32家，省级众创空间88家，规模领跑全省。年末全市共有省级以上科技孵化器93家，孵化面积超460万平方米，省级以上在孵企业超6100家。中科院电子所苏州研究院、纳米真空互联实验站开工建设。清华-苏州环境创新研究院、华中科技大学(苏州)脑空间信息技术研究院、牛津大学-苏州先进研究中心、悉尼大学中国中心相继设立。年末省级以上公共技术服务平台60家，其中国家级15家。新增省级以上工程技术研究中心48家，累计达625家；新增省级以上企业技术中心61家，累计达381家；新增省级以上工程中心（实验室）11家，累计达68家。

创新人才加速聚集。年末全市各类人才总量244.21万人，其中高层次人才20.05万人，高技能人才52.43万人。年末拥有各类专业技术人员163.4万人，比上年增长9.2%。新增国家“千人计划”32人，累计达219人，其中创业类人才120人。新增省“双创人才”104人，累计达683人。

创新成果质量提升。全年专利申请量和授权量分别达106700件和53528件，其中发明专利申请量和授权量分别达47429件和13267件，发明专利申请占比由上年的43.8%提高至44.5%，发明专利授权占比由上年的16.8%提高至24.8%。万人有效发明专利拥有量达到38.25件，比上年增加10.8件。

教育资源优化布局。全年新建和改扩建中小学、幼儿园52所，新增学位6.6万个。全市拥有各级各类学校（含外来工子弟学校）754所，在校学生131.04万人，毕业生26.9万人，专任教师8.2万人。普通高等院校22所，独立学院5所，普通高等学校在校学生21.93万人，毕业生5.93万人。高等教育毛入学率68.5%。成人高等学校在校学生3.06万人，毕业生1.23万人。拥有幼儿园（含民办）754所，在园幼儿32.44万人。

十、文化、卫生和体育

公共文化服务体系进一步完善。年末全市共有文化馆11个、文化站98个、公共图书馆11个、博物馆42个。文化创意产业做大做强。全市有8个国家级、16个省级和51个市级文化产业示范园区（基地），全年文化产业营业总收入超过4800亿元，比上年增长16%。文化保护与传承进一步加强。全市现有市级以上文物保护单位816处，其中全国重点文物保护单位59处、省级112处，国家级历史文化名镇13个、名村5个。推动苏州文化“走出去”，全年共组织文化“走出去”项目47批次。

医疗卫生服务能力持续增强。年末全市拥有各类卫生机构3175个，其中医院206个、卫生院77个。年末卫生机构床位数6.32万张，其中医院病床5.67万张；拥有卫生技术人员7.22万人，其中执业医师和执业助理医师2.77万人、注册护士3.07万人，分别比上年增长5.6%和8.9%。学科建设和人才培养成效显著。全市建成国家级医学重点学科2个，临床重点专科16个，位列全国地级市前列。医药卫生体制改革取得成效，分级诊疗制度初步形成，上下联动、统一协作的健康管理综合服务机制逐步健全。2016年底拥有医联体共19个，成员机构102个；组建家庭医生团队1030个，签约家庭78.31万户，实行社区药品“直通车”制度。苏州科技城医院正式投用，加快整合广济医院、苏州市第五人民医院打造公共医疗中心。

体育事业稳步发展。体育设施建设加快推进。年末全市公共体育设施面积超过3290万平方米，共有全民健身站点6903个、健身步道1653公里。苏州工业园区体育中心抓紧建设，苏州湾体育公园建成开园，环古城河健身步道全面提升。竞技体育实力增强。苏州体育健儿在里约奥运会、残奥会上夺得7枚金牌。昆山成功举办“汤尤杯”世界羽毛球团体锦标赛。全年体育彩票销售39.17亿元。

十一、人口和就业

人口总量基本稳定。年末全市常住人口1064.74万人，其中城镇人口803.88万人。全市户籍人口678.2万人，户籍人口出生率11.2‰，比上年提高1.28个千分点；户籍人口自然增长率4.85‰，比上年上升1.81个千分点。

就业形势保持平稳。全市新增就业17.11万人，开发公益性岗位0.95万个，城镇就业困难人员实现就业1.8万人。城镇登记失业率1.89%。苏州籍应届高校毕业生就业率达到98.52%。全年免费城乡劳动者职业技能培训4.3万人。全力推进大众创业。年末全市共有国家级创业示范基地1家，省级创业示范基地23家，各级创业孵化载体214家。

十二、人民生活和社会保障

居民收入平稳增长。根据抽样调查，全体常住居民人均可支配收入46595元，比上年增长8.4%。其中城镇常住居民人均可支配收入54341元，比上年增长7.8%；农村常住居民人均可支配收入27691元，比上年增长8.3%。

物价水平基本稳定。市区居民消费价格总水平比上年上涨2.7%。八大类商品及服务价格“七升一降”。其中食品烟酒类价格比上年上涨4.3%；衣着类价格上涨2.0%；居住类价格上涨1.7%；生活用品及服务价格上涨2.0%；教育文化和娱乐价格上涨1.4%；医疗保健价格上涨14.0%；其他用品和服务价格上涨2.8%；交通和通信类价格比上年下降2.3%。

市区居民消费价格指数（以上年价格为100）

类　别	2016年
居民消费价格总指数	102.7
服务项目价格指数	104.1
消费品价格指数	101.8
1.食品烟酒	104.3
其中：食　品	105.5
#粮　食	100.5
食用油	99.8
菜	112.3
#鲜　菜	113.5
畜肉类	110.9
水产品	106.6
蛋　类	98.0
干鲜瓜果	100.4
2.衣　着	102.0
3.居　住	101.7
#水电燃料	101.6
4.生活用品及服务	102.0
5.交通和通信	97.7
6.教育文化和娱乐	101.4
7.医疗保健	114.0
8.其他用品和服务	102.8

社会保障体系进一步完善。年末全市企业职工养老保险缴费人数478.46万人，比上年增加8.45万人；企业养老保险享受人数147.06万人。市区企业退休人员月人均增加养老金148元。年末城乡居民社会养老保险参保人数46.37万人，领取基础养老金人数43.16万人。参加城镇职工基本医疗保险人数635.09万人，比上年增加23.37万人；参加居民医疗保险人数276.83万人。参加失业保险人数446.62万人，比上年增加23.09万人。全市城镇职工社会保险覆盖率、城乡居民养老保险和医疗保险覆盖率均保持在99%以上。

全市城乡最低生活保障标准由750元/月提高至810元/月。年末全市1.76万户、共计2.83万人享受低保，全年发放低保金2.06亿元。市区居民基础养老金由每人每月380元上调至430元。全年社会救助支出19.28亿元。年末拥有各类养老机构

226个，养老机构床位总数65301张。全市新开工建设保障性住房42255套，基本建成53812套，为1260户困难家庭发放住房租赁补贴。全市新增缴存公积金职工68.85万人，年末缴存住房公积金职工数达268.69万人，全年职工提取公积金245.72亿元。

强化食品安全监管。在全省率先建成覆盖城乡的食品安全监测预警网络体系。全年累计抽检各类食品5.96万批次，每千人抽检率达5.62批次，动态合格率为98.5%。立案查处食品安全案件2930起。

十三、城市建设和公用事业

全年完成基础设施投资738.1亿元。常嘉高速公路、张家港疏港高速公路建成通车，沪通铁路苏州段建设进展顺利。城市轨道交通加快建设。轨道交通2号线延伸线建成运营，4号线及支线工程试运行、3号线、5号线建设稳步推进。市区人民路综合整治提升工程基本完成。苏州汽车西站综合客运枢纽建设投运。全市建成换乘停车场24处，泊位1万多个。苏州工业园区桑田岛地下综合管廊建成使用，海绵城市试点项目积极推进。1000千伏特高压淮上线东吴变电站投入运行，"城市光网"覆盖到村，"智慧苏州"重点项目加快建设。

全年全社会用电量1382.58亿千瓦时，比上年增长5.4%。其中工业用电量1116.3亿千瓦时，增长3.9%；城乡居民生活用电量108.26亿千瓦时，增长14.5%。全市拥有区域供水厂22座，总供水能力717.5万立方米/日，其中市区（不含吴江，下同）自来水日供水能力达到255万立方米。全年新建、改建城镇生活污水处理厂5座，新增生活污水处理能力11.55万吨/日，生活污水处理能力达到379万吨/日。城镇生活污水处理率达到95.2%，农村生活污水处理率达到75%。市区管道天然气供气总量8.79亿立方米。

年末城市轨道交通运营线路总长85.7公里，全年运营总里程864.6万列公里，线网客流总量15056.7万人次。市区新辟公交线路35条，其中社区巴士线路20条，年末营运线路364条，线路总长7290公里，全年公交运客总量5.63亿人次。年末市区营运出租汽车4803辆。全年新增农村客运（公交）班线24条，行政村农村客运班车通达率、镇村公交开通率均保持100%。

十四、环境保护和节能降耗

生态保护得到加强。全市环保投入641亿元，比上年增长11.2%，占地区生产总值的比重达4.16%。全市生态红线保护面积比2013年增加54.5平方公里，总面积达3260平方公里。生态文明建设"十大工程"重点项目全年完成投资127.1亿元。全市空气质量达标天数（按AQI标准）比例为76.2%。市区$PM_{2.5}$年均浓度比上年下降20.7%。集中式饮用水水源地水质达标率100%。市区新增绿地面积350万平方米，建成区绿化覆盖率42.0%，市区建成区人均公园绿地面积14.71平方米。农村新增林地、绿地624.73公顷，陆地森林覆盖率29.69%。全市建成美丽村庄示范点10个、三星级康居乡村305个。截止2016年底，全市已建成美丽村庄示范点100个，三星级康居乡村690个。

节能减排扎实推进。全面推进工程减排、结构减排和管理减排，实施减排项目181个。劝退、拒批不符合环保要求建设项目132个。整治燃煤小锅炉1802台。主要污染物排放总量削减完成省下达的任务。全市新增三星级以上“能效之星”企业33家，累计达411家。

2016年，苏州经济社会发展取得了新提升、新成效，实现了“十三五”良好开局。但同时也应看到，经济社会发展中依然面临不少困难和矛盾，经济发展新动力仍显不足，科技创新还未成为推动发展的主动力，结构性矛盾比较突出，产业竞争力整体不强，深化改革任务艰巨繁重，民生事业需要进一步加大力度，生态环境建设任务仍需持续发力。新的一年中，全市要以五大发展理念为引领，以提高发展质量和效益为中心，以供给侧结构性改革为主线，聚力创新求突破，聚焦富民见实效，全力推动苏州经济社会发展再上新台阶，努力当好建设“强富美高”新江苏的先行军和排头兵，以优异成绩迎接党的十九大胜利召开。

AN OVERVIEW OF THE 2016 ECONOMIC AND SOCIAL DEVELOPMENT OF SUZHOU MUNICIPALITY

In 2016, in the face of the complexity of the macroeconomic environment, the whole city, under the correct leadership of Suzhou municipal Party committee and municipal government, thoroughly implemented the spirit of the 18th CPC national congress and the third, fourth, fifth and sixth plenary sessions of the 18th CPC central committee, and with the spirit of General Secretary Xi Jinping's series of important speeches and especially of his important speeches during his inspection tour of Jiangsu as the guide, consciously practiced the five development concepts, adhered to the general work tone of progressing while maintaining stability, unswervingly promoted the supply-side structural reform, actively responded to various risks and challenges, and planned as a whole to advance all the work of growing steadily, promoting the reform, adjusting the structure, improving the people's livelihood and preventing risks; as a result, the city's overall economic operation was smooth and steady, steady and progressing, steady and becoming better, the adjustment of economic structure was sped up, the reform and innovation was deepened, the ecological environment continued to improve, the quality of the people's livelihood kept improving and the social development was harmonious and stable.

1. General economy

The economy was generally stable. The total regional GDP of the whole city was 1,547.51 billion yuan, which was 7.5% higher than the previous year calculated at comparable prices. Per capita regional GDP (measured by the permanent population) was 145,600 yuan or $21,900 converted according to the average exchange.

The economic structure continued to be optimized. The service economy accelerated, and the service sector accounted for more than 50% for the first time. In the whole year, the added value of the service industry was 797.58 billion yuan, up 9.7% over the previous year, and accounting for 51.5% of the region's gross domestic product, up 1.6 percentage points over the previous year.

Macro benefits improved stably. Revenue and tax revenue rose steadily, and the year's general public budget revenue reached 173 billion yuan, an increase of 10.8% over the previous year. The tax revenue was 150.58 billion yuan, increased by 12.5%, and the tax revenue accounted for 87% of the general public budget revenue, an increase of 1.2 percentage points over the previous year; the total revenue, the incremental quantity and the proportion of the tax revenue kept the first in the province. Fiscal expenditure was more invested in the area of the people's livelihood, and the general public budget expenditure for the whole year was 161.71 billion yuan, an increase of 5.9% over the previous year. Of it the urban and rural public service expenditure amounted to 121.99 billion yuan, and the urban and rural public service expenditure accounted for 75.4% of the general public expenditure.

The vitality of the market main bodies was effectively stimulated. At the end of the year, the total market main bodies of the whole city reached 1,128,000 households, with a total registered capital of 4.4 trillion yuan, and Suzhou became the first city in the province with a total market bodies of more than 1 million households. The number of the new private enterprises in the whole year was 83,000, an increase of 27.7% over the previous year; the number of the new individual industrial and commercial households was 109,000, an increase of 12.3% over the previous year. The registered capital of the new private enterprises and that of the new individual industrial and commercial households increased by 57.1% and 19.1% respectively over the previous year.

The annual task of "eliminating three, reducing one and adding one" was completed. In the whole year 977 enterprises with backward and inefficient capacity were closed down and eliminated; the direct financing raised by the new enterprises was 139.9 billion yuan; the cost of enterprises reduced was 30 billion yuan; 111 "improving weak links" key projects in infrastructure, ecological environment and so on have completed investment of 20 billion yuan.

2. Agriculture and rural construction

Agricultural production remained stable. The total output value of the city's agriculture, forestry, animal husbandry and fishery was 42.467 billion yuan, down 1.4% from the previous year calculated at comparable prices. The total grain output in the whole year was 976,800 tons, down 9.7% from the previous year, including 289,100 tons of summer grain, down 20.6% and 687,700 tons of autumn grain, down 4.2% from the previous year. The meat output of pigs, cows, sheep and poultry in the whole year was 97,400 tons, down 10.0% from the previous year; the output of poultry eggs was 38,000 tons, down 12.4% from the previous year; the output of aquatic products was 254,900 tons, down 2.7% from the previous year.

Modern agricultural production methods were accelerated. There were 3.5 thousand hectares of newly-built high-standard farmland for the whole year, and there were 5.47 thousand hectares of newly-built modern agricultural parks, with a total area of 75.5 thousand hectares at the end of the year. The proportion of agriculture in moderate scale management was 92% and the total mechanization of agriculture 88.5%. The mode of production and marketing docking was innovated. A batch of platforms for agricultural production and marketing docking were built, and at the end of the year in the city there were five provincial-level agricultural e-commerce demonstration units, 46 agricultural e-commerce "Taobao villages", and in the year the online transactions by agricultural production and business units were more than 2.6 billion yuan.

Steady progress was made in rural reform. By the end of this year, there were 4,407 rural cooperative organizations in the whole city and the share-holding farmers accounted for more than 96%. At the end of this year, the total assets of the rural collective economy were 172 billion yuan and the average annual stable income of the villages was 8,010,000 yuan, up 6.8% and 3.2% respectively over the previous year. There were 618 villages in the city which had completed the registration and certification of rural contracted land.

3. Industries and construction industry

Industrial production remained stable. The total industrial output value of the whole city was 3,576.7 billion yuan, up 0.1% over the previous year, of which the total output value of the above-scale industries was 3,071.4 billion yuan, up 1.1%. In the above-scale industries, the output value of the state-owned and state-controlled industries reached 78.3 billion yuan, an increase of 1.8% over the previous year; the output value of the foreign and Hong Kong, Macao and Taiwan-funded industries was 1,986.8 billion yuan, up 1.3% over the previous year; the output value of the private industries was 1,021.7 billion yuan, up 0.6% over the previous year. The output value of the six industries of electronics, electric, steel, general equipment, chemical industry and automobile industry reached 2,055.2 billion yuan, up 1.7% over the previous year and accounting for 66.9% of the total output value of the above-scale industries.

Advanced manufacturing accelerated. The output value of the emerging manufacturing industries in the whole city was 1,526.5 billion yuan, an increase of 2.2% over the previous year, and accounting for 49.8% of the total output value of the above-scale industries, up 1.1 percentage points over the previous year. The output value of the five emerging industries of industrial robots, photovoltaic, rail transit, new energy vehicles, biotechnology and new medicines was 191.5 billion yuan, an increase of 5.2% over the previous year. The output value of the industrial robot industry was 16.1 billion yuan, an increase of 14.8%; the output value of the photovoltaic industry was 61.5 billion yuan, up 10.3%. The production of high-end products increased rapidly. The production of industrial robots increased by 171.3% over the previous year; the production of sport utility passenger vehicles (suv) increased by 110.7%; the production of Lithium ion battery increased by 67.9%; the production of optoelectronic devices increased by 25%; the production of medical instruments and equipment increased by 29.2%.

Industrial efficiency improved steadily. The comprehensive index of the economic efficiency of the above-scale industries of the whole city was 235.6%, up 13.3 percentage points over the previous year. The main business income of the above-scale industrial enterprises was 3038 billion yuan, an increase of 1.7% over the previous year; their profits were 177.3 billion yuan, up 14.1% over the previous year. The percentage of the loss-incurring above-scale industrial enterprises was 19.3%, down 4.3 percentage points from the previous year. The asset-liability ratio of the above-scale industries was 52.3%, down 0.8 percentage points from the previous year. The industrial production efficiency was improved. The total labor productivity of the above-scale industries was 227,000 yuan / person, an increase of 8.3% over the previous year; the total asset contribution rate was 9.0%, up 0.4 percentage points over the previous year.

The construction industry is basically stable. The total output value of the city's construction industry was 185.6 billion yuan, a decrease of 5.1% from the previous year, of which the output value of construction and installation was 184.2 billion yuan, down 5.1%. The output value of the completed projects was 170.2 billion yuan, up 3.6% over the previous year, and the completion rate was 91.7%. The construction area of the city's construction enterprises above qualifications was 96.82 million square meters, a decrease of 11% from the previous year, of which the newly-started area was 27.3 million square meters, down 1.8%. At the end of the year, there were 1,395 construction enterprises with total contracting and professional contracting qualifications, which had achieved 14.6 billion yuan of profits and taxes, down 2.7% from the previous year. The total labor productivity of the construction industry was 322,900 yuan / person, down 1.1% from the previous year. The construction output value of the projects completed by the city's construction enterprises in other provinces was 51.3 billion yuan, up 19.4% over the previous year.

4. Investment in fixed assets and real estate development

The quality of the investment in fixed assets was improved in its development. The year's total investment in the society's fixed assets was 564.849 billion yuan, down 7.8% from the previous year. From the perspective of the three industries, the investment in the primary industry was 0.091 billion yuan, down 76.4% from the previous year; that in the secondary industry 198.731 billion yuan, down 9.8% from the previous year, of which the industrial investment was 198.229 billion yuan, down 9.9%; that in the tertiary industry was 366.027 billion yuan, down 6.5% from the previous year and accounting for 64.8% of the total investment in the society's fixed assets. The proportion of the private investment was raised. The year's private investment reached 323.793 billion yuan, down 1.4% from the previous year. The private investment accounted for 57.3% of the total investment in the society's fixed assets, up 3.7 percentage points over the previous year.

The proportion of the investment in the "two new's, one transformation" rose. In the whole year, the investment in the emerging industries reached 141.018 billion yuan, accounting for 25% of the total investment in the society's fixed assets and up 1.5 percentage points over the previous year; the investment in the high and new technology industries reached 82.022 billion yuan, accounting for 41.4% of the industrial investment. The investment in industrial technology transformation was 142.703 billion yuan, accounting for 72% of the industrial investment and up 2.6 percentage points over the previous year.

The real estate market developed steadily. In the whole year the investment in the real estate development was 216.324 billion yuan, up 16% over the previous year. The new construction area of commercial housing was 29,665,100 square meters, an increase of 37.8% over the previous year. The construction area of commercial housing was 121,241,000 square meters, an increase of 7.4% over the previous year. The completed construction area of commercial housing was 18,820,700 square meters, an increase of 13.8% over the previous year. The sales area of commercial housing was 24,940,500 square meters, an increase of 16.9% over the previous year, of which the residential sales area was 22,586,000 square meters, up 16.4% over the previous year.

5. Domestic trade and tourism

The consumer market steadily improved. The year's total retail sales of the society's consumer goods were 493.68 billion yuan, an increase of 10.7% over the previous year. Of them, the retail sales of the wholesale and retail businesses were 434.3 billion yuan, up 10.8% over the previous year; the retail sales of the accommodation and catering industries were 59.38 billion yuan, up 9.6 over the previous year. According to the location of the business units, the retail sales of urban consumer goods reached 431.22 billion yuan, up 10.6% over the previous year; the retail sales of rural consumer goods reached 62.46 billion yuan, up 10.8% over the previous year. The sales of consumer goods of the upgrading category were better. In the wholesale and retail sectors above designated size, the retail sales of communication equipment increased by 12.1% over the previous year; the retail sales of furniture were up 13.3% over the previous year; the retail sales of cars were up 10.6% over the previous year.

At the end of the year, there were 18 national-level featured commercial streets, 82 markets with a capital of more than 100 million yuan, and the turnover of the markets reached 605.662 billion yuan, an increase of 8.8% over the previous year. The new business models developed rapidly. The e-commerce turnover in 2016 was 900 billion yuan, up 30% over the previous year. The Internet retail sales in the wholesale and retail businesses above designated size were up 29.1% over the previous year.

The tourism markets were developing healthily. The city's gross tourism revenue was 208.2 billion yuan, an increase of 11.7% over the previous year, of which $2.167 billion was in tourism foreign exchange. In the year, there were 1,613,000 inbound overnight tourists received and 113,004,000 domestic tourists received, up 6.7% and 6.6% respectively over the previous year. At the end of the year, there were six 5A-class scenic districts (11 spots), 36 4A-class scenic districts and 28 five-star hotels in the city. There were 10 tourist resorts at or above provincial level, including 2 national-level ones. Suzhou was a prefecture-level city which became one of the first cities in the country and the only one in the province to establish a "national citywide tourism demonstration zone". Tourist satisfaction and tourism market order index maintained the forefront of the country.

6. Open economy

Foreign trade was basically stable. The total import and export volume of the city .was 1,806.64 billion yuan, of which the export volume was 1081.22 billion yuan and the import volume 725.42 billion yuan. In dollar terms, the total import and export volume of the city was $273.76 billion, of which the export volume was $163.94 billion and the import volume was $109.82 billion. The import and export volume of the city's general trade was $92.407 billion, up 3.1% over the previous year and accounting for 33.8% of the total import and export volume, 4.4 percentage points higher than the previous year. From the export market, the year's exports to the United States were $43.927 billion, down 0.1% from the previous year; the exports to ASEAN were $14.95 billion, down 1.5% from the previous year; the exports to the EU were $33.498 billion, down 3.1% from the previous year; the exports to Japan were $12.736, down 13.2% from the previous year; the exports to countries along the "Belt and Road" accounted for 20.3% of the total export volume of the city, up 1.5 percentage points over the previous year.

Service trade was developing well. The total import and export value of services in the whole city was $14.116 billion, up 15% over the previous year. Service outsourcing was developing smoothly. The total service outsourcing contract amount for the whole year was $12.845 billion, up 7.8% over the previous year; the offshore performance amount of service outsourcing was $6.688 billion, up 6.7% over the previous year.

The level of using foreign investment was raised. 784 foreign investment projects were newly set up for the whole year, and the foreign investment actually used was $6 billion, of which the foreign investment in services actually used accounted for 42.9%, up 4.8 percentage points over the previous year; the foreign investment in strategic emerging industries and high-tech projects actually used accounted for 50%. New achievements had been made in the construction of regional foreign headquarters agglomeration areas, and 30 foreign enterprises with regional headquarters characteristics or sharing functions were newly established in the whole city with a total of more than 260 by the end of the year.

The pace of "going out" quickened. The amount of the Chinese agreement investment in the new batch of overseas investment projects for the whole year was $3.209 billion, up 56.8% over the previous year, of which the amount of the Chinese agreement investment in the tertiary industry projects accounted for 58.6%; the amount of the investment made by private enterprises accounted for 74.9% of the Chinese agreement investment in overseas projects. The turnover of contracted projects with foreign countries was $1.157 billion, an increase of 11.2% over the previous year. The "Belt and Road" strategic effect was further revealed, and the agreement investment in the countries along the "Belt and Road" was $0.599 billion, accounting for 18.7% of the total.

The level of opening to the outside world continued to rise. Suzhou had been approved as a national-level comprehensive pilot zone of cross-border e-commerce and a pilot city for innovative development of services trade. 51 items of pilot experience of free trade zone reform was replicated in our city. At the end of the year, there were 14 national-level development zones, 3 provincial-level development zones, 7 comprehensive bonded zones and 1 bonded port. The transport capacity of the "Suzhou-Manzhouli -Europe" international railway freight train was improved continuously, and in the year accumulated 120 export freight trains were dispatched, and 10,706 TEUs of goods were delivered, which were worth $0.977 billion.

7. Transportation, post and telecommunications

Transportation was developing steadily. At the end of the year, the total mileage of the highways in the whole city was 13,207.5 kilometers, including 598.3 kilometers of expressways. There were 321 million passengers on roads and waterways in the city, down 7.3% from the previous year, and the passenger turnover reached 12,223 million passenger-kilometers, down 7.7% from the previous year. 135 million tons of goods were carried by highways and waterways, and the cargo turnover was 22,455 million tons, up 3.9% and 5.2% respectively over the previous year. The year's number of railway passengers was 40,590,500, an increase of 8.5% over the previous year. The delivery volume of railway goods was 823,200 tons, and the goods reached 1,036,500 tons. The cargo throughput of Suzhou port was 579 million tons, an increase of 7.3% over the previous year, of which 151 million tons of foreign trade goods were handled, up 7.5% over the previous year. The volume of the container traffic in Suzhou port was 5,479,200 TEUs, up 7.4% over the previous year.

Car ownership was growing steadily. At the end of the year, 3,133,000 cars were owned, including 2,684,000 private cars, up 16.6% and 17.1% respectively over the previous year.

The post and telecommunications business was developing rapidly. The year's postal business revenue was 13.414 billion yuan, an increase of 23.6% over the previous year. In the whole year, 850 million express deliveries were sent, an increase of 50.9% over the previous year; the revenue of express delivery business was 11.415 billion yuan, up 28.9% over the previous year. The telecom revenue was 19.264 billion yuan, up 4.0% over the previous year. At the end of the year, the number of fixed telephone users was 2.52 million, and that of mobile phone users 169.06 million, including 10.797 million 4G users. At the end of the year the number of Internet broadband users reached 4,735,200, a net increase of 641,300 users over the end of the previous year.

8. Finance

The financial operations remained stable. At the end of this year, the total number of financial institutions in the city was 774, with 75,000 financial employees and 4.4 trillion yuan in total financial assets. At the end of the year the amount of RMB deposits in the city's financial institutions was 2,586.426 billion yuan, an increase of 220.516 billion yuan over the start of the year and up 9.3%. At the end of the year the amount of RMB loan balance in the city's financial institutions was 2,192.444 billion yuan, an increase of 272.434 billion yuan over the start of the year and up 14.2%.

The insurance business was growing steadily. In the whole year there were 6 newly-started insurance institutions, and at the end of the year there were 81 insurance institutions and 921 branches of various kinds. In the year the insurance premium income was 52.519 billion yuan, an increase of 42.6% over the previous year; the insurance indemnities and payment expenditures were 15.638 billion yuan, an increase of 14.5% over the previous year. The insurance depth and the insurance density reached 3.39% and 4,933 yuan / per person respectively.

The securities business was developing smoothly. At the end of the year there were a total of 2.27 million securities trading accounts in the city. The total hosting market value of the securities institutions was 612.3 billion yuan. In the year the turnover of various securities was 5.32 trillion yuan, and the turnover of the futures markets 3.10 trillion yuan.

The role of capital markets was prominent. In the year there were 13 newly-listed companies, with a total of 113 listed companies at the end of the year and 158.2 billion yuan of accumulated fund. There were 203 newly-listed “new-three-board” companies with a cumulative total of 432 companies. In the year 137.38 billion yuan of bond financing was newly raised, an increase of 68.81 billion yuan over the previous year.

9. Science, technology and education

Scientific and technological innovation was accelerated. The city's fiscal investment in science and technology amounted to 9.52 billion yuan, or 5.9% of the general public budget expenditures. The development expenditure on research and testing accounted for 2.78% of the region's gross domestic product. In the city there were 920 newly-started high and new technology enterprises, with a total of 4,133 ones. The output value of the high and new technology industries was 1,438.2 billion yuan, accounting for 46.9% of the total output value of the above-scale industries and up 1.0 percentage point over the previous year. In the whole year, there were 1,472 newly-started private technology enterprises above the provincial level, the city’s private technology enterprises with a cumulative total of 11,840.

The cultivation of innovation carriers was accelerated. In the year there were 24 newly-started national-level innovation spaces and 41 newly-started provincial-level innovation spaces, with a total of 32 national-level innovation spaces and 88 provincial-level innovation spaces at the end of the year, leading the whole province. At the end of the year there were 93 science and technology incubators at or above the provincial level in the city, with an incubation area of more than 4.6 million square meters, and there were over 6,100 incubated enterprises at or above the provincial level. Suzhou Institute of the Institute of Electronics of the Chinese Academy of Sciences and the Nanometer Vacuum Interconnection Experiment Station started construction. Tsinghua - Suzhou Institute of Environmental Innovation, the Research Institute of Brain Space Information Technology of Huazhong University of Science and Technology (Suzhou), Oxford University - Suzhou Advanced Research Center, Sydney University China Center had been set up one after another. At the end of the year there were 60 public technology service platforms at or above the provincial level, including 15 national-level ones. There were 43 newly-started engineering technology research centers at or above the provincial level, with a total of 625; there were 61 enterprises technology centers at or above the provincial level, with a cumulative total of 38 ones; there were 11 newly-started engineering centers (laboratories) at or above the provincial level, with a total of 68 ones.

The gathering of innovative talents was speeding. At the end of the year there were totally 2,442,100 talents of all kinds in the city, including 200,500 high-level talents and 524,300 highly- skilled ones. At the end of the year there were 1,634,000 professional and technical personnel of all kinds, up 9.2% over the previous year. There were 32 new talents in the national "thousand- talent plan", with a total of 219 ones, including 120 entrepreneurial talents. There were 104 new talents in the provincial "entrepreneurial -innovation program", with a total of 683 ones.

The quality of innovation results improved. In the year there were 106,700 patent applications and 53,528 grants respectively, including 47,429 invention patent applications and 13,267 grants respectively, the proportion of the invention patent applications rose to 44.5% from 43.8% in the previous year, and the proportion of the invention patent grants rose to 24.8% from 16.8% in the previous year. There were 38.25 10,000-person valid invention patents, an increase of 10.8 over the previous year.

The layout of education resources was optimized. In the year, there were 52 schools and kindergartens newly built or rebuilt or expanded with 66,000 new student places. In the city there were 754 schools of all kinds at all levels (including schools for the children of migrant workers), 1,310,400 students, 269,000 school graduates and 82,000 full-time teachers. There were 22 general institutions of higher learning, 5 independent colleges, 219,300 students in the general institutions of higher learning and 59,300 college graduates. The gross enrollment rate of higher education was 68.5%. There were 30,600 students in the adult institutions of higher education and 12,300 graduates. There were 754 kindergartens (including private ones) and 324,400 children in the kindergartens.

10. Culture, health and sports

The public cultural services system was further improved. At the end of the year there were 11 cultural halls, 98 cultural centers, 11 public libraries and 42 museums in the city. The cultural creative industry was doing a great job. There are eight national-level, 16 provincial-level and 51 city-level cultural industry demonstration parks (bases) in the whole city, and the year's total business income of the cultural industry exceeded 480 billion yuan, a rise of 16% over the previous year. Cultural protection and inheritance had been further strengthened. There were 816 cultural relics protection units at or above the city-level in the city, including 59 national-level key cultural relics protection units and 112 provincial-level ones, 13 national-level historical and cultural famous towns and 5 famous villages. The "going out" of Suzhou culture was promoted and in the year 47 batches of cultural "going out" projects were organized.

The capacity of medical and health services continued to grow. At the end of the year there were 3,175 health institutions of all kinds in the city, including 206 hospitals and 77 health centers. At the end of the year there were 63,200 beds in the health institutions, including 56,700 beds in the hospitals; there were 72,200 health technical personnel, including 27,700 practicing doctors and practicing assistant doctors and 30,700 registered nurses, up 5.6% and 8.9% respectively over the previous year. Discipline construction and personnel training had achieved remarkable results. In the city 2 national-level key disciplines of medicine and 16 key clinical specialties had been established, ranking first in the national prefecture-level cities. The reform of the medical and health care system had been effective and the system of grading treatment had been preliminarily formed, and the comprehensive service mechanism of health management which is linked up and down and coordinated, had been gradually improved. At the end of the year, there were 19 medical joint bodies and 102 member agencies; 1,030 family doctor teams had been set up and 783,100 families had signed contracts, and the "through train" system of community medicines had been implemented. Suzhou Science and Technology Town Hospital had been officially put into use, the integration of Guangji Hospital and Suzhou No. Five People's Hospital was speeding up to build a public medical center.

Sports undertakings were developing steadily. The construction of sports facilities was accelerated. At the end of this year, the area of the public sports facilities in the city exceeded 32.9 million square meters, with a total of 6,903 fitness stations and 1,653 kilometers of fitness trails. Suzhou Industrial Park Sports Center was in the process of construction, the Suzhou Bay Sports Park had been completed and was open to the public, and the fitness trails around the ancient city moat was fully promoted. Competitive sports strength was enhanced. Suzhou sports athletes won seven gold medals at the Rio Olympic Games and Paralympic Games. Kunshan successfully hosted the "Thomas and Uber Cups" World Badminton Team Championships. The year's sports lottery sales were 3.917 billion yuan.

11. Population and employment

The total population was basically stable. At the end of the year, there were 10,647,400 permanent residents in the city, including 8,038,800 urban ones. The registered population of the city was 6,782,000, with a birth rate of 11.2‰, up 1.28 per thousand points over the previous year; the natural growth rate of the registered population was 4.85‰, up 1.81 per thousand points over the previous year.

The employment situation remained stable. In the city there were 171,100 new jobs, 9,500 public welfare posts were developed, and in the urban areas 18,000 people with employment difficulties were employed. The registered urban unemployment rate was 1.89%. The employment rate of the recent college graduates of Suzhou nationality reached 98.52%. In the year 43,000 urban and rural workers received free vocational skills training. Public entrepreneurship was forcefully promoted. At the end of the year, there was one national-level entrepreneurship demonstration base, 23 provincial-level entrepreneurship demonstration bases and 214 entrepreneurship incubation carriers at all levels.

12. The people's livelihood and social security

Residents' incomes rose steadily. According to a sample survey, the per capita disposable income of all the permanent residents was 46,595 yuan, an increase of 8.4% over the previous year. Of it the per capita disposable income of the urban permanent residents was 54,341 yuan, an increase of 7.8% over the previous year; that of the rural permanent residents was 27,691 yuan, an increase of 8.3% over the previous year.

Price levels were basically stable. Urban consumer prices rose 2.7% from the previous year. The prices of seven of the eight categories of goods and services rose and those of one of the eight fell. Of them the prices of foods, tobacco and alcohol rose by 4.3% over the previous year; those of clothing rose by 2%; those of housing rose by 1.7%; those of articles for daily use and services rose by 2%; those of education, culture and entertainment rose by 1.4%; those of health care rose by 14%; those of other supplies and services rose by 2.8%; those of transportation and communication fell 2.3% from the previous year.

Urban Consumer Price Index (Previous Year = 100)

Category	2016
General Residents Consumer Price Index	102.7
Price Index of Service	104.1
Price Index of Consumer Goods	101.8
1. Food, Cigarette and Wine	104.3
# Food	105.5
# Grain	100.5
Edible Oil	99.8
Vegetables	112.3
#Fresh Vegetables	113.5
Livestock Meat	110.9
Aquatic Products	106.6
Eggs	98.0
Dried and Fresh Melons and Fruits	100.4
2. Clothing	102.0
3. Residence	101.7
# Light,Water and Fuel	101.6
4. Life Articles and Service	102.0
5. Transportation and Communication	97.7
6. Education Cultural and Recreation	101.4
7. Medical Service	114.0
8. Other Articles and Service	102.8

The social security system had been further improved. At the end of the year in the city there were 4,784,600 enterprise employees paying pension insurance premiums, an increase of 84,500 people over the previous year; there were 1,470,600 enterprise pensioners enjoying pension insurance benefits. The pensions for the urban enterprise retirees were increased by 148 yuan per person per month. At the end of the year there were 463,700 urban and rural residents participating in the social pension insurance, and 431,600 of them were entitled to basic pensions. There were 6,350,900 urban workers participating in the basic medical insurance, an increase of 233,700 workers over the previous year; there were 2,768,300 residents participating in medical insurance. There were 4,466,200 people participating in unemployment insurance, an increase of 230,900 people over the previous year. In the city the coverage of the social insurance for urban workers, and that of the pension insurance and medical insurance for urban and rural residents both kept above 99%.

The minimum living standards for urban and rural residents increased from 750 yuan per month to 810 yuan per month. At the end of the year in the city there were 17,600 households and a total of 28,300 people entitled to basic living allowances, and a total of 206 million yuan for basic living allowances was issued for the whole year. The basic pension for urban residents was raised from 380 yuan per person per month to 430 yuan. In the year the social relief expenditure was 1.928 billion yuan. At the end of the year there were 226 nursing institutions for the aged with a total of 65,301 beds. In the city 42,255 units of low-income housing started construction; 53,812 units were basically completed, and housing rental subsidies were issued for 1,260 families with financial difficulties. In the city there were 688,500 employees who newly started depositing accumulation funds, at the end of the year there were 2,686,900 employees who deposited housing provident funds, and in the year 24.572 billion yuan of accumulation funds was withdrawn by employees.

The supervision over food safety was strengthened. A food safety monitoring and early warning system covering both urban and rural areas was first established in the province. During the whole year 59,600 batches of food were detected, with a rate of 5.62 batches per thousand people and a dynamic pass rate of 98.5%. 2,930 food safety cases were investigated.

13. Urban construction and public utilities

In the year 73.81 billion yuan was invested in infrastructure. The Chang-Jia Expressway and Zhangjiagang Port Expressway were completed and opened to traffic, and the construction of the Suzhou section of Hutong Railway was going well. The construction of urban rail transit was accelerated. The extension line of Rail Transit Line 2 had been completed and was open to traffic, Rail Transit Line 4 and its branch line project were in their pilot run period, and the construction of Rail Transit Line 3 and Rail Transit Line 5 was being steadily promoted. The general improvement project of the city's Renmin Road was basically completed. The integrated passenger transport hub of Suzhou West Bus Station had been completed and was open to operation. In the city 24 parking lots had been completed with more than 10,000 berths. The underground complex in Sangtian Island of Suzhou Industrial Park had been completed and put into use, and the construction of the pilot project of a sponge city was being actively advanced. Dongwu transformer substation of 1,000 kilovolt uhv Huai-Shang line was put into operation, "the city light network" covered all the villages, and the construction of the key projects of "intelligent Suzhou" was accelerated.

In the year the total amount of electricity consumed by the whole society was 138.258 billion KWH, a rise of 5.4% over the previous year. Of it, the amount of electricity consumed by industries was 111.63 billion KWH, up 3.9% and that by urban and rural residents 10.826 billion KWH up 14.5%. In the city there were 22 regional water supply plants, and the total water supply capacity was 7,175,000 cubic meters per day, of which the water supply capacity per day of the urban areas (excluding Wujiang, the same below) reached 2,550,000 cubic meters. In the year 5 sewage treatment plants were newly built or rebuilt, the new sewage treatment capacity was 115,500 tons / day, and the sewage treatment capacity reached 3.79 million tons / day. The sewage treatment rate in the urban areas reached 95.2% and that in the rural areas 75%. In the urban areas the total pipeline gas supply was 879 million cubic meters.

At the end of the year the total length of the urban rail transit lines was 85.7 kilometers, the total operating mileage of the year was 8,646,000 kilometers, and the total passenger flow volume on the lines and in the network was 150.567 million trips. In the urban areas there are 35 newly-started bus routes, including 20 community bus lines, and at the end of the year there were 364 operating lines and the total length of the lines was 7,290 kilometers, and the year's total number of bus passengers was 563 million trips. At the end of the year 4,803 taxis were operated in the urban areas. In the year there were 24 newly-started rural passenger transport (bus) lines, and the rate of the rural passenger bus services to the administrative villages and the opening rate of public transport in the towns and villages both maintained 100 %.

14. Environmental protection and energy saving and reducing energy consumption

Ecological protection was strengthened. The city's environmental investment reached 64.1 billion yuan, an increase of 11.2% over the previous year and accounting for 4.16% of the region's gross domestic product. The ecological red line protection area of the city was 54.5 square kilometers more than 2013, with a total area of 3,260 square kilometers. In the year 12.71 billion yuan was invested in the key "top 10 projects" of the construction of ecological civilization. The ratio of the number of days of the city's air quality up to the standards (according to the AQI standard) was 76.2%. The annual average concentration of PM2.5 in the urban areas fell by 20.7% from the previous year. The rate of the water quality of the concentrated drinking water sources reaching the standard was 100%. In the urban areas there were 3.5 million square meters of new green space areas, the green coverage in the built-up areas was 42.0%, and the per capita park green areas in the built-up urban areas was 14.71 square meters. In the rural areas there were 624.73 hectares of new woodland and green areas, and the forest coverage was 29.69% of the land. In the city 10 beautiful village demonstration points and 305 three-star healthy-living villages were built. By the end of 2016 there were 100 beautiful village demonstration points and 690 three-star healthy-living villages.

Solid progress was made in energy saving and emission reduction. The project emission reduction, structural emission reduction and management emission reduction were comprehensively advanced, and 181 emission-reduction projects implemented. 132 construction projects not meeting the environmental protection requirements were persuaded to quit or refused to grant. 1,802 small coal-fired boilers were eliminated. The tasks of the reduction of the total emissions of major pollutants given by the provincial authorities had been completed. There were 33 new three-star-and-above "Energy-efficiency Star" enterprises in the city, with a total of 411 ones.

In 2016, new progress and new results were made in the economic and social development in Suzhou, and the "13th Five-year Plan" got off to a good start. But at the same time it should also be noted that, in the economic and social development there were still many difficulties and contradictions to face with, the new momentum of economic development was still inadequate, science and technology innovation initiative had not yet become the fresh power to promote the development, structural contradictions were more prominent, the industrial competitiveness on the whole was not strong, the task of deepening the reform was very difficult, efforts needed to be further intensified in the people's livelihood matters, and efforts should be continuously made in the ecological environment construction tasks. In the new year, the whole city should take the five development concepts as the lead, put the improvement of the development quality and efficiency as the center, put the supply-side structural reform as the main line, gather force on innovation in order to make breakthroughs, focus on enriching the people to see practical results, make great efforts to push the economic and social development in Suzhou to a new level, strive to be a good vanguard in building a "strong, rich, beautiful and high" new Jiangsu, and make excellent achievements for the successful convening of the 19th national congress of the Communist Party of China.

一、综　合

CHAPTER 1
GENERAL SURVEY

1 综　合 GENERAL SURVEY

从统计数字看2016年的苏州

SUZHOU IN STATISTICS OF 2016

苏州在全国的地位 POSITION OF SUZHOU IN THE COUNTRY

地区生产总值	Gross Domestic Product	居全国第 7 位	7th Place in the Country
一般公共预算收入	General Public Budget Revenue	居全国第 6 位	6th Place in the Country
进出口总额	Total Imports and Exports	居全国第 4 位	4th Place in the Country

苏州在全省的地位 POSITION OF SUZHOU IN JIANGSU PROVINCE

地区生产总值	Gross Domestic Product	居全省第 1 位	First Place in Jiangsu
财政收入	Financial Revenue	居全省第 1 位	First Place in Jiangsu
进出口总额	Total Imports and Exports	居全省第 1 位	First Place in Jiangsu

苏州的人口 POPULATION OF SUZHOU

年末户籍总人口	Year-end Registered Population	678.20	万人	10 000 persons
年末户籍总户数	Year-end Registered Households	222.44	万户	10 000 households
户籍人口密度	Density of Registered Population	783	人/平方公里	person/sq.km
年末常住人口	Year-end Permanent Population	1 064.74	万人	10 000 persons
常住人口密度	Density of Permanent Population	1 230	人/平方公里	person/sq.km

苏州的经济发展 ECONOMIC DEVELOPMENT OF SUZHOU

		2016年	1979-2016年平均增长(%) Average Growth Rate
地区生产总值　(亿元)	Gross Domestic Product　(100 million yuan)	15 475.09	13.5
# 第三产业	Tertiary Industry	7 975.82	15.0
财政收入	Financial Revenue	3 154.79	17.3
工业总产值	Gross Industrial Output Value	35 766.97	20.2
全社会固定资产投资	Total Value of Investment in Fixed Assets	5 648.49	24.4
社会消费品零售总额	Total Retail Sales of Consumer Goods	4 936.79	17.9
进出口总额　(亿美元)	Total Exports and Imports　(USD 100 million)	2 737.58	–
实际使用外资	Actual Utilization of Foreign Capital	60.03	–

苏州的人均水平
PER CAPITA LEVEL OF SUZHOU

地区生产总值	Gross Domestic Product	145 556	元	yuan
社会消费品零售总额	Total Retail Sales of Consumer Goods	46 435		
一般公共预算收入	General Public Budget Revenue	16 272		
城镇非私营单位在岗职工平均工资	Average Wage of Staff and Works	79 870		
全体常住居民可支配收入	Disposable Income of All the Residents	46 595		
城镇常住居民可支配收入	Disposable Income of Urban Residents	54 341		
农村常住居民可支配收入	Disposable Income of Rural Residents	27 691		
市区拥有道路面积	Per Capita Area of Roads of Urban Residents	34.21	平方米	sp. m
每万人拥有医生数	Number of Doctors Serving Per 10000 Persons	25.98	人	person

苏州的一天
ONE DAY IN SUZHOU

地区生产总值	Gross Domestic Product	423 975	万元	10 000 yuan
一般公共预算收入	General Public Budget Revenue	47 398		
工业总产值	Gross Industrial Output Value	979 917		
全社会固定资产投资额	Total Investment in Fixed Assets	154 753		
社会消费品零售总额	Total Retail Sales of Consumer Goods	135 254		
进出口总额	Total Imports and Exports	75 002	万美元	USD 10 000
#出　口	Exports	44 915		
实际使用外资	Actual Utilization of Foreign Capital	1 645		

行政区划及自然概况

行政区划

苏州简称苏。下辖4个县级市：常熟市，张家港市，昆山市，太仓市；6个区：姑苏区，吴中区，相城区，高新区、虎丘区，工业园区和吴江区。2016年末, 全市共有镇55个、街道41个、行政村1034个、居委会1126个。

位　置

苏州位于长江三角洲中部，在北纬30度47分至32度零2分，东经119度55分至121度20分之间，东邻上海，南连浙江省嘉兴、湖州两市，西傍太湖，与无锡相接，北枕长江。

苏州地理位置优越。京沪高速铁路、沪宁铁路、沪宁和沿江高速公路贯穿东西，京杭大运河和常台高速公路连接南北，境内河港密布，公路四通八达。横卧北侧的长江是重要水运干道。位于长江下游南岸的苏州港是国家一类口岸。

地　势

苏州地处太湖为中心的浅碟形平原的底部，地形以平原为主，全市地势低平，一般高程为海拔3.5至5米。东南部地势低洼，最低点低洼地在海拔2米以下。西南部多小山丘，穹窿山主峰"箬帽峰"，海拔341.7米，有"吴中之巅"之称。

面　积

苏州全市总面积8657.32平方公里。河流、湖泊、滩涂面积占全市土地面积的36.6%。2016年末市区建成区面积为461.65平方公里。

河　流

苏州是著名的江南水乡，拥有各级河道2万多条，大小湖泊300多个，著名的有太湖、阳澄湖、长江、京杭运河等。

气　候

苏州属亚热带湿润性季风海洋性气候，四季分明，气候温和，雨量充沛。2016年平均气温16.9摄氏度，降水量1745.5毫米。

ADMINISTRATIVE DIVISIONS & NATURAL CONDITIONS

Administrative Divisions

Suzhou is called Su in short. It includes four county-level cities: Changshu city, Zhangjiagang city, Kunshan city and Taicang city, and six districts: Gusu District, Wuzhong District,Xiangcheng District, New & Hi-tech, Huqiu District , Industrial Park and Wujiang District. There are 55 totally towns, 41 sub-districts, 1034 villages and 1126 neighborhood committees in Suzhou.

Location

Suzhou lies in the center of Yangtse River Delta, between 30°47′—32°02′E and 119°55′—121°20′N. It borders on Shanghai on the east, Jiaxing and Huzhou of Zhejiang on the south, Taihu Lake and Wuxi on the west and Yangtse on the north.

Suzhou enjoys strategic geographical location. Hu-Ning Railway, Hu-Ning Expressway and the riparian highway runs from east to west; Beijing-Hangzhou Grand Canal and Chang-Tai expressway connect south and north. Suzhou abounds in waterways and highways. Yangtse Rive that lies on the north of the city is a key waterway artery. Suzhou Port on the south bank of the lower reaches of Yangtse is state first-class port.

Typography

Suzhou, at the bottom of a shallow saucer-shaped plain with Lake Tai at its center, is low and even. Average height is 3.5m-5m above sea level. The southeast part is relatively lower, with the lowest point 2m below sea level. The southwest is a hilly area, with the highest point, the peak of Qionglong Hill, 341.7m above sea level.

Area

The total area of Suzhou is 8657.32 sq.km, the river, lake, beach area accounted for 36.6% of the city's land area. At the end of 2016, Built-up Urban Area covers 461.65 sq.km.

Rivers & Lakes

Suzhou is a famous water country region to the south of Yangtse River. It has over 20 000 rivers and over 300 lakes of various size. Famous among them are Taihu Lake, Yangcheng Lake, Yangtse River & Beijing-Hongzhou Canal, etc.

Climate

Suzhou's climate belongs to monsoon of subtropical moist marine climate zone, with distinct four seasons, Suzhou has a mild climate with plenty rainfall. Average temperature of the year is 16.9℃ and annual precipitation is 1745.5S millimeter in 2016.

表1-1

行政区划和土地面积(2016年末)
ADMINISTRATIVE DIVISION AND LAND AREA (END OF 2016)

单位：个　(unit)

地　区	Region	镇 Town	村 Village	街　道 Subdistrict	居委会 Neighborhood Committee	土地面积(平方公里) Area of Land (sq.km)
全　市	**Whole Municipality**	**55**	**1 034**	**41**	**1 126**	**8 657.32**
市　区	**Urban Area**	**22**	**442**	**38**	**609**	**4 652.84**
姑苏区	Gusu District	–	9	17	167	83.42
吴中区	Wuzhong District	7	84	6	105	2 231.46
相城区	Xiangcheng District	4	68	7	76	489.96
高新区、虎丘区	New & Hi-tech Zone, Huqiu District	3	32	3	57	332.37
工业园区	Industrial Park	–	–	4	138	278.19
吴江区	Wujiang District	8	249	1	66	1 237.44
县级市	**Cities at County Level**	**33**	**592**	**3**	**517**	**4 004.48**
常　熟	Changshu	9	215	2	110	1 276.32
张家港	Zhangjiagang	8	153	–	135	986.73
昆　山	Kunshan	10	151	–	195	931.51
太　仓	Taicang	6	73	1	77	809.93

注：全市土地面积根据第二次全国土地调查结果调整，土地面积中含太湖、阳澄湖、淀山湖等大型湖泊水域面积。河流、湖泊、滩涂面积占全市土地面积的36.6%。

Note:The land area of the whole municipality is adjusted according to the result of the second national land survey, includes water area of Taihu Lake,Yangcheng Lake, Dianshan Lake and so on. The river, lake, beach area accounted for 36.6% of the city's land area.

表1-2

市区分月气象情况 (2016年)
MONTHLY CLIMATE CONDITIONS OF URBAN AREA (2016)

月 份	Month	平均气温 (摄氏度) Average Temperature (℃)	降水量 (毫米) Precipitation (mm)	日照时数 (小时) Sunshine Hours (hours)	平均相对湿度 (%) Average Relative Humidity (%)	平均风力 (米/秒) Average Wind Force (m/second)
全 年	**Annual Total**	**17.6**	**1 975.7**	**1 490.5**	**75**	**2.7**
1月	Jan.	4.2	71.9	80.1	73	2.7
2月	Feb.	7.2	31.4	157.9	64	2.9
3月	Mar.	11.4	46.3	121.3	67	3.0
4月	Apr.	17.4	186.9	126.3	74	3.0
5月	May	20.8	192.5	122.3	76	3.0
6月	Jun.	24.4	400.9	87.0	83	2.6
7月	Jul.	30.1	283.6	176.5	75	2.7
8月	Aug.	29.9	31.9	238.7	69	3.0
9月	Sept.	24.7	260.0	130.3	76	2.5
10月	Oct.	19.9	282.9	42.6	83	2.5
11月	Nov.	12.8	131.8	87.0	80	2.3
12月	Dec.	8.9	55.6	120.5	74	2.4

注:本表数据不含吴江区。 Note: The data in this table does not include Wujiang.

表1-3

分地区气象、水文情况 (2016年)
CLIMATE AND HYDROLOGIC CONDITIONS BY REGION (2016)

地 区	Region	年平均气温(摄氏度) Annual Average Temperature (℃)	年极端最高气温(摄氏度) Highest Temperature of the Year (℃)	年极端最低气温(摄氏度) Lowest Temperature of the Year (℃)	年降水量(毫米) Annual Precipitation (mm)	年降水日(天) Raining Days of the Year (day)	年平均气压(百帕) Annual Average Pressure (hPa)
市 区	Urban Area	17.6	39.4	-8.3	1 975.7	143	1 015.5
吴江区	Wujiang District	17.8	39.5	-7.7	1 728.6	147	1 015.8
常 熟	Changshu	17.4	38.8	-8.4	1 823.7	145	1 016.2
张家港	Zhangjiagang	17.1	39.3	-9.0	1 894.5	150	1 015.2
昆 山	Kunshan	17.6	39.8	-8.0	1 510.3	141	1 016.1
太 仓	Taicang	17.1	38.8	-8.0	1 674.7	140	1 015.9

表1-3 续表 Continued

地 区	Region	年无霜期(天) Annual Frost-free Period (day)	年日照时间(小时) Annual Sunshine Hours (hours)	年平均相对湿度(%) Annual Average Relative Humidity (%)	年平均风力(米/秒) Annual Average Wind-force (meter /second)	最高水位(米) Highest Water Level (m)	最低水位(米) Lowest Water Level (m)
市 区	Urban Area	257	1 490.5	75	2.7	4.82	2.99
吴江区	Wujiang District	246	1 790.5	76	1.9	4.18	2.90
常 熟	Changshu	257	1 772.2	77	2.0	3.99	3.06
张家港	Zhangjiagang	242	1 770.5	77	2.1	4.35	3.32
昆 山	Kunshan	242	1 592.7	75	2.0	3.52	2.59
太 仓	Taicang	255	1 935.6	84	2.4	3.76	2.87

注:本表市区数据不含吴江区。 Note: The data in this table does not include Wujiang.

表1-4

重要年份国民经济主要指标

指　　标		Item		1952年	1978年
人　口		**Population**			
年末户籍总人口	(万人)	Year-end Population	(10 000 persons)	352.32	506.27
年末户籍总户数	(万户)	Total Number of Households (year–end)	(10 000 households)	88.33	137.42
劳动力		**Labor Force**			
年末从业人员	(万人)	Employed Persons (year-end)	(10 000 persons)	158.87	301.15
地区生产总值	(亿元)	**Gross Domestic Product**	(100 million yuan)	4.38	31.95
# 第三产业		Tertiary Industry		1.29	5.18
农　业		**Agriculture**			
1.农林牧渔业总产值		Gross Output Value of Farming, Forestry, Animal Husbandry and Fishery			18.75
2.主要农产品产量		Output of Major Farm Products			
粮　食	(万吨)	Grain	(10 000 tons)	133.41	294.26
油　料		Oil-bearing Crops		2.50	9.13
蚕　茧	(吨)	Silkworm Cocoons	(ton)	3 047	3 325
水产品	(万吨)	Aquatic Products	(10 000 tons)	2.15	8.22
猪出栏数	(万头)	Slaughtered Fattened Hogs	(10 000 heads)	22.16	185.66
猪年末存栏数		Hogs in Stock at Year–end		37.98	264.31
工　业		**Industry**			
1.工业总产值	(亿元)	Gross Industrial Output Value	(100 million yuan)		48.51
# 规模以上工业		Gross Industrial Output Value Above Designated Size			
2.规模以上工业企业主要经济指标		The main index of Above Designated Size			
资产总计		Total Assets			
负债合计		Total Liabilities			
主营业务收入		Major Business Revenue			
利税总额		Total Taxes and Profits			
利润总额		Total Profits			
运输邮电		**Transportation and Postal**			
1.全社会公路水运货运量	(万吨)	Total Freight Traffic of Highways and Waterways	(10 000 tons)	209	2 195
2.全社会公路水运客运量	(万人次)	Total Passenger Traffic of Highways and Waterways	(10 000 person-times)	383	3 296
3.邮电业务总收入	(万元)	Postal and Telecommunications Business Volume	(10 000 yuan)	402	1 774
4.函　件(邮政系统)	(万件)	Letters Delivered (post system)	(10 000 pcs)	781	1 732
5.报刊杂志累计数	(万份)	Number of Newspapers and Magazines Circulation	(10 000 copies)	941	7 234

注：1. 公路客运量自2013年起不包括公交车和出租车的运输量；公路货运量自2013年起不包含农用车和拖拉机的运输量。
2. 2010年起，从业人员计算口径调整。
3. 2013年起，邮政业务总收入中包含规模以上快递公司快递业务收入。

MAJOR NATIONAL ECONOMICAL INDICATORS OF IMPORTANT YEARS

1980年	1990年	2000年	2010年	2012年	2013年	2014年	2015年	2016年
518.62	561.02	578.17	637.66	647.81	653.84	661.08	667.01	678.20
142.33	173.36	198.18	211.79	214.04	215.57	217.46	219.23	222.44
317.17	346.74	313.89	687.50	694.30	695.20	693.40	691.40	691.30
40.68	202.14	1 540.68	9 228.91	12 011.65	13 015.70	13 760.89	14 504.07	15 475.09
6.80	43.90	579.62	3 834.30	5 332.87	6 064.60	6 663.93	7 243.24	7 975.82
11.42	58.12	169.30	271.29	337.72	369.82	392.49	415.17	424.67
254.31	283.50	193.95	114.43	116.46	113.12	110.46	108.22	97.68
8.16	14.01	12.61	3.45	2.59	2.42	2.04	1.57	1.34
4 784	9 785	7 291	638	495	396	357	295	237
8.71	21.73	34.51	27.70	28.84	27.70	26.70	26.21	25.49
310.14	193.54	198.50	117.70	113.44	106.15	103.46	94.89	84.46
250.34	154.62	104.75	83.51	84.97	85.98	76.69	66.44	60.34
73.71	563.73	3 620.74	28 483.69	34 528.10	35 685.21	35 772.99	35 717.59	35 766.97
		2 396.51	24 651.67	28 745.54	30 276.29	30 322.17	30 249.25	30 713.99
		2 346.98	19 351.14	23 331.48	25 128.83	26 108.97	26 895.74	28 356.50
		1 422.37	11 143.67	13 474.80	14 323.37	14 400.82	14 268.20	14 838.02
		2 245.72	24 577.51	28 998.80	30 224.92	30 397.27	29 768.65	30 380.18
		184.09	1 988.28	1 816.35	1 937.53	2 074.08	2 075.15	2 388.24
		97.16	1 507.06	1 251.57	1 350.12	1 460.13	1 529.04	1 772.74
2 712	3 211	7 816	13 417	17 325	11 786	12 953	13 005	13 508
4 813	6 764	18 559	56 475	68 998	39 584	39 958	34 645	32 130
2 300	12 818	441 910	1 726 867	2 076 637	2 665 849	2 752 456	2 937 920	3 267 824
2 245	3 051	5 476	27 841	29 167	27 060	25 449	23 258	13 814
9 977	16 246	30 461	30 438	32 157	31 133	30 832	29 367	27 128

Note: 1.The highway passenger transport volume in 2013 did not include that of buses and taxis; The highway freight transport volume in 2013 did not include that of agricultural vehicles and tractors.

2.In 2010,employed person use the new caliber.

3.In 2013 the total postal revenues began to include the business income of above-scale express courier companies.

表1-4 续表 1

指　标	Item	1952年	1978年
国内贸易	**Domestic Trade**		
社会消费品零售总额　(亿元)	Total Retail Sales of Consumer Goods (100 million yuan)	3.12	9.47
对外经济和国际旅游	**Foreign Trade Economy and International Tourism**		
1.进出口总额　(亿美元)	Total Exports and Imports (USD 100 million)	–	–
出口总额	Exports	–	–
进口总额	Imports	–	–
2.使用外资	Utilization of Foreign Capital		
新设外资项目数　(个)	Number of Projects of Signed Contracts (unit)	–	–
新增注册外资金额　(亿美元)	Newly Added Value of Foreign Capital Signed (USD 100 million)	–	–
实际使用外资	Amount of Foreign Capital Actually Used	–	–
# 第三产业	Tertiary Industry	–	–
3.国际旅游	International Tourism		
接待境外游客　(万人次)	Number of Foreign Tourists (10 000 person-times)	–	–
电　力	**Electricity**		
全社会用电量　(亿千瓦时)	Electricity Consumption of the Whole Society (100 million kwh)	0.45	13.88
# 工业用电量	Industrial Consumption of Electricity		
固定资产投资	**Investment in Fixed Assets**		
全社会固定资产投资　(亿元)	Total Value of Investment in Fixed Assets (100 million yuan)		1.40
# 房地产开发投资	Value of Investment in Real Estate Development		
财　政	**Public Finance**		
财政收入　(亿元)	Financial Revenue (100 million yuan)	1.13	8.28
# 一般公共预算收入	General Public Budget Revenue		
财政支出	Financial Expenditures	0.10	1.35
# 一般公共预算支出	General Public Budget Expenditure		

注：1.2013年起接待境外旅游者人数为公安登记统计口径。
2.2014年起，财政收入不含社保基金收入、财政支出不含社保基金支出。

Continued 1

1980年	1990年	2000年	2010年	2012年	2013年	2014年	2015年	2016年
15.67	72.15	428.17	2 402.02	3 240.97	3 662.24	4 099.83	4 461.62	4 936.79
–	1.88	200.70	2 740.76	3 056.92	3 093.48	3 113.06	3 053.50	2 737.58
–	1.55	104.81	1 531.08	1 746.89	1 757.06	1 811.78	1 814.59	1 639.41
–	0.33	95.89	1 209.68	1 310.03	1 336.41	1 301.28	1 238.90	1 098.18
–	164	943	1 537	1 189	936	905	860	784
–	1.44	46.78	169.20	151.68	100.11	85.79	89.39	57.25
–	0.70	28.83	85.35	91.65	86.98	81.20	70.19	60.03
–	–	2.15	23.23	30.24	34.18	30.54	26.74	20.79
8.37	27.84	71.41	265.15	321.87	188.95	190.24	197.20	209.98
20.53	50.77	190.04	1 024.10	1 189.93	1 263.21	1 268.12	1 311.72	1 382.58
	38.14	153.17	855.25	982.66	1 030.61	1 044.14	1 074.20	1 116.30
2.87	55.37	516.43	3 617.82	5 266.49	6 001.94	6 230.67	6 124.43	5 648.49
	1.65	61.18	935.80	1 263.36	1 475.77	1 764.44	1 864.95	2 163.24
9.46	21.47	158.27	1 950.63	2 561.67	2 788.91	2 688.86	2 936.55	3 154.79
		80.39	900.55	1 204.33	1 331.03	1 443.82	1 560.76	1 730.04
1.67	7.99	79.91	1 095.75	1 479.59	1 593.89	1 366.01	1 592.66	1 700.68
		78.11	825.67	1 113.47	1 212.68	1 304.83	1 527.17	1 617.11

Note: 1.In 2013 the number of foreign tourists began to be the public security registration statistics caliber.
2.Starting from 2014, the financial revenue does not contain the social security fund income.

表1-4 续表 2

指 标	Item	1952年	1978年
金 融	**Finance**		
金融机构人民币存款余额(亿元)	Deposit Balance of Financial Institutions (100 million yuan)	0.26	7.37
金融机构人民币贷款余额	Loans Balance of Financial Institutions	0.11	15.45
物价指数(以上年价格为100)	**Price Indices** (The Price of Preceding Year is Taken as 100)		
市区居民消费价格总指数	General Consumer Price Index of Urban Residents		
市区商品零售价格总指数	General Retail Price Index of Urban Area		
人民生活	**People's Livelihood**		
城镇非私营单位在岗职工平均工资 (元)	Average Wages of Urban Non-private Units (yuan)	455	514
农村居民人均可支配收入	Per Capita Net Income of Rural Residents		204
农村居民人均消费支出	Per Capita Living Expenditure of Rural Residents		212
城镇居民人均可支配收入	Per Capita Disposable Income of Urban Households		
城镇居民人均消费支出	Per Capita Living Expenditure of Urban Residents		
住户存款余额 (亿元)	Amount of Household Deposits (100 million yuan)		1.77
教 育	**Education**		
1.专任教师数 (人)	Number of Full-time Teachers (person)	10 573	40 127
2.在校学生数 (万人)	Students Enrollment (10 000 persons)	33.93	96.81
# 普通高等学校 (人)	Institutions of Higher Education (person)	2 349	6 502
中等职业教育学校	Secondary Vocational Education Schools		
技工学校	Skilled Workers' Schools		
普通中学 (万人)	Regular Secondary Schools (10 000 persons)	3.40	32.76
小 学	Primary Schools	29.42	62.96
3.毕业生数	Graduates	2.20	26.27
卫 生	**Health Care**		
卫生机构数 (所)	Number of Health Institutions (unit)	238	971
# 医院、卫生院	Hospitals	16	204
床位数 (张)	Number of Beds (bed)	1 372	14 470
# 医院、卫生院	Hospitals		13 209
卫生技术人员 (人)	Number of Medical Personnel (person)	3 256	12 902
# 医 生	Doctors	2 363	5 434

注：2014年起，教育相关指标包含外来工子弟学校数据，城乡居民人民币储蓄存款余额口径调整为住户存款口径。2013年起在岗职工平均工资调整为城镇非私营单位口径。

Continued 2

1980年	1990年	2000年	2010年	2012年	2013年	2014年	2015年	2016年
15.68	132.20	1 477.01	13 570.35	17 663.50	20 037.58	21 755.17	23 659.10	25 864.26
21.19	134.10	970.60	10 133.15	13 626.86	15 495.24	17 247.94	19 200.10	21 924.44
	103.9	99.9	103.4	102.7	102.1	102.1	101.6	102.7
104.2	103.2	98.5	103.1	101.9	101.2	101.7	100.4	100.5
687	2 450	11 778	45 566	57 622	61 416	66 956	72 291	79 870
271	1 664	5 462	14 657	19 396	21 578	23 560	25 580	27 691
296	1 415	4 073	10 397	14 381	16 251	15 390	16 761	18 820
	2 150	9 274	29 219	37 531	41 143	46 677	50 390	54 341
	1 805	7 027	17 879	23 092	25 197	28 973	31 136	33 305
3.64	73.33	803.70	4 655.56	5 787.75	6 408.32	7 022.63	7 358.04	7 913.85
35 978	40 145	47 908	65 174	68 404	69 739	76 340	79 114	82 015
81.28	71.13	87.69	95.85	98.91	102.70	117.98	124.37	131.04
8 819	16 280	47 701	187 829	192 206	201 926	209 479	214 816	219 347
5 231	25 293	60 185	74 828	64 706	57 936	57 606	59 227	61 202
1 757	5 866	12 346	32 158	27 244	25 069	24 173	23 743	23 593
22.86	21.73	30.47	27.25	26.18	26.69	27.96	29.25	30.98
56.79	44.56	44.84	38.84	44.04	47.24	60.63	65.07	69.37
18.44	14.15	19.26	24.19	22.42	22.63	22.97	25.03	26.86
1 125	1 537	1 319	2 675	2 992	3 007	3 063	3 121	3 175
207	207	197	216	251	263	263	271	283
13 720	18 424	19 504	39 204	46 070	51 663	55 218	59 304	63 241
12 385	16 223	17 582	36 839	43 772	49 341	52 887	56 894	60 847
14 514	22 253	24 881	46 507	57 168	61 051	64 281	68 179	72 166
6 316	10 895	11 594	18 156	23 194	24 296	25 352	26 197	27 667

Note: Starting from 2014, the relevant indicators of education include data from schools for children of migrant workers.Amount of saving deposits in urban and rural areas was adjusted to the scope of the household deposits caliber. In 2013 the average wages of the workers in the post were adjusted to the scope of the urban non-private units caliber.

表1-5

重要年份国民经济主要指标发展速度

指　标	Item	2016年为	
		1952年	1978年
人　口	**Population**		
年末户籍总人口	Year-end Population	192.5	134.0
年末户籍总户数	Total Number of Households (year–end)	251.8	161.9
劳动力	**Labor Force**		
年末从业人员	Employed Persons (year–end)	350.7	185.0
地区生产总值	**Gross Domestic Product**	942.3倍	121.9倍
# 第三产业	Tertiary Industry		201.3倍
农　业	**Agriculture**		
1.农林牧渔业总产值	Gross Output Value of Farming, Forestry, Animal Husbandry and Fishery		14.4倍
2.主要农产品产量	Output of Major Farm Products		
粮　食	Grain	73.2	33.2
油　料	Oil–bearing Crops	53.6	14.7
蚕　茧	Silkworm Cocoons	7.8	7.1
水产品	Aquatic Products	11.9倍	310.1
猪出栏数	Slaughtered Fattened Hogs	381.1	45.5
猪年末存栏数	Hogs in Stock at Year–end	158.9	22.8
工　业	**Industry**		
1.工业总产值	Gross Industrial Output Value		1 089.9倍
# 规模以上	Gross Industrial Output Value Above Designated Size		
2.规模以上工业企业主要经济指标	The main index of Above Designated Size		
资产总计	Total Assets		
负债合计	Total Liabilities		
主营业务收入	Major Business Revenue		
利税总额	Total Taxes and Profits		
利润总额	Total Profits		
运输邮电	**Transportation and Postal**		
1.全社会公路水运货运量	Total Freight Traffic of Highways and Waterways	121.0倍	11.5倍
2.全社会公路水运客运量	Total Passenger Traffic of Highways and Waterways	189.6倍	22.0倍
3.邮电业务总收入	Postal and Telecommunications Business Volume	7 198.7倍	1 631.3倍
4.函　件	Letters Delivered	17.7倍	797.6
5.报刊杂志累计数	Number of Newspapers and Magazines Circulation	28.8倍	375.0

GROWTH RATES OF MAJOR NATIONAL ECONOMICAL INDICATORS OF IMPORTANT YEARS

以下各年的% % of the Following Years								1979-2016年 平均增长% Average Growth Rate %
1980年	1990年	2000年	2010年	2012年	2013年	2014年	2015年	
130.8	120.9	117.3	106.4	104.7	103.7	102.6	101.7	0.8
156.3	128.3	112.2	105.0	103.9	103.2	102.3	101.5	1.3
175.7	160.7	177.5	100.6	99.6	99.5	99.7	100.0	1.6
102.4倍	30.5倍	669.0	169.1	137.2	125.2	115.6	107.5	13.5
164.7倍	50.1倍	803.6	195.0	152.2	135.0	121.5	109.7	15.0
23.7倍	464.6	159.5	117.0	108.1	105.2	102.0	98.6	7.3
38.4	34.5	50.4	85.4	83.9	86.4	88.4	90.3	-2.9
16.4	9.6	10.6	38.9	51.8	55.4	65.7	85.2	-4.9
5.0	2.4	3.3	37.1	47.9	59.8	66.4	80.3	-6.7
292.7	117.3	73.9	92.0	88.4	92.0	95.5	97.3	3.0
27.2	43.6	42.5	71.8	74.5	79.6	81.6	89.0	-2.1
24.1	39.0	57.6	72.3	71.0	70.2	78.7	90.8	-3.8
717.2倍	93.8倍	981.9	125.6	103.6	100.2	100.0	100.1	20.2
		10.7倍	131.0	105.8	101.6	101.3	101.1	
		687.6	148.2	123.3	116.0	110.3	106.1	
		590.2	135.4	113.1	108.2	105.3	104.4	
		10.0倍	126.1	104.5	101.4	100.2	101.7	
		924.7	130.5	133.9	123.7	115.9	111.8	
		13.0倍	122.6	139.0	127.8	119.0	114.1	
932.1	787.3	323.4	158.1	122.4	114.6	104.3	103.9	6.6
15.1倍	10.7倍	391.3	103.2	84.5	81.2	80.4	92.7	8.5
1 258.2倍	225.8倍	654.9	167.6	139.4	123.9	118.7	111.2	21.5
615.3	452.8	252.3	49.6	47.4	51.0	54.3	59.4	5.6
271.9	167.0	89.1	89.1	84.4	87.1	88.0	92.4	3.5

表1-5 续表 1

指 标	Item	2016年为	
		1952年	1978年
国内贸易	**Domestic Trade**		
社会消费品零售总额	Total Retail Sales of Consumer Goods	1 584.9倍	522.1倍
对外经济和国际旅游	**Foreign Trade Economy and International Tourism**		
1.进出口总额	Total Exports and Imports	–	–
出口总额	Exports	–	–
进口总额	Imports	–	–
2.使用外资	Utilization of Foreign Capital		
新设外资项目数	Number of Projects of Signed Contracts	–	–
新增注册外资金额	Newly Added Value of Foreign Capital Signed	–	–
实际使用外资	Amount of Foreign Capital Actually Used	–	–
# 第三产业	Tertiary Industry	–	–
3.国际旅游	International Tourism		
接待境外旅游者人数	Number of Foreign Tourists	–	–
电 力	**Electricity**		
全社会用电量	Electricity Consumption of the Whole Society	3 072.4倍	99.6倍
# 工业用电量	Industrial Consumption of Electricity		
固定资产投资	**Investment in Fixed Assets**		
全社会固定资产投资	Total Value of Investment in Fixed Assets		4 034.6倍
# 房地产开发投资	Value of Investment in Real Estate Development		
财 政	**Public Finance**		
财政收入	Financial Revenue	3 148.3倍	429.7倍
# 一般公共预算收入	General Public Budget Revenue		
财政支出	Financial Expenditures	2.1万倍	1 571.0倍
# 一般公共预算支出	General Public Budget Expenditure		

Continued 1

以下各年的% % of the Following Years								1979-2016年平均增长% Average Growth Rate %
1980年	1990年	2000年	2010年	2012年	2013年	2014年	2015年	
315.6倍	68.5倍	11.5倍	205.9	152.6	135.0	120.6	110.7	17.9
–	1 456.2倍	13.6倍	99.9	89.6	88.5	87.9	89.7	
–	1 057.7倍	15.6倍	107.1	93.8	93.3	90.5	90.3	
–	3 327.8倍	11.5倍	90.8	83.8	82.2	84.4	88.6	
–	478.0	83.1	51.0	65.9	83.8	86.6	91.2	
–	39.8倍	122.4	33.8	37.7	57.2	66.7	64.0	
–	196.2倍	473.2	70.3	65.5	69.0	73.9	85.5	
–	–	966.9	89.5	68.7	60.8	68.1	77.7	
39.7倍	11.9倍	464.9	125.2	103.1	111.1	110.4	106.5	
67.3倍	27.2倍	727.5	135.0	116.2	109.4	109.0	105.4	12.9
	29.3倍	728.8	130.5	113.6	108.3	106.9	103.9	
1 968.1倍	102.0倍	10.9倍	156.1	107.3	94.1	90.7	92.2	24.4
	1 311.1倍	35.4倍	231.2	171.2	146.6	122.6	116.0	
376.1倍	165.7倍	22.5倍	182.4	138.9	127.6	117.3	107.4	17.3
		21.5倍	192.1	143.7	130.0	119.8	110.8	
1 269.9倍	265.4倍	26.5倍	193.5	143.3	133.1	124.5	106.8	21.4
		20.7倍	195.9	145.2	133.3	123.9	105.9	

表1-5 续表 2

指 标	Item	2016年为	
		1952年	1978年
金 融	**Finance**		
金融机构人民币存款余额	Deposit Balance of Financial Institutions	9.7万倍	3 456.7倍
金融机构人民币贷款余额	Loans Balance of Financial Institutions	19.9万倍	1 419.1倍
物价指数	**Price Indices**		
市区居民消费价格总指数	General Consumer Price Index of Urban Residents		
市区商品零售价格总指数	General Retail Price Index of Urban Area		527.3
人民生活	**People's Livelihood**		
城镇非私营单位在岗职工平均工资	Average Wages of Urban Non-private Units	180.8倍	160.1倍
农村居民人均可支配收入	Per Capita Net Income of Rural Residents		136.8倍
农村居民人均消费支出	Per Capita Living Expenditure of Rural Residents		103.7倍
城镇居民人均可支配收入	Per Capita Disposable Income of Urban Households		
城镇居民人均消费支出	Per Capita Living Expenditure of Urban Residents		
住户存款余额	Amount of Household Deposits		4 299.7倍
教 育	**Education**		
1.专任教师数	Number of Full-time Teachers	736.6	194.1
2.在校学生数	Students Enrollment	354.1	124.1
# 普通高等学校	Institutions of Higher Education	93.4倍	33.7倍
中等职业教育学校	Secondary Vocational Education Schools		22.3倍
技工学校	Skilled Workers' Schools		20.0倍
普通中学	Regular Secondary Schools	894.2	92.8
小 学	Primary Schools	202.4	94.6
3.毕业生数	Graduates	11.6倍	97.0
卫 生	**Health Care**		
卫生机构数	Number of Health Institutions	13.3倍	327.0
# 医院、卫生院	Hospitals	17.7倍	138.7
床位数	Number of Beds	46.1倍	437.0
# 医院、卫生院	Hospitals		460.6
卫生技术人员	Number of Medical Personnel	22.2倍	559.3
# 医 生	Doctors	11.7倍	509.1

Continued 2

以下各年的%	% of the Following Years							1979-2016年平均增长% Average Growth Rate %
1980年	1990年	2000年	2010年	2012年	2013年	2014年	2015年	
1 624.7倍	192.7倍	17.2倍	187.7	144.2	127.1	118.9	109.3	23.9
1 034.7倍	163.5倍	22.6倍	216.4	160.9	141.5	127.1	114.2	21.0
	342.6	146.2	117.4	108.7	106.5	104.4	102.7	
495.6	232.4	121.8	110.9	104.0	102.7	101.0	100.5	
119.8倍	33.6倍	698.6	180.6	142.8	130.0	119.3	110.5	14.3
102.9倍	16.8倍	510.8	190.3	143.8	129.3	117.5	108.3	13.8
74.3倍	15.5倍	539.6	211.4	152.8	135.2	122.3	112.3	13.0
	26.4倍	612.2	178.0	138.6	126.4	116.4	107.8	
	17.3倍	443.1	174.2	134.8	123.6	115.0	107.0	
2 090.8倍	103.8倍	946.9	163.5	131.5	118.8	117.2	107.6	24.6
216.5	194.0	162.6	119.5	113.9	111.7	107.4	103.7	1.8
147.8	168.9	137.0	125.3	121.5	117.0	111.1	105.4	0.6
24.9倍	13.5倍	459.8	116.8	114.1	108.6	104.7	102.1	9.7
11.7倍	242.0	101.7	81.8	94.6	105.6	106.2	103.3	8.5
13.4倍	402.2	191.1	73.4	86.6	94.1	97.6	99.4	8.2
133.0	139.9	99.8	111.6	116.1	113.9	110.8	105.9	-0.2
104.9	133.7	132.8	153.3	135.2	126.1	114.4	106.6	-0.1
138.1	180.0	132.3	105.3	113.6	112.6	116.9	107.3	-0.1
282.2	206.6	240.7	118.7	106.1	105.6	103.7	101.7	3.2
136.7	136.7	143.7	131.0	112.7	107.6	107.6	104.4	0.9
460.9	343.3	324.2	161.3	137.3	122.4	114.5	106.6	4.0
491.3	375.1	346.1	165.2	139.0	123.3	115.1	106.9	4.1
497.2	324.3	290.0	155.2	126.2	118.2	112.3	105.8	4.6
438.0	253.9	238.6	152.4	119.3	113.9	109.1	105.6	4.4

表1-6

部分年份国民经济主要比例关系
MAJOR PROPORTIONS IN NATIONAL ECONOMY OF PARTIAL YEARS

单位：% (%)

指　　标	Item	2012年	2013年	2014年	2015年	2016年
一、常住人口城乡比例	**Ratio of Urban Population and Rural Population in Total Resident Population by Type of Industry**					
城镇人口	Urban Population	72.3	73.2	74.0	74.9	75.5
乡村人口	Rural Population	27.7	26.8	26.0	25.1	24.5
二、常住人口从业人员三次产业比例	**Ratio of Total Resident Population by Type of Industry**					
第一产业	Primary Industry	3.7	3.6	3.5	3.4	3.4
第二产业	Secondary Industry	61.5	61.3	60.5	60.0	59.6
第三产业	Tertiary Industry	34.8	35.1	36.0	36.6	37.0
三、地区生产总值中三次产业比例	**Ratio of GDP by Type of Industry**					
第一产业	Primary Industry	1.5	1.5	1.5	1.5	1.5
第二产业	Secondary Industry	54.1	51.9	50.1	48.6	47.0
第三产业	Tertiary Industry	44.4	46.6	48.4	49.9	51.5
四、农林牧渔业总产值中各业比例	**Ratio in Total Output of Farming, Forestry, Animal Husbandry and Fishery**					
农　业	Agriculture	40.0	40.8	41.2	41.6	42.1
林　业	Forestry	6.0	6.2	6.2	6.2	5.8
牧　业	Animal Husbandry	11.9	10.8	9.9	9.3	8.8
渔　业	Fishery	31.6	31.3	31.2	31.2	32.1
农林牧渔服务业	Farming, Forestry, Animal Husbandry, Fishery and Service Industry	10.5	10.9	11.5	11.7	11.2
五、规模以上工业轻重工业产值比例	**Ratio of Light and Heavy Industries in Total Industrial Output Above Designated Size**					
轻工业	Light Industry	25.7	26.1	25.8	25.2	25.1
重工业	Heavy Industry	74.3	73.9	74.2	74.8	74.9

表1-6 续表　Continued

单位：%　　(%)

指　　标	Item	2012年	2013年	2014年	2015年	2016年
六、建筑业总产值比例	**Ratio of Gross Output Value of Construction**					
# 建筑工程	Construction	89.9	91.2	92.0	92.1	91.8
安装工程	Installation	9.1	7.6	7.2	7.2	7.5
七、社会消费品零售总额比例	**Ratio of Total Retail Sales of Consumer Goods**					
# 批发和零售业	Wholesale and Retail Sale Trades	87.3	87.3	87.3	87.9	88.0
住宿和餐饮业	Accommodation and Catering Trade	11.8	11.8	11.7	12.1	12.0
八、进出口比例	**Ratio of Imports and Exports**					
出口额	Exports	57.1	56.8	58.2	59.4	59.9
进口额	Imports	42.9	43.2	41.8	40.6	40.1
九、实际使用外资中三次产业比例	**Ratio of Amount of Foreign Capital Actually Utilized of Foreign Funded Enterprises by Type of Industry**					
第一产业	Primary Industry	0.1	0.1	0.1	0.1	0.1
第二产业	Secondary Industry	66.9	60.6	62.3	61.8	57.0
第三产业	Tertiary Industry	33.0	39.3	37.6	38.1	42.9
十、专利授权量比例	**Ratio of Number of Patent Applications Granted**					
发　明	Inventions	4.4	5.4	9.6	16.8	24.8
实用新型	Utility Models	22.0	36.8	58.5	57.7	64.7
外　观	Designs	73.6	57.8	31.9	25.5	10.5
十一、税收占公共财政预算收入比例	**Proportion of Public Budget that Income Taxes Accounting For**	**85.0**	**85.5**	**86.2**	**85.8**	**87.0**

表1-7

部分年份国民经济主要指标日均水平
MAJOR DAILY INDICATORS OF NATIONAL ECONOMY OF PARTIAL YEARS

指 标	Item	2012年	2013年	2014年	2015年	2016年
地区生产总值 (万元)	Gross Domestic Product (10 000 yuan)	329 086	356 595	377 011	397 372	423 975
农林牧渔业总产值	Gross Output Value of Farming, Forestry, Animal Husbandry and Fishery	9 253	10 132	10 753	11 375	11 635
工业总产值	Gross Industrial Output Value	945 975	977 677	980 082	978 564	979 917
一般公共预算收入	General Public Budget Revenue	32 995	36 467	39 557	42 761	47 398
粮食产量 (吨)	Yield of Grain Crops (ton)	3 191	3 099	3 026	2 965	2 676
水产品产量	Output of Aquatic Products	790	759	732	718	698
生铁产量	Pig Iron	61 089	67 572	75 228	74 651	71 913
钢材产量	Steel Products	111 217	123 599	109 966	114 609	109 150
笔记本计算机产量 (万台)	Laptop Computer (10 000 unit)	20.49	18.72	16.78	13.41	11.11
发电量 (万千瓦时)	Power Generation (10 000 kwh)	25 023	27 273	271 22	26 963	27 943
社会消费品零售总额 (万元)	Total Retail Sales of Consumer Goods (10 000 yuan)	88 794	100 335	112 324	122 236	135 254
全社会固定资产投资额	Total Fixed Assets Investment	144 287	164 437	170 703	167 793	154 753
竣工住宅建筑面积 (平方米)	Floor Space of Residential Buildings Completed (sq.m)	48 869	40 183	39 541	40 862	40 596
进出口总额 (万美元)	Total Exports and Imports (USD 10 000)	83 751	84 753	85 289	83 658	75 002
# 出 口	Exports	47 860	48 139	49 638	49 715	44 915
市区公共汽车客运总量(万人次)	Passenger Traffic of Buses in Urban Area (10 000 person-times)	191.00	187.82	189.90	183.81	169.64
市区家庭天然气用量 (万立方米)	Household Natural Gas Consumption in Urban Area (10 000 cu.m)	39.47	53.05	50.07	63.63	66.26
汽车上牌数 (辆)	Number of Vehicles Registration (coach)	821	937	1 026	1 122	1 354
快 递 (万件)	Number of Express (10 000 pcs)		77.63	101.21	154.47	233.13
出生人数 (人)	Birth Population (person)	187	185	211	180	206
死亡人数	Death Population	123	122	121	125	117
结 婚 (对)	Marriages (couple)	171	172	159	153	132
离 婚	Divorces	46	45	54	55	59

注：此表日均指标按每年365天计算。

Note：The major daily indicators in this table are calculated by 365 days per year.

表1-8

部分年份国民经济主要指标人均水平
MAJOR PER CAPITA INDICATORS OF NATIONAL ECONOMY OF PARTIAL YEARS

指　标	Item	2012年	2013年	2014年	2015年	2016年
地区生产总值　(元)	Gross Domestic Product　(yuan)	114 029	123 209	129 925	136 702	145 556
农林牧渔业总产值	Gross Output Value of Farming, Forestry, Animal Husbandry and Fishery	3 206	3 501	3 706	3 913	3 994
工业总产值	Gross Industrial Output Value	327 781	337 803	337 755	336 641	336 418
一般公共预算收入	General Public Budget Revenue	11 433	12 600	13 632	14 710	16 272
一般公共预算支出	General Public Budget Expenditure	10 570	11 480	12 320	14 394	15 210
粮食产量　(公斤)	Grain　(kg)	111	107	104	102	92
水产品产量	Aquatic Products	27	26	25	25	24
生铁产量	Pig Iron	2 117	2 335	2 593	2 568	2 469
钢材产量	Steel Products	3 854	4 271	3 790	3 943	3 747
笔记本计算机产量　(台)	Laptop Computer　(unit)	7.10	6.47	5.78	4.61	3.82
发电量　(千瓦时)	Power Generation　(kwh)	8 670	9 448	9 347	9 276	9 593
社会消费品零售总额　(元)	Total Retail Sales of Consumer Goods　(yuan)	30 767	34 667	38 709	42 051	46 435
全社会固定资产投资额	Total Fixed Assets Investment	49 996	56 816	58 828	57 723	53 129
进出口总额　(美元)	Total Exports and Imports　(USD)	29 020	29 283	29 392	28 779	25 749
# 出　口	Exports	16 583	16 633	17 106	17 103	15 420
卫生机构床位数　(张/万人)	Number of Beds in Health Institutions　(unit/10 000 persons)	43.67	48.84	52.07	55.86	59.48
卫生技术人员　(人/万人)	Number of Medical Technical Personnel　(person/10 000 persons)	54.19	57.71	60.62	64.22	67.88
# 医　生	Doctors	21.99	22.97	23.91	24.68	25.98
全体常住居民可支配收入(元)	Disposable Income of the Resident Population　(yuan)			39 780	42 987	46 595
全体常住居民消费支出	Consumer Spending of the Resident Population			24 920	26 847	28 983
城镇常住居民可支配收入	Disposable Income of the Urban Residents	37 531	41 143	46 677	50 390	54 341
城镇常住居民消费支出	Consumer Spending of the Urban Residents	23 092	25 197	28 973	31 136	33 305
农村常住居民可支配收入	Disposable Income of the Rural Residents	19 396	21 578	23 560	25 580	27 691
农村常住居民消费支出	Consumer Spending of the Rural Residents	14 381	16 251	15 390	16 761	18 820
住户存款余额	Deposits of Households at Year-end	54 519	60 365	66 151	69 311	74 436

注：此表人均指标按常住人口计算。居民收支为抽样调查数据。

Note: The per capita indicators in this table are calculated by the resident population. The income and expenditure of the residents were the survey data.

表1-9

苏州市国民经济主要指标在全省的地位 (2016年)
POSITION OF SUZHOU'S MAJOR NATIONAL ECONOMICAL INDICATORS IN THE PROVINCE (2016)

指标	Item	苏州 Suzhou City	江苏 Jiangsu Province	苏州占江苏的比重(%) Percentage of Suzhou in Jiangsu
年末户籍总人口（万人）	Total Population (year-end) (10 000 persons)	678.20	7 775.66	8.7
年末常住总人口	Resident Population (year-end)	1 064.74	7 998.60	13.3
# 城镇人口	Urban Population	803.88	5 416.65	14.8
地区生产总值（亿元）	Gross Domestic Product (100 million yuan)	15 475.09	76 086.17	20.3
农林牧渔业总产值	Gross Output Value of Farming, Forestry, Animal Husbandry and Fishery	424.67	7 235.06	5.9
主要农产品产量	Output of Major Farm Products			
粮　食（万吨）	Grain (10 000 tons)	97.68	3 466.01	2.8
油　料	Oil-bearing Crops	1.34	131.93	1.0
水产品	Aquatic Products	25.49	523.15	4.9
牛　奶	Cow Milk	10.30	59.01	17.4
规模以上工业总产值（亿元）	Gross Industrial Output Value Above Designated Size (100 million yuan)	30 713.99	157 640.23	19.5
# 高新技术产业产值	The High-tech Industry Output Value	14 381.65	67 124.65	21.4
主要工业产品产量	Output of Major Industrial Products			
发电量（亿千瓦时）	Electricity (100 million kwh)	1 019.93	4 667.73	21.9
钢　材（万吨）	Steel Products (10 000 tons)	3 983.98	13 469.72	29.6
粗　钢	Raw Steel	3 177.78	11 080.49	28.7
农用化肥	Agricultural Chemical Fertilizers	40.32	207.17	19.5
纱	Yarn	65.33	536.86	12.2
布（亿米）	Cloth (100 million meters)	8.85	91.46	9.7
全社会用电量（亿千瓦时）	Electricity Consumption (100 million kwh)	1 382.58	5 458.95	25.3
# 工业用电量	Industry	1 116.30	4 081.42	27.4
社会消费品零售总额（亿元）	Total Retail Sales of Consumer Goods (100 million yuan)	4 936.79	28 707.12	17.2
全社会固定资产投资	Investment in Fixed Assets	5 648.49	49 663.21	11.4

表1-9 续表　　Continued

指　　标	Item	苏　州 Suzhou City	江　苏 Jiangsu Province	苏州占江苏的比重(%) Percentage of Suzhou in Jiangsu
进出口总额　（亿美元）	Total Exports and Imports　(USD 100 million)	2 737.58	5 096.12	53.7
出口总额	Total Exports	1 639.41	3 193.44	51.3
进口总额	Total Imports	1 098.18	1 902.68	57.7
新增注册外资金额	Newly Added Value of Foreign Capital Signed	57.25	431.39	13.3
实际使用外资	Amount of Foreign Capital Actually Used	60.03	245.43	24.5
一般公共预算收入　（亿元）	General Public Budget Revenue　(100 million yuan)	1 730.04	8 121.23	21.3
一般公共预算支出	General Public Budget Expenditure	1 617.11	9 981.96	16.2
金融机构人民币存款余额	Deposit Balance of Financial Institutions at Year-end	25 864.26	121 106.58	21.4
金融机构人民币贷款余额	Loans Balance of Financial Institutions at Year-end	21 924.44	91 107.60	24.1
普通高等学校在校学生　（万人）	Students Enrollment of Institutions of Higher Education (10 000 persons)	21.93	174.58	12.6
中等职业教育学校在校学生	Students Enrollment of Specialized Secondary Schools	6.12	65.25	9.4
普通中学在校学生	Students Enrollment of Regular Secondary Schools	30.98	290.10	10.7
小学在校学生	Students Enrollment of Primary Schools	69.37	522.20	13.3
卫生机构　（所）	Health Institutions　(unit)	3 175	32 135	9.9
#医　院	Hospitals	206	1 679	12.3
卫生院、社区卫生服务中心	Rural Township Hospitals, Neighborhood Medical Service Station	160	1 585	10.1
卫生机构床位数　（万张）	Number of Beds in Health Institutions　(10 000 units)	6.32	44.31	14.3
卫生技术人员　（万人）	Number of Medical Personnel　(10 000 persons)	7.22	51.71	14.0
#医　生	Doctors	2.77	20.47	13.5
注册护士	Professional Nurse	3.07	22.12	13.9
全体常住居民人均可支配收入(元)	Per Capita Disposable Income of the Resident Population　(yuan)	46 595	32 070	–
城镇常住居民人均可支配收入	Per Capita Disposable Income of the Urban Residents	54 341	40 152	–
农村常住居民人均可支配收入	Per Capita Disposable Income of the Rural Residents	27 691	17 606	–

表1-10

历年地区生产总值
GROSS DOMESTIC PRODUCT OVER THE YEARS

单位：亿元 (100 million yuan)

年份 Year	地区生产总值 Gross Domestic Product	第一产业 Primary Industry	第二产业 Secondary Industry	工业 Industry	建筑业 Construction	第三产业 Tertiary Industry	人均生产总值(元) Per Capita GDP (yuan)	人均生产总值(美元) Per Capita GDP (USD)
1952	4.38	2.01	1.09	1.06	0.03	1.29	126	
1965	10.78	4.95	3.74	3.56	0.18	2.10	254	
1970	15.03	6.26	6.16	5.61	0.55	2.62	325	
1975	23.32	8.18	10.98	10.08	0.91	4.15	471	
1978	31.95	8.97	17.79	16.69	1.10	5.18	634	
1980	40.68	10.03	23.85	22.61	1.24	6.80	787	
1985	91.91	18.07	56.67	52.59	4.08	17.17	1 714	584
1990	202.14	35.00	123.24	112.52	10.71	43.90	3 617	756
1991	235.10	35.76	147.22	134.46	12.76	52.11	4 178	785
1992	359.69	40.56	230.77	209.80	20.97	88.35	6 360	1 153
1993	525.96	50.16	336.06	305.05	31.01	139.74	9 258	1 607
1994	720.90	68.46	442.89	404.88	38.01	209.55	12 639	1 466
1995	903.11	80.37	543.41	499.12	44.29	279.33	15 784	1 890
1996	1 002.14	88.18	567.96	513.36	54.60	346.00	17 474	2 102
1997	1 132.59	88.16	636.42	577.12	59.30	408.01	19 713	2 378
1998	1 250.01	88.01	701.95	632.48	69.47	460.05	21 733	2 625
1999	1 358.43	88.14	764.07	691.54	72.53	506.22	23 592	2 850
2000	1 540.68	90.96	870.10	790.83	79.27	579.62	26 692	3 224
2001	1 760.28	91.41	999.89	912.11	87.78	668.98	30 384	3 671
2002	2 080.37	91.72	1 211.52	1 106.87	104.65	777.13	35 733	4 317
2003	2 801.56	75.75	1 771.86	1 586.61	185.25	953.95	47 693	5 762
2004	3 450.00	77.00	2 268.00	2 068.00	200.00	1 105.00	57 992	7 007
2005	4 138.21	82.08	2 681.54	2 520.33	161.21	1 374.59	55 667	6 796
2006	4 900.63	94.80	3 152.03	2 978.55	173.48	1 653.80	62 526	7 843
2007	5 850.11	105.26	3 632.03	3 442.20	189.83	2 112.82	69 151	9 094
2008	7 078.09	121.17	4 257.90	4 025.30	232.60	2 699.02	78 875	11 357
2009	7 740.20	129.01	4 547.12	4 265.47	281.65	3 064.07	83 696	12 252
2010	9 228.91	140.80	5 253.81	4 916.49	337.32	3 834.30	93 043	13 744
2011	10 716.99	161.03	5 957.74	5 555.33	402.41	4 598.22	102 129	15 812
2012	12 011.65	176.53	6 502.25	6 055.10	447.15	5 332.87	114 029	18 064
2013	13 015.70	193.29	6 757.81	6 266.07	492.82	6 064.60	123 209	19 896
2014	13 760.89	203.98	6 892.98	6 360.14	533.96	6 663.93	129 925	21 151
2015	14 504.07	215.71	7 045.12	6 490.44	555.80	7 243.24	136 702	21 948
2016	15 475.09	221.81	7 277.46	6 709.02	569.78	7 975.82	145 556	21 913

注：1.2005年起人均地区生产总值按常住人口计算，下同。
2.2013年、2014年数据根据第三次经济普查口径调整。
Note:1. In 2005, per capita GDP began to be calculated according to the resident population, the same below.
2.The data of 2013 and 2014 has been adjusted in accord with the third economic census.

表1-11

历年地区生产总值构成
PROPORTIONS IN GROSS DOMESTIC PRODUCT OVER THE YEARS

单位：% (%)

年 份 Year	地 区 生产总值 Gross Domestic Product	第一产业 Primary Industry	第二产业 Secondary Industry	工 业 Industry	建筑业 Construction	第三产业 Tertiary Industry
1952	100.0	45.9	24.8	24.2	0.6	29.3
1965	100.0	45.9	34.6	33.0	1.6	19.5
1970	100.0	41.6	41.0	37.3	3.6	17.4
1975	100.0	35.1	47.1	43.2	3.9	17.8
1978	100.0	28.1	55.7	52.2	3.4	16.2
1980	100.0	24.7	58.6	55.6	3.0	16.7
1985	100.0	19.7	61.6	57.2	4.4	18.7
1990	100.0	17.3	61.0	55.7	5.3	21.7
1991	100.0	15.2	62.6	57.2	5.4	22.2
1992	100.0	11.3	64.2	58.3	5.8	24.5
1993	100.0	9.5	63.9	58.0	5.9	26.6
1994	100.0	9.5	61.4	56.2	5.3	29.1
1995	100.0	8.9	60.2	55.3	4.9	30.9
1996	100.0	8.8	56.7	51.2	5.5	34.5
1997	100.0	7.8	56.2	51.0	5.2	36.0
1998	100.0	7.0	56.2	50.6	5.6	36.8
1999	100.0	6.5	56.2	50.9	5.3	37.3
2000	100.0	5.9	56.5	51.3	5.2	37.6
2001	100.0	5.2	56.8	51.8	5.0	38.0
2002	100.0	4.4	58.2	53.2	5.0	37.4
2003	100.0	2.7	63.2	56.6	6.6	34.1
2004	100.0	2.2	65.7	59.9	5.8	32.1
2005	100.0	2.0	64.8	60.9	3.9	33.2
2006	100.0	1.9	64.3	60.8	3.5	33.8
2007	100.0	1.8	62.1	58.8	3.3	36.1
2008	100.0	1.7	60.2	56.9	3.3	38.1
2009	100.0	1.7	58.7	55.1	3.6	39.6
2010	100.0	1.5	56.9	53.2	3.7	41.6
2011	100.0	1.5	55.6	51.8	3.8	42.9
2012	100.0	1.5	54.1	50.4	3.7	44.4
2013	100.0	1.5	51.9	48.1	3.8	46.6
2014	100.0	1.5	50.1	46.2	3.9	48.4
2015	100.0	1.5	48.6	44.8	3.8	49.9
2016	100.0	1.5	47.0	43.3	3.7	51.5

表1-12

历年地区生产总值指数

INDICES OF GROSS DOMESTIC PRODUCT OVER THE YEARS

(以上年为100，按可比价格计算 Takes Preceding Year as 100, Calculated at Comparable Price)

单位：% (%)

年 份 Year	地 区 生产总值 Gross Domestic Product	第一产业 Primary Industry	第二产业 Secondary Industry	工 业 Industry	建筑业 Construction	第三产业 Tertiary Industry	人均生产总值 Per Capita GDP
1979	104.0	86.2	107.0	106.6	113.4	124.1	102.6
1980	114.5	103.9	124.1	126.1	96.4	98.5	113.2
1981	107.5	94.7	110.5	109.9	121.8	112.7	106.4
1982	107.5	115.6	106.8	105.9	120.9	101.6	106.3
1983	111.2	95.6	113.0	112.2	124.3	123.1	110.5
1984	126.3	135.3	126.5	126.0	132.5	117.4	126.1
1985	130.0	96.3	138.8	139.4	131.9	132.9	129.6
1986	108.1	111.1	106.5	105.0	126.9	112.2	107.2
1987	116.4	100.1	120.4	118.1	146.0	114.2	115.2
1988	116.8	99.4	121.7	120.2	135.6	109.3	115.7
1989	95.5	96.4	94.0	95.7	80.5	101.7	94.6
1990	113.5	108.6	116.3	117.7	103.9	104.9	112.5
1991	111.9	98.7	114.3	114.4	112.9	109.2	111.2
1992	145.8	109.6	147.7	147.9	145.1	156.7	145.0
1993	125.1	101.6	126.0	128.2	102.4	130.3	124.5
1994	112.1	101.0	109.0	109.3	105.2	125.0	111.7
1995	114.8	111.8	114.5	114.9	108.6	116.5	114.4
1996	106.3	106.3	102.5	101.5	119.8	115.7	106.0
1997	114.2	103.4	114.4	114.8	108.6	116.5	114.0
1998	113.1	100.2	114.6	114.4	117.4	112.8	113.0
1999	112.1	106.2	113.2	113.7	105.1	111.0	112.0
2000	112.6	104.1	112.7	113.1	106.7	113.8	112.3
2001	112.3	101.2	112.6	112.9	109.6	113.6	111.9
2002	114.5	101.1	116.3	116.3	116.3	113.8	114.0
2003	118.0	94.5	121.7	120.3	133.5	115.0	117.0
2004	117.6	99.5	120.4	122.5	105.9	114.5	116.1
2005	115.3	100.7	115.3	115.6	110.3	116.7	112.0
2006	115.8	105.1	115.8	116.3	107.2	116.8	109.8
2007	116.1	104.6	115.6	116.1	107.5	117.8	107.6
2008	113.2	103.5	112.2	112.7	102.0	115.8	106.7
2009	111.5	103.9	110.0	109.5	119.3	114.5	108.2
2010	113.3	103.9	113.3	113.3	112.0	113.7	105.6
2011	112.0	104.4	111.5	111.7	108.1	112.9	105.9
2012	110.1	104.1	107.8	107.4	113.5	113.5	109.7
2013	109.6	102.7	107.5	107.5	106.3	112.7	109.3
2014	108.3	100.0	106.2	106.2	106.6	111.1	108.0
2015	107.5	103.3	104.8	104.4	111.4	110.8	107.3
2016	107.5	99.0	105.4	105.5	104.3	109.7	107.3

表1-13

全市生产总值
GROSS DOMESTIC PRODUCT IN THE WHOLE CITY

项 目	Item	2015年	2016年	增长%（可比价）Increased (%) (at comparable prize)
全市生产总值 (亿元)	**Gross Domestic Product** (100 million yuan)	**14 504.07**	**15 475.09**	**7.5**
按产业分	**Grouped by Industry**			
第一产业	Primary Industry	215.71	221.81	-1.0
第二产业	Secondary Industry	7 045.12	7 277.46	5.4
第三产业	Tertiary Industry	7 243.24	7 975.82	9.7
按行业分	**Grouped by Sector**			
农林牧渔业	Farming, Forestry, Animal Husbandry and Fishery	241.22	247.02	-1.3
工 业	Industry	6 490.44	6 709.02	5.5
建筑业	Construction	555.80	569.78	4.3
交通运输、仓储和邮政业	Transportation, Logistics and Postal	453.18	478.02	5.0
信息传输、软件和信息技术服务业	Information Transmission, Software and Information Technology Services	324.79	390.91	21.2
批发和零售业	Wholesale and Retail Trade Services	1 947.47	2 047.44	5.1
# 零售业	Retail Trade Services	398.26	421.64	5.0
住宿和餐饮业	Accommodation and Catering Services	406.28	439.43	5.6
# 餐饮业	Catering Services	351.19	381.18	5.5
金融业	Financial Industries	1 180.43	1 333.77	13.6
房地产业	Real Estate	896.38	1 015.15	11.2
# 房地产开发经营业	Real Estate Development	507.36	595.67	13.1
租赁和商务服务业	Leasing and Business Services	565.84	668.57	18.7
科学研究和技术服务业	Scientific Research and Technical Services	202.17	216.47	6.1
水利、环境和公共设施管理业	Water Conservancy, Environment and Public Facilities Management	92.78	94.83	1.2
居民服务和其他服务业	Community Service and Other Services	162.98	200.15	24.2
教 育	Education	329.91	359.60	7.5
卫生和社会工作	Health Care and Social Work	215.88	236.35	8.0
文化、体育和娱乐业	Culture, Sports and Entertainment	70.91	73.03	2.1
公共管理和社会组织	Public Administration and Social Organizations	367.61	395.55	6.4
人均生产总值(户籍人口) (元)	**Per Capita GDP** (Household Register Population) (yuan)	**218 420**	**230 077**	**6.1**
人均生产总值(常住人口)	**Per Capita GDP** (the Resident Population)	**136 702**	**145 556**	**7.3**

表1-14

分地区生产总值 (2016年)

项　目		Item		市　区 Urban Area
绝对值	(亿元)	**Absolute Value**	(100 million yuan)	
地区生产总值		**Gross Domestic Product**		**8 008.45**
第一产业		Primary Industry		80.88
第二产业		Secondary Industry		3 685.44
# 工　业		Industry		3 369.62
第三产业		Tertiary Industry		4 242.13
人均地区生产总值(户籍人口)	(元)	Per Capita GDP (Household Register Population)	(yuan)	232 374
人均地区生产总值(常住人口)		Per Capita GDP (The Resident Population)		145 576
构　成	(%)	**Composition**	(%)	
地区生产总值		**Gross Domestic Product**		**100.0**
第一产业		Primary Industry		1.0
第二产业		Secondary Industry		46.0
# 工　业		Industry		42.1
第三产业		Tertiary Industry		53.0
比上年增长	(%)	**Increase Over Last Year**	(%)	
地区生产总值		**Gross Domestic Product**		**7.5**
第一产业		Primary Industry		-1.3
第二产业		Secondary Industry		5.3
# 工　业		Industry		5.4
第三产业		Tertiary Industry		9.6
人均地区生产总值(户籍人口)		Per Capita GDP (Household Register Population)		5.9
人均地区生产总值(常住人口)		Per Capita GDP (The Resident Population)		7.2

GROSS DOMESTIC PRODUCT BY REGION (2016)

# 吴江区 Wujiang District	常熟 Changshu	张家港 Zhangjiagang	昆山 Kunshan	太仓 Taicang
1 628.33	**2 112.39**	**2 317.24**	**3 160.29**	**1 155.13**
42.81	42.76	31.34	30.07	36.76
834.85	1 082.43	1 214.70	1 708.82	583.87
783.74	1 026.16	1 155.30	1 608.39	547.67
750.67	987.20	1 071.20	1 421.40	534.50
198 278	197 708	250 601	392 442	240 015
125 420	139 768	184 744	191 058	162 523
100.0	**100.0**	**100.0**	**100.0**	**100.0**
2.6	2.0	1.4	0.9	3.2
51.3	51.3	52.4	54.1	50.5
48.1	48.6	49.9	50.9	47.4
46.1	46.7	46.2	45.0	46.3
7.5	**7.5**	**7.0**	**7.4**	**7.3**
-0.5	-0.1	0.5	0.3	-3.7
6.0	6.5	4.3	4.8	6.0
6.3	6.7	4.1	4.6	6.1
9.7	8.9	10.5	10.8	9.7
6.8	7.5	6.6	3.8	6.7
7.4	7.4	6.9	7.2	7.0

表1-15

私营企业户数 (2016年末)

单位：户

项　目	Item	全　市 Whole Municipality
私营企业	**Private Enterprises**	**433 650**
农、林、牧、渔业	Farming , Forestry ,Animal Husbandry and Fishery	2 296
采矿业	Mining and Quarrying	11
制造业	Manufacturing	103 814
电力、热力、燃气及水生产和供应业	Electricity, Heat, Gas and Water Production and Supply Industries	283
建筑业	Construction	28 913
批发和零售业	Wholesale and Retail Trade Services	159 331
交通运输、仓储和邮政业	Transportation, Logistics and Postal	11 476
住宿和餐饮业	Accommodation and Catering Services	3 221
信息传输、软件和信息技术服务业	Information Transmission, Software and Information Technology Services	14 154
金融业	Financial Industries	1 534
房地产业	Real Estate	11 550
租赁和商务服务业	Leasing and Business Services	48 338
科学研究和技术服务业	Scientific Research and Technical Services	33 821
水利、环境和公共设施管理业	Water Conservancy, Environment and Public Facilities Management	1 333
居民服务、修理和其他服务业	Resident Services, Repairs and Other Services	7 489
教　育	Education	941
卫生和社会工作	Health and Social Work	597
文化、体育和娱乐业	Culture, Sports and Entertainment	4 540
其他行业	Others	8

NUMBER OF PRIVATE ENTERPRISES (END OF 2016)

(household)

市　区 Urban Area	# 吴江区 Wujiang District	常　熟 Changshu	张家港 Zhangjiagang	昆　山 Kunshan	太　仓 Taicang	本年开业 Opened in This Year	本年注销 Cancelled in This Year
255 674	**46 673**	**34 248**	**39 011**	**82 920**	**21 797**	**82 960**	**7 393**
1 527	451	236	190	216	127	260	34
9	1	–	2	–	–	2	–
51 693	16 513	12 449	12 532	19 697	7 443	9 504	983
120	33	75	40	30	18	94	–
17 238	2 225	1 444	1 693	7 016	1 522	5 972	603
91 613	18 220	11 864	16 228	33 502	6 124	31 987	2 595
6 297	814	931	1 384	1 724	1 140	1 949	189
2 070	244	283	123	636	109	662	110
10 814	676	672	429	1 892	347	3 971	345
1 186	101	138	64	98	48	343	51
6 797	1 101	848	362	2 849	694	2 698	264
34 267	3 035	2 356	2 318	7 702	1 695	10 708	1 267
22 338	1 863	1 447	2 686	5 549	1 801	10 891	611
671	118	198	84	320	60	148	17
4 811	712	866	584	889	339	1 405	200
659	83	27	64	172	19	467	17
257	39	118	50	124	48	145	20
3 301	442	296	178	502	263	1 751	87
6	2	–	–	2	–	3	–

表1-16

私营企业从业人员 (2016年末)

单位：人

项　　目	Item	全　市 Whole Municipality
私营企业	**Private Enterprises**	**4 408 695**
农、林、牧、渔业	Farming , Forestry ,Animal Husbandry and Fishery	18 828
采矿业	Mining and Quarrying	147
制造业	Manufacturing	1 917 235
电力、热力、燃气及水生产和供应业	Electricity, Heat, Gas and Water Production and Supply Industries	4 048
建筑业	Construction	330 861
批发和零售业	Wholesale and Retail Trade Services	988 404
交通运输、仓储和邮政业	Transportation, Logistics and Postal	100 035
住宿和餐饮业	Accommodation and Catering Services	44 327
信息传输、软件和信息技术服务业	Information Transmission, Software and Information Technology Services	96 526
金融业	Financial Industries	16 618
房地产业	Real Estate	125 873
租赁和商务服务业	Leasing and Business Services	364 331
科学研究和技术服务业	Scientific Research and Technical Services	269 449
水利、环境和公共设施管理业	Water Conservancy, Environment and Public Facilities Management	16 715
居民服务、修理和其他服务业	Resident Services, Repairs and Other Services	70 395
教　育	Education	5 188
卫生和社会工作	Health and Social Work	10 779
文化、体育和娱乐业	Culture, Sports and Entertainment	28 895
其他行业	Others	41

EMPLOYMENT OF PRIVATE ENTERPRISES (END OF 2016)

(person)

市 区 Urban Area	# 吴江区 Wujiang District	常 熟 Changshu	张家港 Zhangjiagang	昆 山 Kunshan	太 仓 Taicang	附：注册资金 (万元) Registered Capital (10 000 yuan)
2 399 746	**447 544**	**502 545**	**578 067**	**676 803**	**251 534**	**208 599 971**
11 281	2 631	2 450	1 802	1 759	1 536	637 708
85	10	–	62	–	–	53 503
906 667	256 931	316 631	312 763	258 235	122 939	44 052 643
1 572	367	774	1 136	227	339	358 202
178 521	21 280	25 466	31 272	78 693	16 909	14 903 564
556 817	100 699	79 872	133 505	174 102	44 108	34 370 819
52 625	5 710	7 507	15 621	12 825	11 457	4 701 079
28 685	3 351	4 822	2 140	6 960	1 720	770 132
73 328	3 859	4 208	3 482	12 325	3 183	4 406 830
12 943	657	1 850	776	777	272	15 855 118
77 965	9 906	9 940	5 904	23 767	8 297	10 294 126
254 623	19 344	19 062	23 408	52 475	14 763	57 212 278
166 863	12 994	14 325	31 437	37 215	19 609	16 651 187
8 157	1 061	2 553	1 123	4 069	813	889 170
39 192	5 107	9 976	9 907	8 150	3 170	1 368 622
3 650	454	132	508	781	117	136 106
5 449	325	961	1 876	1 798	695	168 035
21 284	2 837	2 016	1 345	2 643	1 607	1 769 936
39	21	–	–	2	–	913

表1-17

个体劳动者户数 (2016年末)

单位：户

项　目	Item	全　市 Whole Municipality
个体劳动者	**Self-employed Individuals**	**638 639**
农、林、牧、渔业	Farming , Forestry ,Animal Husbandry and Fishery	2 535
采矿业	Mining and Quarrying	9
制造业	Manufacturing	74 678
电力、热力、燃气及水生产和供应业	Electricity, Heat, Gas and Water Production and Supply Industries	67
建筑业	Construction	4 786
批发和零售业	Wholesale and Retail Trade Services	402 166
交通运输、仓储和邮政业	Transportation, Logistics and Postal	12 607
住宿和餐饮业	Accommodation and Catering Services	62 510
信息传输、软件和信息技术服务业	Information Transmission, Software and Information Technology Services	1 240
金融业	Financial Industries	14
房地产业	Real Estate	2 538
租赁和商务服务业	Leasing and Business Services	11 155
科学研究和技术服务业	Scientific Research and Technical Services	2 749
水利、环境和公共设施管理业	Water Conservancy, Environment and Public Facilities Management	321
居民服务、修理和其他服务业	Resident Services, Repairs and Other Services	55 539
教　育	Education	1 295
卫生和社会工作	Health and Social Work	576
文化、体育和娱乐业	Culture, Sports and Entertainment	3 853
其他行业	Others	1

NUMBER OF SELF-EMPLOYED INDIVIDUALS (END OF 2016)

(household)

市 区 Urban Area	# 吴江区 Wujiang District	常 熟 Changshu	张家港 Zhangjiagang	昆 山 Kunshan	太 仓 Taicang	本年开业 Opened in This Year	本年注销 Cancelled in This Year
310 587	**66 835**	**94 741**	**73 583**	**113 780**	**45 948**	**109 366**	**31 072**
1 094	399	411	401	349	280	362	69
3	–	–	2	4	–	–	2
29 483	6 205	13 639	10 153	14 405	6 998	9 773	3 834
17	6	25	11	9	5	2	2
1 265	249	445	615	1 468	993	1 738	121
203 272	46 668	61 719	38 854	70 888	27 433	59 290	18 293
1 455	465	3 617	5 358	1 394	783	2 639	409
32 380	5 029	6 393	7 565	12 112	4 060	18 624	4 542
403	40	98	373	265	101	402	61
1	1	1	–	12	–	14	1
959	28	98	138	909	434	635	161
5 812	1 191	777	1 300	2 543	723	3 202	472
1 683	212	224	250	399	193	619	118
86	11	63	26	96	50	69	9
29 312	5 824	6 780	7 849	8 031	3 567	10 421	2 649
490	75	49	246	450	60	714	61
366	119	18	67	85	40	93	18
2 506	313	384	375	360	228	768	250
–	–	–	–	1	–	1	–

表1-18

个体劳动者从业人员 (2016年末)

单位：人

项　　目	Item	全　市 Whole Municipality
个体劳动者	**Self-employed Individuals**	**1 269 526**
农、林、牧、渔业	Farming , Forestry ,Animal Husbandry and Fishery	6 345
采矿业	Mining and Quarrying	18
制造业	Manufacturing	250 697
电力、热力、燃气及水生产和供应业	Electricity, Heat, Gas and Water Production and Supply Industries	136
建筑业	Construction	12 010
批发和零售业	Wholesale and Retail Trade Services	627 900
交通运输、仓储和邮政业	Transportation, Logistics and Postal	15 210
住宿和餐饮业	Accommodation and Catering Services	180 913
信息传输、软件和信息技术服务业	Information Transmission, Software and Information Technology Services	2 041
金融业	Financial Industries	20
房地产业	Real Estate	5 123
租赁和商务服务业	Leasing and Business Services	20 807
科学研究和技术服务业	Scientific Research and Technical Services	5 958
水利、环境和公共设施管理业	Water Conservancy, Environment and Public Facilities Management	789
居民服务、修理和其他服务业	Resident Services, Repairs and Other Services	124 453
教　育	Education	3 574
卫生和社会工作	Health and Social Work	1 529
文化、体育和娱乐业	Culture, Sports and Entertainment	12 001
其他行业	Others	2

EMPLOYMENT OF SELF-EMPLOYED INDIVIDUALS (END OF 2016)

(person)

市 区 Urban Area	# 吴江区 Wujiang District	常 熟 Changshu	张家港 Zhangjiagang	昆 山 Kunshan	太 仓 Taicang	附：注册资金 (万元) Registered Capital (10 000 yuan)
662 596	**125 284**	**171 360**	**143 070**	**229 703**	**62 797**	**4 965 559**
3 117	1 182	1 057	944	782	445	74 973
9	–	–	2	7	–	65
111 929	20 285	52 261	33 512	37 302	15 693	797 090
37	10	39	32	20	8	617
3 100	586	1 245	2 745	3 246	1 674	58 890
339 383	70 715	79 457	55 816	122 541	30 703	2 585 729
2 315	838	4 128	5 824	2 046	897	89 370
105 761	14 413	15 923	20 572	32 270	6 387	714 533
680	74	150	609	489	113	7 689
2	2	2	–	16	–	95
1 754	34	129	262	2 488	490	15 083
11 301	1 939	1 440	2 146	4 988	932	95 117
3 808	408	442	636	807	265	19 083
266	52	142	85	215	81	4 401
69 752	13 236	13 389	17 127	19 607	4 578	420 212
1 421	262	91	809	1 156	97	13 841
1 067	409	26	123	238	75	6 771
6 894	839	1 439	1 826	1 483	359	62 001
–	–	–	–	2	–	–

主 要 统 计 指 标 解 释

行政区划 指国家对行政区域的划分。根据有关法规规定，我国的行政区域划分如下：(1)全国分为省、自治区、直辖市；(2)省、自治区分为自治州、地区、自治县、市；(3)自治州分为县、自治县、市；(4)县、自治县分为乡、民族乡、镇；(5)直辖市和较大的市分为区、县；(6)国家在必要时设立的特别行政区。

气温 指空气的温度，我国一般以摄氏度为单位表示。气象观测的温度表是放在离地面约1.5米处通风良好的百叶箱里测量的，因此，通常说的气温指的是离地面1.5米处百叶箱中的温度。

相对湿度 指空气中实际水气压与当时气温下的饱和水气压之比。

降水量 指从天空降落到地面的液态或固态(经融化后)水，未经蒸发、渗透、流失而在地面上积聚的深度。

日照时数 指太阳实际照射地面的时数。

国内生产总值(GDP) 指一个国家所有常住单位在一定时期内生产活动的最终成果。对于一个地区来说，称为地区生产总值或地区GDP。国内生产总值有三种表现形态，即价值形态、收入形态和产品形态。从价值形态看，它是所有常住单位在一定时期内生产的全部货物和服务价值与同期投入的全部非固定资产货物和服务价值的差额，即所有常住单位的增加值之和；从收入形态看，它是所有常住单位在一定时期内创造的各项收入之和，包括劳动者报酬、生产税净额、固定资产折旧和营业盈余；从产品形态看，它是所有常住单位在一定时期内最终使用的货物和服务价值与货物和服务净出口价值之和。在实际核算中，国内生产总值有三种计算方法，即生产法、收入法和支出法。三种方法分别从不同的方面反映国内生产总值及其构成。

三次产业 三次产业的划分是世界上较为常用的产业结构分类，根据《国民经济行业分类》（GB/T 4754—2011），三次产业划分是：

第一产业是指农、林、牧、渔业（不含农、林、牧、渔服务业）；

第二产业是指采矿业（不含开采辅助活动），制造业（不含金属制品、机械和设备修理业），电力、热力、燃气及水生产和供应业，建筑业；

第三产业是指除第一产业、第二产业以外的其他行业。

EXPLANATORY NOTES ON MAIN STATISTICAL INDICATORS

Divisions of Administrative Areas refers to the division of administrative areas by the State. The relative laws stipulate that 1) the whole country is divided into provinces, autonomous regions and municipalities directly under the Central Government; 2) provinces and autonomous regions are further divided into autonomous prefectures, counties, autonomous counties and cities; 3) autonomous prefectures are further divided into counties, autonomous counties and cities; 4) counties and autonomous counties are further divided into townships, ethnic townships and towns; 5) municipalities and large cities are divided into districts and counties, 6) the State shall, when necessary, establish special administrative regions.

Temperature refers to the air temperature. China uses centigrade as the unit. The thermometry used for weather observation is put in a breezy shutter, which is 1.5 meters high from the ground. Therefore, the commonly used temperature refers to the temperature in the breezy shutter 1.5 meters away from the ground.

Relative Humidity refers to the ratio of actual water vapour pressure to the saturation water vapour density under the current temperature.

Volume of Precipitation refers to the deepness of liquid state or solid state (thawed) water falling from the sky to the ground that has not been evaporated, infiltrated or run off.

Sunshine Hours refer to the actual hours of sun irradiating the earth, usually expressed in hours.

Gross Domestic Product (GDP) refers to the final products produced by all resident units in a country during a certain period of time. For a region, it is called as Gross Regional Product (GRP) or regional GDP. Gross domestic product is expressed in three different perspectives, namely value, income, and products respectively. GDP in its value perspective refers to the balance of total value of all goods and services produced by all resident units during a certain period of time, minus the total value of input of goods and services of the nature of non-fixed assets; in other words, it is the sum of the value-added of all resident units. GDP from the perspective of income refers to the sum of all kinds of revenue, including Compensation of Employees, Net Taxes on Production, Depreciation of Fixed Assets, and Operating Surplus. GDP from the perspective of products refers to the value of all goods and services for final demand by all resident units plus the net exports of goods and services during a given period of time. In the practice of national accounting, gross domestic product is calculated from three approaches, namely production approach, income approach and expenditure approach, which reflect gross domestic product and its composition from different angles.

The Three Industries Classification of economic activities into three strata of industry is a common practice in the world. In China, according to Industrial classification for National Economic Activities (GB/T 4754—2011), economic activities are categorized into the following three strata of industry:

The primary industry refers to agriculture, forestry, animal husbandry and fishery industries (not including services in support of agriculture, forestry, animal husbandry and fishery industries);

The secondary industry refers to mining and quarrying(not including support activities for mining), manufacturing(not including repair service of metal products, machinery and equipment), production and supply of electricity, heat, gas and water, and construction;

The tertiary industry refers to all other economic activities not included in the primary or secondary industries.

二、人口 劳动力

CHAPTER 2 POPULATION AND LABOR FORCE

2 人口 劳动力 POPULATION AND LABOR FORCE

主要统计指标 MAJOR STATISTICAL INDICATORS

2016年末常住人口	Resident Population	1 064.74	万人	10 000 persons
城镇人口比重	Proportion of Urban Population	75.5	%	
2016年末户籍总户数	Total Households	222.44	万户	10 000 households
比上年增长	Increase Over Last Year	1.5	%	
2016年末户籍总人口	Total Household Population	678.20	万人	10 000 persons
比上年增长	Increase Over Last Year	1.7	%	
2016年末户籍人口中:	In the Household Population			
出生人数	Birth Population	75 303	人	persons
出生率	Birth Rate	11.20	‰	
死亡人数	Death Population	42 685	人	persons
死亡率	Death Rate	6.35	‰	
自然增长人数	Natural Growth Population	32 618	人	persons
自然增长率	Natural Growth Rate	4.85	‰	
2016年末从业人员	Number of Employed Persons	691.30	万人	10 000 persons
比上年增长	Increase Over Last Year	0.0	%	
2016年城镇非私营单位在岗职工平均工资	The Average Wages of The Employees of The Non-private Units	79 870	元	yuan
比上年增长	Increase Over Last Year	10.5	%	

表2-1

全市人口普查主要数据
MAIN DATA OF THE PREVIOUS CENSUS

指 标		Item		1982年 “三普” The Third Census in 1982	1990年 “四普” The Fourth Census in 1990	2000年 “五普” The Fifth Census in 2000	2010年 “六普” The Sixth Census in 2010
常住人口	(万人)	**Resident Population**	(10 000 persons)	**527.53**	**564.36**	**679.22**	**1 045.99**
男		Male		264.87	282.77	336.41	533.45
女		Female		262.66	281.59	342.82	512.54
性别比(女性为100)		Sex Ratio (Female = 100)		100.84	100.42	98.13	104.08
家庭户规模	(人/户)	**Family Size**	(person/household)	**3.50**	**3.51**	**3.15**	**2.84**
各年龄组人口	(万人)	**Population by Age Group**	(10 000 persons)				
0-14岁		Aged 0—14		126.08	105.07	97.88	96.31
15-64岁		Aged 15—64		367.23	413.75	516.25	860.77
65岁及以上		Aged 65 and Over		34.22	45.54	65.09	88.91
劳动适龄人口	(万人)	**Working Age Population**	(10 000 persons)	**326.88**	**370.77**	**469.16**	**779.41**
男（16-59岁）		Male (Aged 16—59)		172.01	194.75	241.46	414.93
女（16-54岁）		Female (Aged 16—54)		154.87	176.02	227.70	364.48
民族人口	(万人)	**Population by Ethnicity**	(10 000 persons)				
汉 族		Han Nationality		527.25	563.79	677.56	1 038.70
占总人口比重	(%)	Proportion	(%)	99.94	99.89	99.76	99.30
少数民族		Minority Nationalities		0.28	0.57	1.66	7.29
占总人口比重	(%)	Proportion	(%)	0.06	0.11	0.24	0.70
各种受教育程度的人口	(万人)	**Population with Various Education Attainments**	(10 000 persons)	**342.56**	**411.63**	**596.41**	**975.11**
小 学		Primary School		191.98	199.25	219.89	226.64
初 中		Junior Secondary School		108.69	149.02	249.88	402.38
高中、中专		Senior Secondary School and Technical Secondary School		37.71	52.82	94.41	199.79
大专及以上		Junior College and Above		4.18	10.55	32.23	146.30
#大学专科		Junior College				20.32	88.49
大学本科		Undergraduate College				11.39	53.21
研究生		Graduate College				0.52	4.60
城乡人口	(万人)	**Population by Residence**	(10 000 persons)				
城镇人口		Urban Population		108.24	146.01	387.73	732.95
乡村人口		Rural Population		419.29	418.35	291.49	313.04

表2-2

分地区常住人口
RESIDENT POPULATION BY REGION

单位：万人 (10 000 persons)

地 区	Region	2015年末 End of 2015		2016年末 End of 2016	
		常住人口 Total Population	城镇人口比重 (%) Proportion of Urban Population (%)	常住人口 Total Population	城镇人口比重 (%) Proportion of Urban Population (%)
全 市	**Whole Municipality**	**1 061.60**	**74.90**	**1 064.74**	**75.50**
市 区	**Urban Area**	**549.21**	**80.83**	**551.03**	**81.40**
姑苏区	Gusu District	95.20	100.00	95.30	100.00
吴中区	Wuzhong District	112.12	71.03	112.40	71.66
相城区	Xiangcheng District	72.87	69.69	73.17	70.14
高新区、虎丘区	New & Hi-tech Zone , Huqiu District	59.08	86.74	59.40	87.54
工业园区	Industrial Park	80.26	98.92	80.78	99.55
吴江区	Wujiang District	129.68	67.62	129.98	68.44
县级市	**Cities at County Level**				
常 熟	Changshu	151.01	67.06	151.26	67.86
张家港	Zhangjiagang	125.31	66.99	125.55	67.76
昆 山	Kunshan	165.12	72.04	165.70	72.44
太 仓	Taicang	70.95	66.28	71.20	66.90

注：常住人口根据当年人口变动情况抽样调查数据推算。
Note:Resident population is calculated according to the change of the population sample survey data.

表2-3

历年年末户籍户数、人口数

单位：人

年 份 Year	全市总人口 Total Population of Whole Municipality	按地区分					
		市 区 Urban Area	# 吴江区 Wujiang District	常熟市 Changshu	张家港市 Zhangjiagang	昆山市 Kunshan	太仓市 Taicang
1949	3 386 027	1 613 652	468 631	681 358	484 098	304 813	302 106
1952	3 523 189	1 671 208	490 870	693 474	497 929	348 754	311 824
1957	3 851 040	1 839 466	539 483	750 452	538 305	382 491	340 326
1962	3 996 505	1 912 708	541 890	773 606	569 442	389 084	351 665
1965	4 295 134	2 057 262	585 879	820 204	618 233	427 467	371 968
1970	4 680 237	2 199 896	657 381	894 054	698 071	483 290	404 926
1975	4 926 040	2 319 193	693 119	939 340	735 534	509 228	422 745
1978	5 062 702	2 392 332	708 187	964 437	756 618	521 320	427 995
1980	5 186 167	2 490 995	716 057	980 263	762 715	523 532	428 662
1985	5 351 145	2 597 103	733 017	998 031	782 712	537 940	435 359
1990	5 610 165	2 732 375	764 187	1 032 888	834 070	564 610	446 222
1995	5 729 088	2 805 659	777 226	1 043 573	850 486	580 504	448 866
1996	5 741 163	2 813 076	776 458	1 043 391	851 988	583 364	449 344
1997	5 749 902	2 818 180	775 609	1 043 260	853 567	585 155	449 740
1998	5 753 485	2 820 759	773 308	1 041 785	853 979	587 509	449 453
1999	5 762 287	2 830 054	771 085	1 039 978	854 137	588 865	449 253
2000	5 781 689	2 843 674	771 822	1 039 064	854 953	594 592	449 406
2001	5 805 252	2 864 844	770 320	1 037 618	853 597	600 279	448 914
2002	5 838 599	2 893 397	769 423	1 036 229	852 718	606 936	449 319
2003	5 909 656	2 940 849	772 186	1 037 962	860 195	619 534	451 116
2004	5 988 510	2 985 027	777 509	1 043 132	868 640	637 157	454 554
2005	6 073 101	3 034 158	783 094	1 047 659	879 033	654 603	457 648
2006	6 160 814	3 089 935	788 438	1 054 825	887 804	666 809	461 441
2007	6 244 311	3 146 191	793 172	1 061 410	893 039	679 846	463 825
2008	6 297 530	3 177 364	795 254	1 065 018	898 430	690 435	466 283
2009	6 332 903	3 199 301	797 240	1 066 417	900 132	699 885	467 168
2010	6 376 558	3 224 328	799 569	1 066 908	905 085	711 333	468 904
2011	6 423 336	3 254 268	801 784	1 067 183	907 868	723 644	470 373
2012	6 478 054	3 289 922	804 868	1 067 798	910 208	737 565	472 561
2013	6 538 372	3 328 982	808 562	1 067 263	914 740	752 926	474 461
2014	6 610 766	3 374 960	814 370	1 068 844	919 816	769 746	477 400
2015	6 670 124	3 412 564	817 952	1 068 211	922 757	787 031	479 561
2016	6 781 957	3 480 163	824 518	1 068 666	926 592	823 547	482 989

YEAR-END HOUSEHOLDS AND POPULATION OVER THE YEARS

(person)

按性别分 By Sex		年平均人口 Average Person Per Year	总户数(户) Total Number of Households (household)	平均每户人口 Average Person	人口密度 (人/平方公里) Density of Population (person/sq.km)
男 Male	女 Female				
1 685 685	1 700 342	3 384 031	815 858	4.15	399
1 768 903	1 754 286	3 467 676	883 279	3.99	415
1 910 677	1 940 363	3 818 428	950 301	4.05	453
1 977 577	2 018 928	3 966 800	1 080 214	3.70	471
2 143 538	2 151 596	4 294 262	1 081 437	3.97	506
2 330 843	2 349 394	4 642 755	1 203 088	3.89	551
2 461 171	2 464 869	4 904 225	1 269 739	3.88	580
2 534 209	2 528 493	5 036 822	1 374 222	3.68	596
2 598 646	2 587 521	5 167 938	1 423 285	3.64	611
2 685 217	2 665 928	5 335 524	1 556 308	3.44	630
2 812 685	2 797 480	5 588 121	1 733 612	3.24	661
2 866 058	2 863 030	5 721 692	1 878 344	3.05	675
2 867 616	2 873 547	5 735 126	1 911 529	3.00	676
2 868 569	2 881 333	5 745 533	1 938 413	2.97	677
2 867 134	2 886 351	5 751 693	1 935 432	2.97	678
2 867 598	2 894 689	5 757 886	1 948 501	2.96	679
2 873 897	2 907 792	5 771 988	1 981 783	2.92	681
2 882 853	2 922 399	5 793 471	1 994 777	2.91	684
2 900 486	2 938 113	5 821 926	2 019 150	2.89	688
2 927 836	2 981 820	5 874 128	2 049 073	2.88	696
2 963 235	3 025 275	5 949 083	2 058 936	2.91	705
3 003 445	3 069 656	6 030 805	2 068 264	2.93	715
3 045 120	3 115 694	6 116 958	2 072 444	2.97	726
3 085 728	3 158 583	6 202 563	2 087 038	2.99	736
3 110 084	3 187 446	6 270 921	2 096 473	3.00	742
3 125 028	3 207 875	6 315 217	2 106 918	3.01	746
3 144 153	3 232 405	6 354 731	2 117 941	3.01	751
3 164 805	3 258 531	6 399 947	2 132 385	3.01	757
3 189 087	3 288 967	6 450 695	2 140 419	3.03	763
3 215 645	3 322 727	6 508 213	2 155 714	3.03	770
3 247 621	3 363 145	6 574 569	2 174 611	3.04	779
3 273 640	3 396 484	6 640 445	2 192 281	3.04	770
3 325 291	3 456 666	6 726 041	2 224 446	3.05	783

表2-4

历年户籍人口自然变动情况
NATURAL CHANGE OF POPULATION OVER THE YEARS

年 份 Year	出 生 Birth		死 亡 Death		自然增长 Natural Growth	
	人数(人) Population (person)	出生率(‰) Birth Rate (‰)	人数(人) Population (person)	死亡率(‰) Death Rate (‰)	人数(人) Population (person)	自然增长率(‰) Natural Growth Rate(‰)
1949	112 250	33.17	36 481	10.78	75 769	22.39
1952	128 700	37.11	32 286	9.31	96 414	27.80
1957	151 343	39.63	42 553	11.14	108 790	28.49
1962	123 893	31.23	45 428	11.45	78 465	19.78
1965	138 504	32.59	36 606	8.61	101 898	23.98
1970	119 799	25.80	31 297	6.74	88 502	19.06
1975	67 435	13.75	31 667	6.46	35 768	7.29
1978	73 308	14.55	32 800	6.51	40 508	8.04
1980	60 835	11.77	33 726	6.53	27 109	5.24
1985	55 305	10.37	36 219	6.79	19 086	3.58
1990	67 998	13.32	37 402	6.69	30 596	6.63
1995	48 803	8.53	40 073	7.00	8 730	1.53
1996	45 040	7.85	40 319	7.03	4 721	0.82
1997	40 304	7.01	39 898	6.94	406	0.07
1998	40 487	7.04	42 125	7.32	-1 638	-0.28
1999	38 122	6.62	39 396	6.84	-1 274	-0.22
2000	44 002	7.62	40 677	7.05	3 325	0.58
2001	36 694	6.33	38 930	6.72	-2 236	-0.39
2002	40 068	6.88	41 634	7.15	-1 566	-0.27
2003	42 786	7.28	42 308	7.20	478	0.08
2004	47 501	7.98	40 814	6.86	6 687	1.12
2005	48 477	8.04	41 385	6.86	7 092	1.18
2006	46 325	7.57	39 111	6.39	7 214	1.18
2007	48 552	7.83	40 503	6.53	8 049	1.30
2008	47 772	7.62	41 743	6.66	6 029	0.96
2009	49 663	7.86	41 427	6.56	8 236	1.30
2010	58 402	9.19	42 866	6.75	15 536	2.44
2011	58 732	9.18	41 956	6.56	16 776	2.62
2012	68 097	10.56	45 010	6.98	23 087	3.58
2013	67 396	10.36	44 478	6.84	22 918	3.52
2014	76 837	11.69	44 178	6.72	32 659	4.97
2015	65 846	9.92	45 691	6.88	20 155	3.04
2016	75 303	11.20	42 685	6.35	32 618	4.85

表2-5

分地区户籍户数与人口情况 (2016年末) HOUSEHOLDS AND POPULATION BY REGION (END OF 2016)

地　区	Region	总户数(户) Total Number of Households (household)	总人口(人) Total Population (person)	按性别分(人) By Sex (person)	
				男 Male	女 Female
全　市	**Whole Municipality**	**2 224 446**	**6 781 957**	**3 325 291**	**3 456 666**
市　区	**Urban Area**	**1 139 296**	**3 480 163**	**1 712 159**	**1 768 004**
姑苏区	Gusu District	280 711	732 135	359 329	372 806
吴中区	Wuzhong District	194 167	647 349	316 558	330 791
相城区	Xiangcheng District	129 005	413 254	201 838	211 416
高新区、虎丘区	New & Hi-tech Zone , Huqiu District	115 026	375 270	186 033	189 237
工业园区	Industrial Park	161 479	487 637	242 440	245 197
吴江区	Wujiang District	258 908	824 518	405 961	418 557
县级市	**Cities at County Level**	**1 085 150**	**3 301 794**	**1 613 132**	**1 688 662**
常　熟	Changshu	326 297	1 068 666	518 301	550 365
张家港	Zhangjiagang	329 524	926 592	454 041	472 551
昆　山	Kunshan	278 473	823 547	407 216	416 331
太　仓	Taicang	150 856	482 989	233 574	249 415

表2-5 续表 1　Continued 1

地　区	Region	年平均人口(人) Average Person Per Year (person)	平均预期寿命 e°x (岁) Average Life-span (age)		
			合　计 Total	男 Male	女 Female
全　市	**Whole Municipality**	**6 726 041**	**82.90**	**80.57**	**85.24**
市　区	**Urban Area**	**3 446 364**	**82.96**	**80.75**	**85.22**
姑苏区	Gusu District	733 248	83.88	81.59	86.28
吴中区	Wuzhong District	639 476	82.54	80.32	84.71
相城区	Xiangcheng District	409 327	81.96	79.32	84.68
高新区、虎丘区	New & Hi-tech Zone , Huqiu District	369 492	82.62	80.26	85.02
工业园区	Industrial Park	473 586	83.12	81.30	84.88
吴江区	Wujiang District	821 235	82.69	80.53	84.93
县级市	**Cities at County Level**	**3 279 677**	**82.85**	**80.38**	**85.28**
常　熟	Changshu	1 068 438	82.43	79.95	84.84
张家港	Zhangjiagang	924 675	82.58	79.87	85.32
昆　山	Kunshan	805 289	83.55	81.32	85.77
太　仓	Taicang	481 275	83.41	81.09	85.64

表2-5 续表 2 Continued 2

地　　区	Region	出生人数（人）Birth Population (person)	出生率（‰）Birth Rate (‰)	死亡人数（人）Death Population (person)	死亡率（‰）Death Rate (‰)
全　　市	**Whole Municipality**	**75 303**	**11.20**	**42 685**	**6.35**
市　区	**Urban Area**	**43 257**	**12.55**	**20 754**	**6.02**
姑苏区	Gusu District	6 398	8.73	5 185	7.07
吴中区	Wuzhong District	8 656	13.54	3 724	5.82
相城区	Xiangcheng District	5 544	13.54	2 573	6.29
高新区、虎丘区	New & Hi-tech Zone , Huqiu District	5 303	14.35	1 843	4.99
工业园区	Industrial Park	8 622	18.21	1 670	3.53
吴江区	Wujiang District	8 734	10.64	5 759	7.01
县级市	**Cities at County Level**	**32 046**	**9.77**	**21 931**	**6.69**
常　熟	Changshu	8 025	7.51	8 167	7.64
张家港	Zhangjiagang	8 895	9.62	6 077	6.57
昆　山	Kunshan	11 313	14.05	4 097	5.09
太　仓	Taicang	3 813	7.92	3 590	7.46

表2-5 续表 3 Continued 3

地　　区	Region	自然增长人数（人）Natural Growth Population (person)	自然增长率（‰）Natural Growth Rate (‰)	迁入人数（人）Number of the Transferred From Outside (person)	迁出人数（人）Number of the Transferred to Outside (person)
全　　市	**Whole Municipality**	**32 618**	**4.85**	**96 472**	**17 253**
市　区	**Urban Area**	**22 503**	**6.53**	**53 682**	**11 026**
姑苏区	Gusu District	1 213	1.66	8 603	2 810
吴中区	Wuzhong District	4 932	7.72	10 019	1 506
相城区	Xiangcheng District	2 971	7.25	5 556	520
高新区、虎丘区	New & Hi-tech Zone , Huqiu District	3 460	9.36	7 954	1 874
工业园区	Industrial Park	6 952	14.68	16 849	3 204
吴江区	Wujiang District	2 975	3.63	4 701	1 112
县级市	**Cities at County Level**	**10 115**	**3.08**	**42 790**	**6 227**
常　熟	Changshu	-142	-0.13	2 818	1 523
张家港	Zhangjiagang	2 818	3.05	3 235	1 463
昆　山	Kunshan	7 216	8.96	32 112	2 394
太　仓	Taicang	223	0.46	4 625	847

表2-6

婚姻登记情况 (2016年)
CONDITIONS OF MARRIAGE REGISTRATION (2016)

地　区	Region	准予结婚登记 (对) Marriage Legally Registered (couple)	初　婚 (人) First Married (person)	再　婚 (人) Re-married (person)	女性晚婚率 (%) Rate of Marriage at Mature Age for Female (%)	离　婚 (对) Divorced (couple)
全　市	**Whole Municipality**	**48 097**	**72 771**	**23 423**	**80.02**	**21 382**
市　区	**Urban Area**	**26 731**	**40 101**	**13 361**	**78.41**	**12 036**
姑苏区	Gusu District	6 013	8 597	3 429	79.71	2 811
吴中区	Wuzhong District	4 315	6 463	2 167	77.90	1 974
相城区	Xiangcheng District	3 152	4 967	1 337	75.41	1 291
高新区、虎丘区	New & Hi-tech Zone , Huqiu District	3 137	5 031	1 243	73.75	1 432
工业园区	Industrial Park	4 515	6 208	2 822	86.90	2 215
吴江区	Wujiang District	5 599	8 835	2 363	76.78	2 313
县级市	**Cities at County Level**	**21 366**	**32 670**	**10 062**	**81.21**	**9 346**
常　熟	Changshu	6 131	9 545	2 717	76.82	2 482
张家港	Zhangjiagang	6 645	10 355	2 935	85.20	2 870
昆　山	Kunshan	5 691	8 501	2 881	82.26	2 715
太　仓	Taicang	2 899	4 269	1 529	74.92	1 279

表2-7

生育情况 (2016年)
CONDITIONS OF BIRTH (2016)

地　区	Region	育龄妇女年末人数 (万人) Number of Woman of Child-bearing Age (10 000 persons)	总和生育率(%) Total Fertility Rate(%)
全　市	**Whole Municipality**	**155.02**	**1.48**
市　区	**Urban Area**	**79.46**	**1.50**
姑苏区	Gusu District	15.01	1.11
吴中区	Wuzhong District	14.89	1.80
相城区	Xiangcheng District	9.28	1.66
高新区、虎丘区	New & Hi-tech Zone , Huqiu District	8.68	1.53
工业园区	Industrial Park	12.36	1.17
吴江区	Wujiang District	19.24	1.59
县级市	**Cities at County Level**	**75.56**	**1.46**
常　熟	Changshu	23.10	1.31
张家港	Zhangjiagang	21.62	1.39
昆　山	Kunshan	19.63	1.80
太　仓	Taicang	11.21	1.31

表2-8

历年按三次产业划分的年末从业人员及构成
NUMBER AND COMPOSITION OF EMPLOYED PERSONS BY INDUSTRY OVER THE YEARS

年份 Year	年末从业人员(万人) Number of Employed Persons (10 000 persons)	第一产业 Primary Industry	第二产业 Secondary Industry	第三产业 Tertiary Industry	构成(%) Composition (%)	第一产业 Primary Industry	第二产业 Secondary Industry	第三产业 Tertiary Industry
1952	158.87	128.58	13.55	16.74	100.0	80.9	8.5	10.6
1957	177.69	144.40	17.95	15.34	100.0	81.3	10.1	8.6
1970	260.61	213.62	30.40	16.59	100.0	81.9	11.7	6.4
1975	282.34	213.12	45.49	23.73	100.0	75.5	16.1	8.4
1978	301.15	187.70	81.57	31.88	100.0	62.3	27.1	10.6
1980	317.17	184.93	98.85	33.39	100.0	58.3	31.2	10.5
1985	349.44	128.37	168.49	52.58	100.0	36.7	48.2	15.1
1990	346.74	103.13	177.84	65.77	100.0	29.7	51.3	19.0
1995	324.45	65.08	178.98	80.39	100.0	20.0	55.2	24.8
1996	323.84	66.21	174.15	83.48	100.0	20.4	53.8	25.8
1997	320.47	66.96	167.69	85.82	100.0	20.9	52.3	26.8
1998	307.52	68.40	153.87	85.25	100.0	22.3	50.0	27.7
1999	311.29	68.50	151.72	91.07	100.0	22.0	48.7	29.3
2000	313.89	65.90	156.27	91.72	100.0	21.0	49.8	29.2
2001	321.96	66.29	158.98	96.69	100.0	20.6	49.4	30.0
2002	323.75	61.66	161.38	100.71	100.0	19.0	49.9	31.1
2003	346.19	55.02	195.31	95.86	100.0	15.9	56.4	27.7
2004	358.82	48.61	211.11	99.10	100.0	13.6	58.8	27.6
2005	393.72	43.38	231.68	118.66	100.0	11.0	58.9	30.1
2006	429.46	35.94	263.71	129.81	100.0	8.4	61.4	30.2
2007	483.40	33.64	307.23	142.53	100.0	7.0	63.5	29.5
2008	495.53	32.11	303.86	159.56	100.0	6.5	61.3	32.2
2009	518.66	29.45	311.04	178.17	100.0	5.7	60.0	34.3
2010(老口径)	554.15	27.83	330.14	196.19	100.0	5.0	59.6	35.4
2010(新口径)	687.50	26.00	427.90	233.60	100.0	3.8	62.2	34.0
2011	691.00	25.60	427.10	238.30	100.0	3.7	61.8	34.5
2012	694.30	25.30	427.10	241.90	100.0	3.7	61.5	34.8
2013	695.20	25.10	425.90	244.20	100.0	3.6	61.3	35.1
2014	693.40	24.50	419.80	249.10	100.0	3.5	60.5	36.0
2015	691.40	23.80	414.50	253.10	100.0	3.4	60.0	36.6
2016	691.30	23.50	412.10	255.70	100.0	3.4	59.6	37.0

注:本表2009年及以前数据为城镇单位从业人员、城镇私营与个体从业人员、农村劳动者之和；2010年起根据常住人口变动、劳动力抽样调查数据推算。
Note: The data in the table in 2009 and before was the sum total of the employees of urban units, the urban private employees and individual self-employed and the rural workers; in 2010 the data began to be the projections based on changes in the resident population and the labor force survey data.

表2-9

分地区从业人员及构成
NUMBER AND COMPOSITION OF EMPLOYED PERSONS BY REGION

地区	Region	2015年末 End of 2015 从业人员(万人) Number of Employed Persons (10 000 persons)	第一产业 Primary Industry	第二产业 Secondary Industry	第三产业 Tertiary Industry	从业人员构成(%) Composition of Employed Persons (%)	第一产业 Primary Industry	第二产业 Secondary Industry	第三产业 Tertiary Industry
全 市	**Whole Municipality**	**691.40**	**23.80**	**414.50**	**253.10**	**100.0**	**3.4**	**60.0**	**36.6**
市 区	**Urban Area**	**347.38**	**10.95**	**201.33**	**135.10**	**100.0**	**3.1**	**58.0**	**38.9**
姑苏区	Gusu District	48.20	0.03	16.73	31.44	100.0	0.1	34.7	65.2
吴中区	Wuzhong District	74.45	5.20	43.33	25.92	100.0	7.0	58.2	34.8
相城区	Xiangcheng District	49.13	1.02	31.01	17.10	100.0	2.1	63.1	34.8
高新区、虎丘区	New & Hi-tech Zone , Huqiu District	36.71	0.54	22.88	13.29	100.0	1.5	62.3	36.2
工业园区	Industrial Park	52.63	0.37	33.50	18.76	100.0	0.7	63.7	35.6
吴江区	Wujiang District	86.26	3.79	53.88	28.59	100.0	4.4	62.5	33.1
县级市	**Cities at County Level**	**344.02**	**12.85**	**213.17**	**118.00**	**100.0**	**3.7**	**62.0**	**34.3**
常 熟	Changshu	104.72	4.00	64.64	36.08	100.0	3.8	61.7	34.5
张家港	Zhangjiagang	77.39	4.47	46.85	26.07	100.0	5.8	60.5	33.7
昆 山	Kunshan	116.08	1.75	74.72	39.61	100.0	1.5	64.4	34.1
太 仓	Taicang	45.83	2.63	26.96	16.24	100.0	5.8	58.8	35.4

表2-9 续表 Continued

地区	Region	2016年末 End of 2016 从业人员(万人) Number of Employed Persons (10 000 persons)	第一产业 Primary Industry	第二产业 Secondary Industry	第三产业 Tertiary Industry	从业人员构成(%) Composition of Employed Persons (%)	第一产业 Primary Industry	第二产业 Secondary Industry	第三产业 Tertiary Industry
全 市	**Whole Municipality**	**691.30**	**23.50**	**412.10**	**255.70**	**100.0**	**3.4**	**59.6**	**37.0**
市 区	**Urban Area**	**347.41**	**10.81**	**200.21**	**136.39**	**100.0**	**3.1**	**57.6**	**39.3**
姑苏区	Gusu District	47.99	0.03	16.44	31.52	100.0	0.1	34.2	65.7
吴中区	Wuzhong District	74.39	5.14	43.08	26.17	100.0	6.9	57.9	35.2
相城区	Xiangcheng District	49.20	1.01	30.88	17.31	100.0	2.0	62.8	35.2
高新区、虎丘区	New & Hi-tech Zone , Huqiu District	36.77	0.53	22.78	13.46	100.0	1.4	62.0	36.6
工业园区	Industrial Park	52.88	0.36	33.46	19.06	100.0	0.7	63.3	36.0
吴江区	Wujiang District	86.18	3.74	53.57	28.87	100.0	4.3	62.2	33.5
县级市	**Cities at County Level**	**343.89**	**12.69**	**211.89**	**119.31**	**100.0**	**3.7**	**61.6**	**34.7**
常 熟	Changshu	104.55	3.95	64.17	36.43	100.0	3.8	61.4	34.8
张家港	Zhangjiagang	77.27	4.41	46.51	26.35	100.0	5.7	60.2	34.1
昆 山	Kunshan	116.27	1.73	74.40	40.14	100.0	1.5	64.0	34.5
太 仓	Taicang	45.80	2.60	26.81	16.39	100.0	5.7	58.5	35.8

表2-10

历年分地区在岗职工人数
NUMBER OF STAFF AND WORKERS BY REGION OVER THE YEARS

单位：万人 (10 000 persons)

年 份 Year	全 市 Whole Municipality	市 区 Urban Area	# 吴江区 Wujiang District	常 熟 Changshu	张家港 Zhangjiagang	昆 山 Kunshan	太 仓 Taicang
1975	50.34	33.41	4.74	5.96	4.80	2.97	3.20
1976	53.26	35.25	5.09	6.38	4.84	3.37	3.42
1977	62.10	40.96	5.64	7.12	5.41	4.86	3.75
1978	60.91	40.90	5.56	7.20	5.32	3.77	3.72
1979	65.95	44.82	5.95	7.67	5.48	3.95	4.03
1980	70.30	47.52	6.43	8.22	5.88	4.27	4.41
1985	85.84	56.78	8.60	9.88	8.07	5.28	5.83
1990	95.43	60.91	9.51	11.98	9.50	6.21	6.83
1995	96.62	58.05	8.88	12.89	11.05	8.48	6.15
1996	94.51	56.40	8.68	12.70	10.33	8.90	6.18
1997	93.69	55.33	8.12	12.88	10.00	9.28	6.20
1998	78.88	44.12	6.91	11.31	8.82	9.04	5.59
1999	76.24	42.42	6.31	10.50	8.56	9.12	5.64
2000	74.09	39.53	5.77	10.34	8.17	10.65	5.40
2001	73.45	38.90	7.14	10.03	8.08	11.23	5.21
2002	74.16	38.22	6.79	9.66	8.12	12.67	5.49
2003	81.09	42.92	7.54	9.59	8.45	13.53	6.60
2004	87.18	46.19	7.76	9.70	9.33	14.16	7.80
2005	100.44	54.35	8.37	10.64	10.15	16.02	9.28
2006	111.39	62.37	8.50	10.42	11.57	16.89	10.14
2007	122.97	68.73	9.13	11.12	12.71	18.69	11.72
2008	118.08	65.77	9.04	10.92	12.45	17.34	11.60
2009	115.80	65.28	9.14	11.18	12.27	16.17	10.90
2010	126.97	72.68	11.04	11.62	13.07	18.32	11.28
2011	129.83	71.92	11.36	12.37	13.88	19.58	12.08
2012	130.40	72.60	11.50	12.22	14.47	19.21	11.90
2013	285.47	145.90	25.22	20.72	28.71	77.92	12.22
2014	307.21	158.02	33.48	25.17	28.78	81.04	14.19
2015	295.79	153.41	32.99	25.03	27.29	76.37	13.69
2016	279.90	141.72	31.34	25.90	26.05	72.46	13.77

注：2012年及以前为原城镇国有集体单位在岗职工，2013年起调整为城镇非私营单位在岗职工。

Note:The workers in the post in 2012 and before were the workers in the post of the urban state-owned and collective units, and in 2013 began to be adjusted to the workers in the post of the urban non-private units.

表2-11

历年分地区在岗职工平均工资
AVERAGE WAGE OF STAFF AND WORKERS BY REGION OVER THE YEARS

单位：元　　(yuan)

年　份 Year	全　市 Whole Municipality	市　区 Urban Area	# 吴江区 Wujiang District	常　熟 Changshu	张家港 Zhangjiagang	昆　山 Kunshan	太　仓 Taicang
1975	489	505	452	450	415	469	502
1976	481	499	448	442	398	464	478
1977	502	513	476	440	421	448	464
1978	514	537	498	472	443	496	522
1979	574	590	548	473	550	531	575
1980	687	704	643	586	654	638	693
1985	1 106	1 107	987	1 156	1 079	1 068	1 100
1990	2 450	2 512	2 393	2 474	2 183	2 352	2 327
1995	6 944	6 917	6 319	7 196	7 163	6 818	6 452
1996	7 742	7 681	7 006	7 920	7 806	7 919	7 570
1997	8 443	8 462	7 687	8 472	8 214	8 598	8 353
1998	9 616	9 947	8 613	9 325	8 907	9 235	9 272
1999	10 583	11 258	9 468	9 801	9 436	9 591	10 211
2000	11 778	12 898	10 324	10 246	10 156	10 658	11 006
2001	13 670	15 231	11 478	11 500	11 777	12 271	12 114
2002	15 924	17 902	13 605	13 590	13 702	14 383	13 334
2003	19 790	22 024	16 919	18 063	17 081	17 602	16 084
2004	22 510	24 991	19 157	20 327	20 226	20 099	18 564
2005	25 016	26 905	22 236	22 994	23 330	22 928	22 078
2006	28 010	29 775	25 911	25 411	26 042	25 989	25 503
2007	31 404	32 952	30 740	28 732	29 089	29 704	30 111
2008	36 090	37 826	35 440	33 420	33 538	33 735	34 716
2009	40 261	42 513	40 303	37 095	36 597	37 394	38 718
2010	45 566	47 780	44 393	41 784	42 518	41 669	45 120
2011	51 660	54 011	49 281	47 917	50 041	46 749	51 045
2012	57 622	59 692	55 949	53 982	56 591	53 461	57 037
2013	61 416	63 595	57 999	58 600	60 629	55 616	61 812
2014	66 956	68 378	60 974	63 675	66 466	59 868	68 252
2015	72 291	74 321	63 011	71 300	70 694	64 254	78 407
2016	79 870	83 293	68 004	80 489	77 976	70 967	87 994

注：2012年及以前为原城镇国有集体单位在岗职工平均工资，2013年开始调整为城镇非私营单位在岗职工平均工资。
Note:The average wages of workers in the post in 2012 and before were the average wages of the workers in the post of the urban state-owned and collective units, and in 2013 began to be adjusted to the average wages of the workers in the post of the urban non-private units.

表2-12 分地区分行业城镇非私营单位从业人员（2016年末）

单位：人

项　目	Item	全　市 Whole Municipality
总　计	**Total**	**2 886 930**
一、按机构类型分	**Grouped by Character of the Units**	
企　业	Enterprises	2 606 954
事　业	Institutions	195 331
机　关	Government Agencies	65 125
其　他	Others	19 520
二、按登记注册类型分	**Grouped by Registration Status**	
内资单位	Domestic Units	1 066 618
国有单位	State-owned Units	288 368
集体单位	Collective-owned Units	43 105
股份合作单位	Share-holding Cooperative Units	4 908
联营单位	Joint Ownership Units	556
有限责任公司	Limited Liability Corporations	488 740
股份有限公司	Share-holding Corporations Ltd.	227 757
其他单位	Other Enterprises	13 184
港澳台商投资单位	Units with Investment from HongKong, Macao and Taiwan	583 103
外商投资单位	Units with Foreign Investment	1 237 209
三、按行业分	**Grouped by Sector**	
农林牧渔业	Farming, Forestry, Animal Husbandry and Fishery	152
采矿业	Mining and Quarrying	531
制造业	Manufacturing	2 007 702
电力、燃气及水的生产和供应业	Power, Gas and Water Production and Supply	14 239
建筑业	Construction	120 005
批发和零售业	Wholesale and Retail Trade Services	104 396
交通运输、仓储和邮政业	Transportation, Logistics and Postal	71 669
住宿和餐饮业	Accommodation and Catering Services	37 929
信息传输、软件和信息技术服务业	Information Transmission, Software and Information Technology Services	38 666
金融业	Financial Industries	61 949
房地产业	Real Estate	56 426
租赁和商务服务业	Renting and Labor Services	43 843
科学研究和技术服务业	Scientific Research and Technical Services	25 641
水利、环境和公共设施管理业	Water Conservancy, Environment and Public Facilities Management	19 943
居民服务和其他服务业	Residents Service and Other Service Trades	6 547
教　育	Education	101 385
卫生和社会工作	Health Care and Social Work	67 356
文化、体育和娱乐业	Culture, Sports and Entertainment	9 013
公共管理和社会组织	Public Administration and Social Organizations	99 538

EMPLOYEES OF URBAN NON-PRIVATE UNITS BY SECTORS AND REGIONS (END OF 2016)

(person)

市　区 Urban Area	常　熟 Changshu	张家港 Zhangjiagang	昆　山 Kunshan	太　仓 Taicang
1 467 058	**265 954**	**269 631**	**740 887**	**143 400**
1 331 252	229 874	237 599	687 369	120 860
95 242	22 978	21 849	41 060	14 202
27 549	8 999	9 745	11 258	7 574
13 015	4 103	438	1 200	764
543 164	125 732	204 955	141 858	50 909
147 529	32 980	37 420	50 420	20 019
17 704	6 432	5 019	9 462	4 488
1 301	1 493	486	1 339	289
213	30	65	248	–
233 023	41 396	145 380	54 873	14 068
133 551	43 262	16 199	23 199	11 546
9 843	139	386	2 317	499
296 759	70 494	22 010	165 232	28 608
627 135	69 728	42 666	433 797	63 883
132	–	6	–	14
531	–	–	–	–
962 933	193 543	154 868	600 413	95 945
6 174	3 064	2 098	1 120	1 783
67 409	5 154	28 088	15 127	4 227
49 032	7 466	14 584	29 015	4 299
37 840	7 017	12 856	9 262	4 694
30 471	877	2 555	2 767	1 259
29 828	692	3 139	4 165	842
40 394	6 262	4 497	6 765	4 031
41 733	1 407	5 401	6 865	1 020
27 493	5 993	3 403	5 043	1 911
17 678	1 388	1 563	3 950	1 062
10 211	2 114	1 553	5 114	951
3 785	127	1 635	785	215
56 631	10 143	10 255	17 248	7 108
34 094	8 729	8 951	10 781	4 801
5 205	1 385	828	1 326	269
45 484	10 593	13 351	21 141	8 969

表2-13

市区分行业城镇非私营单位从业人员 (2016年末)

单位：人

项　目	Item	市　区 Urban Area
总　计	**Total**	**1 467 058**
一、按机构类型分	**Grouped by Character of the Units**	
企　业	Enterprises	1 331 252
事　业	Institutions	95 242
机　关	Government Agencies	27 549
其　他	Others	13 015
二、按登记注册类型分	**Grouped by Registration Status**	
内资单位	Domestic Units	543 164
国有单位	State-owned Units	147 529
集体单位	Collective-owned Units	17 704
股份合作单位	Share-holding Cooperative Units	1 301
联营单位	Joint Ownership Units	213
有限责任公司	Limited Liability Corporations	233 023
股份有限公司	Share-holding Corporations Ltd.	133 551
其他单位	Other Enterprises	9 843
港澳台商投资单位	Units with Investment from HongKong, Macao and Taiwan	296 759
外商投资单位	Units with Foreign Investment	627 135
三、按行业分	**Grouped by Sector**	
农林牧渔业	Farming, Forestry, Animal Husbandry and Fishery	132
采矿业	Mining and Quarrying	531
制造业	Manufacturing	962 933
电力、燃气及水的生产和供应业	Power, Gas and Water Production and Supply	6 174
建筑业	Construction	67 409
批发和零售业	Wholesale and Retail Trade Services	49 032
交通运输、仓储和邮政业	Transportation, Logistics and Postal	37 840
住宿和餐饮业	Accommodation and Catering Services	30 471
信息传输、软件和信息技术服务业	Information Transmission, Software and Information Technology Services	29 828
金融业	Financial Industries	40 394
房地产业	Real Estate	41 733
租赁和商务服务业	Renting and Labor Services	27 493
科学研究和技术服务业	Scientific Research and Technical Services	17 678
水利、环境和公共设施管理业	Water Conservancy, Environment and Public Facilities Management	10 211
居民服务和其他服务业	Residents Service and Other Service Trades	3 785
教　育	Education	56 631
卫生和社会工作	Health Care and Social Work	34 094
文化、体育和娱乐业	Culture, Sports and Entertainment	5 205
公共管理和社会组织	Public Administration and Social Organizations	45 484

EMPLOYEES OF URBAN NON-PRIVATE UNITS BY SECTORS IN URBAN AREA（END OF 2016)

(person)

姑苏区 Gusu District	吴中区 Wuzhong District	相城区 Xiangcheng District	高新区、虎丘区 New Hi-tech Zone & Huqiu District	工业园区 Industrial Park	吴江区 Wujiang District
131 271	**182 357**	**108 935**	**291 202**	**433 745**	**319 548**
94 536	159 241	83 953	282 327	421 977	289 218
30 458	17 844	10 063	5 738	9 747	21 392
6 010	4 909	3 514	2 548	1 809	8 759
267	363	11 405	589	212	179
125 288	73 350	60 581	82 853	105 300	95 792
48 082	23 790	24 903	12 112	8 538	30 104
1 309	3 564	6 831	1 415	1 312	3 273
898	272	70	61	–	–
–	44	72	–	–	97
48 509	35 494	21 307	43 965	45 723	38 025
24 904	8 934	7 112	23 496	44 935	24 170
1 586	1 252	286	1 804	4 792	123
2 620	33 336	16 212	66 362	66 718	111 511
3 363	75 671	32 142	141 987	261 727	112 245
–	94	–	–	–	38
–	–	–	531	–	–
972	115 836	61 870	210 300	314 189	259 766
1 046	920	211	618	1 096	2 283
11 621	8 228	15 319	10 717	14 035	7 489
13 098	6 267	1 309	5 303	20 141	2 914
19 384	3 975	1 465	4 722	5 060	3 234
6 195	2 836	1 419	13 827	4 054	2 140
7 156	17	205	7 484	14 082	884
10 971	459	38	5 595	19 516	3 815
7 849	7 136	1 203	9 521	13 107	2 917
6 112	7 516	25	4 620	7 289	1 931
4 291	3 189	359	3 422	5 482	935
2 565	1 956	299	1 827	101	3 463
1 705	1 051	31	303	390	305
13 332	10 152	6 516	6 688	8 073	11 870
14 178	5 844	2 992	2 917	2 804	5 359
2 930	616	169	894	538	58
7 866	6 265	15 505	1 913	3 788	10 147

表2-14 全市城镇非私营单位从业人员及平均工资（2016年）

项　目	Item	从业人员（人） Number of Employed Persons (person)
总　计	**Total**	**2 886 930**
一、按地区分	**Grouped by Region**	
市　区	Urban Area	1 467 058
姑苏区	Gusu District	131 271
吴中区	Wuzhong District	182 357
相城区	Xiangcheng District	108 935
高新区、虎丘区	New & Hi-tech Zone, Huqiu District	291 202
工业园区	Industrial Park	433 745
吴江区	Wujiang District	319 548
常　熟	Changshu	265 954
张家港	Zhangjiagang	269 631
昆　山	Kunshan	740 887
太　仓	Taicang	143 400
二、按机构类型分	**Grouped by Character of the Units**	
企　业	Enterprises	2 606 954
事　业	Institutions	195 331
机　关	Government Agencies	65 125
其　他	Others	19 520
三、按登记注册类型分	**Grouped by Registration Status**	
内资单位	Domestic Units	1 066 618
国有单位	State-owned Units	288 368
集体单位	Collective-owned Units	43 105
股份合作单位	Share-holding Cooperative Units	4 908
联营单位	Joint Ownership Units	556

EMPLOYEES OF CITY'S URBAN NON-PRIVATE UNIES, AVERAGE WAGES AND MEDIAN WAGES (2016)

	从业人员平均工资		从业人员工资中位数	
# 在岗职工 Fully Employed Staff and Workers	(元) Average Remuneration (yuan)	# 在岗职工 Fully Employed Staff and Workers	(元) Median of Wage (yuan)	# 在岗职工 Fully Employed Staff and Workers
2 799 000	**80 187**	**79 870**	**67 885**	**67 487**
1 417 199	83 392	83 293	70 817	70 834
123 606	93 857	96 736	84 310	84 449
173 560	75 830	76 115	64 080	63 282
106 206	74 265	74 377	66 273	65 878
280 987	78 098	78 028	66 820	65 489
419 441	98 916	97 866	87 025	84 798
313 399	68 206	68 004	59 053	59 053
258 992	81 079	80 489	72 160	68 819
260 515	77 580	77 976	68 571	68 571
724 634	71 884	70 967	63 651	63 015
137 660	87 939	87 994	76 916	78 167
2 535 676	76 118	75 461	64 937	64 788
181 206	113 791	119 006	113 556	120 135
62 713	135 058	137 455	123 713	123 713
19 405	109 545	109 967	87 237	87 237
1 016 271	90 111	91 880	79 331	78 732
274 387	115 684	118 888	113 308	115 006
39 627	85 816	89 829	88 208	95 140
4 669	58 459	59 212	53 012	49 600
422	80 140	96 206	86 491	68 360

表 2-14 续表

项 目	Item	从业人员（人）Number of Employed Persons (person)
有限责任公司	Limited Liability Corporations	488 740
股份有限公司	Share-holding Corporations Ltd.	227 757
其他单位	Other Enterprises	13 184
港澳台商投资单位	Units with Investment from HongKong, Macao and Taiwan	583 103
外商投资单位	Units with Foreign Investment	1 237 209
四、按行业分	**Grouped by Sector**	
农林牧渔业	Farming, Forestry, Animal Husbandry and Fishery	152
采矿业	Mining and Quarrying	531
制造业	Manufacturing	2 007 702
电力、燃气及水的生产和供应业	Power, Gas and Water Production and Supply	14 239
建筑业	Construction	120 005
批发和零售业	Wholesale and Retail Trade Services	104 396
交通运输、仓储和邮政业	Transportation, Logistics and Postal	71 669
住宿和餐饮业	Accommodation and Catering Services	37 929
信息传输、软件和信息技术服务业	Information Transmission, Software and Information Technology Services	38 666
金融业	Financial Industries	61 949
房地产业	Real Estate	56 426
租赁和商务服务业	Renting and Labor Services	43 843
科学研究和技术服务业	Scientific Research and Technical Services	25 641
水利、环境和公共设施管理业	Water Conservancy, Environment and Public Facilities Management	19 943
居民服务和其他服务业	Residents Service and Other Service Trades	6 547
教 育	Education	101 385
卫生和社会工作	Health Care and Social Work	67 356
文化、体育和娱乐业	Culture, Sports and Entertainment	9 013
公共管理和社会组织	Public Administration and Social Organizations	99 538

Continued

# 在岗职工 Fully Employed Staff and Workers	从业人员平均工资 (元) Average Remuneration (yuan)	# 在岗职工 Fully Employed Staff and Workers	从业人员工资中位数 (元) Median of Wage (yuan)	# 在岗职工 Fully Employed Staff and Workers
463 902	71 432	72 476	63 716	64 659
220 688	99 995	100 895	79 331	77 093
12 576	79 763	80 744	70 905	70 905
571 460	66 441	65 964	59 053	59 053
1 211 269	78 151	76 392	67 675	66 673
106	72 144	86 542	63 769	83 531
531	75 941	75 941	75 941	75 941
1 967 892	72 666	71 599	64 788	64 305
14 137	117 107	117 388	111 070	111 153
105 838	59 992	60 914	50 973	52 000
99 419	75 681	73 914	58 724	58 881
70 490	78 995	79 472	78 238	79 041
36 372	45 199	45 205	43 454	43 545
38 470	131 210	131 081	123 306	123 306
60 085	179 409	182 395	174 754	177 335
52 893	81 911	84 539	50 000	51 868
42 313	83 235	83 133	57 023	58 644
25 043	123 618	123 836	113 716	112 069
16 953	65 146	71 480	54 433	62 364
6 276	58 913	59 560	53 370	56 536
94 188	114 782	120 278	113 119	122 103
63 170	111 186	114 307	113 175	117 143
8 231	91 452	95 383	81 187	83 324
96 593	123 808	125 495	114 826	114 826

表2-15

市区城镇非私营单位从业人员平均工资（2016年）
AVERAGE WAGES OF EMPLOYEES OF NON-PRIVATE UNITS IN THE URBAN AREA (2016)

单位：元 (yuan)

项　　目	Item	平均工资 Average Remuneration	# 在岗职工 Fully Employed Staff and Workers
总　　计	**Total**	**83 392**	**83 293**
一、按机构类型分	**Grouped by Character of the Units**		
企　业	Enterprises	80 205	79 822
事　业	Institutions	110 233	114 382
机　关	Government Agencies	145 549	147 109
其　他	Others	87 148	87 548
二、按登记注册类型分	**Grouped by Registration Status**		
内资单位	Domestic Units	94 657	96 574
国有单位	State-owned Units	112 609	115 226
集体单位	Collective-owned Units	74 437	76 644
股份合作单位	Share-holding Cooperative Units	60 743	64 233
联营单位	Joint Ownership Units	85 839	82 319
有限责任公司	Limited Liability Corporations	75 562	77 043
股份有限公司	Share-holding Corporations Ltd.	111 766	112 861
其他单位	Other Enterprises	87 072	88 396
港澳台商投资单位	Units with Investment from HongKong, Macao and Taiwan	65 585	65 556
外商投资单位	Units with Foreign Investment	82 189	80 528
三、按行业分	**Grouped by Sector**		
农林牧渔业	Farming, Forestry, Animal Husbandry and Fishery	63 812	77 115
采矿业	Mining and Quarrying	75 941	75 941
制造业	Manufacturing	74 996	74 147
电力、燃气及水的生产和供应业	Power, Gas and Water Production and Supply	104 654	104 969
建筑业	Construction	65 417	66 554
批发和零售业	Wholesale and Retail Trade Services	77 359	74 087
交通运输、仓储和邮政业	Transportation, Logistics and Postal	80 140	80 416
住宿和餐饮业	Accommodation and Catering Services	43 956	43 931
信息传输、软件和信息技术服务业	Information Transmission, Software and Information Technology Services	138 888	138 631
金融业	Financial Industries	194 388	196 149
房地产业	Real Estate	83 196	85 583
租赁和商务服务业	Renting and Labor Services	89 102	90 914
科学研究和技术服务业	Scientific Research and Technical Services	126 098	126 720
水利、环境和公共设施管理业	Water Conservancy, Environment and Public Facilities Management	71 411	75 648
居民服务和其他服务业	Residents Service and Other Service Trades	66 955	69 039
教　育	Education	107 605	111 608
卫生和社会工作	Health Care and Social Work	103 952	106 890
文化、体育和娱乐业	Culture, Sports and Entertainment	88 934	92 808
公共管理和社会组织	Public Administration and Social Organizations	127 416	128 462

主 要 统 计 指 标 解 释

人口数　指一定时点、一定地区范围内有生命的个人总和。年度统计的年末人口数指每年12月31日24时的人口数。

出生率(又称粗出生率)　指在一定时期内(通常为一年)一定地区的出生人数与同期内平均人数(或期中人数)之比，用千分率表示。本资料中的出生率指年出生率，其计算公式为：

$$出生率=\frac{年出生人数}{年平均人数}\times 1000‰$$

式中：出生人数指活产婴儿，即胎儿脱离母体时(不管怀孕月数)，有过呼吸或其他生命现象。年平均人数指年初、年底人口数的平均数，也可用年中人口数代替。

死亡率(又称粗死亡率)　指在一定时期内(通常为一年)一定地区的死亡人数与同期内平均人数(或期中人数)之比，用千分率表示。本资料中的死亡率指年死亡率，其计算公式为：

$$死亡率=\frac{年死亡人数}{年平均人数}\times 1000‰$$

人口自然增长率　指在一定时期内(通常为一年)人口自然增加数(出生人数减死亡人数)与该时期内平均人数(或期中人数)之比，用千分率表示。计算公式为：

$$人口自然增长率=\frac{本年出生人数-本年死亡人数}{年平均人数}\times 1000‰$$

$$=人口出生率-人口死亡率$$

从业人员　指在一定年龄以上，有劳动能力，为取得劳动报酬或经营收入而从事一定社会劳动的人员。具体指年满16周岁，为取得报酬或经营利润，在调查周内从事了1小时（含1小时）以上劳动的人员；或由于学习、休假等原因在调查周内暂时处于未工作状态，但有工作单位或场所的人员；或由于季节性歇业、单位不景气放假等原因在调查周内暂时处于未工作状态，但不满三个月的人员。

单位从业人员　指在各级国家机关、政党机关、社会团体及企业、事业单位中工作，取得工资或其他形式的劳动报酬的全部人员。包括在岗职工、再就业的离退休人员、民办教师以及在各单位中工作的外方人员和港澳台方人员、兼职人员、借用的外单位人员和第二职业者。不包括离开本单位仍保留劳动关系的职工。各单位的就业人员反映了各单位实际参加生产或工作的全部劳动力。

城镇非私营单位从业人员　指在城镇非私营单位工作，并由单位支付劳动报酬的人员，包括在岗职工和其他就业人员。城镇非私营单位是指城镇地区全部非私营法人单位，具体包括国有单位、城镇集体单位、联营经济、股份制经济、外商投资经济、港澳台投资经济等单位。

职工　指在国有、城镇集体、联营、股份制、外商和港、澳、台投资、其他单位及其附属机构工作，并由其支付工资的各类人员。不包括下列人员：(1)乡镇企业就业人员；(2)私营企业就业人员；(3)城镇个体劳动者；(4)离休、退休、退职人员；(5)再就业的离、退休人员；(6)民办教师；(7)在城镇单位中工作的外方及港、澳、台人员；(8)其他按有关规定不列入职工统计范围的人员。(1998年及以后的数据均为在岗职工数据，其他相关指标如职工工资总额，职工平均工资等指标也从1998年按此口径进行了相应调整)。

国有单位　指资产归国家所有的经济组织。包括按《中华人民共和国企业法人登记管理条例》规定登记注册的非公司制的经济组织，以及中央、地方各级国家机关、事业单位和社会团体。

集体单位 指生产资料归集体所有，并按《中华人民共和国企业法人登记管理条例》规定登记注册的经济组织。

其他单位 包括股份合作单位、联营单位、有限责任公司、股份有限公司、港澳台商投资单位以及外商投资单位等其他登记注册类型单位。

城镇非私营单位在岗职工 指在本城镇地区非私营单位工作，以及有工作岗位，但由于学习、病伤产假等原因暂未工作，仍由单位支付工资的人员。在岗职工还包括：应订立劳动合同而未订立劳动合同人员（如使用的农村户籍人员）；处于试用期人员；编制外招用的人员，如临时人员；派往外单位工作，但工资仍由本单位发放的人员（如挂职锻炼、外派工作等情况）；本单位使用的且由本单位支付工资的劳务派遣人员。

平均工资 指企业、事业、机关单位的职工在一定时期内平均每人所得的货币工资额。它表明一定时期职工工资收入的高低程度，是反映职工工资水平的主要指标。计算公式为:

$$平均工资=\frac{报告期实际支付的全部职工工资总额}{报告期全部职工平均人数}$$

中位数 是指将总体各单位标志值按大小顺序排列，处于中间位置的那个标志值。在许多不易计算平均值的情况下，可用中位数代表总体的一般水平。由于中位数的确定仅取决于它在数列中的位置，因此不受数列中极端标志值的影响。中位数的确定依据提供的具体资料不同而采取相应的方法。

EXPLANATORY NOTES ON MAIN STATISTICAL INDICATORS

Total Population refers to the total number of people alive at a certain point of time within a given area. The annual statistics on total population is taken at midnight, the 31st of December.

Birth Rate (or Crude Birth Rate) refers to the ratio of the number of births to the average population (or mid-period population) during a certain period of time (usually a year), expressed in ‰. Birth rate in the chapter refers to annual birth rate. The following formula is used:

$$\text{Birth Rate} = \frac{\text{Number of Births}}{\text{Annual Average Population}} \times 1000‰$$

Number of births in the formula refers to live births, i.e. when a baby has breathed or showed any vital phenomena regardless of the length of pregnancy.

Annual average population is the average of the number of population at the beginning of the year and that at the end of the year. Sometimes it is substituted by the mid-year population.

Death Rate (or Crude Death Rate) refers to the ratio of the number of deaths to the average population (or mid-period population) during a certain period of time (usually a year), expressed in ‰. Death rate in the chapter refers to annual death rate. The following formula is used:

$$\text{Death Rate} = \frac{\text{Number of Deaths}}{\text{Annual Average Population}} \times 1000‰$$

Natural Growth Rate of Population refers to the ratio of natural increase in population (number of births minus number of deaths) in a certain period of time (usually a year) to the average population (or mid-period population) of the same period, expressed in ‰. The following formula is applied:

$$\begin{array}{c}\text{Natural Growth} \\ \text{Rate of Population}\end{array} = \frac{\text{Number of Births - Number of Deaths}}{\text{Annual Average Population}} \times 1000‰$$

$$= \text{Birth Rate-Death Rate}$$

Employed Persons refers to persons above a specified age who had labour capacity and performed some social work for compensation or business gains. Specifically, it refers to persons, aged 16 and over, who performed some work for compensation or business gains for one hour or more during the reference period; or persons who do not work for the reasons of study or on holiday, but had work units or sites during the reference period; or persons who do not work for the reasons of seasonal closing business, recession etc, but not exceeding three months during the reference period.

Persons Employed in Various Units refer to all the persons working in government agencies of various levels, political and party organizations, social organizations, enterprises and institutions, and receiving wages or other forms of payment. They include fully-employed staff and workers, re-employed retirees, teachers in the schools run by the local people, foreigners and Chinese compatriots from Hong Kong, Macao, and Taiwan working in various units, part-time employees, employees of other units working temporarily at current posts, and employees holding the second job, but do not include persons who have left their working units while keeping their labor contract (employment relation) unchanged. This indicator reflects the total number of laborers actually engaged in production or other operations in various units.

Urban non-private unit employees refer to people who work in urban non-private units and are paid by the units, including staff and workers and other employees. Urban non-private units refer to all non-private legal entities in urban areas, including state -owned units, urban collective units, associated economic units, share economic units, foreign invested economic units, and Hong Kong, Macao and Taiwan invested economic units.

Staff and Workers refer to persons working in, and receive payment from units of state ownership, collective ownership, joint ownership, share holding ownership, foreign ownership, and ownership by entrepreneurs from Hong Kong, Macao, and Taiwan, and other types of ownership and their affiliated units. They do not include 1) persons employed in township enterprises, 2) persons employed in private enterprises, 3) urban self-employed persons, 4) retirees, 5) re-employed retirees, 6) teachers in the schools run by the local people, 7) foreigners and persons from Hong Kong, Macao and Taiwan who work in urban units, and 8) other persons not to be included by relevant regulations. (Data since 1998 refer to fully employed staff and workers. Other related statistics indicators, such as total wage bill and average wage are adjusted since 1998 accordingly).

State-owned Units refer to economic units whose assets are owned by the state, including non-corporation units registered according to *Regulation of the People's Republic of China on the Registration of Enterprises and Corporations*, state organs, institutions and social organizations at the central-level and local levels.

Collective-owned Units refer to economic units registered according to *Regulation of the People's Republic of China on the Registration of Enterprises and Corporations* where the means of production are collectively owned.

Units of Other Types of Ownership refer to units registered with other types of ownership, including cooperative units, joint ownership units, limited liability corporations, share holding corporations, units funded by entrepreneurs from Hong Kong, Macao, and Taiwan, and foreign- funded units.

Urban Non-private Unit Staff and Workers refer to people who work in non-private units in urban areas, and people who have a post, but are temporarily not working because of learning, sick leave, injury leave or maternity leave and other reasons and are still paid by the units. Workers in the post also include people who should have but have not had a labor contract (such as rural workers employed); people who are in probation; people who are recruited outside the preparation of personnel staffing, such as temporary workers; people who are assigned to work outside the unit but are still paid by the unit (things such as training with the post suspended and work assignments outside the unit); and dispatched personnel who are used and paid by the unit.

Average Wage refers to the average wage in money terms per person during a certain period of time for staff and workers in enterprises, institutions, and government agencies, which reflects the general level of wage income during a certain period of time and is calculated as follows:

$$\text{Average Wage} = \frac{\text{Total Wage Bill of Staff and Workers at Reference Time}}{\text{Average Number of Staff and Workers at Reference Time}}$$

The Median refers to the symbol value which is in the middle position of the sequence that is in symbol values size order. In many cases that are not easy to calculate the average, the median of the available median represents the general level of the population. Because the median is determined only by its position in the sequence, so it is not affected by the extreme value of the sequence. The determination of the median is based on the specific information provided by the different ways to take the corresponding.

三、农 业

CHAPTER 3
AGRICULTURE

3 农 业
AGRICULTURE

主要统计指标
MAJOR STATISTICAL INDICATORS

2016年末乡村实有从业人员	Rural Real Employed persons	171.89	万人	10 000 persons
比上年增长	Increase Over Last Year	-0.8	%	
2016年农作物播种面积	Sown Areas Of Farm Crops	241.40	千公顷	1 000 hectares
比上年增长	Increase Over Last Year	-3.5	%	
2016年农林牧渔业总产值	Gross Output Value of Farming, Forestry, Animal Husbandry and Fishery	424.67	亿元	100 million yuan
比上年增长	Increase Over Last Year	2.3	%	
2016年农林牧渔业总产值(可比价格)	Gross Output Value of Farming, Forestry, Animal Husbandry and Fishery (at Comparable Price)	409.42	亿元	100 million yuan
比上年增长	Increase Over Last Year	-1.4	%	
2016年农林牧渔业增加值	Value Added of Farming, Forestry, Animal Husbandry and Fishery	247.02	亿元	100 million yuan
比上年增长	Increase Over Last Year	-1.3	%	
2016年粮食总产量	Total Yield of Grain Crops	97.68	万吨	10 000 tons
比上年增长	Increase Over Last Year	-9.7	%	

表3-1

部分年份农村基本情况
BASIC CONDITIONS OF COUNTRYSIDE OF PARTIAL YEARS

项　目		Item		2012年	2013年	2014年	2015年	2016年
农村组织	(个)	**Village Units**	(unit)					
镇政府		Town Governments		55	55	55	55	55
村民委员会		Number of Villagers' Committees		1 068	1 043	1 041	1 039	1 034
村民小组		Villager Group		27 514	26 992	26 837	26 671	26 454
乡村户数、人口		**Households and Rural Population**						
乡村总户数	(万户)	Number of Households	(10 000 households)	91.42	90.11	89.08	88.32	87.50
乡村总人口	(万人)	Rural Population	(10 000 persons)	296.41	292.41	288.83	286.16	283.23
年末乡村实有从业人员		**Rural Employees of year-end**						
合　计		Total		179.54	176.85	174.76	173.30	171.89
1.按性别分		Grouped by Sex						
男劳动力		Male		92.84	91.11	89.81	89.19	88.65
女劳动力		Female		86.70	85.74	84.95	84.11	83.24
2.按行业分		Grouped by Sector						
农林牧渔业		Farming, Forestry, Animal Husbandry and Fishery		24.22	23.49	22.81	22.26	21.83
农　业		Farming		15.40	14.70	14.29	13.97	13.69
林牧渔业		Forestry, Animal Husbandry and Fishery		8.82	8.79	8.52	8.29	8.14
工　业		Industry		106.84	105.34	105.05	104.31	103.57
建筑业		Construction		10.28	10.05	9.88	10.02	9.66
交通运输、邮电业		Transportation, Postal and Telecommunications Services		5.62	5.52	5.51	5.51	5.48
信息传输、计算机服务和软件业		Information Transmission, Software and Information Technology Services		0.98	1.02	1.11	1.18	1.22
批发和零售业		Wholesale and Retail Trade Services		10.30	10.20	10.22	10.28	10.24
住宿和餐饮业		Accommodation and Catering Services		4.45	4.51	4.50	4.47	4.55
金融保险业		Banking and Insurance		0.77	0.78	0.86	0.88	0.94
房地产、社会服务业		Real Estate and Social Services		2.55	2.58	2.39	2.35	2.31
卫生、体育、社会福利业		Health Care, Sporting and Social Welfare		0.95	0.98	1.04	1.06	1.10
文、教、艺术和广播影视业		Culture, Education and Arts, Radio, Film and Television		0.87	0.88	0.96	0.97	0.97
科研和综合技术服务业		Scientific Research and Polytechnical Services		0.20	0.22	0.22	0.23	0.26
乡镇经济组织管理		Rural Economic Management		1.20	1.20	1.16	1.16	1.19
其　他		Others		10.31	10.08	9.05	8.62	8.57

表3-2

历年年末乡村实有从业人员
RURAL REAL EMPLOYED PERSONS OVER THE YEARS (YEAR-END)

单位：万人　　(10 000 persons)

年　份 Year	全　市 Whole Municipality	市　区 Urban Area	# 吴江区 Wujiang District	常　熟 Changshu	张家港 Zhangjiagang	昆　山 Kunshan	太　仓 Taicang
1949	124.93	45.96	17.08	30.24	20.54	12.66	15.53
1952	130.35	48.80	17.87	30.47	20.79	14.74	15.55
1957	146.38	57.93	22.31	32.48	24.60	16.07	15.30
1962	150.22	60.28	20.73	33.87	23.51	15.72	16.84
1965	176.82	72.24	24.23	38.71	28.78	18.21	18.88
1970	222.22	92.13	32.71	48.02	36.45	23.91	21.71
1975	233.63	97.64	34.39	49.47	36.77	25.55	24.20
1978	244.55	98.51	34.76	52.83	41.78	26.30	25.13
1980	250.74	103.00	36.76	54.20	40.94	26.83	25.77
1985	269.24	112.57	39.61	57.10	44.62	30.19	24.76
1990	260.51	113.95	40.59	57.44	37.52	29.69	21.91
1995	230.96	101.07	37.77	50.02	32.96	26.29	20.62
1996	228.45	99.29	37.14	50.97	32.11	26.06	20.02
1997	224.83	98.27	36.06	49.43	32.05	25.36	19.72
1998	223.14	98.79	35.63	48.67	31.90	24.73	19.05
1999	219.42	96.90	34.56	50.43	31.40	23.19	17.50
2000	213.75	95.34	33.22	49.76	30.17	22.16	16.32
2001	212.22	95.50	32.13	49.47	30.16	21.52	15.57
2002	210.55	94.36	31.85	49.37	30.20	21.29	15.33
2003	209.42	92.50	30.88	49.96	30.35	21.33	15.28
2004	207.60	90.48	32.04	49.24	30.60	22.30	14.98
2005	207.20	89.88	31.99	48.83	30.54	23.14	14.81
2006	206.90	88.59	32.36	48.52	30.92	22.73	16.14
2007	205.49	89.90	32.81	44.63	31.14	22.96	16.86
2008	205.94	89.76	32.40	43.87	33.10	22.60	16.61
2009	199.99	84.68	32.25	42.92	33.49	22.47	16.43
2010	190.42	74.88	31.98	42.42	33.68	22.50	16.94
2011	184.77	73.31	32.67	40.89	32.55	21.39	16.63
2012	179.54	70.82	31.71	39.74	31.61	21.21	16.16
2013	176.85	69.71	31.24	39.16	31.16	20.90	15.92
2014	174.76	68.70	30.78	38.78	30.70	20.85	15.73
2015	173.30	67.76	30.32	38.76	30.45	20.80	15.53
2016	171.89	66.75	29.87	38.42	30.42	20.78	15.52

表3-3

历年农林牧渔业总产值
GROSS OUTPUT VALUE OF FARMING, FORESTRY, ANIMAL HUSBANDRY AND FISHERY OVER THE YEARS

单位：万元 (10 000 yuan)

年 份 Year	总产值 Gross Output Value	农 业 Farming	# 种植业 Planting	林 业 Forestry	牧 业 Animal Husbandry	渔 业 Fishery	农林牧渔服务业 Farming,Forestry,Animal Husbandry,Fishery and Service Industry
1978	187 469	163 707	163 015	557	18 837	4 368	
1979	193 422	162 903	162 044	582	25 343	4 594	
1980	114 163	83 915	82 812	720	23 600	5 928	
1985	274 220	171 637	148 084	3 091	62 215	37 277	
1990	581 222	349 554	290 067	5 025	119 400	107 243	
1991	586 831	364 221	298 524	4 698	115 081	102 831	
1992	687 303	443 730	324 601	7 740	123 611	112 222	
1993	867 634	560 735	410 256	7 712	154 676	144 511	
1994	1 274 976	804 597	618 022	9 990	248 916	211 473	
1995	1 416 173	918 417	697 111	9 834	233 110	254 812	
1996	1 625 939	1 077 094	779 714	6 725	242 010	300 110	
1997	1 650 915	1 071 369	751 572	9 011	231 268	339 267	
1998	1 654 137	1 047 069	693 739	8 789	239 493	358 786	
1999	1 647 033	1 012 489	630 165	11 583	224 721	398 240	
2000	1 692 982	1 001 634	610 779	11 740	231 251	448 357	
2001	1 734 596	962 669	562 869	27 485	247 416	497 026	
2002	1 744 598	901 031	516 749	43 046	245 472	555 049	
2003	1 562 657	561 773	561 773	38 031	232 988	547 683	182 182
2004	1 639 627	589 162	589 162	50 311	249 959	562 791	187 404
2005	1 628 655	577 417	577 417	63 554	217 068	594 059	176 557
2006	1 721 844	663 120	663 120	72 351	214 312	601 890	170 171
2007	1 810 817	663 883	663 883	86 189	274 583	609 590	176 572
2008	2 334 155	878 179	878 179	126 262	330 251	727 964	271 499
2009	2 489 315	940 627	940 627	147 646	347 466	785 044	268 532
2010	2 712 943	1 052 848	1 052 848	161 828	357 452	853 943	286 872
2011	3 098 576	1 210 220	1 210 220	179 825	411 440	978 319	318 772
2012	3 377 237	1 350 458	1 350 458	204 834	402 031	1 066 347	353 567
2013	3 698 219	1 507 763	1 507 763	231 267	400 479	1 156 898	401 812
2014	3 924 922	1 614 539	1 614 539	244 711	388 226	1 226 420	451 026
2015	4 151 748	1 728 527	1 728 527	258 763	387 641	1 293 042	483 775
2016	4 246 673	1 788 110	1 788 110	247 639	373 939	1 360 760	476 225

注：2008年数据根据第二次农业普查、第二次经济普查已作调整。
Note:The 2008 data were adjusted according to the second agricultural census and the second economic census.

表3-4

历年粮食、棉花、油料播种面积
SOWN AREAS OF GRAIN CROPS, COTTON AND OIL-BEARING CROPS OVER THE YEARS

单位：千公顷 (1 000 hectares)

年 份 Year	粮 食 Grain Crops	夏 粮 Summer Grain	秋 粮 Autumn Grain	棉 花 Cotton	油 料 Oil-bearing Crops	# 油菜籽 Rapeseeds
1949	527.02	193.56	333.46	44.58	39.95	39.25
1952	562.96	220.65	342.31	61.73	46.19	45.57
1957	593.95	238.15	355.80	46.05	45.46	44.81
1962	505.48	199.85	305.63	41.46	34.31	33.49
1965	499.19	188.97	310.22	47.56	37.92	37.41
1970	598.12	185.07	413.05	46.50	41.72	41.59
1975	644.58	181.05	463.53	48.30	46.23	46.19
1978	636.61	179.59	457.02	47.76	47.89	47.77
1980	600.83	178.75	422.08	47.39	51.46	51.38
1985	500.49	197.12	303.37	44.50	90.11	89.95
1990	471.29	197.89	273.40	33.21	74.23	74.05
1995	398.73	159.41	239.32	25.40	67.17	66.84
1996	399.25	157.88	241.37	21.06	68.06	67.78
1997	401.03	159.45	241.58	14.87	62.63	62.37
1998	371.31	145.58	225.73	16.22	61.84	61.55
1999	343.52	129.87	213.65	13.33	58.92	58.37
2000	290.33	105.93	184.40	11.29	61.56	60.82
2001	234.05	76.29	157.76	11.92	58.49	57.70
2002	219.07	75.52	143.55	7.63	52.43	51.69
2003	173.56	60.72	112.84	6.58	39.42	38.85
2004	167.61	51.21	116.40	6.35	31.64	31.12
2005	169.85	54.28	115.57	4.46	33.22	32.67
2006	163.26	58.63	104.63	2.97	27.86	27.41
2007	153.45	59.71	93.74	2.39	28.02	27.62
2008	162.43	65.21	97.22	2.37	17.70	17.11
2009	160.07	65.56	94.51	2.02	19.49	18.90
2010	161.72	70.10	91.62	1.59	14.47	13.95
2011	159.65	70.15	89.50	1.39	11.65	11.04
2012	159.66	71.31	88.35	1.18	10.09	9.53
2013	154.27	69.74	84.53	0.96	9.26	8.77
2014	151.29	70.05	81.24	0.80	7.82	7.33
2015	147.82	68.49	79.33	0.60	6.03	5.60
2016	145.01	67.70	77.31	0.45	5.40	5.01

表3-5

历年粮食、棉花、油料总产量
TOTAL YIELD OF GRAIN CROPS, COTTON AND OIL-BEARING CROPS OVER THE YEARS

年份 Year	粮食 (万吨) Grain Crops (10 000 tons)	夏粮 Summer Grain	秋粮 Autumn Grain	棉花 (吨) Cotton (ton)	油料 (吨) Oil-bearing Crops (ton)	#油菜籽 Rapeseeds
1949	84.01	8.98	75.03	4 450	14 420	14 130
1952	133.41	16.81	116.60	14 810	24 950	24 080
1957	135.69	20.73	114.96	16 490	26 410	25 430
1962	152.32	31.09	121.23	14 560	17 250	16 660
1965	210.32	40.55	169.77	40 820	41 120	39 360
1970	223.62	38.27	185.35	35 880	57 060	56 300
1975	241.87	42.96	198.91	37 350	55 780	55 460
1978	294.26	66.70	227.56	36 330	91 320	90 610
1980	254.31	75.64	178.67	35 180	81 620	81 120
1985	238.49	59.02	179.47	42 600	141 020	140 480
1990	283.50	75.74	207.76	36 932	140 129	139 760
1995	265.67	66.26	199.41	40 210	145 608	144 798
1996	279.10	70.06	209.04	36 594	146 606	145 861
1997	279.93	70.24	209.69	22 725	130 213	129 464
1998	239.63	36.57	203.06	24 284	56 462	55 702
1999	225.84	53.21	172.62	9 349	123 902	122 441
2000	193.95	40.61	153.34	11 722	126 066	123 917
2001	159.48	23.93	135.55	12 976	102 529	100 106
2002	146.42	22.30	124.12	7 527	78 093	75 896
2003	112.77	17.90	94.87	6 816	62 418	60 347
2004	117.71	20.44	97.27	7 450	69 234	67 387
2005	110.76	22.76	88.00	4 605	69 593	68 143
2006	111.21	24.38	86.83	3 117	63 019	61 779
2007	94.14	24.66	69.48	2 459	64 107	62 980
2008	113.22	31.39	81.83	2 525	42 571	40 884
2009	112.94	30.84	82.10	2 135	46 632	44 991
2010	114.43	33.12	81.31	1 685	34 468	33 052
2011	115.00	34.92	80.08	1 508	28 907	27 352
2012	116.46	36.71	79.75	1 292	25 882	24 354
2013	113.12	36.50	76.62	1 038	24 209	22 892
2014	110.46	37.15	73.31	882	20 395	19 087
2015	108.22	36.43	71.79	666	15 747	14 603
2016	97.68	28.91	68.77	500	13 409	12 368

表3-6

历年粮食、棉花、油料单产
YIELD OF GRAIN CROPS, COTTON AND OIL-BEARING CROPS PER HECTARE OVER THE YEARS

单位：公斤/公顷 (kg/hectare)

年 份 Year	粮 食 Grain Crops	夏 粮 Summer Grain	秋 粮 Autumn Grain	棉 花 Cotton	油 料 Oil-bearing Crops	# 油菜籽 Rapeseeds
1949	1 594	464	2 250	100	361	360
1952	2 370	762	3 406	240	540	528
1957	2 285	870	3 231	358	581	568
1962	3 013	1 556	3 967	351	503	497
1965	4 213	2 146	5 473	858	1 084	1 052
1970	3 739	2 068	4 487	772	1 368	1 354
1975	3 752	2 373	4 291	773	1 261	1 201
1978	4 022	3 714	4 979	761	1 907	1 897
1980	4 233	4 232	4 233	742	1 586	1 579
1985	4 765	2 994	5 916	957	1 565	1 562
1990	6 015	3 825	7 605	1 112	1 888	1 887
1995	6 663	4 157	8 332	1 583	2 168	2 166
1996	6 990	4 437	8 661	1 738	2 154	2 152
1997	6 980	4 405	8 680	1 528	2 079	2 076
1998	6 454	2 512	8 996	1 497	913	905
1999	6 574	4 097	8 080	701	2 103	2 098
2000	6 680	3 833	8 316	1 038	2 048	2 037
2001	6 814	3 137	8 592	1 089	1 753	1 735
2002	6 684	2 953	8 646	987	1 489	1 468
2003	6 497	2 974	8 408	1 036	1 583	1 553
2004	7 023	3 991	8 356	1 173	2 188	2 165
2005	6 521	4 193	7 615	1 033	2 095	2 086
2006	6 812	4 159	8 299	1 051	2 262	2 254
2007	6 135	4 131	7 412	1 029	2 288	2 280
2008	6 970	4 813	8 417	1 065	2 405	2 389
2009	7 055	4 704	8 686	1 057	2 393	2 380
2010	7 076	4 725	8 874	1 060	2 382	2 369
2011	7 203	4 977	8 948	1 085	2 481	2 478
2012	7 294	5 148	9 027	1 095	2 565	2 556
2013	7 333	5 234	9 064	1 081	2 614	2 610
2014	7 301	5 304	9 023	1 103	2 608	2 604
2015	7 321	5 320	9 049	1 110	2 611	2 608
2016	6 736	4 271	8 895	1 111	2 483	2 469

表3-7

历年蚕桑、茶叶、水果生产情况
STATISTICS ON SILKWORM COCOONS, TEA AND FRUITS OVER THE YEARS

年份 Year	蚕桑 Silkworm Cocoons and Mulberry		茶叶 Tea		水果 Fruits	
	桑园面积（公顷）Mulberry Field Area (hectare)	蚕茧产量（吨）Output of Silkworm Cocoons (ton)	茶园面积（公顷）Tea Field Area (hectare)	总产量（吨）Total Output (ton)	果园面积（公顷）Area of Orchards (hectare)	总产量（吨）Total Output (ton)
1949	7 051	1 797	117	66	1 096	6 785
1952	7 360	3 047	117	77	1 184	7 584
1957	7 191	2 510	121	47	1 321	8 257
1962	5 843	943	208	90	1 517	12 213
1965	5 745	1 917	212	137	1 599	16 236
1970	7 051	4 520	210	190	1 706	19 039
1975	7 046	4 340	314	261	2 098	23 357
1978	6 115	3 325	393	286	2 440	18 653
1980	6 065	4 784	401	286	2 778	17 407
1985	6 868	5 663	417	265	5 771	39 113
1990	7 973	9 785	360	369	4 853	42 280
1995	9 275	12 435	421	262	6 796	62 096
1996	7 092	9 805	422	274	6 070	56 155
1997	7 967	9 020	376	247	5 838	69 391
1998	7 583	8 669	411	253	5 862	44 250
1999	6 834	8 170	409	259	5 785	75 120
2000	6 188	7 291	469	258	6 080	59 203
2001	6 090	7 397	570	249	6 286	78 523
2002	5 333	5 785	679	235	6 523	67 918
2003	4 164	3 437	1 530	399	6 554	79 307
2004	3 918	3 512	1 815	315	6 191	73 084
2005	3 895	2 771	1 955	348	6 708	74 138
2006	3 881	3 008	2 106	381	7 029	76 023
2007	3 879	2 478	2 120	385	7 554	79 767
2008	3 853	1 654	2 207	397	8 712	91 102
2009	3 745	915	2 296	403	9 627	103 064
2010	3 618	638	2 344	338	10 214	96 953
2011	3 474	558	2 400	349	10 791	103 082
2012	3 601	495	2 416	375	10 866	105 993
2013	2 070	396	2 403	383	11 155	110 763
2014	2 067	357	2 400	374	11 343	114 928
2015	2 047	295	2 430	364	11 444	104 156
2016	2 030	237	2 430	357	11 132	95 595

表3-8

历年牧业、渔业生产情况
STATISTICS ON LIVESTOCK AND FISHERY OVER THE YEARS

年 份 Year	猪（万头）Hogs (10 000 heads)			年末存栏 Livestock Being Raised at Year-end			牛奶产量（吨）Output of Cow Milk (ton)	水产品产量（吨）Output of Aquatic Products(ton)
	年末存栏 Hog Being Raised at Year-end	肉猪出栏 Slaughtered Hogs	猪肉产量（吨）Output of Pork (ton)	牛（万头）Cattle and Buffaloes (10 000 heads)	羊（万只）Sheep and Goats (10 000 heads)	家禽（万只）Poultry (10 000 heads)		
1949	23.21	11.80		8.59	18.73	120.23		14 977
1952	37.98	22.16		10.18	26.86	178.32		21 470
1957	81.58	40.40		9.45	41.96	278.11		30 998
1962	71.52	25.67		6.69	58.40	162.37		26 672
1965	155.04	120.68		6.24	42.18	169.81		32 817
1970	214.19	117.68		6.20	49.28	203.55		44 765
1975	245.64	178.35		3.55	47.57	269.22	1 934	61 845
1978	264.31	185.66		2.74	45.58	418.93	2 375	82 249
1980	250.34	310.14	129 457	2.43	48.53	453.57	4 110	87 119
1985	186.01	210.41	110 498	0.79	24.00	1 012.16	10 155	158 774
1990	154.62	193.54	101 418	0.62	41.00	1 048.48	16 069	217 276
1995	111.73	177.46	104 321	0.34	49.38	1 008.51	12 316	284 097
1996	103.64	177.53	104 429	0.50	41.14	986.48	14 101	285 180
1997	103.32	178.19	116 098	0.48	39.63	696.20	16 605	301 319
1998	107.58	191.27	115 847	0.47	36.58	757.76	21 240	307 640
1999	97.15	186.14	106 825	0.59	33.23	816.41	28 293	321 206
2000	104.75	198.50	111 075	0.86	35.92	971.05	43 742	345 139
2001	98.71	204.74	115 631	1.89	36.16	1 109.73	80 453	354 308
2002	88.78	188.12	107 976	2.65	32.12	1 181.12	105 095	357 221
2003	75.89	178.49	93 809	2.47	27.05	1 067.30	100 266	338 707
2004	76.00	160.82	85 617	2.26	21.75	1 060.91	108 812	311 884
2005	73.85	139.91	86 274	2.40	13.08	1 202.80	94 651	316 523
2006	66.05	136.64	99 935	2.29	5.89	929.61	100 547	299 882
2007	70.87	122.24	92 499	2.30	4.67	1 050.83	98 129	292 785
2008	77.93	110.66	79 204	2.68	4.88	1 113.06	91 983	290 637
2009	82.37	117.34	88 876	2.32	6.49	1 120.89	91 019	273 498
2010	83.51	117.70	84 487	2.35	7.90	1 093.48	91 675	277 049
2011	85.34	118.49	86 164	2.34	7.77	991.09	92 577	284 083
2012	84.97	113.44	84 543	2.28	8.58	853.76	92 524	288 433
2013	85.98	106.15	79 751	2.20	9.87	787.92	95 060	276 955
2014	76.69	103.46	75 525	2.39	10.73	656.68	101 224	267 039
2015	66.44	94.89	70 423	2.36	12.96	657.45	113 774	262 057
2016	60.34	84.46	61 778	2.15	10.36	651.87	102 957	254 918

表3-9

农村基本情况（2016年末）

项　　目		Item		全　市 Whole Municipality
农村组织		**Village Units**		
镇政府	(个)	Town Governments	(unit)	55
村民委员会		Number of Villagers' Committees		1 034
乡村户数、人口		**Households and Rural Population**		
乡村总户数	(万户)	Number of Households	(10 000 households)	87.50
乡村总人口	(万人)	Rural Population	(10 000 persons)	283.23
年末乡村实有从业人员		**Rural Employees of year-end**		
合　计		Total		171.89
1.按性别分		Grouped by Sex		
男劳动力		Male		88.65
女劳动力		Female		83.24
2.按行业分		Grouped by Sector		
农林牧渔业		Farming, Forestry, Animal Husbandry and Fishery		21.83
工　业		Industry		103.57
建筑业		Construction		9.66
交通运输、仓储和邮政业		Transportation, Logistics and Postal		5.48
信息传输、计算机服务和软件业		Information Transmission, Software and Information Technology Services		1.22
批发和零售业		Wholesale and Retail Trade Services		10.24
住宿和餐饮业		Accommodation and Catering Services		4.55
金融、保险业		Banking and Insurance		0.94
房地产、社会服务业		Real Estate and Social Services		2.31
卫生、体育、社会福利业		Health Care, Sporting and Social Welfare		1.10
文、教、艺术和广播影视业		Culture, Education and Arts, Radio, Film and Television		0.97
科研和综合技术服务业		Scientific Research and Polytechnical Services		0.26
乡镇经济组织管理		Rural Economic Management		1.19
其　他		Others		8.57

BASIC CONDITIONS OF COUNTRYSIDE (END OF 2016)

市区 Urban Area	# 吴江区 Wujiang District	常熟 Changshu	张家港 Zhangjiagang	昆山 Kunshan	太仓 Taicang
22	8	9	8	10	6
442	249	215	153	151	73
34.29	15.41	17.75	18.47	10.29	6.70
110.84	50.11	57.12	55.93	35.71	23.63
66.75	29.87	38.42	30.42	20.78	15.52
34.76	15.15	19.46	15.91	10.61	7.91
31.99	14.72	18.96	14.51	10.17	7.61
10.66	3.70	3.58	3.05	1.67	2.87
37.08	18.20	23.87	19.81	12.89	9.92
4.55	2.03	1.98	1.45	1.09	0.59
2.03	0.86	1.17	1.29	0.62	0.37
0.46	0.27	0.25	0.20	0.25	0.06
4.54	1.96	2.30	1.69	1.36	0.35
1.87	0.65	0.82	0.73	0.96	0.17
0.32	0.14	0.24	0.14	0.15	0.09
0.42	0.27	0.68	0.37	0.73	0.11
0.34	0.15	0.31	0.16	0.22	0.07
0.30	0.09	0.37	0.10	0.13	0.07
0.07	0.05	0.06	0.06	0.05	0.02
0.48	0.24	0.33	0.22	0.10	0.06
3.63	1.26	2.46	1.15	0.56	0.77

表3-10

农林牧渔业总产值 (2016年) GROSS OUTPUT VALUE OF FARMING, FORESTRY, ANIMAL HUSBANDRY AND FISHERY (2016)

单位：万元　(可比价格　at Comparable Price)　(10 000 yuan)

地　区	Region	总产值 Gross Output Value	农　业 Farming	林　业 Forestry	牧　业 Animal Husbandry	渔　业 Fishery	农林牧渔服务业 Services
全　市	**Whole Municipality**	**4 094 194**	**1 717 672**	**240 841**	**363 797**	**1 306 820**	**465 064**
市　区	Urban Area	1 533 197	495 438	58 198	102 915	683 180	193 466
# 吴江区	Wujiang	741 356	297 634	25 835	64 580	304 841	48 466
常　熟	Changshu	763 103	448 359	30 413	52 113	140 097	92 121
张家港	Zhangjiagang	594 949	334 519	71 326	50 723	59 276	79 105
昆　山	Kunshan	525 407	148 034	46 941	26 427	272 755	31 250
太　仓	Taicang	677 538	291 322	33 963	131 619	151 512	69 122

表3-11

农林牧渔业总产值 (2016年) GROSS OUTPUT VALUE OF FARMING, FORESTRY, ANIMAL HUSBANDRY AND FISHERY (2016)

单位：万元　(10 000 yuan)

地　区	Region	总产值 Gross Output Value	农　业 Farming	林　业 Forestry	牧　业 Animal Husbandry	渔　业 Fishery	农林牧渔服务业 Services
全　市	**Whole Municipality**	**4 246 673**	**1 788 110**	**247 639**	**373 939**	**1 360 760**	**476 225**
市　区	Urban Area	1 597 286	515 266	60 674	107 048	716 190	198 108
# 吴江区	Wujiang	770 100	306 563	26 662	67 163	320 083	49 629
常　熟	Changshu	798 014	475 261	31 386	53 155	143 880	94 332
张家港	Zhangjiagang	611 401	344 889	72 895	51 737	60 876	81 004
昆　山	Kunshan	545 148	153 215	47 974	27 748	284 211	32 000
太　仓	Taicang	694 824	299 479	34 710	134 251	155 603	70 781

表3-12

农林牧渔业增加值（2016年）
VALUE ADDED OF FARMING, FORESTRY, ANIMAL HUSBANDRY AND FISHERY (2016)

单位：万元 (10 000 yuan)

项　目	Item	总产值 Gross Output Value	中间消耗 Depreciation	增加值 Value-added	增加值率(%) Value-adding Rate (%)
总　计	**Total**	**4 246 673**	**1 776 479**	**2 470 194**	**58.2**
农　业	Farming	1 788 110	614 553	1 173 557	65.6
林　业	Forestry	247 639	114 365	133 274	53.8
牧　业	Animal Husbandry	373 939	211 770	162 169	43.4
渔　业	Fishery	1 360 760	611 639	749 121	55.1
农林牧渔服务业	Services	476 225	224 152	252 073	52.9

表3-13

分地区农林牧渔业增加值（2016年）
VALUE ADDED OF FARMING, FORESTRY, ANIMAL HUSBANDRY AND FISHERY BY REGION (2016)

单位：万元 (10 000 yuan)

地　区	Region	增加值 Value-added	农　业 Farming	林　业 Forestry	牧　业 Animal Husbandry	渔　业 Fishery	农林牧渔服务业 Services
全　市	**Whole Municipality**	**2 470 194**	**1 173 557**	**133 274**	**162 169**	**749 121**	**252 073**
市　区	Urban Area	913 436	338 857	31 362	43 715	394 860	104 642
#吴江区	Wujiang	450 319	213 450	15 059	27 440	172 138	22 232
常　熟	Changshu	480 106	309 729	17 464	21 262	79 133	52 518
张家港	Zhangjiagang	349 348	219 894	39 006	22 037	32 502	35 909
昆　山	Kunshan	319 262	104 186	26 386	11 654	158 476	18 560
太　仓	Taicang	408 042	200 891	19 056	63 501	84 150	40 444

表3-14

农作物播种面积（2016年）
SOWN AREAS OF FARM CROPS (2016)

单位：千公顷 (1 000 hectares)

项　目	Item	全　市 Whole Municipality	市　区 Urban Area	#吴江区 Wujiang District	常　熟 Changshu	张家港 Zhang-jiagang	昆　山 Kunshan	太　仓 Taicang
农作物总播种面积	**Total Sown Area**	**241.40**	**55.66**	**38.40**	**68.40**	**51.67**	**21.46**	**44.21**
一、粮食作物	**Grain Crops**	**145.01**	**30.27**	**22.14**	**41.24**	**33.87**	**15.37**	**24.26**
（一）夏收粮食	Summer Grain	67.70	12.64	8.64	20.26	16.54	7.55	10.71
1.夏收谷物	Summer Cereal	66.56	12.59	8.64	20.01	16.38	7.38	10.20
（1）小　麦	Wheat	66.55	12.59	8.64	20.01	16.37	7.38	10.20
（2）元　麦	Hull-less Barley	0.01	–	–		0.01	–	–
（3）大　麦	Barley	–	–	–	–	–	–	–
2.夏收豆类	Summer Beans	1.14	0.05	–	0.25	0.16	0.17	0.51
（二）秋收粮食	Autumn Grain	77.31	17.63	13.50	20.98	17.33	7.82	13.55
1.秋收谷物	Autumn Cereal	74.05	17.53	13.50	20.26	16.20	7.44	12.62
（1）稻　谷	Rice	72.70	17.52	13.50	19.75	16.03	7.34	12.06
#单季晚稻	Single Late Rice	72.70	17.52	13.50	19.75	16.03	7.34	12.06
（2）玉　米	Corn	1.35	0.01	–	0.51	0.17	0.10	0.56
（3）其他谷物	Others	–	–	–	–	–	–	–
2.秋收豆类	Autumn Beans	2.56	0.07	–	0.48	0.96	0.32	0.73
（1）大　豆	Soybeans	2.12	0.05	–	0.37	0.86	0.23	0.61
（2）杂　豆	Others	0.44	0.02	–	0.11	0.10	0.09	0.12
3.秋收薯类	Autumn Tubers	0.70	0.03	–	0.24	0.17	0.06	0.20
二、油　料	**Oil-bearing Crops**	**5.40**	**0.36**	**0.19**	**1.39**	**1.52**	**0.70**	**1.43**
#油菜籽	Rapeseeds	5.01	0.35	0.19	1.33	1.35	0.69	1.29
三、棉　花	**Cotton**	**0.45**	–	–	**0.28**	**0.03**	**0.01**	**0.13**
四、麻　类	**Fiber Crops**	–	–	–	–	–	–	–
五、糖　料	**Sugar Crops**	**0.03**	–	–	–	**0.02**	–	**0.01**
六、药　材	**Crude Drugs**	**0.04**	–	–	–	**0.02**	**0.02**	–
七、蔬菜、瓜类	**Vegetables and Melon Crops**	**81.93**	**22.57**	**13.97**	**24.58**	**12.98**	**4.79**	**17.01**
八、其他农作物	**Others**	**8.54**	**2.46**	**2.10**	**0.91**	**3.23**	**0.57**	**1.37**
#青饲料	Green Fodder	1.56	1.01	1.00	0.02	0.02	0.23	0.28
绿　肥	Green Manure	1.26	1.10	1.10	0.03	0.08	0.01	0.04
附：常年蔬菜地	**In Addition Vegetable Gardens**	**26.40**	**7.60**	**5.10**	**7.80**	**4.24**	**1.25**	**5.51**

表3-15

农产品总产量（2016年）
TOTAL YIELD OF FARM CROPS (2016)

单位：吨 (ton)

项 目	Item	全 市 Whole Municipality	市 区 Urban Area	# 吴江区 Wujiang District	常 熟 Changshu	张家港 Zhang-jiagang	昆 山 Kunshan	太 仓 Taicang
一、粮食作物	**Grain Crops**	**976 826**	**211 055**	**161 500**	**277 560**	**221 652**	**101 255**	**165 304**
（一）夏收粮食	Summer Grain	289 118	51 792	38 258	86 073	74 581	30 374	46 298
1.夏收谷物	Summer Cereal	285 327	51 702	38 258	85 103	74 173	29 734	44 615
（1）小 麦	Wheat	285 282	51 702	38 258	85 103	74 128	29 734	44 615
（2）元 麦	Hull-less Barley	45	–	–	–	45	–	–
（3）大 麦	Barley	–	–	–	–	–	–	–
2.夏收豆类	Summer Beans	3 791	90	–	970	408	640	1 683
（二）秋收粮食	Autumn Grain	687 708	159 263	123 242	191 487	147 071	70 881	119 006
1.秋收谷物	Autumn Cereal	673 870	158 796	123 242	187 358	143 268	68 970	115 478
（1）稻 谷	Rice	665 632	158 737	123 242	184 120	142 250	68 295	112 230
# 单季晚稻	Single Late Rice	665 632	158 737	123 242	184 120	142 250	68 295	112 230
（2）玉 米	Corn	8 238	59	–	3 238	1 018	675	3 248
（3）其他谷物	Others	–	–	–	–	–	–	–
2.秋收豆类	Autumn Beans	9 294	288	–	2 293	2 669	1 416	2 628
（1）大 豆	Soybeans	7 527	221	–	1 704	2 361	1 045	2 196
（2）杂 豆	Others	1 767	67	–	589	308	371	432
3.秋收薯类	Autumn Tubers	4 544	179	–	1 836	1 134	495	900
二、油 料	**Oil-bearing Crops**	**13 409**	**860**	**506**	**3 547**	**3 833**	**1 558**	**3 611**
# 油菜籽	Rapeseeds	12 368	825	506	3 352	3 487	1 543	3 161
三、棉 花	**Cotton**	**500**	–	–	**288**	**27**	**22**	**163**
四、麻 类	**Fiber Crops**	–	–	–	–	–	–	–
五、糖 料	**Sugar Crops**	**1 359**	–	–	–	**942**	–	**417**

表3-16

农产品单产 (2016年)

YIELD OF FARM CROPS PER HECTARE (2016)

单位：公斤/公顷 (kg/hectare)

项　目	Item	全　市 Whole Municipality	市　区 Urban Area	#吴江区 Wujiang District	常　熟 Changshu	张家港 Zhang-jiagang	昆　山 Kunshan	太　仓 Taicang
一、粮食作物	**Grain Crops**	**6 736**	**6 972**	**7 294**	**6 730**	**6 544**	**6 588**	**6 814**
（一）夏收粮食	Summer Grain	4 271	4 097	4 428	4 248	4 509	4 023	4 323
1.夏收谷物	Summer Cereal	4 287	4 107	4 428	4 253	4 528	4 029	4 374
（1）小　麦	Wheat	4 287	4 107	4 428	4 253	4 528	4 029	4 374
（2）元　麦	Hull-less Barley	4 500	–	–	–	4 500	–	–
（3）大　麦	Barley	–	–	–	–	–	–	–
2.夏收豆类	Summer Beans	3 325	1 800	–	3 880	2 550	3 765	3 300
（二）秋收粮食	Autumn Grain	8 895	9 034	9 129	9 127	8 486	9 064	8 783
1.秋收谷物	Autumn Cereal	9 100	9 059	9 129	9 248	8 844	9 270	9 150
（1）稻　谷	Rice	9 156	9 060	9 129	9 323	8 874	9 304	9 306
# 单季晚稻	Single Late Rice	9 156	9 060	9 129	9 323	8 874	9 304	9 306
（2）玉　米	Corn	6 102	5 900	–	6 349	5 988	6 750	5 800
（3）其他谷物	Others	–	–	–	–	–	–	–
2.秋收豆类	Autumn Beans	3 630	4 114	–	4 777	2 780	4 425	3 600
（1）大　豆	Soybeans	3 550	4 420	–	4 605	2 745	4 543	3 600
（2）杂　豆	Others	4 016	3 350	–	5 355	3 080	4 122	3 600
3.秋收薯类	Autumn Tubers	6 491	5 967	–	7 650	6 671	8 250	4 500
二、油　料	**Oil-bearing Crops**	**2 483**	**2 389**	**2 663**	**2 552**	**2 522**	**2 226**	**2 525**
# 油菜籽	Rapeseeds	2 469	2 357	2 663	2 520	2 583	2 236	2 450
三、棉　花	**Cotton**	**1 111**	–	–	**1 029**	**900**	**2 200**	**1 254**
四、麻　类	**Fiber Crops**	–	–	–	–	–	–	–
五、糖　料	**Sugar Crops**	**45 300**	–	–	–	**47 100**	–	**41 700**

表3-17

渔业生产情况 (2016年)
STATISTICS ON FISHERY (2016)

项 目	Item	全 市 Whole Municipality	市 区 Urban Area	#吴江区 Wujiang District	常 熟 Changshu	张家港 Zhang-jiagang	昆 山 Kunshan	太 仓 Taicang
基本情况	**Basic Conditions**							
渔业村数 (个)	Number of Fishing Villages (unit)	47	37	15	–	–	10	–
渔业户数 (户)	Number of Fishing Households (household)	27 830	17 539	5 782	3 766	300	4 412	1 813
#海 洋	Seawater	45	–	–	45	–	–	–
渔业人口 (人)	Population in Fishery (person)	114 566	75 724	18 818	14 542	1 900	17 823	4 577
渔业劳动力	Fishery Labor Force	77 302	53 139	19 338	9 656	889	9 805	3 813
#专业劳动力	Specialized Labor Force	59 475	39 145	12 434	7 843	734	9 000	2 753
#捕捞专业	Fish Catching	7 585	4 875	1 533	582	134	1 500	494
养殖专业	Aquaculture	50 477	32 950	10 569	7 231	585	7 500	2 211
水产品产量 (吨)	**Output of Aquatic Products** (ton)	**254 918**	**139 341**	**80 121**	**36 804**	**16 100**	**41 042**	**21 631**
海洋产品	Seawater Aquatic Products	10 418	–	–	2 832	–	–	7 586
淡水产品	Freshwater Aquatic Products	244 500	139 341	80 121	33 972	16 100	41 042	14 045
捕 捞	Fish Catching	17 684	11 953	2 601	662	800	950	3 319
养 殖	Aquaculture	226 816	127 388	77 520	33 310	15 300	40 092	10 726
渔 船	**Fishing Boat**							
机动渔船 (艘)	Motorized Fishing Boats (unit)	10 781	9 838	2 740	119	67	730	27
(吨)	(ton)	52 193	42 176	9 306	3 431	850	1 665	4 071
(千瓦)	(kw)	124 389	100 120	34 637	5 888	2 035	7 846	8 500
非机动渔船 (艘)	Non-motorized Fishing Boats (unit)	13 571	10 886	1 738	435	98	750	1 402
(载吨)	(ton)	35 862	32 992	6 578	285	26	2 056	503
淡水养殖面积 (千公顷)	**Freshwater Raise Areas**(1 000 hectares)	**69.06**	**43.16**	**22.04**	**11.03**	**2.67**	**9.80**	**2.40**
#池塘面积	Pond Area	36.18	20.20	10.24	6.53	1.92	5.13	2.40

表3-18

牧业生产情况（2016年）
STATISTICS ON LIVESTOCK (2016)

项　目	Item	全　市 Whole Municipality	市　区 Urban Area	#吴江区 Wujiang District	常　熟 Changshu	张家港 Zhang-jiagang	昆　山 Kunshan	太　仓 Taicang
当年出栏数	**Slaughtered Livestock of the Year**							
牛　(万头)	Cattle and Buffaloes (10 000 heads)	–	–	–	–	–	–	–
猪	Hogs	84.46	35.02	22.20	13.22	6.99	8.27	20.96
羊　(万只)	Sheep and Goats (10 000 heads)	11.32	4.22	3.86	1.51	1.39	0.18	4.02
#山　羊	Goats	3.56	0.54	0.40	0.15	1.13	0.16	1.58
家　禽	Poultry	1 663.08	178.96	119.19	57.43	107.53	19.16	1 300.00
兔	Rabbit	3.64	1.59	1.54	–	0.53	–	1.52
年末存栏数	**Livestock Being Raised at Year-end**							
牛　(万头)	Cattle and Buffaloes (10 000 heads)	2.15	0.20	–	0.64	0.39	0.24	0.68
猪	Hogs	60.34	24.05	16.04	11.17	5.12	1.90	18.10
羊　(万只)	Sheep and Goats (10 000 heads)	10.36	3.42	2.96	2.50	1.08	0.16	3.20
#山　羊	Goats	3.04	0.45	0.27	0.35	0.90	0.14	1.20
家　禽	Poultry	651.87	133.34	99.47	50.35	71.67	16.51	380.00
兔	Rabbit	4.10	1.82	1.82	–	0.08	–	2.20
产　量　(吨)	**Output of Meat** (ton)							
牛　肉	Beef	–	–	–	–	–	–	–
猪　肉	Pork	61 778	26 297	16 429	9 252	5 593	5 789	14 847
羊　肉	Mutton	1 982	694	589	370	182	26	710
#山羊肉	Goat Mutton	536	66	42	34	143	23	270
禽　肉	Poultry	33 653	3 619	2 333	994	1 786	470	26 784
兔　肉	Rabbit	95	48	45	–	16	–	31
奶　类	Milk	102 957	9 997	–	26 758	18 749	16 213	31 240
#牛　奶	Cow Milk	102 957	9 997	–	26 758	18 749	16 213	31 240
绵羊毛	Sheep Wool	41.40	20.00	20.00	21.40	–	–	–
蜂　蜜	Honey	397	44	32	188	82	20	63
禽　蛋	Poultry Eggs	38 030	11 564	9 662	3 955	6 548	600	15 363

表3-19

林业、蚕桑、茶叶、水果生产情况（2016年）
STATISTICS ON FORESTRY, SILKWORM COCOONS, TEA AND FRUITS PRODUCTION (2016)

项目	Item	全市 Whole Municipality	市区 Urban Area	#吴江区 Wujiang District	常熟 Changshu	张家港 Zhang-jiagang	昆山 Kunshan	太仓 Taicang
林业	**Forestry**							
造林面积（公顷）	Build Forestry Areas (hectare)	444	136	71	32	69	112	95
四旁植树（万株）	Planting (10 000 plants)	–	–	–	–	–	–	–
育苗面积（公顷）	Raise Seedlings Areas (hectare)	7 191	5 223	3 008	771	834	163	200
木材采伐（万立方米）	Timber Cut (10 000 cu.m)	0.58	0.09	–	0.49	–	–	–
竹材采伐（万根）	Bamboo Cut (10 000 pieces)	1	1	–	–	–	–	–
年末实有林地面积（公顷）	Actual Forestry Areas (year-end) (hectare)	102 133	55 077	19 425	14 694	11 831	12 763	7 768
蚕桑	**Silkworm Cocoons and Mulberry**							
蚕茧产量（吨）	Output of Silkworm Cocoons (ton)	237	237	237	–	–	–	–
年末实有桑园面积（公顷）	Mulberry Field Area (year-end) (hectare)	2 030	2 030	2 030	–	–	–	–
茶叶	**Tea**							
茶叶产量（吨）	Output of Tea (ton)	357	306	–	40	11	–	–
#绿毛茶	Green Tea	242	224	–	11	7	–	–
年末实有茶园面积（公顷）	Tea Field Area (year-end) (hectare)	2 430	2 252	–	131	47	–	–
水果	**Fruits**							
水果产量（吨）	Output of Fruits (ton)	95 595	37 854	10 281	15 931	19 570	12 812	9 428
#柑桔	Citrus	18 098	12 180	6 798	380	4 560	229	750
梨	Pears	11 850	5 553	1 435	930	2 237	2 630	500
葡萄	Grapes	33 606	4 332	1 085	12 274	4 764	6 336	5 900
年末实有果园面积（公顷）	Area of Orchards (year-end) (hectare)	11 132	6 843	788	1 459	1 278	773	779
#柑桔	Citrus	1 544	1 318	422	37	141	12	37
梨	Pears	1 043	516	115	154	173	124	76
葡萄	Grapes	2 373	473	111	817	279	404	401

表3-20 农业机械化、化学化及农田水利化情况 (2016年)

指　标		Item		全　市 Whole Municipality
一、农业机械化情况		**Statistics on Agricultural Machinery**		
（一）机耕面积	(千公顷)	Area Ploughed by Tractors	(1 000 hectares)	169.63
（二）机播面积		Seeded Area by Tractors		133.24
#机插水稻面积		Rice Planted Area by Transplanters		58.76
机播水稻面积		Seeded Rice Area by Tractors		7.10
机播小麦面积		Wheat Area by Tractors		55.71
（三）机械植保面积		Plant Protection Area by Tractors		166.67
（四）机收面积		Harvest Area by Tractors		138.64
#机收水稻面积		Rice Harvest Area by Tractors		69.37
机收小麦面积		Wheat Harvest Area by Tractors		65.73
（五）机械脱粒粮食数量	(万吨)	Amount of Grain Crops Shelling by Thresher	(10 000 tons)	88.83
二、农用化肥、农药施用量		**Use of Agricultural Fertilizers and Insecticides**		
化　肥（折纯量）	(吨)	Chemical Fertilizer (pure)	(ton)	71 147
农　药		Agricultural Chemical Insecticides		3 739
三、农村用电量	(万千瓦时)	**Electricity Consumed in Rural Area**	(10 000 kwh)	**6 097 800**
四、农田水利建设情况		**Irrigation and Water Conservancy**		
有效灌溉面积	(千公顷)	Effective Irrigation Area	(1 000 hectares)	160.57

STATISTICS ON AGRICULTURAL MACHINERY, CHEMICAL APPLICATION AND IRRIGATION OF FARMING LAND (2016)

市 区 Urban Area	# 吴江区 Wujiang District	常 熟 Changshu	张家港 Zhangjiagang	昆 山 Kunshan	太 仓 Taicang
28.17	20.63	48.26	42.10	13.57	37.54
24.94	20.42	33.79	39.10	12.99	22.44
12.13	10.77	16.87	14.04	4.86	10.85
2.33	0.52	0.91	1.74	2.12	–
10.43	7.23	16.01	14.60	6.01	8.67
29.44	21.97	41.12	44.20	14.78	37.13
26.93	19.39	39.89	31.74	14.78	25.30
14.54	10.56	19.75	15.68	7.34	12.06
12.08	8.64	20.01	16.06	7.38	10.20
18.86	14.10	23.58	21.10	9.81	15.48
18 519	9 465	24 406	11 149	7 495	9 578
953	460	1 677	530	295	284
2 214 860	**1 450 900**	**785 163**	**1 505 326**	**1 045 472**	**546 979**
46.32	23.12	35.51	30.65	15.67	32.42

表3-21

主要农业机械拥有量（2016年末）

项　目		Item		全　市 Whole Municipality
一、农业机械总动力	(万千瓦)	**Total Power of Agricultural Machinery**	(10 000 kw)	**163.89**
# 柴油机		Diesel Engines		93.21
电动机		Motor		53.19
二、主要农业机械		**Main Agricultural Machinery**		
1.大中型拖拉机	(台)	Large and Medium Tractors	(unit)	4 377
	(万千瓦)		(10 000 kw)	20.16
2.小型拖拉机	(台)	Mini-tractors	(unit)	1 260
	(万千瓦)		(10 000 kw)	1.07
3.机动水稻插秧机	(台)	Rice Transplanters	(unit)	3 873
4.农用排灌动力机械	(万台)	Machinery for Agricultural Drainage and Irrigation	(10 000 units)	3.49
	(万千瓦)		(10 000 kw)	29.75
# 柴油机	(万台)	Diesel Engines	(10 000 units)	0.36
	(万千瓦)		(10 000 kw)	3.89
电动机	(万台)	Motor	(10 000 units)	3.12
	(万千瓦)		(10 000 kw)	25.82
5.农用水泵	(万台)	Agricultural Water Pump	(10 000 units)	3.61
6.节水灌溉类机械	(套)	Equipment in Water-saving Irrigation	(set)	1 850
7.联合收割机	(台)	Combine Harvesters	(unit)	2 687
8.机动脱粒机		Motorized Huller		14 007
9.渔业机械		Machinery of Fishery		54 223
	(万千瓦)		(10 000 kw)	19.83

POSSESSION OF AGRICULTURAL MACHINERY (END OF 2016)

市 区 Urban Area	# 吴江区 Wujiang District	常 熟 Changshu	张家港 Zhangjiagang	昆 山 Kunshan	太 仓 Taicang
63.02	**41.34**	**32.03**	**29.99**	**18.00**	**20.85**
33.49	19.29	18.38	19.57	9.58	12.20
19.10	15.08	11.96	7.09	7.59	7.45
786	676	1 184	881	431	1 095
3.48	2.71	5.38	4.70	2.12	4.49
429	331	320	260	162	89
0.40	0.30	0.27	0.17	0.14	0.08
961	818	1 300	815	267	530
1.27	1.11	0.72	0.56	0.19	0.76
14.36	11.56	4.60	4.18	2.94	3.67
0.27	0.28	0.04	–	0.03	0.02
3.29	3.08	0.37	–	0.04	0.19
0.97	0.83	0.68	0.56	0.18	0.74
11.03	8.48	4.23	4.18	2.90	3.48
1.36	0.87	0.92	0.44	0.17	0.72
507	–	488	249	176	430
387	267	782	686	236	596
1 871	1 737	10 102	–	–	2 034
27 452	19 623	8 671	2 660	11 842	3 598
12.08	7.22	1.89	0.35	2.74	2.76

表3-22

分乡、镇基本情况 (2016年)

乡、镇 Townships and Towns		行政区域面积（公顷）The Administrative Area (hectare)	年末人口（人）Population Year-end (person)	各类科技人员（人）Scientific and Technical Personnel of All Kinds (person)	年末耕地面积（公顷）Cultivated Area Year-end (hectare)	#高标准农田 High Standard Farmland Area	农机总动力（千瓦）Total Agricultural Machinery Power (kw)
吴中区	**Wuzhong District**						
角　直	Luzhi	9 799	158 570	2 651	2 074	788	9 213
木　渎	Mudu	6 228	282 347	3 764	80	–	900
胥　口	Xukou	3 650	96 657	1 872	228	64	990
东　山	Dongshan	9 600	57 794	850	474	152	44 285
光　福	Guangfu	6 156	48 067	763	1 340	–	22 025
金　庭	Jinting	8 342	45 738	918	779	–	6 753
临　湖	Linhu	5 430	88 542	832	1 795	1 300	17 421
相城区	**Xiangcheng District**						
望　亭	Wangting	4 406	61 481	652	1 138	1 138	14 100
黄　埭	Huangdai	5 600	144 687	1 423	773	773	23 210
渭　塘	Weitang	3 936	74 616	624	937	265	3 100
阳澄湖	Yangchenghu	6 284	63 721	312	1 681	67	22 156
高新区、虎丘区	**New & Hi-tech Zone,Huqiu District**						
浒墅关	Xushuguan	3 000	59 135	595	347	97	1 500
通　安	Tongan	3 698	76 732	420	840	170	1 601
东　渚	Dongzhu	2 002	37 368	230	440	24	8 600
吴江区	**WuJiang District**						
松　陵	Songling	19 872	249 062	8 250	4 491	721	34 202
平　望	Pingwang	13 565	125 262	3 731	4 650	2 800	22 500

STATISTICS ON TOWNS AND TOWNSHIPS (2016)

农作物播种面积(公顷) Sown Area of Farm Crops (hectare)	#粮食作物 Grain Crops	#蔬菜作物 Vegetables Crops	粮食总产量(吨) Total Output of Grain (ton)	蔬菜总产量(吨) Total Output of Vegetables (ton)	肉类总产量(吨) Total Output of Meat (ton)	#猪肉产量 Output of Pork	水产品总产量(吨) Total Output of Aquatic Products (ton)
2 177	975	1 116	6 452	37 198	4 439	4 109	3 407
68	55	13	331	400	295	295	145
215	100	113	698	3 398	2 755	2 413	3 822
287	27	260	239	7 796	3	2	4 961
248	140	81	805	2 598	136	105	3 815
680	93	380	413	11 394	625	455	2 757
2 545	1 326	720	7 762	14 775	7 232	5 316	2 982
1 146	821	266	4 760	6 680	160	160	340
1 019	874	130	6 113	3 439	5 264	4 312	3 461
501	77	227	415	4 213	593	589	1 776
643	422	187	1 441	4 795	1 324	900	8 826
680	547	100	2 926	2 998	1 898	1 556	515
742	287	113	1 755	3 398	160	150	113
164	68	70	429	1 769	400	150	155
4 286	2 227	1 727	18 195	51 771	1 350	1 160	32 000
6 030	3 960	1 094	27 891	29 583	2 591	2 312	11 833

表3-22 续表 1

乡、镇 Townships and Towns		地区生产总值（万元）Gross Domestic Product (10 000 yuan)	第一产业 Primary Industry	第二产业 Secondary Industry	第三产业 Tertiary Industry	企业个数（个）Number of Enterprises (unit)	#规模以上工业 Number of Enterprises Above Designated	企业从业人员(人) Laborers of Enterprises (person)
吴中区	**Wuzhong District**							
甪　直	Luzhi	1 033 541	21 037	486 167	526 337	3 283	129	109 927
木　渎	Mudu	1 590 120	4 225	694 981	890 914	11 023	103	240 988
胥　口	Xukou	1 060 079	28 065	557 666	474 348	2 868	129	62 820
东　山	Dongshan	287 865	26 818	143 589	117 458	626	31	32 950
光　福	Guangfu	311 258	19 455	124 802	167 001	699	21	39 737
金　庭	Jinting	210 810	23 024	26 835	160 951	115	8	27 371
临　湖	Linhu	607 300	24 100	250 400	332 800	1 315	65	56 709
相城区	**Xiangcheng District**							
望　亭	Wangting	455 001	3 408	224 153	227 440	2 467	61	43 019
黄　埭	Huangdai	1 646 642	31 306	960 028	655 308	1 926	159	90 133
渭　塘	Weitang	700 113	6 340	352 332	341 441	2 368	96	48 499
阳澄湖	Yangchenghu	602 054	30 901	290 958	280 195	880	53	43 998
高新区、虎丘区	**New & Hi-tech Zone,Huqiu District**							
浒墅关	Xushuguan	607 000	2 560	415 700	188 740	1 083	82	21 024
通　安	Tongan	326 000	10 200	125 500	190 300	1 682	42	41 200
东　渚	Dongzhu	30 900	2 200	19 600	9 100	203	4	19 490
吴江区	**WuJiang District**							
松　陵	Songling	2 649 508	59 125	843 258	1 747 125	4 150	95	140 578
平　望	Pingwang	1 320 830	20 951	753 816	546 063	1 669	120	65 462

Continued 1

工业总产值（万元）Gross Industrial Output Value (10 000 yuan)	# 规模以上工业 Gross Industrial Output Value Above Designated Size	固定资产投资完成额(万元) Value of Investment in Fixed Assets (10 000 yuan)	进出口总额（万美元）Total Imports and Exports (USD 10 000)	# 出口总额 Total Exports	财政总收入（万元）Total Revenue (10 000 yuan)	# 一般公共预算收入 General Public Budget Revenue	农村常住居民人均可支配收入(元) Per Capita Net Income of Rural Resident (yuan)
1 918 726	1 105 667	129 761	54 459	42 076	282 672	94 529	33 304
1 620 310	810 155	492 133	45 223	36 543	374 500	225 000	34 506
2 235 786	1 707 509	520 419	83 108	58 342	192 673	94 701	34 231
668 158	531 278	96 347	19 799	15 975	41 075	25 572	34 356
435 918	299 138	57 363	5	4	65 388	18 122	36 480
92 214	55 576	31 831	810	810	45 912	9 643	22 005
1 003 900	608 500	348 225	33 736	30 012	76 336	35 436	31 632
895 591	475 905	81 977	16 300	8 755	90 646	42 924	27 215
5 006 452	4 155 356	761 020	100 700	77 604	278 954	111 539	27 418
1 576 038	976 604	378 929	23 900	12 226	135 858	60 604	31 138
1 001 016	382 622	281 021	13 400	12 000	67 568	26 257	31 069
1 798 800	1 618 600	621 500	–	–	350 436	96 259	28 570
619 000	431 800	287 601	23 600	7 000	60 551	37 313	29 356
106 600	27 462	89 000	–	–	27 901	17 194	27 667
1 798 400	1 136 578	2 247 768	141 714	116 192	487 259	310 154	27 448
3 024 688	2 145 826	579 266	36 109	12 156	141 114	73 680	31 900

表3-22 续表 2

乡、镇 Townships and Towns		行政区域面积(公顷) The Administrative Area (hectare)	年末人口(人) Population Year-end (person)	各类科技人员(人) Scientific and Technical Personnel of All Kinds (person)	年末耕地面积(公顷) Cultivated Area Year-end (hectare)	#高标准农田 High Standard Farmland Area	农机总动力(千瓦) Total Agricultural Machinery Power (kw)
盛 泽	Shengze	14 774	198 259	7 011	4 429	1 685	50 082
七 都	Qidu	8 620	82 230	2 008	2 956	211	34 100
震 泽	Zhenze	9 561	89 963	3 920	3 845	1 610	46 200
桃 源	Taoyuan	9 060	79 111	2 126	3 635	79	19 800
黎 里	Lili	25 800	178 504	13 978	8 179	1 228	74 800
常 熟	**Chang Shu**						
虞 山	Yushan	18 900	572 990	52 628	3 770	3 770	16 027
梅 李	Meili	8 084	108 097	1 658	3 112	1 428	8 051
海 虞	Haiyu	10 997	129 183	2 196	3 789	2 100	7 869
古 里	Guli	9 646	105 710	3 233	2 280	2 280	30 921
沙家浜	Shajiabang	7 024	56 102	1 109	1 984	333	9 985
支 塘	Zhitang	12 896	79 184	1 458	5 358	5 358	33 867
董 浜	Dongbang	6 261	55 583	788	3 264	2 812	22 147
辛 庄	Xinzhuang	10 426	112 776	5 860	3 321	222	36 381
尚 湖	Shanghu	11 250	123 834	1 586	4 122	3 200	48 200
张家港	**Zhang Jia Gang**						
杨 舍	Yangshe	15 309	305 332	25 513	3 516	2 236	32 809
塘 桥	Tangqiao	9 427	157 627	7 470	3 895	958	38 965
金 港	JinGang	13 161	319 501	20 010	3 028	2 815	31 947
锦 丰	Jinfeng	11 434	177 936	8 582	4 749	481	34 653
乐 余	Leyu	7 861	90 703	3 523	4 624	4 154	25 237

Continued 2

农作物播种面积(公顷) Sown Area of Farm Crops (hectare)	#粮食作物 Grain Crops	#蔬菜作物 Vegetables Crops	粮食总产量(吨) Total Output of Grain (ton)	蔬菜总产量(吨) Total Output of Vegetables (ton)	肉类总产量(吨) Total Output of Meat (ton)	#猪肉产量 Output of Pork	水产品总产量(吨) Total Output of Aquatic Products (ton)
3 368	3 063	247	25 209	7 396	988	921	3 456
981	516	437	3 570	15 900	1 095	890	6 580
5 158	4 327	673	28 367	20 189	1 106	882	9 300
873	560	313	4 582	9 395	2 993	2 183	1 986
5 230	4 865	327	36 470	9 794	9 350	8 500	30 350
7 062	6 255	650	40 408	13 954	1 714	1 417	1 764
5 553	3 281	1 890	24 201	52 671	2 379	2 117	1 033
7 323	6 307	779	40 456	17 955	778	715	614
4 635	4 248	358	31 389	8 592	3 766	2 986	8 279
179	125	54	1 146	1 826	27	25	9 900
9 317	7 071	1 985	48 517	45 401	7 509	5 969	5 366
8 635	1 306	6 407	8 405	230 807	2 126	1 865	1 782
3 994	3 133	768	20 751	12 593	976	553	9 295
8 532	7 911	419	53 374	9 832	1 508	1 098	5 544
5 718	2 810	2 840	18 446	85 152	1 128	907	1 471
5 158	4 558	479	32 698	19 865	1 225	810	1 385
5 223	3 574	971	22 493	19 743	2 356	1 275	1 316
7 238	4 834	1 636	31 589	58 003	756	448	1 544
8 572	5 800	1 673	37 486	41 143	953	380	1 790

表3-22 续表 3

乡、镇 Townships and Towns		地区生产总值 (万元) Gross Domestic Product (10 000 yuan)	第一产业 Primary Industry	第二产业 Secondary Industry	第三产业 Tertiary Industry	企业个数(个) Number of Enterprises (unit)	#规模以上工业 Number of Enterprises Above Designated	企业从业人员(人) Laborers of Enterprises (person)
盛　泽	Shengze	3 673 298	22 316	1 727 370	1 923 612	15 363	310	144 505
七　都	Qidu	965 100	42 100	533 100	389 900	879	94	51 042
震　泽	Zhenze	1 183 595	59 600	642 405	481 590	1 550	81	48 160
桃　源	Taoyuan	676 722	35 495	349 186	292 041	1 420	97	46 220
黎　里	Lili	2 452 239	63 016	1 381 299	1 007 924	4 483	259	108 578
常　熟	**Chang Shu**							
虞　山	Yushan	8 499 950	15 911	2 033 650	6 450 389	8 390	208	201 895
梅　李	Meili	816 445	36 510	576 970	202 965	1 285	95	59 328
海　虞	Haiyu	894 273	26 142	572 075	296 056	1 619	126	86 929
古　里	Guli	1 548 567	28 186	1 194 671	325 710	1 511	119	80 254
沙家浜	Shajiabang	1 000 640	37 682	747 900	215 058	704	63	52 994
支　塘	Zhitang	713 603	35 198	358 745	319 660	1 737	95	49 793
董　浜	Dongbang	338 535	32 905	168 857	136 773	897	68	43 977
辛　庄	Xinzhuang	993 161	26 566	716 262	250 333	1 617	105	69 230
尚　湖	Shanghu	786 449	23 705	462 325	300 419	1 413	103	73 134
张家港	**Zhang Jia Gang**							
杨　舍	Yangshe	6 760 600	49 900	2 297 200	4 413 500	8 140	292	223 194
塘　桥	Tangqiao	1 659 600	33 192	904 482	721 926	2 135	107	99 077
金　港	JinGang	6 287 200	36 324	3 130 276	3 120 600	12 879	311	207 445
锦　丰	Jinfeng	5 448 500	42 500	4 005 200	1 400 800	3 139	88	106 312
乐　余	Leyu	421 600	30 500	227 600	163 500	1 530	65	44 988

Continued 3

工业总产值(万元) Gross Industrial Output Value (10 000 yuan)	# 规模以上工业 Gross Industrial Output Value Above Designated Size	固定资产投资完成额(万元) Value of Investment in Fixed Assets (10 000 yuan)	进出口总额(万美元) Total Imports and Exports (USD 10 000)	# 出口总额 Total Exports	财政总收入(万元) Total Revenue (10 000 yuan)	# 一般公共预算收入 General Public Budget Revenue	农村常住居民人均可支配收入(元) Per Capita Net Income of Rural Resident (yuan)
7 019 300	5 159 200	1 137 149	195 288	130 779	570 776	282 382	35 443
3 980 200	3 542 400	274 018	31 077	26 050	122 226	60 784	27 448
1 695 000	1 233 700	292 090	33 081	18 700	94 638	63 930	30 650
1 417 800	873 185	200 446	24 425	24 127	93 490	70 600	26 720
5 527 364	3 979 702	617 271	123 652	104 472	1 046 499	223 928	27 448
8 956 000	7 184 691	1 621 923	538 923	434 720	800 854	455 932	31 853
2 912 000	2 500 151	200 914	99 842	87 582	134 307	66 455	32 653
2 233 200	1 779 504	254 255	113 525	90 811	184 155	87 687	33 250
4 711 000	4 312 100	260 413	79 093	73 231	143 458	67 410	29 795
3 262 652	2 773 254	148 604	65 821	63 186	134 317	63 968	31 478
1 542 631	1 133 200	183 994	24 568	21 117	75 813	36 517	32 020
715 260	522 856	140 801	8 844	8 002	40 803	21 323	32 724
3 116 500	2 719 283	331 838	114 628	103 439	125 425	55 663	31 557
1 620 000	1 130 474	68 384	38 781	36 541	88 277	43 454	31 505
8 225 580	6 385 900	2 120 700	684 778	591 217	1 035 454	576 597	33 100
3 220 000	2 750 000	426 500	88 166	72 152	166 027	89 876	34 792
11 059 801	9 905 946	1 676 300	1 168 200	272 800	840 238	415 785	34 538
20 646 730	19 441 400	1 179 100	460 848	272 966	517 179	272 158	33 730
1 013 250	673 522	149 969	27 772	27 010	63 550	32 135	33 808

表3-22 续表 4

乡、镇 Townships and Towns		行政区域面积（公顷）The Administrative Area (hectare)	年末人口（人）Population Year-end (person)	各类科技人员（人）Scientific and Technical Personnel of All Kinds (person)	年末耕地面积（公顷）Cultivated Area Year-end (hectare)	#高标准农田 High Standard Farmland Area	农机总动力（千瓦）Total Agricultural Machinery Power (kw)
凤　凰	Fenghuang	7 877	120 404	9 215	2 732	987	39 668
南　丰	Nanfeng	6 249	78 773	3 457	2 366	1 690	34 845
大　新	Daxin	4 048	69 275	668	1 246	220	15 706
昆　山	**Kun Shan**						
玉　山	Yushan	11 800	234 628	25 623	890	806	11 228
巴　城	Bacheng	15 700	105 385	7 319	1 099	272	28 204
周　市	Zhoushi	7 943	145 306	17 370	790	333	15 038
陆　家	Lujia	3 546	95 010	5 690	365	352	2 531
花　桥	Huaqiao	5 009	122 311	5 812	448	416	4 707
淀山湖	Dianshanhu	6 587	50 504	3 684	877	600	35 900
张　浦	Zhangpu	10 904	137 652	10 675	2 710	1 440	32 532
周　庄	Zhouzhuang	3 605	28 516	1 474	470	340	18 260
千　灯	Qiandeng	7 853	160 882	10 604	1 488	1 100	12 446
锦　溪	Jinxi	9 069	51 683	6 354	1 544	903	42 429
太　仓	**Tai Cang**						
城　厢	Chengxiang	5 295	149 964	19 200	1 919	1 175	23 950
沙　溪	Shaxi	13 240	144 746	8 190	6 153	2 270	29 860
浏　河	Liuhe	6 459	93 421	5 243	3 085	1 868	13 340
浮　桥	Fuqiao	14 444	132 046	2 030	4 395	833	24 840
璜　泾	Huangjing	7 963	83 368	3 423	4 339	2 190	21 581
双　凤	Shuangfeng	6 250	56 774	1 542	2 270	1 955	15 821

Continued 4

农作物播种面积(公顷) Sown Area of Farm Crops (hectare)	#粮食作物 Grain Crops	#蔬菜作物 Vegetables Crops	粮食总产量(吨) Total Output of Grain (ton)	蔬菜总产量(吨) Total Output of Vegetables (ton)	肉类总产量(吨) Total Output of Meat (ton)	#猪肉产量 Output of Pork	水产品总产量(吨) Total Output of Aquatic Products (ton)
4 492	3 137	412	20 910	9 367	1 342	1 273	2 825
5 351	3 307	760	21 402	18 414	4 464	3 596	913
2 284	1 622	360	10 610	3 260	266	266	1 368
1 957	1 638	286	11 210	8 595	992	992	3 883
2 674	1 213	402	7 989	10 388	1 886	1 498	9 334
1 867	780	804	4 888	20 845	442	320	2 727
1 070	782	247	4 938	6 187	41	41	70
603	527	43	3 275	1 026	308	308	2
1 950	1 561	188	10 957	3 245	2 920	2 850	7 533
3 504	2 189	854	13 442	29 231	2 769	1 874	10 095
1 013	759	173	4 820	3 344	18	10	8 967
3 070	2 347	374	15 644	8 763	210	188	2 991
2 293	2 074	159	14 404	3 728	452	388	3 678
3 305	2 196	804	13 407	15 480	14 450	950	1 815
7 820	4 335	2 791	27 268	119 939	10 197	5 540	4 226
3 635	1 425	1 648	10 509	28 041	14 123	13 463	5 849
7 878	4 538	2 540	33 894	88 075	3 615	3 140	5 346
6 876	4 494	1 512	31 948	29 650	2 430	1 310	3 144
3 418	1 575	1 708	11 819	30 742	3 790	2 794	4 188

表3-22 续表 5

乡、镇 Townships and Towns		地区生产总值(万元) Gross Domestic Product (10 000 yuan)	第一产业 Primary Industry	第二产业 Secondary Industry	第三产业 Tertiary Industry	企业个数(个) Number of Enterprises (unit)	#规模以上工业 Number of Enterprises Above Designated	企业从业人员(人) Laborers of Enterprises (person)
凤 凰	Fenghuang	1 000 100	36 600	573 000	390 500	2 102	133	63 867
南 丰	Nanfeng	1 156 600	38 200	776 600	341 800	867	42	48 300
大 新	Daxin	345 200	19 700	192 600	132 900	745	35	35 779
昆 山	**Kun Shan**							
玉 山	Yushan	9 224 454	22 210	3 136 735	6 065 509	7 956	282	156 214
巴 城	Bacheng	1 500 124	46 350	680 591	773 183	3 977	173	82 400
周 市	Zhoushi	2 185 000	13 000	1 243 400	928 600	3 988	194	106 568
陆 家	Lujia	1 410 010	2 844	852 405	554 761	2 425	92	73 023
花 桥	Huaqiao	2 299 532	5 400	373 849	1 920 283	6 443	69	96 600
淀山湖	Dianshanhu	865 000	20 000	399 500	445 500	1 651	119	40 938
张 浦	Zhangpu	2 132 548	40 800	1 356 250	735 498	5 021	253	131 279
周 庄	Zhouzhuang	454 716	8 050	52 665	394 001	1 031	13	19 916
千 灯	Qiandeng	1 697 179	20 073	1 072 835	604 271	4 376	208	104 995
锦 溪	Jinxi	655 053	20 500	290 044	344 509	1 286	58	50 560
太 仓	**Tai Cang**							
城 厢	Chengxiang	1 311 489	39 000	371 304	901 185	2 963	99	77 950
沙 溪	Shaxi	1 238 695	74 314	609 353	555 028	3 452	139	83 783
浏 河	Liuhe	893 400	35 015	398 277	460 108	1 556	97	73 475
浮 桥	Fuqiao	2 901 918	64 500	2 187 052	650 366	2 450	157	86 495
璜 泾	Huangjing	1 062 384	27 506	683 201	351 677	1 486	214	50 697
双 凤	Shuangfeng	361 051	42 966	170 081	148 004	977	83	39 830

Continued 5

工业总产值(万元) Gross Industrial Output Value (10 000 yuan)	# 规模以上工业 Gross Industrial Output Value Above Designated Size	固定资产投资完成额(万元) Value of Investment in Fixed Assets (10 000 yuan)	进出口总额(万美元) Total Imports and Exports (USD 10 000)	# 出口总额 Total Exports	财政总收入(万元) Total Revenue (10 000 yuan)	# 一般公共预算收入 General Public Budget Revenue	农村常住居民人均可支配收入(元) Per Capita Net Income of Rural Resident (yuan)
2 854 040	2 254 700	484 200	117 661	70 196	167 712	86 156	34 450
3 537 600	3 460 500	486 500	176 800	96 800	125 918	64 300	35 341
610 600	455 000	142 900	11 990	11 590	43 590	23 801	31 484
13 600 111	12 440 111	1 607 209	577 500	317 100	1 497 957	686 375	38 570
3 640 627	3 150 173	400 383	161 098	118 500	259 709	161 085	35 270
5 640 128	4 754 988	620 648	145 500	94 200	422 774	228 844	35 901
3 550 939	3 090 880	206 986	141 850	110 600	281 878	141 171	36 556
1 368 661	1 188 751	879 391	138 500	58 600	1 532 211	358 831	36 485
1 850 449	1 534 806	260 404	97 500	81 700	167 560	101 551	33 555
6 751 057	5 562 915	630 367	146 200	75 200	382 463	195 487	36 134
305 240	105 921	88 085	12 456	7 600	45 205	27 352	32 499
5 692 029	4 722 029	560 320	215 000	124 300	291 780	159 598	36 251
1 625 705	1 312 721	207 088	82 100	43 200	119 302	61 044	31 373
1 128 000	859 347	428 000	59 690	37 691	124 666	96 133	29 160
2 487 000	1 866 282	428 831	53 302	40 958	148 782	64 045	34 757
1 304 600	990 637	351 000	35 896	29 260	91 078	50 900	30 382
7 936 000	6 600 001	1 388 430	424 025	159 006	539 688	258 668	30 142
2 764 000	2 073 575	428 059	14 127	12 712	51 284	26 916	37 034
1 228 000	1 002 744	297 355	23 138	20 018	60 618	29 105	26 254

主 要 统 计 指 标 解 释

农林牧渔业总产值 指以货币表现的农、林、牧、渔业全部产品和对农林牧渔业生产活动进行的各种支持性服务活动的价值总量，它反映一定时期内农林牧渔业生产总规模和总成果。1957年以前的农林牧渔业总产值中包括了厩肥和农民自给性手工业(如农民自制衣服、鞋、袜，自己从事粮食初步加工等)。1958年及以后，林业中增加了村及村以下竹木采伐产值；牧业中取消了厩肥产值；副业中取消了农民自给性手工业产值，增加了村及村以下办的工业产值； 渔业中增加了海洋捕捞水产品产值。1980年及以后，在副业中增加了农民家庭兼营工业商品部分的产值。从1984年起村及村以下工业产值划归工业。从1993年起取消副业，将野生动物的捕猎划入牧业，野生植物采集和农民家庭兼营商品性工业划归农业。从2003年起，执行新的国民经济行业分类标准，农林牧渔业总产值中包括了农林牧渔服务业产值。林业中增加了森林采运业产值。农业中取消了家庭兼营商品性工业产值，将野生林产品的采集划归林业。

农林牧渔业总产值的计算方法通常是按农、林、牧、渔业产品及其副产品的产量分别乘以各自单位产品价格求得；少数生产周期较长，当年没有产品或产品产量不易统计的，则采用间接方法匡算其产值；然后将四业产品产值及农林牧渔服务业产值相加即为农林牧渔业总产值。

粮食产量 指全社会的产量。包括国有经济经营的、集体统一经营的和农民家庭经营的粮食产量，还包括工矿企业办的农场和其他生产单位的产量。粮食除包括稻谷、小麦、玉米、高粱、谷子及其他杂粮外，还包括薯类和豆类。其产量计算方法，豆类按去豆荚后的干豆计算；薯类(包括甘薯和马铃薯，不包括芋头和木薯)1963年以前按每4公斤鲜薯折1公斤粮食计算，从1964年开始改为按5公斤鲜薯折1公斤粮食计算。城市郊区作为蔬菜的薯类(如马铃薯等)按鲜品计算，并且不作粮食统计。其他粮食一律按脱粒后的原粮计算。1989年以前全国粮食产量数据主要靠全面报表取得，1989年开始使用抽样调查数据。

棉花产量 指全社会的产量。包括春播棉和夏播棉。产量按皮棉计算。不包括木棉。

油料产量 指全部油料作物的生产量。包括花生、油菜籽、芝麻、向日葵籽、胡麻籽（亚麻籽）和其他油料。不包括大豆、木本油料和野生油料。花生以带壳干花生计算。

水产品产量 指人工养殖的水产品和天然生长的水产品的捕捞量。包括海水的鱼类、虾蟹类、贝类和藻类以及内陆水域的鱼类、虾蟹类和贝类，不包括淡水生植物。水产品产量是通过各级农业和统计部门逐级上报取得数据。1995年及以前，贝类中牡蛎按鲜肉计算；蚶、蛤、蛙按5斤鲜品折1斤计算。1996年以后则统一按鲜品计算。

猪、牛、羊肉产量 指当年出栏并已屠宰、除去头蹄下水后带骨肉(即胴体重)的重量。包括全社会范围内的产量。

期初(末)畜禽存栏头(只)数 指报告期初(末)农村各种合作经济组织和国营农场、农民个人、机关、团体、学校、工矿企业、部队等单位以及城镇居民饲养的大牲畜、猪、羊、家禽等畜禽的存栏数。

农作物播种面积 指实际播种或移植有农作物的面积。凡是实际种植有农作物的面积，不论种植在耕地上还是种植在非耕地上，均包括在农作物播种面积中。在播种季节基本结束后，因遭灾而重新改种和补种的农作物面积，也包括在内。它是反映我国耕地面积利用情况的一个重要指标。目前，农作物播种面积主要包括粮食、棉花、油料、糖料、麻类、烟叶、蔬菜和瓜类、药材和其他农作物九大类。

有效灌溉面积 指具有一定的水源，地块比较平整，灌溉工程或设备已经配套，在一般年景下，当年能够进行正常灌溉的耕地面积。在一般情况下，有效灌溉面积应等于灌溉工程或设备已经配备，能够进行正常灌溉的水田和水浇地面积之和。它是反映我国耕地抗旱能力的一个重要指标。

农用化肥施用量 指本年内实际用于农业生产的化肥数量，包括氮肥、磷肥、钾肥和复合肥。化肥施用量要求按折纯量计算数量。折纯量是指把氮肥、磷肥、钾肥分别按含氮、含五氧化二磷、含氧化钾的百分之百成份进行折算后的数量。复合肥按其所含主要成分折算。公式为：

折纯量=实物量×某种化肥有效成份含量的百分比

农业机械总动力　指主要用于农、林、牧、渔业的各种动力机械的动力总和。包括耕作机械、排灌机械、收获机械、农用运输机械、植物保护机械、牧业机械、林业机械、渔业机械和其他农业机械〔内燃机按引擎马力折成瓦(特)计算、电动机按功率折成瓦(特)计算〕。不包括专门用于乡、镇、村、组办工业、基本建设、非农业运输、科学试验和教学等非农业生产方面用的动力机械与作业机械。这个指标的统计数据主要来源于农机部门。

乡村户数　指长期(一年以上)居住在乡镇(不包括城关镇)行政管理区域内的住户，还包括居住在城关镇所辖行政村范围内的农村住户。户口不在本地而在本地居住一年及以上的住户也包括在本地农村住户内；有本地户口，但举家外出谋生一年以上的住户，无论是否保留承包耕地都不包括在本地农村住户范围内。不包括乡村地区内的国有经济的机关、团体、学校、企业、事业单位的集体户。

乡村人口数　指乡村地区常住居民户数中的常住人口数，即经常在家或在家居住6个月以上，而且经济和生活与本户连成一体的人口。外出从业人员在外居住时间虽然在6个月以上，但收入主要带回家中，经济与本户连为一体，仍视为家庭常住人口；在家居住，生活和本户连成一体的国家职工、退休人员也为家庭常住人口。但是现役军人、中专及以上(走读生除外)的在校学生、以及常年在外(不包括探亲、看病等)且已有稳定的职业与居住场所的外出从业人员，不应当作家庭常住人口。

乡村从业人员　指乡村人口中实际参加生产经营活动并取得实物或货币收入的人员，包括劳动年龄内经常参加劳动的人员，也包括超过劳动年龄但经常参加劳动的人员，但不包括户口在家的在外学生、现役军人和丧失劳动能力的人，也不包括待业人员和家务劳动者。从业人员按从事主业时间最长（时间相同按收入）分为农林牧渔业从业人员、工业从业人员、建筑业从业人员、交通运输业、仓储及邮电通信业从业人员、批零贸易业、餐饮业从业人员、其他非农行业从业人员。

EXPLANATORY NOTES ON MAIN STATISTICAL INDICATORS

Gross Output Value of Agriculture, Forestry, Animal Husbandry and Fishery refers to the total value of products of agriculture, forestry, animal husbandry and fishery, and total value of services in support of agriculture, forestry, animal husbandry and fishery activities. It reflects the total scale and results of agricultural production during a given period. Prior to 1957, China's gross agricultural output value included barnyard manure and handicraft products for self-consumption (clothes, shoes, stockings, and initial grain processing undertaken by peasants). Since 1958, cutting and felling of bamboo and trees by villages and other cooperative organizations under villages have been included in forestry; value of barnyard manure has been excluded from animal husbandry; self consumed handicrafts have not been included from sideline occupations, while the output value of industries run by villages and cooperative organizations under village has been included in sideline occupations; and the output value of fish catches by motor fishing boats has been added to fishery. Since 1980, the value of handicraft products made for sale by individuals in households has been added to sideline occupations. Since 1984, industries run by villages and under villages have been included in the sector of industry. Since 1993, the subdivision of sideline occupations has been cancelled, and the hunting of wild animals has been classified into animal husbandry, and the gathering of wild plants and commodity industry run by rural household have been included in farming. A new industrial classification of economic activities was introduced in 2003. Under the new classification, value of services to agriculture, forestry, animal husbandry and fishery is included in the gross output value of agriculture, value of wood felling and transport is included in forestry, value of industrial output by rural households is not included in agriculture, and the collection of wild forest products is taken from agriculture and included in forestry.

Gross output value of agriculture is obtained by multiplying the output of each product or by-product by its price, resulting in the output value of each single item. For a small number of products, annual output of which is not available or difficult to get due to the long production (growing) process involved, the output value is estimated through an indirect approach. The sum of output values of all products of agriculture, forestry, animal husbandry and fishery and services in support to those industries is then equal to the gross output value of agriculture.

Grain Output refers to the total output in the whole country including grains produced by State farms, collective units, rural households, as well as by farms affiliated to industrial and mining enterprises and other production units. Grain includes rice, wheat, corn, sorghum, millet and other miscellaneous grains as well as tubers and beans. Output of beans refers to dry beans without pods. The output of tubers (sweet potatoes and potatoes, not including taros and cassava) are converted into that of grain at the ratio 4:1, i.e. 4 kilograms of fresh tubers were equivalent to 1 kilogram of grain up to 1963. Since 1964 the ratio for conversion has been 5:1. Tubers supplied as vegetables (such as potatoes) in cities and suburbs are calculated as fresh vegetables and their output is not included in the output of grain. Output of all other grains refers to husked grain. Data on grain production before 1989 were obtained through the Comprehensive Statistical Reporting System. Since 1989, data from sample surveys are used.

Cotton Output refers to cotton production in the whole country including cotton planted in spring and in autumn. Output is measured as the weight of ginned cotton. Kapok is not included.

Output of Oil-bearing Crops refers to the total production of oil-bearing crops of various kinds, including peanuts (dry, in shell), rapeseeds, sesame, sunflower seeds, flax seeds, and other oil-bearing crops. Soybeans, oil-bearing woody plants, and wild oil-bearing crops are not included.

Output of Aquatic Products refers to catches of both artificially cultured and naturally grown aquatic products, including fish, shrimps, crabs and shellfish in sea and inland water as well as seaweed. Freshwater plants are not included.

Output of Pork, Beef, and Mutton refers to the meat of slaughtered hogs, cattle, sheep and goats with head, feet, and offal taken away. Data refers to the production of the whole country.

Number of Livestock or Poultry in Stock at Beginning (or End) of Period refers to the total number of large animals, pigs, sheep, fowls, etc. raised by rural cooperative organizations, State farms, rural individuals, government agencies, schools, industrial and mining enterprises, army, and urban residents at the beginning (or end) of the reference period.

Sown Area of Crops refers to area of land sown or transplanted with crops regardless of being in cultivated area or non-cultivated area. Area of land re-sown due to natural disasters is also included. This is an important indicator that can reflect the utilization condition of the cultivated land in China. At present, the sown area of crops mainly include the following 9 categories of crops: grain, cotton, oil-bearing crops, sugar crops, flax crops, tobacco, vegetables and melons, medicinal materials and other farm crops.

Irrigated Area refers to area of land that are effectively irrigated, i.e. relatively level land, where there are water sources or complete sets of irrigation facilities to lift and move adequate water for irrigation purpose under normal conditions. Under normal situations, irrigated area is the sum of watered fields and irrigated fields where irrigation systems or equipment have been installed for regular irrigation purpose. This important indicator reflects drought resistance capacity of the cultivated land in China.

Consumption of Chemical Fertilizers in Agriculture refers to the quantity of chemical fertilizers applied in agriculture in the year, including nitrogenous fertilizer, phosphate fertilizer, potash fertilizer, and compound fertilizer. The consumption of chemical fertilizers is calculated in terms of volume of effective components by means of converting the gross weight of the respective fertilizers into weight containing effective component (e.g. nitrogen content in nitrogenous fertilizer, phosphorous pentoxide contents in phosphate fertilizer, and potassium oxide contents in potash fertilizer). Compound fertilizer is converted in regard to its major components. The formula is:

Volume of effective component= physical quantity× effective component of certain chemical fertilizer (%)

Total Power of Agricultural Machinery refers to total mechanical power of machinery used in agriculture, forestry, animal husbandry and fishery, including machinery for ploughing, irrigation and drainage, harvesting, transport, plant protection, animal husbandry, forestry and fishery and other agricultural machineries. (For the power of internal combustion engines, it is converted from its horsepower into watts while for electric motors the output power is converted into watts.) Machinery employed for non-agricultural purposes, such as the machines used in township-run and village-run industry, construction, non-agricultural transport, scientific experiments and teaching, are not included. Data are mainly from agricultural machinery agencies.

Number of Households in Villages refers to households resident on a long term basis (i.e. 1 year or more) in administrative districts in townships (not including urban townships), including rural households resident in areas under the jurisdiction of urban townships. Households whose household registration is not in the locality yet resident for one year or more are included among the rural households. Households having local household registration yet the whole household having left for somewhere else for work for one year or more, whether still retaining contracted farmland, are not included among the local rural households. Also not included are collective households associated with institutions of the State economy, organizations, schools and enterprises.

Number of Residents of Villages refers to the number of usual residents in usual resident households in rural areas. These are persons who are regularly at home or are at home for 6 months or more and economically and socially integrated with the household. For persons who are away from home for employment for more than 6 months yet the main income is brought back home and thus economically integrated with the household, the person is still considered as a usual resident of the household. National employee and retired personnel who reside at home and whose living is integrated with the household are also considered as usual residents. However, serving military personnel, students at secondary technical level or above (unless commuting between school and home), employed persons who are regularly elsewhere the year round (except visiting relatives or receiving medical attention) and having a stable job and residence should not be considered as usual resident of the household.

Rural Persons Engaged refer to persons in the rural labour force aged over 16 years who are engaged in actual production and management activities and receive payment in kind or wages, including those covered within the labour force age bracket and regularly participating in production activities, and those who are out of the labour force age bracket yet also participating in production activities regularly. Students studying in other places with their permanent residence registered in local areas, servicemen and persons incapable of working are not included. Also not included are those who are waiting for jobs and those engaged in housework. Persons employed are classified as persons engaged in agriculture, forestry, animal husbandry or fishery activities; persons engaged in industrial activities; persons engaged in construction activities; persons engaged in transport, storage and telecommunications activities; persons engaged in wholesale and retail trade and catering activities; and persons engaged in other non-agriculture activities. In case the person is engaged in more than one type of work, classification is according to the industry in which he works most of the time (where time is the same income would be the criterion).

四、工 业

CHAPTER 4
INDUSTRY

4 工 业
INDUSTRY

主 要 统 计 指 标
MAJOR STATISTICAL INDICATORS

2016年末工业企业单位数	Number of Industrial Enterprises	163 953	个	unit
# 规模以上工业企业	Above Designated Size	9 616	个	unit
2016年工业总产值	Gross Industrial Output Value	35 766.97	亿元	100 million yuan
比上年增长	Increase Over Last Year	0.1	%	
2016年规模以上工业总产值	Gross Industrial Output Value Above Designated Size	30 713.99	亿元	100 million yuan
比上年增长	Increase Over Last Year	1.1	%	
按轻重工业分	Grouped by Light and Heavy Industry			
轻工业	Light Industry	7 695.83	亿元	100 million yuan
重工业	Heavy Industry	23 018.16	亿元	100 million yuan
按企业规模分	Grouped by Size of Enterprises			
大型企业	Large	16 464.17	亿元	100 million yuan
中型企业	Medium-sized	6 496.86	亿元	100 million yuan
小型企业	Small	7 588.95	亿元	100 million yuan
微型企业	Micro	164.01	亿元	100 million yuan

表4-1

历年工业企业单位数、工业总产值
NUMBER AND OUTPUT VALUE OF INDUSTRIAL ENTERPRISES OVER THE YEARS

单位：万元 (10 000 yuan)

年 份 Year	企业单位数(个) Number of Enterprises (unit)	工业总产值 Gross Industrial Output Value 全 市 Whole Municipality	市 区 Urban Area	# 吴江区 Wujiang District	常 熟 Changshu	张家港 Zhangjiagang	昆 山 Kunshan	太 仓 Taicang
1978		485 050	324 779	40 779	71 543	39 525	22 464	26 739
1979		568 074	372 330	50 153	81 270	51 014	28 118	35 342
1980		737 116	458 653	69 878	113 161	79 941	35 805	49 556
1985	31 046	1 891 164	943 476	185 526	348 644	315 300	128 362	155 382
1986	54 428	2 324 775	1 142 154	236 563	433 633	402 930	176 661	169 397
1987	67 299	3 036 865	1 454 227	320 836	565 274	535 849	249 480	232 035
1988	66 687	4 306 836	2 047 716	467 648	788 752	720 695	392 260	357 413
1989	59 818	5 058 307	2 453 367	563 709	874 586	807 090	509 303	413 961
1990	54 221	5 637 287	2 725 421	736 228	970 239	932 662	566 983	441 982
1995	75 854	19 627 449	8 944 876	2 696 328	3 235 916	4 200 560	1 802 991	1 443 106
1996	69 648	22 745 223	10 054 825	2 883 626	3 627 776	4 974 754	2 260 795	1 827 073
1997	77 201	24 224 588	10 824 895	3 028 394	3 621 599	4 993 214	2 700 890	2 083 990
1998	82 263	26 157 900	11 905 551	3 551 356	4 078 000	4 720 555	3 051 788	2 402 006
1999	83 978	30 062 835	14 275 058	3 731 020	4 497 008	4 966 329	3 659 803	2 664 637
2000	87 234	36 207 408	17 619 030	4 131 972	5 578 818	5 599 596	4 306 080	3 103 884
2001	89 439	40 758 099	19 095 203	4 550 114	6 602 696	6 811 218	5 128 749	3 120 233
2002	93 913	51 394 368	24 077 620	6 438 686	8 001 841	8 208 084	7 456 206	3 650 617
2003	103 517	70 107 652	33 693 949	9 011 620	10 384 361	11 009 185	10 672 258	4 347 899
2004	82 565	95 601 322	45 333 212	12 105 415	13 082 757	15 426 095	16 333 095	5 426 163
2005	85 581	121 230 937	54 565 875	14 853 547	16 502 812	20 021 799	23 332 394	6 808 057
2006	91 000	153 159 355	67 809 871	18 552 000	20 501 652	25 017 292	30 828 100	9 002 440
2007	99 812	190 601 250	81 482 095	23 300 000	25 603 688	32 201 183	40 306 451	11 007 833
2008	106 231	221 034 689	90 942 337	26 504 900	29 182 652	37 902 600	50 005 000	13 002 100
2009	112 468	237 045 579	93 827 939	25 122 500	30 106 215	40 021 014	58 032 212	15 058 199
2010	118 080	284 836 867	112 293 666	31 020 000	36 521 562	47 008 700	70 012 900	19 000 039
2011	121 928	333 473 737	132 940 095	37 000 125	42 753 862	54 555 010	80 015 670	23 209 100
2012	132 870	345 281 021	136 450 967	37 910 000	44 055 216	55 208 800	85 205 138	24 360 900
2013	153 809	356 852 132	140 586 862	38 500 000	45 597 148	56 303 500	88 721 006	25 643 616
2014	156 695	357 729 896	142 221 401	38 020 000	45 812 352	56 308 500	87 084 938	26 302 705
2015	162 100	357 175 935	142 515 757	38 310 000	45 543 000	52 558 500	90 002 831	26 555 848
2016	163 953	357 669 740	144 255 850	39 000 000	45 771 000	51 205 000	90 935 290	25 502 600

注：1995年起工业总产值按新口径计算。
Note: The total industrial output value from 1995 is calculated by the new method.

表4-2

历年分地区规模以上工业企业总产值
OUTPUT VALUE OF INDUSTRIAL ENTERPRISES ABOVE DESIGNATED SIZE BY REGION OVER THE YEARS

单位：万元 (10 000 yuan)

年 份 Year	全 市 Whole Municipality	市 区 Urban Area	# 吴江区 Wujiang District	常 熟 Changshu	张家港 Zhangjiagang	昆 山 Kunshan	太 仓 Taicang
1998	16 256 934	7 336 488	1 665 121	2 101 273	3 072 288	2 420 098	1 326 787
1999	19 263 441	9 070 298	1 876 460	2 484 232	3 391 149	2 894 854	1 422 908
2000	23 965 052	11 659 000	2 318 918	3 096 625	4 007 507	3 559 366	1 642 554
2001	27 847 905	13 161 313	2 765 147	3 724 183	5 003 145	4 345 031	1 614 233
2002	34 658 727	15 930 828	3 290 451	4 352 008	6 219 393	6 173 313	1 983 185
2003	49 765 080	23 649 624	4 502 385	5 571 061	8 610 559	9 389 353	2 544 483
2004	73 075 445	35 517 607	8 469 680	7 520 464	12 470 707	14 101 475	3 465 192
2005	99 085 843	45 072 779	11 542 869	11 482 290	16 322 488	21 211 715	4 996 571
2006	125 385 124	54 348 374	14 684 833	15 582 685	20 499 187	27 986 607	6 968 271
2007	159 089 177	66 443 947	19 001 048	20 130 711	27 026 673	36 899 633	8 588 213
2008	186 301 295	76 343 404	21 784 723	22 907 113	31 537 806	45 548 614	9 964 358
2009	202 844 954	79 772 998	21 021 825	23 265 394	34 320 651	53 820 320	11 665 592
2010	246 516 665	97 355 621	26 216 173	28 832 743	39 579 760	65 908 022	14 840 519
2011	277 787 533	110 767 237	29 936 721	32 516 638	44 619 122	72 822 072	17 062 464
2012	287 455 409	111 570 697	29 863 062	33 692 100	47 005 617	76 868 173	18 318 822
2013	302 762 935	116 200 047	30 961 694	35 822 474	49 220 491	81 572 964	19 946 959
2014	303 221 722	118 560 214	30 807 047	36 686 952	48 637 109	78 523 910	20 813 538
2015	302 492 460	118 869 131	30 208 174	36 125 437	44 857 381	82 709 675	19 930 836
2016	307 139 889	120 465 256	31 168 054	36 848 914	45 716 594	83 832 389	20 276 736

注:2011年起规模以上工业企业调整为主营业务收入2000万元以上企业。
Note: In 2011, industrial enterprises above Designated Size refers to enterprise with main business income above 20 million yuan.

表4-3 历年规模以上工业企业单位数、总产值

单位：万元

年 份 Year	企业单位数(个) Number of Enterprises (unit)	工业总产值 Gross Industrial Output Value	按轻重工业分 Grouped by Light and Heavy Industry	
			轻工业 Light Industry	重工业 Heavy Industry
1998	2 994	16 256 934	8 893 282	7 363 652
1999	3 002	19 263 441	10 156 195	9 107 246
2000	3 112	23 965 052	11 436 139	12 528 913
2001	3 735	27 847 905	12 809 043	15 038 862
2002	4 112	34 658 727	15 444 514	19 214 212
2003	4 553	49 765 080	17 678 551	32 086 529
2004	5 044	73 075 445	23 975 758	49 099 687
2005	6 743	99 085 843	33 334 762	65 751 081
2006	7 485	125 385 124	41 050 258	84 334 866
2007	8 632	159 089 177	49 727 549	109 361 628
2008	9 959	186 301 295	53 942 361	132 358 934
2009	13 720	202 844 954	57 460 526	145 384 428
2010	13 538	246 516 665	67 657 641	178 859 024
2011	9 904	277 787 533	73 490 164	204 297 369
2012	10 444	287 455 409	73 916 098	213 539 311
2013	10 776	302 762 935	78 901 611	223 861 324
2014	10 432	303 221 722	78 318 071	224 903 651
2015	10 062	302 492 460	76 331 670	226 160 789
2016	9 616	307 139 889	76 958 330	230 181 558

注:2012年起企业规模按新标准划分为大型、中型、小型和微型。

NUMBER AND OUTPUT VALUE OF INDUSTRIAL ENTERPRISES ABOVE DESIGNATED SIZE OVER THE YEARS

(10 000 yuan)

按企业规模分		Grouped by Size of Enterprises	
大型企业 Large	中型企业 Medium-sized	小型企业 Small	微型企业 Micro
2 995 207	2 609 044	10 652 683	
3 414 152	2 716 347	13 132 942	
3 904 674	3 109 090	16 951 288	
7 135 751	8 218 624	12 493 530	
8 539 021	9 757 505	16 362 201	
16 870 145	19 628 859	13 266 076	
21 811 989	29 610 744	21 652 712	
35 539 278	38 002 461	25 544 104	
47 091 734	45 881 307	32 412 083	
60 631 093	56 618 033	41 840 051	
71 641 117	59 368 646	55 291 532	
85 074 954	61 423 155	56 346 845	
105 149 095	74 590 048	66 777 522	
124 795 596	83 096 116	69 895 821	
157 579 505	55 970 829	69 743 737	4 161 338
164 846 417	59 803 476	75 574 904	2 538 139
159 625 055	63 898 002	77 209 688	2 488 977
164 584 505	62 412 235	73 658 725	1 836 995
164 641 653	64 968 586	75 889 501	1 640 149

Note: From 2012, the enterprise size divide into large, medium-sized, small and micro by new standard.

表4-4

全市工业企业数与总产值 (2016年)

地　　区	Region	全部工业 Total Industry	规模以上工业 Enterprises Above Designated	按轻重工业 Grouped by Light and Heavy Industry 轻工业 Light Industry	重工业 Heavy Industry
工业企业单位数 (个)	**Number of Industrial Enterprises (unit)**	**163 953**	**9 616**	**3 561**	**6 055**
市　区	Urban Area	68 959	4 358	1 538	2 820
姑苏区	Gusu District	2 160	15	2	13
吴中区	Wuzhong District	17 540	835	275	560
相城区	Xiangcheng District	18 727	742	225	517
高新区、虎丘区	New Hi-tech Zone & Huqiu District	7 370	690	153	537
工业园区	Industrial Park	7 713	772	166	606
吴江区	Wujiang District	15 449	1 304	717	587
常　熟	Changshu	26 418	1 309	654	655
张家港	Zhangjiagang	20 341	1 078	468	610
昆　山	Kunshan	35 545	1 851	450	1 401
太　仓	Taicang	12 690	1 020	451	569
工业总产值 (万元)	**Gross Industrial Output Value (10 000 yuan)**	**357 669 740**	**307 139 889**	**76 958 330**	**230 181 558**
市　区	Urban Area	144 255 850	120 465 256	33 690 156	86 775 099
姑苏区	Gusu District	516 200	377 822	41 236	336 587
吴中区	Wuzhong District	16 368 708	12 264 898	4 061 006	8 203 892
相城区	Xiangcheng District	14 850 926	11 040 128	3 359 646	7 680 482
高新区、虎丘区	New Hi-tech Zone & Huqiu District	29 033 216	26 909 294	4 256 382	22 652 912
工业园区	Industrial Park	44 486 800	38 705 059	9 648 476	29 056 583
吴江区	Wujiang District	39 000 000	31 168 054	12 323 411	18 844 643
常　熟	Changshu	45 771 000	36 848 914	14 994 969	21 853 946
张家港	Zhangjiagang	51 205 000	45 716 594	10 675 686	35 040 908
昆　山	Kunshan	90 935 290	83 832 389	10 571 462	73 260 927
太　仓	Taicang	25 502 600	20 276 736	7 026 058	13 250 678

NUMBER AND OUTPUT VALUE OF INDUSTRIAL ENTERPRISES OF THE WHOLE MUNICIPALITY (2016)

按经济类型分 Grouped by Ownership					规模以下工业（含个体工业）Enterprises Below Designated Size (include individual industry)
国有 State-owned	民营 Private and Individual	#私营 Private	外商及港澳台 Enterprises with Investment from Foreign, Hong Kong, Macao and Taiwan	其他 Other	
5	**5 338**	**4 557**	**4 174**	**99**	**154 337**
–	2 276	1 923	2 031	51	64 601
–	11	6	1	3	2 145
–	506	425	323	6	16 705
–	525	460	208	9	17 985
–	287	200	383	20	6 680
–	114	76	653	5	6 941
–	833	756	463	8	14 145
1	957	858	341	10	25 109
1	815	640	255	7	19 263
1	689	598	1 145	16	33 694
2	601	538	402	15	11 670
138 081	**102 173 115**	**52 142 692**	**198 683 746**	**6 144 947**	**50 529 852**
–	34 153 811	21 967 132	84 029 592	2 281 853	23 790 594
–	76 903	47 313	5 499	295 420	138 378
–	5 529 643	3 924 586	6 669 393	65 863	4 103 810
–	7 021 716	4 793 668	3 443 956	574 456	3 810 798
–	3 885 264	1 845 955	22 399 229	624 800	2 123 922
–	3 335 485	1 132 661	34 994 453	375 120	5 781 741
–	14 304 799	10 222 949	16 517 062	346 193	7 831 946
5 969	18 696 484	9 744 404	17 916 858	229 603	8 922 086
27 575	28 604 488	6 611 692	15 254 354	1 830 178	5 488 406
46 101	12 212 377	7 859 606	70 889 326	684 584	7 102 902
58 436	8 505 955	5 959 858	10 593 615	1 118 729	5 225 864

表4-5

规模以上工业企业主要经济指标 (2016年)

单位：万元

项　　目	Item	企业单位数（个）Number of Enterprises (unit)	# 亏损企业 Loss Making Enterprises
总　　计	**Total**	**9 616**	**1 858**
一、按登记注册类型分	**Grouped by Registration Status**		
国有企业	State-owned Enterprises	5	3
集体企业	Collective-owned Enterprises	10	3
股份合作企业	Share-holding Cooperative Enterprises	14	–
联营企业	Joint Ownership Enterprises	4	1
有限责任公司	Limited Liability Corporations	603	108
股份有限公司	Share-holding Corporations Ltd.	245	32
私营企业	Private Enterprises	4 557	738
其他企业	Other Enterprises	4	–
港澳台投资企业	Enterprises with Investment from HongKong, Macao and Taiwan	1 264	294
外商投资企业	Enterprises with Foreign Investment	2 910	679
二、按轻重工业分	**Grouped by Light and Heavy Industry**		
轻工业	Light Industry	3 561	686
重工业	Heavy Industry	6 055	1 172
三、按企业规模分	**Grouped by Size of Enterprises**		
大型企业	Large	407	40
中型企业	Medium-sized	1 529	226
小型企业	Small	7 362	1 495
微型企业	Micro	318	97
四、按行业类别分	**Grouped by Sector**		
有色金属矿采选业	Nonferrous Metals Mining and Processing	–	–
非金属矿采选业	Nonmetal Minerals Mining and Dressing	1	–
农副食品加工业	Agricultural and Sideline Food Processing	45	13
食品制造业	Food Production	55	15
酒、饮料和精制茶制造业	Wine, Beverage and Refined Tea Manufacturing	19	6
烟草制品业	Manufacture of Tobacco	1	–
纺织业	Textile Industry	1 201	221

MAIN ECONOMIC INDICATORS OF INDUSTRIAL ENTERPRISES ABOVE DESIGNATED SIZE (2016)

(10 000 yuan)

工业总产值 Gross Industrial Output Value	工业销售产值 Value of Industrial Products Sales	# 出口交货值 Delivery Value for Export	资产总计 Total Assets	# 流动资产合计 Circulating Funds	# 应收帐款 Net Account Income	# 产成品 Manufactured Products
307 139 889	**303 110 656**	**117 403 015**	**283 565 028**	**171 499 147**	**61 755 308**	**13 418 314**
138 081	138 209	–	494 536	228 745	14 909	954
70 472	69 236	2 512	172 584	159 949	16 221	6 370
203 273	193 293	9 102	268 179	197 105	67 911	45 511
32 108	34 725	1 849	74 946	53 987	4 165	5 556
40 072 137	40 485 077	6 205 365	44 434 662	23 708 557	5 919 888	2 061 394
15 574 019	14 952 140	1 817 504	22 955 474	12 272 653	3 459 605	1 039 779
52 142 692	51 241 040	6 126 186	51 988 198	33 989 320	11 949 921	3 187 780
223 362	223 214	2 583	127 917	48 355	23 419	5 112
52 335 754	51 340 028	22 457 640	48 548 008	29 349 989	11 463 242	1 994 972
146 347 992	144 433 695	80 780 275	114 500 525	71 490 487	28 836 027	5 070 888
76 958 330	75 891 270	21 107 490	73 351 178	44 333 348	12 645 469	4 284 960
230 181 558	227 219 387	96 295 525	210 213 850	127 165 799	49 109 839	9 133 354
164 641 653	162 195 951	84 765 422	128 032 249	76 752 299	27 692 761	5 477 972
64 968 586	64 128 800	19 515 484	74 181 976	42 197 868	14 750 865	3 460 515
75 889 501	75 139 191	12 990 620	79 831 196	51 584 990	18 958 261	4 395 018
1 640 149	1 646 715	131 490	1 519 606	963 990	353 420	84 810
–	–	–	–	–	–	–
18 786	19 011	–	43 001	14 389	1 670	1 552
2 806 076	2 893 728	16 007	1 750 801	1 199 050	272 129	122 780
2 564 858	2 432 086	99 957	1 789 854	918 505	264 361	87 896
512 248	515 112	2 127	663 241	261 607	68 295	19 225
10 660	13 542	–	36 434	2 443	864	–
13 098 751	13 014 763	2 140 288	13 048 543	7 733 157	1 871 405	1 045 372

表4-5 续表 1

单位：万元

项 目	Item	# 固定资产合计 Fixed Assets	固定资产原价 Original Value of Fixed Assets
总 计	**Total**	**76 248 018**	**147 662 053**
一、按登记注册类型分	**Grouped by Registration Status**		
国有企业	State-owned Enterprises	228 403	380 634
集体企业	Collective-owned Enterprises	8 898	34 899
股份合作企业	Share-holding Cooperative Enterprises	47 284	109 328
联营企业	Joint Ownership Enterprises	20 040	36 744
有限责任公司	Limited Liability Corporations	12 743 343	23 124 256
股份有限公司	Share-holding Corporations Ltd.	4 281 049	6 981 279
私营企业	Private Enterprises	11 362 753	19 190 731
其他企业	Other Enterprises	74 087	93 861
港澳台投资企业	Enterprises with Investment from HongKong, Macao and Taiwan	13 909 954	27 446 485
外商投资企业	Enterprises with Foreign Investment	33 572 208	70 263 836
二、按轻重工业分	**Grouped by Light and Heavy Industry**		
轻工业	Light Industry	20 063 936	36 773 438
重工业	Heavy Industry	56 184 082	110 888 615
三、按企业规模分	**Grouped by Size of Enterprises**		
大型企业	Large	34 091 073	71 424 568
中型企业	Medium-sized	22 237 671	39 914 379
小型企业	Small	19 669 452	35 925 929
微型企业	Micro	249 823	397 176
四、按行业类别分	**Grouped by Sector**		
有色金属矿采选业	Nonferrous Metals Mining and Processing	–	–
非金属矿采选业	Nonmetal Minerals Mining and Dressing	19 431	36 188
农副食品加工业	Agricultural and Sideline Food Processing	333 647	645 330
食品制造业	Food Production	615 243	978 103
酒、饮料和精制茶制造业	Wine, Beverage and Refined Tea Manufacturing	342 972	632 162
烟草制品业	Manufacture of Tobacco	31 843	53 257
纺织业	Textile Industry	3 661 282	6 929 129

Continued 1

(10 000 yuan)

累计折旧 Accumulative Total Depreciation	负债合计 Total Liabilities	所有者权益合计 Total Creditors Equity					
			# 实收资本 Total Capital Hold	国家资本 State Capital	集体资本 Collective Capital	法人资本 Corporate Capital	个人资本 Personal Capital
72 598 512	**148 380 223**	**135 020 597**	**75 605 858**	**1 884 255**	**880 610**	**21 247 208**	**10 588 531**
152 231	237 556	254 791	52 915	52 915	–	–	–
26 001	154 956	17 628	12 456	–	12 315	81	60
78 846	133 964	134 215	20 174	–	978	683	18 513
16 705	27 947	47 000	5 743	2 147	2 197	1 400	–
10 591 745	26 461 032	17 965 715	7 992 209	835 524	486 082	5 150 518	1 265 821
2 917 473	10 937 351	12 009 970	4 276 856	138 349	126 211	1 591 908	2 128 876
8 066 428	31 743 795	20 167 808	11 604 116	43 526	138 045	5 539 788	5 805 807
41 947	60 463	67 454	25 898	–	–	25 760	138
13 667 153	23 775 058	24 734 260	13 596 516	175 775	35 009	2 106 712	512 829
37 039 982	54 848 103	59 621 756	38 018 976	636 020	79 774	6 830 358	856 488
17 180 567	40 289 282	33 025 373	19 053 170	408 498	121 346	5 875 714	3 217 067
55 417 944	108 090 941	101 995 225	56 552 688	1 475 757	759 264	15 371 494	7 371 464
37 942 738	68 398 277	59 633 968	27 070 037	759 519	402 719	8 250 160	2 666 095
18 019 915	36 664 927	37 517 037	21 759 478	522 463	230 197	5 893 270	2 625 652
16 482 085	42 416 980	37 414 111	26 379 994	590 450	245 479	6 973 176	5 216 862
153 774	900 039	455 481	396 350	11 823	2 215	130 602	79 922
–	–	–	–	–	–	–	–
17 683	19 241	23 759	10 000	10 000	–	–	–
315 438	855 879	894 921	339 226	70 056	–	47 567	22 683
371 908	1 050 383	739 470	573 976	–	42 981	173 982	46 721
288 863	295 887	367 354	255 629	–	–	99 993	3 542
21 414	4 191	32 244	36 286	36 286	–	–	–
3 336 809	8 181 171	4 851 046	3 044 238	5 644	4 582	878 397	1 148 531

表4-5 续表 2

单位：万元

项　　目	Item	港澳台资本 Capital from Hong Kong, Macao and Taiwan	外商资本 Foreign Invested Capital
总　　计	**Total**	**11 069 569**	**29 935 684**
一、按登记注册类型分	**Grouped by Registration Status**		
国有企业	State-owned Enterprises	–	–
集体企业	Collective-owned Enterprises	–	–
股份合作企业	Share-holding Cooperative Enterprises	–	–
联营企业	Joint Ownership Enterprises	–	–
有限责任公司	Limited Liability Corporations	62 603	191 661
股份有限公司	Share-holding Corporations Ltd.	197 558	93 953
私营企业	Private Enterprises	16 270	60 679
其他企业	Other Enterprises	–	–
港澳台投资企业	Enterprises with Investment from HongKong, Macao and Taiwan	9 283 950	1 482 241
外商投资企业	Enterprises with Foreign Investment	1 509 188	28 107 149
二、按轻重工业分	**Grouped by Light and Heavy Industry**		
轻工业	Light Industry	3 336 827	6 093 718
重工业	Heavy Industry	7 732 742	23 841 966
三、按企业规模分	**Grouped by Size of Enterprises**		
大型企业	Large	4 164 325	10 827 219
中型企业	Medium-sized	3 622 546	8 865 349
小型企业	Small	3 222 312	10 131 715
微型企业	Micro	60 386	111 401
四、按行业类别分	**Grouped by Sector**		
有色金属矿采选业	Nonferrous Metals Mining and Processing	–	–
非金属矿采选业	Nonmetal Minerals Mining and Dressing	–	–
农副食品加工业	Agricultural and Sideline Food Processing	19 372	179 550
食品制造业	Food Production	106 868	203 423
酒、饮料和精制茶制造业	Wine, Beverage and Refined Tea Manufacturing	75 968	76 127
烟草制品业	Manufacture of Tobacco	–	–
纺织业	Textile Industry	424 035	583 049

Continued 2

(10 000 yuan)

主营业务收入 Major Business Revenue	主营业务成本 Major Business Cost	主营业务税金及附加 Pre-tax and Related Payment of Major Business	营业利润 Business Profits	利润总额 Total Profits	亏损企业亏损总额 Total Deficit of Loss-Making Enterprises	利税总额 Total Taxes and Profits	应交增值税 Value Added Tax Payable
303 801 818	**261 696 085**	**1 102 128**	**17 430 529**	**17 727 401**	**1 980 239**	**23 882 390**	**5 041 440**
138 430	106 992	110	7 407	7 470	1 105	9 145	1 564
71 183	65 854	208	-368	-91	1 808	1 957	1 840
190 286	160 951	779	9 887	14 701	–	22 894	7 414
34 868	28 258	232	-1 071	-876	3 150	472	1 116
40 939 517	35 750 570	106 957	1 902 741	1 953 898	294 907	2 778 170	714 020
15 144 998	12 143 390	79 474	1 236 955	1 279 724	97 600	1 757 891	397 446
50 878 249	44 166 070	177 739	2 212 413	2 352 653	248 216	3 634 989	1 103 463
222 913	199 913	395	16 551	17 500	–	24 525	6 631
51 476 725	44 841 326	180 323	3 101 582	3 189 244	296 172	4 202 574	832 569
144 704 651	124 232 762	555 911	8 944 433	8 913 178	1 037 281	11 449 774	1 975 376
75 983 650	63 906 981	310 529	3 930 622	4 129 187	391 947	5 995 042	1 552 879
227 818 167	197 789 105	791 599	13 499 907	13 598 214	1 588 293	17 887 348	3 488 561
160 832 687	142 574 698	483 097	8 703 518	8 609 532	530 967	11 020 161	1 923 530
65 448 040	53 328 344	305 191	4 950 551	5 195 486	535 113	6 956 017	1 452 708
75 864 517	64 250 818	309 567	3 776 137	3 930 345	864 812	5 892 813	1 648 167
1 656 573	1 542 226	4 274	324	-7 962	49 347	13 399	17 036
–	–	–	–	–	–	–	–
19 011	12 814	314	588	2 160	–	4 574	2 101
2 912 847	2 653 979	4 334	97 285	104 009	7 597	141 232	32 874
2 411 618	1 379 501	11 016	76 919	83 649	30 245	151 299	56 378
517 440	418 180	13 252	43 629	45 196	7 340	80 940	22 492
13 542	7 155	130	274	318	–	1 745	1 297
12 988 940	11 835 137	41 801	299 341	329 051	63 734	610 074	239 046

表4-5 续表 3

单位：万元

项　　目	Item	企业单位数（个）Number of Enterprises (unit)	# 亏损企业 Loss Making Enterprises
纺织服装、服饰业	Garments and Apparel Industry	379	80
皮革、毛皮、羽毛及其制品和制鞋业	Leather, Fur, Wool and Shoes Products	55	14
木材加工及木、竹、藤、棕、草制品业	Wood Processing, Wood, Bamboo, Rattan and Coir Products Straw Products	43	8
家具制造业	Furniture Manufacturing	75	15
造纸及纸制品业	Papermaking and Paper Products	146	27
印刷业和记录媒介复制业	Printing and Record Duplicating	157	33
文教、工美、体育和娱乐用品制造业	Stationary,Educational, Industrial arts, Sports and Entertainment products	125	14
石油加工、炼焦及核燃料加工业	Oil Processing, Coking and Nuclear Fuel Processing	22	4
化学原料及化学制品制造业	Raw Chemical Materials and Chemical Products	653	102
医药制造业	Medical and Pharmaceutical Products	107	11
化学纤维制造业	Chemical Fiber Manufacturing	329	86
橡胶和塑料制品业	Rubber and Plastic Products	609	117
非金属矿物制品业	Nonmetal Mineral Products	318	95
黑色金属冶炼及压延加工业	Smelting and Pressing of Ferrous Metals	165	27
有色金属冶炼及压延加工业	Smelting and Pressing of Nonferrous Metals	231	57
金属制品业	Metal Products	650	111
通用设备制造业	General Equipment Manufacture	831	146
专用设备制造业	Special Purposes Equipment Manufacturing	678	132
汽车制造业	Automobile Manufacturing	413	71
铁路、船舶、航空航天和其他运输设备制造业	Railway, Ship, Aerospace and Other Transportation Equipment Manufacturing	119	20
电气机械及器材制造业	Electric Equipment and Machinery Manufacturing	743	130
计算机、通信和其他电子设备制造业	Computer Telecommunications and Other Electronic Equipment Manufacture	1 145	255
仪器仪表制造业	Instruments, Meters Machinery	167	20
其他制造业	Other Products Manufacture	10	3
废弃资源综合利用业	Comprehensive Utilization of Waste Resources	40	16
电力、热力的生产和供应业	Production and Supply of Electricity and Thermal Power	38	1
燃气生产和供应业	Production and Supply of Gas	21	3
水的生产和供应业	Production and Supply of Water	25	5

Continued 3

(10 000 yuan)

工业总产值 Gross Industrial Output Value	工业销售产值 Value of Industrial Products Sales	# 出口交货值 Delivery Value for Export	资产总计 Total Assets	# 流动资产合计 Circulating Funds	# 应收帐款 Net Account Income	# 产成品 Manufactured Products
7 396 559	7 313 635	1 529 024	5 759 339	3 707 404	869 380	466 848
457 795	453 543	308 597	411 837	305 100	90 352	31 500
536 150	555 701	50 657	836 723	489 772	119 731	64 579
915 019	942 052	493 860	859 560	591 824	205 314	55 566
5 402 002	5 386 281	508 565	8 132 037	4 540 123	1 024 079	178 513
2 160 815	2 148 199	508 963	2 252 893	1 340 669	577 853	77 990
2 405 330	2 404 184	944 771	1 938 688	1 253 951	308 769	211 326
1 316 917	1 187 756	461	838 384	487 494	144 657	54 274
19 562 055	19 453 309	3 249 828	23 085 522	12 937 841	4 361 528	979 936
3 055 731	2 864 495	477 311	3 662 676	2 219 935	532 225	292 702
10 405 122	9 987 849	620 433	10 675 551	5 858 617	831 072	722 719
8 577 994	8 515 542	2 515 158	8 352 442	5 108 292	2 212 763	491 761
4 540 573	4 577 401	564 211	6 180 888	4 111 244	2 166 952	287 902
24 348 650	24 727 443	2 859 223	19 537 604	9 389 493	826 891	915 484
5 386 166	5 296 089	606 669	4 199 557	2 687 755	898 146	216 567
7 728 378	7 604 695	1 581 436	9 757 502	5 954 822	2 338 928	467 695
19 520 531	19 402 097	6 457 114	20 388 669	13 747 329	4 806 499	1 077 047
10 281 335	10 122 265	3 513 188	14 052 852	9 186 112	3 150 000	696 277
15 451 801	15 253 570	2 263 671	15 942 030	9 075 507	4 160 205	719 878
2 723 009	2 721 446	1 214 588	2 765 178	1 871 294	698 704	185 487
27 155 191	26 572 800	9 038 694	28 390 251	19 027 406	7 582 052	1 186 807
99 479 097	97 514 079	74 518 536	61 173 678	40 681 207	19 831 099	2 455 329
3 686 932	3 631 942	1 232 153	3 754 328	2 761 573	968 822	277 960
58 977	59 832	15 693	57 311	36 852	13 759	1 713
389 388	379 271	3 580	447 710	269 515	40 079	17 379
3 446 788	3 433 471	–	7 514 980	1 622 359	411 161	–
1 357 653	1 339 557	68 254	2 497 078	1 333 590	76 150	4 122
382 555	373 913	–	2 767 885	772 918	29 413	4 127

表4-5 续表 4

单位：万元

项　　目	Item	# 固定资产合　计 Fixed Assets	固定资产原价 Original Value of Fixed Assets
纺织服装、服饰业	Garments and Apparel Industry	1 360 207	1 861 395
皮革、毛皮、羽毛及其制品和制鞋业	Leather, Fur, Wool and Shoes Products	63 749	145 477
木材加工及木、竹、藤、棕、草制品业	Wood Processing, Wood, Bamboo, Rattan and Coir Products Straw Products	139 904	283 385
家具制造业	Furniture Manufacturing	207 557	360 719
造纸及纸制品业	Papermaking and Paper Products	2 415 802	4 900 140
印刷业和记录媒介复制业	Printing and Record Duplicating	696 831	1 361 956
文教、工美、体育和娱乐用品制造业	Stationary,Educational, Industrial arts, Sports and Entertainment products	374 336	782 569
石油加工、炼焦及核燃料加工业	Oil Processing, Coking and Nuclear Fuel Processing	141 391	222 754
化学原料及化学制品制造业	Raw Chemical Materials and Chemical Products	7 357 788	12 318 170
医药制造业	Medical and Pharmaceutical Products	869 730	1 671 479
化学纤维制造业	Chemical Fiber Manufacturing	3 048 633	5 753 132
橡胶和塑料制品业	Rubber and Plastic Products	2 625 542	5 262 410
非金属矿物制品业	Nonmetal Mineral Products	1 577 420	3 408 312
黑色金属冶炼及压延加工业	Smelting and Pressing of Ferrous Metals	6 739 273	14 905 203
有色金属冶炼及压延加工业	Smelting and Pressing of Nonferrous Metals	906 423	1 833 239
金属制品业	Metal Products	2 025 767	3 526 666
通用设备制造业	General Equipment Manufacture	4 295 850	7 869 442
专用设备制造业	Special Purposes Equipment Manufacturing	3 060 085	5 286 399
汽车制造业	Automobile Manufacturing	4 529 366	7 112 758
铁路、船舶、航空航天和其他运输设备制造业	Railway, Ship, Aerospace and Other Transportation Equipment Manufacturing	650 879	1 130 307
电气机械及器材制造业	Electric Equipment and Machinery Manufacturing	5 081 910	9 317 476
计算机、通信和其他电子设备制造业	Computer Telecommunications and Other Electronic Equipment Manufacture	16 238 859	37 054 398
仪器仪表制造业	Instruments, Meters Machinery	674 980	1 265 676
其他制造业	Other Products Manufacture	17 057	43 277
废弃资源综合利用业	Comprehensive Utilization of Waste Resources	106 703	183 005
电力、热力的生产和供应业	Production and Supply of Electricity and Thermal Power	3 906 019	7 259 413
燃气生产和供应业	Production and Supply of Gas	428 511	628 889
水的生产和供应业	Production and Supply of Water	1 703 030	2 639 842

Continued 4

(10 000 yuan)

累计折旧 Accumulative Total Depreciation	负债合计 Total Liabilities	所有者权益合计 Total Creditors Equity	# 实收资本 Total Capital Hold	国家资本 State Capital	集体资本 Collective Capital	法人资本 Corporate Capital	个人资本 Personal Capital
697 365	3 488 223	2 260 749	746 568	–	950	293 327	273 019
82 264	202 466	209 371	124 527	–	1 596	15 558	15 997
145 079	359 391	477 331	221 500	–	1 000	96 144	23 547
154 575	415 147	444 412	304 452	–	15 146	55 161	45 519
2 498 923	3 830 757	4 301 278	3 107 233	84 002	1 407	920 201	357 886
681 323	1 181 832	1 062 430	574 535	–	8 930	189 764	93 298
415 174	1 012 056	926 631	515 897	–	1 339	169 282	55 339
96 270	316 603	514 730	293 523	–	–	237 079	9 583
5 063 132	10 508 340	12 563 122	7 280 241	134 676	43 583	2 168 026	733 626
795 027	1 579 541	2 083 134	1 478 415	8 333	4 500	284 843	68 678
2 752 215	6 687 507	3 986 865	2 637 789	12 500	475	1 597 356	536 533
2 643 736	3 602 355	4 742 672	3 075 503	5 000	3 696	401 898	304 132
1 838 455	3 408 111	2 758 283	1 977 643	73 700	52 076	404 563	293 810
8 359 610	12 021 209	7 515 479	2 371 053	40 666	29 712	733 230	641 324
930 163	2 244 651	1 950 701	1 427 621	53 138	1 242	215 244	309 493
1 549 591	4 883 963	4 868 879	3 362 934	26 619	60 564	1 137 684	914 760
3 612 149	9 125 227	11 222 890	5 247 850	25 793	70 169	1 687 054	911 895
2 303 696	6 390 718	7 686 879	3 477 287	78 560	65 198	739 562	589 837
2 638 908	8 886 305	7 055 719	4 697 060	46 901	15 639	1 975 808	218 963
527 864	1 382 555	1 382 621	599 213	4 000	6 272	158 708	52 668
4 279 682	15 105 448	13 282 023	6 452 949	62 445	344 651	1 827 927	1 678 263
20 948 731	31 895 862	29 228 141	17 459 231	431 971	37 751	3 395 150	911 389
596 288	1 725 848	2 021 859	853 781	518	1 142	212 337	127 907
26 220	39 047	18 264	33 382	–	–	9 952	2 000
77 833	296 227	151 483	163 391	26 485	–	22 568	46 837
3 362 107	4 287 336	3 227 644	1 901 274	397 207	16 039	837 028	26 045
200 378	1 273 691	1 223 386	345 962	55 274	8 000	82 876	117 806
969 638	1 823 058	944 827	615 690	194 481	41 971	178 940	6 900

表4-5 续表 5

单位：万元

项 目	Item	港澳台资本 Capital from Hong Kong,Macao and Taiwan	外商资本 Foreign Invested Capital
纺织服装、服饰业	Garments and Apparel Industry	72 059	107 213
皮革、毛皮、羽毛及其制品和制鞋业	Leather, Fur, Wool and Shoes Products	25 673	65 703
木材加工及木、竹、藤、棕、草制品业	Wood Processing, Wood, Bamboo, Rattan and Coir Products Straw Products	15 307	85 502
家具制造业	Furniture Manufacturing	84 395	104 232
造纸及纸制品业	Papermaking and Paper Products	737 237	1 006 501
印刷业和记录媒介复制业	Printing and Record Duplicating	91 926	190 618
文教、工美、体育和娱乐用品制造业	Stationary,Educational, Industrial arts, Sports and Entertainment products	135 795	154 142
石油加工、炼焦及核燃料加工业	Oil Processing, Coking and Nuclear Fuel Processing	–	46 861
化学原料及化学制品制造业	Raw Chemical Materials and Chemical Products	978 488	3 221 842
医药制造业	Medical and Pharmaceutical Products	174 514	937 548
化学纤维制造业	Chemical Fiber Manufacturing	323 247	167 678
橡胶和塑料制品业	Rubber and Plastic Products	553 566	1 807 210
非金属矿物制品业	Nonmetal Mineral Products	342 509	810 984
黑色金属冶炼及压延加工业	Smelting and Pressing of Ferrous Metals	315 949	610 173
有色金属冶炼及压延加工业	Smelting and Pressing of Nonferrous Metals	241 784	606 721
金属制品业	Metal Products	309 332	913 975
通用设备制造业	General Equipment Manufacture	387 983	2 164 956
专用设备制造业	Special Purposes Equipment Manufacturing	438 839	1 565 290
汽车制造业	Automobile Manufacturing	200 442	2 239 307
铁路、船舶、航空航天和其他运输设备制造业	Railway, Ship, Aerospace and Other Transportation Equipment Manufacturing	123 173	254 393
电气机械及器材制造业	Electric Equipment and Machinery Manufacturing	683 879	1 855 784
计算机、通信和其他电子设备制造业	Computer Telecommunications and Other Electronic Equipment Manufacture	3 261 194	9 421 775
仪器仪表制造业	Instruments, Meters Machinery	89 122	422 755
其他制造业	Other Products Manufacture	8 131	13 299
废弃资源综合利用业	Comprehensive Utilization of Waste Resources	34 236	33 265
电力、热力的生产和供应业	Production and Supply of Electricity and Thermal Power	585 136	39 820
燃气生产和供应业	Production and Supply of Gas	73 315	8 690
水的生产和供应业	Production and Supply of Water	156 098	37 300

Continued 5

(10 000 yuan)

主营业务收入 Major Business Revenue	主营业务成本 Major Business Cost	主营业务税金及附加 Pre-tax and Related Payment of Major Business	营业利润 Business Profits	利润总额 Total Profits	亏损企业亏损总额 Total Deficit of Loss-Making Enterprises	利税总额 Total Taxes and Profits	应交增值税 Value Added Tax Payable
7 294 538	6 023 262	44 077	433 865	438 411	14 649	608 352	125 819
450 680	397 939	2 607	7 075	8 821	5 071	18 972	7 545
553 860	451 477	5 445	26 890	30 582	6 793	54 431	18 403
945 183	794 023	4 572	45 175	58 818	7 174	82 316	18 825
5 357 559	4 388 191	21 844	355 951	370 052	20 051	565 281	173 374
2 177 939	1 761 608	11 146	163 018	167 992	9 509	250 697	71 534
2 367 477	2 045 334	9 686	107 138	110 220	4 305	167 236	47 330
1 192 638	1 045 130	17 577	77 425	78 443	2 197	143 024	46 863
19 816 509	15 496 080	87 999	1 769 230	1 806 921	191 040	2 427 024	531 626
2 823 439	1 664 629	21 829	292 518	307 004	22 045	496 989	168 001
10 031 402	9 307 159	20 880	246 750	267 478	66 820	454 811	166 447
8 600 793	7 025 847	38 894	596 255	597 163	101 447	850 311	214 139
4 629 140	3 944 061	22 266	178 934	212 454	64 737	397 453	162 645
24 075 134	22 188 259	43 185	705 418	642 924	62 704	1 053 222	367 064
6 704 078	6 272 618	12 070	128 131	132 043	23 640	197 079	52 913
7 547 525	6 339 860	34 788	319 340	365 089	140 652	579 195	179 139
19 394 121	15 246 705	108 032	1 934 602	1 969 395	113 899	2 530 533	452 763
10 133 409	7 888 893	49 937	954 472	993 629	109 881	1 285 689	241 914
15 329 380	12 457 376	161 459	1 225 504	1 248 328	265 347	1 739 834	327 451
2 727 332	2 089 691	13 259	341 308	345 417	11 893	418 982	60 284
26 204 288	22 205 509	79 047	1 762 518	1 786 958	131 387	2 166 418	300 107
97 347 516	89 123 447	168 534	4 041 545	3 943 373	452 633	4 767 613	653 390
3 647 897	2 869 966	17 758	346 159	367 301	18 586	458 880	73 711
59 129	48 759	439	779	758	1 084	3 551	2 354
387 219	354 477	1 118	-5 067	-1 604	16 758	7 417	7 886
3 429 845	2 589 633	26 562	675 849	691 043	322	892 903	173 425
1 331 245	1 118 638	3 658	152 976	155 142	3 631	178 599	19 462
379 147	250 752	2 615	28 736	68 864	3 073	95 717	22 838

表4-6 规模以上国有及国有控股工业企业主要经济指标 (2016年)

单位：万元

项　　目	Item	企业单位数（个）Number of Enterprises (unit)	# 亏损企业 Loss Making Enterprises
总　计	**Total**	**124**	**31**
有色金属矿采选业	Nonferrous Metals Mining and Processing	–	–
非金属矿采选业	Nonmetal Minerals Mining and Dressing	1	–
农副食品加工业	Agricultural and Sideline Food Processing	2	2
酒、饮料和精制茶制造业	Wine, Beverage and Refined tea manufacturing	1	–
烟草制品业	Manufacture of Tobacco	1	–
纺织业	Textile Industry	2	1
纺织服装、服饰业	Garments and Apparel Industry	2	–
造纸及纸制品业	Papermaking and Paper Products	1	–
印刷和记录媒介复制业	Printing and Record Duplicating	–	–
文教、工美、体育和娱乐用品制造业	Printing and Record Duplicating	1	–
石油加工、炼焦及核燃料加工业	Oil Processing, Coking and Nuclear Fuel Processing	1	–
化学原料及化学制品制造业	Raw Chemical Materials and Chemical Products	16	3
医药制造业	Medical and Pharmaceutical Products	1	–
橡胶和塑料制品业	Rubber and Plastic Products	2	1
非金属矿物制品业	Nonmetal Mineral Products	12	4
黑色金属冶炼及压延加工业	Smelting and Pressing of Ferrous Metals	3	2
有色金属冶炼及压延加工业	Smelting and Pressing of Nonferrous Metals	4	1
金属制品业	Manufacture of Metal Products	4	2
通用设备制造业	General Equipment Manufacture	11	5
专用设备制造业	For Special Purposes Equipment Manufacturing	7	1
汽车制造业	Automobile Manufacturing	3	–
铁路、船舶、航空航天和其他运输设备制造业	Transport Equipment Manufacturing	1	–
电气机械及器材制造业	Electric Equipment and Machinery Manufacturing	4	2
计算机、通信和其他电子设备制造业	Computer Telecommunications and Other Electronic Equipment Manufacture	13	4
仪器仪表制造业	Instruments, Meters Machinery	2	–
废弃资源综合利用业	Comprehensive Utilization of Waste Resources	1	1
电力、热力的生产和供应业	Production and Supply of Electricity and Thermal Power	11	–
燃气生产和供应业	Production and Supply of Gas	7	1
水的生产和供应业	Production and Supply of Water	10	1

MAIN ECONOMIC INDICATORS OF STATE-OWNED ENTERPRISES AND SHARE HOLDING INDUSTRIAL ENTERPRISES ABOVE DESIGNATED SIZE (2016)

(10 000 yuan)

工业总产值 Gross Industrial Output Value	工业销售产值 Value of Industrial Products Sales	# 出口交货值 Delivery Value for Export	资产总计 Total Assets	# 流动资产合计 Circulating Funds	# 固定资产合计 Fixed Assets	累计折旧 Accumulative Depreciation	负债合计 Total Liabilities
7 833 593	**7 580 124**	**1 313 824**	**11 226 160**	**4 486 613**	**5 178 577**	**4 149 563**	**6 219 445**
–	–	–	–	–	–	–	–
18 786	19 011	–	43 001	14 389	19 431	17 683	19 241
33 666	32 657	–	31 151	24 929	4 316	4 713	22 761
37 047	36 958	355	90 349	58 054	28 783	61 957	7 808
10 660	13 542	–	36 434	2 443	31 843	21 414	4 191
18 489	18 862	1 016	29 498	15 988	9 234	6 522	44 497
15 487	15 776	–	19 509	13 547	4 818	6 484	6 598
96 148	92 066	–	142 097	97 496	41 410	128 865	6 553
–	–	–	–	–	–	–	–
28 583	28 185	–	36 273	20 144	7 619	12 800	11 569
268 377	143 633	–	78 808	55 574	23 234	24 240	16 476
1 081 445	1 076 794	249 293	1 909 113	741 296	853 135	430 292	1 138 430
28 854	32 359	–	44 359	27 385	1 689	4 761	32 131
59 225	56 347	7 962	35 312	22 566	5 652	13 499	19 977
304 113	310 718	19 091	389 149	234 988	121 235	77 516	183 954
237 882	259 586	18 071	197 961	94 273	92 231	165 343	177 100
1 017 869	886 554	1 187	223 921	153 928	54 971	25 610	174 912
65 711	63 908	5 976	230 337	129 401	86 586	51 716	179 377
274 520	283 157	102 523	458 761	259 729	123 363	53 475	219 711
448 115	442 686	10 637	574 393	383 912	84 245	48 325	362 699
48 023	49 115	4 433	83 590	51 742	20 459	12 414	44 296
8 045	7 089	–	18 663	17 603	44	385	4 765
39 708	38 629	49	117 820	39 711	20 718	1 972	78 891
1 544 923	1 549 983	890 880	2 029 956	909 377	846 486	865 405	1 192 515
23 318	22 854	2 351	22 869	17 281	4 725	5 073	10 091
53 307	53 470	–	58 516	42 917	2 131	1 007	42 838
1 427 285	1 427 285	–	2 097 592	317 748	1 512 540	1 410 037	894 586
450 985	433 478	–	734 065	449 451	142 064	101 504	325 138
193 023	185 424	–	1 492 664	290 743	1 035 617	596 553	998 344

表4-6 续表

单位：万元

项 目	Item	所有者权益合 计 Creditors Equity	# 实收资本 Total Capital Hold
总 计	**Total**	**4 988 011**	**3 236 510**
有色金属矿采选业	Nonferrous Metals Mining and Processing	-	-
非金属矿采选业	Nonmetal Minerals Mining and Dressing	23 759	10 000
农副食品加工业	Agricultural and Sideline Food Processing	8 391	14 645
酒、饮料和精制茶制造业	Wine, Beverage and Refined tea manufacturing	82 541	73 154
烟草制品业	Manufacture of Tobacco	32 244	36 286
纺织业	Textile Industry	-14 999	9 500
纺织服装、服饰业	Garments and Apparel Industry	12 910	2 306
造纸及纸制品业	Papermaking and Paper Products	135 544	84 000
印刷和记录媒介复制业	Printing and Record Duplicating	-	-
文教、工美、体育和娱乐用品制造业	Printing and Record Duplicating	24 705	7 939
石油加工、炼焦及核燃料加工业	Oil Processing, Coking and Nuclear Fuel Processing	62 333	-
化学原料及化学制品制造业	Raw Chemical Materials and Chemical Products	770 682	223 717
医药制造业	Medical and Pharmaceutical Products	12 228	9 720
橡胶和塑料制品业	Rubber and Plastic Products	15 335	11 131
非金属矿物制品业	Nonmetal Mineral Products	205 624	98 840
黑色金属冶炼及压延加工业	Smelting and Pressing of Ferrous Metals	20 860	87 823
有色金属冶炼及压延加工业	Smelting and Pressing of Nonferrous Metals	49 008	54 107
金属制品业	Manufacture of Metal Products	50 960	71 004
通用设备制造业	General Equipment Manufacture	222 109	119 338
专用设备制造业	For Special Purposes Equipment Manufacturing	211 694	121 770
汽车制造业	Automobile Manufacturing	39 294	27 422
铁路、船舶、航空航天和其他运输设备制造业	Transport Equipment Manufacturing	13 898	10 000
电气机械及器材制造业	Electric Equipment and Machinery Manufacturing	36 740	34 990
计算机、通信和其他电子设备制造业	Computer Telecommunications and Other Electronic Equipment Manufacture	837 442	1 111 170
仪器仪表制造业	Instruments, Meters Machinery	12 779	7 196
废弃资源综合利用业	Comprehensive Utilization of Waste Resources	15 679	20 000
电力、热力的生产和供应业	Production and Supply of Electricity and Thermal Power	1 203 006	654 144
燃气生产和供应业	Production and Supply of Gas	408 927	63 080
水的生产和供应业	Production and Supply of Water	494 320	273 229

Continued

(10 000 yuan)

主营业务收入 Major Business Revenue	主营业务成本 Major Business Cost	主营业务税金及附加 Pre-tax and Related Payment of Major Business	营业利润 Business Profits	利润总额 Total Profits	亏损企业亏损总额 Total Deficit of Loss-Making Enterprises	利税总额 Total Taxes and Profits	应交增值税 Value Added Tax Payable
8 880 087	**7 746 613**	**33 368**	**445 901**	**507 003**	**101 299**	**820 840**	**276 712**
–	–	–	–	–	–	–	–
19 011	12 814	314	588	2 160	–	4 574	2 101
33 058	31 158	52	-1 604	-1 699	1 699	-1 196	451
36 958	25 439	4 784	3 319	3 408	–	11 259	3 067
13 542	7 155	130	274	318	–	1 745	1 297
20 307	18 687	83	-1 268	-1 178	1 565	-648	448
15 776	8 887	183	1 099	1 172	–	3 058	1 702
93 113	57 886	1 001	14 229	15 169	–	24 502	8 332
–	–	–	–	–	–	–	–
28 366	24 895	103	825	825	–	1 727	800
141 501	125 291	2 550	5 112	5 152	–	33 874	26 032
1 088 009	958 987	2 307	32 179	36 320	1 983	60 791	21 987
33 934	14 579	404	-294	227	–	3 994	3 364
56 280	48 826	174	-343	365	473	2 462	1 924
323 969	261 880	1 700	14 418	15 830	3 442	30 070	12 541
251 834	244 315	228	-16 234	-19 869	20 116	-17 681	1 961
2 188 696	2 172 602	118	4 207	4 452	52	4 791	221
64 984	67 054	243	-49 312	-49 133	50 506	-48 624	266
283 423	241 593	2 290	1 363	5 349	13 060	23 752	15 936
438 719	367 983	2 835	26 579	29 749	491	44 782	12 198
48 600	37 172	316	1 885	2 139	–	4 372	1 917
7 089	4 718	65	1 116	1 146	–	1 788	577
39 908	34 628	58	14	937	847	1 762	766
1 540 529	1 342 025	1 094	75 795	92 096	6 021	147 988	54 798
22 854	17 045	136	296	325	–	1 216	756
53 470	53 257	3	-485	-405	405	-398	4
1 409 645	1 101 918	9 892	270 231	277 001	–	372 414	83 658
437 808	353 900	1 463	60 454	62 734	212	73 662	9 141
188 705	111 920	844	1 459	22 416	426	34 805	10 469

表4-7 规模以上民营工业企业主要经济指标 (2016年)

单位：万元

项　目	Item	企业单位数（个）Number of Enterprises (unit)	# 亏损企业 Loss Making Enterprises
总　计	**Total**	**5 338**	**861**
农副食品加工业	Agricultural and Sideline Food Processing	24	7
食品制造业	Food Production	25	6
酒、饮料和精制茶制造业	Wine, Beverage and Refined tea manufacturing	4	1
纺织业	Textile Industry	992	171
纺织服装、服饰业	Garments and Apparel Industry	277	49
皮革、毛皮、羽毛及其制品和制鞋业	Leather, Fur, Wool and Shoes Products	25	3
木材加工及木、竹、藤、棕、草制品业	Wood Processing, Wood, Bamboo, Rattan and Coir Products Straw Products	30	4
家具制造业	Furniture Manufacturing	38	3
造纸及纸制品业	Papermaking and Paper Products	82	7
印刷业和记录媒介复制业	Printing and Record Medium Reproduction	106	17
文教、工美、体育和娱乐用品制造业	Stationary,Educational, Industrial arts, Sports and Entertainment products	64	6
石油加工、炼焦及核燃料加工业	Petroleum Processing, Coking and Nucleus Fuel Machining Trade	17	4
化学原料及化学制品制造业	Raw Chemical Materials and Chemical Products	299	35
医药制造业	Medical and Pharmaceutical Products	66	4
化学纤维制造业	Chemical Fiber	299	78
橡胶和塑料制品业	Rubber and Plastic Products	322	46
非金属矿物制品业	Nonmetal Mineral Products	188	42
黑色金属冶炼及压延加工业	Smelting and Pressing of Ferrous Metals	111	12
有色金属冶炼及压延加工业	Smelting and Pressing of Nonferrous Metals	149	34
金属制品业	Metal Products	428	61
通用设备制造业	General Equipment Manufacture	407	58
专用设备制造业	Special Purposes Equipment Manufacturing	333	44
汽车制造业	Automobile Manufacturing	133	15
铁路、船舶、航空航天和其他运输设备制造业	Railway, Ship, Aerospace and Other Transportation Equipment Manufacturing	38	7
电气机械及器材制造业	Electric Equipment and Machinery Manufacturing	417	66
计算机、通信和其他电子设备制造业	Computer Telecommunications and Other Electronic Equipment Manufacture	329	61
仪器仪表造业	Instruments, Meters, Machinery	72	5
其他制造业	Other Industry	2	–
废弃资源综合利用业	Comprehensive Utilization of Waste Resources	22	9
电力、热力的生产和供应业	Production and Supply of Electric Power and Heat Energy	20	1
燃气生产和供应业	Production and Supply of Gas	8	2
水的生产和供应业	Production and Supply of Water	11	3

MAIN ECONOMIC INDICATORS OF PRIVATE AND INDIVIDUAL INDUSTRIAL ENTERPRISES ABOVE DESIGNATED SIZE (2016)

(10 000 yuan)

工业总产值 Gross Industrial Output Value	工业销售产值 Value of Industrial Products Sales	# 出口交货值 Delivery Value for Export	资产总计 Total Assets	# 流动资产合计 Circulating Funds	# 固定资产合计 Fixed Assets	累计折旧 Accumulative Depreciation	负债合计 Total Liabilities
102 173 115	**101 295 586**	**13 720 355**	**111 362 302**	**67 050 485**	**24 481 441**	**18 802 523**	**64 797 756**
451 472	453 758	3 031	250 337	179 154	57 784	42 973	156 942
482 544	470 088	24 136	317 968	179 930	111 952	97 753	128 210
118 492	117 229	–	136 295	68 628	46 901	22 732	34 765
10 342 535	10 250 606	1 404 456	9 595 506	5 594 334	2 608 406	2 271 123	6 247 568
6 388 466	6 304 334	871 591	4 942 475	3 124 499	1 193 331	479 621	3 089 051
223 135	222 101	133 167	209 105	156 889	21 423	29 282	114 007
305 238	307 061	6 115	489 896	228 669	68 174	77 444	201 498
344 272	343 456	99 807	331 907	242 072	59 964	40 403	200 898
1 117 935	1 128 783	20 355	953 719	451 784	148 832	109 424	404 601
1 126 516	1 117 564	177 767	1 121 227	670 419	368 604	295 990	673 418
830 782	782 223	296 462	793 595	499 207	145 335	119 068	500 716
633 848	634 682	461	405 969	165 822	45 818	18 024	168 448
7 115 513	7 035 917	819 152	9 171 043	5 623 665	2 098 904	915 804	4 287 500
990 015	982 687	172 471	1 076 492	625 908	283 196	171 792	592 637
8 115 787	7 768 641	358 571	7 367 344	4 455 705	1 697 238	1 941 545	5 029 272
2 676 525	2 650 167	482 492	2 316 678	1 603 958	508 693	340 636	1 266 916
1 748 640	1 751 043	89 932	2 695 833	2 048 365	401 264	377 414	1 789 858
15 915 718	16 767 994	2 319 743	14 640 751	7 209 049	4 515 516	5 196 068	9 262 426
2 293 296	2 273 266	211 210	1 823 733	1 178 520	297 564	235 702	1 086 647
4 700 855	4 585 037	645 185	6 060 230	3 611 452	1 042 805	645 852	3 317 901
5 451 059	5 394 435	835 050	7 071 555	4 302 911	1 333 616	814 207	3 163 823
2 982 876	2 917 914	669 096	5 029 813	3 059 457	963 200	549 327	2 672 196
3 946 739	3 865 603	306 609	3 734 547	2 623 632	680 820	365 696	2 587 408
443 327	433 046	52 908	757 674	502 133	182 178	85 983	469 679
12 447 420	11 919 106	1 452 879	15 541 089	9 948 585	2 546 895	1 507 585	9 022 494
8 506 423	8 413 839	2 114 029	9 714 417	6 252 864	1 855 680	1 083 808	5 268 490
1 145 762	1 091 983	148 342	1 564 852	1 183 241	208 258	89 496	747 792
18 330	18 141	5 340	10 172	6 530	3 483	4 172	5 005
211 466	200 551	–	267 518	150 167	69 165	37 976	204 515
814 673	812 507	–	2 344 739	618 064	810 922	709 129	1 622 073
184 950	184 361	–	134 466	113 923	9 330	13 043	109 520
98 506	97 464	–	491 357	370 952	96 192	113 453	371 483

表4-7 续表

单位：万元

项　　目	Item	所有者权益合　计 Creditors Equity	# 实收资本 Total Capital Hold
总　计	**Total**	**46 471 455**	**21 720 452**
农副食品加工业	Agricultural and Sideline Food Processing	93 395	43 075
食品制造业	Food Production	189 758	146 791
酒、饮料和精制茶制造业	Wine, Beverage and Refined tea manufacturing	101 530	4 042
纺织业	Textile Industry	3 340 931	1 678 362
纺织服装、服饰业	Garments and Apparel Industry	1 843 059	465 964
皮革、毛皮、羽毛及其制品和制鞋业	Leather, Fur, Wool and Shoes Products	95 098	36 518
木材加工及木、竹、藤、棕、草制品业	Wood Processing, Wood, Bamboo, Rattan and Coir Products Straw Products	288 397	119 942
家具制造业	Furniture Manufacturing	131 007	76 067
造纸及纸制品业	Papermaking and Paper Products	549 117	226 939
印刷业和记录媒介复制业	Printing and Record Medium Reproduction	447 807	219 096
文教、工美、体育和娱乐用品制造业	Stationary,Educational, Industrial arts, Sports and Entertainment products	292 879	131 109
石油加工、炼焦及核燃料加工业	Petroleum Processing, Coking and Nucleus Fuel Machining Trade	230 471	189 193
化学原料及化学制品制造业	Raw Chemical Materials and Chemical Products	4 870 471	2 339 052
医药制造业	Medical and Pharmaceutical Products	483 854	263 909
化学纤维制造业	Chemical Fiber	2 336 893	1 356 665
橡胶和塑料制品业	Rubber and Plastic Products	1 049 755	533 950
非金属矿物制品业	Nonmetal Mineral Products	891 898	596 455
黑色金属冶炼及压延加工业	Smelting and Pressing of Ferrous Metals	5 377 409	1 080 682
有色金属冶炼及压延加工业	Smelting and Pressing of Nonferrous Metals	732 882	383 670
金属制品业	Metal Products	2 739 109	1 879 563
通用设备制造业	General Equipment Manufacture	3 884 126	1 811 612
专用设备制造业	Special Purposes Equipment Manufacturing	2 356 450	1 120 004
汽车制造业	Automobile Manufacturing	1 147 137	554 512
铁路、船舶、航空航天和其他运输设备制造业	Railway, Ship, Aerospace and Other Transportation Equipment Manufacturing	287 995	154 277
电气机械及器材制造业	Electric Equipment and Machinery Manufacturing	6 518 008	3 017 221
计算机、通信和其他电子设备制造业	Computer Telecommunications and Other Electronic Equipment Manufacture	4 445 922	2 267 329
仪器仪表造业	Instruments, Meters, Machinery	810 440	264 000
其他制造业	Other Industry	5 167	3 500
废弃资源综合利用业	Comprehensive Utilization of Waste Resources	63 002	74 208
电力、热力的生产和供应业	Production and Supply of Electric Power and Heat Energy	722 665	587 843
燃气生产和供应业	Production and Supply of Gas	24 946	35 671
水的生产和供应业	Production and Supply of Water	119 874	59 233

Continued

(10 000 yuan)

主营业务收入 Major Business Revenue	主营业务成本 Major Business Cost	主营业务税金及附加 Pre-tax and Related Payment of Major Business	营业利润 Business Profits	利润总额 Total Profits	亏损企业亏损总额 Total Deficit of Loss-Making Enterprises	利税总额 Total Taxes and Profits	应交增值税 Value Added Tax Payable
100 275 983	**86 166 435**	**335 814**	**5 015 920**	**5 207 128**	**568 604**	**7 570 309**	**2 025 231**
464 737	419 967	719	13 894	15 270	2 871	21 269	5 265
477 006	397 092	2 099	20 831	21 308	1 491	36 927	13 520
116 598	77 548	2 154	27 603	27 831	47	35 394	5 410
10 216 472	9 390 498	31 692	204 915	231 310	38 057	458 420	195 252
6 296 716	5 159 034	38 276	413 218	396 033	9 430	546 573	112 246
218 712	192 312	1 178	5 183	5 929	305	10 705	3 597
304 493	256 998	2 578	10 126	13 739	3 190	26 248	9 931
339 571	275 744	1 812	19 941	24 365	831	37 248	11 016
1 122 131	1 006 775	2 736	31 257	33 680	1 473	62 130	25 715
1 117 465	948 111	4 343	67 355	72 978	1 491	106 182	28 862
790 060	680 637	3 940	45 471	48 461	803	71 380	18 979
639 673	608 539	399	5 956	6 419	2 197	10 828	4 010
6 954 755	5 023 638	28 432	884 857	914 116	44 068	1 167 644	224 886
979 666	775 057	4 723	63 859	67 462	4 906	104 398	32 213
7 827 455	7 338 921	15 918	158 912	175 782	42 911	306 259	114 553
2 635 689	2 237 528	10 115	131 174	135 671	9 321	200 536	54 635
1 753 888	1 523 462	7 763	50 172	78 479	13 158	139 813	53 482
16 064 724	14 615 790	27 769	471 506	403 732	4 732	677 921	246 372
2 359 594	2 216 882	5 281	27 373	32 546	8 696	60 945	23 112
4 513 168	3 863 983	18 724	170 498	180 905	51 051	307 178	107 405
5 355 104	4 246 161	25 357	380 138	407 755	22 930	618 423	185 149
2 896 378	2 184 462	16 054	286 526	310 138	43 624	422 144	95 863
3 880 245	3 430 883	12 254	62 211	49 692	133 394	132 538	70 407
437 332	335 340	2 121	29 998	34 595	7 520	49 327	12 611
11 620 055	9 848 391	28 661	679 178	720 098	46 958	930 067	181 025
8 455 304	7 243 754	27 088	485 526	499 606	53 746	670 953	144 123
1 098 747	763 857	6 557	136 155	152 293	4 090	193 271	34 367
18 139	15 899	110	401	409	–	1 334	815
209 585	192 394	586	-5 099	-2 965	11 164	1 472	3 834
830 071	649 096	5 705	124 509	129 288	322	136 179	1 186
183 032	173 519	140	394	350	3 419	1 409	905
99 416	74 165	533	11 882	19 855	410	25 197	4 486

表4-8 规模以上外商和港澳台商投资工业企业主要经济指标 (2016年)

单位：万元

指 标	Item	企业单位数(个) Number of Enterprises (unit)	# 亏损企业 Loss Making Enterprises
总 计	**Total**	**4 174**	**973**
农副食品加工业	Agricultural and Sideline Food Processing	19	4
食品制造业	Food Production	30	9
酒、饮料和精制茶制造业	Wine, Beverage and Refined tea manufacturing	14	5
纺织业	Textile Industry	207	49
纺织服装、服饰业	Garments and Apparel Industry	100	31
皮革、毛皮、羽毛及其制品和制鞋业	Leather, Fur, Wool and Shoes Products	30	11
木材加工及木、竹、藤、棕、草制品业	Timber Processing, Bamboo, Cane, Palm Fiber and Straw Products	13	4
家具制造业	Furniture Manufacturing	37	12
造纸及纸制品业	Papermaking and Paper Products	63	20
印刷业和记录媒介复制业	Printing and Record Medium Reproduction	51	16
文教、工美、体育和娱乐用品制造业	Stationary,Educational, Industrial arts, Sports and Entertainment products	61	8
石油加工、炼焦及核燃料加工业	Petroleum Processing, Coking and Nucleus Fuel Machining Trade	4	-
化学原料及化学制品制造业	Raw Chemical Materials and Chemical Products	339	64
医药制造业	Medical and Pharmaceutical Products	40	7
化学纤维制造业	Chemical Fiber	30	8
橡胶和塑料制品业	Rubber and Plastic Products	287	71
非金属矿物制品业	Nonmetal Mineral Products	118	49
黑色金属冶炼及压延加工业	Smelting and Pressing of Ferrous Metals	51	13
有色金属冶炼及压延加工业	Smelting and Pressing of Nonferrous Metals	79	22
金属制品业	Metal Products	219	49
通用设备制造业	Ordinary Equipment Manufactory Trade	415	85
专用设备制造业	Special Purposes Equipment Manufacturing	339	87
汽车制造业	Automobile Manufacturing	277	56
铁路、船舶、航空航天和其他运输设备制造业	Railway, Ship, Aerospace and Other Transportation Equipment Manufacturing	81	13
电气机械及器材制造业	Electric Equipment and Machinery	322	62
计算机、通信和其他电子设备制造业	Computer Telecommunications and Other Electronic Equipment Manufacture	809	193
仪器仪表制造业	Instruments, Meters Machinery	94	15
其他制造业	Others Industry	8	3
废弃资源综合利用业	Comprehensive Utilization of Waste Resources	17	6
电力、热力的生产和供应业	Production and Supply of Electric Power and Heat Energy	7	-
燃气生产和供应业	Production and Supply of Gas	7	-
水的生产和供应业	Production and Supply of Water	6	1

MAIN ECONOMIC INDICATORS OF INDUSTRIAL ENTERPRISES ABOVE DESIGNATED SIZE WITH FOREIGN INVESTMENT AND INVESTMENT FROM HONG KONG, MACAO AND TAIWAN (2016)

(10 000 yuan)

工业总产值 Gross Industrial Output Value	工业销售产值 Value of Industrial Products Sales	# 出口交货值 Delivery Value for Export	资产总计 Total Assets	# 流动资产合计 Circulating Funds	# 固定资产合计 Fixed Assets	累计折旧 Accumulative Depreciation	负债合计 Total Liabilities
198 683 746	**195 773 723**	**103 237 914**	**163 048 532**	**100 840 476**	**47 482 163**	**50 707 135**	**78 623 161**
2 320 937	2 407 313	12 976	1 469 312	994 967	271 547	267 751	676 176
2 082 314	1 961 999	75 821	1 471 886	738 575	503 292	274 156	922 173
356 709	360 924	1 772	436 597	134 926	267 288	204 174	253 314
2 737 728	2 745 295	734 817	3 423 539	2 122 835	1 043 642	1 059 165	1 889 106
992 606	993 525	657 433	797 355	569 358	162 058	211 260	392 574
234 660	231 441	175 430	202 732	148 212	42 326	52 982	88 459
230 913	248 640	44 542	346 827	261 103	71 730	67 635	157 893
570 747	598 597	394 053	527 653	349 752	147 593	114 173	214 249
4 187 919	4 165 431	488 211	7 036 221	3 990 843	2 225 561	2 260 634	3 419 603
1 034 299	1 030 635	331 196	1 131 666	670 250	328 226	385 333	508 414
1 574 549	1 621 961	648 309	1 145 093	754 744	229 001	296 107	511 340
414 691	409 441	–	353 607	266 098	72 339	54 006	131 680
11 471 164	11 447 084	2 245 086	12 151 859	6 646 303	4 476 816	3 792 765	5 138 390
2 036 861	1 849 449	304 840	2 541 825	1 566 642	584 846	618 474	954 773
2 289 335	2 219 208	261 861	3 308 207	1 402 912	1 351 396	810 670	1 658 234
5 901 469	5 865 374	2 032 666	6 035 764	3 504 334	2 116 850	2 303 100	2 335 439
2 487 819	2 515 640	455 188	3 095 906	1 827 891	1 054 921	1 383 525	1 434 299
8 195 050	7 699 864	521 409	4 698 893	2 086 171	2 131 526	2 998 198	2 581 682
2 110 346	2 171 615	395 458	2 160 461	1 361 592	555 927	669 598	990 270
2 987 318	2 976 339	936 143	3 607 696	2 289 879	948 791	879 091	1 508 198
13 803 636	13 733 188	5 520 302	12 889 089	9 192 718	2 841 091	2 745 618	5 752 453
6 960 244	6 871 565	2 833 455	8 721 095	5 892 648	2 053 319	1 715 825	3 544 814
11 457 039	11 338 853	1 952 629	12 123 893	6 400 133	3 828 087	2 260 799	6 254 602
2 279 681	2 288 399	1 161 680	2 007 504	1 369 161	468 700	441 881	912 876
14 668 063	14 615 065	7 585 766	12 731 343	9 039 110	2 514 298	2 770 125	6 004 063
90 527 453	88 654 586	72 303 225	50 581 272	33 993 325	14 073 079	19 810 050	26 160 091
2 524 551	2 523 672	1 081 460	2 171 113	1 565 415	462 105	502 378	971 186
40 647	41 691	10 353	47 139	30 322	13 574	22 048	34 042
124 615	125 250	3 580	121 676	76 432	35 408	38 850	48 874
1 204 829	1 193 679	–	3 072 649	686 546	1 582 557	1 242 941	1 770 676
738 927	738 927	68 254	1 665 530	783 162	293 897	93 070	856 358
136 629	129 075	–	973 133	124 118	730 376	360 753	546 861

表4-8 续表

单位：万元

项　　目	Item	所有者权益合　计 Creditors Equity	# 实收资本 Total Capital Hold
总　计	**Total**	**84 356 016**	**51 615 492**
农副食品加工业	Agricultural and Sideline Food Processing	793 135	281 506
食品制造业	Food Production	549 712	427 185
酒、饮料和精制茶制造业	Wine, Beverage and Refined tea manufacturing	183 283	178 433
纺织业	Textile Industry	1 525 113	1 356 376
纺织服装、服饰业	Garments and Apparel Industry	404 780	278 299
皮革、毛皮、羽毛及其制品和制鞋业业	Leather, Fur, Wool and Shoes Products	114 273	88 009
木材加工及木、竹、藤、棕、草制品业	Timber Processing, Bamboo, Cane, Palm Fiber and Straw Products	188 934	101 559
家具制造业	Furniture Manufacturing	313 405	228 384
造纸及纸制品业	Papermaking and Paper Products	3 616 617	2 796 295
印刷业和记录媒介复制业	Printing and Record Medium Reproduction	614 623	355 439
文教、工美、体育和娱乐用品制造业	Stationary,Educational, Industrial arts, Sports and Entertainment products	633 752	384 788
石油加工、炼焦及核燃料加工业	Petroleum Processing, Coking and Nucleus Fuel Machining Trade	221 926	104 330
化学原料及化学制品制造业	Raw Chemical Materials and Chemical Products	7 012 479	4 758 772
医药制造业	Medical and Pharmaceutical Products	1 587 052	1 204 786
化学纤维制造业	Chemical Fiber	1 649 973	1 281 124
橡胶和塑料制品业	Rubber and Plastic Products	3 692 917	2 541 552
非金属矿物制品业	Nonmetal Mineral Products	1 660 761	1 282 348
黑色金属冶炼及压延加工业	Smelting and Pressing of Ferrous Metals	2 117 209	1 202 548
有色金属冶炼及压延加工业	Smelting and Pressing of Nonferrous Metals	1 170 191	991 651
金属制品业	Metal Products	2 098 059	1 438 528
通用设备制造业	Ordinary Equipment Manufactory Trade	7 119 691	3 323 271
专用设备制造业	Special Purposes Equipment Manufacturing	5 202 191	2 303 675
汽车制造业	Automobile Manufacturing	5 869 288	4 115 126
铁路、船舶、航空航天和其他运输设备制造业	Railway, Ship, Aerospace and Other Transportation Equipment Manufacturing	1 094 626	444 936
电气机械及器材制造业	Electric Equipment and Machinery	6 727 275	3 400 738
计算机、通信和其他电子设备制造业	Computer Telecommunications and Other Electronic Equipment Manufacture	24 371 511	14 788 592
仪器仪表制造业	Instruments, Meters Machinery	1 199 926	583 449
其他制造业	Others Industry	13 097	29 882
废弃资源综合利用业	Comprehensive Utilization of Waste Resources	72 802	69 183
电力、热力的生产和供应业	Production and Supply of Electric Power and Heat Energy	1 301 973	659 288
燃气生产和供应业	Production and Supply of Gas	809 172	262 011
水的生产和供应业	Production and Supply of Water	426 272	353 428

Continued

(10 000 yuan)

主营业务收入 Major Business Revenue	主营业务成本 Major Business Cost	主营业务税金及附加 Pre-tax and Related Payment of Major Business	营业利润 Business Profits	利润总额 Total Profits	亏损企业亏损总额 Total Deficit of Loss-Making Enterprises	利税总额 Total Taxes and Profits	应交增值税 Value Added Tax Payable
196 181 376	**169 074 088**	**736 234**	**12 046 015**	**12 102 422**	**1 333 453**	**15 652 348**	**2 807 945**
2 415 052	2 202 854	3 563	84 996	90 439	3 027	121 160	27 158
1 934 612	982 409	8 917	56 087	62 341	28 753	114 371	42 858
363 883	315 193	6 314	12 707	13 957	7 293	34 287	14 016
2 752 162	2 425 952	10 026	95 694	98 920	24 112	152 302	43 346
982 045	855 341	5 618	19 548	41 205	5 219	58 722	11 870
231 967	205 627	1 428	1 892	2 892	4 766	8 267	3 947
249 367	194 480	2 868	16 765	16 844	3 603	28 184	8 472
605 612	518 278	2 760	25 234	34 453	6 343	45 068	7 809
4 142 315	3 323 530	18 108	310 466	321 202	18 578	478 648	139 327
1 060 474	813 497	6 803	95 663	95 014	8 019	144 515	42 673
1 577 417	1 364 697	5 746	61 667	61 758	3 502	95 856	28 352
411 465	311 300	14 629	66 358	66 872	–	98 321	16 821
11 880 230	9 598 171	57 744	855 994	860 890	144 989	1 207 664	288 940
1 809 839	874 992	16 703	228 953	239 316	17 139	388 597	132 425
2 203 946	1 968 237	4 962	87 839	91 696	23 908	148 552	51 895
5 965 103	4 788 319	28 779	465 081	461 492	92 127	649 775	159 504
2 551 284	2 158 720	12 803	114 345	118 145	48 136	227 570	96 622
7 758 576	7 328 153	15 188	250 145	259 062	37 855	392 982	118 732
2 184 875	1 911 987	6 765	96 540	95 046	14 893	131 472	29 614
2 989 981	2 433 698	15 908	182 488	217 463	54 949	303 504	70 096
13 764 281	10 767 305	80 410	1 551 616	1 554 990	79 209	1 887 032	251 628
6 908 248	5 423 326	32 290	650 714	663 869	65 765	834 955	138 677
11 400 535	8 989 321	148 889	1 161 409	1 196 498	131 953	1 602 924	255 127
2 290 000	1 754 351	11 138	311 310	310 823	4 373	369 655	47 673
14 544 324	12 322 489	50 328	1 083 325	1 065 923	83 582	1 234 589	118 316
88 451 153	81 479 276	140 905	3 547 588	3 424 793	398 354	4 077 894	510 017
2 532 863	2 093 553	11 101	209 808	214 782	14 496	264 761	38 822
40 990	32 860	329	378	349	1 084	2 217	1 539
124 164	108 826	529	517	1 767	5 189	6 343	4 048
1 190 129	838 618	10 965	281 109	284 754	–	384 310	88 581
734 369	607 756	2 285	95 913	95 839	–	107 972	9 848
130 114	80 972	1 436	23 869	39 032	2 237	49 880	9 195

表4-9

规模以上工业高新技术产业主要经济指标 (2016年)
MAIN ECONOMIC INDICATORS OF HI-TECH MANUFACTURING INDUSTRY ABOVE THE DESIGNATED SIZE(2016)

项　　目		Item		全　市 Whole Municipality
企业单位数	(个)	Number of Enterprises	(unit)	2 955
从业人员平均人数	(人)	Average Employees	(person)	1 358 433
工业总产值	(万元)	Gross Industrial Output Value Total	(10 000 yuan)	143 816 456
航空航天制造业		Aviation and Aerospace		696 577
电子计算机及办公设备制造业		Computer and Manufacturing of Office Appliance		16 360 542
电子及通讯设备制造业		Electronics and Communications Equipment		66 899 362
医药制造业		Biomedical Manufacturing		4 658 685
仪器仪表制造业		Instrument Manufacturing		2 048 474
智能装备制造业		Intelligent Equipment Manufacturing Industry		25 082 027
新材料制造业		New Material Production Industry		21 991 709
新能源制造业		New Energy Manufacturing		6 079 080
资产总计		Total Assets		129 400 094
负债合计		Total Liabilities		65 190 001
所有者权益合计		Total Creditors Equity		64 116 766
# 实收资本		Total Capital Hold		35 689 663
主营业务收入		Major Business Revenue		142 664 810
利税总额		Total Taxes and Profits		10 897 548
利润总额		Total Profits		8 505 962
产销率	(%)	Proportion of Products Sold	(%)	98.43

表4-10

规模以上工业新兴产业主要经济指标（2016年）
MAIN ECONOMIC INDICATORS OF EMERGING INDUSTRIES ABOVE DESIGNATED SIZE(2016)

项目		Item		全市 Whole Municipality
企业单位数	(个)	Number of Enterprises	(unit)	2 588
从业人员平均人数	(人)	Average Employees	(person)	1 275 968
工业总产值	(万元)	Gross Industrial Output Value Total	(10 000 yuan)	152 652 549
新型平板显示		New Flat Panel Displays		28 936 985
新材料		New Materials		39 767 938
智能电网和物联网		Smart Grid and Internet Of Things		16 054 356
高端装备制造		High-End Equipment Manufacturing		34 284 163
节能环保		Energy Saving and Environmental Protection		10 077 893
新能源		New Energy		11 627 964
生物技术和新医药		Biotechnology and New Medicines		7 285 647
集成电路		Integrated Circuit		4 617 603
资产总计		Total Assets		149 792 768
负债合计		Total Liabilities		75 936 315
所有者权益合计		Total Creditors Equity		73 809 654
# 实收资本		Total Capital Hold		40 640 758
主营业务收入		Major Business Revenue		153 482 442
利税总额		Total Taxes and Profits		12 970 689
利润总额		Total Profits		9 919 502
产销率	(%)	Proportion of Products Sold	(%)	97.78

表4-11 规模以上工业企业主要经济效益指标 (2016年)

单位：%

项 目	Item	总资产贡献率 Total Assets Contribution Ratio
总 计	**Total**	**9.03**
一、按轻重工业分	**Grouped by Light and Heavy Industry**	
轻工业	Light Industry	8.94
重工业	Heavy Industry	9.06
二、按行业类别分	**Grouped by Sector**	
有色金属矿采选业	Nonferrous Metals Mining and Processing	–
非金属矿采选业	Nonmetal Minerals Mining and Dressing	10.98
农副食品加工业	Agricultural and Sideline Food Processing	8.33
食品制造业	Food Production	8.89
酒、饮料和精制茶制造业	Wine, Beverage and Refined tea manufacturing	13.09
烟草制品业	Manufacture of Tobacco	4.79
纺织业	Textile Industry	5.91
纺织服装、服饰业	Garments and Apparel Industry	11.48
皮革、毛皮、羽毛及其制品和制鞋业	Leather, Fur, Wool Products	5.52
木材加工及木、竹、藤、棕、草制品业	Wood Processing, Wood, Bamboo, Rattan and Coir Products Straw Products	7.18
家具制造业	Furniture Manufacturing	10.05
造纸及纸制品业	Papermaking and Paper Products	7.48
印刷业和记录媒介的复制	Printing and Record Duplicating	11.54
文教、工美、体育和娱乐用品制造业	Stationary,Educational, Industrial Arts, Sports and Entertainment Products	9.05
石油加工、炼焦及核燃料加工业	Oil Processing, Coking and Nuclear Fuel Processing	17.46

MAIN INDICATORS OF ECONOMIC BENEFIT OF INDUSTRIAL ENTERPRISES ABOVE DESIGNATED SIZE (2016)

(%)

规模以上工业 Enterprises Above Designated Size				# 民营工业 Private and Individual	
成本费用利润率 Rate Between Profit and Cost	资产负债率 Assets Liability Ratio	固定资产净值率 New Value Added in Fixed Asset	产销率 Proportion of Products Sold	总资产贡献率 Total Assets Contribution Ratio	成本费用利润率 Rate Between Profit and Cost
6.06	**52.33**	**50.83**	**98.69**	**7.82**	**5.27**
5.58	54.93	53.28	98.61	9.08	4.83
6.23	51.42	50.02	98.71	7.29	5.51
–	–	–	–	–	–
11.40	44.75	51.13	101.20	–	–
3.67	48.88	51.12	103.12	9.37	3.33
3.54	58.69	61.98	94.82	12.01	4.66
9.47	44.61	54.31	100.56	26.50	29.77
1.87	11.50	59.79	127.03	–	–
2.41	62.70	51.84	99.36	6.10	2.11
6.40	60.57	62.54	98.88	12.00	6.73
1.99	49.16	43.45	99.07	6.64	2.77
5.73	42.95	48.80	103.65	6.15	4.65
6.46	48.30	57.15	102.95	12.05	7.51
7.21	47.11	49.00	99.71	7.20	3.07
8.29	52.46	49.97	99.42	10.19	6.88
4.75	52.20	46.95	99.95	9.53	6.26
7.04	37.76	56.78	90.19	3.56	1.01

表4-11 续表 1

单位：%

项 目	Item	# 民营工业 资产负债率 Assets Liability Ratio
总 计	**Total**	**58.19**
一、按轻重工业分	**Grouped by Light and Heavy Industry**	
轻工业	Light Industry	61.51
重工业	Heavy Industry	56.80
二、按行业类别分	**Grouped by Sector**	
有色金属矿采选业	Nonferrous Metals Mining and Processing	–
非金属矿采选业	Nonmetal Minerals Mining and Dressing	–
农副食品加工业	Agricultural and Sideline Food Processing	62.69
食品制造业	Food Production	40.32
酒、饮料和精制茶制造业	Wine, Beverage and Refined tea manufacturing	25.51
烟草制品业	Manufacture of Tobacco	–
纺织业	Textile Industry	65.11
纺织服装、服饰业	Garments and Apparel Industry	62.50
皮革、毛皮、羽毛及其制品业	Leather, Fur, Wool Products	54.52
木材加工及木、竹、藤、棕、草制品业	Wood Processing, Wood, Bamboo, Rattan and Coir Products Straw Products	41.13
家具制造业	Furniture Manufacturing	60.53
造纸及纸制品业	Papermaking and Paper Products	42.42
印刷业和记录媒介的复制	Printing and Record Duplicating	60.06
文教、工美、体育和娱乐用品制造业	Stationary,Educational,Industrial arts, Sports and Entertainment products	63.09
石油加工、炼焦及核燃料加工业	Oil Processing, Coking and Nuclear Fuel Processing	41.49

Continued 1

(%)

Private and Individual		# 外商和港澳台商 Enterprises with Investment from Foreign ,Hong Kong,Macao and Taiwan				
固定资产净值率 New Value Added in Fixed Asset	产销率 Proportion of Products Sold	总资产贡献率 Total Assets Contribution Ratio	成本费用利润率 Rate Between Profit and Cost	资产负债率 Assets Liability Ratio	固定资产净值率 New Value Added in Fixed Asset	产销率 Proportion of Products Sold
55.90	**99.14**	**9.91**	**6.50**	**48.22**	**48.10**	**98.54**
54.64	98.07	8.99	6.31	49.14	52.12	99.08
56.52	99.73	10.20	6.55	47.93	46.99	98.40
–	–	–	–	–	–	–
–	–	–	–	–	–	–
56.68	100.51	8.40	3.86	46.02	50.15	103.72
52.82	97.42	8.21	3.27	62.65	64.44	94.22
67.35	98.93	9.10	3.96	58.02	56.72	101.18
–	–	–	–	–	–	–
53.16	99.11	5.42	3.70	55.18	48.71	100.28
67.55	98.68	8.22	4.35	49.23	43.21	100.09
42.19	99.54	4.37	1.26	43.63	44.13	98.63
46.80	100.60	8.64	7.07	45.53	50.92	107.68
59.31	99.76	8.79	5.88	40.60	56.33	104.88
57.22	100.97	7.34	8.12	48.60	49.47	99.46
53.86	99.21	12.88	9.82	44.93	46.51	99.65
54.15	94.16	8.72	3.99	44.65	43.37	103.01
71.76	100.13	27.83	20.18	37.24	51.54	98.73

表4-11 续表 2

单位：%

项　　目	Item	总资产贡献率 Total Assets Contribution Ratio
化学原料及化学制品制造业	Raw Chemical Materials and Chemical Products	11.30
医药制造业	Medical and Pharmaceutical Products	13.81
化学纤维制造业	Chemical Fiber Manufacturing	5.98
橡胶和塑料制品业	Rubber and Plastic Products	10.63
非金属矿物制品业	Nonmetal Mineral Products	7.03
黑色金属冶炼及压延加工业	Smelting and Pressing of Ferrous Metals	6.54
有色金属冶炼及压延加工业	Smelting and Pressing of Nonferrous Metals	5.68
金属制品业	Metal Products	6.53
通用设备制造业	General Equipment Manufacture	12.62
专用设备制造业	Special Purposes Equipment Manufacturing	9.56
汽车制造业	Automobile Manufacturing	11.17
铁路、船舶、航空航天和其他运输设备制造业	Railway, Ship, Aerospace and Other Transportation Equipment Manufacturing	15.68
电气机械及器材制造业	Electric Equipment and Machinery Manufacturing	8.38
计算机、通信和其他电子设备制造业	Computer Telecommunications and Other Electronic Equipment Manufacture	7.96
仪器仪表制造业	Instruments, Meters Machinery	12.38
其他制造业	Other Products Manufacture	7.79
废弃资源综合利用业	Comprehensive Utilization of Waste Resources	2.77
电力、热力的生产和供应业	Manufacture and Supply of Electricity and Thermal Power	13.40
燃气生产和供应业	Manufacture and Supply of Gas	7.42
水的生产和供应业	Manufacture and Supply of Water	4.73

Continued 2

(%)

规模以上工业 Enterprises Above Designated Size				# 民营工业 Private and Individual	
成本费用利润率 Rate Between Profit and Cost	资产负债率 Assets Liability Ratio	固定资产净值率 New Value Added in Fixed Asset	产销率 Proportion of Products Sold	总资产贡献率 Total Assets Contribution Ratio	成本费用利润率 Rate Between Profit and Cost
9.85	45.52	58.90	99.44	13.71	14.62
12.00	43.13	52.44	93.74	10.71	7.34
2.64	62.64	52.16	95.99	5.99	2.20
7.41	43.13	49.76	99.27	9.46	5.37
4.72	55.14	46.06	100.81	5.82	4.55
2.59	61.53	43.91	101.56	5.91	2.41
1.99	53.45	49.26	98.33	4.66	1.38
4.97	50.05	56.06	98.40	5.78	4.09
11.15	44.76	54.10	99.39	9.27	8.02
10.55	45.48	56.42	98.45	9.23	11.44
8.68	55.74	62.90	98.72	4.26	1.28
14.40	50.00	53.30	99.94	8.14	8.41
7.17	53.21	54.07	97.86	7.20	6.41
4.20	52.14	43.46	98.02	7.45	6.15
10.82	45.97	52.89	98.51	12.44	15.81
1.31	68.13	39.41	101.45	13.44	2.31
-0.41	66.16	57.47	97.40	2.41	-1.38
23.42	57.05	53.69	99.61	7.31	17.81
12.52	51.01	68.14	98.67	0.95	0.19
15.29	65.86	63.27	97.74	5.43	19.26

表4-11 续表 3

单位：%

项 目	Item	# 民营工业 资产负债率 Assets Liability Ratio
化学原料及化学制品制造业	Raw Chemical Materials and Chemical Products	46.75
医药制造业	Medical and Pharmaceutical Products	55.05
化学纤维制造业	Chemical Fiber Manufacturing	68.26
橡胶和塑料制品业	Rubber and Plastic Products	54.69
非金属矿物制品业	Nonmetal Mineral Products	66.39
黑色金属冶炼及压延加工业	Smelting and Pressing of Ferrous Metals	63.26
有色金属冶炼及压延加工业	Smelting and Pressing of Nonferrous Metals	59.58
金属制品业	Metal Products	54.75
通用设备制造业	General Equipment Manufacture	44.74
专用设备制造业	Special Purposes Equipment Manufacturing	53.13
汽车制造业	Automobile Manufacturing	69.28
铁路、船舶、航空航天和其他运输设备制造业	Railway, Ship, Aerospace and Other Transportation Equipment Manufacturing	61.99
电气机械及器材制造业	Electric Equipment and Machinery Manufacturing	58.06
计算机、通信和其他电子设备制造业	Computer Telecommunications and Other Electronic Equipment Manufacture	54.23
仪器仪表制造业	Instruments, Meters Machinery	47.79
其他制造业	Other Products Manufacture	49.21
废弃资源综合利用业	Comprehensive Utilization of Waste Resources	76.45
电力、热力的生产和供应业	Manufacture and Supply of Electricity and Thermal Power	69.18
燃气生产和供应业	Manufacture and Supply of Gas	81.45
水的生产和供应业	Manufacture and Supply of Water	75.60

Continued 3

(%)

Private and Individual		# 外商和港澳台商 Enterprises with Investment from Foreign ,Hong Kong,Macao and Taiwan				
固定资产净值率 New Value Added in Fixed Asset	产销率 Proportion of Products Sold	总资产贡献率 Total Assets Contribution Ratio	成本费用利润率 Rate Between Profit and Cost	资产负债率 Assets Liability Ratio	固定资产净值率 New Value Added in Fixed Asset	产销率 Proportion of Products Sold
69.50	98.88	10.52	7.76	42.28	53.63	99.79
62.34	99.26	15.17	14.91	37.56	48.84	90.80
46.05	95.72	5.97	4.28	50.12	62.37	96.94
59.53	99.02	11.09	8.34	38.69	47.90	99.39
51.11	100.14	7.90	4.79	46.33	43.24	101.12
45.40	105.35	9.15	3.32	54.94	41.56	93.96
55.49	99.13	6.71	4.46	45.84	45.38	102.90
60.83	97.54	8.79	7.61	41.81	51.67	99.63
61.75	98.96	14.70	12.64	44.63	50.68	99.49
63.29	97.82	9.74	10.38	40.65	53.73	98.73
64.61	97.94	13.34	11.43	51.59	62.61	98.97
67.59	97.68	18.53	15.64	45.47	48.92	100.38
62.66	95.76	9.88	7.82	47.16	47.33	99.64
63.06	98.91	8.15	4.01	51.72	41.38	97.93
69.60	95.31	12.40	8.89	44.73	47.79	99.97
45.50	98.97	6.57	0.87	72.22	38.11	102.57
64.04	94.84	5.24	1.47	40.17	47.68	100.51
53.29	99.73	14.49	30.31	57.63	56.01	99.07
41.70	99.68	7.04	14.26	51.42	75.95	100.00
45.78	98.94	6.00	26.83	56.20	66.34	94.47

表4-12

分地区规模以上工业企业主要经济指标 (2016年)

单位：万元

项　　目	Item	企业单位数(个) Number of Enterprises (unit)	# 亏损企业 Loss Making Enterprises	工业总产值 Gross Industrial Output Value
全　　市	**Whole Municipality**	**9 616**	**1 858**	**307 139 889**
按地区分	**Grouped by Region**			
市　区	Urban Area	4 358	749	120 465 256
常　熟	Changshu	1 309	252	36 848 914
张家港	Zhangjiagang	1 078	240	45 716 594
昆　山	Kunshan	1 851	378	83 832 389
太　仓	Taicang	1 020	239	20 276 736
在市区中	**In Urban Area**			
姑苏区	Gusu District	15	2	377 822
吴中区	Wuzhong District	835	145	12 264 898
相城区	Xiangcheng District	742	122	11 040 128
高新区、虎丘区	New Hi-tech Zone & Huqiu District	690	122	26 909 294
工业园区	Industrial Park	772	129	38 705 059
吴江区	Wujiang District	1 304	229	31 168 054

MAIN ECONOMIC INDICATORS OF INDUSTRIAL ENTERPRISES ABOVE DESIGNATED SIZE BY REGION (2016)

(10 000 yuan)

工业销售产值 Value of Industrial Products Sales	# 出口交货值 Delivery Value for Export	资产总计 Total Assets	# 流动资产合计 Circulating Funds	# 固定资产合计 Fixed Assets	累计折旧 Accumulative Depreciation
303 110 656	**117 403 015**	**283 565 028**	**171 499 147**	**76 248 018**	**72 598 512**
117 627 279	47 988 015	119 880 101	76 188 609	29 377 911	28 545 966
36 218 838	9 907 386	39 393 725	22 120 661	11 707 693	8 136 160
45 774 768	6 162 382	47 468 072	25 096 696	13 947 325	13 769 098
83 712 650	50 266 537	55 734 926	36 372 669	15 020 831	17 249 329
19 777 121	3 078 695	21 088 205	11 720 512	6 194 257	4 897 959
375 766	3 600	728 217	268 150	279 276	160 033
12 204 315	4 011 864	13 650 244	9 149 906	2 891 645	2 612 411
10 897 500	2 552 039	11 091 520	6 920 030	2 785 409	2 247 533
25 435 275	14 983 938	21 974 509	14 912 220	4 327 270	5 311 557
38 258 191	17 345 955	39 400 590	24 809 275	10 618 274	11 574 342
30 456 232	9 090 619	33 035 020	20 129 029	8 476 038	6 640 090

表4-12 续表

单位：万元

项　　目	Item	负债合计 Total Liabilities	所有者权益合计 Creditors Equity	# 实收资本 Total Capital Hold
全　市	**Whole Municipality**	**148 380 223**	**135 020 597**	**75 605 858**
按地区分	**Grouped by Region**			
市　区	Urban Area	59 982 642	59 852 207	34 220 627
常　熟	Changshu	21 890 438	17 412 762	10 984 460
张家港	Zhangjiagang	27 774 820	19 687 142	8 708 373
昆　山	Kunshan	27 795 471	27 922 601	15 723 519
太　仓	Taicang	10 936 852	10 145 885	5 968 878
在市区中	**In Urban Area**			
姑苏区	Gusu District	287 739	440 478	134 299
吴中区	Wuzhong District	7 173 657	6 476 576	4 367 564
相城区	Xiangcheng District	6 018 505	5 073 003	3 200 141
高新区、虎丘区	New Hi-tech Zone & Huqiu District	10 560 630	11 385 445	6 527 319
工业园区	Industrial Park	17 562 862	21 829 307	11 811 738
吴江区	Wujiang District	18 379 250	14 647 398	8 179 566

Continued

(10 000 yuan)

主营业务收入 Major Business Revenue	主营业务成本 Major Business Cost	主营业务税金及附加 Pre-tax and Related Payment of Major Business	利税总额 Total taxes and Profits	利润总额 Total Profits	亏损企业亏损总额 Total Deficit of Loss-Making Enterprises	应交增值税 Value Added Tax Payable
303 801 818	**261 696 085**	**1 102 128**	**23 882 390**	**17 727 401**	**1 980 239**	**5 041 440**
117 257 504	98 423 918	456 873	9 969 977	7 583 632	879 401	1 922 470
36 331 374	30 525 934	232 367	3 242 994	2 357 570	322 016	650 856
46 836 662	41 952 924	113 944	2 616 436	1 770 787	262 423	731 369
83 693 938	74 460 151	198 118	5 889 528	4 468 133	400 024	1 222 122
19 682 339	16 333 159	100 826	2 163 455	1 547 279	116 375	514 623
365 229	304 308	931	42 145	30 472	1 090	9 795
12 149 783	10 067 928	51 916	995 105	705 016	131 518	236 831
10 653 259	9 169 842	43 836	747 165	520 096	94 104	182 768
25 516 744	21 970 221	85 204	1 842 259	1 495 212	159 886	260 838
38 411 825	30 414 059	176 722	4 047 149	3 183 478	342 935	685 883
30 160 663	26 497 559	98 264	2 296 154	1 649 358	149 869	546 355

表4-13

分地区、分经济类型规模以上工业企业主要经济效益指标 (2016年)

单位：%

项　　目	Item	经济效益综合指数 Comprehensive Index on Economic Return	总资产贡献率 Ratio of Total Assets to Industrial Output Value
总　　计	**Total**	**235.63**	**9.03**
按地区分	**Grouped by Region**		
市　区	Urban Area	223.57	8.83
常　熟	Changshu	236.28	8.96
张家港	Zhangjiagang	280.80	6.61
昆　山	Kunshan	240.47	10.81
太　仓	Taicang	274.27	11.06
在市区中	**In Urban Area**		
姑苏区	Gusu District	224.91	5.71
吴中区	Wuzhong District	188.22	7.76
相城区	Xiangcheng District	196.55	7.33
高新区、虎丘区	New Hi-tech Zone & Huqiu District	260.04	8.61
工业园区	Industrial Park	277.66	10.54
吴江区	Wujiang District	178.52	7.94
按经济类型分	**Grouped by Ownership**		
国有经济	State-owned	268.82	8.29
民营经济	Private and Individual	207.26	7.82
外商及港澳台经济	Enterprises with Investment from Foreign ,Hong Kong,Macao and Taiwan	233.59	9.91

MAIN INDICATORS OF ECONOMIC BENEFIT INDUSTRIAL ENTERPRISES ABOVE DESIGNATED SIZE BY REGION AND OWNERSHIP (2016)

(%)

成本费用利润率 Rate Between Profit and Cost	资产负债率 Assets Liability Ratio	固定资产净值率 New Value Added in Fixed Asset	产销率 Proportion of Products Sold	资本保值增值率 Rate of the Preserved Value and Increased Value of Capital	流动资产周转次数(次) Number of Times of Turnover of Circulating Fund (time)
6.06	**52.33**	**50.83**	**98.69**	**107.89**	**1.81**
6.80	50.04	50.43	97.64	107.73	1.56
6.82	55.57	58.19	98.29	104.27	1.67
3.71	58.51	49.94	100.13	114.34	1.99
5.60	49.87	46.21	99.86	106.78	2.33
8.28	51.86	55.64	97.54	106.74	1.72
8.42	39.51	63.57	99.46	106.15	1.42
6.07	52.55	52.41	99.51	106.21	1.35
4.98	54.26	55.06	98.71	107.28	1.58
6.18	48.06	44.87	94.52	108.93	1.73
8.89	44.58	47.38	98.85	107.37	1.58
5.66	55.64	55.82	97.72	108.25	1.52
5.77	55.40	55.13	96.76	100.06	2.05
5.27	58.19	55.90	99.14	111.03	1.56
6.50	48.22	48.10	98.54	106.95	1.97

表4-14 分地区大中型工业企业主要经济指标 (2016年)

项目		Item		全市 Whole Municipality
企业单位数	(个)	Number of Enterprises	(unit)	1 936
# 亏损企业		Loss Making Enterprises		266
工业总产值	(万元)	Gross Industrial Output Value	(10 000 yuan)	229 610 239
工业销售产值		Value of Industrial Products Sales		226 324 751
# 出口交货值		Delivery Value for Export		104 280 906
资产总计		Total Assets (year-end)		202 214 225
# 流动资产合计		Circulating Funds		118 950 167
# 应收帐款		Net Account Income		42 443 626
产成品		Manufactured Products		8 938 487
固定资产合计		Fixed Assets		56 328 743
固定资产原价		Original Value of Fixed Assets		111 338 947
累计折旧		Accumulative Total Depreciation		55 962 653
固定资产净值		Net Value of Fixed Assets		55 376 295
负债合计		Total Liabilities		105 063 204
所有者权益合计		Total Creditors Equity		97 151 005
实收资本		Total Capital Hold		48 829 514
国家资本		State Capital		1 281 983
集体资本		Collective Capital		632 916
法人资本		Corporate Capital		14 143 430
个人资本		Personal Capital		5 291 747
港澳台资本		Capital from Hong Kong, Macao and Taiwan		7 786 871
外商资本		Foreign Capital		19 692 569
主营业务收入		Major Business Revenue		226 280 727
主营业务成本		Major Business Cost		195 903 042
主营业务税金及附加		Pre-tax and Related Payment of Major Business		788 288
营业利润		Business Profits		13 654 068
利税总额		Total Taxes and Profits		17 976 177
# 利润总额		Total Profits		13 805 017
本年应交增值税		Value Added Tax Payable		3 376 237
成本费用利润率	(%)	Rate Between Profit and Cost	(%)	6.35
资产负债率		Assets Liability Ratio		51.96
工业产销率		Proportion of Products Sold		98.57
总资产贡献率		New Value Added in Fixed Asset		9.48

MAIN INDICATORS OF ECONOMIC BENEFIT OF LARGE AND MEDIUM INDUSTRIAL ENTERPRISES BY REGION (2016)

市 区 Urban Area	# 吴江区 Wujiang District	常 熟 Changshu	张家港 Zhangjiagang	昆 山 Kunshan	太 仓 Taicang
932	258	213	158	496	137
122	32	36	24	67	17
87 860 000	22 308 648	26 343 734	36 189 252	68 287 725	10 929 529
85 304 550	21 675 058	25 806 986	36 249 331	68 218 938	10 744 946
41 434 057	8 008 236	8 387 327	5 052 979	47 417 428	1 989 114
83 744 460	22 823 096	27 978 268	37 111 129	41 272 128	12 108 240
52 040 572	13 525 181	15 202 191	18 872 626	26 614 920	6 219 859
19 609 461	4 674 684	5 583 958	3 353 847	12 136 710	1 759 650
3 700 182	1 024 009	1 256 435	1 734 611	1 812 078	435 181
20 943 047	5 817 496	8 478 369	11 269 444	11 650 757	3 987 127
42 001 382	10 510 465	13 806 512	22 674 647	25 439 128	7 417 278
21 275 860	4 744 238	5 697 777	11 590 821	13 945 173	3 453 023
20 725 522	5 766 227	8 108 735	11 083 826	11 493 956	3 964 255
41 366 427	12 242 572	15 178 347	21 700 960	20 605 898	6 211 572
42 378 023	10 580 522	12 799 920	15 410 168	20 666 227	5 896 667
22 129 633	5 317 206	7 548 461	5 585 918	10 479 262	3 086 240
418 137	62 632	200 672	127 644	517 922	17 608
138 736	22 923	359 910	44 211	45 059	45 000
5 895 867	1 862 468	2 257 496	2 539 738	2 273 683	1 176 646
2 679 523	1 012 261	811 480	1 018 727	547 897	234 120
3 083 300	1 170 014	1 645 026	107 254	1 926 923	1 024 368
9 914 070	1 186 909	2 273 877	1 748 345	5 167 779	588 498
84 724 868	21 317 377	25 879 046	37 038 713	67 961 283	10 676 817
71 394 714	18 746 909	21 605 787	33 502 161	60 857 479	8 542 902
316 384	68 656	188 988	82 155	144 911	55 850
5 493 600	1 239 734	1 770 469	1 370 760	3 950 550	1 068 689
7 196 796	1 716 893	2 441 025	1 977 855	4 865 174	1 495 328
5 672 147	1 280 194	1 823 892	1 353 611	3 827 640	1 127 727
1 204 456	367 840	426 341	541 910	891 817	311 713
7.05	6.25	7.44	3.56	5.93	11.31
49.40	53.64	54.25	58.48	49.93	51.30
97.09	97.16	97.96	100.17	99.90	98.31
9.06	8.49	9.39	6.47	11.99	13.20

表4-15

规模以下工业企业主要经济指标（2016年）
MAIN ECONOMIC INDICATORS OF INDUSTRIAL ENTERPRISES BELOW DESIGNATED SIZE (2016)

单位：万元 (10 000 yuan)

地区或类别	Type	企业单位数 (个) Number of Enterprises (unit)	主营业务收入 Major Business Revenue	资产总计 Total Assets at the Year end	实收资本 Actual Capital Hold	全部从业人员 (人) Total Employees (person)
合　计	**Total**	**94 860**	**41 912 513**	**65 942 662**	**29 977 579**	**1 308 637**
市　区	Urban Area	46 569	21 629 896	29 747 397	14 091 994	589 507
# 吴江区	Wujiang District	9 635	5 720 363	8 112 850	3 435 596	136 720
常　熟	Changshu	9 089	4 746 238	9 524 013	4 462 301	153 312
张家港	Zhangjiagang	11 100	5 193 658	6 853 542	2 527 219	181 157
昆　山	Kunshan	21 054	7 355 769	16 441 167	7 366 834	285 591
太　仓	Taicang	7 048	2 986 952	3 376 543	1 529 231	99 070
集体企业	**Collective-owned Enterprises**	**363**	**162 964**	**766 221**	**164 509**	**4 874**
市　区	Urban Area	94	64 380	517 708	115 896	1 761
# 吴江区	Wujiang District	–	–	–	–	–
常　熟	Changshu	75	20 907	88 260	22 966	905
张家港	Zhangjiagang	31	54 703	46 504	5 032	894
昆　山	Kunshan	115	21 073	92 951	19 856	892
太　仓	Taicang	48	1 901	20 798	759	422
股份合作企业	**Share-holding Cooperative Enterprises**	**380**	**189 830**	**325 140**	**92 577**	**3 557**
市　区	Urban Area	264	151 106	182 496	43 472	2 217
# 吴江区	Wujiang District	–	–	–	–	–
常　熟	Changshu	11	3 439	8 924	1 770	175
张家港	Zhangjiagang	69	18 735	42 670	34 667	716
昆　山	Kunshan	20	6 731	84 049	9 504	177
太　仓	Taicang	16	9 819	7 001	3 164	272
股份制企业	**Share-holding Enterprises**	**5 196**	**2 308 086**	**5 750 275**	**2 361 833**	**61 015**
市　区	Urban Area	3 085	1 412 902	2 403 325	1 032 966	32 481
# 吴江区	Wujiang District	122	93 850	191 035	15 885	1 498

注：本表规模以下工业企业不含个体工业数据。 Note: The table below scale industrial enterprises do not contain individual business data.

表4-15 续表 Continued

单位：万元 (10 000 yuan)

地区或类别	Type	企业单位数(个) Number of Enterprises (unit)	主营业务收入 Major Business Revenue	资产总计 Total Assets at the Year end	实收资本 Actual Capital Hold	全部从业人员(人) Total Employees (person)
常 熟	Changshu	39	22 790	435 957	207 700	1 293
张家港	Zhangjiagang	1 473	686 289	1 015 238	434 198	21 945
昆 山	Kunshan	531	124 155	1 858 815	670 070	4 113
太 仓	Taicang	68	61 950	36 940	16 899	1 183
私营企业	**Joint Ownership Enterprises**	**79 065**	**31 579 802**	**40 952 319**	**16 306 402**	**1 016 018**
市 区	Urban Area	37 443	15 751 868	19 288 335	8 612 858	441 308
# 吴江区	Wujiang District	8 886	5 074 487	6 284 980	2 280 823	117 542
常 熟	Changshu	8 601	4 375 945	5 944 148	2 390 900	135 750
张家港	Zhangjiagang	9 116	3 952 718	4 667 708	1 320 877	143 851
昆 山	Kunshan	17 852	5 305 909	8 719 037	3 290 452	218 036
太 仓	Taicang	6 053	2 193 362	2 333 091	691 315	77 074
外商及港澳台商投资企业	**Enterprises with Foreign Investment or Investment from Hongkong, Macao and Taiwan**	**7 934**	**6 625 396**	**16 024 037**	**10 240 473**	**203 547**
市 区	Urban Area	4 092	3 431 094	6 067 224	3 723 063	93 933
# 吴江区	Wujiang District	585	539 426	1 605 830	1 122 780	17 095
常 熟	Changshu	353	314 860	2 674 714	1 720 710	15 029
张家港	Zhangjiagang	403	479 644	1 075 989	731 935	13 657
昆 山	Kunshan	2 273	1 817 749	5 285 257	3 251 741	61 399
太 仓	Taicang	813	582 049	920 853	813 024	19 529
其他企业	**Other Enterprises**	**1 922**	**1 046 435**	**2 124 671**	**811 786**	**19 625**
市 区	Urban Area	1 591	818 546	1 288 309	563 739	17 807
# 吴江区	Wujiang District	42	12 600	31 005	16 108	585
常 熟	Changshu	10	8 297	372 010	118 255	160
张家港	Zhangjiagang	8	1 569	5 433	510	94
昆 山	Kunshan	263	80 152	401 058	125 211	974
太 仓	Taicang	50	137 871	57 861	4 071	590

表4-16

规模以上工业主要产品产量 (2016年)

产品名称		Name of Products		全 市 Whole Municipality
饲 料	(吨)	Fodder	(ton)	1 077 883
精制食用植物油		Refined Edible Vegetable Oil		1 103 969
乳制品		Dairy Products		179 524
大 米		Rice		38 932
饮料酒	(千升)	Drinks	(1 000 liters)	417 297
纱	(吨)	Yarn	(ton)	653 344
布	(万米)	Cloth	(10 000 meters)	88 473
绒线（毛线）	(吨)	Knitting Wool	(ton)	56 905
毛机织物（呢绒）	(万米)	Wool Fabrics	(10 000 meters)	8 833
印染布		Printing and Dyeing Cloth		153 619
蚕丝及交织机织物(含蚕丝≥50%)		Silk and Woven Fabrics (Including Silk ≥ 50%)		228
服 装	(万件)	Garment	(10 000 pieces)	61 039
皮革鞋靴	(万双)	Leather Footwear	(10 000 pairs)	842
人造板	(立方米)	Artificial Board	(cu.m)	867 923
家 具	(件)	Furniture	(piece)	6 769 529
机制纸及纸板（外购原纸加工除外）	(吨)	Machine Made Paper	(ton)	6 610 321
焦 炭	(万吨)	Coke	(10 000 tons)	541
硫酸（折100%）	(吨)	Sulfuric Acid (100%)	(ton)	2 083 785
纯碱（碳酸钠）		Soda Ash		879 724
合成氨(无水氨）		Synthetic Ammonia		776 924
农用氮、磷、钾化学肥料总计(折纯)		Agricultural Chemical Fertilizers (Pure)		403 242
化学农药原药(折有效成分100%)		Chemicals and Pesticides (Active Ingredient 100% Discount)		13 079
涂 料		Paint		708 579
初级形态的塑料		Primary form of Plastic		1 064 072

MAJOR PRODUCTS OUTPUT OF INDUSTRIAL ENTERPRISES ABOVE DESIGNATED SIZE (2016)

市 区 Urban Area	# 吴江区 Wujiang District	常 熟 Changshu	张家港 Zhangjiagang	昆 山 Kunshan	太 仓 Taicang
96 329	46 965	10 107	971 447	–	–
52 812	52 812	49 398	984 417	17 342	–
152 296	–	–	27 229	–	–
–	–	–	38 932	–	–
194 076	–	–	57 013	166 208	–
107 516	99 403	37 331	444 118	2 233	62 146
48 695	42 061	1 266	23 091	9 225	6 197
1 459	–	4 691	50 755	–	–
45	–	251	8 536	–	–
41 813	15 415	65 552	43 140	3 114	–
228	212	–	–	–	–
22 002	6 997	11 743	17 937	6 188	3 168
833	826	–	–	9	–
85 171	–	756 023	16 046	10 683	–
1 736 712	1 153 824	138 256	1 311 358	3 413 440	169 763
2 108 241	–	1 344 291	74 993	207 493	2 875 303
–	–	–	541	–	–
–	–	214 515	1 854 352	14 918	–
–	–	–	621 366	258 358	–
–	–	–	641 509	135 415	–
–	–	–	329 086	74 156	–
–	–	–	8 896	–	4 183
316 186	36 023	–	182 661	200 554	9 177
474 979	92 478	66 079	320 088	68 800	134 126

表4-16 续表 1

产品名称		Name of Products		全 市 Whole Municipality
化学药品原药	(吨)	Original Drug Chemicals (Chemical Medicine)	(ton)	12 355
化学纤维		Chemical Fiber		6 844 818
橡胶轮胎外胎	(条)	Tires	(piece)	65 684 582
塑料制品	(吨)	Plastic Products	(ton)	1 028 314
水　泥		Cement		9 362 983
平板玻璃	(重量箱)	Plate Glass	(wt.cases)	12 921 731
生　铁	(吨)	Pig Iron	(ton)	26 248 401
粗　钢		Raw Steel		31 777 815
钢　材		Rolled Steel		39 839 848
金属切削机床	(台)	Metal-cutting Machines	(unit)	24 009
# 数控金属切削机床		CNC Metal Cutting Machine		3 297
阀　门	(吨)	Valves	(ton)	147 067
滚动轴承	(万套)	Rolling Bearing	(10 000 sets)	103 732
模　具	(套)	Mould	(set)	1 153 717
汽　车	(辆)	Trucks	(coach)	106 440
改装汽车		Refit Trucks		139 387
两轮脚踏自行车		Two-wheel Pedal Bicycles		3 761 444
交流电动机	(千瓦)	Alternating Current Motor	(kw)	8 186 517
变压器	(千伏安)	Transformer	(kva)	15 102 039
通信及电子网络用电缆	(对千米)	Communication Cables	(pair km)	7 522 177
电力电缆	(千米)	Electric Power Cables	(km)	1 964 489
光　缆	(芯千米)	Optic Fiber	(core kilometer)	47 550 803
锂离子电池	(只)	Lithium-Ion Batteries	(piece)	351 382 230
家用电冰箱(家用冷冻冷藏箱)	(台)	Household Refrigerator (Household Refrigerated Freezers)	(unit)	980 061
家用冷柜(家用冷冻箱)		Household Refrigerators (Household Freezers)		724 032

Continued 1

市 区 Urban Area	# 吴江区 Wujiang District	常 熟 Changshu	张家港 Zhangjiagang	昆 山 Kunshan	太 仓 Taicang
5 484	190	999	675	2 830	2 368
5 159 186	4 222 498	235 350	689 488	–	760 794
1 413 996	–	12 601 940	4 804 528	46 864 118	–
240 661	57 142	91 653	381 895	264 842	49 263
3 158 694	2 781 594	–	3 000 128	1 242 396	1 961 765
3 727 066	–	–	–	8 945 714	248 951
435 045	–	–	25 813 356	–	–
473 133	–	2 870 089	28 434 593	–	–
860 821	197 312	5 363 100	33 526 961	88 966	–
6 026	761	–	7 103	10 880	–
1 826	–	–	–	1 471	–
137 691	738	–	–	9 376	–
25 796	–	5 365	13 593	14 341	44 637
25 831	266	700 875	2 200	424 637	174
17 831	–	88 609	–	–	–
529	–	1 895	735	136 228	–
–	–	–	114 584	2 892 436	754 424
2 139 635	844 939	–	536 755	–	5 510 127
15 096 344	10 816 326	–	–	5 695	–
6 261 180	6 212 500	90 873	1 132 776	37 169	179
1 066 245	212 091	608 865	14 979	274 400	–
39 489 823	39 489 823	7 450 448	–	610 532	–
48 853 533	48 802 064	108 651 037	127 274 127	66 603 533	–
934 982	–	45 079	–	–	–
–	–	724 032	–	–	–

表4-16 续表 2

产品名称		Name of Products		全 市 Whole Municipality
房间空气调节器	(台)	Room Air Conditioner	(unit)	3 856 732
家用电风扇		Household Electric Fan		798 060
家用吸排油烟机		Household Smoke Absorbers		285 130
家用洗衣机		Household Washing Machines		3 074 348
家用吸尘器		Household Dust Catcher		46 378 443
家用燃气灶具		Household Gas Utensile		236 878
家用燃气热水器		Household Water Heater		265 943
移动通信手持机(手机)		Mobile Phone		49 260 966
微型计算机设备		Micro-Computer Equipment		51 254 557
# 笔记本计算机		Laptop Computer		40 561 447
显示器		Monitors		39 050 199
# 平板显示器		Flat Panel Displays		24 325 268
集成电路	(万块)	Integrated Circuit	(10 000 pieces)	160 722
光电子器件	(万只、片、套)	Optoelectronic Devices	(10 000 pieces,sets)	2 540 692
# 发光二极管(LED管)	(万只)	Light Emitting Diode (LED)	(10 000 units)	2 235 041
电子元件		Electronic Components		111 297 690
印制电路板	(平方米)	Printed Circuit Board	(sq.m)	64 330 074
彩色电视机	(台)	Color TV Sets	(unit)	13 060 201
# 液晶(LCD)电视机		Liquid Crystal (LCD) TV Sets		13 060 201
工业自动调节仪表与控制系统	(台、套)	Industrial Automatically-Adjusting Instrumentation and Control System	(unit,set)	2 107 962
照相机	(台)	Cameras	(unit)	11 110 613
# 数码照相机		Digital Camera		5 122 054
发电量	(亿千瓦时)	Power Generation	(100 million kwh)	1 020

Continued 2

市 区 Urban Area	# 吴江区 Wujiang District	常 熟 Changshu	张家港 Zhangjiagang	昆 山 Kunshan	太 仓 Taicang
3 726 358	–	–	–	130 374	–
638 000	–	–	–	160 060	–
–	–	–	–	285 130	–
3 074 348	–	–	–	–	–
46 303 196	1 330 629	75 247	–	–	–
–	–	–	–	236 878	–
–	–	–	–	265 943	–
10 946 531	7 465 259	–	–	38 314 435	–
7 964 281	–	–	–	43 290 276	–
2 973 118	–	–	–	37 588 329	–
39 050 199	6 333 785	–	–	–	–
24 325 268	6 333 785	–	–	–	–
160 271	87 665	–	–	451	–
2 496 977	2 103 489	6 516	1 973	29 793	5 433
2 235 041	1 971 520	–	–	–	–
109 483 619	790 494	1 542 486	2 081	256 792	12 712
33 722 583	274 298	717 195	–	29 890 297	–
9 610 246	5 137 075	–	–	3 449 955	–
9 610 246	5 137 075	–	–	3 449 955	–
2 104 439	201 091	–	3 183	257	83
8 168 453	1 035 208	–	–	2 942 160	–
2 179 894	1 035 208	–	–	2 942 160	–
256	53	313	160	20	270

表4-17

全市工业主营业务收入百强企业（2016年）
TOP 100 ENTERPRISES OF THE MAJOR BUSINESS REVENUE (2016)

序号 No.	企业名称 Name of Enterprises	所在地区 Location	序号 No.	企业名称 Name of Enterprises	所在地区 Location
1	江苏沙钢集团有限公司	张家港市	26	华芳集团有限公司	张家港市
2	仁宝信息技术（昆山）有限公司	昆山市	27	舍弗勒（中国）有限公司	太仓市
3	仁宝电子科技（昆山）有限公司	昆山市	28	苏州市相城区江南化纤集团有限公司	相城区
4	名硕电脑（苏州）有限公司	高新区、虎丘区	29	江苏恒力化纤股份有限公司	吴江区
5	世硕电子（昆山）有限公司	昆山市	30	常熟阿特斯阳光电力科技有限公司	常熟市
6	纬创资通（昆山）有限公司	昆山市	31	江苏国望高科纤维有限公司	吴江区
7	仁宝资讯工业（昆山）有限公司	昆山市	32	正新橡胶（中国）有限公司	昆山市
8	波司登股份有限公司	常熟市	33	苏州三星电子有限公司	工业园区
9	江苏永钢集团有限公司	张家港市	34	金红叶纸业集团有限公司	工业园区
10	张家港宏昌钢板有限公司	张家港市	35	苏州三星电子液晶显示科技有限公司	工业园区
11	纬新资通（昆山）有限公司	昆山市	36	苏州三星电子电脑有限公司	工业园区
12	达富电脑（常熟）有限公司	常熟市	37	中利科技集团股份有限公司	常熟市
13	康准电子科技（昆山）有限公司	昆山市	38	长春化工（江苏）有限公司	常熟市
14	张家港联合铜业有限公司	张家港市	39	澳洋集团有限公司	张家港市
15	亨通集团有限公司	吴江区	40	昆山专用汽车制造厂有限公司	昆山市
16	张家港荣盛炼钢有限公司	张家港市	41	江苏骏马集团有限责任公司	张家港市
17	通力电梯有限公司	昆山市	42	南亚电子材料（昆山）有限公司	昆山市
18	博世汽车部件（苏州）有限公司	工业园区	43	高创（苏州）电子有限公司	吴江区
19	奇瑞捷豹路虎汽车有限公司	常熟市	44	伟创力电子技术（苏州）有限公司	工业园区
20	中粮东海粮油工业（张家港）有限公司	张家港市	45	中达电子（江苏）有限公司	吴江区
21	张家港浦项不锈钢有限公司	张家港市	46	玖龙纸业（太仓）有限公司	太仓市
22	苏州佳世达电通有限公司	高新区、虎丘区	47	牧田（昆山）有限公司	昆山市
23	瑞仪光电（苏州）有限公司	吴江区	48	江苏隆力奇集团有限公司	常熟市
24	常熟市龙腾特种钢有限公司	常熟市	49	金龙联合汽车工业（苏州）有限公司	工业园区
25	纬视晶光电（昆山）有限公司	昆山市	50	昆山德力铜业有限公司	昆山市

表4-17 续表 Continued

序 号 No.	企业名称 Name of Enterprises	所在地区 Location	序 号 No.	企业名称 Name of Enterprises	所在地区 Location
51	江苏华昌（集团）有限公司	张家港市	76	久保田农业机械（苏州）有限公司	工业园区
52	富士康（昆山）电脑接插件有限公司	昆山市	77	上海华电电力发展有限公司望亭发电厂	相城区
53	康硕电子（苏州）有限公司	高新区、虎丘区	78	晶端显示器件（苏州）有限公司	工业园区
54	佳能（苏州）有限公司	高新区、虎丘区	79	罗技科技（苏州）有限公司	高新区、虎丘区
55	中利腾晖光伏科技有限公司	常熟市	80	乐金电子（昆山）有限公司	昆山市
56	康宝莱（中国）保健品有限公司	工业园区	81	苏州紫翔电子科技有限公司	工业园区
57	好孩子儿童用品有限公司	昆山市	82	利乐包装（昆山）有限公司	昆山市
58	苏州长城开发科技有限公司	工业园区	83	昆山丘钛微电子科技有限公司	昆山市
59	富翔精密工业（昆山）有限公司	昆山市	84	太仓东华能源燃气有限公司	太仓市
60	江苏盛虹科技股份有限公司	吴江区	85	苏州大立光电有限公司	吴江区
61	张家港康得新光电材料有限公司	张家港市	86	张家港协鑫集成科技有限公司	张家港市
62	苏州市欧菲光科技有限公司	相城区	87	中达电子零组件（吴江）有限公司	吴江区
63	江苏梦兰集团有限公司	常熟市	88	天弘（苏州）科技有限公司	工业园区
64	苏州乐轩科技有限公司	高新区、虎丘区	89	仁宝视讯电子（昆山）有限公司	昆山市
65	江苏常熟发电有限公司	常熟市	90	德尔福电子（苏州）有限公司	工业园区
66	微盟电子（昆山）有限公司	昆山市	91	中磊电子（苏州）有限公司	工业园区
67	苏州三星电子家电有限公司	工业园区	92	达明电子（常熟）有限公司	常熟市
68	四海电子（昆山）有限公司	昆山市	93	江苏通润机电集团有限公司	常熟市
69	伟创力电脑(苏州)有限公司	吴中区	94	华冠通讯（江苏）有限公司	吴江区
70	圣美精密工业（昆山）有限公司	昆山市	95	苏州阿特斯阳光电力科技有限公司	高新区、虎丘区
71	烨辉（中国）科技材料有限公司	常熟市	96	克诺尔车辆设备（苏州）有限公司	高新区、虎丘区
72	亚旭电子科技（江苏）有限公司	吴江区	97	苏州协鑫光伏科技有限公司	高新区、虎丘区
73	江苏宝洁有限公司	太仓市	98	芬欧汇川(中国)有限公司	常熟市
74	万都底盘部件（苏州）有限公司	高新区、虎丘区	99	雅鹿集团股份有限公司	太仓市
75	苏州璨宇光电有限公司	吴江区	100	三一重机有限公司	昆山市

表4-18

全市工业利税总额百强企业（2016年）
TOP 100 ENTERPRISES OF THE TOTAL TAXES AND PROFITS (2016)

序　号 No.	企业名称 Name of Enterprises	所在地区 Location	序　号 No.	企业名称 Name of Enterprises	所在地区 Location
1	通力电梯有限公司	昆山市	26	纬新资通（昆山）有限公司	昆山市
2	奇瑞捷豹路虎汽车有限公司	常熟市	27	华润电力（常熟）有限公司	常熟市
3	博世汽车部件（苏州）有限公司	工业园区	28	利乐包装（昆山）有限公司	昆山市
4	波司登股份有限公司	常熟市	29	艾默生环境优化技术（苏州）有限公司	工业园区
5	江苏沙钢集团有限公司	张家港市	30	太仓港协鑫发电有限公司	太仓市
6	仁宝信息技术（昆山）有限公司	昆山市	31	江苏科林集团有限公司	吴江区
7	江苏宝洁有限公司	太仓市	32	惠氏制药有限公司	吴中区
8	仁宝电子科技（昆山）有限公司	昆山市	33	德尔福电子（苏州）有限公司	工业园区
9	张家港康得新光电材料有限公司	张家港市	34	江苏通润机电集团有限公司	常熟市
10	张家港宏昌钢板有限公司	张家港市	35	江苏国望高科纤维有限公司	吴江区
11	纬创资通（昆山）有限公司	昆山市	36	张家港浦项不锈钢有限公司	张家港市
12	仁宝资讯工业（昆山）有限公司	昆山市	37	富翔精密工业（昆山）有限公司	昆山市
13	舍弗勒（中国）有限公司	太仓市	38	常熟开关制造有限公司（原常熟开关厂）	常熟市
14	江苏常熟发电有限公司	常熟市	39	丰田汽车（常熟）零部件有限公司	常熟市
15	江苏永钢集团有限公司	张家港市	40	张家港保税区康得菲尔实业有限公司	张家港市
16	克诺尔车辆设备（苏州）有限公司	高新区、虎丘区	41	卫材（中国）药业有限公司	工业园区
17	江苏恒力化纤股份有限公司	吴江区	42	江苏理文造纸有限公司	常熟市
18	正新橡胶（中国）有限公司	昆山市	43	常熟阿特斯阳光电力科技有限公司	常熟市
19	玖龙纸业（太仓）有限公司	太仓市	44	莱克电气股份有限公司	高新区、虎丘区
20	亨通集团有限公司	吴江区	45	江苏隆力奇集团有限公司	常熟市
21	牧田（昆山）有限公司	昆山市	46	康力电梯股份有限公司	吴江区
22	上海华电电力发展有限公司望亭发电厂	相城区	47	常熟市龙腾特种钢有限公司	常熟市
23	华能太仓发电有限责任公司	太仓市	48	名硕电脑（苏州）有限公司	高新区、虎丘区
24	昆山龙腾光电有限公司	昆山市	49	三星电子（苏州）半导体有限公司	工业园区
25	南亚电子材料（昆山）有限公司	昆山市	50	中利科技集团股份有限公司	常熟市

表4-18 续表 Continued

序 号 No.	企业名称 Name of Enterprises	所在地区 Location	序 号 No.	企业名称 Name of Enterprises	所在地区 Location
51	天齐锂业（江苏）有限公司	张家港市	76	日立汽车系统（苏州）有限公司	工业园区
52	苏州三星显示有限公司	工业园区	77	耐世特汽车系统（苏州）有限公司	工业园区
53	埃克森美孚（太仓）石油有限公司	太仓市	78	苏州三星电子有限公司	工业园区
54	万都底盘部件（苏州）有限公司	高新区、虎丘区	79	芬欧汇川(中国)有限公司	常熟市
55	金红叶纸业集团有限公司	工业园区	80	华芳集团有限公司	张家港市
56	富士和机械工业（昆山）有限公司	昆山市	81	瑞仪光电（苏州）有限公司	吴江区
57	三一重机有限公司	昆山市	82	威特电梯部件（苏州）有限公司	吴江区
58	江苏盛虹科技股份有限公司	吴江区	83	苏州协鑫光伏科技有限公司	高新区、虎丘区
59	优美科汽车催化剂（苏州）有限公司	工业园区	84	牧田（中国）有限公司	昆山市
60	AW（苏州）汽车零部件有限公司	吴中区	85	大陆汽车系统（常熟）有限公司	常熟市
61	定颖电子（昆山）有限公司	昆山市	86	贝克曼库尔实验系统（苏州）有限公司	工业园区
62	膳魔师（中国）家庭制品有限公司	昆山市	87	江苏新泰材料科技股份有限公司	常熟市
63	国华太仓发电有限公司	太仓市	88	通鼎互联信息股份有限公司	吴江区
64	大金空调（苏州）有限公司	工业园区	89	中达电子零组件（吴江）有限公司	吴江区
65	康美包（苏州）有限公司	工业园区	90	盛虹集团有限公司	吴江区
66	三菱电机汽车部件（中国）有限公司	常熟市	91	苏州三星电子电脑有限公司	工业园区
67	苏州三星电子液晶显示科技有限公司	工业园区	92	苏州碧迪医疗器械有限公司	工业园区
68	NGK（苏州）环保陶瓷有限公司	高新区、虎丘区	93	和舰科技（苏州）有限公司	工业园区
69	维益食品（苏州）有限公司	工业园区	94	碧辟（中国）工业油品有限公司	太仓市
70	博格华纳汽车零部件（江苏）有限公司	太仓市	95	苏州百特医疗用品有限公司	工业园区
71	苏州东瑞制药有限公司	吴中区	96	哈曼汽车电子系统(苏州)有限公司	工业园区
72	特灵空调系统（中国）有限公司	太仓市	97	莱顿汽车部件（苏州）有限公司	工业园区
73	金华盛纸业（苏州工业园区）有限公司	工业园区	98	易程（苏州）新技术股份有限公司	高新区、虎丘区
74	苏州汇川技术有限公司	吴中区	99	澳洋集团有限公司	张家港市
75	佳能（苏州）有限公司	高新区、虎丘区	100	SEW-传动设备（苏州）有限公司	工业园区

表4-19

全市工业利润总额百强企业（2016年）
TOP 100 ENTERPRISES OF THE TOTAL PROFITS (2016)

序　号 No.	企业名称 Name of Enterprises	所在地区 Location	序　号 No.	企业名称 Name of Enterprises	所在地区 Location
1	通力电梯有限公司	昆山市	26	南亚电子材料（昆山）有限公司	昆山市
2	博世汽车部件（苏州）有限公司	工业园区	27	上海华电电力发展有限公司望亭发电厂	相城区
3	仁宝信息技术（昆山）有限公司	昆山市	28	华润电力（常熟）有限公司	常熟市
4	奇瑞捷豹路虎汽车有限公司	常熟市	29	艾默生环境优化技术（苏州）有限公司	工业园区
5	波司登股份有限公司	常熟市	30	太仓港协鑫发电有限公司	太仓市
6	仁宝电子科技（昆山）有限公司	昆山市	31	德尔福电子（苏州）有限公司	工业园区
7	江苏宝洁有限公司	太仓市	32	莱克电气股份有限公司	高新区、虎丘区
8	纬创资通（昆山）有限公司	昆山市	33	常熟开关制造有限公司（原常熟开关厂）	常熟市
9	张家港康得新光电材料有限公司	张家港市	34	常熟阿特斯阳光电力科技有限公司	常熟市
10	仁宝资讯工业（昆山）有限公司	昆山市	35	名硕电脑（苏州）有限公司	高新区、虎丘区
11	江苏沙钢集团有限公司	张家港市	36	三星电子（苏州）半导体有限公司	工业园区
12	舍弗勒（中国）有限公司	太仓市	37	张家港保税区康得菲尔实业有限公司	张家港市
13	张家港宏昌钢板有限公司	张家港市	38	利乐包装（昆山）有限公司	昆山市
14	江苏永钢集团有限公司	张家港市	39	丰田汽车（常熟）零部件有限公司	常熟市
15	江苏常熟发电有限公司	常熟市	40	张家港浦项不锈钢有限公司	张家港市
16	克诺尔车辆设备（苏州）有限公司	高新区、虎丘区	41	天齐锂业（江苏）有限公司	张家港市
17	牧田（昆山）有限公司	昆山市	42	苏州三星显示有限公司	工业园区
18	纬新资通（昆山）有限公司	昆山市	43	江苏国望高科纤维有限公司	吴江区
19	正新橡胶（中国）有限公司	昆山市	44	康力电梯股份有限公司	吴江区
20	江苏恒力化纤股份有限公司	吴江区	45	江苏理文造纸有限公司	常熟市
21	亨通集团有限公司	吴江区	46	万都底盘部件（苏州）有限公司	高新区、虎丘区
22	玖龙纸业（太仓）有限公司	太仓市	47	三一重机有限公司	昆山市
23	江苏科林集团有限公司	吴江区	48	昆山龙腾光电有限公司	昆山市
24	华能太仓发电有限责任公司	太仓市	49	芬欧汇川(中国)有限公司	常熟市
25	富翔精密工业（昆山）有限公司	昆山市	50	富士和机械工业（昆山）有限公司	昆山市

表4-19 续表 Continued

序　号 No.	企业名称 Name of Enterprises	所在地区 Location	序　号 No.	企业名称 Name of Enterprises	所在地区 Location
51	中利科技集团股份有限公司	常熟市	76	烨辉（中国）科技材料有限公司	常熟市
52	大金空调（苏州）有限公司	工业园区	77	康美包（苏州）有限公司	工业园区
53	江苏通润机电集团有限公司	常熟市	78	三菱电机汽车部件（中国）有限公司	常熟市
54	惠氏制药有限公司	吴中区	79	常熟三爱富中昊化工新材料有限公司	常熟市
55	卫材（中国）药业有限公司	工业园区	80	张家港沙洲电力有限公司	张家港市
56	苏州协鑫光伏科技有限公司	高新区、虎丘区	81	维益食品（苏州）有限公司	工业园区
57	膳魔师（中国）家庭制品有限公司	昆山市	82	苏州百特医疗用品有限公司	工业园区
58	优美科汽车催化剂（苏州）有限公司	工业园区	83	牧田（中国）有限公司	昆山市
59	埃克森美孚（太仓）石油有限公司	太仓市	84	江苏新泰材料科技股份有限公司	常熟市
60	耐世特汽车系统（苏州）有限公司	工业园区	85	康普通讯技术（中国）有限公司	工业园区
61	佳能（苏州）有限公司	高新区、虎丘区	86	和舰科技（苏州）有限公司	工业园区
62	国华太仓发电有限公司	太仓市	87	日立汽车系统（苏州）有限公司	工业园区
63	苏州三星电子有限公司	工业园区	88	苏州安洁科技股份有限公司	吴中区
64	瑞仪光电（苏州）有限公司	吴江区	89	贝克曼库尔实验系统（苏州）有限公司	工业园区
65	特灵空调系统（中国）有限公司	太仓市	90	易程（苏州）新技术股份有限公司	高新区、虎丘区
66	江苏盛虹科技股份有限公司	吴江区	91	苏州碧迪医疗器械有限公司	工业园区
67	博格华纳汽车零部件（江苏）有限公司	太仓市	92	威特电梯部件（苏州）有限公司	吴江区
68	苏州东瑞制药有限公司	吴中区	93	苏州西门子电器有限公司	高新区、虎丘区
69	AW（苏州）汽车零部件有限公司	吴中区	94	苏州汇川技术有限公司	吴中区
70	中达电子零组件（吴江）有限公司	吴江区	95	天顺风能（苏州）股份有限公司	太仓市
71	哈曼汽车电子系统(苏州)有限公司	工业园区	96	澳洋集团有限公司	张家港市
72	江苏隆力奇集团有限公司	常熟市	97	苏州纽威阀门股份有限公司	高新区、虎丘区
73	金华盛纸业（苏州工业园区）有限公司	工业园区	98	苏州三星电子电脑有限公司	工业园区
74	NGK（苏州）环保陶瓷有限公司	高新区、虎丘区	99	莱顿汽车部件（苏州）有限公司	工业园区
75	大陆汽车系统（常熟）有限公司	常熟市	100	常熟市龙腾特种钢有限公司	常熟市

表4-20

全市工业资产总计百强企业 (2016年)
TOP 100 ENTERPRISES OF THE TOTAL ASSETS (2016)

序 号 No.	企业名称 Name of Enterprises	所在地区 Location	序 号 No.	企业名称 Name of Enterprises	所在地区 Location
1	江苏沙钢集团有限公司	张家港市	26	江苏盛虹科技股份有限公司	吴江区
2	亨通集团有限公司	吴江区	27	金华盛纸业（苏州工业园区）有限公司	工业园区
3	江苏永钢集团有限公司	张家港市	28	江苏常熟发电有限公司	常熟市
4	波司登股份有限公司	常熟市	29	达富电脑（常熟）有限公司	常熟市
5	金红叶纸业集团有限公司	工业园区	30	江苏国望高科纤维有限公司	吴江区
6	张家港宏昌钢板有限公司	张家港市	31	仁宝信息技术（昆山）有限公司	昆山市
7	张家港康得新光电材料有限公司	张家港市	32	纬新资通（昆山）有限公司	昆山市
8	通力电梯有限公司	昆山市	33	苏州东山精密制造股份有限公司	吴中区
9	澳洋集团有限公司	张家港市	34	三一重机有限公司	昆山市
10	观致汽车有限公司	常熟市	35	苏州天沃科技股份有限公司	张家港市
11	太仓港协鑫发电有限公司	太仓市	36	长春化工（江苏）有限公司	常熟市
12	苏州胜利精密制造科技股份有限公司	高新区、虎丘区	37	苏州市相城区江南化纤集团有限公司	相城区
13	苏州三星电子液晶显示科技有限公司	工业园区	38	常熟阿特斯阳光电力科技有限公司	常熟市
14	奇瑞捷豹路虎汽车有限公司	常熟市	39	芬欧汇川(中国)有限公司	常熟市
15	名硕电脑（苏州）有限公司	高新区、虎丘区	40	金龙联合汽车工业（苏州）有限公司	工业园区
16	博世汽车部件（苏州）有限公司	工业园区	41	江苏骏马集团有限责任公司	张家港市
17	中利腾晖光伏科技有限公司	常熟市	42	舍弗勒（中国）有限公司	太仓市
18	中利科技集团股份有限公司	常熟市	43	世硕电子（昆山）有限公司	昆山市
19	张家港沙洲电力有限公司	张家港市	44	上海华电电力发展有限公司望亭发电厂	相城区
20	南亚电子材料（昆山）有限公司	昆山市	45	常熟市龙腾特种钢有限公司	常熟市
21	友达光电(昆山)有限公司	昆山市	46	道康宁（张家港）有限公司	张家港市
22	江苏恒力化纤股份有限公司	吴江区	47	纬创资通（昆山）有限公司	昆山市
23	江苏华昌（集团）有限公司	张家港市	48	中粮东海粮油工业（张家港）有限公司	张家港市
24	玖龙纸业（太仓）有限公司	太仓市	49	攀华集团有限公司	张家港市
25	东华能源股份有限公司	张家港市	50	正新橡胶（中国）有限公司	昆山市

表4-20 续表　Continued

序　号 No.	企业名称 Name of Enterprises	所在地区 Location	序　号 No.	企业名称 Name of Enterprises	所在地区 Location
51	伟创力电子技术（苏州）有限公司	工业园区	76	香塘集团有限公司	太仓市
52	张家港浦项不锈钢有限公司	张家港市	77	和舰科技（苏州）有限公司	工业园区
53	华芳集团有限公司	张家港市	78	张家港荣盛炼钢有限公司	张家港市
54	长江润发集团有限公司	张家港市	79	张家港富瑞特种装备股份有限公司	张家港市
55	苏州佳世达电通有限公司	高新区、虎丘区	80	常熟风范电力设备股份有限公司	常熟市
56	瑞仪光电（苏州）有限公司	吴江区	81	礼来苏州制药有限公司	工业园区
57	张家港扬子江石化有限公司	张家港市	82	江苏银河电子股份有限公司	张家港市
58	富翔精密工业（昆山）有限公司	昆山市	83	常熟市汽车饰件股份有限公司	常熟市
59	昆山龙腾光电有限公司	昆山市	84	康力电梯股份有限公司	吴江区
60	通鼎互联信息股份有限公司	吴江区	85	仁宝资讯工业（昆山）有限公司	昆山市
61	烨辉（中国）科技材料有限公司	常熟市	86	江苏梦兰集团有限公司	常熟市
62	天顺风能（苏州）股份有限公司	太仓市	87	雅鹿集团股份有限公司	太仓市
63	纬视晶光电（昆山）有限公司	昆山市	88	昆山丘钛微电子科技有限公司	昆山市
64	江苏隆力奇集团有限公司	常熟市	89	苏州三星显示有限公司	工业园区
65	高创（苏州）电子有限公司	吴江区	90	国巨电子（中国）有限公司	高新区、虎丘区
66	苏州三星电子电脑有限公司	工业园区	91	特灵空调系统（中国）有限公司	太仓市
67	牧田（昆山）有限公司	昆山市	92	六丰金属科技(昆山)有限公司	昆山市
68	昆山国显光电有限公司	昆山市	93	苏州春兴精工股份有限公司	工业园区
69	苏州阿特斯阳光电力科技有限公司	高新区、虎丘区	94	江苏鹿港文化股份有限公司	张家港市
70	永鼎集团有限公司	吴江区	95	张家港协鑫集成科技有限公司	张家港市
71	苏州市欧菲光科技有限公司	相城区	96	苏州纽威阀门股份有限公司	高新区、虎丘区
72	三星电子（苏州）半导体有限公司	工业园区	97	华能太仓发电有限责任公司	太仓市
73	沪士电子股份有限公司	昆山市	98	富士康（昆山）电脑接插件有限公司	昆山市
74	江苏理文造纸有限公司	常熟市	99	康准电子科技（昆山）有限公司	昆山市
75	江苏常铝铝业股份有限公司	常熟市	100	张家港华兴电力有限公司	张家港市

表4-21

苏州的驰名商标（2016年末）

（行政认定）

LIST OF RENOWNED AND DISTINGUISHED BRANDS IN SUZHOU (END OF 2016)

(ADMINISTRATIVE RECOGNITION)

商标名称 Brand Name	主要产品 Main Product	注册单位 Registered Units	认定时间 Time of Recognition	所在地区 Location
春花	吸尘器	苏州春花国际贸易有限公司	2000	市 区
亨通光电	通信电缆等	江苏亨通光电股份有限公司	2004	市 区
DER	地板等	德尔国际家居股份有限公司	2005	市 区
BenQ	液晶显示器、扫描仪	明基电通股份有限公司	2007	市 区
通鼎光电	电缆，光缆	江苏通鼎光电股份有限公司	2007	市 区
羅普斯金LPSK	金属建筑材料	苏州罗普斯金铝业股份有限公司	2007	市 区
罗技	计算机鼠标器、计算机周边设备	罗技科技(苏州)有限公司	2008	市 区
迪欧UNDC及图	咖啡馆、餐厅	迪欧餐饮管理有限公司	2008	市 区
七宝及图	电线、电缆	江苏七宝光电集团有限公司	2009	市 区
盛虹及图SHENGHONG	布、织物	盛虹集团有限公司	2009	市 区
洞庭山碧螺春及图	茶叶	苏州市吴中区洞庭（山）碧螺春茶业协会	2009	市 区
SJEC	升降机（电梯）、升降设备	苏州江南嘉捷电梯股份有限公司	2010	市 区
科林kelin及图	除尘器	科林环保设备股份有限公司	2010	市 区
桑罗	服装、领带、围巾	江苏华佳投资集团有限公司	2010	市 区
雅士利	油漆、涂料（油漆）	雅士利涂料（苏州）有限公司	2011	市 区
苏净及图	空气净化装置和机器、水净化装置、洁净工作台(系列)	江苏苏净集团有限公司	2011	市 区
水天堂	咖啡馆、自助餐厅、饭店	江苏水天堂餐饮管理有限公司	2011	市 区
恒远HENGYUAN及图	弹力丝(纺织用)；长丝	恒力集团有限公司	2011	市 区
大卫及图	地板，木板材条	苏州大卫木业有限公司	2011	市 区
环球及图	套筒滚子链	苏州环球集团有限公司	2011	市 区
牛头NIU TOU及图	纤维纺织原料、纺织品纤维	江苏江南高纤股份有限公司	2011	市 区
二叶ERYE及图	西药	苏州二叶制药有限公司	2011	市 区
雷允上及图	中药成药	雷允上药业有限公司	2012	市 区
第3394728号图形	物理学设备和仪器、材料检验仪器和机器	苏州东菱振动试验仪器有限公司	2012	市 区
丁家宜	洗面奶、化妆品	珈侬生化科技（中国）有限公司	2012	市 区
金螳螂	室内装饰、外墙装饰（玻璃幕墙）	苏州金螳螂建筑装饰股份有限公司	2012	市 区
同 程	旅行预定、旅行社（不包括预定旅馆）、旅客陪同	苏州同程旅游网络科技有限公司	2012	市 区
康 力	电梯、自动梯、可移动楼梯	康力电梯股份有限公司	2012	市 区
吴通WUTONG及图	连接器(数据处理设备)	江苏吴通通讯股份有限公司	2012	市 区
SEALL	货物传送、运输信息、海上运输等	苏州物流中心有限公司	2013	市 区

表4-21 续表 1 Continued 1

商标名称 Brand Name	主要产品 Main Product	注册单位 Registered Units	认定时间 Time of Recognition	所在地区 Location
稻香村DXC	果子面包、糕点	苏州稻香村食品工业有限公司	2013	市 区
巨峰及图	涂料、油漆、清漆等	苏州巨峰电气绝缘系统股份有限公司	2013	市 区
LZY	电源材料；电线连接物；电器联接器	苏州路之遥科技股份有限公司	2014	市 区
松鹤楼	餐馆	苏州松鹤楼餐饮食文化有限公司	2014	市 区
红蚂蚁RED ANT及图	室内装饰设计；建筑咨询；建筑制图等	江苏红蚂蚁装饰设计工程有限公司	2014	市 区
大象及图	清漆、调合漆	江苏大象东亚制漆有限公司	2014	市 区
神王SHEN WANG 及图	钢丝；金属绳；金属绳索	江苏神王集团有限公司	2014	市 区
纽威	金属阀门（非机器零件）；金属水管阀；金属管道等	苏州纽威阀门股份有限公司	2015	市 区
海格HIGER	汽车；汽车底盘；车轮等	金龙联合汽车工业（苏州）有限公司	2015	市 区
邻里中心+图形	广告；推销(替他人)；替他人作中介(替其它企业购买商品或服务)等	苏州工业园区邻里中心发展有限公司	2015	市 区
德胜洋楼TECSUN	非金属建筑结构、非金属建筑材料、非金属屋顶材料等	德胜（苏州）洋楼有限公司	2015	市 区
美瑞德MEIRUID	室内装潢，室内装潢修理，室内外油漆等	苏州美瑞德建筑装饰有限公司	2015	市 区
明港MINGGANG及图	混凝土建筑构件、水泥管、水泥柱等	吴江市明港道桥工程有限公司	2015	市 区
静思园及图	观光旅游	吴江静思园	2015	市 区
帝奥	电梯；自动梯；可移动楼梯等	苏州帝奥电梯有限公司	2015	市 区
老相食	豆腐；豆腐制品；牛奶制品等	苏州金记食品有限公司	2015	市 区
金宏气体JINHONG GAS及图	氮;氢;液体二氧化碳等	苏州金宏气体股份有限公司	2015	市 区
天烨	金属锻造	苏州天烨集团有限公司	2016	市 区
波司登	服装、皮鞋	波司登股份有限公司	1999	常熟市
梦兰	纺织品	江苏梦兰集团公司	2000	常熟市
隆力奇	纯蛇粉	江苏隆力奇生物科技股份有限公司	2001	常熟市
阪神	冷冻箱	江苏白雪电器股份有限公司	2004	常熟市
BaiXue	冷冻设备等	江苏白雪电器股份有限公司	2004	常熟市
龙达飞LongDafei	服装	江苏龙达飞投资实业有限公司	2006	常熟市
隆力奇及图	化妆品等	江苏隆力奇生物科技股份有限公司	2007	常熟市
雪中飞	羽绒服装	波司登股份有限公司	2007	常熟市
TORIN及图	第7类：千斤顶	江苏通润机电集团有限公司	2009	常熟市
第1273835号图形	第9类：断路器	常熟开关制造有限公司	2009	常熟市
洲艳ZhouYan图形	服装等	江苏洲艳服饰有限公司	2009	常熟市

表4-21 续表 2　　Continued 2

商标名称 Brand Name	主要产品 Main Product	注册单位 Registered Units	认定时间 Time of Recognition	所在地区 Location
通润及图	千斤顶、货车用千斤顶	江苏通润机电集团有限公司	2010	常熟市
千仞岗	服装、羽绒服装	常熟市千仞岗制衣有限公司	2010	常熟市
Enox	化学试剂	江苏强盛化工有限公司	2011	常熟市
阿里山	加工过的坚果、加工过的瓜子	江苏阿里山食品有限公司	2011	常熟市
月龙YUELONG	衣物、茄克、裤子、西服制服、童装、运动衣、皮衣（服装）	江苏月龙服饰有限公司	2011	常熟市
扬帆SETSAIL	针织服装	江苏扬帆服饰有限公司	2011	常熟市
龙星LongXing及图	纺织机械、针织机械、手套机	常熟市金龙机械有限公司	2012	常熟市
金丝狐Jinsihu及图	服装（休闲男装）	江苏金丝狐服饰有限公司	2012	常熟市
冰洁	羽绒服装;服装	波司登国际服饰（中国）有限公司	2013	常熟市
csc	轴承及轴承用钢珠	常熟长城轴承有限公司	2013	常熟市
金辰JINCHEN及图	布、印花棉布、纺织织物	江苏金辰针纺织有限公司	2014	常熟市
梦兰MENGLAN及图	床罩、被子、被罩等	江苏梦兰集团有限公司	2014	常熟市
zl图形	电线，电缆	中利科技集团股份有限公司	2015	常熟市
菊花	味精等	张家港市新菊味精有限公司	2002	张家港市
华芳	纺织纱等	华芳集团有限公司	2004	张家港市
沙洲SZ及图	黄酒	江苏张家港酿酒有限公司	2008	张家港市
沙钢及图	钢型材、金属建筑材料	江苏沙钢集团有限公司	2008	张家港市
港洋及图	精纺呢绒	江苏港洋实业股份有限公司	2009	张家港市
AAA SANEIPAI及图	轴承	张家港市AAA轴承有限公司	2010	张家港市
沙洲优黄	黄酒	江苏张家港酿酒有限公司	2012	张家港市
捷星及图	电梯空心导轨	长江润发机械股份有限公司	2012	张家港市
浩波HOPE	双乙烯酮	苏州浩波科技股份有限公司	2012	张家港市
港星	轻钢龙骨	张家港市新港星科技有限公司	2012	张家港市
联冠及图	塑料挤出机、塑料混合机、塑料切粒机	江苏联冠科技发展有限公司	2012	张家港市
圣达因	罐车、槽车、汽车	张家港中集圣达因低温装备有限公司	2013	张家港市
金宇及图	钠盐、肥料、化学制剂等	江苏华昌化工股份有限公司	2013	张家港市
梁丰	巧克力；咖啡；茶等	江苏梁丰食品集团有限公司	2013	张家港市
TX	涤纶长丝	张家港欣欣高纤股份有限公司	2014	张家港市
鹿港	呢绒；棉织品；毛布料	江苏鹿港科技股份有限公司	2014	张家港市

表4-21 续表 3 Continued 3

商标名称 Brand Name	主要产品 Main Product	注册单位 Registered Units	认定时间 Time of Recognition	所在地区 Location
澳洋AOYANG及图	呢绒、布、毛料等	澳洋集团有限公司	2015	张家港市
NNANKANG	轮胎、内胎、汽车轮胎等	南港（张家港保税区）橡胶工业有限公司	2015	张家港市
伊思贝得 Itsbetter	服装；领带；帽等	江苏东渡纺织集团有限公司	2015	张家港市
正大富通	车辆用液压系统等	江苏正大富通股份有限公司	2016	张家港市
好孩子	儿童车等	好孩子儿童用品有限公司	1999	昆山市
AB	内衣裤等	江苏AB集团股份有限公司	2000	昆山市
捷安特	自行车	巨大机械工业股份有限公司	2004	昆山市
旗舰及图	办公用纸等	亚龙纸制品(昆山)有限公司	2006	昆山市
哈森HARSONE及图	皮鞋	昆山珍兴鞋业有限公司	2006	昆山市
并蒂莲	服装	昆山并蒂莲服装有限公司	2008	昆山市
多威DOWIN	运动鞋	昆山多威体育用品有限公司	2008	昆山市
冠軍	瓷砖等	信益陶瓷(中国)有限公司	2010	昆山市
樱花SAKURA及图	排油烟机、电热水器、厨房炉灶	樱花卫厨（中国）股份有限公司	2011	昆山市
南寶NANPAO	油漆、涂料	南宝树脂化学工厂股份有限公司	2011	昆山市
MIYOU及图	粉碎机（机器）、机械密封件	密友集团有限公司	2012	昆山市
MAXXIS	车轮胎；汽车轮胎；车辆轮胎	正新橡胶(中国)有限公司	2012	昆山市
摩卡MOCCA	咖啡	瑞昶贸易股份有限公司	2012	昆山市
玛吉斯	轮胎	正新橡胶(中国)有限公司	2013	昆山市
周庄zhouzhuang及图	旅行社（不包括预定旅馆）、旅客陪同、观光旅游等	江苏水乡周庄旅游股份有限公司	2013	昆山市
膳魔師	不锈钢锅具；保温瓶；热水瓶	膳魔师(中国)家庭制品有限公司	2013	昆山市
协孚	仿皮、仿皮革、皮	昆山协孚人造皮有限公司	2014	昆山市
巴城陽澄湖	蟹(活)	昆山市巴城镇阳澄湖蟹业协会	2015	昆山市
雅鹿	服装	苏州雅鹿控股股份有限公司	2001	太仓市
太仓及图	肉松	太仓肉松食品有限公司	2008	太仓市
第1080023号图形	聚氯乙烯树脂、合成树脂塑料	江苏德威新材料股份有限公司	2010	太仓市
安佑	动物饲料；家畜饲料等	安佑（中国）动物营养研发有限公司	2012	太仓市
口水娃及图	精致坚果仁、熟制豆、水果蜜饯等	苏州口水娃食品有限公司	2015	太仓市
蓝冰	衬衫、羽绒服、体闲服等	苏州雅鹿控股股份有限公司	2015	太仓市
Frognie Zila	工作服、皮衣（服饰）、羽绒服装等	苏州佛朗尼齐拉服饰有限公司	2015	太仓市

主要统计指标解释

工业 指从事自然资源的开采，对采掘品和农产品进行加工和再加工的物质生产部门。具体包括：(1)对自然资源的开采，如采矿、晒盐等(但不包括禽兽捕猎和水产捕捞)；(2)对农副产品的加工、再加工，如粮油加工、食品加工、缫丝、纺织、制革等；(3)对采掘品的加工、再加工，如炼铁、炼钢、化工生产、石油加工、机器制造、木材加工等，以及电力、自来水、煤气的生产和供应等；(4)对工业品的修理、翻新，如机器设备的修理、交通运输工具(如汽车)的修理等。

工业统计调查单位为独立核算法人工业企业。

独立核算法人工业企业指从事工业生产经营活动的单位。独立核算法人工业企业应同时具备以下条件：①依法成立，有自己的名称、组织机构和场所，能够承担民事责任；②独立拥有和使用资产，承担负债，有权与其他单位签订合同；③独立核算盈亏，并能够编制资产负债表。

本年鉴中涉及的企业登记注册类型：

国有及国有控股企业 指国有企业加上国有控股企业。国有企业(即原全民所有制工业或国营工业)指企业全部资产归国家所有，并按《中华人民共和国企业法人登记管理条例》规定登记注册的非公司制的经济组织。包括国有企业、国有独资公司和国有联营企业。1957年以前的公私合营和私营工业，后均改造为国营工业，1992年改为国有工业，这部分工业的资料不单独分列时，均包括在国有企业内。国有控股企业是对混合所有制经济的企业进行的“国有控股”分类。它是指这些企业的全部资产中国有资产(股份)相对其他所有者中的任何一个所有者占资(股)最多的企业。该分组反映了国有经济控股情况。

集体企业 指企业资产归集体所有，并按《中华人民共和国企业法人登记管理条例》规定登记注册的经济组织。是社会主义公有制经济的组成部分。包括城乡所有使用集体投资举办的企业，以及部分个人通过集资自愿放弃所有权并依法经工商行政管理机关认定为集体所有制的企业。

股份合作企业 指以合作制为基础，由企业职工共同出资入股，吸收一定比例的社会资产投资组建，实行自主经营，自负盈亏，共同劳动，民主管理，按劳分配与按股分红相结合的一种集体经济组织。

联营企业 指两个及两个以上相同或不同所有制性质的企业法人或事业单位法人，按自愿、平等、互利的原则，共同投资组成的经济组织。联营企业包括：

国有联营企业指国有企业与国有企业间的联营；

集体联营企业指集体企业与集体企业间的联营；

国有与集体联营企业指国有企业与集体企业间的联营。

有限责任公司 指根据《中华人民共和国公司登记管理条例》规定登记注册，由两个以上，五十个以下的股东共同出资，每个股东以其所认缴的出资额对公司承担有限责任，公司以其全部资产对其债务承担责任的经济组织。

有限责任公司包括国有独资公司以及其他有限责任公司。

股份有限公司 指根据《中华人民共和国企业法人登记管理条例》规定登记注册，其全部注册资本由等额股份构成并通过发行股票筹集资本，股东以其认购的股份对公司承担有限责任，公司以其全部资产对其债务承担责任的经济组织。

私营企业 指由自然人投资设立或由自然人控股，以雇佣劳动为基础的营利性经济组织。包括按照《公司法》、《合伙企业法》、《私营企业暂行条例》以及《个人独资企业法》规定登记注册的私营有限责任公司、私营股份有限公司、私营合伙企业和私营独资企业。

港、澳、台商投资企业　指企业注册登记类型中的港、澳、台资合资、合作、独资经营企业和股份有限公司之和。

外商投资企业　指企业注册登记类型中的中外合资、合作经营企业、外资企业和外商投资股份有限公司之和。

"三资"企业　指港、澳、台商投资企业和外资企业的简称。

轻工业　指主要提供生活消费品和制作手工工具的工业。按其所使用的原料不同，可分为两大类：(1)以农产品为原料的轻工业，是指直接或间接以农产品为基本原料的轻工业。主要包括食品制造、饮料制造、烟草加工、纺织、缝纫、皮革和毛皮制作、造纸以及印刷等工业；(2)以非农产品为原料的轻工业，是指以工业品为原料的轻工业。主要包括文教体育用品、化学药品制造、合成纤维制造、日用化学制品、日用玻璃制品、日用金属制品、手工工具制造、医疗器械制造、文化和办公用机械制造等工业。

重工业　指为国民经济各部门提供物质技术基础的主要生产资料的工业。按其生产性质和产品用途，可以分为下列三类：(1)采掘(伐)工业，是指对自然资源的开采，包括石油开采、煤炭开采、金属矿开采、非金属矿开采等工业；(2)原材料工业，指向国民经济各部门提供基本材料、动力和燃料的工业。包括金属冶炼及加工、炼焦及焦炭、化学、化工原料、水泥、人造板以及电力、石油和煤炭加工等工业；(3)加工工业，是指对工业原材料进行再加工制造的工业。包括装备国民经济各部门的机械设备制造工业、金属结构、水泥制品等工业，以及为农业提供的生产资料如化肥、农药等工业。

根据上述划分原则，修理业中以重工业产品为修理作业对象的划为重工业，反之划为轻工业。

工业总产值

(1)定义：

工业总产值是以货币形式表现的，工业企业在一定时期内生产的工业最终产品或提供工业性劳务活动的总价值量。它反映一定时间内工业生产的总规模和总水平。

(2)计算原则：

工业生产的原则，即凡是企业在报告期生产的经检验合格的产品，不管是否在报告期销售，均包括在内。

最终产品的原则，即凡是计入工业总产值的产品，必须是本企业生产的经检验合格的，不需要再进行任何加工的最终产品。如果企业有中间产品(半成品)对外销售，则对外销售的中间产品应视为企业的最终产品。

工厂法原则，即工业总产值是以工业企业作为基本计算(核算)单位，即按企业的最终产品计算工业总产值。按这种方法计算的工业总产值，不允许同一产品价值在企业内部重复计算，不能把企业内部各个车间(分厂)生产的成果相加，但允许企业间的重复计算。

(3)内容及计算方法：

1995年全国工业普查对工业总产值(原规定)的内容及计算原则和方法做了某些修订，修订后的工业总产值(新规定)包括三项内容：即本期生产成品价值、对外加工费收入、在制品半成品期末期初差额价值三部分。

本期生产成品价值：指企业本期生产，并在报告期内不再进行加工，经检验、包装入库的全部工业成品(半成品)价值合计，包括企业生产的自制设备及提供给本企业在建工程、其他非工业部门和福利部门等单位使用的成品价值。本期生产成品价值为按自备原材料生产的产品的数量乘以本期不含增值税(销项税额)的产品实际销售平均单价计算；会计核算中按成本价格转帐的自制设备和自产自用的成品，按成本价格计算生产成品价值。生产成品价值中不包括用定货者来料加工的成品(半成品)价值。

对外加工费收入：指企业在报告期内完成的对外承接的工业品加工(包括用定货者来料加工产品)的加工费收入和对外工业修理作业所取得的加工费收入。对外加工费收入按不含增值税(销项税额)的价格计算，可根据会计"产品销售收入"科目的有关资料取得。

对于本企业对内非工业部门提供的加工修理、设备安装的劳务收入，如果企业会计核算基础较好，能取得这部分资料，而且这部分价值所占比重较大，应包括在对外加工费收入中。

自制半成品在制品期末期初差额价值：指企业报告期在制品期末减期初的差额价值，本指标一般可以从会计核算资料中取得。如果会计产品成本核算中不计算半成品、在制品的成本，则总产值中也不包括这部分价值，反之则包括。

(4)工业总产值统计范围变化和计算方法修订情况：

1984年以前工业总产值不包括村办工业，村办工业总产值划归农业。1984年以后工业总产值包括村办工业。

1995年工业普查对工业总产值计算方法做了修订，即从1995年始按新修订(新规定)方法计算工业总产值。新规定与原规定的区别如下：

全价与加工费的计算原则不同：新规定为凡自备原材料，不论其生产繁简程度如何，一律按全价计算工业总产值；凡来料加工，允许按加工费计算工业总产值。原规定则视生产加工的繁简程度不同，规定哪些行业按全价，哪些行业按加工费计算工业总产值。

自制半成品、在产品期末期初差额价值的计算原则不同：新规定要求，凡会计产品成本核算时计算了成本的差额价值，总产值中就应包括，否则可不包括；原规定则按生产周期六个月的界限区分，凡生产周期六个月以上的企业，总产值计算中应包括这部分差额价值，否则可不包括。

计算价格不同：新规定按不含增值税(销项税额)的价格计算；原规定则按含增值税(销项税额)的价格计算。

资产总计 指企业过去的交易或者事项形成的、由企业拥有或者控制的、预期会给企业带来经济利益的资源。资产一般按流动性（资产的变现或耗用时间长短）分为流动资产和非流动资产。其中流动资产可分为货币资金、交易性金融资产、应收票据、应收账款、预付款项、其他应收款、存货等；非流动资产可分为长期股权投资、固定资产、无形资产及其他非流动资产等。根据会计“资产负债表”中“资产总计”项目的期末余额数填报。

执行2006年《企业会计准则》或2011年《小企业会计准则》的企业：资产总计=流动资产合计+非流动资产合计；执行其他企业会计制度的企业资产包括流动资产、长期投资、固定资产、无形资产和其他资产等。

流动资产 指企业可以在一年内或者超过一年的一个生产周期内变现或者耗用的资产，包括现金及各种存款、短期投资，应收及预付款项、存货等。

固定资产原价 指企业在建造、购置、安装、改建、扩建、技术改造某项固定资产时所支出的全部货币总额。它一般包括买价、包装费、运杂费和安装费等。

负债合计 指企业过去的交易或者事项形成的，预期会导致经济利益流出企业的现时义务。负债一般按偿还期长短分为流动负债和非流动负债。根据会计“资产负债表”中“负债合计”项目的期末余额数填报。

执行2006年《企业会计准则》或2011年《小企业会计准则》的企业：负债合计=流动负债合计+非流动负债合计；执行其他企业会计制度的企业负债包括流动负债和长期负债。

所有者权益 指企业投资人对企业净资产的所有权。企业净资产等于企业全部资产减去全部负债后的余额，包括企业投资人对企业的最初投入的实际到位的资产及资本公积金、盈余公积金和未分配利润。所有者权益合计数小于零，表示企业资不抵债。

主营业务收入 根据会计“主营业务收入”科目的期末贷方余额（结转前）填报。执行2006年《企业会计准则》或2011《小企业会计准则》的企业，如未设置该科目，以“营业收入”代替填报。

主营业务成本 根据会计“主营业务成本”科目的期末借方余额（结转前）填报。执行2006年《企业会计准则》或2011《小企业会计准则》的企业，如未设置该科目，以“营业成本”代替填报。

主营业务税金及附加 根据会计“主营业务税金及附加”科目的期末借方余额（结转前）填报。执行2006年《企业会计准则》或2011《小企业会计准则》的企业，如未设置该科目，以“营业税金及附加”代替填报。

利润总额 指企业在一定会计期间的经营成果，是生产经营过程中各种收入扣除各种耗费后的盈余，反映企业在报告期内实现的盈亏总额。根据会计“利润表”中“利润总额”项目的本期金额数填报。执行2006年《企业会计准则》或2011年《小企业会计准则》的企业，利润总额为营业利润加上营业外收入，减去营业外支出后的金额；执行其他企业会计制度的企业，利润总额为营业利润加上投资收益、政府补助、营业外收入，再减去营业外支出后的金额。

应交增值税 指按照税法规定，针对销售货物或提供加工、修理修配劳务以及进口货物实现的增值额，企业在报告期内应交纳的税金。

从业人员平均人数　是指报告期内每天拥有的从业人员人数。其计算公式为：

$$季平均人数=\frac{季内各月平均人数之和}{3}$$

$$月平均人数=\frac{报告月内每天实有人数之和}{报告月日历日数}$$

$$年平均人数=\frac{年内各月平均人数之和}{12}$$

总资产贡献率　反映企业全部资产的获利能力，是企业经营业绩和管理水平的集中体现，是评价和考核企业盈利能力的核心指标。计算公式为：

$$总资产贡献率(\%)=\frac{利润总额+税金总额+利息支出}{平均资金总额}\times 100\%$$

公式中：税金总额为产品销售税金及附加与应交增值税之和；平均资产总额为期初期末资产之和的算术平均值。

资产负债率　该指标既反映企业经营风险的大小，也反映企业利用债权人提供的资金从事经营活动的能力。计算公式为：

$$资产负债率(\%)=\frac{负债总额}{资产总额}\times 100\%$$

资产与负债均为报告期期末数。

流动资产周转次数　指一定时期内流动资产完成的周转次数，反映投入工业企业流动资金的周转速度。计算公式为：

$$流动资产周转次数=\frac{产品销售收入}{全部流动资产平均余额}$$

公式中：全部流动资产平均余额为期初和期末的流动资产之和的算术平均值。

成本费用利润率　反映企业投入的生产成本及费用的经济效益，同时也反映企业降低成本所取得的经济效益。计算公式为：

$$成本费用利润率(\%)=\frac{利润总额}{成本费用总额}\times 100\%$$

公式中：成本费用总额为产品销售成本、销售费用、管理费用、财务费用之和。

产品销售率　该指标反映工业产品已实现销售的程度，是分析工业产销衔接情况，研究工业产品满足社会需求的指标。计算公式为：

$$产品销售率(\%)=\frac{工业销售产值}{工业总产值(现价)}\times 100\%$$

资产保值增值率　该指标反映企业净资产的变动状况，是企业发展能力的集中体现。计算公式为：

$$资本保值增值率=\frac{报告期期末所有者权益}{上年同期期末所有者权益}\times 100\%$$

所有者权益等于资产总计减负债总计。

固定资产净值率　指企业固定资产净值与固定资产原值的比率，是反映固定资产新旧程度的一种指标。计算公式为：

$$固定资产净值率=\frac{固定资产净值}{固定资产原值}\times 100\%$$

EXPLANATORY NOTES ON MAIN STATISTICAL INDICATORS

Industry refers to the material production sector which is engaged in the extraction of natural resources and processing and reprocessing of minerals and agricultural products, including (1) extraction of natural resources, such as mining, salt production (but not including hunting and fishing); (2) processing and reprocessing of farm and sideline produces, such as rice husking, flour milling, wine making, oil pressing, silk reeling, spinning and weaving, and leather making; (3) manufacture of industrial products, such as steel making, iron smelting, chemicals manufacturing, petroleum processing, machine building, timber processing; water and gas production and electricity generation and supply; (4)repairing of industrial products such as the repairing of machinery and means of transport (including cars).

In industrial statistics surveys, the units of enquiry are corporate industrial enterprises with independent accounting systems.

Corporate industrial enterprises with independent accounting systems refer to enterprises engaging in industrial production activities, which meet the following requirements: (1) They are established legally, having their own names, organizations, location and able to take civil liability; (2) They possess and use their assets independently, assume liabilities and are entitled to sign contracts with other units; (3) They are financially independent and compile their own balance sheets.

Enterprises covered in the industrial statistics in the Yearbook include the following categories by their registration:

State-owned and State-holding Enterprises refer to state-owned enterprises plus State-holding enterprises. State-owned enterprises (originally known as State-run enterprises with ownership by the whole society) are non-corporate economic entities registered in accordance with the *Regulation of the People's Republic of China on the Management of Registration of Legal Enterprises*, where all assets are owned by the State. Included in this category are State-owned enterprises, State-funded corporations and State-owned joint-operation enterprises. Joint State-private industries and private industries, which existed before 1957, were transformed into state-run industries since 1957, and into State-owned industries after 1992. Statistics on those enterprises are included in the State-owned industries instead of being grouped them separately. State-holding enterprises are a sub-classification of enterprises with mixed ownership, referring to enterprises where the percentage of State assets (or shares by the State) is larger than any other single share holder of the same enterprise. This sub-classification illustrates the control of the State over a particular industry.

Collective-owned Enterprises refer to economic entities registered in accordance with the *Regulation of the People's Republic of China on the Management of Registration of Legal Enterprises*, where assets are owned collectively. Collective enterprises constitute an integral part of the socialist economy with public ownership. They include urban and rural enterprises invested collectively, and some enterprises registered in industrial and commercial administration agency as collective units where funds are pooled together by individuals who voluntarily give up their right of ownership.

Share-holding Cooperative Enterprises refer to economic units set up on a cooperative basis, with funding partly from employees of the enterprise and partly from outside investment, where the operation and management is decided by all the members who also participate in the production, and the distribution of income is based both on work (labour input) and on shares (capital input).

Joint-operation Enterprises refer to economic units that are established by joint investment by two or more corporate enterprises or institutions of the same or different types of ownership on voluntary, equal and mutual-beneficial basis. They include:

a) State-owned joint-operation enterprises (joint operation between State-owned enterprises);

b) Collective joint-operation enterprises (joint operation between collective enterprises; and

c) State-collective joint-operation enterprises (joint operation between state and collective enterprises).

Limited Liability Corporations refer to economic units registered in accordance with the *Regulation of the People's Republic of China on the Management of Registration of Corporations*, with capital from 2 to 49 investors, each investor bears limited liability to the corporation depending on his/her holding of shares, and the corporation bears liability to its debt to the maximum of its total assets.

Share-holding Corporations Ltd. refer to economic units registered in accordance with the *Regulation of the People's Republic of China on the Management of Registration of Corporate Enterprises*, with total registered capital divided into equal shares and raised through issuing stocks. Each investor bears limited liability to the corporation depending on the holding of shares, and the corporation bears liability to its debt to the maximum of its total assets.

Private Enterprises refer to economic units invested or controlled (by holding the majority of the shares) by natural persons who hire labours for profit-making activities. Included in this category are private limited liability corporations, private shareholding corporations Ltd., private partnership enterprises and private sole investment enterprises registered in accordance with the *Corporation Law, Partnership Enterprise Law, Tentative Regulation on Private Enterprises and Sole Proprietorship Enterprise Law.*

Enterprises with Funds from Hong Kong, Macao and Taiwan refers to all industrial enterprises registered as the joint-venture, cooperative, sole (exclusive) investment industrial enterprises and limited liability corporations with funds from Hong Kong, Macao and Taiwan.

Foreign Funded Enterprises refer to all industrial enterprises registered as the joint-venture, cooperative, sole (exclusive) investment industrial enterprises and limited liability corporations with foreign funds.

Enterprises with Hong Kong, Macao, Taiwan and Foreign Fund refer to all the enterprises with funds from Hong Kong, Macao, Taiwan and foreign funded enterprises.

Light Industry refers to the industry that produces consumer goods and hand tools. It consists of two categories, depending on the materials used:

(1) Industries using farm products as raw materials. These are the branches of light industry which directly or indirectly use farm products as basic raw materials, including the manufacture of food and beverages, tobacco processing, textile, clothing, fur and leather manufacturing, paper making, printing, etc.

(2) Industries using non-farm products as raw materials. These are the branches of light industry which use manufactured goods as raw materials, including the manufacture of cultural, educational articles and sports goods, chemicals, synthetic fibre, chemical products for daily use, glass products for daily use, metal products for daily use, hand tools, medical apparatus and instruments, and the manufacture of cultural and office machinery.

Heavy Industry refers to the industry which produces capital goods, and provides various sectors of the national economy with necessary material and technical basis for production. It consists of the following three branches according to the purpose of production or the use of products:

(1) Mining, quarrying and logging industry, which refers to the industry that extracts natural resources, including extraction of petroleum, coal, metal and non-metal ores.

(2) Raw materials industry refers to the industry that provides various sectors of the national economy with raw materials, fuels and power. It includes smelting and processing of metals, coking and coke chemistry, chemical materials and building materials such as cement, plywood, and power, petroleum refining and coal dressing.

(3) Manufacturing industry which refers to the industry that processes raw materials. It includes machine-building industries which equip sectors of the national economy; industries producing metal structure and cement products; and industries producing means of agricultural production, such as chemical fertilizers and pesticides.

In accordance with the above principles of classification, the repairing trades, which are engaged primarily in repairing products of heavy industry, are classified as heavy industry while those which are engaged in repairing products of light industry are classified as light industry.

Gross Industrial Output Value

(1) Definition: Gross industrial output value is the total volume of final industrial products produced and industrial services provided during a given period. It reflects the total achievements and overall scale of industrial production during a given period.

(2) Principles for calculation:

Statistics on industrial production follow the principle that all products produced by the enterprises and accepted through quality check during the reference period are to be included no matter whether they are sold or not during the reference period.

Determination of final products follows the principle that all products that are included in the calculation of gross industrial output value are the final products of the enterprise which have been accepted through quality check and require no further processing. If an enterprise has intermediate (semi-finished) products to sell, these intermediate products are considered as the final products of the enterprise.

Gross industrial output value is calculated following the principle of factory approach, i.e. industrial enterprise is used as the basic accounting unit in calculating the gross industrial output value. By this approach, value of the same product is not to be double-counted, and the output value of different workshops (branch factories) within the enterprise should not be added. However, this approach allows the possibility of double counting between enterprises.

(3) Content and method of calculation: The old definition of gross industrial output value was modified during the 1995 National Industrial Census. The revised (new) definition of gross industrial output value consists of 3 components: value of the finished products during the reference period, income from processing for external parties, and value of change in semi-finished

products between the end and the beginning of the reference period.

Value of finished products during the reference period: refers to the value of all finished (semi-finished) industrial products that are produced during the reference period without the need for further processing, checked for acceptance, packed and put into the warehouse of the enterprise, including the value of own-produced equipment and the value of products provided to the projects under construction of the enterprise, and to other non-industrial or welfare units. Value of finished products during the reference period is calculated by the quantity of products produced using own materials multiplied by the average unit prices at which products are sold (excluding value-added tax). Own-produced equipment and products produced for own use are valued at cost prices as in the case of enterprise accounting. Value of finished products does not include the value of finished products (semi-finished products) that are produced using the materials from the clients who place the orders.

Income from external processing: refers to income from contracted external processing of industrial products (including processing of industrial products using materials from the clients), and the income from industrial repairing work provided to other parties. Income from external processing is calculated using information from the item "products sales income" in the enterprise accounting at the prices with value-added tax excluded.

For income from services such as processing, repairing and installation of equipment provided to non-industrial units within the enterprise, if the accounting work of the enterprise is good enough to separate it from other records, and the share of such services is significant, it should also be included in the income from external processing.

Value of change in semi-finished products between the end and the beginning of the reference period: refers to the value of change in semi-finished products between the end and the beginning of the reference period, which generally can be obtained from accounting records of enterprises. If the enterprise accounting excludes the cost of semi-finished products, then it should not be included in the gross industrial output value, and the reverse if otherwise.

(4) Changes in the scope and method of calculation of the gross industrial output value

Prior to 1984, the value of rural industry run by villages was classified into agriculture instead of industry. Since 1984, it has been included in the gross industrial output value. Method of calculation for the gross industrial output value was modified in the industrial census in 1995. The difference in the new method as compared with the old one is outlined below:

Principle in using full value vs. processing fee: The new method stipulates that all products produced using own materials are to be calculated with full value in reporting the gross industrial output value irrespective of the complexity of production, and for external processing, it allows calculation using processing fee. In the old method, however, the use of full value or processing fee was determined by the degree of complexity of production in different branches of industries.

Principle in determining the value of change in semi-finished products: The new method requires that value of change in semi-finished products should be included in the gross industrial output value if it is included in the accounting record of the enterprise, otherwise it should not be included. In the old method, it is determined by the type of enterprises in terms of production cycle. If the production cycle is over 6 months, the value of change in semi-finished products is included in the gross industrial output value, otherwise it is not.

Difference in prices: The new method uses prices excluding value-added tax in the calculation of gross industrial output value, while the old method used prices including value-added tax.

Total Assets refers to the resources formed by an enterprise's past transactions or events, owned or controlled by the enterprise, and expected to bring economic benefits to the enterprise. Assets are generally divided into current assets and non-current assets according to the liquidity (assets into cash or consumed time length). Current assets can be divided into monetary funds, tradable financial assets, notes receivable, accounts receivable, prepayments, other receivables, inventory, etc.; non-current assets can be divided into long-term equity investments, fixed assets, intangible assets and other non-current assets, etc. Total assets are to be filled according to the term-end balance of the "total assets" item in the accounting "balance sheet".

An enterprise which carries out "The Accounting Standards for Enterprises" (2006) or "The Accounting Standards for Small Businesses" (2011): total assets = total current assets + total non-current assets; the assets of an enterprise which carries out other enterprise accounting systems include current assets, long-term investments, fixed assets, intangible assets and other assets, etc.

Working Capital refers to capital that an enterprise can cash or use during one year or one production cycle that may exceed one year, including cash and savings deposits of various forms, short-term investment, money receivable and prepaid money, inventories, etc.

Original Value of Fixed Assets refers to the total value, in monetary terms, that an enterprise spent on fixed assets, through construction, purchase, installation, transformation, expansion or technical upgrading. Generally, it covers cost of purchase, packing, transportation and installation, etc.

Total liabilities refers to the present obligations formed by an enterprise's past transactions or events and expected to lead to the economic benefits from the enterprise. Liabilities are generally divided into current liabilities and non-current liabilities according to the length of the payback period. Total assets are to be filled according to the term-end balance of the "total liabilities" item in the accounting "balance sheet".

An enterprise which carries out "The Accounting Standards for Enterprises" (2006) or "The Accounting Standards for Small Businesses" (2011): total liabilities = total current liabilities + total non-current liabilities; the liabilities of an enterprise which carries out other enterprise accounting systems include current liabilities and long-term liabilities.

Owner's Equity refers to the ownership of net assets of enterprise by its investors. Net assets equal total assets minus total liabilities of the enterprise, including the actual assets invested into the enterprise by investors, accumulation of capital and operating surplus and non-distributed profits. The enterprise's assets are less than its liabilities if the sum of owner's equity is smaller than zero.

Revenue from Principal Business is to be filled out according to the term-end credit balance (before carrying over) of the accounting "the main business income" subject. The enterprises which implement the 2006 "Enterprise Accounting Standards" or 2011 "Small Enterprise Accounting Standards", if they have not set up the subject, can fill out with the "operating income" instead.

Cost of Principal Business is to be filled out according to the term-end debit balance (before carrying over) of the accounting "the main business costs" subject. The enterprises which implement the 2006 "Enterprise Accounting Standards" or 2011 "Small Enterprise Accounting Standards", if they have not set up the subject, can fill out with the "operating costs" instead.

Tax and Extra Charges from Principal Business are to be filled out according to the term-end debit balance (before carrying over) of the accounting "the main business tax and surcharges" subjects. The enterprises which implement the 2006 "Enterprise Accounting Standards" or 2011 "Small Enterprise Accounting Standards", if they have not set up the subject, can fill out with the "business tax and surcharges" instead.

Total profit refers to the operating results of an enterprise in a certain accounting period, and is the surplus of the income of various kinds after the deduction of the cost of various kinds in the process of production and operation and reflects the total profit and loss which the enterprise realizes in the reporting period. Total profit is to be filled according to the current amount of the "total profit" item in the accounting "profit sheet". The total profit of an enterprise which carries out "The Accounting Standards for Enterprises" (2006) or "The Accounting Standards for Small Businesses" (2011) is the amount of operating profit plus non-operating income after the deduction of non-operating expenses; the total profit of an enterprise which carries out other enterprises accounting systems is the amount of operating profit plus return on investment, government subsidies and non-operating income after the deduction of non-operating expenses.

Value-added Tax Payable in the Current Year refers to taxes which an enterprise shall pay during the reporting period in accordance with the provisions of the tax law, and targeted on the appreciation value realized by the sale of goods or the provision of processing, repairs and replacement services, and imported goods.

Average Annual Number of Employed Persons Employed persons refer to all those who are employed in enterprises and receive remunerations there from, including currently working employees, retirees who are re-employed, teachers of local-run schools, as well as foreigners, staff from Hong Kong, Macao and Taiwan, part-time employees and persons with second job who are employed by the enterprise, and employees of other units temporarily working in the enterprises, but excluding former employees who left the enterprise with their employment records still being kept by the enterprises.

Average number of employed persons refers to the number of employee everyday during the reference period, calculated with the following formula:

$$\text{Monthly average number} = \frac{\text{sum of actual employees everyday in reference month}}{\text{number of calendar dates in reference month}}$$

$$\text{Quarterly average number} = \frac{\text{sum of monthly average number in reference quarter}}{3}$$

$$\text{Annual average number} = \frac{\text{sum of monthly average number in reference year}}{12}$$

Ratio of Profits, Taxes and Interests to Average Assets reflects the profit-making capability of all assets of the enterprise and is a key indicator manifesting the performance and management and evaluating the profit-making potential of the enterprise. It is calculated as follows:

$$\text{Ratio of Profits, Taxes and Interests to Average Assets (\%)} = \frac{\text{total profits} + \text{total taxes} + \text{interest payment}}{\text{average assets}} \times 100\%$$

In the above formula, total taxes is the sum of tax and extra charges on the sales of products and value-added tax payable; and average assets is the arithmetic mean of the sum of beginning assets and ending assets.

Ratio of Debts to Assets reflects both the operation risk and the capability of the enterprise in making use of the capital from the creditors. It is calculated as follows:

$$\text{Ratio of Debts to Assets (\%)} = \frac{\text{total debts}}{\text{total assets}} \times 100\%$$

Both assets and debts are figures at the end of the reference period.

Turnover of Working Capital refers to the number of times of turnover of working capital in a given period of time, which reflects the speed of the turnover of working capital of industrial enterprises, and is calculated as follows:

$$\text{Turnover of Working Capital} = \frac{\text{sales revenue of products}}{\text{average balance of total working capital}}$$

In the above formula, average balance of total working capital refers to the arithmetic mean of the sum of working capital at the beginning and at the end of the reference period.

Ratio of Profits to Total Industrial Costs refers to the ratio of profits realized in a given period to the total costs in the same period, which reflects the economic efficiency of input cost and is calculated as follows:

$$\text{Ratio of Profits to Total Industrial Cost (\%)} = \frac{\text{total profits}}{\text{total costs}} \times 100\%$$

Total costs in the above formula are the sum of cost of products sold, marketing cost, management cost and financial cost.

Sales Ratio of Products is an indicator reflecting the actual sale of industrial products, analyzing the production-selling and supply-demand relations. It is calculated as:

$$\text{Sales Ratio of Products (\%)} = \frac{\text{value of industrial sales}}{\text{gross industrial output value (current prices)}} \times 100\%$$

Asset Value Increment Rate The index reflects the status of changes of the net assets of an enterprise, and is the concentrated reflection of the enterprise's development ability. The calculation formula is:

$$\text{Asset Value Increment Rate} = \frac{\text{The owner's equity at the end of the reporting period}}{\text{The owner's equity at the end of the same period last year}} \times 100\%$$

An owner's equity is equal to the total assets minus total liabilities.

Rate of Net Value of Fixed Assets refers to the ratio of the net value of the fixed assets of an enterprise and the value of its fixed assets, and is a measure reflecting the old and new conditions of the fixed assets. The calculation formula is:

$$\text{Rate of Net Value of Fixed Assets} = \frac{\text{The net value of the fixed assets}}{\text{The value of the fixed assets}} \times 100\%$$

五、建 筑 业

CHAPTER 5
CONSTRUCTION

5 建 筑 业
CONSTRUCTION

主 要 统 计 指 标
MAJOR STATISTICAL INDICATORS

2016年末建筑企业数	Number of Construction Enterprise	1 395	个	unit
2016年建筑业总产值	Gross Output Value of Construction	1 855.90	亿元	100 million yuan
比上年增长	Increase Over Last Year	-5.1	%	
2016年竣工产值	Output Value of Buildings Completed	1 702.03	亿元	100 million yuan
比上年增长	Increase Over Last Year	3.6	%	
2016年房屋建筑施工面积	Floor Space of Buildings Under Construction	9 681.78	万平方米	10 000 sq.m.
比上年增长	Increase Over Last Year	-11.0	%	
2016年房屋建筑竣工面积	Floor Space of Buildings Completed	3 569.78	万平方米	10 000 sq.m.
比上年增长	Increase Over Last Year	-11.1	%	
2016年建筑业全员劳动生产率	Overall Labor Productivity of Construction	32.29	万元/人	10 000 yuan/person
比上年增长	Increase Over Last Year	-1.1	%	

表5-1 分地区、分行业建筑业生产情况 (2016年)

指标		Item		全市 Whole Municipality	市区 Urban Area
企业数	(个)	Number of Enterprises	(unit)	1 395	855
签订的合同额	(万元)	Contractual Value	(10 000 yuan)	30 015 335	21 038 040
建筑业总产值		Gross Output Value of Construction		18 559 005	13 043 448
# 装饰装修产值		Decorate and Materials Construction		4 017 586	3 632 701
# 在外省完成的产值		Output Value of Buildings Completed outside of Jiangsu province		5 128 840	4 656 500
# 建筑工程		Construction		17 031 156	12 021 123
安装工程		Installation		1 388 760	907 994
其他产值		Others		139 090	114 331
竣工产值		Output Value of Buildings Completed		17 020 284	11 478 057
房屋建筑施工面积	(万平方米)	Floor Space of Buildings Under Construction	(10 000 sq.m)	9 681.78	5 008.77
# 本年新开工		Beginning Projects in this Year		2 729.66	1 298.64
# 投标承包		Floor Space of Biding System		8 042.91	4 060.52
房屋建筑竣工面积		Floor Space of Buildings Completed		3 569.78	1 962.49
从业人员平均人数	(人)	Average Employed Persons	(person)	574 709	362 838
全员劳动生产率	(万元/人)	Overall Labor Productivity	(10 000 yuan/person)	32.29	35.95

STATISTICS ON CONSTRUCTION BY REGION AND SECTOR (2016)

按地区分 Grouped by Region					按行业分 Grouped by Sector			
# 吴江区 Wujiang District	常熟 Changshu	张家港 Zhangjiagang	昆山 Kunshan	太仓 Taicang	房屋建筑业 Housing Construction	土木工程建筑业 Civil Engineering Construction	建筑安装业 Installation of Lines, Pipelines and Equipment	建筑装饰和其他建筑业 Decoration and Other Construction
145	141	121	193	85	372	361	297	365
1 520 766	1 915 067	2 534 081	3 878 709	649 439	13 251 334	9 668 489	1 827 431	5 268 082
1 090 677	1 349 952	1 287 043	2 417 045	461 519	7 459 960	5 402 155	1 386 110	4 310 780
66 286	174 907	30 274	144 382	35 322	130 272	6 569	19 219	3 861 526
42 873	66 807	110 736	258 892	35 906	552 551	2 176 863	307 333	2 092 093
995 143	1 233 957	1 132 665	2 213 639	429 773	7 387 480	5 043 484	382 117	4 218 075
61 913	114 595	150 608	197 027	18 536	19 353	301 275	993 800	74 331
33 622	1 400	3 770	6 378	13 210	53 128	57 395	10 193	18 374
1 259 762	1 492 092	1 568 236	2 123 728	358 171	7 980 355	4 126 716	1 093 617	3 819 596
956.56	1 236.79	1 430.52	1 655.30	350.40	9 493.46	106.18	76.68	5.46
221.82	456.27	343.65	548.34	82.75	2 675.82	40.53	12.21	1.10
643.69	1 082.47	1 330.94	1 349.51	219.47	7 925.85	87.58	24.30	5.18
450.76	491.93	530.75	505.68	78.93	3 492.77	51.00	20.50	5.51
46 477	46 808	47 817	89 972	27 274	295 236	103 060	48 020	128 393
23.47	28.84	26.92	26.86	16.92	25.27	52.42	28.87	33.57

表5-2

分登记注册类型建筑业生产情况（2016年）

指　　标		Item		总　计 Total	国有企业 State-owned Enterprises
企业数	(个)	Number of Enterprises	(unit)	1 395	6
签订的合同额	(万元)	Contractual Value	(10 000 yuan)	30 015 335	32 643
建筑业总产值		Gross Output Value of Construction		18 559 005	20 692
# 装饰装修产值		Decorate and Materials Construction		4 017 586	–
# 在外省完成的产值		Output Value of Buildings Completed outside of Jiangsu province		5 128 840	–
# 建筑工程		Construction		17 031 156	150
安装工程		Installation		1 388 760	20 542
其他产值		Others		139 090	–
竣工产值		Output Value of Buildings Completed		17 020 284	21 194
房屋建筑施工面积	(万平方米)	Floor Space of Buildings Under Construction	(10 000 sq.m)	9 681.78	–
# 本年新开工		Beginning Projects in this Year		2 729.66	–
# 投标承包		Floor Space of Biding System		8 042.91	–
房屋建筑竣工面积		Floor Space of Buildings Completed		3 569.78	–
从业人员平均人数	(人)	Average Employed Persons	(person)	574 709	796
全员劳动生产率	(万元/人)	Overall Labor Productivity	(10 000 yuan/person)	32.29	25.99

STATISTICS ON CONSTRUCTION BY TYPE OF REGISTRATION (2016)

集体企业 Collective-owned Enterprises	股份合作企业 Share-holding Cooperative Enterprises	有限责任公司 Limited Liability Corporations	股份有限公司 Share-holding Corporations Ltd.	私营企业 Private Enterprises	港澳台商投资企业 Enterprises With Investment From HongKong, Macao and Taiwan	外商投资企业 Enterprises with Foreign Investment
5	3	164	42	1 149	13	13
120 554	20 512	13 115 948	3 562 417	12 589 298	173 025	400 938
113 967	19 145	6 618 905	2 822 318	8 639 949	141 837	182 193
86 556	–	253 062	2 374 365	1 303 394	210	–
33 218	813	2 190 872	1 719 523	1 043 825	10 684	129 905
109 725	3 216	6 201 069	2 754 758	7 830 320	111 385	20 533
–	14 565	408 085	67 412	686 217	30 279	161 660
4 243	1 364	9 750	148	123 413	173	–
116 275	18 455	5 664 723	2 734 071	8 234 844	123 968	106 754
26.11	3.20	3 453.02	258.37	5 867.83	54.81	18.44
8.84	2.40	806.66	65.62	1 829.64	9.25	7.25
26.11	1.52	3 251.54	234.21	4 478.60	50.46	0.47
11.51	1.52	1 149.16	171.47	2 215.17	12.00	8.94
3 146	200	141 455	63 797	354 966	3 956	6 393
36.23	95.73	46.79	44.24	24.34	35.85	28.50

表5-3

分地区、分行业建筑业财务状况 (2016年)

单位：万元

指 标	Item	全 市 Whole Municipality	按… 市 区 Urban Area	#吴江区 WujiangDistrict
年末资产负债	**Asset and Liabilities at Year-end**			
流动资产	Circulating Assets	20 872 206	12 794 082	1 321 253
# 存 货	Stocks	5 043 454	2 478 621	365 323
固定资产小计	Fixed Assets	1 180 106	750 776	80 381
固定资产原价	Original Value of Fixed Assets	1 977 129	1 227 723	138 242
累计折旧	Accumulative Total Depreciation	925 642	555 577	66 391
# 本年折旧	Depreciation Within the Year	126 721	78 298	7 769
在建工程	Project Under Construction	83 105	53 258	4 539
资产总计	Total Assets	23 569 468	14 642 388	1 463 369
流动负债	Liquid Liabilities	15 405 903	9 483 301	851 554
非流动负债合计	Total Non Liquid Liabilities	311 484	256 792	37 587
负债合计	Total Liabilities	15 813 988	9 770 310	894 713
所有者权益	Creditors' Equity	7 751 211	4 867 809	568 656
# 实收资本	Actual Capital Hold	3 972 465	2 419 655	330 350
国家资本	State Capital	148 823	105 627	758
集体资本	Collective Capital	92 710	32 828	5 080
法人资本	Corporation Capital	1 103 925	750 518	71 454
个人资本	Individual Capital	2 491 982	1 412 307	242 801
港、澳、台资本	Capital from HongKong, Macao and Taiwan	32 356	29 276	10 258
外商资本	Foreign Capital	102 669	89 098	–
损益及分配	**Expenditure, Income and Distribution**			
主营业务收入	Main Business Income	20 307 791	13 491 861	1 218 221
主营业务成本	Main Business Cost	18 088 039	12 008 254	1 071 435
主营业务税金及附加	Main Business Taxes and Surcharges	362 744	211 660	26 648
其他业务利润	Profits of Other Business	37 008	21 569	421
管理费用	Management Fee	810 816	556 707	47 339
财务费用	Financial Expenses	105 809	52 539	8 515
营业利润	Operating Profit	844 993	557 963	51 980
利润总额	Total Profit	862 217	574 505	52 139
应交所得税	Income Tax Payable	186 233	117 159	13 905
工资、福利费	**Wages and Welfare Expenses**			
应付职工薪酬(本年贷方累计发生额)	Employee Compensation Payable (the Cumulative Amount of Credits)	2 784 766	1 811 297	195 083

FINANCIAL CONDITIONS OF CONSTRUCTION BY REGION AND SECTOR (2016)

(10 000 yuan)

地区分 Grouped by Region				按行业分 Grouped by Sector			
常熟 Changshu	张家港 Zhangjiagang	昆山 Kunshan	太仓 Taicang	房屋建筑业 Housing Construction	土木工程建筑业 Civil Engineering Construction	建筑安装业 Installation of Lines, Pipelines and Equipment	建筑装饰和其他建筑业 Decoration and Other Construction
2 024 244	2 028 377	3 396 168	629 336	8 368 231	6 139 236	1 927 515	4 437 224
639 684	587 852	1 147 941	189 357	2 501 002	1 515 819	616 305	410 328
82 971	107 404	176 066	62 890	372 759	431 060	122 571	253 717
158 690	205 102	295 925	89 689	604 156	812 585	183 177	377 211
83 822	103 943	140 314	41 987	264 972	426 800	90 383	143 487
8 648	13 438	19 299	7 038	38 350	53 461	12 877	22 032
5 263	-4 296	14 733	14 146	17 586	25 393	24 742	15 384
2 173 190	2 217 149	3 810 613	726 129	9 193 247	6 947 239	2 182 496	5 246 487
1 449 358	1 565 291	2 512 534	395 420	6 396 209	4 546 798	1 341 972	3 120 924
26 268	2 956	25 137	332	92 883	141 919	3 937	72 745
1 535 561	1 573 836	2 537 691	396 591	6 534 875	4 702 181	1 352 696	3 224 237
637 629	643 312	1 272 923	329 538	2 658 372	2 245 058	825 531	2 022 250
312 849	350 140	716 621	173 200	1 604 477	1 214 494	435 441	718 054
7 003	12 744	23 435	15	15 504	112 624	14 004	6 692
31 226	11 600	11 877	5 179	26 846	41 733	11 356	12 775
90 118	98 447	121 356	43 486	409 443	372 166	135 949	186 367
184 502	227 350	545 530	122 292	1 143 879	672 281	227 107	448 716
–	–	3 080	–	4 138	7 720	20 499	–
–	–	11 343	2 228	4 668	7 970	26 527	63 504
1 669 772	1 617 716	2 963 995	564 446	8 379 308	6 021 882	1 544 526	4 362 075
1 483 854	1 440 612	2 670 476	484 843	7 680 508	5 403 708	1 288 710	3 715 113
41 184	31 667	63 824	14 409	180 923	105 493	26 785	49 542
1 070	3 808	9 220	1 342	12 774	9 851	8 194	6 189
58 185	68 021	97 080	30 823	252 703	246 430	132 586	179 098
13 388	18 927	15 980	4 974	63 042	18 502	3 943	20 322
73 103	63 356	128 809	21 762	201 943	242 119	87 011	313 920
73 774	64 965	127 758	21 215	208 700	244 942	90 017	318 559
17 434	17 363	29 360	4 918	52 931	55 892	23 850	53 560
250 320	219 005	395 244	108 900	1 409 746	481 616	163 839	729 565

表5-4

分登记注册类型建筑业财务状况（2016年）

单位：万元

指　　标	Item	总　计 Total	国有企业 State-owned Enterprises
年末资产负债	**Asset and Liabilities at Year-end**		
流动资产	Circulating Assets	20 872 206	31 848
# 存　货	Stocks	5 043 454	8 294
固定资产小计	Fixed Assets	1 180 106	17 863
固定资产原价	Original Value of Fixed Assets	1 977 129	5 830
累计折旧	Accumulative Total Depreciation	925 642	2 138
# 本年折旧	Depreciation Within the Year	126 721	236
在建工程	Project Under Construction	83 105	13 970
资产总计	Total Assets	23 569 468	54 282
流动负债	Liquid Liabilities	15 405 903	30 261
非流动负债合计	Total Non Liquid Liabilities	311 484	–
负债合计	Total Liabilities	15 813 988	30 261
所有者权益	Creditors' Equity	7 751 211	24 022
# 实收资本	Actual Capital Hold	3 972 465	16 403
国家资本	State Capital	148 823	14 903
集体资本	Collective Capital	92 710	–
法人资本	Corporation Capital	1 103 925	1 500
个人资本	Individual Capital	2 491 982	–
港、澳、台资本	Capital from HongKong, Macao and Taiwan	32 356	–
外商资本	Foreign Capital	102 669	–
损益及分配	**Expenditure, Income and Distribution**		
主营业务收入	Main Business Income	20 307 791	27 986
主营业务成本	Main Business Cost	18 088 039	22 420
主营业务税金及附加	Main Business Taxes and Surcharges	362 744	493
其他业务利润	Profits of Other Business	37 008	921
管理费用	Management Fee	810 816	2 623
财务费用	Financial Expenses	105 809	-45
营业利润	Operating Profit	844 993	3 415
利润总额	Total Profit	862 217	3 530
应交所得税	Income Tax Payable	186 233	758
工资、福利费	**Wages and Welfare Expenses**		
应付职工薪酬(本年贷方累计发生额)	Employee Compensation Payable (the Cumulative Amount of Credits)	2 784 766	3 552

FINANCIAL CONDITIONS OF CONSTRUCTION BY TYPE OF REGISTRATION (2016)

(10 000 yuan)

集体企业 Collective-owned Enterprises	股份合作制企业 Share-holding Cooperative Enterprises	有限责任公司 Limited Liability Corporations	股份有限公司 Share-holding Corporations Ltd.	私营企业 Private Enterprises	港澳台商投资企业 Enterprises With Investment From HongKong, Macao and Taiwan	外商投资企业 Enterprises with Foreign Investment
90 159	7 447	6 413 329	3 379 698	10 368 029	327 783	253 914
18 760	1 268	1 889 433	296 224	2 711 410	53 960	64 106
2 123	251	305 648	174 736	640 172	26 087	13 226
12 817	943	598 715	234 191	1 065 638	40 174	18 821
10 694	691	309 776	77 214	501 181	15 081	8 867
325	97	37 554	11 825	73 468	2 420	796
–	–	13 092	16 065	36 861	994	2 123
92 591	7 698	7 058 212	4 065 768	11 641 308	368 627	280 982
53 229	3 849	5 365 924	2 489 889	7 096 252	237 668	128 832
–	–	94 080	106 661	73 038	37 655	50
53 229	3 849	5 460 770	2 598 357	7 263 281	275 360	128 882
39 362	3 849	1 597 443	1 467 411	4 373 758	93 266	152 100
19 338	2 000	793 717	421 165	2 621 542	47 917	50 384
11 504	4	117 898	–	4 515	–	–
3 107	200	48 420	5 615	35 368	–	–
4 402	–	314 394	106 768	676 726	–	134
325	1 797	313 004	245 277	1 903 933	20 273	7 374
–	–	–	–	1 000	19 836	11 520
–	–	–	63 504	–	7 808	31 357
112 058	19 168	6 954 905	2 960 806	9 850 147	152 815	229 906
77 750	17 182	6 375 315	2 509 609	8 769 876	132 811	183 075
833	344	111 169	30 059	215 580	2 601	1 664
1 582	3	12 436	1 702	19 994	209	163
2 668	938	264 705	101 449	405 400	10 131	22 903
1 926	1	10 888	14 435	76 308	2 597	-300
5 985	702	227 541	238 962	343 033	3 312	22 044
5 962	701	234 247	242 052	347 347	3 840	24 539
1 512	350	55 037	38 394	82 306	1 259	6 616
19 062	785	733 885	477 871	1 509 592	15 818	24 202

表5-5

劳务分包建筑企业生产经营情况 (2016年)
BUSINESS STATUS OF SUBCONTRACTING CONSTRUCTION ENTERPRISES (2016)

单位：万元 (10 000 yuan)

类　别	Type	企业数(个) Number of Enterprises (unit)	建筑业总产值 Gross Output Value of Construction	营业收入合计 Total Business Revenue	#主营业务收入 Major Business Revenue	资产合计 Total Assets	负债合计 Total Liabilities
全　市	**Whole Municipality**	**81**	**374 205**	**360 897**	**360 156**	**145 174**	**117 767**
按地区分	**Grouped by Region**						
市　区	Urban Area	22	190 345	192 761	192 070	56 914	47 170
# 吴江区	Wujiang District	1	80	75	75	68	9
常　熟	Changshu	10	6 414	6 158	6 108	10 775	8 033
张家港	Zhangjiagang	41	163 803	155 521	155 521	69 532	56 120
昆　山	Kunshan	5	9 668	2 482	2 482	6 317	5 881
太　仓	Taicang	3	3 975	3 975	3 975	1 636	564
按行业分	**Grouped by Sector**						
房屋建筑业	Housing Construction	25	94 989	93 286	92 545	51 629	41 923
土木工程建筑业	Civil Engineering Construction	2	69 810	65 260	65 260	6 460	5 166
建筑安装业	Construction Installation	5	5 908	3 791	3 791	2 173	1 227
建筑装饰和其他建筑业	Decoration and Other Construction	49	203 498	198 560	198 560	84 912	69 451

表5-5 续表 Continued

单位：万元 (10 000 yuan)

类　别	Type	实收资本 Actual Capital Hold	利润总额 Total Profits	税金及附加 Taxes and Extra Charges Project Settlement Accounts	从业人员(人) Number of Employed Persons (person)	计算劳动生产率人数(人) Number of Persons Overall Labor Productivity (person)	应付职工薪酬 Deal with the employee payment
全　市	**Whole Municipality**	**16 079**	**4 353**	**9 894**	**48 063**	**44 669**	**230 250**
按地区分	**Grouped by Region**						
市　区	Urban Area	5 042	2 858	5 575	18 337	14 948	95 840
# 吴江区	Wujiang District	50	5	3	20	19	64
常　熟	Changshu	1 968	15	153	629	329	1 389
张家港	Zhangjiagang	8 437	1 232	3 945	26 075	26 739	121 346
昆　山	Kunshan	430	98	67	2 850	2 495	11 101
太　仓	Taicang	202	150	153	172	158	575
按行业分	**Grouped by Sector**						
房屋建筑业	Housing Construction	6 206	1 073	2 225	11 377	12 204	53 261
土木工程建筑业	Civil Engineering Construction	200	347	1 927	12 360	7 669	69 810
建筑安装业	Construction Installation	580	24	99	913	793	3 576
建筑装饰和其他建筑业	Decoration and Other Construction	9 093	2 909	5 643	23 413	24 003	103 603

表5-6

全市建筑业总产值三十强企业（2016年）
TOP 30 ENTERPRISES OF THE GROSS OUTPUT VALUE OF CONSTRUCTION (2016)

序 号 No.	企业名称 Name of Enterprises	所在地区 Location	资质等级 Qualification Grade
1	苏州金螳螂建筑装饰股份有限公司	工业园区	专业承包一级
2	中亿丰建设集团股份有限公司	相城区	总承包特级
3	中铁四局集团第二工程有限公司	相城区	总承包一级
4	中交一公局第二工程有限公司	高新区、虎丘区	总承包一级
5	中铁二十局集团第一工程有限公司	高新区、虎丘区	总承包一级
6	苏州第一建筑集团有限公司	姑苏区	总承包特级
7	中铁十局集团第五工程有限公司	高新区、虎丘区	总承包一级
8	江苏金土木建设集团有限公司	常熟市	总承包一级
9	苏州美瑞德建筑装饰有限公司	姑苏区	专业承包一级
10	苏州柯利达装饰股份有限公司	高新区、虎丘区	专业承包一级
11	振华集团（昆山）建设工程有限公司	昆山市	总承包一级
12	苏州嘉盛建设工程有限公司	吴中区	总承包特级
13	苏州狮山建筑安装工程有限公司	相城区	总承包一级
14	苏州交通工程集团有限公司	相城区	总承包一级
15	吴江市建设工程（集团）有限公司	吴江区	总承包一级
16	天合建设集团有限公司	昆山市	总承包一级
17	江苏兴港建设集团有限公司	张家港市	总承包一级
18	苏州苏明装饰股份有限公司	相城区	专业承包一级
19	江苏城南建设集团有限公司	昆山市	总承包一级
20	江苏金厦建设集团有限公司	张家港市	总承包一级
21	昆山市金都建设有限公司	昆山市	总承包一级
22	苏州工业设备安装集团有限公司	姑苏区	总承包一级
23	苏州第五建筑集团有限公司	姑苏区	总承包一级
24	苏州建鑫建设集团有限公司	高新区、虎丘区	总承包一级
25	江苏永联精筑建设集团有限公司	张家港市	总承包一级
26	江苏南方雄狮建设工程有限公司	吴中区	专业承包二级
27	亚翔系统集成科技（苏州）股份有限公司	工业园区	专业承包一级
28	苏州建设（集团）有限责任公司	姑苏区	总承包一级
29	江苏苏鑫装饰(集团)公司	相城区	专业承包一级
30	苏州电力建设工程有限公司	姑苏区	总承包二级

主要统计指标解释

建筑业统计单位 指从事房屋、构筑物建造和设备安装活动的法人企业。建筑业法人企业应具有建筑业资质并能够独立核算，同时其应具备以下条件：①依法成立，有自己的名称、组织机构和场所，能够承担民事责任；②独立拥有和使用资产，承担负债，有权与其他单位签订合同；③独立核算盈亏，能够编制资产负债表。

建筑业总产值 是以货币形式表现的建筑业企业在一定时期内生产的建筑业产品和提供的服务的总和。建筑业总产值包括：

(1) 建筑工程产值：指列入建筑工程预算内的各种工程价值。

(2) 安装工程产值：指设备安装工程价值，不包括被安装设备本身的价值。

(3) 其他产值：建筑业总产值中除建筑工程、安装工程以外的产值。包括房屋构筑物修理产值、非标准设备制造产值、总包企业向分包企业收取的管理费以及不能明确划分的施工活动所完成的产值。

a.房屋构筑物修理产值：指房屋和构筑物修理所完成的产值，但不包括被修理房屋、构筑物本身价值和生产设备的修理产值。

b.非标准设备制造产值：指加工制造没有定型的非标准生产设备的加工费和原材料价值(如化工厂、炼油厂用的各种罐、槽，矿井生产统一使用的各种漏斗、三角槽、阀门等)以及附属加工厂为本企业承建工程制作的非标准设备的价值。

房屋建筑施工面积 指在报告期内施过工的全部房屋建筑面积，包括本期新开工的房屋面积、上期施工跨入本期继续施工的房屋面积、上期停缓建在本期恢复施工的房屋面积、本期竣工的房屋面积及本期施工后又停缓建的房屋面积。

房屋建筑竣工面积 指在报告期内房屋建筑按照设计要求全部完工，达到了使用条件，经验收鉴定合格，正式移交使用单位的房屋建筑面积。

主营业务收入 指企业(或单位)按承包工程实现的工程价款结算收入，以及向发包单位收取的除工程价款以外的按规定列作营业收入的各种款项，如临时设施费、劳动保险费、施工机械调迁费等以及向发包单位收取的各种索赔款。

EXPLANATORY NOTES ON MAIN STATISTICAL INDICATORS

Statistical Unit in the Construction Industry refers to a corporate enterprise engaged in the construction of buildings and structures and in the installation of equipment. A corporate construction enterprise should have qualification certificates with independent accounting system, and should meet the following 3 requirements: a) being set up in line with relevant legal basis, having its full name, organization and location, and capable of taking civil liabilities; b) independently possessing and using its assets and assuming its liabilities, and entitled to sign contracts with other institutions; and c) making independent accounts of its profits and losses, and capable of compiling its own balance sheet.

Gross Output Value of Construction refers to total of construction products and services, expressed in money terms, produced or rendered by construction and installation enterprises during a given period of time. It includes:

(1) Output value of construction projects: the value of projects covered by the project budgets;

(2) Output value of installation projects: the value of the installation of equipment, (excluding the value of the equipment to be installed);

(3) Other output values: the output value of construction industry apart from that of construction projects and installation projects. It includes: output value of repair of buildings and structures; output value of non-standard equipment manufacturing; overhead expenses received by contracted enterprises from the sub-contracted enterprises and the completed output value of construction activities for which there is no clear definition.

a. Output value of repair of buildings and structures: the value created through the repairs of buildings or structures. It does not include the value of buildings or structures being repaired and the value of the repair of production equipment;

b. Output value of manufactured non-standard equipment: the value of non-standard production equipment, including raw materials and manufacturing cost, made for the construction project (i.e., chemical plant; kettles or tanks used by refineries; various fillers, triangle tanks, valves used by mines). It also includes the output value of equipment manufactured by subsidiary workshops.

Floor Space of Buildings Under Construction refers to floor space of buildings under construction during the reference period, including the floor space of buildings for which construction has newly started; buildings for which construction has started earlier and is continuing during the reference period; and buildings for which construction has been suspended earlier but has restarted during the reference period; buildings completed during the reference period; and buildings under construction but construction has subsequently been during the reference period.

Floor Space of Buildings Completed refers to the floor space of buildings that are completed in the reference period in accordance with the requirements of the design, up to the standard for being put into use, and having been checked and accepted by departments concerned as qualified ones.

Main Business Income refers to the income received by the construction enterprise from the contracted project through settlement procedures, and other charges to the contractor as operational costs in addition to the value of the project, such as temporary facility fee, labour insurance premium , moving cost of construction equipment, as well as various types of claims to the contractor.

六、运输 邮电业

CHAPTER 6
TRANSPORTATION，POST AND TELECOMMUNICATION

6 运输 邮电业 TRANSPORTATION, POST AND TELECOMMUNICATION

主要统计指标 MAJOR STATISTICAL INDICATORS

2016年全社会公路水运客运量	Total Passenger Traffic of Highways and Waterways	32 130	万人次	10 000 person-times
比上年增长	Increase Over Last Year	-7.3	%	
2016年全社会公路水运货运量	Total Freight Traffic of Highways and Waterways	13 508	万吨	10 000 tons
比上年增长	Increase Over Last Year	3.9	%	
2016年苏州港货物吞吐量	Cargo Handled at Suzhou Ports	57 937	万吨	10 000 tons
比上年增长	Increase Over Last Year	7.3	%	
2016年苏州港集装箱吞吐量	Volume of Container Handled at Suzhou Ports	547.92	万标箱	10 000 teu
比上年增长	Increase Over Last Year	7.4	%	
2016年末私家车拥有量	Number of Private Motor Vehicles	268.40	万辆	10 000 coach
比上年增长	Increase Over Last Year	17.1	%	
2016年邮电业务总收入	Total Revenue of Postal and Telecommunication Services	326.78	亿元	100 million yuan
比上年增长	Increase Over Last Year	11.2	%	

表6-1

部分年份全社会交通运输量
TOTAL TRAFFIC OF PARTIAL YEARS

项　　目	Item	2012年	2013年	2014年	2015年	2016年
铁　路	**Railway**					
旅客发送量 (万人次)	Number of Passengers Dispatched (10 000 person-times)	2 627.98	3 035.07	3 496.38	3 742.43	4 059.05
市　区	Urban Area	1 868.00	2 170.39	2 547.67	2 751.06	2 992.96
昆　山	Kunshan	759.98	864.68	948.72	991.37	1 066.09
货物发送量 (万吨)	Volume of Freight Dispatched (10 000 tons)	93.78	83.53	67.17	66.78	82.32
市　区	Urban Area	75.65	69.99	54.47	58.17	72.30
昆　山	Kunshan	18.13	13.53	12.70	8.61	10.02
货物到达量	Volume of Freight Arrived	311.43	195.79	154.67	111.62	103.65
市　区	Urban Area	272.94	163.29	125.51	88.40	85.35
昆　山	Kunshan	38.49	32.50	29.16	23.22	18.30
公　路	**Highways**					
客运量 (万人次)	Passenger Traffic (10 000 person-times)	68 895	39 050	39 432	34 110	31 589
货运量 (万吨)	Freight Traffic (10 000 tons)	16 441	10 799	11 855	11 814	12 287
旅客周转量 (万人公里)	Passenger-kilometers (10 000 person-km)	3 076 263	1 368 347	1 374 907	1 318 903	1 217 335
货物周转量 (万吨公里)	Freight Ton-kilometers (10 000 ton-km)	1 357 255	1 435 496	1 579 367	1 665 643	1 732 654
水　运	**Waterways**					
客运量 (万人次)	Passenger Traffic (10 000 person-times)	103	534	526	535	541
货运量 (万吨)	Freight Traffic (10 000 tons)	884	987	1 098	1 191	1 221
旅客周转量 (万人公里)	Passenger-kilometers (10 000 person-km)	1 128	4 878	4 847	4 925	4 974
货物周转量 (万吨公里)	Freight Ton-kilometers (10 000 ton-km)	347 829	381 818	425 701	469 519	512 808
地方港口吞吐量 (万吨)	Cargo Handled at Local Ports (10 000 tons)	48 302	50 939	55 033	61 092	65 032
# 苏州港港口吞吐量	Cargo Handled at Suzhou Port	42 801	45 435	47 792	53 990	57 937

注：1、公路客运量自2013年起不包括公交车和出租车的运输量；　2、公路货运量自2013年起不包含农用车和拖拉机的运输量。
Note:1. The highway passenger transport volume in 2013 did not include that of buses and taxis.
2. The highway freight transport volume in 2013 did not include that of agricultural vehicles and tractors.

表6-2

部分年份公路和航道通航里程
LENGTH OF HIGHWAYS AND NAVIGABLE INLAND WATERWAYS OF PARTIAL YEARS

项 目	Item	2012年	2013年	2014年	2015年	2016年
一、公路总里程 (公里)	**Total Length of Highways (km)**	**13 089.5**	**13 155.2**	**13 212.1**	**13 238.8**	**13 207.5**
1. 按技术等级分	Rated by Technical Standards					
高 速	Express-way	535.1	550.2	550.2	550.2	598.3
一 级	A Qualification	1 652.8	1 672.3	1 706.7	1 704.3	1 748.8
二 级	B Qualification	3 900.6	4 044.3	4 114.4	4 149.3	4 099.7
三 级	C Qualification	2 891.1	2 373.5	2 407.4	2 405.4	2 366.9
四 级	D Qualification	4 110.0	4 514.7	4 433.4	4 429.6	4 393.8
2.按行政等级分	Grouped by Grade of Administration					
国 道	State Highway	496.3	496.0	496.0	496.0	824.6
省 道	Provincial Highway	794.1	809.2	928.6	928.6	639.8
县 道	County Highway	1 751.6	1761.9	1 634.5	1 629.6	1 650.7
乡 道	Rural Highway	4 060.0	4 069.7	4 083.8	4 091.6	4 055.4
村 道	Village Highway	5 947.8	5 978.7	6 029.5	6 053.3	5 997.4
专用公路	Specialized Highway	39.7	39.7	39.7	39.7	39.7
3. 按路面标准分	Grouped by Standard of Road Surface					
高 级	High	12 879.8	13 001.1	13 085.3	13 115.4	13 181.5
中级、低级	Medium and Low	209.7	154.1	126.8	123.4	25.9
二、公路桥梁 (座)	**Highway Bridges (unit)**	**9 690**	**9 720**	**9 704**	**9 721**	**9 754**
(米)	**(m)**	**490 011**	**503 054**	**500 193**	**493 695**	**550 356**
三、内河航道通航里程 (公里)	**Length of Navigable Inland Waterways (km)**	**2 760.0**	**2 760.0**	**2 787.0**	**2 786.0**	**2 786.0**
# 水深 1 米以上里程	Depths of One Meter and Over	2 611.9	2 611.9	2 638.9	2 638.4	2 638.4
四、通航河流上建筑物 (座)	**Construction in Navigable Waterways (unit)**	**108**	**110**	**110**	**110**	**111**
1.永久性闸坝	Permanent Gate and Dam	47	49	49	49	49
2.船 闸	Lock Gate	7	7	7	7	8
3.套 闸	Gate Set	54	54	54	54	54
五、内河航道上设立的航标	**Navigation Mark in Inland Waterways**	**158**	**171**	**171**	**159**	**159**
# 发光的	Luminary	139	153	158	159	159

表6-3

部分年份全社会船舶数
TOTAL NUMBER OF TRANSPORT VESSELS OF PARTIAL YEARS

指　标		Item		2012年	2013年	2014年	2015年	2016年
客　船	(艘)	**Passenger Ship**	(unit)	**119**	**132**	**122**	**147**	**147**
	(客位)		(seat)	4 937	5 368	5 292	10 939	11 458
	(千瓦)		(kw)	10 676	12 231	12 451	21 919	22 894
货　船	(艘)	**Cargo Ship**	(unit)	**215**	**242**	**208**	**187**	**167**
	(吨位)		(ton)	106 564	114 229	116 486	130 030	135 664
	(千瓦)		(kw)	60 142	65 614	65 847	63 885	63 341
拖　船	(艘)	**Tug Boat**	(unit)	**5**	**7**	**5**	**2**	**6**
	(千瓦)		(kw)	967	1 455	1 064	440	11 474
驳　船	(艘)	**Barges**	(unit)	**42**	**42**	**41**	**27**	**36**
	(吨位)		(ton)	4 748	4 748	6 560	4 960	13 040

注：原既可装货也可以载客的渡船作为货船统计，从2015年起纳入客船统计。
Note: The ferry which can carry both goods and passengers was as the cargo ship statistics, from 2015 onwards, the ferry is as the passenger ship statistics.

表6-4

分地区机动车拥有量(2016年末)
CIVIL MOTOR VEHICLES BY REGION (END OF 2016)

单位：辆 (coach)

地　区　Region	机动车总计 Total Motor Vehicles	# 汽 车 Vehicles	# 私家客车 Personal Passenger Vehicles	# 私家货车 Personal Freight Trucks	年末汽车驾驶员(人) The Number of Car Drivers (person)	年内汽车上牌数 The number of Auto Registration in 2016	年内汽车驾驶员领证(人) Driver's license number in 2016 (persons)
全　市 Whole Municipality	**3 277 867**	**3 132 583**	**2 659 977**	**24 071**	**3 469 682**	**494 050**	**286 977**
市　区　Urban Area	1 760 579	1 709 359	1 453 405	10 162	1 812 688	274 984	149 742
#吴江区 Wujiang District	338 791	307 783	270 345	5 411	370 995	48 250	32 237
常　熟　Changshu	421 622	391 406	341 338	3 840	524 921	52 492	35 505
张家港　Zhangjiagang	359 096	336 502	286 575	5 449	392 896	44 725	26 784
昆　山　Kunshan	513 619	498 754	414 226	1 753	481 310	93 480	50 590
太　仓　Taicang	222 951	196 562	164 433	2 867	257 867	28 369	24 356

表6-5

历年全社会客运情况
TOTAL PASSENGER TRAFFIC OVER THE YEARS

年份 Year	客运量(万人次) Passenger Traffic (10 000 person-times)	公路 Highways	水运 Waterways	旅客周转量(万人公里) Passenger-kilometers (10 000 person-km)	公路 Highways	水运 Waterways	铁路旅客发送量(万人次) Number of Passengers Dispatched on Railway (10 000 person-times)
1949	56	45	11	1 486	1 299	187	
1952	383	167	216	8 651	3 232	5 419	
1957	2 270	1 887	383	26 754	18 024	8 730	
1962	1 486	845	641	39 595	23 076	16 519	366.45
1965	1 101	676	425	24 381	15 425	8 956	208.86
1970	1 724	1 054	670	33 280	21 241	12 039	226.06
1975	2 919	2 091	828	55 339	39 726	15 613	316.63
1978	3 296	2 477	819	64 766	48 775	15 991	356.44
1980	4 813	4 034	779	96 041	74 404	21 637	520.21
1985	6 757	6 340	417	188 795	165 851	22 944	745.40
1990	6 764	6 516	247	232 799	218 521	14 278	755.78
1995	18 945	18 840	104	628 147	620 152	7 995	917.64
1996	11 272	11 234	39	561 389	556 970	4 419	830.68
1997	15 672	15 639	32	581 201	577 878	3 323	800.61
1998	14 291	14 255	36	660 212	656 940	3 272	792.30
1999	16 845	16 752	93	820 104	816 339	3 765	883.25
2000	18 559	18 447	112	1 013 554	1 009 983	3 571	940.23
2001	19 508	19 394	114	1 064 044	1 060 708	3 336	1 043.47
2002	21 031	20 935	96	1 199 190	1 196 358	2 832	1 161.83
2003	22 921	22 835	86	1 518 126	1 515 701	2 425	1 211.27
2004	25 292	25 265	27	1 792 342	1 791 228	1 114	1 481.92
2005	30 707	30 703	4	1 919 138	1 918 713	425	1 663.78
2006	35 186	35 182	4	2 149 435	2 149 035	400	1 707.07
2007	40 163	40 163	-	2 498 592	2 498 592	-	1 625.41
2008	45 386	45 386	-	2 855 005	2 855 005	-	1 893.33
2009	39 338	39 263	75	1 679 103	1 678 269	834	1 939.87
2010	56 475	56 392	83	2 412 841	2 411 917	924	2 044.68
2011	63 793	63 699	94	2 746 339	2 745 297	1 042	2 274.68
2012	68 998	68 895	103	3 077 391	3 076 263	1 128	2 627.98
2013老口径	71 798	71 696	102	3 212 308	3 211 241	1 067	3 035.07
2013新口径	39 584	39 050	534	1 373 225	1 368 347	4 878	
2014	39 958	39 432	526	1 379 754	1 374 907	4 847	3 496.38
2015	34 645	34 110	535	1 323 828	1 318 903	4 925	3 742.43
2016	32 130	31 589	541	1 222 309	1 217 335	4 974	4 059.05

注：新口径公路客运量不包括公交车和出租车的运输量。
Note:The new caliber of passenger traffic of highways didn’t include that of buses and taxis.

表6-6

历年全社会货运情况
TOTAL FREIGHT TRAFFIC OVER THE YEARS

单位：万吨 (10 000 tons)

年份 Year	货运量 Freight Traffic	公路 Highways	水运 Waterways	货物周转量 (万吨公里) Freight Ton-kilometers (10 000 ton-km)	公路 Highways	水运 Waterways	铁路货物发送量 Volume of Freight Dispatched on Railway	铁路货物到达量 Volume of Freight Arrived on Railway
1949	55	1	54	2 419	26	2 393		
1952	209	34	175	8 995	257	8 738		
1957	365	21	344	19 991	287	19 704		
1962	501	78	422	19 753	883	18 870	35.03	141.85
1965	777	108	668	35 314	1 128	34 186	41.61	222.96
1970	926	122	805	56 138	1 432	54 706	52.33	250.44
1975	1 645	226	1 419	92 848	3 392	89 456	79.54	317.52
1978	2 195	329	1 866	115 434	6 086	109 348	87.28	465.79
1980	2 712	399	2 313	138 610	8 663	129 947	92.93	541.90
1985	6 041	871	5 170	258 795	24 060	234 735	124.05	630.52
1990	3 211	746	2 465	208 573	26 187	182 386	116.43	557.97
1995	8 561	4 746	3 815	496 290	190 242	306 048	164.13	740.91
1996	8 296	4 810	3 486	508 238	216 659	291 579	158.88	704.22
1997	7 237	4 373	2 864	449 609	231 801	217 808	157.91	661.83
1998	6 201	3 060	3 142	386 075	151 758	234 317	134.70	608.19
1999	6 870	3 738	3 132	500 869	218 030	282 839	154.98	561.22
2000	7 816	4 567	3 248	458 916	245 987	212 929	159.37	391.51
2001	7 988	4 738	3 250	464 030	254 699	209 331	174.53	564.09
2002	8 350	5 010	3 340	478 850	275 550	203 300	164.44	703.81
2003	7 354	5 389	1 965	454 889	334 060	120 829	165.94	838.26
2004	8 833	6 941	1 892	522 670	397 170	125 500	167.72	800.78
2005	10 393	7 762	2 631	684 229	515 208	169 021	145.92	741.27
2006	11 099	8 891	2 208	746 045	590 016	156 029	147.15	644.36
2007	11 834	9 958	1 876	820 219	656 395	163 824	131.30	632.35
2008	12 631	10 863	1 768	902 918	733 993	168 925	127.61	494.50
2009	11 370	10 820	550	1 032 213	887 006	145 207	118.40	452.66
2010	13 417	12 768	649	1 237 387	1 037 797	199 590	90.94	400.06
2011	15 602	14 798	804	1 498 375	1 200 220	298 155	93.00	406.34
2012	17 325	16 441	884	1 705 084	1 357 255	347 829	93.78	311.43
2013老口径	18 504	17 568	936	1 818 741	1 445 420	373 321	83.53	195.79
2013新口径	11 786	10 799	987	1 817 314	1 435 496	381 818		
2014	12 953	11 855	1 098	2 005 068	1 579 367	425 701	67.17	154.67
2015	13 005	11 814	1 191	2 135 162	1 665 643	469 519	66.78	111.62
2016	13 508	12 287	1 221	2 245 462	1 732 654	512 808	82.32	103.65

注：新口径公路货运量不包含农用车和拖拉机的运输量。
Note: The new caliber of Freight traffic of highways didn't include that of agricultural vehicles and tractors.

表6-7

分地区客运量（2016年）
PASSENGER TRAFFIC BY REGION (2016)

地　区	Region	客运量（万人次）Passenger Traffic (10 000 person-times)	公　路 Highways	水　运 Waterways	旅客周转量（万人公里）Passenger-kilometers (10 000 person-km)	公　路 Highways	水　运 Waterways
全　市	**Whole Municipality**	**32 130**	**31 589**	**541**	**1 222 309**	**1 217 335**	**4 974**
市　区	Urban Area	18 355	18 088	267	699 576	697 120	2 456
# 吴江区	Wujiang District	3 218	3 173	44	122 686	122 277	409
常　熟	Changshu	3 583	3 528	55	136 426	135 920	506
张家港	Zhangjiagang	3 228	3 129	98	121 506	120 602	905
昆　山	Kunshan	4 101	4 048	53	156 445	155 959	486
太　仓	Taicang	2 864	2 796	68	108 357	107 735	622

表6-8

分地区货运量（2016年）
FREIGHT TRAFFIC BY REGION (2016)

地　区	Region	货运量（万吨）Freight Traffic (10 000 tons)	公　路 Highways	水　运 Waterways	货物周转量（万吨公里）Freight-kilometers (10 000 ton-km)	公　路 Highways	水　运 Waterways
全　市	**Whole Municipality**	**13 508**	**12 287**	**1 221**	**2 245 462**	**1 732 654**	**512 808**
市　区	Urban Area	7 272	6 773	499	1 164 845	955 082	209 763
# 吴江区	Wujiang District	1 142	1 040	101	189 413	146 697	42 717
常　熟	Changshu	1 457	1 275	182	256 305	179 815	76 490
张家港	Zhangjiagang	1 830	1 599	231	322 073	225 454	96 620
昆　山	Kunshan	1 440	1 339	102	231 398	188 754	42 645
太　仓	Taicang	1 509	1 302	208	270 840	183 550	87 290

表6-9

苏州港码头泊位和吞吐量（2016年）
NUMBER OF BERTHS AND THROUGHPUT OF SUZHOU PORT (2016)

项　　目	Item	合　计 Total	常熟港区 Changshu Port	张家港港区 Zhangjiagang Port	太仓港区 Taicang Port
码头泊位个数　（个）	**Number of Berths　(unit)**	**290**	**52**	**162**	**76**
# 万吨级以上	10 000 Ton Class	128	21	73	34
# 公用码头	Public Berths	153	32	58	63
# 集装箱码头	Containen Berths	19	3	4	12
货物吞吐量　（万吨）	**Cargo at Ports Throughput (10 000 tons)**	**57 937**	**8 665**	**26 068**	**23 204**
# 外　贸	Freight Trade	15 142	1 567	6 103	7 472
集装箱吞吐量(万标箱)	**International Containes (10 000TEU)**	**547.92**	**41.45**	**98.33**	**408.14**
重　量　（万吨）	Weight　(10 000 tons)	7 697.41	461.15	1 317.98	5 918.28
# 货　物	Freight	6 598.36	378.24	1 122.92	5 097.20

注：标箱指折合20英尺标准箱，英文缩写TEU。　Note:TEU is the abbreviation, Which refers to 20-foot equivalent unit.

表6-10

苏州港集装箱吞吐量（2016年）
VOLUME OF CONTAINER HANDLED OF SUZHOU PORT (2016)

项　　目	Item	合　计 Total	其　中 of which		按航线分 Grouped by Routes		
			进　港 In-Port	出　港 Out-Port	国际航线 International Routes	内支线 Ports of In-land Rivers	国内航线 Domestic Routes
箱量合计　（标箱）	**Total Containers (TEU)**	**5 479 223**	**2 712 148**	**2 767 075**	**522 078**	**1 967 856**	**2 989 290**
空箱小计	Light Case Subtotal	1 181 355	529 101	652 253	158 785	275 384	747 186
# 45英尺箱（箱）	45-foot equivalent unit (unit)	3 242	105	3 137	–	252	2 990
40英尺箱	40-foot equivalent unit	351 397	130 284	221 113	54 932	85 647	210 818
20英尺箱	20-foot equivalent unit	471 178	268 234	202 944	48 833	103 523	318 822
重箱小计　（标箱）	Heavy Case Subtotal (TEU)	4 297 869	2 183 047	2 114 822	363 293	1 692 472	2 242 104
# 45英尺箱（箱）	45-foot equivalent unit (unit)	1 010	871	139	3	942	65
40英尺箱	40-foot equivalent unit	1 163 651	619 396	544 255	130 463	621 988	411 200
20英尺箱	20-foot equivalent unit	1 967 752	942 027	1 025 725	101 818	446 376	1 419 558
重量合计　（吨）	**Total Weight　(ton)**	**76 974 127**	**39 906 743**	**37 067 384**	**4 067 556**	**24 103 186**	**48 803 385**
# 货　重	Freight Weight	65 983 579	34 457 462	31 526 117	3 006 326	20 264 335	42 712 918

表6-11

苏州港进出港口货物分类流向一览（2016年）
FREIGHT HANDLED AT SUZHOU PORT BY DIRECTION (2016)

单位：万吨 (10 000 tons)

类别	Type	总计 Total	总计中 In Total		总计中 In Total	
			进港 Arrival	出港 Departure	外贸 Foreign Trade	内贸 Domestic Trade
总计	**Total**	**57 936.59**	**35 570.35**	**22 366.24**	**15 141.98**	**42 794.61**
1.煤炭及其制品	Coal and Its Products	16 149.81	10 838.00	5 311.81	779.21	15 370.60
2.石油、天然气及制品	Petroleum, Natural Gas and Related Products	738.77	479.65	259.11	279.92	458.85
#成品油	Product Oil	–	–	–	–	–
3.金属矿石	Metal Ores	16 379.75	11 047.52	5 332.23	5 309.39	11 070.36
#铁矿石	Iron Ore	15 312.41	10 199.51	5 112.90	5 055.35	10 257.06
4.钢铁	Iron and Steel	3 790.51	753.04	3 037.47	1 312.63	2 477.88
#钢材	Rolled Steel	2 929.15	243.05	2 686.10	905.63	2 023.52
5.矿物性建筑材料	Mineral Building Materials	4 353.83	2 815.83	1 538.00	–	4 353.83
6.水泥	Cement	139.91	33.56	106.36	29.61	110.30
7.木材	Timber	1 625.23	1 350.86	274.37	1 338.72	286.52
#原木	Log	1 134.90	933.75	201.14	920.63	214.27
8.非金属矿石	Nonmetal Ores	103.22	92.22	11.00	28.84	74.38
9.化学肥料及农药	Chemical Fertilizers and Pesticides	312.35	157.16	155.19	152.21	160.14
10.盐	Salt	13.05	11.35	1.70	0.57	12.48
11.粮食	Grain	844.96	596.10	248.85	442.73	402.22
#黄豆	Bean	604.80	460.02	144.78	374.65	230.15
12.机械、设备、电器	Machine, Equipment and Wiring	188.32	7.52	180.80	148.82	39.51
13.化工原料及制品	Chemical Industry Materials and Products	2 294.23	1 627.91	666.32	1 296.60	997.63
14.有色金属	Nonferrous Metals	0.41	0.41	–	–	0.41
15.轻工、医药产品	Products of Light Industry and Medicine & Pharmacy	572.54	384.00	188.54	366.44	206.09
16.农林牧渔业产品	The Output of Agricultural Products	439.40	171.50	267.90	126.98	312.42
17.其他	Others	9 990.31	5 203.71	4 786.59	3 529.31	6 460.99

表6-12

邮政电信基本情况（2016年）

项　目		Item		全　市 Whole Municipality
一、邮电业务总收入	(亿元)	**Business Income of Post & Telecommunications**	(100 million yuan)	**326.78**
电信业务总收入		Business Income of Telecommunications		192.64
邮政业务总收入		Business Income of Post		134.14
# 快递业务收入		Business Income of Express		114.15
二、邮政行业分类业务量		**Business Volume of Postal Service**		
函　件(邮政系统)	(万件)	Number of Letters (Postal System)	(10 000 pcs)	13 814
包　裹	(万件)	Number of Package	(10 000 pcs)	59.73
快递业务量	(万件)	Business Volume of Express	(10 000 pcs)	85 093
订销报刊杂志累计数	(万份)	Number of Newspapers and Magazines Circulation	(10 000 copies)	27 128
邮政储蓄余额	(亿元)	Postal Savings Balance	(100 million yuan)	495.25
三、电信业务主要指标		**Main Indicators on Telecommunications**		
电话交换机总容量	(门)	Total Capacity of Urban and Rural Telephone Exchanges	(line)	3 802 786
固定电话用户	(户)	Fixed Telephone Subscribers	(household)	2 519 943
普通电话		Telephones		2 427 301
公用电话		Public Telephone		92 642
移动电话用户	(户)	Number of Mobile Telephone Subscribers	(household)	16 906 242
# 3G用户		3G users		1 499 128
# 4G用户		4G users		10 796 569
互联网用户	(户)	International Exchange Network Users	(household)	16 770 131
# 宽带用户		Subscriber of Broad Band		4 735 246
# 用3G业务的互联网用户数		3G service users		1 279 509
# 用4G业务的互联网用户数		4G service users		10 646 456
# 用上网卡的互联网用户数		Spending NIC users		108 796

注：邮政业务总收入中包含规模以上快递公司快递业务收入，但未包括邮政储蓄银行直接营业收入。

POSTS AND TELECOMMUNICATIONS (2016)

市 区 Urban Area	# 吴江区 Wujiang District	常 熟 Changshu	张家港 Zhangjiagang	昆 山 Kunshan	太 仓 Taicang
188.75	**32.62**	**41.65**	**24.45**	**56.70**	**15.23**
106.93	21.71	21.83	17.88	35.52	10.48
81.82	10.91	19.82	6.57	21.18	4.75
71.54	8.59	16.48	4.58	18.15	3.40
11 486	263	650	346	996	336
33.97	3.27	2.46	4.25	15.88	3.17
43 039	8 137	22 239	3 159	14 226	2 430
14 652	2 278	4 286	2 602	3 553	2 034
225.53	73.35	96.73	55.71	83.85	33.43
2 288 803	342 039	401 736	313 859	605 883	192 505
1 392 508	257 140	330 484	243 156	400 824	152 971
1 338 445	242 276	315 896	235 045	389 849	148 066
54 063	14 864	14 588	8 111	10 975	4 905
9 167 907	1 903 496	2 025 936	1 716 974	2 995 526	999 900
816 721	155 211	181 153	156 491	250 350	94 411
5 887 977	1 215 242	1 246 536	1 062 883	1 965 288	633 884
8 982 380	1 847 502	2 021 945	1 694 743	3 051 232	1 019 830
2 407 005	513 158	630 272	509 896	876 614	311 459
702 000	126 301	148 776	124 638	221 407	82 688
5 806 173	1 198 260	1 230 516	1 051 100	1 938 709	619 958
67 099	9 773	12 381	9 108	14 489	5 719

Note: Business volume of post contain business volume of express company above designated size , but not contain the postal savings bank direct operating income.

主 要 统 计 指 标 解 释

公路里程 指在一定时期内实际达到《公路工程[WTBZ]技术标准JTJ01-88》规定的等级公路，并经公路主管部门正式验收交付使用的公路里程数。包括大中城市的郊区公路以及通过小城镇街道部分的公路里程和桥梁、渡口的长度，不包括大中城市的街道、厂矿、林区生产用道和农业生产用道的里程。两条或多条公路共同经由同一路段，只计算一次，不得重复计算里程长度。该指标可以反映公路建设的发展规模，也是计算运输网密度等指标的基础资料。

内河航道里程 也称内河通航里程，指在一定时期内，能通航运输船舶及排筏的天然河流、湖泊水库、运河及通航渠道的长度。包括全年季节性通航累计三个月以上的航道，不包括仅供零散流放竹、木排的河道。该指标可以反映内河水运网的规模、水平和发展情况。

货(客)运量 指在一定时期内，各种运输工具实际运送的货物(旅客)数量。货运按吨计算，客运按人计算。货物不论运输距离长短、货物类别，均按实际重量统计。旅客不论行程远近或票价多少，均按一人一次客运量统计；半价票、儿童票也按一人统计。

货物(旅客)周转量 指在一定时期内，由各种运输工具运送的货物(旅客)数量与其相应运输距离的乘积之总和。该指标可以反映运输业生产的总成果，也是编制和检查运输生产计划，计算运输效率、劳动生产率以及核算运输单位成本的主要基础资料。计算货物周转量通常按发出站与到达站之间的最短距离，也就是计费距离计算。计算公式为：

货物（旅客）周转量=Σ（货物（旅客）运输量×运输距离）

民用汽车拥有量 指报告期末，在公安交通管理部门按照《机动车注册登记工作规范》，已注册登记领有民用车辆牌照的全部汽车数量。汽车拥有量统计的主要分类：根据汽车结构分为载客汽车、载货汽车及其他汽车；根据汽车所有者不同分为个人(私人)汽车、单位汽车；根据汽车的使用性质分为营运汽车、非营运汽车；根据汽车大小规格不同载客汽车分为大型、中型、小型和微型，载货汽车分为重型、中型、轻型和微型。

移动电话用户 指在电信运营企业营业网点办理开户登记手续，通过移动电话交换机进入移动电话网，占用移动电话号码的各类电话用户。包括GSM数字移动电话用户、CDMA数字移动电话用户和电信运营企业发行的报告期末已激活充值的能异地漫游的各种智能卡用户。

快递业务量 企业收寄的各类快递业务总数量，由受理用户委托的企业负责统计。

快递业务量=国内同城快递业务量+国内异地快递业务量+港澳台快递业务量+国际快递业务量。

EXPLANATORY NOTES ON MAIN STATISTICAL INDICATORS

Length of Highways refers to the length of highways which are built in conformity with the grades specified by the highway engineering standard [Highways WTBZ-Technical Standard JTJ01-88]formulated by the Ministry of Communications, and have been formally checked and accepted by the departments of highways and put into use. The length of highways includes that of the suburb highways at large and medium-sized cities, highways passing through streets at small cities and towns, and also the length of bridges and ferry piers. It does not include the length of streets in big and medium-sized cities and highways built for the production purpose at factories, mines, forest areas and agricultural areas. If two or more highways go the same section of the way, the length of the section is only calculated for once and no duplication is allowed. The length of highways is an indicator to show the development of the scale of highway construction and to provide essential information to calculate the transport network density.

Length of Navigable Inland Waterways is an indicator reflecting the size and development of inland water network. It refers to the length of the natural rivers, lakes, reservoirs, canals, and ditches open to navigation during a given period, which enables transportation by ships and rafts. It includes the channels open to navigation for over an accumulated period of 3 months in a year, yet this does not include the river courses which are only used to float odd logs and bamboo rafts. This indicator can reflect the scale, level and development situation of the inland waterway network.

Freight (Passenger) Traffic refers to the volume of freight (passenger) transported with various means within a specific period of time. Freight transport is calculated in tons and passenger traffic is calculated in terms of number of persons. Freight transport is calculated in terms of the actual weight of the goods and takes no account of the type of freight and distance of travel. Passenger traffic is calculated by the principle that one person can be counted only once in one trip and takes no account of the travelling distance and ticket price. The passengers who travel with a half price ticket or a child's ticket is also calculated as one person.

Freight Ton-kilometres (Passenger-kilometres) refers to the sum of the product of the volume of transported cargo (passengers) multiplied by the transport distance. It is an important indicator to reflect the achievement of the transportation industry. This is an important indicator to show the total results of the transport industry; to prepare and examine the transport plan; and to serve as the main basic data for calculating the efficiency, labour productivity and unit cost of transport. Normally, the shortest distance between the departure station and the destination station (i.e., the payable distance) is the basis in calculating the freight ton-kilometres. The formula is as follows:

$$\begin{matrix}\text{Freight ton-kilometres}\\ \text{(passenger-kilometres)}\end{matrix} = \sum \begin{matrix}\text{freight}\\ \text{(passenger)traffic}\end{matrix} \times \begin{matrix}\text{distance of}\\ \text{transportation}\end{matrix}$$

Possession of Civil Motor Vehicles refer to the total numbers of vehicles that are registered and received vehicles license tags according to the *Work Standard for Motor Vehicles Registration* formulated by the Transport Management Office under the department of public security at the end of the reference period. They are divided into categories. According to the structure of motor vehicles, they are divided into passenger vehicles, trucks and others; according to ownership into private vehicles and vehicles for the unit's use; according to kind of usage into working vehicles and non-working vehicles; and according to size of vehicles into large passenger vehicles, medium-sized passenger vehicles, small passenger vehicles and mini passenger vehicles, heavy trucks, light-heavy trucks, light trucks and mini-trucks.

Mobile Telephone Subscribers refer to persons who have gone through registration procedures in the operation points of enterprises engaged in telecommunications and are hence connected with the mobile telephone communication network through the mobile telephone switchboards and occupy mobile phone numbers. Included are GSM digital mobile phone subscribers, CDMA digital mobile phone subscribers and subscribers to intelligent phone cards with roaming facility issued by telecommunications enterprises and which have been subscribed to and activated at the end of the reference period.

Business volume of express the total number of express services received by enterprises, count by enterprises who was entrusted by the user. Business volume of express= domestic express delivery business volume of same city + domestic express delivery business volume of different city + Hong Kong, Macao and Taiwan express business volume + International express delivery business volume.

七、贸易餐饮业

CHAPTER 7
TRADE AND CATERING BUSINESS

7 贸易餐饮业 TRADE AND CATERING BUSINESS

主要统计指标 MAJOR STATISTICAL INDICATORS

2016年社会消费品零售总额	Total Retail Sales of Consumer Goods	4 936.79	亿元	100 million yuan
比上年增长	Increase Over Last Year	10.7	%	
2016年批发和零售业零售额	Wholesale and Retail Sale Trades	4 343.02	亿元	100 million yuan
比上年增长	Increase Over Last Year	10.8	%	
2016年住宿和餐饮业零售额	Accommodation and Catering Trade	593.77	亿元	100 million yuan
比上年增长	Increase Over Last Year	9.6	%	
2016年限额以上批发和零售业	Enterprises Above Designated Size in Wholesale and Retail Trades			
商品购进总额	Total Purchases	10 008.69	亿元	100 million yuan
商品销售总额	Total Sales	11 563.37	亿元	100 million yuan
商品年末库存总额	Inventory (year-end)	581.13	亿元	100 million yuan
2016年限额以上住宿业营业总额	Total Business Turnover of Hotel Accommodation Above Designated Size	75.90	亿元	100 million yuan
2016年限额以上餐饮业营业总额	Total Business Turnover of Catering Trade Above Designated Size	74.70	亿元	100 million yuan
2016年亿元以上商品交易市场商品成交总额	Total Business Turnover of Transaction Markets Over 100 Million Yuan	6 056.62	亿元	100 million yuan
比上年增长	Increase Over Last Year	8.8	%	

表7-1

历年分地区社会消费品零售总额
TOTAL RETAIL SALES OF CONSUMER GOODS OVER THE YEARS BY REGION

单位：万元 (10 000 yuan)

年 份 Year	全 市 Whole Municipality	市 区 Urban Area	# 吴江区 Wujiang District	常 熟 Changshu	张家港 Zhangjiagang	昆 山 Kunshan	太 仓 Taicang
1949	23 818	15 576	3 604	2 867	1 562	2 067	1 746
1952	31 193	18 652	4 125	5 004	2 319	2 663	2 555
1957	35 788	22 027	3 615	5 863	2 533	2 627	2 738
1962	42 967	26 191	5 011	7 294	3 187	3 383	2 912
1965	48 564	27 345	5 103	8 510	4 977	3 912	3 820
1970	51 397	28 185	5 397	8 636	5 299	4 922	4 355
1975	77 612	44 546	8 102	12 415	8 418	6 140	6 093
1978	94 747	51 986	10 208	15 313	13 233	6 924	7 291
1980	156 707	84 305	17 124	26 894	20 571	11 114	13 823
1985	370 485	194 924	42 027	69 891	44 214	30 366	31 090
1990	721 514	375 196	72 891	147 881	75 660	65 017	57 760
1995	2 423 094	1 217 029	207 724	507 723	285 642	247 284	165 416
2000	4 281 714	2 293 890	345 989	756 715	458 523	516 558	256 028
2001	4 914 382	2 652 807	393 390	847 521	522 342	609 046	282 666
2002	5 713 157	3 113 126	456 687	975 385	600 748	703 170	320 728
2003	6 640 502	3 633 803	526 263	1 108 282	705 690	831 572	361 155
2004	7 768 800	4 255 432	613 551	1 296 788	820 809	980 079	415 692
2005	9 343 000	5 103 568	762 873	1 509 313	996 237	1 226 497	507 385
2006	11 236 000	6 099 528	952 656	1 764 594	1 211 273	1 536 685	623 920
2007	13 706 000	7 378 277	1 207 675	2 099 770	1 494 469	1 955 155	778 329
2008	17 488 000	9 318 800	1 620 000	2 629 000	1 949 000	2 557 000	1 034 200
2009	20 268 405	10 774 312	1 874 029	3 045 857	2 261 813	2 980 480	1 205 943
2010	24 020 199	12 759 030	2 229 679	3 601 883	2 678 564	3 566 414	1 414 308
2011	28 295 794	14 987 098	2 636 452	4 262 612	3 164 556	4 209 816	1 671 712
2012	32 409 679	16 820 177	3 080 430	4 995 373	3 707 280	4 936 190	1 950 659
2013	36 622 357	18 953 775	3 567 589	5 644 322	4 138 019	5 699 233	2 187 008
2014	40 998 329	21 337 066	3 924 952	6 186 745	4 583 222	6 500 862	2 390 434
2015	44 616 214	23 117 215	4 222 992	6 756 392	4 948 748	7 146 845	2 647 014
2016	49 367 885	25 585 002	4 676 567	7 407 789	5 351 641	8 150 370	2 873 083

表7-2

部分年份分行业社会消费品零售总额
TOTAL RETAIL SALES OF CONSUMER GOODS OF PARTIAL YEARS BY SECTOR

单位：万元 (10 000 yuan)

年 份 Year	社会消费品零售总额 Total Retail Sales of Consumer Goods	# 批发和零售业 Wholesale and Retail Sale Trades	# 住宿和餐饮业 Accommodation and Catering Trade
1990	721 514	654 249	39 794
1995	2 423 094	2 177 435	207 724
2000	4 281 714	3 760 650	488 204
2001	4 914 382	4 290 204	590 511
2002	5 713 157	4 959 154	721 325
2003	6 640 502	5 753 184	852 147
2004	7 768 800	6 720 264	1 010 942
2005	9 343 000	8 119 628	1 179 960
2006	11 236 000	9 774 077	1 424 519
2007	13 706 000	11 924 334	1 749 650
2008	17 488 000	15 021 411	2 459 714
2009	20 268 405	17 792 291	2 256 499
2010	24 020 199	21 075 139	2 725 445
2011	28 295 794	24 764 557	3 213 714
2012	32 409 679	28 303 744	3 827 257
2013	36 622 357	31 972 397	4 303 595
2014	40 998 329	35 803 949	4 807 120
2015	44 616 214	39 196 633	5 419 581
2016	49 367 885	43 430 180	5 937 705

表7-3

分地区社会消费品零售总额 (2016年)
TOTAL RETAIL SALES OF CONSUMER GOODS BY REGION (2016)

单位：万元 (10 000 yuan)

地 区 Region	社会消费品零售总额 Total Retail Sales of Consumer Goods	# 个 体 Individual	按行业分 Grouped by Sector	
			批发和零售业 Wholesale and Retail Sale Trades	住宿和餐饮业 Accommodation and Catering Trade
全 市 Whole Municipality	**49 367 885**	**19 978 823**	**43 430 180**	**5 937 705**
市 区 Urban Area	25 585 002	8 317 391	22 961 813	2 623 189
# 吴江区 Wujiang District	4 676 567	2 558 587	4 062 158	614 410
常 熟 Changshu	7 407 789	3 975 735	6 783 190	624 600
张家港 Zhangjiagang	5 351 641	2 997 974	4 575 443	776 198
昆 山 Kunshan	8 150 370	2 816 961	6 639 273	1 511 097
太 仓 Taicang	2 873 083	1 870 762	2 470 462	402 621

表7-4

分月社会消费品零售总额（2016年）
RETAIL SALES OF CONSUMER GOODS BY MONTH (2016)

单位：万元 (10 000 yuan)

月份	Month	全市 Whole Municipality	市区 Urban Area	# 吴江区 Wujiang District	常熟 Changshu	张家港 Zhangjiagang	昆山 Kunshan	太仓 Taicang
总计	**Total**	**49 367 885**	**25 585 002**	**4 676 567**	**7 407 789**	**5 351 641**	**8 150 370**	**2 873 083**
一季度	**1st Quarter**	**12 189 825**	**6 432 335**	**1 196 165**	**1 801 969**	**1 308 244**	**1 927 138**	**720 139**
1月	Jan.	3 884 527	2 076 182	381 876	571 108	406 890	597 668	232 680
2月	Feb.	4 233 606	2 262 756	416 193	622 430	443 455	651 376	253 590
3月	Mar.	4 071 692	2 093 397	398 096	608 432	457 899	678 094	233 870
二季度	**2nd Quarter**	**11 636 740**	**5 971 732**	**1 103 356**	**1 835 173**	**1 239 421**	**1 902 119**	**688 295**
4月	Apr.	3 621 811	1 865 134	367 063	581 608	374 140	581 970	218 959
5月	May.	4 013 562	2 082 963	354 801	619 329	439 806	640 141	231 323
6月	June	4 001 367	2 023 635	381 492	634 236	425 475	680 008	238 013
三季度	**3rd Quarter**	**11 987 307**	**6 202 612**	**1 133 068**	**1 817 238**	**1 277 262**	**1 988 425**	**701 770**
7月	July	3 909 186	2 003 231	382 020	601 561	423 648	642 945	237 801
8月	Aug.	4 032 622	2 099 003	366 821	605 507	418 431	677 947	231 734
9月	Sept.	4 045 499	2 100 378	384 227	610 170	435 183	667 533	232 235
四季度	**4th Quarter**	**13 554 013**	**6 978 323**	**1 243 978**	**1 953 409**	**1 526 714**	**2 332 688**	**762 879**
10月	Oct.	4 502 160	2 346 972	408 732	672 947	506 218	719 707	256 316
11月	Nov.	4 510 396	2 320 776	393 764	639 369	499 674	794 943	255 634
12月	Dec.	4 541 457	2 310 575	441 482	641 093	520 822	818 038	250 929

表7-5 限额以上批发和零售、住宿和餐饮法人企业基本情况 (2016年)

BASIC CONDITION OF WHOLESALE AND RETAIL, ACCOMMODATION AND CATERING CORPORATE ENTERPRISES ABOVE THE DESIGNATED SIZE (2016)

项　目	Item	法人企业数(个) Number of Corporation (unit)	零售或餐饮营业面积(平方米) Floor Space of Retail or Catering Business (sq.m)	年末从业人员(人) Year-end Employees (person)
总　计	**Total**	**3 625**	**6 777 049**	**253 838**
市　区	Urban Area	1 721	4 086 115	133 680
# 吴江区	Wujiang District	518	402 342	17 592
常　熟	Changshu	447	674 653	20 831
张家港	Zhangjiagang	706	590 694	30 974
昆　山	Kunshan	581	1 199 280	59 284
太　仓	Taicang	170	226 307	9 069
一、批发和零售业小计	**Wholesale Trades and Retail Sales**	**3 228**	**5 710 300**	**186 695**
按行业分	**Grouped by Sector**			
批发业	Wholesale Trades	2 357	1 109 241	86 536
零售业	Retail Sales	871	4 601 059	100 159
按地区分	**Grouped by Region**			
市　区	Urban Area	1 473	3 365 574	85 387
# 吴江区	Wujiang District	481	300 520	13 207
常　熟	Changshu	408	577 692	17 066
张家港	Zhangjiagang	674	500 336	25 877
昆　山	Kunshan	522	1 085 210	51 591
太　仓	Taicang	151	181 488	6 774
二、住宿和餐饮业小计	**Accommodation and Catering Trade**	**397**	**1 066 749**	**67 143**
按行业分	**Grouped by Sector**			
住宿业	Accommodation	204	541 083	31 684
餐饮业	Catering Trade	193	525 666	35 459
按地区分	**Grouped by Region**			
市　区	Urban Area	248	720 541	48 293
# 吴江区	Wujiang District	37	101 822	4 385
常　熟	Changshu	39	96 961	3 765
张家港	Zhangjiagang	32	90 358	5 097
昆　山	Kunshan	59	114 070	7 693
太　仓	Taicang	19	44 819	2 295

表7-6

限额以上批发和零售业商品购进、销售、库存总额（2016年）

单位：万元

项　　目	Item	购进总额 Total Purchases
总　　计	**Total**	**100 086 932**
一、批发业	**Wholesale Trades**	**79 671 814**
# 国有及国有控股	State-owned and State Holding Majority Shares	10 104 219
1. 按地区分	**Grouped by Region**	
市　区	Urban Area	28 155 881
# 吴江区	Wujiang District	13 312 769
常　熟	Changshu	6 591 203
张家港	Zhangjiagang	33 923 696
昆　山	Kunshan	5 080 238
太　仓	Taicang	5 920 796
2. 按登记注册类型分	**Grouped by Registration Status**	
国有企业	State-owned Enterprises	1 110 764
集体企业	Collective-owned Enterprises	49 455
股份合作企业	Share-holding Cooperative Enterprises	1 426
联营企业	Joint Ownership Enterprises	–
有限责任公司	Limited Liability Corporations	34 062 781
股份有限公司	Share-holding Cooperative Ltd.	1 214 180
私营企业	Private Enterprises	34 684 369
其他企业	Other Enterprises	4 230
港澳台商投资企业	Enterprises with Investment from HongKong, Macao and Taiwan	4 856 297
外商投资企业	Enterprises with Foreign Investment	3 688 312
3. 按主要行业分	**Grouped by Sector**	
农畜产品批发	Wholesale of Farm and Animal Products	490 853
食品、饮料及烟草制品批发	Wholesale of Food, Beverages and Tobaccos	3 640 453
纺织、服装及日用品批发	Wholesale of Textiles, Garments and Daily Articles	19 501 229
# 服装批发	Wholesale of Garments	1 933 261
文化、体育用品及器材批发	Wholesale of Cultural, Sports and Appliances Goods	1 232 274

TOTAL PURCHASES，SALES AND INVENTORY OF WHOLESALE AND RETAIL TRADE ABOVE DESIGNATED SIZE (2016)

(10 000 yuan)

#进 口 Imports	销售总额 Total Sales	批 发 Wholesale	#出 口 Exports	零 售 Retail Sale	年末库存总额 Inventory (year-end)
4 324 474	**115 633 683**	**91 889 065**	**7 818 092**	**23 744 619**	**5 811 252**
3 710 401	**92 199 156**	**89 097 241**	**7 817 943**	**3 101 915**	**3 992 812**
56 684	14 125 514	13 242 313	2 122 432	883 201	644 924
1 308 434	32 900 741	30 905 701	2 357 325	1 995 040	1 207 823
147 264	13 889 334	13 752 450	878 215	136 884	147 012
42 460	7 561 736	7 413 887	664 903	147 849	398 955
1 771 293	38 788 019	38 311 733	4 290 130	476 286	1 458 248
336 675	6 199 765	5 795 000	401 574	404 765	497 292
251 539	6 748 896	6 670 921	104 011	77 975	430 494
–	4 379 163	4 248 986	2 072 422	130 177	202 731
–	49 276	49 276	20 112	–	5 472
–	1 968	1 968	–	–	2 295
–	–	–	–	–	–
1 661 406	35 870 353	34 677 369	2 339 360	1 192 984	1 268 945
15 822	1 348 735	1 207 809	117 991	140 925	121 026
770 400	36 967 538	36 081 200	2 749 949	886 338	1 403 009
–	4 886	4 886	–	–	1 878
345 717	6 306 049	6 041 865	136 684	264 184	459 987
917 058	7 271 189	6 783 883	381 425	487 307	527 471
2 301	537 296	523 783	359	13 512	39 248
159 427	4 685 769	4 578 983	15 389	106 787	226 283
278 223	26 752 070	25 837 675	4 577 601	914 395	1 020 047
92 861	7 310 852	6 724 826	3 067 104	586 026	381 552
7 936	1 482 898	1 434 879	120 365	48 019	221 077

表7-6 续表 1

单位：万元

项　目	Item	购进总额 Total Purchases
医药及医疗器材批发	Wholesale of Medicines and Medical Appliances	1 002 478
矿产品、建材及化工产品批发	Wholesale of Mineral Products, Building Materials and Chemical Products	42 303 559
机械设备、五金交电及电子产品批发	Wholesale of Machinery, Hardware, Transport, Electric and Electronic Equipment	9 831 805
# 农业机械批发	Wholesale Agricultural Machinery	20 064
汽车、摩托车及零配件批发	Wholesale of Motor Vehicles, Motorcycles and Parts	3 242 926
五金、交电批发	Wholesale of Hardware, Transport and Electric	749 740
家用电器批发	Wholesale Household Appliances	2 795 289
计算机、软件及辅助设备批发	Wholesale of Computers, Software and Appliances	289 375
贸易经纪与代理	Trade Management and Agency	539 675
其他批发	Other Wholesale	1 129 487
二、零售业	**Retail Trades**	**20 415 118**
# 国有及国有控股	State-owned and State Holding Majority Shares	3 750 973
1. 按地区分	**Grouped by Region**	
市　区	Urban Area	10 966 717
# 吴江区	Wujiang District	1 240 813
常　熟	Changshu	1 659 156
张家港	Zhangjiagang	1 235 317
昆　山	Kunshan	6 172 492
太　仓	Taicang	381 437
2. 按登记注册类型分	**Grouped by Registration Status**	
国有企业	State-owned Enterprises	25 695
集体企业	Collective-owned Enterprises	44 802
股份合作企业	Share-holding Cooperative Enterprises	7 107
联营企业	Joint Ownership Enterprises	8 643
有限责任公司	Limited Liability Corporations	6 055 235
股份有限公司	Share-holding Cooperative Ltd.	2 140 291
私营企业	Private Enterprises	6 738 297

Continued 1

(10 000 yuan)

# 进 口 Imports	销售总额 Total Sales	批 发 Wholesale	# 出 口 Exports	零 售 Retail Sale	年末库存总额 Inventory (year-end)
271 523	1 213 145	1 031 807	36 247	181 338	134 843
2 160 992	44 483 229	43 614 512	2 104 473	868 717	1 550 377
707 722	11 266 755	10 379 122	624 507	887 633	677 641
–	21 619	21 619	10 978	–	489
22 345	3 965 229	3 920 954	37 747	44 276	81 822
73 634	863 176	828 679	235 007	34 497	74 866
6 779	2 868 014	2 155 006	16 964	713 009	237 104
25 150	317 486	303 023	3 335	14 462	31 281
78 992	568 270	568 270	318 612	–	6 662
43 285	1 209 724	1 128 210	20 391	81 514	116 635
614 073	**23 434 527**	**2 791 823**	**149**	**20 642 704**	**1 818 440**
4 243	3 912 029	961 546	–	2 950 484	188 456
337 418	12 548 217	1 157 618	–	11 390 600	965 618
94 742	1 320 662	16 264	149	1 304 398	129 148
82 438	1 971 674	146 275	–	1 825 399	137 542
108 917	1 477 329	119 622	–	1 357 707	153 540
64 217	7 023 120	1 359 168	–	5 663 952	523 035
21 083	414 187	9 141	–	405 046	38 705
4 243	32 624	424	–	32 200	3 295
–	52 484	4 713	–	47 771	3 554
–	10 068	1 731	–	8 337	149
–	9 079	–	–	9 079	48
191 902	6 994 540	561 183	–	6 433 358	436 033
1 949	2 353 215	395 474	–	1 957 741	109 037
326 736	7 711 154	296 761	149	7 414 393	748 428

表7-6 续表 2

单位：万元

项　目	Item	购进总额 Total Purchases
其他企业	Other Enterprises	7 043
港澳台商投资企业	Enterprises with Investment from HongKong, Macao and Taiwan	3 643 385
外商投资企业	Enterprises with Foreign Investment	1 744 619
3.按主要行业分	**Grouped by Sector**	
综合零售	Retail of Integrated	5 023 050
百货零售	Retail of Consumer Goods	881 185
超级市场零售	Retail of Supermarket	4 138 391
其他综合零售	Others Retail of Integrated	3 473
食品、饮料及烟草制品专门零售	Retail of Food, Beverages and Tobaccos	210 830
纺织、服装及日用品专门零售	Retail of Textiles, Garments and Daily Articles	390 905
文化、体育用品及器材专门零售	Retail of Culture, Sports Articles and Equipment	247 578
医药及医疗器材专门零售	Retail of Medicines and Medical Appliances	1 597 210
汽车、摩托车、燃料及零配件专门零售	Retail of Motor Vehicles, Motorcycles, Fuels and Parts	9 816 573
#汽车零售	Retail of Motor Vehicles	7 254 241
家用电器及电子产品专门零售	Retail of Household Appliances and Electronic Products	899 424
#家用电器零售	Retail of Household Appliances	606 234
计算机、软件及辅助设备零售	Retail of Computers, Software and Appliances	48 415
五金、家具及室内装修材料专门零售	Retail of Hardware Furniture and Materials for Ornament	98 016
无店铺及其他零售	Retail of Non-shop and Others	2 131 532
4.按经营方式分	**Grouped by Means of Operation**	
独立商店	Independent Shop	10 322 805
连锁商店总店	Central Shop of Chain Shops	6 013 727
连锁门店	Outlets of Chain Shops	770 079
其　他	Others	3 308 507
5.按零售业态分	**Grouped by Retail Size**	
百货商店	Department Store	958 565
超级市场	Supermarket	4 180 099
专业店	Special Store	7 065 949
专卖店	Monopoly Store	5 439 236
其　他	Others	2 771 269

Continued 2

(10 000 yuan)

#进口 Imports	销售总额 Total Sales	批发 Wholesale	#出口 Exports	零售 Retail Sale	年末库存总额 Inventory (year-end)
–	8 207	–	–	8 207	163
6 979	4 273 804	1 355 049	–	2 918 755	420 972
82 264	1 989 352	176 489	–	1 812 863	96 762
301	6 336 931	1 331 264	–	5 005 667	481 102
301	1 584 945	294	–	1 584 651	35 958
–	4 744 829	1 330 970	–	3 413 859	444 513
–	7 157	–	–	7 157	630
2 184	262 393	7 093	–	255 300	21 173
6 694	615 936	88 385	149	527 551	95 220
–	330 275	7 850	–	322 425	86 352
12 794	1 671 692	468 101	–	1 203 591	136 099
590 666	10 704 240	810 336	–	9 893 904	863 435
590 666	8 090 817	199 084	–	7 891 733	766 939
165	962 469	40 035	–	922 435	53 198
165	616 935	12 294	–	604 640	21 033
–	53 159	12 492	–	40 667	5 079
246	115 444	4 079	–	111 365	11 368
1 023	2 435 149	34 682	–	2 400 467	70 493
559 935	12 364 472	442 935	149	11 921 537	1 102 643
–	6 560 279	1 857 839	–	4 702 440	493 199
617	873 626	5 837	–	867 789	59 846
53 520	3 636 150	485 212	–	3 150 938	162 753
301	1 704 287	294	–	1 703 993	53 365
–	4 809 631	1 330 970	–	3 478 661	449 491
193 899	7 749 981	748 000	149	7 001 981	682 421
356 835	6 043 703	515 660	–	5 528 042	516 892
63 038	3 126 926	196 900	–	2 930 026	116 271

表7-7

限额以上住宿和餐饮业经营情况 (2016年)

项　目	Item	营业总额 (万元) Total Business Turnover (10 000 yuan)
总　计	**Total**	**1 506 089**
一、住宿业	**Accommodation**	**759 041**
# 国有及国有控股	State-owned and State Holding Majority Shares	226 145
1. 按地区分	**Grouped by Region**	
市　区	Urban Area	562 747
# 吴江区	Wujiang District	62 127
常　熟	Changshu	55 829
张家港	Zhangjiagang	54 803
昆　山	Kunshan	49 661
太　仓	Taicang	36 002
2. 按登记注册类型分	**Grouped by Registration Status**	
国有企业	State-owned Enterprises	99 278
集体企业	Collective-owned Enterprises	14 058
股份合作企业	Share-holding Cooperative Enterprises	777
联营企业	Joint Ownership Enterprises	829
有限责任公司	Limited Liability Corporations	285 022
股份有限公司	Share-holding Cooperative Ltd.	43 354
私营企业	Private Enterprises	163 872
其他企业	Other Enterprises	-
港澳台商投资企业	Enterprises with Investment from HongKong, Macao and Taiwan	58 355
外商投资企业	Enterprises with Foreign Investment	93 497
3. 按主要行业分	**Grouped by Sector**	
旅游饭店	Tourist Hotel	701 179
一般旅馆	Regular Hotel	47 306
其他住宿服务	Other Accommodation Service	10 556
4. 按星级分	**Grouped by Star Rated**	
五　星	Five Star	255 254
四　星	Four Star	143 557
三　星	Three Star	34 920
二　星	Two Star	3 769
一　星	One Star	234
其　他	Other	321 307

BUSINESS CONDITION OF ACCOMMODATION AND CATERING ENTERPRISES ABOVE DESIGNATED SIZE(2016)

客房收入 Room Rate Revenues	餐费收入 Catering Revenues	商品销售收入 Commodity Sales Revenues	其他收入 Others Revenues	年末拥有床位数 (个) Year-end Guest Beds (unit)	年末拥有餐位数 (个) Dining Seats by the Year end (unit)
426 177	**994 330**	**22 688**	**62 895**	**79 146**	**308 151**
363 458	**338 809**	**11 022**	**45 753**	**67 168**	**135 909**
93 272	109 034	3 096	20 743	18 380	44 535
276 401	241 941	9 277	35 128	45 469	89 687
21 898	36 609	581	3 040	5 141	16 581
26 520	25 454	492	3 364	6 597	13 064
16 750	35 222	133	2 698	4 419	15 109
26 600	20 941	710	1 409	7 099	11 804
17 186	15 251	411	3 154	3 584	6 245
39 886	49 697	651	9 045	7 967	19 690
4 198	9 656	76	129	1 231	3 240
504	273	–	–	190	110
240	590	–	–	132	400
127 064	131 350	7 887	18 721	21 671	57 335
22 123	18 961	100	2 170	4 153	4 504
90 892	64 161	1 405	7 414	20 762	35 990
–	–	–	–	–	–
26 492	27 688	545	3 629	5 173	9 073
52 060	36 433	357	4 646	5 889	5 567
324 449	326 343	10 447	39 940	57 638	128 279
31 465	10 885	552	4 405	8 735	6 975
7 544	1 581	24	1 408	795	655
113 357	128 972	1 642	11 284	14 425	36 600
59 052	71 785	2 917	9 802	14 091	43 968
16 081	11 485	398	6 956	6 164	9 685
924	2 089	–	757	400	1 220
234	–	–	–	116	–
173 811	124 478	6 065	16 954	31 972	44 436

表7-7 续表

项　目	Item	营业总额 (万元) Total Business Turnover (10 000 yuan)
二、餐饮业	**Catering Services**	**747 048**
#国有及国有控股	State-owned and State Holding Majority Shares	27 608
1. 按地区分	**Grouped by Region**	
市　区	Urban Area	549 756
# 吴江区	Wujiang District	26 877
常　熟	Changshu	21 015
张家港	Zhangjiagang	47 620
昆　山	Kunshan	119 924
太　仓	Taicang	8 732
2. 按登记注册类型分	**Grouped by Registration Status**	
国有企业	State-owned Enterprises	6 132
集体企业	Collective-owned Enterprises	952
股份合作企业	Share-holding Cooperative Enterprises	-
联营企业	Joint Ownership Enterprises	-
有限责任公司	Limited Liability Corporations	115 040
股份有限公司	Share-holding Cooperative Ltd.	23 245
私营企业	Private Enterprises	266 477
其他企业	Other Enterprises	9 920
港澳台商投资企业	Enterprises with Investment from HongKong, Macao and Taiwan	42 899
外商投资企业	Enterprises with Foreign Investment	282 382
3. 按主要行业分	**Grouped by Sector**	
正餐服务	Dinner	396 480
快餐服务	Fast Food	249 374
饮料及冷饮服务	Beverage and Cold Drink Services	46 121
其他餐饮服务	Other	55 073
4. 按经营方式分	**Grouped by Management Forms**	
独立经营	Independent-stores	359 210
连锁经营总店	Chain-stores-General	237 397
连锁经营分店	Chain-stores-Branch	93 281
其　他	Other	57 160

Continued

				年末拥有床位数(个) Year-end Guest Beds (unit)	年末拥有餐位数(个) Dining Seats by the Year end (unit)
客房收入 Room Rate Revenues	餐费收入 Catering Revenues	商品销售收入 Commodity Sales Revenues	其他收入 Others Revenues		
62 719	**655 521**	**11 665**	**17 142**	**11 978**	**172 242**
9 368	16 091	203	1 945	1 147	5 983
22 909	511 568	4 185	11 094	3 764	126 162
5 639	20 130	122	987	1 519	9 275
2 277	18 190	338	210	855	6 618
10 428	35 308	579	1 305	2 089	12 595
25 236	84 092	6 553	4 043	4 668	22 671
1 870	6 364	9	489	602	4 196
754	4 194	158	1 026	336	1 115
146	682	–	125	97	350
–	–	–	–	–	–
–	–	–	–	–	–
29 267	75 515	821	9 437	4 430	21 742
–	21 797	1 448	–	–	6 628
20 739	234 087	8 753	2 899	5 099	93 230
2 272	7 473	12	164	298	3 500
9 542	29 416	456	3 485	1 718	8 108
–	282 357	18	7	–	37 569
62 719	315 387	3 464	14 910	11 978	100 307
–	249 293	81	–	–	41 056
–	44 086	188	1 847	–	5 177
–	46 755	7 933	385	–	25 702
56 597	279 844	9 160	13 609	10 642	89 055
–	234 939	611	1 847	–	33 070
–	91 773	1 501	7	–	14 853
6 122	48 966	393	1 679	1 336	35 264

表7-8

限额以上批发和零售法人企业主要财务指标 (2016年)

单位：万元

项　目	Item	流动资产合计 Total Circulating Funds	固定资产合计 Total Fixed Assets
总　计	**Total**	**32 554 627**	**2 654 888**
一、批发业	**Wholesale Trades**	**25 836 215**	**1 154 649**
# 国有及国有控股	State-owned and State Holding Majority Shares	4 087 984	356 828
1. 按地区分	**Grouped by Region**		
市　区	Urban Area	9 433 465	432 153
# 吴江区	Wujiang District	2 639 458	112 327
常　熟	Changshu	2 521 423	114 857
张家港	Zhangjiagang	8 837 726	262 171
昆　山	Kunshan	2 447 750	216 046
太　仓	Taicang	2 595 852	129 422
2. 按登记注册类型分	**Grouped by Registration Status**		
国有企业	State-owned Enterprises	1 856 663	220 890
集体企业	Collective-owned Enterprises	16 573	669
股份合作企业	Share-holding Cooperative Enterprises	4 111	383
联营企业	Joint Ownership Enterprises	-	-
有限责任公司	Limited Liability Corporations	8 870 792	200 410
股份有限公司	Share-holding Cooperative Ltd.	433 799	67 108
私营企业	Private Enterprises	8 461 934	350 093
其他企业	Other Enterprises	4 582	630
港澳台商投资企业	Enterprises with Investment from HongKong, Macao and Taiwan	3 068 522	193 082
外商投资企业	Enterprises with Foreign Investment	3 119 239	121 384
3. 按主要行业分	**Grouped by Sector**		
农畜产品批发	Wholesale of Agriculture and Livestock Products	752 600	12 434
食品、饮料及烟草制品批发	Wholesale of Food, Beverages and Tobaccos	1 457 194	109 215
纺织、服装及日用品批发	Wholesale of Textiles, Garments and Daily Articles	8 128 977	519 403
# 服装批发	Wholesale of Garments	3 622 036	303 408
文化、体育用品及器材批发	Wholesale of Cultural, Sports Equipment and Appliances	520 293	12 468

MAIN FINANCIAL INDICATORS OF WHOLESALE AND RETAIL CORPORATION ABOVE DESIGNATED SIZE (2016)

(10 000 yuan)

固定资产原价 Original Value of Fixed Assets	累计折旧 Accumulative Total Depreciation	资产总计 Total Assets	负债总计 Total Liabilities	营业收入 Business Revenue	# 主营业务收入 Major Business Revenue	营业成本 Business Cost	# 主营业务成本 Major Business Cost
4 121 599	**1 593 490**	**40 339 472**	**29 709 119**	**99 591 697**	**98 083 817**	**91 161 335**	**89 894 975**
1 942 887	**801 474**	**30 850 249**	**22 239 188**	**79 401 307**	**78 130 448**	**73 102 667**	**71 892 857**
558 281	201 764	5 095 718	3 250 582	12 568 599	12 190 363	11 294 988	10 974 058
776 696	349 651	11 707 599	7 356 237	27 441 624	26 643 218	25 037 648	24 258 830
159 715	50 481	3 996 296	2 981 761	12 109 896	11 374 066	11 929 212	11 196 760
185 587	72 829	2 807 713	2 278 385	6 346 183	6 314 069	5 737 280	5 725 275
432 227	171 626	10 524 161	8 490 537	34 386 989	34 029 569	33 197 950	32 880 741
327 454	115 659	2 880 245	2 024 449	5 402 949	5 321 665	4 622 866	4 551 713
220 924	91 709	2 930 531	2 089 580	5 823 562	5 821 926	4 506 922	4 476 298
344 224	123 425	2 513 743	1 206 282	4 173 013	3 825 784	3 435 310	3 129 312
2 201	1 532	19 048	17 643	42 116	42 116	41 417	41 417
469	87	6 457	7 585	1 689	1 683	2 065	2 065
–	–	–	–	–	–	–	–
335 860	138 482	10 719 914	8 984 725	31 281 604	30 498 805	30 011 738	29 250 930
100 449	33 412	555 681	321 445	1 178 534	1 178 216	1 060 532	1 060 532
601 392	265 062	9 792 178	7 760 111	32 257 230	32 193 918	31 221 062	31 129 803
1 021	391	5 369	6 315	4 176	4 176	2 967	2 967
310 340	113 440	3 662 456	2 242 319	5 381 856	5 316 844	3 621 302	3 571 249
246 931	125 645	3 575 404	1 692 764	5 081 090	5 068 907	3 706 273	3 704 581
16 017	4 257	784 113	739 195	477 282	477 148	476 780	476 759
185 705	77 004	1 703 279	831 548	4 072 244	4 012 609	3 426 383	3 374 656
870 675	354 373	10 625 151	6 694 085	22 755 224	21 655 587	19 440 765	18 387 864
504 654	203 068	4 585 204	2 487 398	6 434 699	6 074 418	4 718 618	4 402 274
30 454	12 484	546 117	323 350	1 267 503	1 262 177	1 115 872	1 115 260

表7-8 续表 1

单位：万元

项　　目	Item	流动资产合计 Total Circulating Funds	固定资产合计 Total Fixed Assets
医药及医疗器材批发	Wholesale of Medicines and Medical Appliances	494 480	14 273
矿产品、建材及化工产品批发	Wholesale of Mineral Products, Building Materials and Chemical Products	9 589 180	280 822
机械设备、五金交电及电子产品批发	Wholesale of Machinery, Hardware, Transport, Electric and Electronic Equipment	4 317 856	177 163
#农业机械批发	Wholesale Agricultural Machinery	11 454	1 709
汽车、摩托车及零配件批发	Wholesale of Motor Vehicles, Motorcycles and Parts	1 283 197	24 535
五金、交电批发	Wholesale of Hardware, Transport and Electric	370 338	17 107
家用电器批发	Wholesale Household Appliances	772 538	40 615
计算机、软件及辅助设备批发	Wholesale of Computer, Software and Assistant Equipment	85 100	5 159
贸易经纪与代理	Trade Management and Agency	125 150	1 262
其他批发	Other Wholesale	450 485	27 610
二、零售业	**Retail Trades**	**6 718 412**	**1 500 239**
# 国有及国有控股	State-owned and State Holding Majority Shares	1 622 873	198 443
1. 按地区分	**Grouped by Region**		
市　区	Urban Area	3 986 307	995 750
# 吴江区	Wujiang District	281 632	42 347
常　熟	Changshu	453 573	96 546
张家港	Zhangjiagang	504 290	124 413
昆　山	Kunshan	1 688 231	252 201
太　仓	Taicang	86 012	31 329
2. 按登记注册类型分	**Grouped by Registration Status**		
国有企业	State-owned Enterprises	14 426	243
集体企业	Collective-owned Enterprises	14 649	3 682
股份合作企业	Share-holding Cooperative Enterprises	5 108	161
联营企业	Joint Ownership Enterprises	280	291
有限责任公司	Limited Liability Corporations	2 094 923	379 536
股份有限公司	Share-holding Cooperative Ltd.	1 095 471	191 362
私营企业	Private Enterprises	2 409 893	323 661

Continued 1

(10 000 yuan)

固定资产原价 Original Value of Fixed Assets	累计折旧 Accumulative Total Depreciation	资产总计 Total Assets	负债总计 Total Liabilities	营业收入 Business Revenue	# 主营业务收入 Major Business Revenue	营业成本 Business Cost	# 主营业务成本 Major Business Cost
27 068	16 015	520 589	356 390	1 049 737	1 046 732	944 591	942 878
493 523	221 747	10 944 979	9 062 437	38 741 609	38 686 891	37 637 322	37 559 031
258 263	82 917	5 003 463	3 769 563	9 407 530	9 360 250	8 495 857	8 471 876
2 766	1 067	13 342	4 149	21 646	20 941	19 016	18 899
32 138	7 611	1 349 263	1 360 781	3 164 938	3 154 195	2 757 412	2 757 164
28 789	11 899	407 286	278 545	760 830	760 339	692 947	692 796
58 489	18 225	974 877	689 026	2 437 243	2 430 547	2 300 640	2 299 930
7 834	2 681	94 038	56 233	300 562	277 950	284 706	263 096
3 533	2 287	130 099	108 085	524 123	523 942	509 314	509 314
57 649	30 390	592 460	354 537	1 106 056	1 105 113	1 055 783	1 055 220
2 178 713	**792 016**	**9 489 223**	**7 469 931**	**20 190 391**	**19 953 369**	**18 058 669**	**18 002 118**
279 239	119 306	2 028 659	1 558 759	3 548 002	3 491 658	3 250 515	3 233 859
1 331 083	434 649	5 762 446	4 419 032	10 973 635	10 826 199	9 837 482	9 808 824
72 699	31 064	350 595	270 742	1 039 500	1 028 320	942 000	939 957
160 785	68 482	645 999	482 659	1 696 944	1 678 830	1 518 617	1 513 590
200 234	76 528	770 129	598 824	1 243 716	1 230 468	1 124 446	1 122 065
442 645	194 574	2 183 587	1 872 432	5 895 318	5 853 336	5 236 523	5 224 050
43 966	17 783	127 062	96 984	380 777	364 537	341 600	333 589
1 556	1 313	15 948	4 030	23 610	23 438	18 738	18 691
8 000	4 319	19 188	6 372	45 982	45 765	39 648	39 642
441	281	5 269	527	8 605	8 605	6 906	6 906
575	284	571	17	7 760	7 760	7 387	7 387
535 289	211 220	2 926 391	2 379 649	6 127 432	6 049 309	5 395 411	5 381 244
239 098	90 793	1 387 490	1 097 727	2 070 476	2 056 292	1 900 256	1 898 889
539 971	230 604	3 046 141	2 425 573	6 629 568	6 546 149	6 014 434	5 989 531

表7-8 续表 2

单位：万元

项　目	Item	流动资产合计 Total Circulating Funds	固定资产合计 Total Fixed Assets
其他企业	Other Enterprises	570	143
港澳台商投资企业	Enterprises with Investment from HongKong, Macao and Taiwan	853 624	478 121
外商投资企业	Enterprises with Foreign Investment	229 468	123 040
3. 按主要行业分	**Grouped by Sector**		
综合零售	Retail of Integrated	1 333 000	761 682
百货零售	Retail of Consumer Goods	439 917	475 024
超级市场零售	Retail of Supermarket	891 708	286 559
其他综合零售	Others Retail of Integrated	1 375	99
食品、饮料及烟草制品专门零售	Wholesale of Foodstuff, Drink and Tobacco	94 988	22 305
纺织、服装及日用品专门零售	Wholesale of Textiles, Garments, Shoes and Hats	204 694	52 912
文化、体育用品及器材专门零售	Wholesale of Cultural, Sports Equipments and Appliances	198 556	38 074
医药及医疗器材专门零售	Wholesale of Medicines and Medical Appliances	645 652	32 991
汽车、摩托车、燃料及零配件专门零售	Wholesale of Timber	3 034 792	515 389
# 汽车零售	Wholesale of Timber	1 905 071	348 208
家用电器及电子产品专门零售	Retail of Textiles, Garments, Shoes and Hats	234 123	27 152
# 家用电器零售	Retail of Daily Sundry Articles	173 012	25 804
计算机、软件及辅助设备零售	Retail of Computer, Software and Assistant Equipments	26 572	433
五金、家具及室内装修材料专门零售	Retail of Hardware Furniture and Materials for Ornament	31 466	3 594
无店铺及其他零售	Retail of Non-shop and Others	941 142	46 140
4. 按经营方式分	**Grouped by Means of Operation**		
独立商店	Independent shop	3 185 290	865 654
连锁商店总店	Central shop of chain shops	2 013 916	389 913
连锁门店	Chain Shop Outlets	98 396	39 375
其　他	Others	1 420 810	205 297
5. 按零售业态分	**Grouped by Retail Size**		
百货商店	Department Store	511 373	465 019
超级市场	Supermarket	905 783	323 677
专业店	Special Store	2 074 147	330 656
专卖店	Monopoly Store	2 190 437	313 551
其　他	Others	1 036 671	67 336

Continued 2

(10 000 yuan)

固定资产原价 Original Value of Fixed Assets	累计折旧 Accumulative Total Depreciation	资产总计 Total Assets	负债总计 Total Liabilities	营业收入 Business Revenue	# 主营业务收入 Major Business Revenue	营业成本 Business Cost	# 主营业务成本 Major Business Cost
262	119	714	378	2 755	2 755	2 402	2 402
666 109	188 690	1 548 855	1 256 229	3 567 819	3 540 297	3 132 144	3 124 830
187 412	64 394	538 658	299 428	1 706 385	1 673 001	1 541 343	1 532 597
1 063 937	364 423	2 541 765	2 107 289	5 376 684	5 287 978	4 664 757	4 658 511
589 608	175 729	1 126 646	792 005	1 368 482	1 312 469	1 135 137	1 129 888
473 863	188 327	1 413 645	1 313 775	4 002 219	3 969 780	3 524 149	3 523 160
465	367	1 475	1 509	5 983	5 729	5 471	5 463
39 599	17 367	129 406	66 515	225 383	220 402	185 030	182 578
81 762	29 020	395 546	351 006	443 482	439 446	330 669	330 402
75 346	37 633	310 180	198 149	294 721	286 290	229 378	229 319
53 582	20 590	764 581	556 815	1 471 491	1 463 066	1 334 853	1 330 496
748 703	282 463	4 014 301	3 070 820	9 518 145	9 416 765	8 856 828	8 823 258
520 282	182 409	2 589 631	2 020 994	7 149 606	7 066 034	6 675 559	6 648 160
37 384	10 235	290 083	167 613	844 412	831 793	759 947	755 474
33 405	7 604	222 771	130 537	546 315	543 477	504 846	504 727
1 489	1 056	29 092	15 818	48 663	45 297	42 037	39 956
10 262	6 749	36 879	25 027	94 016	93 970	77 982	77 952
68 138	23 537	1 006 481	926 697	1 922 056	1 913 660	1 619 226	1 614 128
1 304 392	499 783	4 820 019	3 590 895	10 778 516	10 631 170	9 702 706	9 663 668
577 887	225 276	2 711 983	2 225 431	5 846 035	5 792 121	5 236 307	5 227 412
55 998	18 824	159 842	120 386	362 776	348 730	302 414	301 585
240 436	48 133	1 797 379	1 533 219	3 203 064	3 181 349	2 817 242	2 809 455
597 426	193 354	1 226 007	849 658	1 454 846	1 396 506	1 210 742	1 205 462
513 724	191 357	1 493 378	1 386 699	4 055 538	4 022 035	3 562 167	3 561 193
542 171	216 243	2 844 417	1 976 897	6 965 049	6 884 303	6 351 948	6 326 837
432 655	164 137	2 676 105	2 162 037	5 199 233	5 142 876	4 762 781	4 741 992
92 737	26 925	1 249 317	1 094 641	2 515 725	2 507 650	2 171 032	2 166 635

表7-8 续表 3

单位：万元

项　目	Item	所有者权益合　计 Total Creditors Equity	营业税金及附加 Taxes and Extra Charges from Business	#主营业务税金及附加 Taxes and Extra Charges from Major Business
总　计	**Total**	**10 630 353**	**307 127**	**304 284**
一、批发业	**Wholesale Trades**	**8 611 061**	**261 824**	**260 491**
# 国有及国有控股	State-owned and State Holding Majority Shares	1 845 137	182 735	181 572
1. 按地区分	**Grouped by Region**			
市　区	Urban Area	4 351 362	203 681	203 031
# 吴江区	Wujiang District	1 014 535	4 420	4 338
常　熟	Changshu	529 328	9 991	9 966
张家港	Zhangjiagang	2 033 623	14 787	14 302
昆　山	Kunshan	855 797	11 263	11 098
太　仓	Taicang	840 951	22 102	22 095
2. 按登记注册类型分	**Grouped by Registration Status**			
国有企业	State-owned Enterprises	1 307 462	170 887	170 322
集体企业	Collective-owned Enterprises	1 405	7	7
股份合作企业	Share-holding Cooperative Enterprises	-1 129	6	6
联营企业	Joint Ownership Enterprises	–	–	–
有限责任公司	Limited Liability Corporations	1 735 189	22 478	21 877
股份有限公司	Share-holding Cooperative Ltd.	234 236	3 709	3 709
私营企业	Private Enterprises	2 032 068	16 151	16 022
其他企业	Other Enterprises	-946	7	7
港澳台商投资企业	Enterprises with Investment from HongKong, Macao and Taiwan	1 420 137	27 537	27 537
外商投资企业	Enterprises with Foreign Investment	1 882 640	21 043	21 005
3. 按主要行业分	**Grouped by Sector**			
农畜产品批发	Wholesale of Agriculture and Livestock Products	44 918	128	128
食品、饮料及烟草制品批发	Wholesale of Food, Beverages and Tobaccos	871 732	166 727	166 727
纺织、服装及日用品批发	Wholesale of Textiles, Garments and Daily Articles	3 931 066	53 524	52 994
# 服装批发	Wholesale of Garments	2 097 806	25 213	24 729
文化、体育用品及器材批发	Wholesale of Cultural, Sports Equipment and Appliances	222 767	6 301	6 301

Continued 3

(10 000 yuan)

其他业务利润 Other Business Profits	销售费用 Cost Related With Sale	管理费用 Managerial Cost	财务费用 Financing Activities Cost	营业利润 Business Profits	利润总额 Total Profits	应交增值税 Value Added Tax Payable
244 086	**3 450 992**	**2 370 965**	**469 689**	**1 866 256**	**2 086 140**	**875 968**
67 707	**2 271 838**	**1 760 363**	**359 907**	**1 621 019**	**1 821 389**	**596 126**
15 662	426 301	137 270	952	491 940	524 159	100 335
25 626	705 393	690 050	134 527	719 944	798 010	208 697
5 752	57 623	57 506	113 916	-49 585	-23 650	18 788
19 704	390 175	85 639	21 158	93 705	105 324	27 269
5 233	419 267	228 532	158 349	290 967	347 797	98 814
16 160	430 016	159 717	19 962	166 499	192 438	107 940
984	326 988	596 426	25 911	349 904	377 820	153 406
828	138 897	116 113	-6 608	279 457	296 167	66 152
–	286	211	357	-162	-164	61
6	10	107	24	-524	-555	66
–	–	–	–	–	–	–
23 897	630 569	125 631	133 482	313 522	356 451	135 740
233	66 847	16 985	6 580	28 092	33 037	14 363
14 518	445 672	329 879	184 531	74 790	132 406	130 055
–	715	449	114	-76	-76	67
18 934	610 036	670 643	26 233	427 267	476 683	208 603
9 292	378 808	500 346	15 195	498 653	527 441	41 019
112	4 236	3 692	970	-10 251	7 842	754
12 128	231 173	53 335	-9 920	206 651	215 419	81 456
10 158	972 630	1 243 318	135 803	895 652	997 220	232 017
4 518	519 744	568 926	8 367	575 009	604 863	51 713
4 639	82 762	23 174	1 187	37 822	48 738	28 914

表7-8 续表 4

单位：万元

项目	Item	所有者权益合计 Total Creditors Equity	营业税金及附加 Taxes and Extra Charges from Business	#主营业务税金及附加 Taxes and Extra Charges from Major Business
医药及医疗器材批发	Wholesale of Medicines and Medical Appliances	164 199	1 169	1 169
矿产品、建材及化工产品批发	Wholesale of Mineral Products, Building Materials and Chemical Products	1 882 542	15 688	14 961
机械设备、五金交电及电子产品批发	Wholesale of Machinery, Hardware, Transport, Electric and Electronic Equipment	1 233 901	17 210	17 132
# 农业机械批发	Wholesale Agricultural Machinery	9 194	97	22
汽车、摩托车及零配件批发	Wholesale of Motor Vehicles, Motorcycles and Parts	-11 517	7 953	7 953
五金、交电批发	Wholesale of Hardware, Transport and Electric	128 741	1 980	1 980
家用电器批发	Wholesale Household Appliances	285 852	2 291	2 291
计算机、软件及辅助设备批发	Wholesale of Computer, Software and Assistant Equipment	37 805	346	345
贸易经纪与代理	Trade Management and Agency	22 014	65	65
其他批发	Other Wholesale	237 923	1 014	1 014
二、零售业	**Retail Trades**	**2 019 292**	**45 303**	**43 793**
# 国有及国有控股	State-owned and State Holding Majority Shares	469 900	6 584	5 990
1. 按地区分	**Grouped by Region**			
市　区	Urban Area	1 343 415	26 337	25 162
# 吴江区	Wujiang District	79 853	1 672	1 626
常　熟	Changshu	163 339	3 931	3 802
张家港	Zhangjiagang	171 305	3 119	3 100
昆　山	Kunshan	311 155	11 034	10 858
太　仓	Taicang	30 078	881	871
2. 按登记注册类型分	**Grouped by Registration Status**			
国有企业	State-owned Enterprises	11 917	86	66
集体企业	Collective-owned Enterprises	12 815	94	94
股份合作企业	Share-holding Cooperative Enterprises	4 741	47	47
联营企业	Joint Ownership Enterprises	554	5	5
有限责任公司	Limited Liability Corporations	546 742	15 786	15 203
股份有限公司	Share-holding Cooperative Ltd.	289 763	4 751	4 612
私营企业	Private Enterprises	620 568	14 572	14 252

Continued 4

(10 000 yuan)

其他业务利润 Other Business Profits	销售费用 Cost Related With Sale	管理费用 Managerial Cost	财务费用 Financing Activities Cost	营业利润 Business Profits	利润总额 Total Profits	应交增值税 Value Added Tax Payable
1 899	46 437	29 545	6 092	22 337	22 580	5 847
12 796	395 707	208 096	203 126	261 309	302 119	152 314
25 462	518 698	176 168	18 346	190 741	209 782	88 422
618	282	1 480	-121	998	1 337	130
11 076	317 728	26 925	522	58 843	66 054	9 512
847	20 781	26 888	353	18 761	18 379	6 548
6 854	82 376	27 055	3 690	24 214	26 127	22 817
731	4 940	5 335	935	4 172	4 407	3 145
114	6 704	5 089	983	1 953	2 167	493
400	13 490	17 946	3 320	14 806	15 523	5 908
176 379	**1 179 153**	**610 601**	**109 782**	**245 238**	**264 751**	**279 843**
9 253	165 002	34 401	8 407	84 761	90 676	34 596
91 962	626 265	314 000	71 423	111 777	125 008	164 130
7 490	62 370	18 618	7 535	9 838	9 171	18 546
18 574	84 357	48 810	10 428	38 448	39 916	22 419
26 042	71 166	44 811	11 067	2 673	4 195	16 029
33 155	380 086	191 100	12 173	87 942	90 945	72 011
6 646	17 280	11 880	4 691	4 399	4 688	5 254
–	1 007	1 412	-132	2 482	2 545	699
265	1 808	2 713	107	1 808	1 852	1 039
–	149	145	34	1 324	1 324	385
–	192	6	–	170	170	50
54 226	423 262	185 673	37 637	87 906	94 202	88 795
16 042	77 892	36 527	5 964	48 116	52 809	28 591
77 336	317 617	201 308	51 025	52 591	57 298	94 250

表7-8 续表 5

单位：万元

项 目	Item	所有者权益合 计 Total Creditors Equity	营业税金及附加 Taxes and Extra Charges from Business	#主营业务税金及附加 Taxes and Extra Charges from Major Business
其他企业	Other Enterprises	335	5	5
港澳台商投资企业	Enterprises with Investment from HongKong, Macao and Taiwan	292 626	7 039	6 662
外商投资企业	Enterprises with Foreign Investment	239 231	2 920	2 849
3. 按主要行业分	**Grouped by Sector**			
综合零售	Retail of Integrated	434 476	16 135	15 810
百货零售	Retail of Consumer Goods	334 641	9 372	9 047
超级市场零售	Retail of Supermarket	99 870	6 749	6 749
其他综合零售	Others Retail of Integrated	-34	14	14
食品、饮料及烟草制品专门零售	Wholesale of Foodstuff, Drink and Tobacco	62 891	658	658
纺织、服装及日用品专门零售	Wholesale of Textiles, Garments, Shoes and Hats	44 540	2 290	2 289
文化、体育用品及器材专门零售	Wholesale of Cultural, Sports Equipment and Appliances	112 031	4 638	4 514
医药及医疗器材专门零售	Wholesale of Medicines and Medical Appliances	207 766	2 523	2 517
汽车、摩托车、燃料及零配件专门零售	Wholesale of Timber	943 481	13 355	12 742
# 汽车零售	Wholesale of Timber	568 637	9 380	8 913
家用电器及电子产品专门零售	Retail of Textiles, Garments, Shoes and Hats	122 470	1 264	1 234
# 家用电器零售	Retail of Daily Sundry Articles	92 234	734	734
计算机、软件及辅助设备零售	Retail of Computer, Software and Assistant Equipment	13 274	164	142
五金、家具及室内装修材料专门零售	Retail of Hardware Furniture and Materials for Ornament	11 852	368	348
无店铺及其他零售	Retail of Non-shop and Others	79 784	4 073	3 682
4. 按经营方式分	**Grouped by Means of Operation**			
独立商店	Independent shop	1 229 124	26 673	25 823
连锁商店总店	Central shop of chain shops	486 553	10 384	10 217
连锁门店	Chain Shop Outlets	39 455	1 541	1 465
其 他	Others	264 160	6 706	6 289
5. 按零售业态分	**Grouped by Retail Size**			
百货商店	Department Store	376 349	10 149	9 804
超级市场	Supermarket	106 679	6 843	6 843
专业店	Special Store	867 520	13 245	12 206
专卖店	Monopoly Storo	514 068	10 347	10 244
其 他	Others	154 676	4 719	4 697

Continued 5

(10 000 yuan)

其他业务利润 Other Business Profits	销售费用 Cost Related With Sale	管理费用 Managerial Cost	财务费用 Financing Activities Cost	营业利润 Business Profits	利润总额 Total Profits	应交增值税 Value Added Tax Payable
–	127	88	–	133	133	40
14 582	250 829	141 052	9 422	37 568	41 167	29 600
13 929	106 270	41 678	5 724	13 141	13 251	36 393
67 696	427 189	237 885	22 287	21 030	29 119	55 836
53 307	94 231	109 526	20 511	-3 662	610	27 353
14 143	332 680	127 998	1 766	24 842	28 650	28 441
246	278	361	10	-150	-141	42
1 879	18 574	11 915	754	9 081	9 689	5 223
2 537	83 716	31 608	6 610	-9 608	-7 953	12 521
9 357	33 484	20 237	3 218	4 600	6 500	5 542
8 151	62 230	29 003	7 100	44 020	43 269	26 840
74 964	288 701	166 023	67 767	157 122	161 370	136 549
70 534	207 224	141 106	63 247	79 650	82 869	107 163
8 126	61 126	13 903	1 377	8 298	8 897	8 904
4 220	30 425	5 587	575	5 441	5 758	5 366
692	1 676	3 309	262	1 341	1 501	963
1	5 949	3 964	53	5 869	5 868	1 528
3 669	198 185	96 064	615	4 826	7 992	26 901
132 446	529 735	325 385	88 872	137 110	147 641	176 089
18 248	377 523	148 839	3 324	84 667	87 347	54 064
10 358	41 656	17 964	1 789	-2 579	-856	6 172
15 327	230 240	118 413	15 796	26 040	30 618	43 518
57 156	98 764	108 334	20 999	3 517	7 976	29 964
14 894	342 667	138 510	3 118	18 197	22 024	30 170
59 714	276 395	164 814	41 616	147 456	152 340	109 621
41 112	237 368	93 165	36 685	70 657	76 345	71 965
3 503	223 959	105 779	7 364	5 411	6 065	38 123

表7-9 限额以上住宿和餐饮法人企业主要财务指标 (2016年)

单位：万元

项　目	Item	流动资产合计 Total Circulating Funds	固定资产合计 Total Fixed Assets
总　计	**Total**	**1 076 523**	**1 675 315**
一、住宿业	**Accommodation**	**770 123**	**1 460 861**
1. 按地区分	**Grouped by Region**		
市　区	Urban Area	539 016	1 041 482
# 吴江区	Wujiang District	53 185	198 074
常　熟	Changshu	67 782	144 716
张家港	Zhangjiagang	45 628	78 345
昆　山	Kunshan	69 647	148 781
太　仓	Taicang	48 051	47 537
2. 按登记注册类型分	**Grouped by Registration Status**		
国有企业	State-owned Enterprises	53 147	322 561
集体企业	Collective-owned Enterprises	27 687	12 509
股份合作企业	Share-holding Cooperative Enterprises	–	–
联营企业	Joint Ownership Enterprises	457	98
有限责任公司	Limited Liability Corporations	357 097	560 096
股份有限公司	Share-holding Cooperative Ltd.	83 281	165 567
私营企业	Private Enterprises	189 332	221 744
其他企业	Other Enterprises	–	–
港澳台商投资企业	Enterprises with Investment from HongKong, Macao and Taiwan	32 037	98 430
外商投资企业	Enterprises with Foreign Investment	27 084	79 857
3. 按星级分	**Grouped by Sear Rated**		
# 五　星	Five Star	263 444	553 742
四　星	Four Star	130 630	283 271
三　星	Three Star	56 099	43 815
二　星	Two Star	5 872	1 509

MAIN FINANCIAL INDICATORS OF ACCOMMODATION AND CATERING CORPORATION ABOVE DESIGNATED SIZE (2016)

(10 000 yuan)

固定资产原价 Original Value of Fixed Assets	累计折旧 Accumulative Total Depreciation	资产总计 Total Assets	负债总计 Total Liabilities	营业收入 Business Revenue	#主营业务收入 Major Business Revenue	营业成本 Business Cost	#主营业务成本 Major Business Cost
2 401 558	**823 448**	**3 742 877**	**2 618 324**	**1 223 977**	**1 212 625**	**505 845**	**501 580**
2 050 251	**682 997**	**3 027 517**	**2 024 014**	**578 393**	**570 963**	**187 346**	**185 811**
1 492 997	502 934	2 221 198	1 396 838	415 344	411 596	128 080	127 219
233 642	78 266	278 686	236 211	52 723	52 693	16 250	16 250
163 528	51 595	248 633	220 257	46 511	45 238	17 590	17 205
144 263	68 487	189 241	136 887	40 237	39 369	15 286	15 118
179 989	37 657	247 714	170 180	40 893	39 931	15 214	15 163
69 475	22 323	120 731	99 852	35 407	34 829	11 175	11 106
364 968	83 770	532 563	241 909	68 771	67 426	21 050	20 831
30 300	18 078	53 040	39 308	12 136	12 136	4 421	4 421
–	–	–	–	–	–	–	–
688	590	555	310	798	798	237	237
810 220	281 027	1 373 365	804 278	247 660	244 456	79 271	78 614
200 545	35 048	280 717	265 978	31 849	31 687	14 763	14 758
311 707	103 682	518 356	475 570	137 816	135 209	48 540	47 887
–	–	–	–	–	–	–	–
153 206	54 776	144 876	90 294	38 757	38 644	7 529	7 529
178 617	106 024	124 045	106 366	40 607	40 607	11 534	11 534
868 746	319 002	1 046 672	749 502	174 134	173 096	45 337	45 173
357 801	125 403	764 140	307 436	134 140	131 075	55 632	55 006
75 601	31 786	133 025	64 316	34 882	33 967	13 460	13 412
3 006	1 496	7 450	6 039	3 756	3 756	1 589	1 589

表7-9 续表 1

单位：万元

项　目	Item	流动资产合计 Total Circulating Funds	固定资产合计 Total Fixed Assets
二、餐饮业	**Catering Services**	**306 400**	**214 454**
1. 按地区分	**Grouped by Region**		
市　区	Urban Area	230 890	119 999
# 吴江区	Wujiang District	7 517	41 532
常　熟	Changshu	15 261	3 547
张家港	Zhangjiagang	15 105	37 526
昆　山	Kunshan	42 516	52 041
太　仓	Taicang	2 627	1 340
2. 按登记注册类型分	**Grouped by Registration Status**		
国有企业	State-owned Enterprises	1 857	92
集体企业	Collective-owned Enterprises	193	25
股份合作企业	Share-holding Cooperative Enterprises	–	–
联营企业	Joint Ownership Enterprises	–	–
有限责任公司	Limited Liability Corporations	99 430	59 423
股份有限公司	Share-holding Cooperative Ltd.	56 989	409
私营企业	Private Enterprises	104 166	92 957
其他企业	Other Enterprises	324	151
港澳台商投资企业	Enterprises with Investment from HongKong, Macao and Taiwan	22 421	45 309
外商投资企业	Enterprises with Foreign Investment	21 020	16 088
3. 按主要行业分	**Grouped by Sector**		
正　餐	Dinner	259 569	191 667
快　餐	Fast Food	11 219	15 486
饮料及冷饮服务	Beverage and Cold Drink Services	16 581	5 449
其他餐饮业	Other	19 031	1 852

Continued 1

(10 000 yuan)

固定资产原价 Original Value of Fixed Assets	累计折旧 Accumulative Total Depreciation	资产总计 Total Assets	负债总计 Total Liabilities	营业收入 Business Revenue	#主营业务收入 Major Business Revenue	营业成本 Business Cost	#主营业务成本 Major Business Cost
351 307	**140 452**	**715 361**	**594 310**	**645 584**	**641 662**	**318 499**	**315 769**
211 826	94 907	476 847	356 050	497 673	495 758	247 090	244 902
57 576	16 088	57 924	46 373	23 549	23 518	11 105	11 100
8 994	5 449	31 123	37 456	20 574	20 162	11 711	11 443
55 613	18 086	78 728	71 215	31 808	31 618	11 751	11 725
72 571	21 019	123 459	121 727	87 462	86 110	43 724	43 530
2 304	991	5 203	7 862	8 068	8 015	4 223	4 170
269	177	1 948	1 055	3 242	3 042	1 423	1 229
45	20	218	23	944	944	486	486
–	–	–	–	–	–	–	–
–	–	–	–	–	–	–	–
108 523	52 549	184 018	197 389	103 964	103 725	39 611	39 185
1 199	851	64 151	62 678	23 280	23 245	9 234	9 234
133 700	40 831	266 185	230 404	252 287	250 520	140 099	139 152
573	421	2 037	6 925	5 553	5 553	3 220	3 220
71 540	26 231	95 466	69 602	32 100	31 688	8 553	8 553
35 460	19 371	101 338	26 235	224 215	222 946	115 874	114 711
301 960	113 851	595 671	536 981	340 852	338 950	146 098	145 378
34 572	19 087	59 815	28 466	241 762	240 585	131 045	129 882
9 855	4 406	35 639	17 510	10 910	10 498	2 770	2 770
4 920	3 108	24 235	11 353	52 061	51 630	38 586	37 740

表7-9 续表 2

单位：万元

项　　目	Item	所有者权益合计 Total Creditors Equity	营业税金及附加 Taxes and Extra Charges from Business	#主营业务税金及附加 Taxes and Extra Charges from Major Business
总　计	**Total**	**1 124 554**	**26 453**	**26 425**
一、住宿业	**Accommodation**	**1 003 503**	**12 688**	**12 668**
1. 按地区分	**Grouped by Region**			
市　区	Urban Area	824 360	9 200	9 189
# 吴江区	Wujiang District	42 475	1 136	1 136
常　熟	Changshu	28 376	938	938
张家港	Zhangjiagang	52 354	862	862
昆　山	Kunshan	77 535	857	857
太　仓	Taicang	20 878	830	822
2. 按登记注册类型分	**Grouped by Registration Status**			
国有企业	State-owned Enterprises	290 654	1 632	1 632
集体企业	Collective-owned Enterprises	13 732	239	239
股份合作企业	Share-holding Cooperative Enterprises	–	–	–
联营企业	Joint Ownership Enterprises	244	18	18
有限责任公司	Limited Liability Corporations	569 087	5 619	5 608
股份有限公司	Share-holding Cooperative Ltd.	14 739	624	624
私营企业	Private Enterprises	42 786	3 011	3 007
其他企业	Other Enterprises	–	–	–
港澳台商投资企业	Enterprises with Investment from HongKong Macao and Taiwan	54 582	761	755
外商投资企业	Enterprises with Foreign Investment	17 679	786	786
3. 按星级分	**Grouped by Sear Rated**			
# 五　星	Five Star	297 170	3 401	3 401
四　星	Four Star	456 704	3 079	3 070
三　星	Three Star	68 709	758	758
二　星	Two Star	1 412	151	151

Continued 2

(10 000 yuan)

其他业务利润 Other Business Profits	销售费用 Cost Related With Sale	管理费用 Managerial Cost	财务费用 Financing Activities Cost	营业利润 Business Profits	利润总额 Total Profits
6 787	**380 820**	**325 979**	**51 606**	**-56 035**	**-53 407**
3 936	**200 937**	**225 987**	**40 395**	**-78 470**	**-75 615**
1 147	152 986	168 978	28 284	-61 775	-61 446
59	23 803	19 067	2 400	-9 893	-9 350
888	14 044	17 688	3 099	-6 835	-5 570
1 197	16 271	10 077	3 354	-5 596	-4 596
213	10 382	15 732	3 725	-4 966	-4 877
492	7 255	13 512	1 934	702	874
712	23 011	28 655	2 571	-8 155	-3 736
–	6 539	879	844	-786	-775
–	–	–	–	–	–
23	468	92	1	5	1
1 917	86 044	94 073	9 938	-15 890	-20 046
117	12 790	15 542	11 398	-23 380	-22 268
280	45 390	49 782	9 185	-18 921	-19 044
–	–	–	–	–	–
109	14 633	17 033	2 383	-3 579	-2 626
777	12 062	19 930	4 075	-7 765	-7 120
1 629	63 097	83 824	13 635	-35 016	-31 162
1 416	38 563	46 251	4 417	-3 585	-7 273
157	10 760	9 882	1 530	-700	-1 621
–	1 722	206	39	50	50

表7-9 续表 3

单位：万元

项　目	Item	所有者权益合计 Total Creditors Equity	营业税金及附加 Taxes and Extra Charges from Business	#主营业务税金及附加 Taxes and Extra Charges from Major Business
二、餐饮业	**Catering Services**	**121 051**	**13 765**	**13 757**
1. 按地区分	**Grouped by Region**			
市　区	Urban Area	120 798	10 582	10 573
# 吴江区	Wujiang District	11 551	554	554
常　熟	Changshu	-6 333	614	614
张家港	Zhangjiagang	7 513	647	647
昆　山	Kunshan	1 732	1 771	1 771
太　仓	Taicang	-2 660	152	152
2. 按登记注册类型分	**Grouped by Registration Status**			
国有企业	State-owned Enterprises	894	70	62
集体企业	Collective-owned Enterprises	194	19	19
股份合作企业	Share-holding Cooperative Enterprises	–	–	–
联营企业	Joint Ownership Enterprises	–	–	–
有限责任公司	Limited Liability Corporations	-13 371	2 122	2 121
股份有限公司	Share-holding Cooperative Ltd.	1 472	480	480
私营企业	Private Enterprises	35 781	5 531	5 531
其他企业	Other Enterprises	-4 888	375	375
港澳台商投资企业	Enterprises with Investment from HongKong Macao and Taiwan	25 865	674	674
外商投资企业	Enterprises with Foreign Investment	75 104	4 495	4 495
3. 按主要行业分	**Grouped by Sector**			
正　餐	Dinner	58 690	7 968	7 959
快　餐	Fast Food	31 350	4 962	4 962
饮料及冷饮服务	Beverage and Cold Drink Services	18 129	210	210
其他餐饮业	Other	12 882	626	626

Continued 3

(10 000 yuan)

其他业务利润 Other Business Profits	销售费用 Cost Related With Sale	管理费用 Managerial Cost	财务费用 Financing Activities Cost	营业利润 Business Profits	利润总额 Total Profits
2 851	**179 883**	**99 992**	**11 212**	**22 436**	**22 208**
1 273	149 068	54 257	7 255	29 357	29 762
745	7 131	5 737	1 123	-2 105	-2 237
144	3 889	4 040	329	-9	14
274	12 630	12 770	1 813	-7 696	-7 649
1 159	12 307	26 321	1 775	1 723	627
–	1 989	2 604	40	-940	-545
5	1 138	553	4	54	50
–	274	159	–	6	6
–	–	–	–	–	–
–	–	–	–	–	–
-81	38 517	24 339	3 945	-4 438	-4 973
68	7 801	4 165	1 072	597	650
2 242	59 757	40 388	3 159	3 503	3 720
–	1 242	475	10	231	237
412	14 834	8 476	2 732	-3 168	-3 226
204	56 321	21 438	290	25 652	25 743
2 047	109 570	72 126	10 573	-5 151	-5 707
164	56 572	22 889	295	25 855	26 166
510	5 335	1 972	258	365	367
130	8 406	3 005	87	1 367	1 382

表7-10

连锁总店经营情况 (2016年)

项 目	Item	连锁总店数(个) Number of Chain Shops (unit)
总 计	**Total**	**50**
一、零售业	**Retail Trades**	**44**
1.按登记注册类型分	**Grouped by Registration Status**	
内资企业	Domestic Funded Enterprises	39
# 有限责任公司	Limited Liability Corporations	24
私营企业	Private Enterprises	14
港澳台商投资企业	Enterprises with Investment from HongKong, Macao and Taiwan	3
外商投资企业	Enterprises with Foreign Investment	2
2.按连锁经营业务分	**Grouped by Scope of Business**	
# 综合零售	Retail of Integrated	16
食品、饮料及烟草制品专门零售	Retail of Food, Beverages and Tobaccos	7
医疗及医疗器材专门零售	Retail of Medicines and Medical Appliances	12
家用电器及电子产品专门零售	Retail of Household Appliances and Electronic Products	3
3.按零售业态分	**Grouped by Retail Size**	
# 便利店	Convenience Store	4
超 市	Supermarket	9
专业店	Special Store	19
专卖店	Monopoly Store	7
二、住宿业	**Accommodation**	**1**
三、餐饮业	**Catering Services**	**5**
正 餐	Dinner	–
快 餐	Fast Food	1
饮料及冷饮服务	Beverage and Cold Drink Services	1
其 他	Other	3
附：外省在苏连锁门店	**Number of Chain Shops in Suzhou of Other Provinces**	–

BASIC STATISTICS OF CENTRAL SHOPS OF CHAIN STORES (2016)

连锁门店数(个) Number of Chain Shop Outlets (unit)	直营店 Factory Outlet	加盟店 Join-in Outlet	从业人员(人) Total Employment (person)	销售总额(营业额)(万元) Total Sales Business Income (10 000 yuan)	# 商品零售额 Retail Sale Trade
3 195	**2 241**	**954**	**48 713**	**5 549 958**	**4 042 967**
2 881	**1 927**	**954**	**35 128**	**5 309 610**	**3 807 360**
2 655	1 701	954	20 685	1 324 581	1 266 864
2 144	1 409	735	16 729	1 040 564	985 727
507	288	219	3 913	282 739	279 858
45	45	–	12 348	3 092 675	1 824 336
181	181	–	2 095	892 354	716 160
1 381	647	734	25 360	3 966 551	2 648 690
237	237	–	1 163	56 706	53 826
681	681	–	3 686	160 759	157 904
18	18	–	665	188 421	188 421
62	62	–	394	11 811	11 811
1 274	540	734	12 361	850 430	800 908
755	747	8	4 638	367 970	362 656
564	352	212	3 035	82 734	79 854
5	**5**	–	**115**	**2 951**	**58**
309	**309**	–	**13 470**	**237 397**	**235 550**
–	–	–	–	–	–
246	246	–	11 948	215 998	215 998
22	22	–	579	7 726	5 879
41	41	–	943	13 673	13 673
49	**49**	–	**4 094**	**422 229**	**307 609**

表7-11

亿元以上商品交易市场基本情况（2016年）
GENERAL INFORMATION OF COMMODITY EXCHANGE MARKET WITH TOTAL SALE OVER 100 MILLION YUAN (2016)

项　目	Item	市场数(个) Number of Markets (unit)	年末已出租摊位数(个) Year-end Number of Hired Booths (unit)	商品成交额(万元) Transaction Value (10 000 yuan)	# 商品零售额 Consumer Goods Retail Sale
总　计	**Total**	**82**	**77 306**	**60 566 239**	**8 465 028**
一、按经营环境分	**Grouped by Form of Operation Environment**				
露天式	Open Air	5	1 372	147 530	47 016
封闭式	Seal Off	61	64 581	40 247 084	7 466 761
其　他	Others	16	11 353	20 171 625	951 251
二、按经营方式分	**Grouped by Form of Operation**				
批　发	Whole sale	50	67 589	58 329 062	6 615 236
零　售	Retail Sale	32	9 717	2 237 177	1 849 792
三、按市场类别分	**Grouped by Category of Market**				
综合市场	Integrated Market	23	11 365	5 964 525	1 808 643
生产资料综合市场	General Market	-	-	-	-
工业品综合市场	Industrial Products	1	390	12 655	5 062
农产品综合市场	Farm and Side-line Products	18	9 447	4 071 454	1 104 470
其他综合市场	Others	4	1 528	1 880 416	699 111
专业市场	Special Market	59	65 941	54 601 714	6 656 385
# 建材市场	Building Materials	6	2 262	314 389	206 507
金属材料市场	Metal Material	7	2 547	12 943 916	3 512
粮油市场	Grain and Oil	3	476	1 670 952	4 015
肉食禽蛋市场	Meat, Poultry and Eggs	4	988	410 682	116 875
水产品市场	Aquatic Products	5	1 383	528 038	472 530
蔬菜市场	Vegetables	2	1 183	120 882	17 721
食品饮料烟酒市场	Food, Beverage and Tobacco	1	408	502 386	25 966
纺织品服装鞋帽市场	Textile Products, Garments, Shoes and Hats	3	33 703	28 271 831	3 977 645
小商品市场	Small Commodities	1	2 321	670 000	201 000
家具市场	Furniture	5	4 417	990 901	150 041
汽车市场	Vehicles	3	325	887 288	844 968

主 要 统 计 指 标 解 释

社会消费品零售总额 指企业（单位、个体户）通过交易直接售给个人、社会集团非生产、非经营用的实物商品金额，以及提供餐饮服务所取得的收入金额。个人包括城乡居民和入境人员，社会集团包括机关、社会团体、部队、学校、企事业单位、居委会或村委会等。

批发和零售业商品购进、销售、库存额 指各种登记注册类型的批发和零售业企业(单位)以本企业(单位)为总体的，从国内、国外市场购进的商品总量，销售和出口的商品总量，库存的商品总量等情况。该指标可以反映商品流转过程中商品的购进、销售、库存之间的比例关系和存在的问题。

商品购进额 指从本企业以外的单位和个人购进（包括从国外直接进口）作为转卖或加工后转卖的商品金额（含增值税）。商品购进包括：（1）从工农业生产者、批发和零售业企业、住宿和餐饮业企业、出版社或报社的出版发行部门和其他服务业企业购进的商品；（2）从机关团体、事业单位购进的商品；（3）从海关、市场管理部门购进的缉私和没收的商品；（4）从居民收购的废旧商品等。不包括：（1）企业为本单位自身经营用，不是作为转卖而购进的商品，如材料物资、包装物、低值易耗品、办公用品等；（2）未通过买卖行为而收入的商品，如接受其他部门移交的商品、借入的商品、收入代其他单位保管的商品、其他单位赠送的样品、加工回收的成品等；（3）经本单位介绍，由买卖双方直接结算，本单位只收取手续费的业务；（4）销售退回和买方拒付货款的商品；（5）商品溢余。

商品销售额 指对本单位以外的单位和个人出售的商品金额（包括售给本单位消费用的商品，含增值税）。商品销售包括（1）售给城乡居民和社会集团消费用的商品；（2）售给农业、工业、建筑业、服务业等国民经济各行业用于生产、经营用的商品，包括售予批发和零售业作为转卖或加工后转卖的商品；（3）对国（境）外直接出口的商品。不包括：（1）未通过买卖行为付出的商品，如随机构变动移交给其他企业单位的商品、借出的商品、归还受其他单位委托代保管的商品、付出的加工原料和赠送给其他单位的样品等；（2）经本单位介绍，由买卖双方直接结算，本单位只收取手续费的业务；（3）购货退回的商品；（4）商品损耗和损失；（5）出售本单位自用的废旧物资。

商品库存额 对于批发和零售业法人单位和个体经营户，是指报告期末取得所有权的全部商品金额（含增值税）；对于批发和零售业产业活动单位，是指报告期末实际在库且归属法人具有所有权的全部商品金额（含增值税）。库存商品包括：(1)存放在本单位(如门市部、批发站、采购站、经营处)的仓库、货场、货柜和货架中的商品；(2)挑选、整理、包装中的商品；(3)已记入购进而尚未运到本单位的商品，即发货单或银行承兑凭证已到而货未到的商品；(4)寄放他处的商品，如因购货方拒绝付款而暂时存在购货方的商品；(5)委托其他单位代销(未作销售或调出)尚未售出的商品；(6)代其他单位购进尚未交付的商品。不包括：所有权不属于本单位的商品；委托外单位加工的商品；外贸企业代理其他单位从国外进口，尚未付给订货单位的商品；代国家储备部门保管的商品。

住宿业 指为旅行者提供短期留宿场所的活动，有些单位只提供住宿，也有些单位提供住宿、饮食、商务、娱乐一体的服务，不包括主要按月或按年长期出租房屋住所的活动。

餐饮业 指通过即时制作加工、商业销售和服务性劳动等，向消费者提供食品和消费场所及设施的服务。

住宿和餐饮业营业额 指住宿和餐饮业单位在经营活动中因提供服务或销售商品等取得的收入。包括：客房收入、餐费收入、商品销售额（含增值税）和其他收入。其中，客房收入指住宿和餐饮业单位在经营活动中因提供住宿服务取得的收入。餐费收入指本单位为顾客提供就餐服务取得的收入，包括：经烹饪、调制加工后出售的各种食品，如主食、炒菜、凉拌菜等的收入。

亿元以上商品交易市场 指年成交额在亿元及以上的商品交易市场。商品交易市场是指经有关部门和组织批准设立，有固定场所、设施，有经营管理部门和监管人员，若干市场经营者入内，常年或实际开业三个月以上，集中、公开、独立地进行生活消费品、生产资料等现货商品交易以及提供相关服务的交易场所，包括各类消费品市场、生产资料市场等。

连锁总店（总部） 指负责连锁企业资源（商号、商誉、经营模式、服务标准、管理模式等等）的开发、配置、控制或使用等功能的企业核心管理机构。连锁经营是指经营同类商品或服务，使用统一商号的若干店铺，在同一总店（总部）的管理下，采取统一采购或特许经营等方式，实现规模效益的组织形式，包括直营连锁、特许连锁和自愿连锁三种形式。其中，直营连锁是指连锁店铺由连锁公司全资或控股开设，在总部的直接控制下，开展统一经营的连锁经营形式；特许连锁是指拥有注册商标、企业标志、专利、专有技术等经营资源的企业（特许人），以合同形式将其拥有的经营资源许可其他经营者（被特许人）使用，被特许人按合同约定在统一的经营模式下开展经营，并向特许人支付特许经营费用的连锁经营形式；自愿连锁是指若干个店铺或企业自愿组合起来，在不改变各自资产所有权关系的情况下，以同一个品牌形象面对消费者，以共同进货为纽带开展的连锁经营形式。

EXPLANATORY NOTES ON MAIN STATISTICAL INDICATORS

Total Retail Sales of Consumer Goods refer to the amount obtained by enterprises (units, self-employed individuals) through direct sales of non-production and non-business physical commodity to individuals, social institutions, and revenue from providing catering services. Individuals include rural and urban households, population from abroad, social institutions include government agencies, social organizations, military units, schools, institutions, neighbourhood (village) committees.

Purchase, Sales and Stock of Commodities by Wholesale and Retail Trades refer to the total volume of commodities purchased, total volume of sales and exports, and the stock of commodities by wholesale and retail enterprises (establishments) of different status of registration from domestic and overseas markets. This indicator reflects the relationship among purchase, sales and stock of commodities in the circulation of goods and reveals the existing problems.

Total Purchases of Commodities refer to the total value of purchases of commodities by enterprises (establishments) from other establishments or individuals (including direct import from abroad) for the purpose of re-selling, either with or without further processing of the commodities purchased. The commodities include: (1) commodities purchased from agricultural and industrial producer, wholesaler, retailer, publishing house and other service business; (2) commodities purchased from institutions and government departments; (3) confiscated goods purchased from the customs authorities or market management agencies; (4) second-hand goods and wastes purchased from residents; The commodities exclude (1) commodities purchased by enterprises (establishments) for use in their own business operation, commodities obtained without buying or selling procedures such as materials, consumable goods of low value, office appliance, etc. (2) received goods without trading, such as goods handed over from others, borrowed goods, preserved goods for others, donated goods from others, processed and retrieved goods, etc. (3) goods of direct settlement between buyer and seller with handling fees introduced by others, (4) goods returned or refused to pay by the buyer, (5) excessive goods.

Total Sales of Commodities refer to value of commodities sold by the establishments to other establishments and individuals (including goods sold for self consumption, including the value-added tax). The commodities include: (1) commodities sold to urban and rural residents and social groups for their consumption; (2) commodities sold to establishments in all industries for their production and operation, including agriculture, industry, construction, and catering services including commodities sold to wholesale and retail establishments for re-selling, with or without further processing; and (3) commodities for direct export to abroad. Excluded are (1) extended commodities without trading, such as goods handed over to other enterprises and institutions because of the change of organizations, lent goods, returned goods preserved for others, extended processing materials and samples donated to others, (2) goods of direct settlement between buyer and seller with handling fees introduced by others, (3) goods returned after purchase, (4) damaged and spoiled goods, (5) waste and used goods of self use,

Total Stock of Commodities For the legal entities and self-employed individuals engaged in wholesale and retail trade, it refers to total value (including VAT) of commodities possessed at the end of the reference period; and for wholesale and retail establishments, it refers to the value (including VAT) of all commodities actually in stock and owned by their legal persons at the end of reference period. The commodities in stock includes: (1) commodities located in storage, garages, counters, and shelves of operating places of wholesale and retail trades (such as sale stores, wholesale centres, procurement stations and operating offices); (2) commodities in the process of being selected, sorted, and packed; (3) commodities not arrived but recorded as purchase in the account, i.e. commodities not arrived but payment receipts for the commodities from the sellers or the banks arrived; (4) commodities deposited in other places rather than places mentioned above, for instance: commodities in the hold of purchasers temporarily due to the refusal of payment; (5) commodities entrusted to other units to sell but not sold yet; (6) commodities purchased for other units but not delivered yet. Commodities not included as stock are those not owned by the enterprises (units), commodities on commission for processing, imported commodities of agency of foreign trade enterprise but not yet delivered to ordering units and finally those put in stock on behalf of the state reserves units.

Hotel Services refer to the accommodation services provided to visitors. Some units may provide only accommodation while others provide a combination of accommodation, meals, business services and/or recreational facilities. It excludes activities related to the provision of long-term primary residences in facilities such as apartments typically leased on a monthly or annual basis.

Catering Services refer to the activities of providing foods, serving locations and facilities to customers through instant processing, commercial sales and service-type labor.

Business Revenue refers to revenue of hotels and catering services received from providing services or selling commodities through business activities, including income from hotels, from catering services, from selling of commodities (including VAT) and from other services. Income from hotels refers to income of hotels and catering services by providing lodging services through business activities. Income from catering services refers to income from providing catering services, including selling of cooked or prepared foods, such as staple food, cooked dishes, or cold dishes.

Large Commodity Markets with Transaction Value over 100 Million Yuan refers to the commodity markets with an annual transaction at and above 100 million. The commodity market refers to the markets approved and managed by related departments, where there are fixed sites, facilities, managers and administration offices, where there are a certain number of traders to operate for three month and above or all the year, where the commodities including the articles for daily consumption and capital goods and services are traded in a centralized, independent and open way. Such market includes markets of daily goods and market of capital goods, etc.

Chain Head Stores (headquarter) refer to the core leading stores responsible for development, allocation, administration and utilization of resources (name of stores, brand of stores, operation model, service standard, management way, etc.) of chain stores. Chain stores refers to the stores engaged in providing homogeneous commodities or services, with the central leadership of head store (headquarters) and guided by common policies, conduct centralized purchase and distributed selling of commodities, in order to gain better efficiency through standardized operation. The chain stores include regular chain stores, franchise chain stores and voluntary chain stores.

Regular Chain store refers to chain stores that are invested or controlled by the headquarters. They operate under direct and unified management from the headquarters.

Franchise chain store refers to the chain stores (franchisees) which are franchised with operation resources such as trade marks, names, patent and operation know-how by the franchisors in form of contract and pay the operation fees to the franchisors.

Voluntary chain store refers to the stores operate jointly on the voluntary bases while maintaining their status of independent legal entities with full ownership of their assets. They sell goods of same brand from same channel of resource to the consumers.

八、对外经济 国际旅游

CHAPTER 8
FOREIGN TRADE ECONOMY AND INTERNATIONAL TOURISM

8 对外经济　国际旅游
FOREIGN TRADE ECONOMY AND INTERNATIONAL TOURISM

主 要 统 计 指 标
MAJOR STATISTICAL INDICATORS

2016年进出口总额	Total Imports and Exports	2 737.58	亿美元	USD 100 million
比上年增长	Increase Over Last Year	-10.3	%	
2016年出口总额	Total Exports	1 639.41	亿美元	USD 100 million
比上年增长	Increase Over Last Year	-9.7	%	
2016年进口总额	Total Imports	1 098.18	亿美元	USD 100 million
比上年增长	Increase Over Last Year	-11.4	%	
2016年新增注册外资金额	Value of Foreign Capital Signed Contracts	57.25	亿美元	USD 100 million
比上年增长	Increase Over Last Year	-36.0	%	
2016年实际使用外资金额	Value of Foreign Capital Actually Used	60.03	亿美元	USD 100 million
比上年增长	Increase Over Last Year	-14.5	%	
2016年接待境外旅游者	Number of Received Foreign Tourists	209.98	万人次	10 000 person-times
比上年增长	Increase Over Last Year	6.5	%	

表8-1

历年进出口总额及外贸依存度
TOTAL IMPORTS AND EXPORTS, FOREIGN TRADE DEPENDENCY OVER THE YEARS

单位：万美元 (USD 10 000)

年 份 Year	进出口总额 Total Imports and Exports	出 口 Exports	进 口 Imports	外贸依存度 (%) Foreign Trade Dependency(%)	出口依存度 Export Dependency	进口依存度 Import Dependency
1990	18 816	15 524	3 292	4.5	3.7	0.8
1991	38 002	31 002	7 000	8.6	7.0	1.6
1992	117 704	95 704	22 000	18.1	14.7	3.4
1993	195 860	84 077	111 783	21.5	9.2	12.3
1994	281 844	141 979	139 865	33.7	17.0	16.7
1995	459 223	233 491	225 732	42.5	21.6	20.9
1996	688 155	349 698	338 457	57.1	29.0	28.1
1997	863 611	464 677	398 934	63.2	34.0	29.2
1998	964 922	520 735	444 187	63.9	34.5	29.4
1999	1 255 482	692 776	562 706	76.5	42.2	34.3
2000	2 007 036	1 048 095	958 941	107.8	56.3	51.5
2001	2 366 160	1 230 679	1 135 481	111.3	57.9	53.4
2002	3 639 008	1 852 061	1 786 947	144.8	73.7	71.1
2003	6 566 313	3 263 377	3 302 936	194.0	96.4	97.6
2004	10 320 051	5 077 384	5 242 667	247.6	121.8	125.8
2005	14 058 895	7 277 472	6 781 423	278.3	144.1	134.2
2006	17 426 360	9 468 488	7 957 872	283.5	154.0	129.5
2007	21 179 567	11 888 422	9 291 145	275.3	154.5	120.8
2008	22 852 565	13 172 260	9 680 305	224.2	129.2	95.0
2009	20 144 633	11 408 529	8 736 104	177.8	100.7	77.1
2010	27 407 639	15 310 849	12 096 790	201.0	112.3	88.7
2011	30 086 256	16 723 345	13 362 911	181.3	100.8	80.5
2012	30 569 196	17 468 868	13 100 328	160.6	91.8	68.8
2013	30 934 780	17 570 638	13 364 142	147.2	83.6	63.6
2014	31 130 567	18 117 763	13 012 804	139.0	80.9	58.1
2015	30 534 957	18 145 930	12 389 027	131.1	77.9	53.2
2016	27 375 823	16 394 054	10 981 769	117.5	70.4	47.1

表8-2

分地区进出口总额(2016年)
TOTAL IMPORTS AND EXPORTS VALUE BY REGION (2016)

单位：万美元 (USD 10 000)

类别和地区	Type and Region	进出口总额 Total Imports and Exports	出口 Exports	进口 Imports
全市	**Whole Municipality**	**27 375 823**	**16 394 054**	**10 981 769**
市区	Urban Area	14 325 881	8 463 123	5 862 758
姑苏区	Gusu District	200 784	178 516	22 268
吴中区	Wuzhong District	766 023	517 620	248 403
相城区	Xiangcheng District	415 605	307 844	107 761
高新区、虎丘区	New & Hi-tech Zone, Huqiu District	3 401 773	2 276 584	1 125 189
工业园区	Industrial Park	7 428 200	3 780 565	3 647 635
吴江区	Wujiang District	2 113 495	1 401 994	711 501
常熟	Changshu	1 985 323	1 335 629	649 693
张家港	Zhangjiagang	2 741 674	1 420 227	1 321 447
昆山	Kunshan	7 226 553	4 632 104	2 594 449
太仓	Taicang	1 096 391	542 970	553 421
一、国有企业	**State-owed Enterprises**	**1 344 886**	**1 130 657**	**214 229**
市区	Urban Area	942 140	820 335	121 805
姑苏区	Gusu District	63 576	61 330	2 246
吴中区	Wuzhong District	109	59	51
相城区	Xiangcheng District	–	–	–
高新区、虎丘区	New & Hi-tech Zone, Huqiu District	11 596	10 623	974
工业园区	Industrial Park	866 859	748 324	118 535
吴江区	Wujiang District	–	–	–
常熟	Changshu	4 356	3 805	551
张家港	Zhangjiagang	377 269	292 588	84 680
昆山	Kunshan	8 148	7 722	427
太仓	Taicang	12 973	6 207	6 766
二、外商及港澳台投资企业	**Enterprises with Investment from Foreign ,Hong Kong, Macao and Taiwan**	**20 585 448**	**11 693 172**	**8 892 277**
市区	Urban Area	11 329 666	6 078 657	5 251 010
姑苏区	Gusu District	2 380	891	1 489
吴中区	Wuzhong District	501 634	302 965	198 670
相城区	Xiangcheng District	235 941	162 846	73 095
高新区、虎丘区	New & Hi-tech Zone, Huqiu District	3 178 684	2 152 532	1 026 152
工业园区	Industrial Park	5 983 391	2 662 103	3 321 288
吴江区	Wujiang District	1 427 636	797 320	630 316
常熟	Changshu	1 449 366	871 369	577 998
张家港	Zhangjiagang	819 796	337 945	481 851
昆山	Kunshan	6 175 867	4 015 015	2 160 852
太仓	Taicang	810 752	390 186	420 566

表8-2 续表 Continued

单位：万美元 (USD 10 000)

类别和地区	Type and Region	进出口总额 Total Imports and Exports	出口 Exports	进口 Imports
三、集体企业	**Collective-owned Enterprises**	**612 368**	**417 155**	**195 213**
市　区	Urban Area	62 408	60 209	2 199
姑苏区	Gusu District	34 035	33 126	909
吴中区	Wuzhong District	16 178	15 859	319
相城区	Xiangcheng District	5 864	5 864	–
高新区、虎丘区	New & Hi-tech Zone, Huqiu District	2 615	2 549	67
工业园区	Industrial Park	3 714	2 811	903
吴江区	Wujiang District	2	–	2
常　熟	Changshu	32 132	20 111	12 022
张家港	Zhangjiagang	473 104	305 946	167 158
昆　山	Kunshan	6 329	2 355	3 974
太　仓	Taicang	38 395	28 535	9 860
四、私营企业	**Private Enterprises**	**4 815 866**	**3 139 412**	**1 676 454**
市　区	Urban Area	1 982 909	1 497 434	485 475
姑苏区	Gusu District	100 773	83 149	17 624
吴中区	Wuzhong District	239 754	192 612	47 142
相城区	Xiangcheng District	173 798	139 134	34 664
高新区、虎丘区	New & Hi-tech Zone, Huqiu District	208 872	110 876	97 996
工业园区	Industrial Park	573 891	367 026	206 865
吴江区	Wujiang District	685 821	604 637	81 184
常　熟	Changshu	499 238	440 115	59 123
张家港	Zhangjiagang	1 071 501	483 743	587 758
昆　山	Kunshan	1 027 975	600 106	427 869
太　仓	Taicang	234 243	118 014	116 229
五、其　他	**Others**	**17 252**	**13 657**	**3 596**
市　区	Urban Area	8 756	6 488	2 269
姑苏区	Gusu District	20	20	–
吴中区	Wuzhong District	8 347	6 126	2 221
相城区	Xiangcheng District	2	–	2
高新区、虎丘区	New & Hi-tech Zone, Huqiu District	5	5	–
工业园区	Industrial Park	345	300	45
吴江区	Wujiang District	37	37	–
常　熟	Changshu	230	230	–
张家港	Zhangjiagang	4	4	–
昆　山	Kunshan	8 234	6 907	1 327
太　仓	Taicang	28	28	–
总计中：一般贸易	**In Total: Ordinary Trade**	**9 240 687**	**5 298 996**	**3 941 690**
加工贸易	**Processing Trade**	**14 677 912**	**9 333 592**	**5 344 320**

表8-3

分国别(地区)进出口总额 (2016年)
TOTAL IMPORTS AND EXPORTS VALUE BY COUNTRY AND REGION (2016)

单位：万美元 (USD 10 000)

国别和地区	Country and Region	进出口总额 Total Imports and Exports	出口 Exports	进口 Imports
总计	**Total**	**27 375 823**	**16 394 054**	**10 981 769**
亚洲	**Asia**	**15 101 924**	**6 815 734**	**8 286 190**
# 中国香港	HongKong, China	1 477 556	1 445 453	32 103
印度	India	445 630	408 268	37 362
日本	Japan	2 536 635	1 273 597	1 263 039
马来西亚	Malaysia	698 309	244 502	453 808
新加坡	Singapore	451 597	259 130	192 468
韩国	Republic of Korea	3 039 414	859 102	2 180 312
泰国	Thailand	559 597	290 246	269 351
阿拉伯联合酋长国	United Arab Emirates	202 498	158 517	43 981
中国台湾	Taiwan, China	2 746 996	655 473	2 091 524
非洲	**Africa**	**283 939**	**240 663**	**43 276**
欧洲	**Europe**	**4 755 336**	**3 595 933**	**1 159 404**
# 比利时	Belgium	144 702	112 357	32 345
英国	United Kingdom	522 051	446 148	75 903
德国	Germany	1 039 857	580 788	459 069
法国	France	294 833	199 834	94 999
意大利	Italy	255 802	174 140	81 662
荷兰	Netherlands	959 111	926 957	32 155
西班牙	Spain	210 376	147 738	62 638
芬兰	Finland	62 547	37 585	24 962
瑞士	Switzerland	81 861	33 433	48 428
南美洲	**South America**	**1 269 001**	**747 100**	**521 901**
# 巴西	Brazil	474 649	154 812	319 837
北美洲	**North America**	**5 371 666**	**4 682 971**	**688 696**
# 加拿大	Canada	376 519	290 219	86 300
美国	United States	4 995 110	4 392 720	602 390
大洋洲	**Oceania**	**593 430**	**311 654**	**281 776**
# 澳大利亚	Australia	524 668	273 931	250 737
总计中：东盟组织	**In Total: Association of Southeast Asian Nations**	**2 941 040**	**1 494 983**	**1 446 056**
欧盟组织	**European Union**	**4 402 236**	**3 349 783**	**1 052 453**

表8-4

分商品类章进出口总额 (2016年)
TOTAL IMPORTS AND EXPORTS OF GOODS OF SUB-CATEGORY CHAPTERS (2016)

单位：万美元 (USD 10 000)

商品名称	Item	进出口总额 Total Imports and Exports	出口 Exports	进口 Imports
总计	**Total**	**27 375 823**	**16 394 054**	**10 981 769**
活动物, 动物产品	Live Animals, Animal Products	48 128	2 612	45 516
植物产品	Vegetable Products	407 023	7 405	399 618
动, 植物油, 脂, 蜡及其分解产品	Animal or Vegetable Fats and Oils and their Cleavage Products	46 785	2 032	44 753
食品, 饮料, 酒及醋, 烟草及制品	Prepared Foodstuffs; Beverages, Spirits And Vinegar; Tobacco and Manufactured Tobacco Substitutes	27 645	18 160	9 485
矿产品	Mineral Products	423 229	3 480	419 748
化学工业及其相关工业的产品	Products of The Chemical or Industries Allied	1 165 179	446 251	718 928
塑料及其制品, 橡胶及其制品	Plastics and Articles Thereof Rubber and Articles Thereof	1 102 272	486 109	616 162
生皮, 皮革, 毛皮及其制品	Raw Hides and Skins, Leather, Fur Skins and Articles Thereof	67 644	57 229	10 415
木及木制品, 其他编结材料制品	Wood and Articles of Wood; Other Plaiting Materials	62 428	19 297	43 131
纸浆, 纸, 纸板及其制品	Pulp of Paper，Paper and Paperboard and Articles Thereof	371 160	149 753	221 407
纺织原料及纺织制品	Textiles and Textile Articles	1 822 720	1 615 691	207 028
鞋帽伞杖鞭, 羽毛制品, 人造花	Footwear, Headgear, Umbrellas, Sun Umbrellas, Walking-Sticks, Seat-Sticks, Feathers and Articles Made ; Artificial Flowers	159 472	65 688	93 784
石料及其制品, 陶瓷玻璃及制品	Articles of Stone, Ceramic Products; Glass and Glassware	203 189	94 289	108 900
珍珠, 宝石, 贵金属, 仿首饰, 硬币	Pearls, Precious , Precious Metals, Imitation Jewelry ; Coin	41 791	11 486	30 305
贱金属及其制品	Base Metals and Articles of Base Metal	1 383 114	897 135	485 979
机器, 电子产品, 电气设备及零件	Machinery, Electronic Products, Electrical Equipment and Parts	16 519 158	10 409 027	6 110 132
车辆, 航空器, 船舶及运输设备	Vehicles, Aircraft, Vessels And Associated Transport Equipment	664 955	491 526	173 429
光学, 检测, 医疗设备, 钟表, 乐器	Optical, Detection, Medical Equipment, Clocks and Watches, and Musical Instruments	2 180 273	966 368	1 213 904
武器, 弹药及其零件, 附件	Arms and Ammunition; Parts and Accessories Thereof	287	287	–
杂项制品	Miscellaneous Manufactured Articles	669 675	641 312	28 363
艺术品, 收藏品及古物	Works of Art, Collectors' Pieces and Antiques	143	122	21
特殊交易品及未分类商品	Special Transaction Goods and Unclassified Goods	9 554	8 794	759
总计中：机电产品	**In Total: Mechanical and electrical products**	**20 350 549**	**12 679 289**	**7 671 261**
高新技术产品	**High-tech products**	**14 042 777**	**8 379 209**	**5 663 568**

表8-5

历年使用外资情况
FOREIGN CAPITAL ACTUALLY USED OVER THE YEARS

单位：万美元 (USD 10 000)

年 份 Year	批准外资项目数(个) Number of Foreign Invested Enterprises Contracts Approved (unit)	新增注册外资金额 Newly Added Value of Foreign Capital Signed	实际使用外资金额 Amount of Foreign Capital Actually Used	历年累计开业外资企业数(个) Accumulative Total of Enterprises with Foreign Investment that Have that Have Entered Production or Operation The Years (unit)
1979~1984	63	2 691	…	
1985	55	8 730	1 070	
1986	32	3 035	1 409	
1987	65	3 719	5 826	9
1988	131	5 233	6 918	32
1989	175	9 457	6 954	99
1990	164	14 361	6 954	172
1991	442	39 104	11 862	325
1992	3 069	476 095	85 973	1 804
1993	2 655	509 644	150 899	3 322
1994	1 270	463 143	219 086	4 379
1995	905	565 119	237 779	
1996	747	459 904	230 467	
1997	648	441 203	249 531	5 151
1998	520	431 694	307 180	4 285
1999	571	356 819	288 691	4 479
2000	943	467 787	288 338	4 761
2001	1 362	723 014	302 183	4 955
2002	2 465	1 006 655	481 398	5 511
2003	2 399	1 249 606	680 511	6 230
2004	2 282	1 470 260	503 314	7 028
2005	2 181	1 533 971	511 607	8 004
2006	2 281	1 592 383	610 462	10 218
2007	2 022	1 836 349	716 471	12 506
2008	1 462	1 638 953	813 262	12 253
2009	1 426	1 583 786	822 653	13 262
2010	1 537	1 691 980	853 511	14 127
2011	1 516	1 702 391	891 222	14 675
2012	1 189	1 516 828	916 490	15 138
2013	936	1 001 077	869 805	16 609
2014	905	857 856	811 978	16 859
2015	860	893 925	701 920	17 054
2016	784	572 513	600 300	17 214

注：2004年及以往年份实际利用外资为苏州市商务局上报数。2004年统计口径调整，2005年及以后年份数据为国家商务部反馈数。2013年起，合同外资更名为新增注册外资。2014年起，实际利用外资更名为实际使用外资。（下同）

Note: In 2004 and the previous year ,the data of foreign capital actually used in the table were report number by Suzhou Municipal Bureau of Commerce , the statistical caliber has been adjust. In 2005 they were feedback number by The State Department of Commerce. Starting from 2013, the contracted foreign investment was renamed as the newly registered foreign investment. Starting from 2014, the foreign investment actually utilized is renamed to the foreign investment actually used. (Same below)

表8-6

外商及港澳台商直接投资（2016年）

指　　标	Item	全　市 Whole Municipality
新设外资项目数　　(个)	**Number of Projects of Signed Contracts**　　(unit)	
本年新设项目数	Number of Projects of Signed Contracts in 2016	784
独资经营	Solely Owned Enterprises	577
合资经营	Joint Venture Enterprises	204
合作经营	Cooperative Operation Enterprises	2
股份有限公司	Share-holding Corporations Ltd.	1
历年累计批准项目数	Accumulative Total of Approved Enterprises The Years	25 122
批准外商注册外资金额　　(万美元)	**Amount of Foreign Investment Contracts**　　(USD 10 000)	
本年新增注册外资	Amount of Foreign Investment Contracts Approved in 2016	572 513
独资经营	Solely Owned Enterprises	464 930
合资经营	Joint Venture Enterprises	82 728
合作经营	Cooperative Operation Enterprises	155
股份有限公司	Share-holding Corporations Ltd.	24 700
历年累计注册外资	Accumulative Foreign Contracts Investment The Years	19 001 613
实际使用外资金额　　(万美元)	**Foreign Capital Actually Used**　　(USD 10 000)	
本年实际使用外资	Foreign Capital Actually Used in 2016	600 300
独资经营	Solely Owned Enterprises	470 320
合资经营	Joint Venture Enterprises	103 112
合作经营	Cooperative Operation Enterprises	14 481
股份有限公司	Share-holding Corporations Ltd.	12 387
历年累计实际使用外资	Total Amount of Foreign Capital Actually Used The Years	12 132 742
历年累计已开业投产的外资企业数　(个)	**Accumulative Total of Enterprises with Foreign Investment that Have Entered Production or Operation The Years**　(unit)	**17 214**

DIRECT INVESTMENT FROM FOREIGN, HONG KONG, MACAO AND TAIWAN (2016)

市 区 Urban Area	# 吴 江 Wujiang	常 熟 Changshu	张家港 Zhangjiagang	昆 山 Kunshan	太 仓 Taicang
443	61	50	49	193	49
315	45	32	35	155	40
126	15	18	13	38	9
1	–	–	1	–	–
1	1	–	–	–	–
13 812	2 651	1 388	1 470	6 632	1 820
276 302	111 095	103 217	45 292	85 410	62 292
234 632	72 673	73 542	41 652	74 858	40 246
37 199	37 490	29 373	-942	7 115	9 983
-1 175	–	–	1 183	147	–
5 646	932	302	3 399	3 290	12 063
10 715 945	2 104 344	1 898 567	1 310 152	3 671 546	1 405 403
331 211	61 640	63 004	60 402	89 626	56 057
271 968	39 613	32 712	53 431	79 689	32 520
45 198	22 027	29 314	6 579	9 711	12 310
13 860	–	–	392	–	229
185	–	978	–	226	10 998
6 317 073	1 182 022	1 309 391	1 225 288	2 371 049	909 941
7 927	**1 496**	**1 449**	**1 807**	**4 180**	**1 851**

表8-7

外商及港澳台商投资企业国别(地区)分组 (2016年)
ENTERPRISES WITH INVESTMENT FROM FOREIGN，HONG KONG，MACAO AND TAIWAN BY COUNTRY (REGION)(2016)

单位：万美元 (USD 10 000)

地 区	Region	新设外资项目数(个) Number of Projects of Signed Contracts (unit)	新增注册外资金额 Newly Added Value of Foreign Capital Signed	实际使用外资金额 Amount of Foreign Capital Actually Used
总 计	**Total**	**784**	**572 513**	**600 300**
分国别合计	**Sum by Country**	**784**	**572 513**	**484 938**
中国香港	HongKong,China	126	181 053	184 844
中国澳门	Macao,China	4	2 817	360
中国台湾	Taiwan,China	185	40 177	25 968
新加坡	Singapore	39	1 574	25 288
马来西亚	Malaysia	5	4 742	8 084
日 本	Japan	32	5 319	35 663
韩 国	Republic of Korea	87	52 965	17 690
泰 国	Thailand	–	20	77
澳大利亚	Australia	5	237	355
法 国	France	7	4 980	2 629
意大利	Italy	9	5 229	3 916
德 国	Germany	47	16 975	12 061
英 国	United Kingdom	9	7 924	7 919
丹 麦	Denmark	1	540	105
瑞 士	Switzerland	3	6 549	7 624
荷 兰	Netherlands	8	8 234	3 115
西班牙	Spain	5	629	2 002
美 国	United States	65	30 809	76 228
加拿大	Canada	22	8 490	2 156
维尔京群岛	Virgin Islands	8	8 417	9 916
开曼群岛	Cayman Islands	4	11 393	11 801
萨摩亚	Samoan	36	32 020	19 326
毛里求斯	Mauritius	1	8 052	1 605
文 莱	Brunei	2	1 620	731
其 他	Others	74	131 748	25 475
总计中：东盟组织	**In Total: Association of Southeast Asian Nations**	**47**	**6 965**	**34 406**
欧盟组织	**European Union**	**109**	**54 938**	**34 994**
总计中：外方股东境外中长期贷款	**In Total: Offshore Medium and Long Term Loans by Foreign Shareholders**	**–**	**–**	**115 362**

表8-8

外商及港澳台商投资企业行业分组（2016年） ENTERPRISES WITH INVESTMENT FROM FOREIGN，HONG KONG，MACAO AND TAIWAN BY SECTOR (2016)

单位：万美元 (USD 10 000)

行　业	Sector	新设外资项目数（个）Number of Projects of Signed Contracts (unit)	新增注册外资金额 Newly Added Value of Foreign Capital Signed	实际使用外资金额 Amount of Foreign Capital Actually Used
总　计	**Total**	**784**	**572 513**	**600 300**
行业合计	**Sum by Sector**	**784**	**572 513**	**484 938**
第一产业	**Primary Industry**	**1**	**-15**	**570**
第二产业	**Secondary Industry**	**229**	**355 677**	**276 489**
工　业	Industry	221	347 811	275 906
#机　械	Machinery	100	114 921	73 441
仪器、办公用品	Equipment and office supplies	3	3 669	2 530
电子通讯	Electronic communications	20	44 541	50 505
电气器材	Electronic Equipment	24	36 110	23 704
化　工	Chemical	9	52 974	47 516
建　材	Building Materials	1	6 881	5 073
冶　金	Metallurgy	1	10 146	17 360
塑料制品	Plastic Products	13	10 152	2 609
纺织服装	Textile and Apparel	6	3 128	2 868
食品加工	Food processing	9	16 892	5 033
建筑业	Construction	8	7 866	501
第三产业	**Tertiary Industry**	**554**	**216 851**	**207 879**
交通运输业	Transportation	15	29 713	18 750
#仓储业	Logistics	7	21 659	17 529
房地产业	Real Estate	16	4 366	93 280
信息传输、计算机服务业	Information Transmission, Computer Services	8	890	217
软件业	Software	19	3 611	1 802
批发和零售业	Wholesale and Retail Trades	285	87 205	31 800
住宿和餐饮业	Hotels and Catering Services	22	7 660	3 214
文化、体育、娱乐业	Culture, Sports and Entertainment	6	362	13
租赁和商务服务业	Leasing and Business Services	91	48 071	44 468
科技和技术服务业	Scientific Research, Technical Service	70	6 533	5 655
卫生、教育	Health and Education	2	5 850	1 677
其　他	Others	20	22 590	7 002
总计中：外方股东境外中长期贷款	**In Total: Offshore Medium and Long Term Loans by Foreign Shareholders**	–	–	**115 362**

表8-9

国家级、省级开发区建设发展情况（2016年）

开发区名称	Development Zones	新设外资项目数（个）Number of Foreign Invested Enterprises Contracts Approved (unit)	新增注册外资（万美元）Newly Added Foreign Investment (USD 10 000)
总　　计	**Total**	**621**	**465 378**
一、国家级开发区	**State Development Zones**	**583**	**435 399**
苏州工业园区	Suzhou Industrial Park	238	39 049
苏州高新技术产业开发区	Suzhou New and Hi-tech Development Zone	70	83 152
昆山经济技术开发区	Kunshan Economic and Technological Development Zone	72	34 475
张家港保税区	Zhangjiagang Bonded Area	15	13 512
苏州太湖国家旅游度假区	Suzhou Taihu National Tourism and Vacation Zone	2	372
昆山国家高新技术产业开发区	Kunshan New and Hi-tech industrial Development Zone	40	25 598
常熟经济技术开发区	Changshu Economic and Technological Development Zone	23	79 250
吴江经济技术开发区	Wujiang Economic and Technological Development Zone	29	37 909
太仓港经济技术开发区	Taicang Economic and Technological Development Zone	26	48 341
张家港经济技术开发区	Zhangjiagang Economicand Technological Development Zone	24	21 741
吴中经济技术开发区	Wuzhong Economic and Technological Development Zone	13	14 376
苏州浒墅关经济开发区	Xushuguan Economic Development Zone	30	14 476
苏州相城经济开发区	Xiangcheng Economic Development Zone	11	19 638
常熟高新技术产业开发区	Changshu New and Hi-tech Industrial Development Zone	20	17 986
二、省级开发区	**Provincial Development Zones**	**38**	**29 979**
昆山旅游度假区	Kunshan Tourism and Holiday Zone	12	7 277
汾湖高新技术产业开发区	Foho New and Hi-tech Industrial Development Zone	13	16 809
昆山花桥经济开发区	Kunshan Huaqiao Economic Development Zone	13	5 893

注：苏州高新技术开发区中包含浒墅关经济开发区数据，下同。

CONSTRUCTION OF STATE AND PROVINCIAL DEVELOPMENT ZONES (2016)

实际使用外资 (万美元) Foreign Capital Actually Used (USD 10 000)	业务总收入 (万元) Total Business Revenue (10 000 yuan)	财政收入 (万元) Financial Revenue (10 000 yuan)	# 一般公共预算收入 General Public Budget Revenue	出口额 (万美元) Exports (USD 10 000)	进口额 (万美元) Imports (USD 10 000)
397 951	**455 597 723**	**28 351 164**	**11 495 122**	**13 999 873**	**9 811 025**
381 247	**419 221 462**	**24 878 935**	**10 417 820**	**13 632 185**	**9 600 559**
105 070	78 525 610	6 596 673	2 881 030	3 582 222	3 422 620
46 647	42 938 000	4 545 787	1 298 028	2 153 273	996 953
30 968	71 688 465	2 465 220	1 060 491	3 629 013	1 933 505
28 364	43 081 141	803 554	415 800	281 458	889 794
331	1 533 801	103 502	62 313	15 490	8 554
15 772	28 810 000	1 757 666	847 460	464 075	315 014
46 077	32 681 178	1 456 843	675 688	718 763	437 419
31 556	17 313 790	1 505 887	408 000	842 218	570 048
35 748	25 255 012	1 616 417	747 977	390 525	454 280
10 432	28 502 314	1 423 619	695 173	682 374	129 376
13 869	15 493 428	1 140 855	565 003	290 782	180 866
1 736	12 691 405	882 235	180 890	116 137	98 970
9 589	19 595 498	760 007	408 551	264 098	98 127
6 824	13 803 225	702 905	352 306	317 894	164 003
16 704	**36 376 261**	**3 472 229**	**1 077 302**	**367 688**	**210 466**
10 186	14 745 863	613 814	349 545	154 311	96 579
2 527	6 914 614	1 046 499	223 928	124 036	25 032
3 991	14 715 784	1 811 916	503 829	89 341	88 855

Note: The data of Suzhou New and Hi-tech Development Zone includes the data of Xushuguan Economic Development Zone, same as the following.

表8-10 国家级、省级开发区建设发展情况（至2016年累计）

开发区名称	Development Zones	已开发面积（平方公里） Area of Development (sq.km)	全社会固定资产投资（亿元） Total Value of Investment in Fixed Assets (100 million yuan)
总　计	**Total**	**840.71**	**33 937.75**
一、国家级开发区	**State Development Zones**	**752.70**	**30 939.68**
苏州工业园区	Suzhou Industrial Park	175.80	7 300.84
苏州高新技术产业开发区	Suzhou New and Hi-tech Development Zone	91.90	4 288.55
昆山经济技术开发区	Kunshan Economic and Technological Development Zone	58.44	2 779.94
张家港保税区	Zhangjiagang Bonded Area	53.06	1 488.23
苏州太湖国家旅游度假区	Suzhou Taihu National Tourism and Vacation Zone	20.00	388.95
昆山国家高新技术产业开发区	Kunshan New and Hi-tech industrial Development Zone	31.72	1 459.94
常熟经济技术开发区	Changshu Economic and Technological Development Zone	48.69	2 891.38
吴江经济技术开发区	Wujiang Economic and Technological Development Zone	51.04	1 632.81
太仓港经济技术开发区	Taicang Economic and Technological Development Zone	71.47	2 581.24
张家港经济技术开发区	Zhangjiagang Economicand Technological Development Zone	38.55	1 739.63
吴中经济技术开发区	Wuzhong Economic and Technological Development Zone	48.55	1 768.90
苏州浒墅关经济开发区	Xushuguan Economic Development Zone	45.50	809.49
苏州相城经济开发区	Xiangcheng Economic Development Zone	32.21	1 610.31
常熟高新技术产业开发区	Changshu New and Hi-tech Industrial Development Zone	31.27	1 008.96
二、省级开发区	**Provincial Development Zones**	**88.01**	**2 998.07**
昆山旅游度假区	Kunshan Tourism and Holiday Zone	12.60	514.46
汾湖高新技术产业开发区	Foho New and Hi-tech Industrial Development Zone	20.15	1 188.99
昆山花桥经济开发区	Kunshan Huaqiao Economic Development Zone	55.26	1 294.62

CONSTRUCTION OF STATE AND PROVINCIAL DEVELOPMENT ZONES (BY 2016)

基础设施投入 (亿元) Investment In Infrastructure (100 million yuan)	期末内资企业数 (个) Number of Domestic Enterprise by Year End (unit)	内资企业注册资本额 (亿元) Registered Capital of Domestic Enterprise (100 million yuan)	期末注册外资企业数(个) Number of Enterprises with Foreign Investment that Have Registered by Year End (unit)	实际到账外资额 (亿美元) Foreign Capital Actually Used (USD 100 million)	期末从业人数 (万人) Number of Employee Persons by Year End (10 000 persons)
4 904.09	**205 678**	**17 920.37**	**17 374**	**999.10**	**392.56**
4 481.19	**184 871**	**16 479.34**	**14 958**	**923.15**	**345.36**
798.77	56 141	5 462.77	4 510	253.80	75.64
686.79	19 770	2 344.18	1 845	123.73	33.80
312.33	17 500	1 427.07	1 624	96.35	51.85
275.99	10 809	737.64	620	43.44	11.63
92.43	2 068	456.67	115	3.67	9.32
153.57	23 999	676.75	918	55.19	47.28
345.32	8 696	1 095.35	524	84.51	20.33
323.71	6 458	517.07	929	60.12	19.86
345.01	9 784	686.74	1 384	68.82	13.40
536.07	9 718	685.42	473	30.40	18.67
338.30	9 480	1 347.07	765	37.47	11.90
286.97	2 086	263.89	284	19.28	10.93
176.60	7 730	713.82	715	28.78	19.02
96.30	2 718	328.79	536	36.87	12.66
422.90	**20 807**	**1 441.03**	**2 416**	**75.95**	**47.20**
74.26	7 602	404.21	1 296	28.89	22.74
132.27	2 900	541.89	510	26.21	12.76
216.37	10 305	494.93	610	20.85	11.70

表8-11

部分年份对外承包工程及服务外包
OVERSEAS CONTRACTING PROJECT AND SERVICE OUTSOURCING OF PARTIAL YEAR

单位：万美元 (USD 10 000)

年份 Year	对外承包工程 Overseas Contracting Project			服务外包 Services Outsourcing	
	签订合同金额 Contracted Value	实际营业额 Value of Business Fulfilled	当年外派劳务人员(人次) Persons Sent Abroad in the year (person-times)	接包合同额 Access Package Contract Amount	离岸执行额 Offshore Executive Amount
1990	2 249	1 100	399		
1991	1 643	1 661	627		
1992	3 079	3 398	1 290		
1993	5 202	4 461	1 827		
1994	7 861	6 004	1 790		
1995	8 113	8 093	1 850		
1996	8 346	8 093	1 876		
1997	10 025	9 269	1 951		
1998	9 559	10 233	2 232		
1999	10 733	11 271	2 545		
2000	12 199	12 122	3 625		
2001	14 535	13 555	3 787		
2002	18 386	16 997	3 127		
2003	24 860	22 580	3 205		
2004	40 672	38 585	3 273		
2005	41 379	39 811	2 595		
2006	49 278	42 668	2 691		
2007	34 526	30 757	2 148		
2008	38 930	37 033	2 368		
2009	55 579	43 968	1 955	144 887	89 096
2010	91 294	57 046	1 599	226 842	126 934
2011	95 097	76 850	1 361	356 994	201 346
2012	102 574	83 716	2 776	559 619	305 409
2013	108 334	90 721	1 912	863 852	462 365
2014	134 712	95 434	723	1 038 857	548 585
2015	187 982	104 098	1 733	1 191 593	626 608
2016	151 083	115 723	700	1 284 545	668 847

注：2013年及之前对外承包工程各项指标中包含劳务合作数据。
Note: The indicators of the foreign contracted projects in 2013 and prior to it included the labor cooperation data.

表8-12

分地区对外承包工程（2016年） CONTRACTED PROJECTS WITH FOREIGN COUNTRIES BY REGIONS (2016)

地　　区	Region	签订合同金额（万美元） Contractual Value (USD 10 000)	实际营业额（万美元） Value of Business Fulfilled (USD 10 000)	当年外派人员（人） Persons Sent Abroad in the Year (person)
全　市	**Whole Municipality**	**151 083**	**115 723**	**700**
市　区	Urban Area	65 431	32 807	15
# 吴江区	Wujiang District	59 986	20 099	-
常　熟	Changshu	16 056	18 727	-
张家港	Zhangjiagang	27 800	26 400	-
昆　山	Kunshan	36 267	32 707	685
太　仓	Taicang	5 529	5 082	-

表8-13

分地区服务外包情况（2016年） SERVICE OUTSOURCING BY REGION(2016)

地　　区	Region	新增企业(个) The New Enterprise (unit)	接包合同额(万美元) Access Package Contract Amount (USD 10 000)	离岸执行额(万美元) Offshore Executive Amount (USD 10 000)	新受训人员(人) The New Trainees (person)
全　市	**Whole Municipality**	**387**	**1 284 545**	**668 847**	**34 343**
市　区	Urban Area	314	979 436	562 100	16 951
# 吴江区	Wujiang District	10	17 815	11 447	741
常　熟	Changshu	4	31 611	19 244	97
张家港	Zhangjiagang	11	35 142	13 215	473
昆　山	Kunshan	44	159 769	46 826	16 514
太　仓	Taicang	14	78 587	27 462	308

表8-14

部分年份海外企业情况
OVERSEAS BUSINESS CONDITIONS IN PART OF THE YEAR

年 份 Year	境外企业数（个） Number of Newly Approved Foreign Enterprises (unit)		新批中方境外投资额（万美元） New Registered Oversea Investment from China (USD 10 000)
	新 增 Newly Added	累计实有 Total	
2000	2	74	320
2001	5	79	285
2002	8	85	187
2003	7	91	453
2004	32	110	4 793
2005	42	134	8 211
2006	51	185	10 566
2007	50	235	13 023
2008	63	298	20 526
2009	111	377	32 224
2010	118	495	47 446
2011	138	589	70 048
2012	187	744	122 163
2013	159	871	161 851
2014	209	1 034	170 029
2015	252	1 235	204 754
2016	334	1 509	320 896

表8-15

分地区海外企业情况 (2016年)
OVERSEAS BUSINESS CONDITIONS BY REGION(2016)

地 区	Region	境外企业数（个） Number of Newly Approved Foreign Enterprises (unit)		新批中方境外投资额（万美元） New Registered Oversea Investment from China (USD 10 000)
		新 增 Newly Added	累计实有 Total	
全 市	**Whole Municipality**	**334**	**1 509**	**320 896**
市 区	Urban Area	219	845	215 011
# 吴江区	Wujiang District	28	136	56 624
常 熟	Changshu	25	171	21 351
张家港	Zhangjiagang	39	234	51 889
昆 山	Kunshan	28	154	8 179
太 仓	Taicang	23	105	24 466

表8-16

人民币对主要外币年平均汇价（中间价）
AVERAGE EXCHANGE RATE OF RMB YUAN AGAINST MAIN CONVERTIBLE CURRENCIES (MIDDLE PRICE)

单位：人民币元 (RMB yuan)

年 份 Year	100美元 100 US Dollars	100日元 100 Japanese Yen	100港元 100 Hong Kong Dollars	100欧元 100 Euro
1985	293.66	1.25	37.57	
1986	345.28	2.07	44.22	
1987	372.21	2.58	47.74	
1988	372.21	2.91	47.70	
1989	376.51	2.74	48.28	
1990	478.32	3.32	61.39	
1991	532.33	3.96	68.45	
1992	551.46	4.36	71.24	
1993	576.20	5.20	74.41	
1994	861.87	8.44	111.53	
1995	835.10	8.92	107.96	
1996	831.42	7.64	107.51	
1997	828.98	6.86	107.09	
1998	827.91	6.35	106.88	
1999	827.83	7.29	106.66	
2000	827.84	7.69	106.18	
2001	827.70	6.81	106.08	
2002	827.70	6.62	106.07	800.58
2003	827.70	7.15	106.24	936.13
2004	827.68	7.66	106.23	1 029.00
2005	819.17	7.45	105.30	1 019.53
2006	797.18	6.86	102.62	1 001.90
2007	760.40	6.46	97.46	1 041.75
2008	694.51	6.74	89.19	1 022.27
2009	683.10	7.30	88.12	952.70
2010	676.95	7.73	87.13	897.25
2011	645.88	8.11	82.97	900.11
2012	631.25	7.90	81.38	810.67
2013	619.28	6.33	79.85	822.19
2014	614.28	5.82	79.22	816.51
2015	622.84	5.16	80.34	691.41
2016	664.23	6.12	85.58	734.26

表8-17

部分年份国际旅游情况

项目		Item		1990年
一、旅游外汇收入	（万美元）	**Foreign Exchange Earnings of Tourism**	(USD 10 000)	**1 581**
二、接待境外游客	（万人次）	**Number of Foreign Tourists**	(10 000 person-times)	**27.84**
三、接待过夜境外游客		**Number of Foreign Tourists Staying Overnight**		**26.16**
外国人		Foreigners		8.07
港澳台同胞		Compatriots from HongKong, Macao and Taiwan		17.34
四、境外游客过夜人天数	（万人天）	**Person-days of Foreign Tourists Staying Overnight**	(10 000 person-days)	**31.93**
外国人		Foreigners		11.38
港澳台同胞		Compatriots from HongKong, Macao and Taiwan		19.75
五、接待过夜外国人分国别	（人次）	**Foreign Tourists Staying Overnight by Country**	(person-time)	
#日　本		Japan		31 321
新加坡		Singapore		2 494
泰　国		Thailand		
印度尼西亚		Indonesia		
马来西亚		Malaysia		
美　国		United States		5 864
加拿大		Canada		
英　国		United Kingdom		2 314
法　国		France		3 606
德　国		Germany		2 367
意大利		Italy		
瑞　士		Switzerland		
澳大利亚		Australia		
六、接待能力		**Reception Capacity**		
星级宾馆	（家）	Star-rated Hotels	(unit)	12
星级宾馆床位	（张）	Number of Beds Star-rated Hotels	(unit)	3 212
附：旅游总收入	（亿元）	**The Total Income of Tourism**	(100 million yuan)	
# 国内旅游收入		Earnings form Domestic Tourism		
接待国内旅游人数	（万人次）	**Number of Received Domestic Tourists**	(10 000 person-times)	

注：2013年起国家旅游局对入境旅游统计口径进行调整，以社会住宿设施床位数为基础，并以公安部门的接待境外人员数据进行校核。

INTERNATIONAL TOURISM OF PARTIAL YEARS

2000年	2010年	2012年	2013年	2014年	2015年	2016年
20 135	**125 059**	**164 723**	**135 687**	**170 463**	**200 183**	**216 708**
71.41	**265.15**	**321.87**	**188.95**	**190.24**	**197.20**	**209.98**
55.73	**207.53**	**249.22**	**144.21**	**145.32**	**151.20**	**161.28**
37.58	147.23	179.54	94.89	82.75	84.43	91.08
18.15	60.30	69.68	49.32	62.57	66.77	70.20
88.32	**668.01**	**827.97**	**582.72**	**593.83**	**627.03**	**676.13**
62.67	453.03	556.73	383.47	304.48	309.80	334.84
25.65	214.98	271.24	199.25	289.35	317.23	341.29
114 870	426 352	465 723	206 290	198 511	158 794	161 423
19 217	57 832	85 797	29 584	31 136	29 961	26 873
7 595	24 363	30 524	11 102	8 756	6 059	8 195
4 688	21 808	32 217	14 863	17 658	12 342	11 809
36 570	59 078	74 408	47 714	48 859	29 117	24 024
36 027	192 581	244 889	77 551	83 013	125 740	130 890
4 312	43 358	65 485	20 993	27 698	21 520	14 109
10 823	44 071	56 541	21 559	24 124	22 367	17 798
20 920	38 428	44 846	26 782	22 571	18 193	15 650
10 604	68 084	110 010	43 212	44 555	65 468	63 816
7 555	20 422	33 796	16 874	15 106	18 233	17 195
1 926	5 808	8 509	3 896	3 898	4 296	3 484
5 779	33 131	42 449	14 432	18 575	13 510	12 916
67	159	144	142	132	123	110
14 816	41 183	36 657	38 658	35 850	39 414	37 511
141.88	**1 018.19**	**1 376.24**	**1 522.90**	**1 697.78**	**1 863.60**	**2 082.01**
125.22	917.76	1 254.38	1 419.09	1 574.81	1 728.79	1 932.50
1 496.05	**7 004.88**	**8 624.43**	**9 416.33**	**10 028.84**	**10 605.45**	**11 300.37**

Note: In 2013 the National Tourism Administration began to adjust the caliber of inbound tourism statistics, and it is based on the number of beds of the society's accommodation facilities and checked with the data of foreign tourists received in the police department.

表8-18

四星级及以上饭店、宾馆一览（2016年末）
LIST OF HOTELS ABOVE 4-STAR STANDARD (END OF 2016)

单位 Hotels and Restaurants	地址 Address	电话 Telephone Number	星级标准 Standard	客房数(间) Number of Guest Rooms (room)
苏州吴宫泛太平洋酒店	苏州市姑苏区新市路259号	65103388	五星	481
苏州雅都大酒店	苏州市姑苏区三香路488号	68291888	五星	327
苏州国泰南园宾馆	苏州市姑苏区十全街655号	67786778	五星	233
苏州万豪酒店	苏州市姑苏区干将西路1296号	82258888	五星	293
苏州怡景太湖高尔夫酒店	苏州市吴中区太湖国家旅游度假区墅里路2号	66217777	五星	118
苏州新城花园酒店	苏州市高新区狮山路1号	68250228	五星	457
苏州香格里拉大酒店	苏州市高新区塔园路168号	68080168	五星	390
苏州中茵皇冠假日酒店	苏州市工业园区星港街168号	67616688	五星	344
苏州工业园区金鸡湖大酒店	苏州市工业园区国宾路168号	62887878	五星	159
苏州工业园区阳澄湖澜廷度假酒店	苏州市工业园区阳澄湖半岛	62988888	五星	200
苏州金鸡湖凯宾斯基酒店	苏州市工业园区国宾路1号	62897888	五星	458
苏州维景国际大酒店	苏州市工业园区金鸡湖大道1355号	62800666	五星	475
苏州同里湖大饭店	苏州市吴江区九里湖路8号	63337888	五星	491
吴江东恒盛国际大酒店	苏州市吴江区文苑路88号	63928888	五星	422
吴江海悦花园大酒店	苏州市吴江区经济开发区运东大道1168号	63438888	五星	510
常熟虞山饭店	常熟市北门大街8号	52118888	五星	291
常熟天铭国际大酒店	常熟市海虞北路12号	52877777	五星	316
常熟皇冠假日酒店	常熟市开元大道6号	52729999	五星	269
常熟裕坤国贸酒店	常熟市珠江路176号	52988888	五星	286
常熟金海华丽嘉酒店	常熟市西门大街73号	52188888	五星	192
张家港国贸酒店	张家港市人民中路42号	58687788	五星	515
张家港华芳金陵国际酒店	张家港市长安中路388号	58811999	五星	398

表8-18 续表 1 Continued 1

单 位 Hotels and Restaurants	地 址 Address	电 话 Telephone Number	星级标准 Standard	客房数(间) Number of Guest Rooms (room)
张家港馨苑度假村	张家港市长安南路279号	58818888	五星	227
昆山一醉皇冠酒店	昆山市前进中路216号	57338888	五星	239
昆山阳澄湖滨商务度假酒店	昆山市马鞍山西路3668号	57800888	五星	200
昆山马穆拉卡酒店	昆山市前进中路387号	57885788	五星	387
太仓花园酒店	太仓市人民北路11号	53531888	五星	251
太仓锦江国际大酒店	太仓市上海东路89号	53580000	五星	316
苏州胥城大厦	苏州市姑苏区三香路333号	68286688	四星	395
苏州凯莱大酒店	苏州市姑苏区干将东路535号	65218855	四星	294
苏州雅戈尔富宫大酒店	苏州市姑苏区宫巷63号	65159998	四星	201
苏州冠云大酒店	苏州市姑苏区桐泾北路538号	68018118	四星	169
苏州市会议中心酒店	苏州市姑苏区道前街100号	65226691	四星	381
苏州园外楼饭店	苏州市姑苏区留园路477号	85888588	四星	182
苏州三元宾馆	苏州市姑苏区人民路887号	65113608	四星	96
苏州独墅湖书香世家会所酒店	苏州市吴中区通达路2699号	62795888	四星	184
苏州中华园大饭店	苏州市吴中区金山南路168号	66256666	四星	127
苏州山水度假村	苏州市吴中区东山镇西泾山	66399888	四星	130
苏州苏苑饭店	苏州市吴中区东吴北路130号	66018888-6635	四星	271
苏州南亚宾馆	苏州市相城区阳澄湖东路1号	65761688	四星	276
苏州金澄大酒店	苏州市相城区兴太路260号	65431888	四星	175
苏州桃园度假村	苏州市高新区金山东路68号	68018888	四星	210
苏州金龙大酒店	苏州市高新区玉山路28号	68253538-416	四星	143
苏州工业园区建屋国际酒店	苏州市工业园区星湖街金鸡湖商业广场	62966666	四星	177

表8-18 续表 2 Continued 2

单 位 Hotels and Restaurants	地 址 Address	电 话 Telephone Number	星级标准 Standard	客房数(间) Number of Guest Rooms (room)
苏州商旅美居酒店	苏州市工业园区凤里街336号	62967888	四星	193
苏州戴斯酒店	苏州市工业园区渔泾路9号	62995888	四星	171
吴江宾馆	苏州市吴江区鲈乡南路2155号	63420888	四星	232
吴江新世纪国际酒店	苏州市吴江区平望镇平波台3号	65059888	四星	79
吴江汇丰国际花园酒店	苏州市吴江区震泽镇南东路699号	63779888	四星	74
吴江盛世锦江国际大酒店	苏州市吴江区盛泽镇盛泽大道88号	63139999	四星	158
吴江汉唐国际酒店	苏州市吴江区鲈乡南路1433号	63115555	四星	90
吴江松陵饭店	苏州市吴江区中山北路51号	63472888	四星	175
吴江盛虹万丽国际酒店	苏州市吴江区盛泽镇哈密路199号	63037888	四星	126
常熟虞城大酒店	常熟市海虞南路64号	52777777	四星	280
常熟森林大酒店	常熟市虞山北路79号	52102888	四星	200
常熟时风国际假日酒店	常熟市海虞南路68号	52228888	四星	100
常熟凯悦国际酒店	常熟市东南开发区金都路1号	52111805	四星	144
张家港沙洲宾馆	张家港市暨阳中路170号	58810888	四星	242
张家港江南花园酒店	张家港市金港镇长江中路132号	58812569	四星	146
张家港市长江大酒店	张家港市金港镇长江西路99号	58318518	四星	200
昆山宾馆	昆山市人民北路99号	57888000	四星	196
昆山嘉顿国际饭店	昆山市马鞍山东路18号	57558888	四星	214
昆山威尼斯假日酒店	昆山市民权路18号	57016888	四星	240
太仓陆渡宾馆	太仓市陆渡镇号郑和中路78号	53459890	四星	244
太仓娄东宾馆	太仓市县府街6号	53712222	四星	284
太仓世代大酒店	太仓市县府东街30号	53587778	四星	112

表8-19 国际友好城市一览（2016年末）
LIST OF INTERNATIONAL SISTER CITIES OF SUZHOU (END OF 2016)

友好城市	Sister Cities	缔结时间 Time of Establishment of Relationship
苏州市	**Suzhou**	
意大利威尼斯市	Venice, Italy	1980年03月24日
加拿大维多利亚市	Victoria, Canada	1980年10月20日
日本池田市	Ikeda, Japan	1981年06月06日
日本金泽市	Kanazawa, Japan	1981年06月13日
美国波特兰市	Portland, USA	1988年06月07日
罗马尼亚图尔恰县	Tulcea, Romania	1995年09月20日
韩国全州市	Chonju, Republic of Korea	1996年03月21日
拉脱维亚里加市	Riga, Latvia	1997年09月22日
埃及伊斯梅利亚市	Ismailia, Egypt	1998年03月03日
法国格勒诺布尔市	Grenoble, France	1998年09月20日
荷兰奈梅亨市	Nijmegen, The Netherlands	1999年09月23日
丹麦埃斯比约市	Esbjerg, Denmark	2002年08月20日
巴西阿雷格里港市	Porto Alegre, Brazil	2004年06月22日
马达加斯加塔那那利佛市	Antananarivo, Madagascar	2005年11月29日
德国康斯坦茨市	Konstanz, Germany	2007年10月18日
新西兰陶波市	Taupo, New Zealand	2008年02月07日
澳大利亚洛根市	Logan, Australia	2009年11月09日
瑞典克鲁努贝里地区	Region Kronoberg, Sweden	2012年08月22日
波兰新松奇市	Nowy Sacz, Poland	2016年06月14日
刚果（布）黑角市	Pointe-Noire, Republic of the Congo	2016年07月05日
马尔代夫马累市	Male, Maldives	2016年07月15日
姑苏区	**Gusu District**	
马耳他桑塔露西亚市	Santa Lucija, Malta	2001年11月09日
吴中区	**Wuzhong District**	
德国里萨市	Riesa, Germany	1999年08月16日
新西兰罗托鲁瓦市	Rotorua, New Zealand	2000年02月18日
美国南湖市	Southlake, USA	2014年12月05日
相城区	**Xiangcheng District**	
韩国荣州市	Yongju, Republic of Korea	1998年04月23日
瑞典维克舍市	Vaxjo, Sweden	2014年10月16日

表8-19 续表 Continued

友好城市	Sister Cities	缔结时间 Time of Establishment of Relationship
吴江区	**Wujiang District**	
法国布尔昆-雅里昂市	Bourgoin - Jallieu, France	1993年10月07日
澳大利亚达博市	Dubbo, Australia	1995年06月07日
日本千叶市	Chiba, Japan	1996年10月10日
韩国华城市	Hwa Sung County, Republic of Korea	2000年09月27日
日本内滩町市	Uchinada, Japan	2006年10月08日
南非莫哈林市	Mogale, South Africa	2006年11月14日
美国马伯洛市	Marlboro Township,USA	2011年12月09日
常熟市	**Changshu**	
日本绫部市	Ayabe, Japan	1989年05月12日
日本萨摩川内市	Satsuma Sendai, Japan	1991年07月26日
澳大利亚汤斯维尔市	Townsville, Australia	1995年04月30日
美国惠蒂尔市	Whitter, USA	1995年05月12日
法国布莱斯特市	Brest, France	1996年07月16日
加拿大本拿比市	Burnaby, Canada	2009年07月20日
摩洛哥索维拉市	Essaouira, Morocco	2013年05月20日
韩国务安郡	MUAN-GUN, Republic of Korea	2016年10月21日
张家港市	**Zhangjiagang**	
澳大利亚波特兰市	Portland, Australia	1995年08月08日
日本丸龟市	Marugame, Japan	1999年05月28日
俄罗斯维亚基马市	Vyazama, Russia	2004年10月11日
美国丽浪多	Redondo Beach, USA	2007年05月21日
昆山市	**Kunshan**	
美国南艾尔蒙地市	South Elmonte, USA	1993年06月07日
纳米比亚赫鲁特方丹市	Grootfontein, Namibia	2003年07月21日
日本馆林市	Tatebayashi, Japan	2006年05月16日
澳大利亚彭里斯市	Australia, Penrith	2013年10月31日
芬兰许温凯市	Hyvinkaa, Finland	2016年05月20日
太仓市	**Taicang**	
意大利罗索里纳市	Rosolina, Italy	2000年02月23日
英国威勒尔市	Wirral, UK	2013年12月18日

主 要 统 计 指 标 解 释

进出口总额 指实际进出我国国境的货物总金额。包括对外贸易实际进出口货物，来料加工装配进出口货物，国家间、联合国及国际组织无偿援助物资和赠送品，华侨、港澳台同胞和外籍华人捐赠品，租赁期满归承租人所有的租赁货物，进料加工进出口货物，边境地方贸易及边境地区小额贸易进出口货物，中外合资企业、中外合作经营企业、外商独资经营企业进出口货物和公用物品，到、离岸价格在规定限额以上的进出口货样和广告品(无商业价值、无使用价值和免费提供出口的除外)，从保税仓库提取在中国境内销售的进口货物，以及其他进出口货物。该指标可以观察一个国家在对外贸易方面的总规模。我国规定出口货物按离岸价格统计，进口货物按到岸价格统计。

使用外资 指我国各级政府、部门、企业和其他经济组织通过对外借款、吸收外商直接投资以及用其他方式筹措的境外现汇、设备、技术等。

外商直接投资 指外国企业和经济组织或个人(包括华侨、港澳台胞以及我国在境外注册的企业)按我国有关政策、法规，用现汇、实物、技术等在我国境内开办外商独资企业、与我国境内的企业或经济组织共同举办中外合资经营企业、合作经营企业或合作开发资源的投资(包括外商投资收益的再投资)，以及经政府有关部门批准的项目投资总额内企业从境外借入的资金。

外商其他投资 指除对外借款和外商直接投资以外的各种利用外资的形式。包括企业在境内外股票市场公开发行的以外币计价的股票（目前主要是在香港证券市场发行的H股和在境内证券市场发行的B股）发行价总额，国际租赁进口设备的应付款，补偿贸易中外商提供的进口设备、技术、物料的价款，加工装配贸易中外商提供的进口设备、物料的价款。

对外直接投资 指我国国内投资者以现金、实物、无形资产等方式在国外及港澳台地区设立、购买国（境）外企业，并以控制该企业的经营管理权为核心的经济活动。

对外承包工程 指各对外承包公司以招标议标承包方式承揽的下列业务：(1)承包国外工程建设项目；(2)承包我国对外经援项目；(3)承包我国驻外机构的工程建设项目；(4)承包我国境内利用外资进行建设的工程项目；(5)与外国承包公司合营或联合承包工程项目时我国公司分包部分；(6)对外承包兼营的房屋开发业务。对外承包工程的营业额是以货币表现的本期内完成的对外承包工程的工作量，包括以前年度签订的合同和本年度新签订的合同在报告期内完成的工作量。

对外劳务合作 指以收取工资的形式向业主或承包商提供技术和劳动服务的活动。我国对外承包公司在境外开办的合营企业，中国公司同时又提供劳务的，其劳务部分也纳入劳务合作统计。劳务合作营业额按报告期内向雇主提交的结算数(包括工资、加班费和奖金等)统计。

旅游人数

(1)入境旅游人数：指报告期内来我国观光、度假、探亲访友、就医疗养、购物、参加会议或从事经济、文化、体育、宗教活动的外国人、港澳台同胞等入境游客。统计时，外国人、港澳台同胞每入境一次统计1人次。入境旅游人数包括入境过夜游客和入境一日游游客。

(2)出境人数：指中国（大陆）居民因公或因私出境前往其他国家、中国香港特别行政区、澳门特别行政区和台湾省观光、度假、探亲访友、就医疗养、购物、参加会议或从事经济、文化、体育、宗教活动的人数，即出境游客。统计时，按每出境一次统计1人次。

(3)国内旅游人数：指在报告期内在中国（大陆）观光游览、度假、探亲访友、就医疗养、购物、参加会议或从事经济、文化、体育、宗教活动的中国（大陆）居民人数，其出游的目的不是通过所从事的活动谋取报酬。统计时，国内游客按每出游一次统计1人次。

国际旅游(外汇)收入 指入境游客在中国（大陆）境内旅行、游览过程中用于交通、参观游览、住宿、餐饮、购物、娱乐等全部花费。

国内旅游收入 指国内游客在国内旅行、游览过程中用于交通、参观游览、住宿、餐饮、购物、娱乐等全部花费。

星级饭店 指设备、设施、服务符合《旅游饭店星级的划分与评定》（GB/T14308-2003），通过相关旅游管理部门评定，并取得星级饭店称号的饭店（含预备星级饭店）。

EXPLANATORY NOTES ON MAIN STATISTICAL INDICATORS

Total Imports and Exports at Customs refer to the real value of commodities imported and exported across the border of China. They include the actual imports and exports through foreign trade, imported and exported goods under the processing and assembling trades and materials, supplies and gifts as aid given gratis between governments and by the United Nations and other international organizations, and contributions donated by overseas Chinese, compatriots in Hong Kong and Macao and Chinese with foreign citizenship, leasing commodities owned by tenant at the expiration of leasing period, the imported and exported commodities processed with imported materials, commodities trading in border areas, the imported and exported commodities and articles for public use of the Sino-foreign joint ventures, cooperative enterprises and ventures with sole foreign investment. Also included is import or export of samples and advertising goods for which CIF or FOB value are beyond the permitted ceiling (excluding goods of no trading or use value and free commodities for export), imported goods sold in China from bonded warehouses and other imported or exported goods. The indicator of the total imports and exports at customs can be used to observe the total size of external trade in a country. In accordance with the stipulation of the Chinese government, imports are calculated at CIF, while exports are calculated at FOB.

Utilization of Foreign Capitals refers to remittance, equipment and technology financed from abroad, by loans, foreign direct investment and other forms undertaken by the Chinese governments at all levels, by various departments, enterprises and other economic units.

Foreign Direct Investment refers to the investments inside China by foreign enterprises and economic organizations or individuals (including overseas Chinese, compatriots from Hong Kong, Macao and Taiwan, and Chinese enterprises registered abroad), following the relevant policies and laws of China, for the establishment of ventures exclusively with foreign own investment, Sino-foreign joint ventures and cooperative enterprises or for co-operative exploration of resources with enterprises or economic organizations in China. It includes the re- investment of the foreign entrepreneurs with the profits gained from the investment and the funds that enterprises borrow from abroad in the total investment of projects which are approved by the relevant department of the government.

Other Foreign Investment refers to all forms of utilization of foreign capitals other than foreign borrowings and foreign direct investment. It includes the total value of stock shares in foreign currencies issued by enterprises at domestic or foreign stock exchanges (now mainly consisting of H shares issued at Hong Kong Security Market and B shares issued at domestic security markets), rent payable for the imported equipment through international leasing arrangement, cost of imported equipment, technology and materials provided by foreign counterparts in compensation trade and processing and assembly trade.

Overseas Direct Investment refers to enterprises set up or bought by domestic investors in foreign countries and in Hong Kong, Macao and Taiwan, and the economic activities centring on operation and management of those enterprises are under the control of domestic investors.

Overseas Contracted Project refers to projects undertaken by Chinese contractors (project contracting companies) through bidding process. They include: (1) overseas civil engineering construction projects financed by foreign investors; (2) overseas projects financed by the Chinese government through its foreign aid programs; (3) construction projects of Chinese diplomatic missions, trade offices and other institutions stationed abroad; (4) construction projects in China financed by foreign investment; (5) sub-contracted projects to be taken by Chinese contractors through a joint umbrella project with foreign contractor(s); (6) housing development projects. The business income from international contracted projects is the work volume of contracted projects completed during the reference period, expressed in monetary terms, including completed work on projects signed in previous years.

Overseas Labour Services refer to the activities of providing technology and labour services to employers or contractors in the forms of receiving salaries and wages. Labour services providing by contractual joint ventures of Chinese international contracting corporations should be included in the statistics of service co-operation with foreign countries. The business income of labour service cooperation is the income in the form of wages and salaries, overtime pay, bonuses and other remuneration received from the employers during the reference period.

Number of Tourists

(1) Visitor arrivals refer to the number of foreigners, Chinese compatriots from Hong Kong, Macao and Taiwan Chinese (mainland) who come to China (mainland) for sight-seeing, vacation, visiting relatives, medical treatment, shopping, attending conference, or to engage in economic, cultural, sports and religious activities. In compiling statistics, each time of entering China is counted as one person-time. The number of overseas visitor arrivals includes inbound overnight tourists and one-day tourists.

(2) Number of Chinese residents going abroad refer to the number of Chinese (mainland) residents going to other countries, Hong Kong Special Administrative region, Macao Special Administrative region and Taiwan for on official or private purposes, for sight-seeing, vacation, visiting relatives, medical treatment, shopping, attending conference, or to engage in economic, cultural, sports and religious activities. In compiling statistics, each time of leaving is counted as one person-time.

(3) Number of domestic tourists refers to the number Of Chinese (mainland) residents who travel within China (mainland) for sight-seeing, vacation, visiting relatives, medical treatment, shopping, attending conference, or to engage in economic, cultural, sports and religious activities. In compiling statistics, each time of travelling is counted as one person-time.

Foreign Exchange Earnings from International Tourism refer to the total expenditure of foreigners, overseas Chinese, Chinese compatriots from Hong Kong, Macao and Taiwan during their stay in the mainland of China on transportation,sighting, accommodation, food, shopping and entertainment.

Income from Domestic Tourism refer to expenditure of domestic tourists on transportation, sighting, accommodation, food, shopping and entertainment while they travel.

Star-rated Hotels refer to hotels rated with stars as assessed by the relevant tourism authorities according to GB/T14308-2003 standard with reference to their infrastructure, facilities and service levels.

九、服务业

CHAPTER 9
SERVICES

9 服务业 SERVICES

主要统计指标 MAJOR STATISTICAL INDICATORS

2016年服务业税收	Tax of Services	1 288.87	亿元	100 million yuan
比上年增长	Increase Over Last Year	11.1	%	
2016年服务业投资	Investment of Services	3 660.27	亿元	100 million yuan
比上年增长	Increase Over Last Year	-6.5	%	
2016年服务业实际使用外资	Actual Use of Foreign Investment by Services	20.79	亿美元	USD 100 million
比上年增长	Increase Over Last Year	-22.3	%	
2016年服务业用电量	Services Consumption of Electricity	143.63	亿千瓦时	100 million kwh
比上年增长	Increase Over Last Year	12.8	%	
服务业集聚区	Service Area	87	个	unit
# 省　级	Provincial Level	23	个	unit

表9-1

规模以上服务业法人单位主要指标 (2016年)

单位：万元

项　目	Item	单位数(个) Number of Enterprises (unit)	固定资产原价 Original Value of Fixed Assets
总　计	**Total**	**2 629**	**22 812 947**
1. 按地区分	**Grouped by Region**		
市　区	Urban Area	1 387	15 594 322
# 吴江区	Wujiang District	132	539 755
常　熟	Changshu	225	1 513 882
张家港	Zhangjiagang	335	1 834 666
昆　山	Kunshan	505	2 253 675
太　仓	Taicang	177	1 616 401
2. 按登记注册类型分	**Grouped by Registration Status**		
国有企业	State-owned Enterprises	54	811 322
集体企业	Collective-owned Enterprises	62	524 032
股份合作企业	Share-holding Cooperative Enterprises	3	39 172
联营企业	Joint Ownership Enterprises	–	–
有限责任公司	Limited Liability Corporations	674	11 579 290
股份有限公司	Share-holding Cooperative Ltd.	95	3 609 256
私营企业	Private Enterprises	1 469	1 900 225
其他企业	Other Enterprises	24	119 666
港澳台商投资企业	Enterprises with Investment from HongKong, Macao and Taiwan	84	2 202 191
外商投资企业	Enterprises with Foreign Investment	164	2 027 794
3. 按主要行业分	**Grouped by Sector**		
交通运输、仓储和邮政业	Transportation, Storage and Postal Services	808	9 796 614
道路运输业	Road Transport	401	5 852 216
水上运输业	Water Transport	45	1 726 507
装卸搬运和运输代理业	Handling and Transportation Agency	250	899 887
仓储业	Warehousing	96	1 195 522
邮政业	Postal Services	16	122 482
信息传输、软件和信息技术服务业	Information Transmission, Software and IT Services	271	4 180 422
电信、广播电视和卫星传输服务	Telecommunications, Radio and Television and Satellite Transmission Services	13	3 668 676
互联网和相关服务	Internet and Related Services	15	58 591
软件和信息技术服务业	Software and IT Services	243	453 155

MAIN INDICATORS OF CORPORATE UNITS OF ABOVE-SCALE SERVICES (2016)

(10 000 yuan)

本年折旧 Depreciation Charge of the Year	资产总计 Total Assets	负债总计 Total Liabilities	营业收入 Business Revenue	营业成本 Business Cost	所有者权益合计 Total Creditors Equity	营业税金及附加 Taxes and Extra Charges from Business
1 206 958	**95 438 654**	**52 682 823**	**23 437 071**	**17 323 639**	**42 755 831**	**185 239**
815 735	57 150 473	31 377 616	13 854 058	9 973 973	25 772 858	110 284
53 481	2 305 357	1 492 144	648 457	561 298	813 213	7 199
76 876	9 816 335	5 562 883	1 833 762	1 235 812	4 253 452	18 286
119 511	7 413 356	3 798 519	1 976 449	1 588 514	3 614 838	15 792
126 392	16 938 009	9 612 845	4 864 383	3 802 054	7 325 163	33 351
68 444	4 120 481	2 330 960	908 420	723 286	1 789 521	7 528
28 337	7 510 170	4 267 945	709 832	595 717	3 242 225	8 705
25 336	3 534 383	2 783 227	179 747	109 584	751 156	4 689
1 898	38 491	23 627	6 133	3 015	14 864	216
–	–	–	–	–	–	–
465 207	61 926 735	34 558 071	6 218 524	4 700 934	27 368 664	88 277
284 033	4 933 272	2 268 685	2 860 600	1 510 765	2 664 587	7 736
158 309	8 313 433	5 103 384	8 942 145	7 336 459	3 210 049	51 421
14 545	256 750	101 293	131 882	80 529	155 456	443
115 084	2 599 298	1 285 759	1 124 402	673 418	1 313 539	6 470
114 210	6 326 122	2 290 832	3 263 808	2 313 218	4 035 290	17 283
410 517	18 646 846	9 980 432	5 647 960	4 732 505	8 666 414	28 380
226 268	12 232 286	6 763 213	2 216 421	2 013 755	5 469 074	12 159
71 678	2 043 445	946 797	452 061	299 280	1 096 649	1 247
60 128	1 848 190	873 908	1 499 741	1 222 460	974 282	7 043
47 935	2 315 135	1 272 735	940 236	744 261	1 042 400	5 924
4 508	207 790	123 781	539 501	452 750	84 010	2 006
319 036	6 543 700	3 335 713	5 024 787	2 916 327	3 207 986	18 067
274 768	2 120 472	1 446 046	1 984 011	988 789	674 427	1 935
6 138	973 990	119 624	297 872	151 264	854 366	432
38 129	3 449 238	1 770 044	2 742 904	1 776 274	1 679 194	15 700

表9-1 续表1

单位：万元

项　目	Item	单位数(个) Number of Enterprises (unit)	固定资产原价 Original Value of Fixed Assets
房地产业	Real Estate	244	599 462
物业管理	Property Management	223	576 663
房地产中介服务	Real Estate Services	19	21 123
自有房地产经营活动	Business Activities with Own Real Estate	2	1 676
租赁和商务服务业	Leasing and Business Services	525	4 873 714
租赁业	Leasing Industry	28	126 276
商务服务业	Business Services	497	4 747 439
科学研究和技术服务业	Scientific Research and Technical Services	383	1 572 584
研究和试验发展	Research and Experimental Development	51	332 508
专业技术服务业	Professional Technical Services	297	711 918
科技推广和应用服务业	Technology Promotion and Application Services	35	528 158
水利、环境和公共设施管理业	Water, Environment and Public Facilities Management Industry	111	557 990
水利管理业	Water Conservancy	5	143 549
生态保护和环境治理业	Ecological Protection and Environmental Management Industry	18	60 868
公共设施管理业	Public Facilities Management	88	353 573
居民服务、修理和其他服务业	Resident Services, Repairs and Other Services	102	102 107
居民服务业	Resident Services	24	35 935
机动车、电子产品和日用产品修理业	Motor Vehicles, Electronics and Household Goods Repair Industry	43	35 754
其他服务业	Other Services	35	30 418
教　育	Education	56	145 005
教　育	Education	56	145 005
卫生和社会工作	Health and Social Work	63	425 674
卫　生	Health	61	419 460
社会工作	Social Work	2	6 214
文化、体育和娱乐业	Culture, Sports and Entertainment	66	559 374
新闻和出版业	Press and Publishing	5	90 608
广播、电视、电影和影视录音制作业	Radio, Television, Film and Video Recording Production Industry	30	37 386
文化艺术业	Culture and Arts	9	18 891
体　育	Physical Education	12	232 289
娱乐业	Entertainment	10	180 201

Continued 1

(10 000 yuan)

本年折旧 Depreciation Charge of the Year	资产总计 Total Assets	负债总计 Total Liabilities	营业收入 Business Revenue	营业成本 Business Cost	所有者权益合计 Total Creditors Equity	营业税金及附加 Taxes and Extra Charges from Business
26 342	2 004 714	1 286 848	744 078	501 961	717 865	23 355
24 893	1 806 775	1 181 636	661 155	452 464	625 139	21 181
1 346	69 504	28 951	79 218	48 733	40 553	1 841
103	128 435	76 261	3 705	764	52 173	333
221 203	56 250 362	31 383 213	7 830 328	6 234 945	24 867 149	70 125
15 458	285 257	197 038	91 099	61 244	88 219	1 162
205 745	55 965 105	31 186 175	7 739 230	6 173 700	24 778 930	68 963
115 603	4 787 738	2 098 062	2 418 877	1 672 328	2 689 676	18 676
23 337	958 773	381 005	360 718	236 819	577 768	1 619
51 271	2 053 632	907 619	1 552 258	1 053 960	1 146 013	13 275
40 995	1 775 332	809 438	505 901	381 549	965 894	3 783
37 031	4 848 068	3 237 494	550 152	407 567	1 610 574	15 125
5 668	378 006	298 962	40 128	22 643	79 044	734
4 317	252 170	145 317	82 839	52 111	106 853	761
27 046	4 217 892	2 793 215	427 185	332 813	1 424 677	13 630
5 925	385 835	250 560	356 421	271 227	135 275	4 492
1 563	148 826	104 073	83 925	46 955	44 753	145
2 038	134 442	84 101	104 405	83 797	50 341	610
2 324	102 567	62 386	168 091	140 475	40 181	3 737
17 784	269 194	147 740	201 958	122 936	121 454	2 725
17 784	269 194	147 740	201 958	122 936	121 454	2 725
21 454	517 022	349 850	461 177	325 147	167 172	213
21 152	513 838	341 843	459 122	324 684	171 995	203
303	3 183	8 007	2 055	462	-4 824	9
32 063	1 185 177	612 911	201 334	138 697	572 266	4 082
2 855	111 926	87 053	24 329	24 072	24 874	158
8 797	140 908	75 211	64 640	45 988	65 697	1 268
897	23 163	17 048	27 525	22 371	6 116	198
9 972	238 093	75 027	32 027	20 690	163 066	1 059
9 543	671 087	358 573	52 812	25 578	312 513	1 399

表9-1 续表2

单位：万元

项　　目	Item	销售费用 Cost Related With Sale	管理费用 Managerial Cost
总　　计	**Total**	**1 386 348**	**2 695 609**
1. 按地区分	**Grouped by Region**		
市　区	Urban Area	933 474	1 716 104
# 吴江区	Wujiang District	15 401	92 665
常　熟	Changshu	133 275	168 793
张家港	Zhangjiagang	68 889	208 120
昆　山	Kunshan	216 436	504 454
太　仓	Taicang	34 273	98 137
2. 按登记注册类型分	**Grouped by Registration Status**		
国有企业	State-owned Enterprises	15 241	115 750
集体企业	Collective-owned Enterprises	6 028	51 559
股份合作企业	Share-holding Cooperative Enterprises	1 088	1 397
联营企业	Joint Ownership Enterprises	–	–
有限责任公司	Limited Liability Corporations	258 891	766 026
股份有限公司	Share-holding Cooperative Ltd.	340 255	260 662
私营企业	Private Enterprises	493 815	815 839
其他企业	Other Enterprises	6 044	26 473
港澳台商投资企业	Enterprises with Investment from HongKong, Macao and Taiwan	68 448	224 058
外商投资企业	Enterprises with Foreign Investment	196 536	433 846
3. 按主要行业分	**Grouped by Sector**		
交通运输、仓储和邮政业	Transportation, Storage and Postal Services	133 600	548 808
道路运输业	Road Transport	54 037	202 301
水上运输业	Water Transport	3 784	56 540
装卸搬运和运输代理业	Handling and Transportation Agency	30 492	132 412
仓储业	Warehousing	29 487	113 394
邮政业	Postal Services	15 801	44 161
信息传输、软件和信息技术服务业	Information Transmission, Software and IT Services	514 278	643 742
电信、广播电视和卫星传输服务	Telecommunications, Radio And Television and Satellite Transmission Services	252 195	85 616
互联网和相关服务	Internet and Related Services	89 888	51 605
软件和信息技术服务业	Software and IT Services	172 195	506 520

Continued 2

(10 000 yuan)

财务费用 Financing Activities Cost	投资收益 Income from Investment	营业利润 Business Profits	利润总额 Total Profits	应交所得税 Income Tax Payable	应付职工薪酬 Employee Salary payable	应交增值税 Value Added Tax Payable	从业人员平均人数(人) Average Employment (person)
540 367	**384 897**	**1 697 210**	**2 507 890**	**541 015**	**3 615 403**	**365 831**	**415 410**
325 303	149 577	967 327	1 506 031	354 862	2 274 348	211 218	238 443
27 142	3 873	-49 457	14 925	8 161	89 215	6 830	13 946
73 827	116 006	324 772	400 413	66 430	246 632	41 848	31 526
35 621	41 384	129 106	150 086	32 879	286 770	36 930	40 454
75 798	76 894	246 301	405 208	66 235	647 618	57 572	84 495
29 817	1 036	29 704	46 152	20 609	160 036	18 263	20 492
29 917	33 398	-18 373	38 928	5 289	199 810	6 292	17 188
14 813	1 841	-4 994	11 161	3 897	46 738	1 383	6 003
294	–	122	158	–	1 087	2	117
–	–	–	–	–	–	–	–
374 271	147 147	188 903	761 469	165 526	1 174 122	121 189	126 727
17 371	11 651	744 409	782 409	170 534	322 202	30 426	26 662
54 538	41 127	242 076	295 242	90 360	1 260 813	107 242	186 901
2 717	–	18 259	18 033	1 185	29 875	72	4 376
32 741	2 807	135 067	153 012	24 892	156 092	34 130	14 510
13 704	146 927	391 741	447 480	79 332	424 664	65 096	32 926
211 385	57 557	82 724	556 482	117 038	896 677	77 027	104 230
135 495	40 497	-142 284	251 107	59 980	465 926	40 689	55 140
27 631	1 352	64 960	77 771	19 018	63 495	12 409	6 585
13 461	10 610	114 104	123 110	17 503	160 654	9 468	18 992
35 282	5 323	20 844	79 451	18 823	84 646	12 287	10 259
-484	-226	25 099	25 043	1 713	121 956	2 174	13 254
6 582	50 364	972 093	1 028 609	206 967	873 426	133 321	75 222
-326	74	651 268	648 730	154 145	148 895	43 524	8 028
645	11 869	16 471	17 668	2 967	63 655	443	4 280
6 263	38 421	304 354	362 211	49 856	660 875	89 354	62 914

表9-1 续表3

单位：万元

项　　目	Item	销售费用 Cost Related With Sale	管理费用 Managerial Cost
房地产业	Real Estate	48 025	131 320
物业管理	Property Management	34 390	118 901
房地产中介服务	Real Estate Services	13 617	12 030
自有房地产经营活动	Business Activities with Own Real Estate	18	389
租赁和商务服务业	Leasing and Business Services	471 049	639 976
租赁业	Leasing Industry	7 039	14 824
商务服务业	Business Services	464 010	625 152
科学研究和技术服务业	Scientific Research and Technical Services	96 633	442 763
研究和试验发展	Research and Experimental Development	15 724	89 652
专业技术服务业	Professional Technical Services	64 150	250 299
科技推广和应用服务业	Technology Promotion and Application Services	16 759	102 812
水利、环境和公共设施管理业	Water, Environment and Public Facilities Management Industry	26 454	70 884
水利管理业	Water Conservancy	4 404	4 225
生态保护和环境治理业	Ecological Protection and Environmental Management Industry	2 732	12 684
公共设施管理业	Public Facilities Management	19 319	53 975
居民服务、修理和其他服务业	Resident Services, Repairs and Other Services	15 209	46 577
居民服务业	Resident Services	7 394	16 921
机动车、电子产品和日用产品修理业	Motor Vehicles, Electronics and Household Goods Repair Industry	6 310	12 166
其他服务业	Other Services	1 505	17 490
教　育	Education	25 318	38 515
教　育	Education	25 318	38 515
卫生和社会工作	Health and Social Work	23 212	87 895
卫　生	Health	22 688	86 268
社会工作	Social Work	524	1 627
文化、体育和娱乐业	Culture, Sports and Entertainment	32 570	45 131
新闻和出版业	Press and Publishing	1 512	8 321
广播、电视、电影和影视录音制作业	Radio, Television, Film and Video Recording Production Industry	13 145	6 592
文化艺术业	Culture and Arts	2 545	5 512
体　育	Physical Education	1 793	12 650
娱乐业	Entertainment	13 574	12 056

Continued 3

(10 000 yuan)

财务费用 Financing Activities Cost	投资收益 Income from Investment	营业利润 Business Profits	利润总额 Total Profits	应交所得税 Income Tax Payable	应付职工薪酬 Employee Salary Payable	应交增值税 Value Added Tax Payable	从业人员平均人数（人） Average Employment (Person)
23 352	5 554	29 284	50 820	14 176	334 295	8 783	72 396
18 871	5 553	25 934	48 161	11 425	285 704	7 980	67 973
214	1	2 813	2 825	1 789	48 434	802	4 388
4 268	–	538	-166	963	157	–	35
239 856	234 081	352 034	522 705	120 316	609 090	80 529	70 995
6 689	243	-2 335	-2 989	-138	11 002	1 439	1 820
233 167	233 838	354 369	525 694	120 453	598 088	79 090	69 175
20 588	11 112	195 688	241 729	51 598	516 338	46 621	39 786
4 368	4 567	25 004	35 830	5 281	94 409	1 409	5 199
5 342	6 854	180 525	188 481	40 024	361 585	31 297	31 489
10 877	-309	-9 841	17 418	6 293	60 344	13 915	3 098
20 317	6 209	16 161	22 744	6 423	69 571	9 688	11 747
3 755	31	5 402	5 199	1 278	6 050	840	421
4 598	–	8 712	13 106	1 274	8 577	5 865	1 038
11 965	6 178	2 047	4 439	3 871	54 944	2 984	10 288
1 981	-10	17 202	18 459	4 623	73 872	3 486	11 983
1 995	–	8 788	9 200	1 840	14 333	26	2 120
359	7	1 409	1 736	817	15 406	2 578	2 642
-374	-16	7 006	7 522	1 967	44 133	882	7 221
2 115	181	16 676	18 843	4 355	76 748	1 088	7 957
2 115	181	16 676	18 843	4 355	76 748	1 088	7 957
8 272	62	20 537	23 012	7 556	109 914	6	14 313
8 246	62	21 132	23 470	7 502	108 730	–	14 033
26	–	-595	-458	55	1 184	6	280
5 919	19 788	-5 190	24 489	7 963	55 473	5 283	6 781
1 039	20 161	9 323	11 288	–	12 708	565	819
3 299	-141	-5 623	-3 797	1 048	9 523	3 377	1 570
286	–	-3 522	584	85	5 143	478	498
982	-232	-5 143	-2 828	615	12 980	411	1 687
312	–	-225	19 240	6 215	15 120	452	2 207

表9-2

全市规模以上服务业营业收入三十强企业 (2016年)
TOP 30 ABOVE-SCALE SERVICE ENTERPRISES OF OPERATING INCOME (2016)

序　号 No.	单位名称 Name of Enterprises	地　区 Region	行业类别 Category of Employment
1	同程国际旅行社有限公司	工业园区	商务服务业
2	恩斯克投资有限公司	昆山市	商务服务业
3	中国移动通信集团江苏有限公司苏州分公司	姑苏区	电信、广播电视和卫星传输服务
4	中国电信股份有限公司苏州分公司	姑苏区	电信、广播电视和卫星传输服务
5	住友橡胶（中国）有限公司	常熟市	商务服务业
6	八爪鱼在线旅游发展有限公司	工业园区	商务服务业
7	华为数字技术（苏州）有限公司	工业园区	软件和信息技术服务业
8	江苏吴中集团有限公司	吴中区	商务服务业
9	江苏设计谷科技有限公司	昆山市	专业技术服务业
10	苏州爱康能源工程技术股份有限公司	张家港市	科技推广和应用服务业
11	中国联合网络通信有限公司苏州市分公司	高新区、虎丘区	电信、广播电视和卫星传输服务
12	苏州蜗牛数字科技股份有限公司	工业园区	软件和信息技术服务业
13	苏州工业园区顺丰速运有限公司	工业园区	邮政业
14	苏州邮政局	姑苏区	邮政业
15	江苏白杨湾物流中心有限公司	昆山市	装卸搬运和运输代理业
16	热风投资有限公司	昆山市	商务服务业
17	玖隆钢铁物流有限公司	张家港市	道路运输业
18	苏州市华谊商务有限公司	高新区、虎丘区	商务服务业
19	华住酒店管理有限公司	昆山市	商务服务业
20	江苏沿江高速公路有限公司	常熟市	道路运输业
21	苏州苏嘉杭高速公路有限公司	工业园区	道路运输业
22	苏州新浒投资发展有限公司	高新区、虎丘区	商务服务业
23	同程网络科技股份有限公司	工业园区	互联网和相关服务
24	阿特斯（中国）投资有限公司	高新区、虎丘区	商务服务业
25	昆山银桥控股集团有限公司	昆山市	商务服务业
26	张家港港务集团有限公司	张家港市	装卸搬运和运输代理业
27	吴江市力良农电服务有限公司	吴江区	其他服务业
28	苏州九龙医院有限公司	工业园区	卫　生
29	苏州热工研究院有限公司	姑苏区	研究和试验发展
30	张家港保税科技股份有限公司	张家港市	商务服务业

表9-3

全市规模以上服务业资产三十强企业（2016年）
TOP 30 ABOVE-SCALE SERVICE ENTERPRISES OF ASSETS(2016)

序 号 No.	单位名称 Name of Enterprises	地 区 Region	行业类别 Category of Employment
1	苏州城市建设投资发展有限责任公司	姑苏区	商务服务业
2	苏州市轨道交通集团有限公司	姑苏区	道路运输业
3	昆山国创投资集团有限公司	昆山市	商务服务业
4	江苏省吴中经济技术发展总公司	吴中区	商务服务业
5	苏州高新区国有资产经营公司	高新区、虎丘区	商务服务业
6	江苏省太仓港港口开发建设投资公司	太仓市	公共设施管理业
7	常熟市发展投资有限公司	常熟市	商务服务业
8	张家港保税区张保实业有限公司	张家港市	商务服务业
9	昆山市创业控股有限公司	昆山市	商务服务业
10	昆山银桥控股集团有限公司	昆山市	商务服务业
11	常熟市滨江城市建设经营投资有限责任公司	常熟市	商务服务业
12	苏州元禾控股有限公司	工业园区	商务服务业
13	苏州高新区城乡一体化建设发展有限公司	高新区、虎丘区	商务服务业
14	苏州国际发展集团有限公司	姑苏区	商务服务业
15	江苏沿江高速公路有限公司	常熟市	道路运输业
16	常熟东南资产经营投资有限公司	常熟市	商务服务业
17	同程网络科技股份有限公司	工业园区	互联网和相关服务
18	中国电信股份有限公司苏州分公司	姑苏区	电信、广播电视和卫星传输服务
19	中国移动通信集团江苏有限公司苏州分公司	姑苏区	电信、广播电视和卫星传输服务
20	住友橡胶（中国）有限公司	常熟市	商务服务业
21	江苏吴中集团有限公司	吴中区	商务服务业
22	恩斯克投资有限公司	昆山市	商务服务业
23	苏州市营财投资集团公司	姑苏区	商务服务业
24	苏州市吴中区胥口镇集体资产经营公司	吴中区	商务服务业
25	常熟服装城集团有限公司	常熟市	商务服务业
26	阿特斯（中国）投资有限公司	高新区、虎丘区	商务服务业
27	苏州高新区城市建设投资发展有限公司	高新区、虎丘区	商务服务业
28	苏州历史文化名城保护集团有限公司	姑苏区	商务服务业
29	苏州文化博览中心有限公司	工业园区	商务服务业
30	苏州新浒投资发展有限公司	高新区、虎丘区	商务服务业

表9-4 全市规模以上服务业利润总额三十强企业（2016年）

TOP 30 ABOVE-SCALE SERVICE ENTERPRISES OF TOTAL PROFITS(2016)

序　号 No.	单位名称 Name of Enterprises	地　区 Region	行业类别 Category of Employment
1	中国移动通信集团江苏有限公司苏州分公司	姑苏区	电信、广播电视和卫星传输服务
2	中国电信股份有限公司苏州分公司	姑苏区	电信、广播电视和卫星传输服务
3	住友橡胶（中国）有限公司	常熟市	商务服务业
4	华为数字技术（苏州）有限公司	工业园区	软件和信息技术服务业
5	江苏沿江高速公路有限公司	常熟市	道路运输业
6	恩斯克投资有限公司	昆山市	商务服务业
7	苏州苏嘉杭高速公路有限公司	工业园区	道路运输业
8	江苏白杨湾物流中心有限公司	昆山市	装卸搬运和运输代理业
9	六和机械投资（中国）有限公司	昆山市	商务服务业
10	苏州元禾控股有限公司	工业园区	商务服务业
11	苏州电视广告有限公司	姑苏区	商务服务业
12	苏州蜗牛数字科技股份有限公司	工业园区	软件和信息技术服务业
13	中国联合网络通信有限公司苏州市分公司	高新区、虎丘区	电信、广播电视和卫星传输服务
14	华住酒店管理有限公司	昆山市	商务服务业
15	苏州美生元信息科技有限公司	相城区	软件和信息技术服务业
16	张家港保税区张保实业有限公司	张家港市	商务服务业
17	苏州汽车客运集团有限公司	姑苏区	道路运输业
18	玖隆钢铁物流有限公司	张家港市	道路运输业
19	江苏广和慧云科技股份有限公司	常熟市	软件和信息技术服务业
20	苏州乐园发展有限公司	高新区、虎丘区	娱乐业
21	歌斐资产管理有限公司	昆山市	商务服务业
22	苏州市UL美华认证有限公司	工业园区	专业技术服务业
23	常熟市发展投资有限公司	常熟市	商务服务业
24	苏州城市建设投资发展有限责任公司	姑苏区	商务服务业
25	张家港港务集团有限公司	张家港市	装卸搬运和运输代理业
26	太仓武港码头有限公司	太仓市	水上运输业
27	苏州市农业担保有限公司	姑苏区	商务服务业
28	苏州市吴中国盛国有资产经营管理有限公司	吴中区	商务服务业
29	苏州邮政局	姑苏区	邮政业
30	江苏国泰新点软件有限公司	常熟市	软件和信息技术服务业

表9-5

服务业集聚区发展情况 (2016年)
DEVELOPMENT OF THE SERVICE AREA(2016)

服务业集聚区名称 Service Area	地　区 Region	入区企业数(家) Enterprises Entered Service Area (households)
全　市(87个)		**76 968**
一、省级服务业集聚区(23个)		**42 549**
苏州市吴中科技创业园	吴中区	230
吴中区检验检测产业集聚区	吴中区	35
中国珍珠宝石城	相城区	689
苏州高新区综合保税区	高新区、虎丘区	224
苏州科技城服务业集聚区	高新区、虎丘区	633
江苏苏州高新区人力资源服务产业园	高新区、虎丘区	70
苏州工业园区国际科技服务业集聚区	工业园区	598
苏州工业园区现代物流集聚区	工业园区	324
东方丝绸市场	吴江区	7 011
吴江汾湖商务服务业集聚区	吴江区	4 100
吴江丝绸创业设计产业园	吴江区	128
吴江现代物流集聚区	吴江区	39
中国常熟服装城	常熟市	3 500
常熟国家大学科技园	常熟市	627
张家港保税物流集聚区	张家港市	4 842
江苏化工品交易中心	张家港市	2 952
张家港玖隆钢铁物流园区	张家港市	1 824
江苏扬子江冶金物流集聚区	张家港市	2 400
昆山花桥国际商务城	昆山市	10 915
昆山软件服务业集聚区	昆山市	342
昆山综合保税区保税物流集聚区	昆山市	60
天镜湖文化科技产业园	太仓市	136
太仓物流园区	太仓市	870
二、市级服务业集聚区(64个)		**34 419**
苏州市平江科技创业园	姑苏区	54
苏州市沧浪科技创业园	姑苏区	142
江苏苏州大学科技创业园	姑苏区	80
苏州工投科技创业园	姑苏区	155

表9-5 续表 1　Continued 1

服务业集聚区名称 Service Area	地　区 Region	入区企业数(家) Enterprises Entered Service Area (households)
传化公路港－苏州物流基地	姑苏区	667
平江路休闲旅游特色街	姑苏区	377
苏州山塘历史街区	姑苏区	102
东弘科技创业园	姑苏区	166
苏州市粮食批发交易市场	吴中区	250
金枫路创新创意产业街区	吴中区	1 280
江苏吴中出口加工区现代物流集聚区	吴中区	80
凯马广场汽车街	吴中区	1 110
江苏蠡口国际家具城	相城区	3 920
望亭国际物流园	相城区	97
太平羽绒服装城	相城区	75
通灵金属市场	相城区	450
苏州西交漕湖科技园	相城区	110
苏州阳澄湖数字文化创意产业园	相城区	160
苏州小样青年社区	相城区	79
苏州留学人员创业园	高新区、虎丘区	288
苏州国家环保高新技术产业园	高新区、虎丘区	169
博济科技创业园	高新区、虎丘区	323
苏州市高新区狮山中心商务区	高新区、虎丘区	10 310
苏州西部生态休闲文化创意集聚区	高新区、虎丘区	611
苏州高新区知识产权服务业集聚区	高新区、虎丘区	76
苏州高新区科技金融服务集聚区	高新区、虎丘区	32
苏州生物产业园服务业集聚区	工业园区	452
月亮湾商务区	工业园区	193
苏州2.5产业园	工业园区	125
苏州工业园区云彩创新孵化器集聚区	工业园区	290
阳澄湖半岛休闲旅游集聚区	工业园区	70
东沙湖股权投资中心	工业园区	416
苏州工业园区金鸡湖景区	工业园区	253
吴江市再生资源回收利用市场	吴江区	213

表9-5 续表 2 Continued 2

服务业集聚区名称 Service Area	地 区 Region	入区企业数(家) Enterprises Entered Service Area (households)
吴江科技创业园	吴江区	170
盛泽商务集聚区	吴江区	86
同里古镇文化休闲旅游区	吴江区	1 400
盛泽丝绸现代物流中心	吴江区	43
江苏省汾湖高新技术产业开发区科技创业园	吴江区	187
苏州湾科技城	吴江区	104
苏州盛泽纺织科技创业园	吴江区	82
东太湖科技金融城	吴江区	217
常熟经济开发区高新技术创业中心	常熟市	295
常熟国际物流园	常熟市	562
常熟虞山尚湖旅游度假区	常熟市	95
沙家浜江南水乡影视产业园	常熟市	121
常熟纺织服装创意产业园	常熟市	70
常熟汽车汽配商贸城	常熟市	2 000
张家港保税区纺织品原料市场	张家港市	1 200
张家港市金港物流中心	张家港市	121
张家港名贵木材国际交易中心	张家港市	353
张家港软件（动漫）产业园	张家港市	82
张家港众益危化品物流园区	张家港市	39
张家港保税港区进口汽车物流园	张家港市	280
昆山文化创意产业园	昆山市	572
昆山阳澄湖科技园	昆山市	211
昆山商贸城	昆山市	2 067
千灯现代商贸物流园	昆山市	9
太仓LOFT工业设计产业集聚区	太仓市	43
太仓科技创业园暨留学人员创业园	太仓市	322
太仓软件园	太仓市	88
太仓市生物医药产业园	太仓市	75
太仓森茂汽车城	太仓市	282
太仓市天镜湖私募基金创业基地	太仓市	68

主 要 统 计 指 标 解 释

规模以上服务业法人单位 指年营业收入1000万元及以上，或年末从业人员50人及以上服务业法人单位，包括：交通运输、仓储和邮政业，信息传输、软件和信息技术服务业，租赁和商务服务业，科学研究和技术服务业，水利、环境和公共设施管理业，教育，卫生和社会工作；以及物业管理、房地产中介服务、自有房地产经营活动和其他房地产业等行业；以及年营业收入500万元及以上，或年末从业人员50人及以上服务业法人单位，包括：居民服务、修理和其他服务业，文化、体育和娱乐业。

现代服务业集聚区 指以某一服务产业为主体，相关服务产业相配套，产业特色鲜明，空间相对集中，具有资源集合、产业集群、服务集成功能，现代服务业集聚度达到一定水平的区域。

省级服务业集聚区 指根据《江苏省省级现代服务业集聚区认定和管理暂行办法》，符合省发展改革委《关于加快建设现代服务业集聚区的意见》（苏发改服务发［2007］52号）第三条规定，并满足下列条件的现代服务业产业园区：

(1) 有园区发展规划和产业布局规划，边界清晰、形态突出，目标明确；

(2) 有一定的公共服务支撑体系，能够为入区企业提供投融资、合作交流、人才培训、信息管理、技术创新、知识产权保护、检验检测等公共服务；

(3) 有专门的管理机构，专职管理人员不少于3人，实行统一管理，一站式服务；

(4) 建筑面积10000平方米以上，对通过中心城市主城区改造、工业企业“退二进三”、老建筑保护性开发等利用城市存量资产开发的园区，可适当降低标准；

(5) 经省级以上有关部门批准或经省发展改革委批复园区发展规划，并已列入市级现代服务业集聚区。

不同形态的集聚区还应同时满足下列条件：

中央商务区

(1) 城市功能核心区，主要以金融、保险、证券、商务、商贸等企业为主体，高级酒店、商务设施配套；

(2) 企业总部或地区总部集中，拥有跨国公司或国际性金融机构区域性业务总部，或国内行业百强企业总部；

(3) 交通条件便利，通达性良好。

创意产业园

(1) 有较齐备的基础设施和生产环境；能够为创意企业开展创意研发、设计生产和流通交易等活动提供适宜的硬件环境保障；

(2) 产业特色鲜明，具有符合创意产业生产规律的产业形态，拥有注册创意及相关产业链配套企业20家以上，能够引领相关创意产业的发展；

(3) 拥有一定数量的自主知识产权，原创产品占有一定的市场份额，有良好的品牌影响力。

科技创业园

(1) 具有创业企业发展所需的技术支撑体系及相配套的基础设施，能够为企业提供一定的商务、信息、咨询、技术服务；

(2) 实际运营2年以上，经营状况良好；

(3) 产业特色鲜明，注册科技类企业达20家以上。

软件园

(1) 具有软件产业发展的技术支撑体系及相配套的基础设施和通信网络设施；

(2) 注册软件企业数不少于20家，有一定的产业规模；

(3) 拥育一定比例的自主知识产权，并具备一定的软件出口能力。

现代物流园

(1) 依托港口、空港、站场、道口等交通枢纽或正业开发区，具备良好的基础设施条件和信息服务功能；

(2) 至少拥有三种以上物流功能（仓储、加工、包装、分拣、货代、搬运装卸、配送等），并初步具备金融、保险、税务和后勤服务等基本配套服务；

(3) 注册第三方物流企业10家以上。

产品交易市场

(1) 符合全省统一规划，依托当地特色产业或商品集散能力强的优势，采取有形和无形相结合，主要从事工农业产品、材料及其他重要生产资料的批发；

(2) 具有产品展示、交易结算、仓储运输、质量检测、加工配送等功能和条件，初步具备商品集散、加工、交易、价格形成、信息发布和电子商务等功能；

(3) 年商品成交额处于全省同类市场前5名，覆盖全省、辐射华东地区以至全国家，外向度处于同类市场领先地位。

通过认定的现代服务业产业园区，由省发展改革委授予“江苏省现代服务业集聚区”。

市级服务业集聚区 指根据《苏州市现代服务业集聚区认定暂行办法》，通过苏州市级现代服务业集聚区的申报和认定，获批成为苏州市“现代服务业集聚区”的服务业产业园区。

EXPLANATORY NOTES ON MAIN STATISTICAL INDICATORS

The Corporate Unit of Above-scale Services refers to a corporate unit of the service industry employing 50 people or more, or earning annual revenues of 10 million yuan or above, including: transportation, storage and postal services, information transmission, software and IT services, leasing and business services, scientific research and technical services, water, environment and public facilities management, education, health care and social work, property management, real estate services ,business activities with one's own real estate and other real estate industries and so on; also a corporate unit of the service industry employing 50 people or more, or earning annual revenues of 5 million yuan or above, including: resident services, repairs and other services, culture, sports and entertainment.

The Modern Service Area refers to an area with a service industry as the main and related service industries supporting, with distinctive industrial features and relatively concentrated space, with the functions of resources collection, industrial clusters and service integration, and with a certain level of modern services gathering.

The Provincial Service Area refers to a modern service industrial park that should be in accordance with the "Jiangsu's interim measures of recognizing and managing the provincial modern service area" and in line with Article III of the provincial Development and Reform Commission's "Opinions on speeding up the construction of modern service areas" (Su Development and Reform Services [2007] No. 52), and meets the following conditions:

(1) It has industrial park development planning and layout planning, clear boundaries, prominent forms, and clear objectives;

(2) It has a certain public service support system, and can provide the enterprises in the area with such public services as investment and financing, cooperation and exchange, personnel training, information management, technological innovation, intellectual property protection, and inspection and testing;

(3) It has a special management agency with at least three full-time managers, unified management and one-stop service;

(4) It has a building area of over 10,000 square meters. However, to the parks that develop with the city's existing assets such as the transformation of the main city area of the central city, industrial enterprises "two retreat and three advance", and the protective development of old buildings, it may be appropriate to reduce the standard;

(5) It has its development plan approved by the relevant departments above the provincial level or by the Provincial Development and Reform Commission, and has been included in the municipal modern service area.

Clustering areas of different forms should also meet the following conditions:

Central Business District

(1) The core area of urban functions is an area with finance, insurance, securities, business, commerce and other enterprises as the main, and with luxury hotels and business facilities supporting;

(2) It has centralized corporate headquarters or regional headquarters, regional business headquarters of multinational corporations or international financial institutions, or the headquarters of the top 100 domestic industrial enterprises;

(3) Transportation is convenient and accessibility good.

Creative Industrial Park

(1) It has a more complete infrastructure and production environments, and can provide creative enterprises with appropriate hardware environment for such activities as carrying out innovative research and development, designing production and distribution transactions;

(2) It has distinctive industrial features, has industrial forms in line with the production laws of creative industries, has more than 20 companies with registered creativity and related industrial chain supporting, and can lead the development of related creative industries;

(3) It has a certain number of independent intellectual property rights, and original products occupy a certain market share and a good brand influence.

Technology Park

(1) It has the necessary technical support system for the development of entrepreneurial enterprises and supporting infrastructure, and can provide enterprises with a certain business, information, consulting and technology services;

(2) It has actually operated for more than 2 years, and the operating conditions are good;

(3) It has distinctive industrial features, and the registered tech enterprises amounted to more than 20 .

Software Park

(1) It has a technical support system and supporting infrastructure and communications network facilities for the development of the software industry;

(2) It has at least 20 registered software companies with a certain scale of the industry;

(3) It has and will cultivate a certain proportion of independent intellectual property rights, and has a certain software export capacity.

Modern Logistics Park

(1) It relies on transportation hubs such as ports, airports, stations and crossings or a positive industry development zone, and has good infrastructure conditions and information services;

(2) It has at least three or more logistics functions (storage, processing, packing, sorting, forwarding, handling, distribution, etc.), and initially has the finance, insurance, tax, and logistics support services, and other basic services;

(3) It has registered more than 10 third-party logistics companies.

Products Market

(1) It complies with the province's unified planning, relies on the advantages of local specialties industries or commodity distribution capability, combines the tangible and the intangible, and is mainly engaged in the wholesale of agricultural and industrial products, materials and other important means of production;

(2) It has such functions and conditions as product display, transaction clearing, warehousing and transportation, quality testing, processing and distribution, and initially has such functions as commodity distribution, processing, trade, price formation, information dissemination and e-commerce;

(3) It has the annual commodity turnover among the province’s top five similar markets, covering the whole province, and spreading over East China and even the whole country, and its outgoing degrees are in the leading position of similar markets.

The modern service industrial park that has been recognized will be awarded “Jiangsu Modern Service Area” by the provincial Development and Reform Commission.

The Municipal Service Area refers to a service industry park that should be in accordance with the “Suzhou’s interim measures of recognizing the municipal service area”, has been declared and recognized as a Suzhou’s municipal modern service area, and approved as Suzhou’s “modern service area”.

十、能源消费

CHAPTER 10
CONSUMPTION OF ENERGY

10 能源消费 CONSUMPTION OF ENERGY

主要统计指标 MAJOR STATISTICAL INDICATORS

2016年规模以上工业企业能源消费总量	Total Energy Consumption of Industry Above Designated Size	8 485.04	万吨标准煤	10 000 tons of SCE
# 原　煤	Raw Coal	5 293.07	万吨	10 000 tons
焦　炭	Coke	1 228.83	万吨	10 000 tons
汽　油	Gasoline	6.63	万吨	10 000 tons
柴　油	Diesel Oil	15.17	万吨	10 000 tons
燃料油	Fuel Oil	12.40	万吨	10 000 tons
热　力	Heat	108 628 412	百万千焦	1 million kilo-joule
电　力	Electricity	919.68	亿千瓦时	100 million kwh
2016年全社会用电量	Total Consumption of Electricity	1 382.58	亿千瓦时	100 million kwh
比上年增长	Increase Over Last Year	5.4	%	
2016年工业用电量	Industrial Consumption of Electricity	1 116.30	亿千瓦时	100 million kwh
比上年增长	Increase Over Last Year	3.9	%	
2016年第三产业用电量	Tertiary Industry Consumption of Electricity	143.63	亿千瓦时	100 million kwh
比上年增长	Increase Over Last Year	12.8	%	
2016年城乡居民生活用电量	Consumption of Electricity for Non-production Purposes	108.26	亿千瓦时	100 million kwh
比上年增长	Increase Over Last Year	14.5	%	

表10-1 全市规模以上工业企业能源购进、消费及库存量（2016年）

ENERGY PURCHASES, CONSUMPTION AND STOCK OF INDUSTRIAL ENTERPRISES OF WHOLE MUNICIPALITY ABOVE DESIGNATED SIZE(2016)

能源品种		Type of Energy		购进量 Purchases	消费量 Consumption	# 工业生产 Industrial Production	#用于原材料 Raw Materials	年末库存量 Stock (year-end)
能源合计	(吨标准煤)	**Total Energy**	(ton of SCE)	**69 229 790**	**84 850 372**	**84 376 647**	**1 222 584**	**2 088 010**
原　煤	(吨)	Raw Coal	(ton)	53 341 196	52 930 655	52 901 085	1 057 485	2 138 644
洗精煤		Washing Coal		7 712 472	7 678 792	7 678 792	–	285 379
其他洗煤		Other Washed Coals		5 612	5 739	5 677	–	146
煤制品		Coal Products		206 920	206 630	206 630	–	1 686
焦　炭		Coke		6 942 129	12 288 290	12 288 290	–	289 912
其他焦化产品		Other Coking Products		312 444	308 426	308 426	308 246	20 821
焦炉煤气	(万立方米)	Coke Oven Gas	(10 000 cu.m)	–	223 481	223 481	–	–
高炉煤气		Blast-furnace Gas		190	4 004 367	4 004 367	–	–
转炉煤气		Converter Gas		–	203 952	203 952	–	–
发生炉煤气		Furnace Gas		–	–	–	–	–
天然气		Natural Gas		402 347	401 984	399 996	730	–
液化天然气	(吨)	LNG	(ton)	41 699	41 696	40 951	315	3
汽　油		Gasoline		67 138	66 250	10 549	257	276
煤　油		Kerosene		2 393	2 442	2 422	41	170
柴　油		Diesel Oil		151 860	151 720	87 778	29	5 354
燃料油		Fuel Oil		126 712	123 981	123 694	–	15 896
液化石油气		LPG		8 805	8 820	8 455	–	439
润滑油		Lubricating Oil		2 164	2 089	2 077	160	156
石　蜡		Paraffin wax		376	357	357	13	21
溶剂油		Solvent Oil		659	640	640	–	33
石油焦		Petroleum coke		–	–	–	–	–
石油沥青		Petroleum Asphalt		–	–	–	–	–
其他石油制品		Other Petroleum Products		3 751	3 753	3 753	1 592	3
热　力	(百万千焦)	Heat	(1 million kilo-joule)	74 787 743	108 628 412	107 576 381	–	–
电　力	(万千瓦时)	Electricity	(10 000 kwh)	7 674 214	9 196 802	9 021 293	–	–
城市生活垃圾用于燃料	(吨)	City Waste For Fuel	(Ton)	1 165 978	1 167 062	1 167 062	–	–
生物质废料用于燃料		Biomass Waste For Fuel		41 785	39 851	39 606	–	1 109
余热余压	(百万千焦)	Heat and Pressure	(1 million kilo-joule)	–	24 687 812	24 687 812	–	–
其他工业废料用于燃料	(吨)	Other Industrial Waste For Fuel	(Ton)	9 001	9 001	9 001	–	–
其他燃料	(吨标准煤)	Other Fuels	(ton of SCE)	10 723	11 260	11 257	–	50

表10-2 市区规模以上工业企业能源购进、消费及库存量（2016年）

ENERGY PURCHASES, CONSUMPTION AND STOCK OF INDUSTRIAL ENTERPRISES OF URBAN AREA ABOVE DESIGNATED SIZE(2016)

能源品种		Type of Energy		购进量 Purchases	消费量 Consumption	# 工业生产 Industrial Production	#用于原材料 Raw Materials	年末库存量 Stock (year-end)
能源合计	(吨标准煤)	**Total Energy**	(ton of SCE)	**16 426 516**	**17 221 718**	**17 024 386**	**381 665**	**254 532**
原　煤	(吨)	Raw Coal	(ton)	11 518 565	11 496 002	11 489 950	–	258 410
洗精煤		Washing Coal		–	–	–	–	–
其他洗煤		Other Washed Coals		4 060	4 139	4 139	–	146
煤制品		Coal Products		201 982	201 762	201 762	–	1 595
焦　炭		Coke		264 825	230 377	230 377	–	42 388
其他焦化产品		Other Coking Products		312 444	308 426	308 426	308 246	20 821
焦炉煤气	(万立方米)	Coke Oven Gas	(10 000 cu.m)	–	–	–	–	–
高炉煤气		Blast-furnace Gas		–	32 665	32 665	–	–
转炉煤气		Converter Gas		–	–	–	–	–
发生炉煤气		Furnace Gas		–	–	–	–	–
天然气		Natural Gas		246 566	245 743	244 661	730	–
液化天然气	(吨)	LNG	(ton)	3 285	3 282	2 764	315	3
汽　油		Gasoline		25 737	25 813	4 542	257	142
煤　油		Kerosene		841	832	817	41	28
柴　油		Diesel Oil		49 563	48 957	23 551	29	901
燃料油		Fuel Oil		44 104	42 779	42 686	–	5 916
液化石油气		LPG		1 072	1 072	1 018	–	137
润滑油		Lubricating Oil		1 414	1 392	1 392	156	92
石　蜡		Paraffin wax		376	357	357	13	21
溶剂油		Solvent Oil		9	9	9	–	1
石油焦		Petroleum coke		–	–	–	–	–
石油沥青		Petroleum Asphalt		–	–	–	–	–
其他石油制品		Other Petroleum Products		2 067	2 069	2 069	1 592	3
热　力	(百万千焦)	Heat	(1 million kilo-joule)	23 946 981	36 473 417	36 220 436	–	–
电　力	(万千瓦时)	Electricity	(10 000 kwh)	2 912 349	3 169 812	3 087 068	–	–
城市生活垃圾用于燃料	(吨)	City Waste For Fuel	(Ton)	770 441	770 441	770 441	–	–
生物质废料用于燃料		Biomass Waste For Fuel		9 973	8 131	8 106	–	167
余热余压	(百万千焦)	Heat and Pressure	(1 million kilo-joule)	–	2 042 688	2 042 688	–	–
其他工业废料用于燃料	(吨)	Other Industrial Waste For Fuel	(Ton)	8 700	8 700	8 700	–	–
其他燃料	(吨标准煤)	Other Fuels	(ton of SCE)	10 692	10 692	10 692	–	1

表10-3

分地区规模以上工业企业能源消费量 (2016年)

能源品种		Type of Energy		全 市 Whole Municipality	市 区 Urban Area
能源合计	(吨标准煤)	**Total Energy**	(ton of SCE)	**84 850 372**	**17 221 718**
原 煤	(吨)	Raw Coal	(ton)	52 930 655	11 496 002
洗精煤		Washing Coal		7 678 792	–
其他洗煤		Other Washed Coals		5 739	4 139
煤制品		Coal Products		206 630	201 762
焦 炭		Coke		12 288 290	230 377
其他焦化产品		Other Coking Products		308 426	308 426
焦炉煤气	(万立方米)	Coke Oven Gas	(10 000 cu.m)	223 481	–
高炉煤气		Blast-furnace Gas		4 004 367	32 665
转炉煤气		Converter Gas		203 952	–
发生炉煤气		Furnace Gas		–	–
天然气		Natural Gas		401 984	245 743
液化天然气	(吨)	LNG	(ton)	41 696	3 282
汽 油		Gasoline		66 250	25 813
煤 油		Kerosene		2 442	832
柴 油		Diesel Oil		151 720	48 957
燃料油		Fuel Oil		123 981	42 779
液化石油气		LPG		8 820	1 072
润滑油		Lubricating Oil		2 089	1 392
石 蜡		Paraffin wax		357	357
溶剂油		Solvent Oil		640	9
石油焦		Petroleum coke		–	–
石油沥青		Petroleum Asphalt		–	–
其他石油制品		Other Petroleum Products		3 753	2 069
热 力	(百万千焦)	Heat	(1 million kilo-joule)	108 628 412	36 473 417
电 力	(万千瓦时)	Electricity	(10 000 kwh)	9 196 802	3 169 812
城市生活垃圾用于燃料	(吨)	City Waste For Fuel	(Ton)	1 167 062	770 441
生物质废料用于燃料		Biomass Waste For Fuel		39 851	8 131
余热余压	(百万千焦)	Heat and Pressure	(1 million kilo-joule)	24 687 812	2 042 688
其他工业废料用于燃料	(吨)	Other Industrial Waste For Fuel	(Ton)	9 001	8 700
其他燃料	(吨标准煤)	Other Fuels	(ton of SCE)	11 260	10 692

ENERGY CONSUMPTION OF INDUSTRIAL ENTERPRISES ABOVE DESIGNATED SIZE BY REGION (2016)

# 吴江区 Wujiang District	常熟 Changshu	张家港 Zhangjiagang	昆山 Kunshan	太仓 Taicang
6 147 785	**15 507 971**	**37 139 270**	**4 148 973**	**10 832 441**
3 808 200	16 310 416	10 333 327	1 696 944	13 093 967
–	–	7 678 792	–	–
2 280	1 549	51	–	–
199 053	1 973	2 895	–	–
2 727	1 102 345	10 954 347	687	535
–	–	–	–	–
–	–	223 481	–	–
–	299 180	3 672 522	–	–
–	–	203 952	–	–
–	–	–	–	–
86 292	33 062	63 356	45 935	13 888
99	2 364	26 297	9 649	103
4 322	9 693	4 622	18 691	7 432
584	414	568	563	66
9 154	21 460	30 930	31 807	18 566
3 898	1 882	6 928	71 424	967
91	373	684	5 682	1 009
10	157	17	500	23
–	–	–	–	–
–	138	86	407	–
–	–	–	–	–
–	–	–	–	–
328	1 502	132	–	50
21 990 188	19 968 231	24 360 591	8 695 232	19 130 941
1 250 097	1 271 627	2 520 850	1 395 053	839 460
–	–	–	395 050	1 571
4 458	1 388	24 322	3 887	2 122
146 164	–	22 645 124	–	–
–	–	–	274	26
–	3	–	561	3

表10-4

全市规模以上工业企业分行业能源消费量 (2016年)

行　　业	Sector	综合能源消费量 (吨标准煤) Overall Consumption Volume of Energy (ton of SCE)	原　煤 (吨) Raw Coal (ton)
总　　计	**Total**	**52 844 112**	**52 930 655**
有色金属矿采选业	Nonferrous Metals Mining and Dressing	404	–
非金属矿采选业	Nonmetal Minerals Mining and Dressing	2 667	–
农副食品加工业	Farming and Side-line Food Processing Trade	197 261	11 291
食品制造业	Food Production	102 095	2 353
酒、饮料和精制茶制造业	Wine, Beverage and Refined tea manufacturing	77 226	19 414
烟草制品业	Manufacture of Tobacco	3 990	–
纺织业	Textile Industry	3 078 745	1 891 948
纺织服装、服饰业	Garments and Apparel Industry	179 181	128 892
皮革、毛皮、羽绒及其制品业	Leather, Furs, Down and Related Products	16 983	4 736
木材加工及竹、藤、棕、草制品业	Timber Processing, Bamboo, Cane, Palm Fiber &Straw Products	43 647	38 350
家具制造业	Furniture Manufacturing	21 336	–
造纸及纸制品业	Papermaking and Paper Products	2 801 517	3 842 038
印刷和记录媒介复制业	Printing and Record Medium Reproduction	88 690	10 775
文教工美体育和娱乐用品制造业	Stationary,Educational,Industrial arts, Sports and Entertainment products	122 646	109 022
石油加工、炼焦和核燃料加工业	Petroleum Processing, Coking and Nuclear Fuel Processing	11 720	6 550
化学原料及化学制品制造业	Raw Chemical Materials and Chemical Products	3 993 876	2 522 620
医药制造业	Medical and Pharmaceutical Products	189 102	238 134
化学纤维制造业	Chemical Fiber	2 032 098	1 487 600
橡胶和塑料制品业	Rubber and Plastic Products	776 460	138 105
非金属矿物制品业	Nonmetal Mineral Products	788 537	181 001
黑色金属冶炼及压延加工业	Smelting and Pressing of Ferrous Metals	17 925 697	4 345 063
有色金属冶炼及压延加工业	Smelting and Pressing of Nonferrous Metals	369 617	6 912
金属制品业	Metal Products	464 571	26 411
通用设备制造业	Ordinary Machinery	420 000	31 390
专用设备制造业	Equipment for Special Purposes	231 954	860
汽车制造业	Automobile Manufacturing	595 002	–
铁路船舶航空航天和其他运输设备制造业	Railway, Ship, Aerospace and other transportation equipment manufacturing	72 748	1 347
电气机械及器材制造业	Electric Equipment and Machinery	552 209	4 272
计算机通信和其他电子设备制造业	Computer Telecommunications and Other Electronic Equipment Manufacture	2 328 142	588 669
仪器仪表制造业	Instruments, Meters Machinery	63 169	215
其他制造业	Others Industry	6 486	2 720
废弃资源综合利用业	Comprehensive Utilization of Waste Resources	43 827	8 267
金属制品、机械和设备修理业	Metal Products, Machinery and Equipment Repair	–	–
电力、热力生产和供应业	Production and Supply of Electric Power and Heat Energy	15 156 261	37 281 701
燃气生产和供应业	Production and Supply of Gas	5 702	–
水的生产和供应业	Production and Supply of Water	80 544	–

注:综合能源消费量=各种能源工业生产消费量合计-能源加工厂转换-能源回收利用。

TOTAL ENERGY CONSUMPTION OF INDUSTRIAL ENTERPRISES ABOVE DESIGNATED SIZE BY SECTOR (2016)

洗精煤 (吨) Washing Coal (ton)	焦炭 (吨) Coke (ton)	汽油 (吨) Gasoline (ton)	柴油 (吨) Diesel Oil (ton)	燃料油 (吨) Fuel Oil (ton)	液化石油气 (吨) Liquefied Petroleum Gas (ton)	热力 (百万千焦) Heat (1 million kilo-joule)	电力 (万千瓦时) Electricity (10 000 kwh)
7 678 792	**12 288 290**	**66 250**	**151 720**	**123 981**	**8 820**	**108 628 412**	**9 196 802**
–	–	–	–	–	–	–	329
–	–	27	100	–	–	–	1 612
–	–	96	905	618	41	3 732 560	39 041
–	–	223	1 072	124	34	924 244	25 994
–	–	91	502	–	–	633 686	22 194
–	–	–	–	–	–	84 205	980
–	–	4 409	7 251	5 203	91	28 379 418	860 001
–	–	3 631	3 751	57	19	681 264	46 674
–	–	505	436	85	–	72 153	8 224
–	–	221	621	–	–	–	10 035
–	–	361	981	1	103	6 805	13 272
–	–	1 485	11 659	24	727	32 109 338	530 399
–	–	1 531	1 795	223	297	35 180	53 931
–	–	836	531	81	–	605 138	40 174
–	–	63	132	–	–	98 056	2 264
–	–	5 087	9 885	1 260	122	19 053 578	1 095 120
–	–	408	207	–	–	1 504 015	60 299
–	–	1 528	1 612	2 520	–	7 716 046	800 659
–	–	3 028	5 767	1 148	8	4 133 571	339 495
–	–	1 434	44 400	101 494	24	796 470	207 836
7 678 792	12 280 514	1 433	19 030	76	562	421 088	1 392 844
–	530	789	1 962	7 819	99	480 939	145 360
–	411	5 545	7 914	1 374	1 675	350 816	215 602
–	1 538	6 502	4 963	360	791	172 786	263 035
–	103	6 279	2 794	16	699	285 243	162 986
–	–	2 279	3 629	69	1 330	600 496	302 988
–	–	630	456	–	1 261	3 610	35 607
–	78	6 014	3 784	188	606	138 578	406 766
–	–	9 565	9 809	1 186	322	4 678 858	1 484 814
–	–	1 111	459	–	9	23 159	37 261
–	–	180	32	–	–	35 987	2 527
–	5 115	199	1 014	–	1	8 793	18 894
–	–	–	–	–	–	–	–
–	–	215	3 813	55	–	625 908	505 882
–	–	427	362	–	–	–	4 146
–	–	120	92	–	–	236 424	59 556

Note: Comprehensive energy consumption= All kinds of energy consumption of industrial production–energy conversion by energy plants-Energy recycling

表10-5

市区规模以上工业企业分行业能源消费量（2016年）

行　　业	Sector	综合能源消费量（吨标准煤）Overall Consumption Volume of Energy (ton of SCE)	原　煤（吨）Raw Coal (ton)
总　计	**Total**	**11 353 536**	**11 496 002**
有色金属矿采选业	Nonferrous Metals Mining and Dressing	404	–
非金属矿采选业	Nonmetal Minerals Mining and Dressing	2 667	–
农副食品加工业	Farming and Side-line Food Processing Trade	27 268	7 182
食品制造业	Food Production	56 174	31
酒、饮料和精制茶制造业	Wine, Beverage and Refined tea manufacturing	44 276	9 520
烟草制品业	Manufacture of Tobacco	–	–
纺织业	Textile Industry	1 874 444	1 205 591
纺织服装、服饰业	Garments and Apparel Industry	31 770	5 796
皮革、毛皮、羽绒及其制品业	Leather, Furs, Down and Related Products	2 574	97
木材加工及竹、藤、棕、草制品业	Timber Processing, Bamboo, Cane, Palm Fiber &Straw Products	13 967	6 774
家具制造业	Furniture Manufacturing	10 128	–
造纸及纸制品业	Papermaking and Paper Products	539 633	743 437
印刷和记录媒介复制业	Printing and Record Medium Reproduction	35 464	5 544
文教工美体育和娱乐用品制造业	Stationary,Educational,Industrial arts, Sports and Entertainment products	10 659	3 174
石油加工、炼焦和核燃料加工业	Petroleum Processing, Coking and Nucleus Fuel Machining Trade	6 620	6 550
化学原料及化学制品制造业	Raw Chemical Materials and Chemical Products	631 394	49 494
医药制造业	Medical and Pharmaceutical Products	78 821	11 642
化学纤维制造业	Chemical Fiber	1 158 381	787 773
橡胶和塑料制品业	Rubber and Plastic Products	199 484	11 237
非金属矿物制品业	Nonmetal Mineral Products	289 695	65 658
黑色金属冶炼及压延加工业	Smelting and Pressing of Ferrous Metals	398 598	62 853
有色金属冶炼及压延加工业	Smelting and Pressing of Nonferrous Metals	123 890	979
金属制品业	Metal Products	145 785	11 656
通用设备制造业	Ordinary Machinery	155 311	13 851
专用设备制造业	Equipment for Special Purposes	106 692	212
汽车制造业	Automobile Manufacturing	141 625	–
铁路船舶航空航天和其他运输设备制造业	Railway, Ship, Aerospace and other transportation equipment manufacturing	18 238	–
电气机械及器材制造业	Electric Equipment and Machinery	301 900	4 156
计算机通信和其他电子设备制造业	Computer Telecommunications and Other Electronic Equipment Manufacture	998 484	26
仪器仪表制造业	Instruments, Meters Machinery	19 221	–
其他制造业	Others Industry	24	–
废弃资源综合利用业	Comprehensive Utilization of Waste Resources	17 320	8 267
金属制品、机械和设备修理业	Metal Products, Machinery and Equipment Repair	–	–
电力、热力生产和供应业	Production and Supply of Electric Power and Heat Energy	3 858 892	8 474 502
燃气生产和供应业	Production and Supply of Gas	2 167	–
水的生产和供应业	Production and Supply of Water	51 568	–

ENERGY CONSUMPTION OF INDUSTRIAL ENTERPRISES ABOVE DESIGNATED SIZE BY SECTOR IN URBAN AREA (2016)

洗精煤 (吨) Washing Coal (ton)	焦 炭 (吨) Coke (ton)	汽 油 (吨) Gasoline (ton)	柴 油 (吨) Diesel Oil (ton)	燃料油 (吨) Fuel Oil (ton)	液化石油气 (吨) Liquefied Petroleum Gas (ton)	热 力 (百万千焦) Heat (1 million kilo-joule)	电 力 (万千瓦时) Electricity (10 000 kwh)
–	**230 377**	**25 813**	**48 957**	**42 779**	**1 072**	**36 473 417**	**3 169 812**
–	–	–	–	–	–	–	329
–	–	27	100	–	–	–	1 612
–	–	41	154	618	15	156 435	7 922
–	–	173	403	124	–	252 940	14 235
–	–	26	100	–	–	263 854	15 334
–	–	–	–	–	–	–	–
–	–	1 689	907	206	32	21 275 522	496 760
–	–	1 002	525	54	5	197 618	13 749
–	–	80	88	46	–	2 275	1 715
–	–	57	228	–	–	–	5 497
–	–	79	750	–	–	–	5 338
–	–	533	2 127	24	13	4 192 828	109 312
–	–	648	688	223	20	7 395	20 476
–	–	208	65	–	–	–	4 868
–	–	–	–	–	–	–	718
–	–	1 715	3 325	–	–	1 130 315	133 214
–	–	149	96	–	–	861 274	29 706
–	–	1 113	1 077	2 073	–	4 932 886	432 853
–	–	1 315	1 670	48	2	591 812	127 307
–	–	724	22 812	37 830	–	2 947	76 185
–	229 194	286	590	76	–	54 249	95 559
–	125	207	627	20	–	92 477	60 812
–	129	2 177	3 029	1 205	582	117 183	71 607
–	929	3 488	1 415	149	135	92 741	96 091
–	–	2 284	818	7	13	186 806	73 267
–	–	641	1 560	21	63	210 393	77 463
–	–	132	45	–	–	18	12 335
–	–	2 644	1 187	–	–	115 139	230 574
–	–	3 846	3 132	–	192	910 442	753 687
–	–	261	20	–	–	4 544	15 682
–	–	–	–	–	–	–	20
–	–	60	277	–	–	8 109	4 217
–	–	–	–	–	–	–	–
–	–	7	935	55	–	625 908	143 154
–	–	188	207	–	–	–	1 204
–	–	13	–	–	–	187 307	37 010

表10-6

主要工业产品单位产量能耗（2016年）
THE ENERGY CONSUMPTION OF MAJOR INDUSTRIAL PRODUCTS (2016)

项目		Item		数值 Numerical Value
吨纱（线）混合数生产用电量	（千瓦时/吨）	Electricity Consumption Per Ton on Production of Yarn	(kwh/ton)	1 855.9
万米布混合数生产用电量	（千瓦时/万米）	Electricity Consumption Per 10000 Meters Cloth	(kwh/10 000 meters)	7 204.2
万米印染布综合能耗	（千克标准煤/万米）	Comprehensive Energy Consumption Per 10000 Meter Dyed Fabric	(kg of SCE/10 000 meters)	2 095.1
万米丝织品用电量	（千瓦时/万米）	Electricity Consumption Per 10000 Meter Silk Fabric	(kwh/10 000 meters)	3 481.6
万米丝织品综合能耗	（千克标准煤/万米）	Comprehensive Energy Consumption Per 10000 Meter Silk Fabric	(kg of SCE/10 000 meters)	804.1
机制纸及纸板耗电	（千瓦时/吨）	Electricity Consumption Per Ton of Machine Finish Paper and Paper Board	(kwh/ton)	647.6
机制纸及纸板综合能耗	（千克标准煤/吨）	Comprehensive Energy Consumption Per Ton of Machine Finish Paper and Paper Board	(kg of SCE/ton)	301.5
天然碱法单位纯碱生产综合能耗		Total Energy Consumption of Natural Alkaline Unit Soda Production		172.1
单位合成氨生产综合能耗		Comprehensive Energy Consumption Per Ton on Synthetic Ammonia Production		1 275.6
吨涤纶用电量（长丝）	（千瓦时/吨）	Electricity Consumption Per Ton Terylene Production (Long Fibre)	(kwh/ton)	749.9
吨涤纶综合能耗（长丝）	（千克标准煤/吨）	Comprehensive Energy Consumption Per Ton Terylene Production (Long Fibre)	(kg of SCE/ton)	205.3
吨水泥综合能耗		Comprehensive Energy Consumption Per Ton Cement Production		3.9
每重量箱平板玻璃综合能耗	（千克标准煤/重量箱）	Comprehensive Energy Consumption Per Weighing Tank of Sheet Glass Production	(kg of SCE/weighing tank)	11.0
吨钢综合能耗	（千克标准煤/吨）	Comprehensive Energy Consumption Per Ton Steel Production	(kg of SCE/ton)	566.4
吨钢耗电	（千瓦时/吨）	Electricity Consumption Per Ton Steel Production	(kwh/ton)	398.8
电厂火力发电标准煤耗	（克标准煤/千瓦时）	Standard Coal Consumption of Thermal Power Generation of Power Plants	(g of SCE/kwh)	281.4
电厂火力供电标准煤耗		Standard Coal Consumption of Thermal Power Supply of Power Plants		294.7
发电厂用电率	（%）	Electricity Consumption of Power Plants	(%)	4.5

表10-7

全市规模以上工业企业用水情况（2016年）
WATER CONSUMPTION OF INDUSTRIAL ENTERPRISES ABOVE DESIGNATED SIZE (2016)

行　　业	Sector	工业取水总量（万立方米）Total Industrial Water ($10\ 000\ M^3$)	重复用水量（万立方米）Repetitive Water Consumption ($10\ 000\ M^3$)
总　计	**Total**	**261 662**	**839 863**
有色金属矿采选业	Nonferrous Metals Mining and Dressing	2	16
非金属矿采选业	Nonmetal Minerals Mining and Dressing	62	32
农副食品加工业	Farming and Side-line Food Processing Trade	410	4
食品制造业	Food Production	462	8
酒、饮料和精制茶制造业	Wine, Beverage and Refined tea manufacturing	788	198
烟草制品业	Manufacture of Tobacco	23	–
纺织业	Textile Industry	16 048	2 962
纺织服装、服饰业	Garments and Apparel Industry	2 607	62
皮革、毛皮、羽绒及其制品业	Leather, Furs, Down and Related Products	176	9
木材加工及竹、藤、棕、草制品业	Timber Processing, Bamboo, Cane, Palm Fiber &Straw Products	94	1
家具制造业	Furniture Manufacturing	268	1
造纸及纸制品业	Papermaking and Paper Products	5 730	70 467
印刷和记录媒介复制业	Printing and Record Medium Reproduction	363	–
文教工美体育和娱乐用品制造业	Stationary,Educational,Industrial arts, Sports and Entertainment products	772	10
石油加工、炼焦和核燃料加工业	Petroleum Processing, Coking and Nuclear Fuel Processing	20	2
化学原料及化学制品制造业	Raw Chemical Materials and Chemical Products	8 805	67 618
医药制造业	Medical and Pharmaceutical Products	828	3 169
化学纤维制造业	Chemical Fiber	1 962	12 057
橡胶和塑料制品业	Rubber and Plastic Products	1 602	222
非金属矿物制品业	Nonmetal Mineral Products	1 683	521
黑色金属冶炼及压延加工业	Smelting and Pressing of Ferrous Metals	10 963	485 661
有色金属冶炼及压延加工业	Smelting and Pressing of Nonferrous Metals	827	668
金属制品业	Metal Products	1 870	134
通用设备制造业	Ordinary Machinery	1 712	288
专用设备制造业	Equipment for Special Purposes	1 446	1 661
汽车制造业	Automobile Manufacturing	1 436	436
铁路船舶航空航天和其他运输设备制造业	Railway, Ship, Aerospace and other transportation equipment manufacturing	408	9
电气机械及器材制造业	Electric Equipment and Machinery	3 085	20 463
计算机通信和其他电子设备制造业	Telecommunications Equipment, Computer and Other Electronic Equipment Manufacture	14 648	22 182
仪器仪表制造业	Instruments, Meters Machinery	269	318
其他制造业	Others Industry	67	–
废弃资源综合利用业	Comprehensive Utilization of Waste Resources	67	540
金属制品、机械和设备修理业	Metal Products, Machinery and Equipment Repair	–	–
电力、热力生产和供应业	Production and Supply of Electric Power and Heat Energy	13 448	149 538
燃气生产和供应业	Production and Supply of Gas	24	–
水的生产和供应业	Production and Supply of Water	168 688	605

表10-8

部分年份分行业用电情况
ENERGY CONSUMPTION BY SECTOR OF PARTIAL YEARS

单位：万千瓦时 (10 000 kwh)

年 份 Year	全社会用电量 Electricity Consumption	全行业用电量 Electricity by Sector	第一产业 Primary Industry	第二产业 Secondary Industry	# 工业 Industry	第三产业 Tertiary Industry	城乡居民生活用电 Electricity Consumption by Urban and Rural Residents
1986	348 398	335 660	47 455	278 290	276 982	9 915	12 738
1987	414 500	398 870	61 251	324 947	323 435	12 672	15 630
1988	465 355	447 053	69 520	356 585	354 553	20 948	18 302
1989	473 882	450 438	68 532	361 120	359 404	20 786	23 444
1990	507 687	479 512	70 821	383 297	381 394	25 394	28 175
1991	576 975	543 672	78 876	438 278	436 385	26 518	33 303
1992	680 698	639 687	91 190	516 370	513 597	32 127	41 011
1993	781 374	730 783	101 470	588 418	581 777	40 895	50 591
1994	892 271	819 691	116 611	649 052	639 885	54 028	72 580
1995	998 485	907 323	131 909	716 671	707 424	58 743	91 162
1996	1 126 972	1 023 750	131 616	825 147	815 410	66 987	103 222
1997	1 233 419	1 119 353	136 434	894 080	884 124	88 839	114 066
1998	1 327 589	1 204 818	132 671	973 282	960 857	98 865	122 771
1999	1 538 193	1 409 790	114 363	1 198 521	1 186 270	96 906	128 403
2000	1 900 439	1 730 448	69 778	1 547 146	1 531 665	113 524	169 991
2001	2 259 217	2 072 342	63 833	1 878 092	1 861 413	130 417	186 875
2002	2 735 800	2 555 864	37 781	2 361 451	2 339 938	156 632	179 936
2003	3 576 083	3 333 262	38 653	3 084 335	3 041 342	210 274	242 821
2004	4 544 696	4 261 961	37 838	3 944 098	3 868 402	280 025	282 735
2005	5 660 372	5 314 255	29 646	4 908 405	4 835 611	376 204	346 117
2006	6 864 926	6 436 636	29 352	5 949 106	5 884 112	458 178	428 290
2007	8 072 735	7 587 350	30 980	7 020 584	6 957 336	535 786	485 385
2008	8 484 230	7 917 897	30 956	7 255 717	7 183 172	631 224	566 333
2009	8 799 436	8 198 015	30 730	7 457 042	7 385 410	710 243	601 421
2010	10 241 031	9 514 098	30 044	8 630 199	8 552 481	853 855	726 933
2011	11 316 316	10 544 566	31 281	9 556 668	9 461 876	956 617	771 750
2012	11 899 281	11 034 355	34 268	9 933 221	9 826 579	1 066 866	864 926
2013	12 632 099	11 640 896	37 996	10 430 709	10 306 099	1 172 191	991 204
2014	12 681 174	11 807 895	36 104	10 574 610	10 441 426	1 197 181	873 279
2015	13 117 154	12 171 484	39 854	10 857 998	10 741 986	1 273 632	945 670
2016	13 825 799	12 743 177	44 976	11 261 852	11 162 958	1 436 349	1 082 622

表10-9

部分年份分地区全社会用电情况
TOTAL ELECTRICITY CONSUMPTION BY REGION OF PARTIAL YEARS

单位：万千瓦时 (10 000 kwh)

年 份 Year	全 市 Whole Municipality	市 区 Urban Area	# 吴江区 Wujiang District	常 熟 Changshu	张家港 Zhangjiagang	昆 山 Kunshan	太 仓 Taicang
1978	138 808	91 452	12 024	15 924	10 263	11 097	10 072
1979	165 231	108 676	14 743	18 882	12 099	13 169	12 405
1980	205 298	133 206	18 852	24 936	16 812	14 943	15 401
1985	311 110	172 271	29 680	45 483	42 084	24 123	27 149
1986	348 398	189 125	33 246	52 006	50 851	27 392	29 024
1987	414 500	219 416	41 139	63 993	61 649	34 773	34 669
1988	465 355	241 398	46 794	70 985	71 934	40 868	40 170
1989	473 882	245 460	48 363	72 402	71 737	43 131	41 152
1990	507 687	261 706	51 440	77 178	79 486	47 193	42 124
1991	576 975	290 322	59 824	86 428	95 583	55 643	48 999
1992	680 698	332 054	72 093	98 870	127 698	64 764	57 312
1993	781 374	377 816	88 287	114 514	153 527	71 894	63 623
1994	892 271	439 174	111 226	126 616	174 599	81 084	70 798
1995	998 485	495 962	124 318	140 406	192 717	92 293	77 107
1996	1 126 972	547 926	138 220	153 003	239 546	104 768	81 729
1997	1 233 419	591 387	153 872	166 149	263 076	123 566	89 241
1998	1 327 589	639 045	164 801	169 582	284 233	143 046	91 683
1999	1 538 193	728 939	177 281	215 680	320 260	170 913	102 401
2000	1 900 439	901 274	236 722	265 272	387 696	219 556	126 641
2001	2 259 217	1 037 898	302 808	314 308	493 471	263 767	149 773
2002	2 735 800	1 240 050	394 185	356 277	614 238	347 936	177 299
2003	3 576 083	1 611 285	544 873	431 064	826 736	477 193	229 805
2004	4 544 696	2 007 707	741 799	538 955	1 060 249	618 148	317 295
2005	5 660 372	2 415 752	894 024	665 584	1 388 054	798 771	389 621
2006	6 864 926	2 868 272	1 057 185	784 605	1 712 749	1 021 111	475 222
2007	8 072 735	3 369 140	1 254 637	922 355	1 967 880	1 231 591	576 003
2008	8 484 230	3 563 320	1 295 607	980 504	2 018 468	1 319 483	602 455
2009	8 799 436	3 647 936	1 351 511	1 064 578	2 143 411	1 322 036	621 475
2010	10 241 031	4 283 235	1 590 285	1 246 016	2 384 474	1 619 135	708 171
2011	11 316 316	4 780 971	1 881 632	1 413 760	2 595 963	1 746 314	779 308
2012	11 899 281	5 140 791	2 103 025	1 473 379	2 655 946	1 819 148	810 017
2013	12 632 099	5 492 795	2 241 800	1 559 753	2 783 828	1 900 279	895 444
2014	12 681 174	5 454 612	2 168 444	1 552 047	2 830 481	1 943 532	900 502
2015	13 117 154	5 679 415	2 294 076	1 623 840	2 899 183	2 004 999	909 717
2016	13 825 799	6 069 996	2 424 055	1 723 339	2 888 066	2 175 123	969 275

表10-10

全社会用电情况 (2016年)

单位：万千瓦时

行　　业	Sector	全　市 Whole Municipality
全社会用电量总计	**Total Electricity Consumption**	**13 825 799**
一、全行业用电合计	**Total Electricity by Sector**	**12 743 177**
按产业分	**Grouped by Industry**	
第一产业	Primary Industry	44 976
第二产业	Secondary Industry	11 261 852
第三产业	Tertiary Industry	1 436 349
按行业分	**Grouped by Sector**	
（一）农、林、牧、渔业	Farming, Forestry, Animal Husbandry and Fishery	44 976
（二）工　业	Industry	11 162 958
采矿业	Mining and Quarrying	2 705
制造业	Manufacturing	10 255 606
1.食品、饮料和烟草制造业	Food ,Beverage and Tobacco Manufacturing	116 409
2.纺织业	Textile Industry	2 202 551
3.服装鞋帽、皮革羽绒及其制品业	Garments, Shoes, Leather and Feather Products	180 789
4.木材加工及制品和家具制品业	Wood Processing and Related Products and Furniture Manufacture	72 313
5.造纸及纸制品业	Papermaking and Paper Products	202 048
6.印刷业和记录媒介复制业	Printing and Record Duplicating	50 437
7.文体用品制造业	Stationary, Educational and Sports Goods	21 074
8.石油加工、炼焦及核燃料加工业	Oil Processing, Coking and Nuclear Fuel Processing	13 093
9.化学原料及化学制品制造业	Raw Chemical Materials and Chemical Products	868 882
10.医药制造业	Medical and Pharmaceutical Products	74 652
11.化学纤维制造业	Chemical Fiber Manufacturing	349 255
12.橡胶和塑料制品业	Rubber and Plastic Products	580 993
13.非金属矿物制品业	Nonmetal Mineral Products	219 768
14.黑色金属冶炼及压延加工业	Smelting and Pressing of Ferrous Metals	1 236 866
15.有色金属冶炼及压延加工业	Smelting and Pressing of Nonferrous Metals	66 128
16.金属制品业	Metal Products	605 552

TOTAL ELECTRICITY CONSUMPTION (2016)

(10 000 kwh)

市 区 Urban Area	# 吴江区 Wujiang District	常 熟 Changshu	张家港 Zhangjiagang	昆 山 Kunshan	太 仓 Taicang
6 069 996	**2 424 055**	**1 723 339**	**2 888 066**	**2 175 123**	**969 275**
5 488 978	**2 305 345**	**1 585 606**	**2 779 980**	**1 981 968**	**906 645**
20 432	13 950	7 469	3 476	6 232	7 367
4 606 724	2 170 141	1 449 967	2 659 247	1 727 293	818 621
861 822	121 254	128 170	117 257	248 443	80 657
20 432	13 950	7 469	3 476	6 232	7 367
4 547 831	2 159 071	1 441 828	2 649 070	1 711 220	813 009
2 380	–	–	198	111	16
4 177 197	2 041 411	1 186 914	2 514 672	1 615 528	761 295
50 713	17 363	7 192	29 890	17 651	10 963
1 303 013	1 184 971	254 137	339 633	31 400	274 368
92 852	59 103	40 140	13 088	17 849	16 860
33 595	16 967	9 775	6 898	13 900	8 145
41 611	8 263	78 091	8 964	22 272	51 110
22 192	1 565	2 031	2 396	21 440	2 378
5 456	1 898	2 545	3 167	8 367	1 539
398	361	21	1 465	50	11 159
92 765	27 522	116 628	512 297	126 016	21 176
48 957	5 495	9 725	7 258	5 008	3 704
227 523	194 739	56 518	47 802	1 594	15 818
245 541	66 717	53 800	68 878	155 530	57 244
94 054	51 088	12 487	34 527	50 715	27 985
34 745	166	88 002	1 091 212	397	22 510
16 590	6 333	6 630	26 308	4 726	11 874
238 989	69 756	134 408	140 637	52 299	39 219

表10-10 续表

单位：万千瓦时

行　　业	Sector	全市 Whole Municipality
17.通用及专用设备制造业	General and Special Equipment Manufacture	734 611
18.交通运输、电气、电子设备制造业	Transportation, Electrical, Electronic Equipment Manufacturing	2 417 286
19.工艺品及其他制造业	Artworks and Other Products Manufacture	216 209
20.废弃资源和废旧材料回收加工业	Waste Resources and Materials Recycling and Processing	26 690
电力、燃气及水的生产和供应业	Power, Gas and Water Production and Supply	904 647
1.电力、热力的生产和供应业	Production and Supply of Electricity and Thermal Power	783 171
2.燃气生产和供应业	Production and Supply of Gas	8 248
3.水的生产和供应业	Production and Supply of Water	113 228
工业总计中：轻工业	In Total: Light Industry	4 058 301
重工业	Heavy Industry	7 104 657
（三）建筑业	Construction	98 894
（四）交通运输、仓储和邮政业	Transportation, Warehousing and Post	131 762
交通运输业	Transportation	93 042
仓储业	Warehousing	36 082
邮政业	Post Industry	2 638
（五）信息传输、计算机服务和软件业	Information Transmission, Computer Services and Software Industries	76 851
（六）商业、住宿和餐饮业	Wholesale, Retail Trade Services, Accommodation and Catering Services	430 038
批发和零售业	Wholesale and Retail Trade Services	311 633
住宿和餐饮业	Accommodation and Catering Services	118 405
（七）金融、房地产、商务及居民服务业	Banking, Real Estate, Business and Community Service	403 252
# 金融业	Financial Industries	25 346
房地产业	Real Estate	261 692
（八）公共事业及管理组织	Public Administration and Social Organizations	394 446
# 教育、文化、体育和娱乐业	Education, Culture, Sports and Entertainment	116 892
卫生、社会保障和社会福利业	Health Care, Social Security and Social Welfare	63 102
二、城乡居民生活用电合计	**Total Electricity Consumption by Urban and Rural Residents**	**1 082 622**
城镇居民	Urban Residents	635 630
乡村居民	Rural Residents	446 992

Continued

(10 000 kwh)

市 区 Urban Area	# 吴江区 Wujiang District	常 熟 Changshu	张家港 Zhangjiagang	昆 山 Kunshan	太 仓 Taicang
259 016	61 488	95 428	82 278	204 194	93 695
1 216 852	259 404	184 515	85 522	850 438	79 959
146 313	6 200	32 378	3 591	29 094	4 833
6 022	2 012	2 463	8 861	2 588	6 756
368 254	117 660	254 914	134 200	95 581	51 698
303 980	96 851	234 537	121 404	78 521	44 729
2 751	274	428	3 669	748	652
61 523	20 535	19 949	9 127	16 312	6 317
2 238 178	1 545 890	566 777	521 477	269 442	462 427
2 309 653	613 181	875 051	2 127 593	1 441 778	350 582
58 893	11 070	8 139	10 177	16 073	5 612
59 718	5 626	7 124	10 188	40 308	14 424
42 267	4 034	2 597	6 626	30 956	10 596
15 858	1 348	4 252	3 343	8 963	3 666
1 593	244	275	219	389	162
37 924	6 008	6 614	6 500	20 542	5 271
234 864	46 094	51 321	42 483	78 808	22 562
165 296	32 486	40 225	30 793	59 839	15 480
69 568	13 608	11 096	11 690	18 969	7 082
278 053	24 279	25 345	24 942	58 238	16 674
16 205	2 149	2 724	2 295	2 319	1 803
196 798	15 765	15 463	11 808	29 534	8 089
251 263	39 247	37 766	33 144	50 547	21 726
79 488	7 440	9 138	9 022	14 431	4 813
37 830	5 782	6 777	7 931	7 263	3 301
581 018	**118 710**	**137 733**	**108 086**	**193 155**	**62 630**
406 445	46 398	50 585	41 032	113 684	23 884
174 573	72 312	87 148	67 054	79 471	38 746

主 要 统 计 指 标 解 释

工业企业能源消费量 指工业企业在工业生产活动和非工业生产活动中消费的能源，包括工业生产活动中作为燃料、动力、原料、辅助材料使用的能源，生产工艺中使用的能源，用于能源加工转换的能源；非工业生产活动中使用的能源。具体包括：

1.用于本企业产品生产、工业性作业和其他生产性活动的能源；

2.用于技术更新改造措施、新技术研究和新产品试制以及科学试验等方面的能源；

3.用于经营维修、建筑及设备大修理、机电设备和交通运输工具等方面的能源；

4.用于劳动保护的能源；

5.生产交通运输工具的企业(如造船厂、汽车制造厂)，向成品轮船、汽车中添加动力用油，应算作企业的能源消费，但不作为工业生产消费，应作为非工业生产消费和交通运输工具消费。

6.其他非生产消费的能源。

不包括：

1.由仓库发到车间，但在报告期最后一天没有消费的能源。这部分能源应在办理假退料手续后计入库存量。

2.拨到外单位，委托外单位加工用的能源。

3.调出本单位或借给外单位的能源。

工业生产能源消费量 指工业企业为进行工业生产活动所消费的能源。主要包括：

1.用于本企业产品生产、工业性作业的能源，包括用作原料、材料、燃料、动力的能源；作为能源加工转换企业，还包括用作加工转换的能源(这部分能源不能理解为用作原材料，用作原材料的概念见后面的解释)；

2.产品生产过程中作为辅助材料使用的能源；

3.生产工艺过程使用的能源；

4.新技术研究、新产品试制、科学试验使用的能源；

5.为了工业生产活动而在进行的各种修理过程中使用的能源；

6.生产区内的劳动保护用能等。

非工业生产能源消费量 指在工业企业能源消费中，除“工业生产能源消费”以外的能源消费，即非工业生产用能和工业企业附属的不从事工业生产活动的非独立核算单位用能。比如本企业施工单位进行技术更新改造、维修等过程用能，非生产区的劳动保护用能，科研单位、农场、车队、学校、医院、食堂、托儿所等单位用能。但是必须注意，上述单位如果是独立核算的，其用能既不能包括在“工业企业能源消费”中，亦不能包括在“非工业生产能源消费”中。

生产交通运输工具的企业(如造船厂、汽车制造厂)，向成品轮船、汽车中添加动力用油，应算作企业的非工业生产消费。

能源库存量 指能源使用企业(单位)在报告期的某时间点所拥有的、用于企业(单位)消费或转卖(不包括本企业自己生产的)的各种能源的库存量。

能源使用企业(单位)的能源库存统计范围，是企业购进和调入(加工来料和借入)的、在报告期某一时点尚未消费或转卖、存放在原材料、能源供应仓库(或场地)、车间、工地中的各种能源。

EXPLANATORY NOTES ON MAIN STATISTICAL INDICATORS

Energy Consumption of Industrial Enterprise refers to the energy consumed by an industrial enterprise in its industrial and non-industrial production activities, which includes the energy used as fuel, power, raw materials, and auxiliary materials in its industrial production activities, that used in its production technology, and that used in energy processing and conversion; the energy used in its non-industrial production activities. Specifically it includes:

1. The energy used in the enterprise's production of products, industrial work and other production activities;

2. The energy used for technical renovation measures, new technology research and new product trial production, scientific experiments, and so on;

3. The energy used for operation and maintenance, building and equipment repair, mechanical and electrical equipment, means of transport, and so on;

4. The energy used for labor protection;

5. In enterprises producing means of transport (e.g., shipyards, automobile factories), the power oil added to such finished products as ships and cars should be classified as the energy consumption of the enterprise, and it is not treated as industrial production consumption but should be as non-industrial production consumption and the consumption of means of transport.

6. Other non-production consumption energies.

It does not include:

1. The energy sent from the warehouse to the workshop but not yet consumed in the last day of the reporting period. This part of the energy should be included in the inventory after the false material return formalities.

2. The energy transferred to other units and used for processing by them.

3. The energy brought out of this unit or lent to other units.

Industrial Production Energy Consumption refers to the energy consumed by an industrial enterprise for its industrial production activities. It mainly includes:

1. The energy used by the enterprise for its production and industrial operation, including the energy used as raw materials, materials, fuel and power; in an energy processing and conversion enterprise, it also includes the energy used for processing and conversion (this part of the energy cannot be understood as raw materials, and as to the concept of energy used as a raw material, see the explanation below);

2. The energy used as auxiliary materials during the production of products;

3. The energy used in the process of production;

4. The energy used for new technology research, new product trial production and scientific experiments;

5. The energy used in the process of repairs of all kinds for industrial production activities;

6. The energy used for labor protection in the production area, and so on.

Non-industrial Production Energy Consumption refers to the energy consumption except the "industrial production energy consumption" in the energy consumption of an industrial enterprise, namely, the energy used in its non-industrial production and in its affiliated non-independent accounting units not engaged in industrial production activities. For example, the energy used in the process of technical upgrading, maintenance and so on by the construction units of the enterprise, the energy used for labor protection in the non-production area, and the energy used in scientific research units, farms, car teams, schools, hospitals, canteens, nurseries and other units. But it must be noted that if the above units are independent business accounting units, the energy used by them can neither be included in the "industrial enterprise energy consumption", nor in the "non-industrial production energy consumption".

In enterprises producing means of transport (e.g., shipyards, automobile factories), the power oil added to such finished products as ships and cars should be classified as the non-industrial production energy consumption of the enterprise.

Energy Stocks refers to the inventory of the energies of various kinds owned by an energy-using enterprise (unit) at a certain point in time during the reporting period and used for its consumption or reselling (not including the energy produced by the enterprise itself).

The energy inventory statistics scope of an energy-using enterprise (unit) is the energies of various kinds which the enterprise buys and brings in (processing supplied materials and borrowing), has not yet consumed or resold at a certain point in time during the reporting period, and stores in the warehouses (or sites) for raw materials and energy supply, workshops, and construction sites.

十一、固定资产投资

CHAPTER 11
INVESTMENT IN FIXED ASSETS

11 固定资产投资 INVESTMENT IN FIXED ASSETS

主 要 统 计 指 标 MAJOR STATISTICAL INDICATORS

2016年全社会固定资产投资额	Total Value of Investment in Fixed Assets	5 648.49	亿元	100 million yuan
比上年增长	Increase Over Last Year	-7.8	%	
2016年工业投资额	Industrial Investment	1 982.29	亿元	100 million yuan
比上年增长	Increase Over Last Year	-9.9	%	
2016年服务业投资额	Tertiary Industry Investment	3 660.27	亿元	100 million yuan
比上年增长	Increase Over Last Year	-6.5	%	
2016年房地产开发投资额	Value of Investment in Real Estate Development	2 163.24	亿元	100 million yuan
比上年增长	Increase Over Last Year	16.0	%	
2016年民间投资额	Private Investment	3 237.93	亿元	100 million yuan
比上年增长	Increase Over Last Year	-1.4	%	
2016年外资投资额	Enterprises with Foreign Investment	998.91	亿元	100 million yuan
比上年增长	Increase Over Last Year	-10.7	%	

表11-1

历年全社会固定资产投资完成额

单位：万元

年 份 Year	全 市 Whole Municipality	按地区分 Grouped by Region					
		市 区 Urban Area	# 吴江区 Wujiang District	常 熟 Changshu	张家港 Zhangjiagang	昆 山 Kunshan	太 仓 Taicang
1990	553 691	253 932	68 648	105 992	93 632	60 830	39 305
1991	803 288	370 601	103 363	158 605	114 416	90 126	69 540
1992	1 543 906	612 895	135 277	328 248	359 525	140 505	102 733
1993	2 718 565	1 185 428	180 264	429 146	542 526	330 320	231 145
1994	3 076 978	1 356 598	217 474	413 504	580 270	470 065	256 541
1995	3 340 991	1 574 996	211 232	383 553	670 679	479 444	232 319
1996	3 805 873	2 011 104	321 946	442 400	555 130	577 948	219 291
1997	4 051 760	2 172 709	230 727	445 330	601 212	562 505	270 004
1998	4 501 061	2 569 089	264 224	506 488	444 469	573 897	407 118
1999	4 751 365	2 671 338	331 525	531 468	481 840	598 705	468 014
2000	5 164 346	3 027 810	621 844	550 168	543 846	638 316	404 206
2001	5 648 539	3 138 199	703 355	703 995	685 043	683 494	437 808
2002	8 128 145	4 061 464	1 060 739	1 162 638	1 150 731	1 153 000	600 312
2003	14 089 329	7 588 970	1 721 190	1 821 089	1 801 076	1 766 358	1 111 836
2004	15 547 986	8 330 734	1 897 918	1 965 100	1 955 030	1 910 868	1 386 254
2005	18 701 431	9 968 338	2 131 580	2 341 375	2 334 337	2 348 141	1 709 240
2006	21 069 898	11 182 879	2 360 556	2 593 063	2 486 481	2 805 816	2 001 659
2007	23 663 595	12 486 968	2 656 766	2 911 910	2 811 570	3 210 071	2 243 076
2008	26 111 595	13 592 361	2 932 522	3 178 027	3 160 398	3 700 316	2 480 493
2009	29 673 482	15 286 269	3 386 178	3 608 902	3 635 092	4 300 572	2 842 647
2010	36 178 211	18 651 157	4 170 136	4 406 523	4 459 095	5 306 914	3 354 522
2011	45 020 211	23 276 099	5 216 865	5 353 678	5 828 073	6 461 539	4 100 822
2012	52 664 852	26 859 457	6 300 746	6 354 752	7 029 782	7 700 434	4 720 427
2013	60 019 428	31 541 738	7 213 614	7 152 070	7 705 555	8 420 018	5 200 047
2014	62 306 662	34 197 405	7 572 883	6 504 377	7 800 216	8 500 504	5 304 160
2015	61 244 251	34 265 426	7 205 664	6 312 157	7 560 469	8 106 097	5 000 102
2016	56 484 864	31 563 905	6 810 230	5 449 065	7 247 656	7 574 238	4 650 000

TOTAL FIXED ASSETS INVESTMENT OVER THE YEARS

(10 000 yuan)

按产业分 Grouped by Industry				基础设施投资 Infrastructure Investment	民间投资 Private Investment	外资投资 Foreign Investment
第一产业 Primary Industry	第二产业 Secondary Industry	# 工 业 Industry	第三产业 Tertiary Industry			
14 976	3 219 770	3 200 143	1 929 600	1 136 156	2 098 565	1 840 875
24 289	3 521 830	3 400 106	2 102 420	1 242 678	2 979 960	1 775 825
31 168	5 109 445	5 095 013	2 987 532	1 788 191	4 035 864	2 331 114
29 163	8 456 066	8 423 117	5 604 100	4 127 901	6 299 125	4 291 620
30 527	8 714 648	8 695 765	6 802 811	4 175 242	7 824 699	4 464 037
21 525	10 506 332	10 491 501	8 173 574	4 881 033	8 795 983	5 811 660
21 962	11 635 037	11 598 665	9 412 899	4 770 675	10 223 735	6 230 337
36 481	12 186 580	12 062 876	11 440 534	4 556 100	12 061 831	8 107 918
48 021	12 775 782	12 676 938	13 287 792	5 142 200	12 910 914	9 180 967
64 613	13 050 274	12 933 066	16 558 595	6 769 853	15 677 012	7 684 425
83 258	15 648 515	15 548 129	20 446 438	7 322 092	20 399 903	8 125 763
88 022	18 918 951	18 806 853	26 013 238	7 636 059	25 981 532	9 976 988
100 052	21 848 885	21 764 295	30 715 915	7 753 049	29 522 385	10 876 385
67 126	24 343 062	24 312 799	35 609 240	10 305 956	32 591 070	12 225 141
43 160	23 081 032	23 049 631	39 182 470	10 221 487	33 217 850	11 745 885
38 617	22 042 446	22 005 198	39 163 188	10 709 269	32 843 605	11 184 472
9 110	19 873 097	19 822 925	36 602 657	7 380 930	32 379 317	9 989 136

表11-2　分地区全社会固定资产投资完成额(2016年)

单位：万元

项　目	Item	全　市 Whole Municipality
总　计	**Total**	**56 484 864**
按建设性质分	**Grouped by Type of Construction**	
新　建	New Construction	16 894 756
扩　建	Expansion	7 488 734
改　建	Reconstruction	3 671 482
其　他	Others	28 429 892
按构成分	**Grouped by Use of Funds**	
建筑工程	Construction	28 008 229
安装工程	Installation	2 764 459
设备工器具购置	Purchase of Equipment and Instruments	15 709 662
其他费用	Others	10 002 514
按登记注册类型分	**Grouped by Registration Status**	
国有企业	State-owed Enterprises	6 360 234
集体企业	Collective-owned Enterprises	1 355 604
股份合作企业	Share-holding Cooperative Enterprises	54 523
联营企业	Joint Ownership Enterprises	53 214
有限责任公司	Limited Liability Corporations	18 420 887
股份有限公司	Share-holding Corporations Ltd.	1 109 258
私营个体经济	Individuals	18 019 335
其　他	Others	229 286
港澳台商投资企业	Enterprises with Investment from HongKong, Macao and Taiwan	4 080 522
外商投资企业	Enterprises with Foreign Investment	6 802 001
按产业分	**Grouped by Industry**	
第一产业	Primary Industry	9 110
第二产业	Secondary Industry	19 873 097
#工　业	Industry	19 822 925
第三产业	Tertiary Industry	36 602 657

TOTAL FIXED ASSETS INVESTMENT BY REGION (2016)

(10 000 yuan)

市　区 Urban Area	# 吴江区 Wujiang District	常　熟 Changshu	张家港 Zhangjiagang	昆　山 Kunshan	太　仓 Taicang
31 563 905	**6 810 230**	**5 449 065**	**7 247 656**	**7 574 238**	**4 650 000**
9 688 554	1 370 746	1 963 147	2 125 750	1 468 240	1 649 065
2 958 565	1 604 055	879 824	2 312 450	765 173	572 722
1 462 540	652 119	289 082	1 061 143	520 758	337 959
17 454 246	3 183 310	2 317 012	1 748 313	4 820 067	2 090 254
15 073 970	3 418 551	3 001 216	3 682 147	4 289 934	1 960 962
1 647 492	168 597	155 442	428 762	353 559	179 204
7 040 378	1 725 643	1 722 927	2 572 817	2 310 038	2 063 502
7 802 065	1 497 439	569 480	563 930	620 707	446 332
4 156 986	878 002	750 916	576 174	337 042	539 116
624 934	187 606	238 070	339 545	87 781	65 274
37 171	–	17 352	–	–	–
12 890	3 860	40 324	–	–	–
10 513 236	1 633 477	1 485 881	3 125 275	2 774 752	521 743
757 022	131 434	60 970	148 639	74 566	68 061
9 800 944	2 644 535	1 558 683	2 408 326	2 008 807	2 242 575
95 271	55 482	535	110 961	20 475	2 044
2 283 282	773 861	600 220	278 810	644 717	273 493
3 282 169	501 973	696 114	259 926	1 626 098	937 694
9 110	910	–	–	–	–
8 255 103	2 305 823	2 437 263	3 856 723	2 725 515	2 598 493
8 204 931	2 304 746	2 437 263	3 856 723	2 725 515	2 598 493
23 299 692	4 503 497	3 011 802	3 390 933	4 848 723	2 051 507

表11-2 续表 1

单位：万元

项　　目	Item	全　市 Whole Municipality
按行业分	**Grouped by Sector**	
农林牧渔业	Farming, Forestry, Animal Husbandry and Fishery	9 110
采矿业	Mining and Quarrying	12 321
制造业	Manufacturing	18 307 643
农副食品加工业	Farm and Sideline Products	54 113
食品制造业	Food Production	128 363
酒、饮料和精制茶制造业	Wine, Beverage and Refined tea manufacturing	31 050
烟草制品业	Tobacco Production	4 835
纺织业	Textile Industry	1 198 560
纺织服装和服饰业	Garments and Apparel Industry	170 474
皮革毛皮羽毛及其制品和制鞋业	Leather, Fur, Wool and shoes Products	26 132
木材加工及木、竹、藤、棕、草制品业	Wood Processing, Wood, Bamboo, Rattan and Coir Products Straw Products	60 867
家具制造业	Furniture Manufacturing	153 271
造纸及纸制品业	Papermaking and Paper Products	231 228
印刷业和记录媒介复制业	Printing and Record Duplicating	172 632
文教体育用品制造业	Stationary, Educational and Sports Goods	113 105
石油加工、炼焦及核燃料加工	Petroleum Processing, Coking and Nuclear Fuel Processing	53 009
化学原料及化学制品制造业	Raw Chemical Materials and Chemical Products	1 387 222
医药制造业	Medical and Pharmaceutical Products	298 142
化学纤维制造业	Chemical Fiber Manufacturing	698 367
橡胶和塑料制品业	Rubber and Plastic Products	681 359
非金属矿物制品业	Nonmetal Mineral Products	384 126
黑色金属冶炼及压延加工业	Smelting and Pressing of Ferrous Metals	384 354
有色金属冶炼及压延加工业	Smelting and Pressing of Nonferrous Metals	254 672
金属制品业	Metal Products	905 237
通用设备制造业	General Equipment Manufacture	1 676 373
专用设备制造业	Special Purposes Equipment Manufacturing	1 889 398
汽车制造业	Automobile Manufacturing	1 292 134
铁路船舶航空航天和其他运输设备制造业	Railway, Ship, Aerospace and Other Transportation Equipment Manufacturing	122 468
电气机械及器材制造业	Electric Equipment and Machinery Manufacturing	1 997 691
计算机、通信和其他电子设备制造业	Computer Telecommunications and Other Electronic Equipment Manufacture	3 459 750
仪器仪表制造业	Instruments, Meters Machinery	292 147
其他制造业	Other Products Manufacture	103 981

Continued 1

(10 000 yuan)

市 区 Urban Area	# 吴江区 Wujiang District	常 熟 Changshu	张家港 Zhangjiagang	昆 山 Kunshan	太 仓 Taicang
9 110	910	–	–	–	–
12 321	–	–	–	–	–
7 729 533	2 211 625	2 243 735	3 260 983	2 576 326	2 497 066
6 880	6 880	4 850	3 800	30 013	8 570
59 904	10 600	18 240	4 300	13 989	31 930
14 890	14 890	400	4 000	8 200	3 560
–	–	–	–	–	4 835
725 810	619 506	147 928	249 072	6 280	69 470
73 196	11 901	46 467	20 700	12 816	17 295
16 162	4 600	4 320	–	–	5 650
42 547	18 500	11 700	–	3 800	2 820
111 819	17 351	2 577	17 200	5 160	16 515
64 356	31 725	16 760	15 500	34 149	100 463
59 107	5 494	18 778	4 200	63 776	26 771
37 423	17 461	–	39 293	28 939	7 450
3 898	–	5 462	–	–	43 649
214 308	30 290	434 798	462 314	99 350	176 452
158 229	10 386	14 263	16 713	12 193	96 744
498 788	417 488	17 884	34 100	5 132	142 463
205 656	46 135	46 581	116 205	151 808	161 109
164 737	34 341	28 469	67 398	14 801	108 721
77 310	26 853	66 281	206 840	1 300	32 623
75 169	27 400	34 720	61 700	60 433	22 650
297 242	86 678	134 893	170 210	72 778	230 114
637 026	162 047	144 669	306 704	206 601	381 373
754 024	89 550	98 651	501 238	236 201	299 284
327 657	58 882	454 126	244 775	115 772	149 804
39 817	–	15 002	10 200	22 128	35 321
1 006 270	233 204	215 074	463 458	155 634	157 255
1 804 031	221 404	234 854	155 262	1 167 556	98 047
211 168	3 189	1 635	27 978	17 042	34 324
16 470	2 520	21 703	24 773	30 475	10 560

表11-2 续表 2

单位：万元

项　目	Item	全　市 Whole Municipality
废弃资源综合利用业	Comprehensive Utilization of Waste Resources	82 583
电力、煤气及水的生产和供应业	Power, Gas and Water Production and Supply	1 502 961
建筑业	Construction	50 172
批发和零售业	Wholesale and Retail Trade Services	452 882
交通运输、仓储和邮政业	Transportation, Logistics and Postal	3 273 823
住宿和餐饮业	Accommodation and Catering Services	212 064
信息传输、软件和信息技术服务业	Information Transmission, Computer Services and Software Industries	659 635
金融业	Financial Industries	232 873
房地产业	Real Estate	23 085 458
租赁和商务服务业	Leasing and Business Services	2 316 109
科学研究和技术服务业	Scientific Research and Technical Services	582 158
水利、环境和公共设施管理业	Water Conservancy, Environment and Public Facilities Management	2 747 079
居民服务和其他服务业	Community Service and Other Services	48 452
教　育	Education	442 123
卫生和社会工作	Health Care and Social Work	315 339
文化、体育和娱乐业	Culture, Sports and Entertainment	1 334 582
公共管理和社会组织	Public Administration and Social Organizations	840 749
本年资金来源合计	**Total**	**98 760 404**
1.上年末结余资金	Balance of Last Year	19 213 108
2.本年资金来源小计	Total Fund for This Year	79 547 296
(1) 国家预算内资金	State Budgetary Appropriation	1 339 717
(2) 国内贷款	Domestic Loans	11 226 806
(3) 债　券	Bonds	–
(4) 利用外资	Foreign Investment	1 571 755
(5) 自筹资金	Fundraising	32 896 656
(6) 其他资金来源	Others	32 512 362
本年新增固定资产	**Newly Increased Fixed Assets this year**	**36 823 082**
房屋建筑面积　(万平方米)	**Floor Space of Buildings**　(10 000 sq. m)	
施工房屋建筑面积	Floor space of Buildings under Construction	15 857.37
# 住　宅	Residential Buildings	8 994.12
竣工房屋建筑面积	Floor Space of Buildings Completed	3 111.69
# 住　宅	Residential Building	1 481.76

Continued 2

(10 000 yuan)

市 区 Urban Area	# 吴江区 Wujiang District	常 熟 Changshu	张家港 Zhangjiagang	昆 山 Kunshan	太 仓 Taicang
25 639	2 350	2 650	33 050	–	21 244
463 077	93 121	193 528	595 740	149 189	101 427
50 172	1 077	–	–	–	–
236 997	43 939	17 698	21 253	34 851	142 083
1 918 011	123 041	687 839	98 884	224 551	344 538
200 054	91 361	–	3 150	3 100	5 760
618 616	9 780	–	7 054	23 415	10 550
195 840	15 085	1 100	13 033	–	22 900
14 499 181	3 156 668	1 645 736	2 145 870	3 825 304	969 367
1 364 587	190 303	57 400	394 084	235 336	264 702
487 481	21 766	40 097	11 170	5 000	38 410
1 426 292	593 957	425 699	396 762	313 585	184 741
10 755	4 453	12 418	15 409	550	9 320
302 941	64 126	44 688	12 245	73 823	8 426
243 701	45 144	33 642	1 009	35 987	1 000
1 237 756	33 243	29 619	42 688	20 306	4 213
499 159	110 631	15 866	228 322	51 905	45 497
60 551 156	**11 298 070**	**8 780 508**	**7 862 525**	**15 276 195**	**6 290 020**
13 329 625	1 485 275	1 384 305	1 149 656	2 886 442	463 080
47 221 531	9 812 795	7 396 203	6 712 869	12 389 753	5 826 940
724 103	300 947	590 869	20 745	4 000	–
7 951 895	1 023 513	724 736	635 547	1 630 962	283 666
–	–	–	–	–	–
403 848	245 083	414 493	97 345	567 282	88 787
17 715 456	4 080 951	3 229 257	4 179 881	3 867 810	3 904 252
20 426 229	4 162 301	2 436 848	1 779 351	6 319 699	1 550 235
17 842 284	**4 283 860**	**3 652 229**	**4 884 080**	**6 869 267**	**3 575 222**
8 145.02	2 203.20	1 352.47	1 492.43	4 064.32	803.13
4 391.85	1 125.97	723.60	1 063.12	2 391.01	424.55
1 305.15	489.98	292.16	268.93	1 001.32	244.13
613.32	109.64	140.81	150.85	511.79	65.00

表11-3

分月全社会固定资产投资完成额(2016年)

单位：万元

项　　目	Item	1~2月 From Jan. to Feb.	1~3月 From Jan. to Mar.
全社会固定资产投资	**Total Value of Investment in Fixed Assets**	**7 207 646**	**12 522 961**
# 亿元以上项目	Projects with More than 100 Million Yuan	3 047 293	4 892 925
# 本年新开工项目	New Projects	1 737 197	3 671 913
# 基础设施投资	Investment in Infrastructure	892 457	1 475 292
# 新兴产业投资	Investment in Emerging Industries	1 290 224	2 660 537
按地区分	**Grouped by Region**		
市　区	Urban Area	4 196 094	6 974 720
# 姑苏区	Gusu District	188 258	413 998
吴中区	Wuzhong District	666 013	1 229 986
相城区	Xiangcheng District	533 510	952 820
高新区、虎丘区	New & Hi-tech Zone , Huqiu District	631 956	1 166 131
工业园区	Industrial Park	1 142 599	1 515 607
吴江区	Wujiang District	748 688	1 271 295
常　熟	Changshu	660 344	1 223 444
张家港	Zhangjiagang	1 003 748	1 766 847
昆　山	Kunshan	1 008 288	1 787 584
太　仓	Taicang	339 172	770 366
按产业分	**Grouped by Industry**		
第一产业	Primary Industry	1 500	2 150
第二产业	Secondary Industry	2 500 679	4 501 736
# 工　业	Industry	2 499 166	4 497 584
# 六大支柱行业投资	Investment in the Six Pillar Industries	1 500 938	2 531 665
工业技改投资	Investment in Industrial Technical Reformation	1 481 724	3 064 182
高新技术产业投资	Investment in Hi-tech Manufacturing Industries	1 158 599	1 843 340
第三产业	Tertiary Industry	4 705 467	8 019 075
按投资主体分	**Grouped by Investment Subjects**		
国有投资	State-owned Investment	1 684 142	2 993 644
民间投资	Private Investment	3 971 101	7 019 043
# 私营个体经济	Value of Investment in Fixed Assets Private and Individuals	2 187 628	3 962 659
外资投资	Foreign Investment	1 552 403	2 510 274

TOTAL FIXED ASSETS INVESTMENT BY MONTH(2016)

(10 000 yuan)

1~4月 From Jan. to Apr.	1~5月 From Jan. to May	1~6月 From Jan. to Jun.	1~7月 From Jan. to Jul.	1~8月 From Jan. to Aug.	1~9月 From Jan. to Sept.	1~10月 From Jan. to Oct.	1~11月 From Jan. to Nov.	1~12月 From Jan. to Dec.
17 199 809	**22 810 903**	**29 801 074**	**34 535 903**	**39 118 073**	**44 629 754**	**49 199 263**	**54 156 274**	**56 484 864**
6 710 657	8 671 269	11 249 790	12 945 712	14 476 270	16 342 459	17 801 682	19 482 545	20 503 434
5 282 684	7 555 699	10 196 437	12 177 553	13 996 767	16 246 861	18 236 102	20 334 261	20 999 665
2 040 118	2 810 207	3 758 791	4 303 751	4 859 713	5 735 228	6 298 632	7 168 979	7 380 930
4 090 678	5 442 620	7 152 904	8 582 281	9 789 052	11 048 383	12 207 261	13 283 136	14 101 760
9 430 315	12 364 359	16 485 047	19 104 350	21 635 068	24 911 287	27 400 850	30 235 223	31 563 905
617 639	810 774	1 133 761	1 298 833	1 531 660	1 779 334	1 967 128	2 217 112	2 303 224
1 681 919	2 181 701	2 868 065	3 314 926	3 736 185	4 438 178	4 936 083	5 386 566	5 616 691
1 377 209	1 814 088	2 498 399	2 950 202	3 288 145	3 675 424	4 034 098	4 565 547	4 762 081
1 601 566	2 092 840	2 643 194	3 087 255	3 513 445	4 138 339	4 603 444	5 105 884	5 300 553
1 953 730	2 454 360	3 049 214	3 528 453	3 886 267	4 247 965	4 591 090	5 016 924	5 231 004
1 651 340	2 341 866	3 378 322	3 934 232	4 609 376	5 426 553	5 971 546	6 529 530	6 810 230
1 675 866	2 198 762	2 816 070	3 262 675	3 681 004	4 215 352	4 715 555	5 249 146	5 449 065
2 492 288	3 304 901	4 185 197	4 695 631	5 288 161	5 893 340	6 434 172	6 953 044	7 247 656
2 450 775	3 268 056	4 045 390	4 728 703	5 342 192	6 011 173	6 627 486	7 265 082	7 574 238
1 150 565	1 674 825	2 269 370	2 744 544	3 171 648	3 598 602	4 021 200	4 453 779	4 650 000
2 700	5 047	6 027	6 627	7 257	7 932	8 300	9 110	9 110
6 065 059	8 260 914	10 784 580	12 480 660	13 999 180	15 817 797	17 490 168	19 122 802	19 873 097
6 056 042	8 246 968	10 765 318	12 457 225	13 967 366	15 782 126	17 452 544	19 079 135	19 822 925
3 273 278	4 378 680	5 669 279	6 583 118	7 351 861	8 195 030	8 943 113	9 730 584	10 103 950
4 517 343	6 030 798	7 807 519	9 114 053	10 166 322	11 394 424	12 629 380	13 736 327	14 270 280
2 336 467	2 971 076	3 767 578	4 357 333	6 014 879	6 707 995	7 358 367	7 944 536	8 202 185
11 132 050	14 544 942	19 010 467	22 048 616	25 111 636	28 804 025	31 700 795	35 024 362	36 602 657
4 147 572	5 277 465	7 042 523	8 119 383	9 291 296	11 076 043	12 225 498	13 600 206	14 116 411
9 729 225	13 188 615	17 333 145	20 154 376	22 900 508	25 696 356	28 416 215	31 144 118	32 379 317
5 406 833	7 182 173	9 523 171	11 247 000	12 557 657	14 216 787	15 891 572	17 392 142	18 019 335
3 323 012	4 344 823	5 425 406	6 262 144	6 926 269	7 857 355	8 557 550	9 411 950	9 989 136

表11-4

分地区新兴产业投资额 (2016年)

项　目	Item	全　市 Whole Municipality
在建项目数　(个)	**Construction Projects in Total　(unit)**	**2 812**
新型平板显示	New Flat Panel Displays	241
新材料	New Materials	637
智能电网和物联网	Smart Grid and Internet Of Things	210
高端装备制造	High-End Equipment Manufacturing	933
节能环保	Energy Saving and Environmental Protection	229
新能源	New Energy	169
生物和新医药	Biotechnology and New Medicines	218
软件和集成电路	Software and Integrated Circuit	175
按行业分	**Grouped by sector**	
# 工业新兴产业	Emerging Industries	2 596
服务业新兴产业	Emerging Service Industries	215
在建项目本年完成投资　(万元)	**Investment in Construction Projects Completed This Year　(10 000 yuan)**	**14 101 760**
新型平板显示	New Flat Panel Displays	2 296 677
新材料	New Materials	3 334 193
智能电网和物联网	Smart Grid and Internet Of Things	1 009 343
高端装备制造	High-End Equipment Manufacturing	3 966 673
节能环保	Energy Saving and Environmental Protection	958 889
新能源	New Energy	900 000
生物和新医药	Biotechnology and New Medicines	978 336
软件和集成电路	Software and Integrated Circuit	657 649
按行业分	**Grouped by sector**	
# 工业新兴产业	Emerging Industries	12 904 416
服务业新兴产业	Emerging Service Industries	1 195 447

INVESTMENT OF EMERGING INDUSTRIES BY REGION(2016)

市 区 Urban Area	# 吴江区 Wujiang District	常 熟 Changshu	张家港 Zhangjiagang	昆 山 Kunshan	太 仓 Taicang
1 615	**298**	**164**	**408**	**324**	**301**
179	20	7	5	47	3
361	117	51	103	56	66
137	23	9	20	40	4
477	96	59	145	113	139
110	22	4	63	23	29
71	7	21	37	17	23
126	9	9	33	13	37
154	4	4	2	15	–
1 426	297	161	393	320	296
188	1	3	15	4	5
6 830 824	**1 260 229**	**1 365 127**	**2 725 960**	**1 843 451**	**1 336 398**
1 251 242	103 859	61 242	172 303	792 090	19 800
1 416 716	603 153	539 755	812 319	287 820	277 583
648 161	73 028	128 976	87 950	121 485	22 771
1 738 936	275 468	511 156	716 224	418 527	581 830
376 537	123 489	5 950	394 920	72 165	109 317
276 311	54 072	66 143	311 870	66 434	179 242
523 333	17 753	41 355	226 874	40 919	145 855
599 588	9 407	10 550	3 500	44 011	–
5 771 586	1 259 563	1 345 287	2 656 476	1 831 791	1 299 276
1 057 341	666	19 840	69 484	11 660	37 122

表11-5

全社会民间固定资产投资额 (2016年)

单位：万元

项　目	Item	全　市 Whole Municipality
总　计	**Total**	**32 379 317**
按建设性质分	**Grouped by Type of Construction**	
新　建	New Construction	7 048 162
扩　建	Expansion	4 765 893
改　建	Reconstruction	2 145 117
其　他	Others	18 420 145
按工程构成分	**Grouped by Use of Funds**	
建筑工程	Construction	15 280 843
安装工程	Installation	1 509 184
设备工器具购置	Purchase of Equipment and Instruments	9 582 828
其他费用	Others	6 006 462
按登记注册类型分	**Grouped by Registration Status**	
集体企业	Collective-owned Enterprises	1 355 604
股份合作企业	Share-holding Cooperative Enterprises	54 523
联营企业	Joint Ownership Enterprises	6 360
有限责任公司	Limited Liability Corporations	11 307 937
股份有限公司	Share-holding Corporations Ltd.	617 954
私营个体经济	Individuals	18 019 335
其　他	Others	229 286
港澳台商投资企业	Enterprises with Investment from HongKong, Macao and Taiwan	174 002
外商投资企业	Enterprises with Foreign Investment	614 316
按产业分	**Grouped by Industry**	
第一产业	Primary Industry	6 153
第二产业	Secondary Industry	12 552 064
# 工　业	Industry	12 501 892
第三产业	Tertiary Industry	19 821 100
按行业分	**Grouped by Sector**	
农林牧渔业	Farming, Forestry, Animal Husbandry and Fishery	6 153
采矿业	Mining and Quarrying	–
制造业	Manufacturing	11 776 427
电力、煤气及水的生产和供应业	Power, Gas and Water Production and Supply	725 465

WHOLE SOCIETY'S PRIVATE INVESTMENT IN FIXED ASSETS(2016)

(10 000 yuan)

市　区 Urban Area	# 吴江区 Wujiang District	常　熟 Changshu	张家港 Zhangjiagang	昆　山 Kunshan	太　仓 Taicang
16 429 436	**3 929 370**	**3 072 103**	**5 918 260**	**4 080 390**	**2 879 128**
2 821 925	582 983	915 530	1 684 578	563 414	1 062 715
1 684 767	1 161 799	376 030	1 974 804	372 053	358 239
689 380	253 385	169 812	939 432	156 228	190 265
11 233 364	1 931 203	1 610 731	1 319 446	2 988 695	1 267 909
7 121 647	1 737 927	1 630 734	2 699 019	2 618 301	1 211 142
633 439	120 776	83 534	394 874	269 546	127 791
4 205 862	1 208 720	976 901	2 369 406	727 930	1 302 729
4 468 488	861 947	380 934	454 961	464 613	237 466
624 934	187 606	238 070	339 545	87 781	65 274
37 171	–	17 352	–	–	–
6 360	3 860	–	–	–	–
5 234 386	813 062	901 879	2 860 560	1 906 683	404 429
337 405	120 364	60 970	148 639	36 095	34 845
9 800 944	2 644 535	1 558 683	2 408 326	2 008 807	2 242 575
95 271	55 482	535	110 961	20 475	2 044
120 591	3 117	46 214	–	2 365	4 832
172 374	101 344	248 400	50 229	18 184	125 129
6 153	–	–	–	–	–
5 010 796	1 600 217	1 427 013	3 525 945	909 251	1 679 059
4 960 624	1 599 140	1 427 013	3 525 945	909 251	1 679 059
11 412 487	2 329 153	1 645 090	2 392 315	3 171 139	1 200 069
6 153	–	–	–	–	–
–	–	–	–	–	–
4 845 601	1 583 499	1 415 617	2 952 226	897 079	1 665 904
115 023	15 641	11 396	573 719	12 172	13 155

表11-5 续表

单位：万元

项　目	Item	全　市 Whole Municipality
建筑业	Construction	50 172
批发和零售业	Wholesale and Retail Trade Services	354 420
交通运输、仓储和邮政业	Transportation, Logistics and Postal	304 877
住宿和餐饮业	Accommodation and Catering Services	156 490
信息传输、软件和信息技术服务业	Information Transmission, Software and Information Technology Services	359 704
金融业	Financial Industries	19 048
房地产业	Real Estate	15 611 164
租赁和商务服务业	Leasing and Business Services	1 061 761
科学研究和技术服务业	Scientific Research and Technical Services	427 795
水利、环境和公共设施管理业	Water Conservancy, Environment and Public Facilities Management	880 450
居民服务和其他服务业	Community Service and Other Services	39 090
教　育	Education	86 482
卫生和社会工作	Health Care and Social Work	51 323
文化、体育和娱乐业	Culture, Sports and Entertainment	196 444
公共管理和社会组织	Public Administration and Social Organizations	253 052
本年资金来源合计	**Total**	**56 900 433**
1.上年末结余资金	Balance of Last Year	9 846 463
2.本年资金来源小计	Total Fund for This Year	47 053 970
(1) 国家预算内资金	State Budgetary Appropriation	33 076
(2) 国内贷款	Domestic Loans	5 988 302
(3) 债　券	Bonds	-
(4) 利用外资	Foreign Investment	104 750
(5) 自筹资金	Fundraising	18 935 174
(6) 其他资金来源	Others	21 992 668
本年新增固定资产	**Newly Increased Fixed Assets this year**	**20 295 513**
房屋建筑面积 (万平方米)	**Floor Space of Buildings** (10 000 sq.m)	
施工房屋建筑面积	Floor Space of Buildings Under Construction	10 728.75
# 住　宅	Residential Buildings	6 458.93
竣工房屋建筑面积	Floor Space of Buildings Completed	1 963.70
# 住　宅	Residential Building	946.76

Continued

(10 000 yuan)

市区 Urban Area	# 吴江区 Wujiang District	常熟 Changshu	张家港 Zhangjiagang	昆山 Kunshan	太仓 Taicang
50 172	1 077	–	–	–	–
169 045	21 089	17 698	20 054	11 113	136 510
61 366	4 110	48 532	51 758	66 512	76 709
144 480	91 361	–	3 150	3 100	5 760
319 685	9 780	–	7 054	23 415	9 550
17 948	15 085	1 100	–	–	–
9 114 747	1 789 506	1 237 321	1 615 299	2 870 204	773 593
477 427	117 003	37 700	364 007	110 948	71 679
340 418	3 466	40 097	11 020	–	36 260
334 309	166 608	202 164	213 732	75 957	54 288
10 755	4 453	7 835	11 180	–	9 320
64 557	18 500	20 775	–	1 150	–
24 353	2 100	22 667	1 009	2 294	1 000
182 772	18 724	4 785	3 733	1 554	3 600
132 635	67 368	4 416	90 319	3 882	21 800
32 239 089	**6 971 467**	**5 793 292**	**5 984 212**	**8 710 553**	**4 173 287**
6 385 558	1 127 531	1 083 148	811 318	1 336 746	229 693
25 853 531	5 843 936	4 710 144	5 172 894	7 373 807	3 943 594
27 863	5 300	3 613	1 600	–	–
4 168 435	529 028	376 017	394 209	858 868	190 773
–	–	–	–	–	–
11 102	5 992	80 538	4 100	9 010	–
9 081 622	2 883 711	1 969 252	3 442 296	2 028 296	2 413 708
12 564 509	2 419 905	2 280 724	1 330 689	4 477 633	1 339 113
9 097 726	**2 422 937**	**1 994 486**	**4 107 048**	**3 010 158**	**2 086 095**
4 979.24	1 541.61	1 015.28	1 182.03	2 949.47	602.72
2 798.53	777.60	566.26	873.14	1 871.43	349.56
778.27	371.80	194.33	249.07	586.41	155.62
352.25	78.29	110.53	142.14	303.32	38.52

表11-6

建设项目投资完成额 (2016年)

单位：万元

项　　目	Item	全　市 Whole Municipality
总　　计	**Total**	**34 852 424**
按建设性质分	**Grouped by Type of Construction**	
新　建	New Construction	16 894 756
扩　建	Expansion	7 488 734
改　建	Reconstruction	3 671 482
其　他	Others	6 797 452
按工程构成分	**Grouped by Use of Funds**	
建筑工程	Construction	14 861 818
安装工程	Installation	1 318 992
设备工器具购置	Purchase of Equipment and Instruments	15 583 991
其他费用	Others	3 087 623
按登记注册类型分	**Grouped by Registration Status**	
国有企业	State-owed Enterprises	5 886 475
集体企业	Collective-owned Enterprises	1 257 278
股份合作企业	Share-holding Cooperative Enterprises	26 721
联营企业	Joint Ownership Enterprises	53 214
有限责任公司	Limited Liability Corporations	8 093 988
# 国有独资	State-owned Sole Investment	1 782 337
股份有限公司	Share-holding Corporations Ltd.	840 061
私营个体经济	Individuals	10 782 329
其　他	Others	204 400
港澳台商投资企业	Enterprises with Investment from HongKong, Macao and Taiwan	2 210 140
外商投资企业	Enterprises with Foreign Investment	5 497 818
按行业分	**Grouped by Sector**	
农林牧渔业	Farming, Forestry, Animal Husbandry and Fishery	9 110
采矿业	Mining and Quarrying	12 321
制造业	Manufacturing	18 307 643
电力、煤气及水的生产和供应业	Power, Gas and Water Production and Supply	1 502 961
建筑业	Construction	50 172
批发和零售业	Wholesale and Retail Trade Services	452 882
交通运输、仓储和邮政业	Transportation, Logistics and Postal	3 273 823

THE FIXED ASSETS OF CONSTRUCTION PROJECTS INVESTMENT(2016)

(10 000 yuan)

市 区 Urban Area	# 吴江区 Wujiang District	常 熟 Changshu	张家港 Zhangjiagang	昆 山 Kunshan	太 仓 Taicang
17 751 951	**3 915 088**	**4 011 917**	**5 609 540**	**3 776 277**	**3 702 739**
9 688 554	1 370 746	1 963 147	2 125 750	1 468 240	1 649 065
2 958 565	1 604 055	879 824	2 312 450	765 173	572 722
1 462 540	652 119	289 082	1 061 143	520 758	337 959
3 642 292	288 168	879 864	110 197	1 022 106	1 142 993
7 788 260	2 072 807	1 920 852	2 453 035	1 305 072	1 394 599
813 998	24 482	85 305	300 456	24 055	95 178
6 961 614	1 720 691	1 712 451	2 565 846	2 288 837	2 055 243
2 188 079	97 108	293 309	290 203	158 313	157 719
3 784 227	728 716	750 916	491 174	337 042	523 116
548 808	187 606	238 070	339 545	65 581	65 274
9 369	–	17 352	–	–	–
12 890	3 860	40 324	–	–	–
3 930 693	358 847	639 714	2 465 028	762 368	296 185
1 500 334	86 024	86 974	24 878	164 351	5 800
575 905	78 286	59 548	125 794	26 053	52 761
5 542 347	1 638 212	1 015 811	1 709 341	795 783	1 719 047
95 271	55 482	535	89 575	16 975	2 044
826 197	503 128	576 876	129 157	408 608	269 302
2 426 244	360 951	672 771	259 926	1 363 867	775 010
9 110	910	–	–	–	–
12 321	–	–	–	–	–
7 729 533	2 211 625	2 243 735	3 260 983	2 576 326	2 497 066
463 077	93 121	193 528	595 740	149 189	101 427
50 172	1 077	–	–	–	–
236 997	43 939	17 698	21 253	34 851	142 083
1 918 011	123 041	687 839	98 884	224 551	344 538

表11-6 续表

单位：万元

项　　目	Item	全　市 Whole Municipality
住宿和餐饮业	Accommodation and Catering Services	212 064
信息传输、软件和信息技术服务业	Information Transmission, Software and Information Technology Services	659 635
金融业	Financial Industries	232 873
房地产业	Real Estate	1 453 018
租赁和商务服务业	Leasing and Business Services	2 316 109
科学研究和技术服务业	Scientific Research and Technical Services	582 158
水利、环境和公共设施管理业	Water Conservancy, Environment and Public Facilities Management	2 747 079
居民服务和其他服务业	Community Service and Other Services	48 452
教　育	Education	442 123
卫生和社会工作	Health Care and Social Work	315 339
文化、体育和娱乐业	Culture, Sports and Entertainment	1 334 582
公共管理和社会组织	Public Administration and Social Organizations	840 749
本年资金来源合计	**Total**	**35 123 781**
1.上年末结余资金	Balance of Last Year	2 274 508
2.本年资金来源小计	Total Fund for This Year	32 849 273
(1) 国家预算内资金	State Budgetary Appropriation	1 339 717
(2) 国内贷款	Domestic Loans	3 888 044
(3) 债　券	Bonds	-
(4) 利用外资	Foreign Investment	1 571 578
(5) 自筹资金	Fundraising	24 929 567
(6) 其他资金来源	Others	1 120 367
本年新增固定资产	**Newly Increased Fixed Assets this year**	**25 394 704**
房屋建筑面积 (万平方米)	**Floor Space of Buildings** (10 000 sq.m)	
施工房屋建筑面积	Floor Space of Buildings Under Construction	3 733.27
# 住　宅	Residential Buildings	439.38
竣工房屋建筑面积	Floor Space of Buildings Completed	1 229.62
# 住　宅	Residential Building	78.97

Continued

(10 000 yuan)

市 区 Urban Area	# 吴江区 Wujiang District	常 熟 Changshu	张家港 Zhangjiagang	昆 山 Kunshan	太 仓 Taicang
200 054	91 361	–	3 150	3 100	5 760
618 616	9 780	–	7 054	23 415	10 550
195 840	15 085	1 100	13 033	–	22 900
687 227	261 526	208 588	507 754	27 343	22 106
1 364 587	190 303	57 400	394 084	235 336	264 702
487 481	21 766	40 097	11 170	5 000	38 410
1 426 292	593 957	425 699	396 762	313 585	184 741
10 755	4 453	12 418	15 409	550	9 320
302 941	64 126	44 688	12 245	73 823	8 426
243 701	45 144	33 642	1 009	35 987	1 000
1 237 756	33 243	29 619	42 688	20 306	4 213
499 159	110 631	15 866	228 322	51 905	45 497
18 011 100	**3 893 363**	**4 158 943**	**4 686 941**	**4 587 636**	**3 679 161**
1 282 100	48 747	202 197	345 252	433 049	11 910
16 729 000	3 844 616	3 956 746	4 341 689	4 154 587	3 667 251
724 103	300 947	590 869	20 745	4 000	–
2 750 773	352 664	237 139	160 122	689 267	50 743
–	–	–	–	–	–
403 671	245 083	414 493	97 345	567 282	88 787
12 207 360	2 867 202	2 610 912	3 842 996	2 753 464	3 514 835
643 093	78 720	103 333	220 481	140 574	12 886
11 808 662	**3 471 967**	**2 849 718**	**3 951 543**	**3 587 659**	**3 197 122**
1 848.93	582.86	404.63	484.73	724.16	270.81
22.18	8.38	45.27	341.26	12.70	17.97
502.34	335.16	139.46	89.32	321.26	177.25
13.21	–	23.52	27.29	–	14.96

表11-7

建设项目投资新增固定资产额 (2016年)

单位：万元

项 目	Item	全 市 Whole Municipality
总 计	**Total**	**25 394 704**
按建设性质分	**Grouped by Type of Construction**	
新 建	New Construction	10 811 224
扩 建	Expansion	5 133 714
改 建	Reconstruction	2 980 082
其 他	Others	6 469 684
按登记注册类型分	**Grouped by Registration Status**	
国有企业	State-owed Enterprises	4 550 567
集体企业	Collective-owned Enterprises	1 205 375
股份合作企业	Share-holding Cooperative Enterprises	28 978
联营企业	Joint Ownership Enterprises	51 291
有限责任公司	Limited Liability Corporations	4 114 285
股份有限公司	Share-holding Corporations Ltd.	403 026
私营个体经济	Individuals	9 478 117
其 他	Others	229 637
港澳台商投资企业	Enterprises with Investment from HongKong, Macao and Taiwan	1 668 439
外商投资企业	Enterprises with Foreign Investment	3 664 989
按产业分	**Grouped by Industry**	
第一产业	Primary Industry	2 957
第二产业	Secondary Industry	15 459 942
# 工 业	Industry	15 442 743
第三产业	Tertiary Industry	9 931 805

THE NEW FIXED ASSETS OF CONSTRUCTION PROJECTS INVESTMENT(2016)

(10 000 yuan)

市 区 Urban Area	# 吴江区 Wujiang District	常 熟 Changshu	张家港 Zhangjiagang	昆 山 Kunshan	太 仓 Taicang
11 808 662	**3 471 967**	**2 849 718**	**3 951 543**	**3 587 659**	**3 197 122**
5 360 424	1 317 320	1 285 990	1 502 148	1 405 512	1 257 150
1 950 063	1 262 237	400 626	1 626 355	659 812	496 858
1 072 135	606 783	286 452	810 040	491 511	319 944
3 426 040	285 627	876 650	13 000	1 030 824	1 123 170
2 699 030	546 135	580 464	453 045	394 086	423 942
416 954	212 496	300 560	333 520	89 067	65 274
3 426	–	25 552	–	–	–
6 360	3 860	44 931	–	–	–
1 878 584	687 292	309 987	1 170 363	543 881	211 470
238 129	39 670	19 885	69 570	26 053	49 389
4 657 010	1 402 571	798 529	1 608 016	839 231	1 575 331
147 537	140 487	535	39 750	37 771	4 044
575 792	203 527	448 490	71 459	355 090	217 608
1 185 840	235 929	320 785	205 820	1 302 480	650 064
2 957	910	–	–	–	–
5 977 304	1 943 548	1 683 690	2 940 725	2 575 918	2 282 305
5 960 105	1 943 435	1 683 690	2 940 725	2 575 918	2 282 305
5 828 401	1 527 509	1 166 028	1 010 818	1 011 741	914 817

表11-7 续表

单位：万元

项　目	Item	全　市 Whole Municipality
按行业分	**Grouped by Sector**	
农林牧渔业	Farming, Forestry, Animal Husbandry and Fishery	2 957
采矿业	Mining and Quarrying	18 778
制造业	Manufacturing	14 745 161
电力、煤气及水的生产和供应业	Power, Gas and Water Production and Supply	678 804
建筑业	Construction	17 199
批发和零售业	Wholesale and Retail Trade Services	459 526
交通运输、仓储和邮政业	Transportation, Logistics and Postal	2 238 755
住宿和餐饮业	Hoteling and Catering Services	112 662
信息传输、软件和信息技术服务业	Information Transmission, Software and Information Technology Services	369 502
金融业	Financial Industries	3 274
房地产业	Real Estate	896 575
租赁和商务服务业	Leasing and Business Services	1 408 058
科学研究和技术服务业	Scientific Research and Technical Services	519 412
水利、环境和公共设施管理业	Water Conservancy, Environment and Public Facilities Management	1 914 500
居民服务和其他服务业	Community Service and Other Services	37 888
教　育	Education	281 516
卫生和社会工作	Health Care and Social Work	185 895
文化、体育和娱乐业	Culture, Sports and Entertainment	268 858
公共管理和社会组织	Public Administration and Social Organizations	1 226 234

Continued

(10 000 yuan)

市 区 Urban Area	# 吴江区 Wujiang District	常 熟 Changshu	张家港 Zhangjiagang	昆 山 Kunshan	太 仓 Taicang
2 957	910	–	–	–	–
18 778	–	–	–	–	–
5 743 506	1 836 666	1 484 742	2 852 481	2 477 699	2 186 733
197 821	106 769	198 948	88 244	98 219	95 572
17 199	113	–	–	–	–
269 356	19 589	16 648	14 249	15 030	144 243
1 286 274	446 167	495 284	37 226	195 326	224 645
107 902	10 277	–	–	–	4 760
335 262	1 820	–	2 000	21 690	10 550
3 274	–	–	–	–	–
290 441	190 103	120 805	425 030	42 343	17 956
796 923	182 755	24 000	129 220	215 464	242 451
433 692	20 700	34 440	7 870	–	43 410
839 154	394 021	385 953	198 840	328 594	161 959
4 453	4 453	8 685	14 880	550	9 320
163 383	71 434	35 095	12 320	62 292	8 426
137 108	2 100	17 163	–	30 624	1 000
215 135	46 962	11 619	36 950	1 554	3 600
937 904	137 128	16 336	132 233	97 264	42 497

表11-8

重大投资项目情况 (2016年)

项　目	Item	全　市 Whole Municipality
投资项目数	(个) **Number of Projects** (unit)	
重大投资项目	**Major Investment Projects**	**365**
按内外资分	**Grouped by Domestic and Foreign Capitals**	
5亿元以上内资项目	Domestic Projects of More Than 500 Million Yuan	324
1亿美元以上外资项目	Foreign Projects of More Than $100 Million	41
按行业分	**Grouped by Sector**	
工业重大项目	Major Industrial Projects	86
服务业重大项目	Major Service Industry Projects	279
亿元项目	**Projects of More Than 100 Million Yuan**	**1 171**
# 亿元以上工业项目	Industrial Projects of More Than 100 Million Yuan	461
亿元以上服务业项目	Service Industry Projects of More Than 100 Million Yuan	707
亿元以上新开工项目	**New Projects of More Than 100 Million Yuan**	**388**
# 工业新开工项目	New Industrial Projects	214
服务业新开工项目	New Service Industry Projects	173
5亿元以上新开工项目	**New Projects of More Than 500 Million Yuan**	**78**
工业新开工项目	New Industrial Projects	38
服务业新开工项目	New Service Industry Projects	40

THE MAJOR PROJECTS INVESTMENT IN FIXED ASSETS (2016)

市 区 Urban Area	# 吴江区 Wujiang District	常 熟 Changshu	张家港 Zhangjiagang	昆 山 Kunshan	太 仓 Taicang
227	**43**	**25**	**40**	**55**	**18**
205	37	20	38	46	15
22	6	5	2	9	3
33	12	12	16	17	8
194	31	13	24	38	10
603	**146**	**127**	**168**	**185**	**88**
177	59	69	87	77	51
423	86	58	81	108	37
178	**44**	**49**	**67**	**56**	**38**
79	25	33	53	27	22
98	19	16	14	29	16
40	**10**	**8**	**9**	**9**	**12**
14	5	5	8	5	6
26	5	3	1	4	6

表11-8 续表

项　　目	Item	全　市 Whole Municipality
本年完成投资额　(万元)	**Investment Completed This Year**　(10 000 yuan)	
重大投资项目	**Major Investment Projects**	**13 279 673**
按内外资分	**Grouped by Domestic and Foreign Capitals**	
5亿元以上内资项目	Domestic Projects of More Than 500 Million Yuan	10 681 633
1亿美元以上外资项目	Foreign Projects of More Than $100 Million	2 598 040
按行业分	**Grouped by Sector**	
工业重大项目	Major Industrial Projects	4 210 001
服务业重大项目	Major Service Industry Projects	9 069 672
亿元项目	**Projects of More Than 100 Million Yuan**	**20 503 434**
# 亿元以上工业项目	Industrial Projects of More Than 100 Million Yuan	7 924 850
亿元以上服务业项目	Service Industry Projects of More Than 100 Million Yuan	12 550 066
亿元以上新开工项目	**New Projects of More Than 100 Million Yuan**	**5 512 886**
# 工业新开工项目	New Industrial Projects	3 344 229
服务业新开工项目	New Service Industry Projects	2 161 103
5亿元以上新开工项目	**New Projects of More Than 500 Million Yuan**	**2 131 073**
工业新开工项目	New Industrial Projects	1 297 557
服务业新开工项目	New Service Industry Projects	833 516

Continued

市 区 Urban Area	# 吴江区 Wujiang District	常 熟 Changshu	张家港 Zhangjiagang	昆 山 Kunshan	太 仓 Taicang
7 813 274	**1 108 291**	**1 308 315**	**2 058 001**	**1 732 450**	**367 633**
6 636 567	756 439	949 871	2 010 636	912 345	172 214
1 176 707	351 852	358 444	47 365	820 105	195 419
1 306 013	411 850	591 437	1 101 182	971 093	240 276
6 507 261	696 441	716 878	956 819	761 357	127 357
10 735 643	**1 805 911**	**2 543 315**	**3 635 895**	**2 637 281**	**951 300**
2 477 060	729 626	1 399 944	2 133 468	1 352 347	562 031
8 230 065	1 075 321	1 143 371	1 502 427	1 284 934	389 269
2 504 621	**799 515**	**838 057**	**1 160 895**	**506 395**	**502 918**
1 150 602	509 082	588 465	1 014 290	264 599	326 273
1 346 465	290 433	249 592	146 605	241 796	176 645
991 791	**417 812**	**365 630**	**268 136**	**229 411**	**276 105**
408 353	306 417	246 478	264 336	145 673	232 717
583 438	111 395	119 152	3 800	83 738	43 388

表11-9

固定资产投资效果情况 (2016年)
EFFECT OF INVESTMENT IN FIXED ASSETS (2016)

单位：% (%)

项　目	Item	项目建成投产率 Rate of Projects Completed and Put into Use	建设周期(年) Construction Cycle (year)	固定资产交付使用率 Rate of Fixed Assets Put into Use	房屋竣工率 Rate of Buildings Completed	# 住　宅 Residential Buildings
总　计	**Total**	**78.7**	**3.9**	**65.2**	**19.6**	**16.5**
按种类分	**Grouped by Type**					
项目投资	Projects Investment	53.2	2.7	72.9	32.9	18.0
房地产开发	Real Estate Development	–	5.9	52.8	15.5	16.4
按地区分	**Grouped by Region**					
市　区	Urban Area	75.7	4.3	56.5	16.0	14.0
# 吴江区	Wujiang District	85.0	3.7	62.9	22.2	9.7
常　熟	Changshu	86.0	2.9	67.0	21.6	19.5
张家港	Zhangjiagang	75.1	2.7	67.4	18.0	14.2
昆　山	Kunshan	77.3	5.3	90.7	24.6	21.4
太　仓	Taicang	88.6	2.5	76.9	30.4	15.3

表11-10

历年房地产开发投资情况
REAL ESTATE DEVELOPMENT OVER THE YEARS

年　份 Year	投资额(万元) Investment (10 000 yuan)	新增固定资产(万元) Newly Increased Fixed Assets (10 000 yuan)	竣工房屋面积(万平方米) Floor Space of Buildings Completed (10 000 sq.m)	# 住 宅 Residential Housing
1990	16 516	16 049	46.95	40.21
1991	22 578	18 015	44.42	39.15
1992	61 858	32 111	89.12	65.36
1993	336 437	150 033	337.47	282.81
1994	400 268	218 471	378.39	299.81
1995	586 461	364 429	398.24	301.47
1996	501 411	430 700	334.16	250.45
1997	512 313	440 908	354.96	277.46
1998	585 447	541 232	403.23	313.12
1999	601 124	515 846	425.72	349.99
2000	611 792	611 091	444.49	376.30
2001	686 178	701 954	467.24	386.26
2002	1 073 363	829 151	558.05	464.94
2003	1 779 403	1 218 305	825.89	709.15
2004	3 343 245	2 024 119	1 462.78	1 269.29
2005	4 143 333	3 439 283	1 677.29	1 380.58
2006	4 707 472	4 070 670	1 823.12	1 484.16
2007	6 019 565	4 794 361	1 873.29	1 481.42
2008	7 180 805	4 023 663	1 481.24	1 131.91
2009	7 243 408	6 488 907	1 878.68	1 409.81
2010	9 358 018	7 054 660	1 761.08	1 221.53
2011	11 991 278	6 361 455	1 514.52	1 102.41
2012	12 633 597	8 954 225	1 827.56	1 386.17
2013	14 757 684	10 192 954	1 692.51	1 227.53
2014	17 644 440	8 708 742	1 527.19	1 129.36
2015	18 649 472	10 350 854	1 653.14	1 274.57
2016	21 632 440	11 428 378	1 882.07	1 402.80

表11-11

房地产开发投资完成额 (2016年)

单位：万元

项　　目	Item	全　市 Whole Municipality
投资额合计	**Investment**	**21 632 440**
# 住宅投资完成额	Completed Investment Value of Residential Housing	16 552 368
一、按工程构成分	**Grouped by Use of Funds**	
建筑工程	Construction	13 146 411
安装工程	Installation	1 445 467
设备、工器具购置	Purchase of Equipment and Instruments	125 671
其他费用	Others	6 914 891
二、按登记注册类型分	**Grouped by Registration Status**	
国有企业	State-owed Enterprises	473 759
集体企业	Collective-owned Enterprises	98 326
股份合作企业	Share-holding Cooperative Enterprises	27 802
联营经济	Joint Ventures of State-owned and Collective Enterprises	–
国有独资	State-owned Enterprises	1 197 793
其他有限责任公司	Limited Liability Corporations	9 129 106
股份有限公司	Share-holding Corporations Ltd.	269 197
私营个体企业	Private and Individuals Enterprises	7 237 006
港澳台商投资企业	Enterprises with Investment from HongKong, Macao and Taiwan	1 870 382
外商投资企业	Enterprises with Foreign Investment	1 304 183
其　他	Others	24 886
本年资金来源合计	**Total**	**63 636 623**
1.上年末结余资金	Balance of Last Year	16 938 600
2.本年资金来源小计	Total Fund for This Year	46 698 023
(1) 国家预算内资金	State Budgetary Appropriation	–
(2) 国内贷款	Domestic Loans	7 338 762
(3) 债　券	Bonds	–
(4) 利用外资	Foreign Investment	177
(5) 自筹资金	Fundraising	7 967 089
(6) 其他资金来源	Others	31 391 995
本年新增固定资产	**Newly Increased Fixed Assets this year**	**11 428 378**
房屋建筑面积 (万平方米)	**Floor Space of Buildings** (10 000 sq.m)	
施工房屋建筑面积	Floor space of Buildings under Construction	12 124.10
# 住　宅	Residential Buildings	8 554.74
竣工房屋建筑面积	Floor Space of Buildings Completed	1 882.07
# 住　宅	Residential Building	1 402.80

INVESTMENT IN REAL ESTATE DEVELOPMENT (2016)

(10 000 yuan)

市 区 Urban Area	# 吴江区 Wujiang District	常 熟 Changshu	张家港 Zhangjiagang	昆 山 Kunshan	太 仓 Taicang
13 811 954	**2 895 142**	**1 437 148**	**1 638 116**	**3 797 961**	**947 261**
10 601 983	2 227 940	1 093 335	1 306 215	2 853 838	696 997
7 285 710	1 345 744	1 080 364	1 229 112	2 984 862	566 363
833 494	144 115	70 137	128 306	329 504	84 026
78 764	4 952	10 476	6 971	21 201	8 259
5 613 986	1 400 331	276 171	273 727	462 394	288 613
372 759	149 286	–	85 000	–	16 000
76 126	–	–	–	22 200	–
27 802	–	–	–	–	–
–	–	–	–	–	–
610 816	317 481	289 850	76 644	220 483	–
5 971 727	957 149	556 317	583 603	1 791 901	225 558
181 117	53 148	1 422	22 845	48 513	15 300
4 258 597	1 006 323	542 872	698 985	1 213 024	523 528
1 457 085	270 733	23 344	149 653	236 109	4 191
855 925	141 022	23 343	–	262 231	162 684
–	–	–	21 386	3 500	–
42 540 056	**7 404 707**	**4 621 565**	**3 175 584**	**10 688 559**	**2 610 859**
12 047 525	1 436 528	1 182 108	804 404	2 453 393	451 170
30 492 531	5 968 179	3 439 457	2 371 180	8 235 166	2 159 689
–	–	–	–	–	–
5 201 122	670 849	487 597	475 425	941 695	232 923
–	–	–	–	–	–
177	–	–	–	–	–
5 508 096	1 213 749	618 345	336 885	1 114 346	389 417
19 783 136	4 083 581	2 333 515	1 558 870	6 179 125	1 537 349
6 033 622	**811 893**	**802 511**	**932 537**	**3 281 608**	**378 100**
6 296.08	1 620.34	947.84	1 007.70	3 340.17	532.32
4 369.66	1 117.60	678.33	721.86	2 378.32	406.58
802.80	154.82	152.69	179.62	680.06	66.89
600.11	109.64	117.30	123.56	511.79	50.04

表11-12

房地产开发基本情况 (2016年)

项　目		Item		全　市 Whole Municipality
开发企业数	(个)	**Number of Development Enterprises**	(unit)	**1 281**
按资质等级分		**Classified by Qualification**		
一　级		A Qualification		17
二　级		B Qualification		332
三　级		C Qualification		150
四　级		D Qualification		9
暂　定		Provisional		657
其　他		Others		116
从业人员平均人数	(人)	**Number of Employed Persons**	(person)	**29 237**
土地开发及购置	(平方米)	**Land Development and Acquisition**	(sq.m)	
待开发土地面积		Area of Land to be Developed		5 343 736
本年土地购置面积		Acreage of Land Acquired Within the Year		5 573 710
本年土地成交价款	(万元)	Actual Land Price of the Year	(10 000 yuan)	3 662 220
资产及损益情况		**Assets and Expenditure**		
资产总计		Total Assets		133 212 048
负债总计		Total Liabilities		99 327 472
所有者权益		Creditors Equity		33 884 576
实收资本合计		Total Capital Hold		25 336 643
主营业务收入总计		Total from Business Revenue		28 304 296
土地转让收入		Revenue from Land Transfer		153 973
商品房销售收入		Revenue Sale of Housing		26 990 548
房屋出租收入		Income for House Lease		226 385
其他收入		Other Revenue		933 391
主营业务成本		Cost from Major Business		21 784 179
销售费用		Cost Related With Sale		884 672
主营业务税金及附加		Taxes and Extra Charges from Major Business		2 274 639
其他业务利润		Other Business Profits		92 341
管理费用及财务费用		Cost of Management and Financing Activities		965 852
投资收益及营业外收入		Benefits of Investment and Non-Business Income		363 701
营业外支出		Non-Business Expenditure		131 507
利润总额		Total Profits		2 523 286

BASIC CONDITION OF REAL ESTATE DEVELOPMENT (2016)

市 区 Urban Area	# 吴江区 Wujiang District	常 熟 Changshu	张家港 Zhangjiagang	昆 山 Kunshan	太 仓 Taicang
619	**156**	**127**	**89**	**305**	**141**
12	5	1	2	2	–
186	66	24	26	65	31
74	26	7	12	36	21
3	2	2	1	–	3
284	39	80	37	183	73
60	18	13	11	19	13
16 053	**3 799**	**2 217**	**2 041**	**6 719**	**2 207**
2 667 658	623 271	261 585	326 964	1 739 556	347 973
3 469 218	639 901	230 759	825 126	384 997	663 610
2 465 306	508 629	125 937	474 755	315 373	280 849
80 173 938	12 498 370	9 156 521	8 249 522	29 238 295	6 393 772
59 591 243	9 961 287	6 319 432	6 446 294	22 508 949	4 461 556
20 582 695	2 537 083	2 837 089	1 803 229	6 729 347	1 932 217
16 260 517	2 101 805	2 135 745	893 739	4 538 288	1 508 355
16 332 480	3 289 891	2 150 880	1 706 461	6 466 208	1 648 268
10 148	–	–	11 806	26 147	105 872
15 661 965	3 280 175	2 084 242	1 656 725	6 233 821	1 353 796
115 634	5 603	14 764	10 626	78 232	7 130
544 734	4 114	51 874	27 305	128 008	181 470
12 592 138	2 665 906	1 722 325	1 414 628	4 731 093	1 323 995
479 735	85 530	47 809	49 333	258 279	49 516
1 378 964	255 366	156 058	94 959	566 696	77 962
89 649	65 555	6 020	8 647	-13 640	1 665
529 878	64 064	67 109	90 531	224 516	53 819
228 956	7 160	15 333	524	99 633	19 254
64 064	8 985	9 684	17 575	32 270	7 913
1 424 348	221 353	164 418	32 994	789 106	112 420

表11-12 续表

项　目		Item		全　市 Whole Municipality
房屋施工面积	(平方米)	**Floor Space of Buildings under Construction**	(sq. m)	**121 241 028**
1. 住　宅		Residential Buildings		85 547 426
2. 办公楼		Office Buildings		5 666 336
3. 商业营业用房		Commercial Business Premises		14 806 488
4. 其　他		Others		15 220 778
新开工面积		**Floor Space of Starting This Year**		**29 665 143**
1. 住　宅		Residential Buildings		23 101 435
2. 办公楼		Office Buildings		1 005 361
3. 商业营业用房		Commercial Business Premises		2 260 415
4. 其　他		Others		3 297 932
房屋竣工面积		**Floor Space of Buildings Completed**		**18 820 657**
1. 住　宅		Residential Buildings		14 027 963
2. 办公楼		Office Buildings		701 278
3. 商业营业用房		Commercial Business Premises		1 985 887
4. 其　他		Others		2 105 529
商品房销售面积		**Floor Space of Housing Sold**		**24 940 451**
1. 住　宅		Residential Buildings		22 586 049
2. 办公楼		Office Buildings		579 301
3. 商业营业用房		Commercial Business Premises		1 460 182
4. 其　他		Others		314 919
待售面积		**Area Of Land For Sale**		**9 399 989**
1. 住　宅		Residential Buildings		4 225 864
2. 办公楼		Office Buildings		981 177
3. 商业营业用房		Commercial Business Premises		3 522 171
4. 其　他		Others		670 777
商品房销售额	(万元)	**Sales of housing**	(10 000 yuan)	**33 225 427**
1. 住　宅		Residential Buildings		30 707 405
2. 办公楼		Office Buildings		573 221
3. 商业营业用房		Commercial Business Premises		1 762 728
4. 其　他		Others		182 073

Continued

市　区 Urban Area	# 吴江区 Wujiang District	常　熟 Changshu	张家港 Zhangjiagang	昆　山 Kunshan	太　仓 Taicang
62 960 834	**16 203 399**	**9 478 379**	**10 076 986**	**33 401 668**	**5 323 161**
43 696 619	11 175 967	6 783 283	7 218 605	23 783 161	4 065 758
2 883 619	759 851	400 944	436 551	1 685 850	259 372
7 799 092	2 101 546	1 459 513	1 510 628	3 668 348	368 907
8 581 504	2 166 035	834 639	911 202	4 264 309	629 124
18 055 328	**4 178 610**	**1 538 674**	**1 699 122**	**6 772 016**	**1 600 003**
14 260 117	3 473 769	1 203 374	1 189 011	5 008 674	1 440 259
446 904	157 773	99 904	53 172	405 381	–
1 298 285	203 829	119 311	138 131	633 333	71 355
2 050 022	343 239	116 085	318 808	724 628	88 389
8 028 048	**1 548 243**	**1 526 942**	**1 796 151**	**6 800 640**	**668 876**
6 001 065	1 096 380	1 172 993	1 235 624	5 117 902	500 379
183 043	26 348	9 599	284 807	193 356	30 473
796 396	189 152	235 988	142 877	788 302	22 324
1 047 544	236 363	108 362	132 843	701 080	115 700
12 727 538	**3 517 595**	**2 131 530**	**1 966 249**	**6 334 272**	**1 780 862**
11 476 661	3 255 087	1 927 969	1 717 528	5 759 682	1 704 209
267 061	78 049	39 627	80 789	170 899	20 925
781 749	163 213	156 832	117 609	371 488	32 504
202 067	21 246	7 102	50 323	32 203	23 224
4 587 504	**1 088 785**	**1 086 068**	**1 221 234**	**1 733 339**	**771 844**
2 022 191	373 569	467 339	564 828	886 535	284 971
399 329	24 375	28 480	263 393	245 763	44 212
1 889 116	642 019	524 962	320 642	498 635	288 816
276 868	48 822	65 287	72 371	102 406	153 845
20 227 455	**4 412 657**	**2 029 137**	**1 803 942**	**7 324 379**	**1 840 514**
18 797 058	4 149 230	1 851 784	1 618 523	6 662 398	1 777 642
310 195	89 120	24 828	61 123	162 425	14 650
976 787	162 700	149 916	106 063	488 218	41 744
143 415	11 607	2 609	18 233	11 338	6 478

表11-13

全市房地产开发四大指标十强企业 (2016年)

序 号 No.	开发企业名称 Name of Development Enterprises	资质等级 Grouped by Grade	地 区 Region	经济类型 Ownership
一、完成投资额 Investment				
1	常熟市城市经营投资有限公司	二 级	常熟市	国 有
2	苏州开平房地产开发有限公司	暂定二级	吴江区	有限责任公司
3	张家港世茂房地产开发有限公司	暂定二级	张家港市	有限责任公司
4	正荣苏南（苏州）置业发展有限公司	暂定二级	吴中区	有限责任公司
5	正荣苏南（苏州）房地产有限公司	暂定二级	吴中区	有限责任公司
6	绿地集团（吴江）置业有限公司	暂定二级	吴江区	国 有
7	苏州工业园区圣哲房地产有限公司	暂定二级	工业园区	有限责任公司
8	苏南阳光城置业（苏州）有限公司	暂定二级	吴中区	有限责任公司
9	苏州旭悦置业有限公司	暂定二级	工业园区	有限责任公司
10	积水常成（苏州）房地产开发有限公司	暂定二级	相城区	中外合资经营
二、施工房屋面积 Floor Space of Building under Construction				
1	昆山市阳澄湖房产有限责任公司	二 级	昆山市	有限责任公司
2	苏州高龙房产发展有限公司	暂定二级	工业园区	中外合资经营
3	昆山市临丰房产开发有限公司	三 级	昆山市	有限责任公司
4	张家港汇金置业有限公司	暂定二级	张家港市	有限责任公司
5	常熟市城市经营投资有限公司	二 级	常熟市	国 有
6	昆山美吉特置业有限公司	暂定二级	昆山市	有限责任公司
7	苏州科技城城乡一体化发展有限公司	暂定二级	高新区、虎丘区	有限责任公司
8	昆山万科房地产有限公司	暂定二级	昆山市	有限责任公司
9	张家港市锦丰城乡开发投资有限公司	暂定二级	张家港市	有限责任公司
10	江苏中航地产有限公司	二 级	昆山市	国 有

TOP 10 OF REAL ESTATE DEVELOPMENT ENTERPRISES THAT BEST COMPLETED THE FOUR MAJOR INDICATORS (2016)

序号 No.	开发企业名称 Name of Development Enterprises	资质等级 Grouped by Grade	地区 Region	经济类型 Ownership
三、竣工房屋面积	**Floor Space of Building Completed**			
1	昆山瑞成房地产开发有限公司	二 级	昆山市	有限责任公司
2	张家港市锦丰城乡开发投资有限公司	暂定二级	张家港市	有限责任公司
3	昆山美吉特置业有限公司	暂定二级	昆山市	有限责任公司
4	华润置地（昆山）有限公司	二 级	昆山市	港澳台商独资
5	昆山市临丰房产开发有限公司	三 级	昆山市	有限责任公司
6	昆山市乐佳置业有限公司	暂定二级	昆山市	有限责任公司
7	中海海润（苏州）房地产有限公司	二 级	姑苏区	有限责任公司
8	江苏中航地产有限公司	二 级	昆山市	国 有
9	昆山市越秀广电投资发展有限公司	暂定二级	昆山市	有限责任公司
10	苏州工业园区娄葑建发房地产有限公司	二 级	工业园区	有限责任公司
四、销售房屋面积	**Floor Space of Building Sale**			
1	苏南阳光城置业（苏州）有限公司	暂定二级	吴中区	有限责任公司
2	张家港市金厦房地产开发公司	一 级	张家港市	国 有
3	中海海诚（苏州）房地产有限公司	暂定二级	相城区	有限责任公司
4	太仓碧桂园房地产开发有限公司	暂定二级	太仓市	有限责任公司
5	苏州旭高房地产开发有限公司	二 级	高新区、虎丘区	港澳台商独资
6	昆山国浩置业有限公司	暂定二级	昆山市	有限责任公司
7	森隆（昆山）置地有限公司	暂定二级	昆山市	有限责任公司
8	中海海纳（苏州）房地产有限公司	暂定二级	吴中区	港澳台商独资
9	昆山万科房地产有限公司	暂定二级	昆山市	有限责任公司
10	昆山乐建住房开发有限公司	暂定二级	昆山市	国 有

表11-14

建成投产的主要建设项目一览 (2016年)
KEY CONSTRUCTION PROJECTS COMPLETED (2016)

项目名称 Name of Projects	开工年月 Start of Construction	全部建成投产年月 Date of Projects Completed and Put into Use	新增生产能力或效益 Newly Increased Production Capacity and Benefit	累计投资总额(万元) Total Increased (10 000 yuan)
苏州轨道交通2号线延伸线	2012.09	2016.09	全长15.6公里，设13座车站，北延线1.82公里，东延线13.47公里	723 457
常嘉高速公路昆山至吴江段	2013.05	2016.12	六车道高速公路28.45公里，设计时速120公里	411 000
张家港疏港高速公路	2013.09	2016.10	六车道高速公路19.57公里，设计时速120公里	310 600
苏州市南环汇邻广场	2013.12	2016.06	总建筑面积约15万平方米	160 000
苏州安博金阊新城国际物流园区	2015.03	2016.12	总建筑面积约11万平方米	57 300
苏州高新区永旺梦乐城	2014.05	2016.08	建筑面积16万平方米，用地面积9.77万平方米商业综合体	150 000
苏州科技城医院及公共卫生中心	2015.10	2016.01	建筑面积为17.8万平方米，床位800张大型综合性三甲医院	120 000
苏州高新区宜家家居商场项目	2015.06	2016.07	建筑面积约6.56万平方米家居商场	56 000
苏州宇臻仓储有限公司仓储项目	2015.09	2016.12	总建筑面积为18.18万平方米，其中仓库17.9万平方米	47 536
第九届江苏省园艺博览会博览园工程	2014.03	2016.05	主展馆建筑面积4.2万平方米，绿化景观132.4万平方米	242 700
苏州南环西延二期工程	2012.08	2016.12	新建道路3.6公里，高架道路宽26米，地面路幅宽50-72米	180 000
第九届江苏省园博园周边道路工程	2015.04	2016.12	共建成4条道路，新建道路8.1公里，改造道路19公里	80 132
苏州圆融房地产开发有限公司(圆融新生活广场)	2014.02	2016.08	总建筑面积23.19万平方米	126 000
苏州市广济医院(苏州心理卫生中心)	2015.01	2016.12	总建筑面积34.53万平方米	92 600
苏州百汇大酒店	2010.01	2016.04	总建筑面积8.69万平方米	72 592
苏州新中天置业有限公司(中翔元和市民广场)	2013.05	2016.05	总建筑面积7.22万平方米	68 000
苏州勇进置业有限公司(永金商业广场)	2014.03	2016.10	总建筑面积13.3万平方米	50 000
苏州工业园区永旺梦乐城	2013.01	2016.02	总建筑面积21.59万平方米	117 025
苏州工业园区苏悦广场南广场项目	2013.03	2016.06	总建筑面积9.38万平方米	116 184
苏州工业园区苏悦广场北广场项目	2013.03	2016.06	总建筑面积5.79万平方米	71 789
苏州工业园区绿点科技-生产线设备项目	2015.05	2016.12	年产11700千件电脑配件	68 155
苏州工业园区景城邻里中心	2012.11	2016.10	总建筑面积9.66万平方米	56 849
苏州工业园区菁源公寓楼	2013.10	2016.06	总建筑面积6.8万平方米	45 288
苏州工业园区国泰万润办公楼	2013.08	2016.12	总建筑面积4.2万平方米	37 300
苏州工业园区微软定制大楼	2014.08	2016.08	总建筑面积4.4万平方米	35 964
苏州工业园区同程网研发办公楼	2013.01	2016.06	总建筑面积1.8万平方米	30 889

表11-14 续表 Continued

项目名称 Name of Projects	开工年月 Start of Construction	全部建成投产年月 Date of Projects Completed and Put into Use	新增生产能力或效益 Newly Increased Production Capacity and Benefit	累计投资总额(万元) Total Increased (10 000 yuan)
吴江东西快速干线工程	2013.07	2016.09	全长29.8公里，设计速度100km/h，共设桥梁32座	365 022
江苏派利帝纺织科技有限公司新建项目	2013.04	2016.10	建筑面积12.38万平方米，年产15万锭环锭紧密纺纱	140 487
吴江盛泽东方国际纺织城	2014.05	2016.10	项目总建筑面积17.28万平方米	112 637
吴江区生活垃圾焚烧发电项目	2015.05	2016.09	焚烧处理生活垃圾1500吨/日，年发电量1.5亿千瓦时	66 000
苏州湾实验小学新建项目	2015.06	2016.09	总建筑面积7万平方米，其中小学面积5.77万平方米	39 652
常熟生益科技有限公司新建覆铜板粘结片生产项目	2015.03	2016.11	年产1100万平方米覆铜板及2400万米商品粘结片	78 800
长春化工（江苏）有限公司年产16800吨铜箔扩建项目	2015.11	2016.12	年产16800吨铜箔	73 560
常熟飞煌工业设施发展有限公司高智能化起重机及设施项目	2014.09	2016.12	年产高智能化起重机1000台等	60 747
常熟阿科玛氟化工生产F1234yf技术改造项目	2014.09	2016.03	建筑面积7378平方米，年产7000吨四氟丙烯	43 310
常熟三爱富中昊六氟丙烯等产品技术改造项目	2014.03	2016.06	年产1万吨六氟丙烯、15万吨副产盐酸等	45 344
常熟威仕科大衡金属材料科技有限公司轻量化工用金属板项目	2016.04	2016.12	年产42万吨轻量化车用金属板	42 289
张家港扬子江石化有限公司年产120万吨丙乙烯项目	2013.01	2016.12	年产120万吨丙乙烯	361 400
张家港市曼巴特购物广场	2012.01	2016.12	总建筑面积约66.84万平方米商业综合体	303 030
张家港市百家桥小区拆迁安置房	2013.01	2016.01	总建筑面积约31.70万平方米安置房	200 000
张家港市滨江新城投资发展有限公司滨江大厦	2010.06	2016.12	总建筑面积15万平方米	74 133
张家港市水利局老海坝节点综合整治工程	2014.07	2016.06	防洪工程，总长约7250米，横向治理宽度约165—255米	54 296
张家港保税区多元机械设备制造有限公司扩建生产车间项目	2016.01	2016.12	年产200台建筑机械	45 600
昆山国显光电有限公司第5.5代有源矩阵有机发光显器件生产项目	2014.01	2016.12	玻璃基板加工能力每月4000片。	261 162
昆山富士康电发新一代数据传输器增资项目建设	2013.03	2016.12	年产新一代数据传输连接器6500万件	180 331
昆山神舟电脑有限公司厂房及设备项目	2009.01	2016.12	年产笔记本电脑360万台	95 219
昆山市高新商贸虹祺路商业街	2014.06	2016.12	建筑面积8.59万平方米	68 970
昆山花桥国际商务城博览中心新展馆	2014.12	2016.05	总建筑面积5.91万平方米，4-7号展厅及中展厅	63 200
圣厦药品食品包装新材料（昆山）有限公司包装材料生产项目	2012.06	2016.12	年产通用软包装材料4.25万吨及建造厂房3.8万平方米	50 000
和泰物流设施发展（苏州）有限公司新建物流仓储用房	2014.03	2016.12	物流仓储用房11.51万平方米	42 217
太仓图辉仓储管理有限公司新建物流园项目	2016.01	2016.09	新增仓储面积11.99万平方米	35 661

主 要 统 计 指 标 解 释

全社会固定资产投资 是以货币形式表现的在一定时期内全社会建造和购置固定资产的工作量以及与此有关的费用的总称。该指标是反映固定资产投资规模、结构和发展速度的综合性指标,又是观察工程进度和考核投资效果的重要依据。全社会固定资产投资按登记注册类型可分为国有、集体、个体、联营、股份制、外商、港澳台商、其他等，由建设项目投资和房地产开发投资两部分组成。

建设项目投资 指各种登记注册类型的企业、事业、行政单位及个体户进行的计划总投资(或实际需要总投资)500万元及500万元以上的建设项目投资。

房地产开发投资 指各种登记注册类型的房地产开发公司、商品房建设公司及其他房地产开发法人单位和附属于其他法人单位实际从事房地产开发或经营活动的单位统一开发的包括统代建、拆迁还建的住宅、厂房、仓库、饭店、宾馆、度假村、写字楼、办公楼等房屋建筑物和配套的服务设施，土地开发工程（如道路、给水、排水、供电、供热、通讯、平整场地等基础设施工程）的投资；不包括单纯的土地交易活动。

固定资产投资的资金来源 根据固定资产投资的资金来源不同，分为国家预算内资金、国内贷款、利用外资、自筹资金和其他资金。

(1)国家预算内资金：分为财政拨款和财政安排的贷款两部分。包括中央财政的基本建设基金(分经营性基金和非经营性基金两部分)、专项支出(如煤代油专项等)、收回再贷、贴息资金，财政安排的挖潜改造和新产品试制支出、城建支出、商业部门简易建筑支出、不发达地区发展基金等资金中用于固定资产投资的资金；地方财政中由国家统筹安排的资金等。

(2)国内贷款：指报告期固定资产投资单位向银行及非银行金融机构借入的用于固定资产投资的各种国内借款，包括银行利用自有资金及吸收的存款发放的贷款、上级主管部门拨入的国内贷款、国家专项贷款、地方财政专项资金安排的贷款、国内储备贷款、周转贷款等。

(3)利用外资：指报告期收到的用于固定资产建造和购置的国外资金(包括设备、材料、技术在内)。包括对外借款(外国政府、国际金融组织贷款、出口信贷、外国银行商业贷款、对外发行债券和股票)、外商直接投资及外商其他投资。不包括我国自有外汇资金(国家外汇、地方外汇、留成外汇、调剂外汇和中国银行自有资金发行的外汇贷款等)。计算利用外资时，需要折算成人民币，折算中所使用的外汇汇率按现汇计算，即按使用外汇时的汇率计算。

(4)自筹资金：指固定资产投资单位报告期收到的，由各地区、各部门及企、事业单位筹集用于固定资产投资的预算外资金，包括中央各部门、各级地方和企、事业单位的自筹资金。

(5)其他资金：指在报告期收到的除以上各种资金之外其他用于固定资产投资的资金，包括企业或金融机构通过发行各种债券筹集到的资金、群众集资、个人资金、无偿捐赠的资金及其他单位拨入的资金等。

固定资产投资按国民经济行业分 根据建设项目建成投产后的主要产品或主要用途及社会经济活动性质来确定国民经济行业。一般情况下，一个建设项目或一个企业、事业单位只能属于一种国民经济行业。

固定资产投资按隶属关系分 是按建设单位或企业、事业、行政单位的主管上级机关确定的。

（1）中央：是指中共中央、人大常委会和国务院各部、委、局、总公司以及直属机构直接领导的建设项目和企业、事业、行政单位。这些单位的固定资产投资计划由国务院各部门直接编制和下达，建设中所需物资、主要设备以及建设中的问题都由中央有关部门安排和解决。

（2）地方：是由省（自治区、直辖市）、地区（州、盟、省辖市）、县（旗、县级市）三级政府及业务主管部门直接领导和管理的建设项目、企业、事业、行政单位。地方项目还包括不隶属以上各级政府及主管部门的建设项目和企业、事业单位，如外商投资企业和无主管部门的企业等。

固定资产投资按建设性质分 根据整个建设项目情况来确定。建设项目的性质一般分为新建、扩建、改建和技术改造、迁建、恢复。房地产开发单位、农村投资、城镇工矿区私人建房投资不划分建设性质。

(1)新建：一般指从无到有开始建设的企业、事业和行政单位或建设项目。现有企业、事业、行政单位一般不属于新建。但如有的单位原有基础很小，经过建设后新增的固定资产价值超过该企、事业、行政单位原有固定资产价值(原值)三倍以上的也应作为新建。

(2)扩建：指在厂内或其他地点，为扩大原有产品的生产能力(或效益)或增加新的产品生产能力，而增建主要的生产车间(或主要工程)、分厂、独立的生产线。行政、事业单位在原单位增建业务用房(如学校增建教学用房、医院增建门诊部、病房等)也作为扩建。

现有企、事业单位为扩大原有主要产品生产能力或增加新的产品生产能力，增建一个或几个主要生产车间(或主要工程)、分厂，同时进行一些更新改造工程的，也应作为扩建。

(3)改建和技术改造：指现有企业、事业单位，对原有设施进行技术改造或更新(包括相应配套的辅助性生产、生活福利设施) 的建设项目。现有企业、事业单位为适应市场变化的需要，而改变企业的主要产品种类(如军工企业转产民用品等) 的建设项目，应作为改建。原有产品生产作业线由于各工序(车间)之间能力不平衡，为填平补齐充分发挥原有生产能力而增建不增加本企业主要产品设计能力的车间，也应作为改建。技术改造是指企业、事业单位在现有基础上，用先进的技术代替落后的技术，用先进的工艺和装备代替落后的工艺和装备，以改变企业落后的技术经济面貌，实现以内涵为主的扩大再生产，达到提高产品质量、促进产品更新换代、节约能源、降低消耗、扩大生产规模、全面提高社会经济效益的目的。技术改造具体包括以下内容：机器设备和工具的更新改造；生产工艺改革、节约能源和原材料的改造；厂房建筑和公共设施的改造；劳动条件和生产环境的改造等。

固定资产投资按构成分 固定资产投资活动按其工作内容和实现方式分为建筑安装工程，设备、工具、器具购置，其他费用三个部分。

(1)建筑安装工程(建筑安装工作量)：指各种房屋、建筑物的建造工程和各种设备、装置的安装工程。包括各种房屋建造工程；各种用途设备基础和各种工业窑炉的砌筑工程及金属结构工程；为施工而进行的各种准备工作和临时工程以及完工后的清理工作等；铁路、道路的铺设，矿井的开凿及石油管道的架设等；水利工程；防空地下建筑等特殊工程；列入房屋工程预算内的暖气、卫生、通风、照明、煤气等设备的价值及装设油饰工程；列入建筑工程预算内的各种管道(蒸汽、压缩空气、石油、给排水等管道)、电力、电讯电缆导线等的敷设工程；以及各种机械设备的安装工程；为测定安装工程质量，对设备进行的试运工作；房地产开发单位进行的商品房屋开发建设工程、土地开发工程。

在安装工程中，不包括被安装设备本身的价值。

(2)设备、工具、器具购置：指建设单位或企、事业单位购置或自制的，达到固定资产标准的设备、工具、器具的价值。新建单位及扩建单位的新建车间，按照设计或计划要求购置或自制的全部设备、工具、器具，不论是否达到固定资产标准均计入“设备、工具、器具购置”中。

(3)其他费用：指在固定资产建造和购置过程中发生的，除上述几项内容以外的各种应分摊计入固定资产的费用。

施工项目 指报告期内进行过建筑或安装施工活动的项目。凡是报告期内施过工的建设项目，不论施工时间长短，均作为施工项目统计。施工项目个数可以反映一定时期固定资产投资的实际规模，与同期全部建成投产项目个数相比，可以从建设速度的角度反映固定资产投资的效果。根据建设项目施工活动的不同性质，施工项目又分为：本年正式施工项目、本年收尾项目和以前年度全部停缓建项目。

全部建成投产项目 工业项目指设计文件规定形成生产能力的主体工程及其相应配套的辅助设施全部建成，经负荷试运转，证明具备生产设计规定合格产品的条件，并经过验收鉴定合格或达到竣工验收标准，与生产性工程配套的生活福利设施可以满足近期正常生产的需要，正式移交生产的建设项目。非工业项目指设计文件规定的主体工程和相应的配套工程全部建成，能够发挥设计规定的全部效益，经验收鉴定合格或达到竣工验收标准，正式移交使用的建设项目。

新增生产能力(或工程效益) 指通过固定资产投资活动而增加的设计能力(或工程效益)，该指标是以实物形态表现的反映固定资产投资成果的指标，也是考核投资经济效果的重要依据之一。

新增生产能力(或工程效益)一般有以下几种表现形式：

(1)用产品数量表示，以工程在单位时间内(一般是一年)所能生产的产品数量(即年产量)表示。如原煤开采用万吨/年表示，化学农药用吨 / 年表示，拖拉机制造用台 / 年表示等。某些化工产品由于含量差别较大，按其设计含量计算折合量表示，如硫酸、纯碱、烧碱等。

(2)用单位时间内所能处理的原料数量表示，以工程每天(或小时)所能处理原料的数量表示。如机制糖工程日处理原料吨，食用植物油日处理原料吨，城市污水处理能力用万吨 / 日表示等。

(3)用新增加的主要设备的数量或容量表示，如新增棉布织机、丝织机等台数，毛纺锭等锭数，发电厂新增发电机组容量用千瓦表示等。

(4)用建筑物容积、容量、面积、长度表示，是非工业项目或工程新增效益的一种表现形式。如铁路投产里程、新建公路、水库容量、粮食仓库、学校学生席位、医院病床、有效灌溉面积等。

根据工程的特点，有时需要用两种或两种以上的复合计量单位表示新增生产能力(或工程效益)，如新增内燃机生产能力同时用年产台数、千瓦数表示等。

为了规范新增生产能力(或工程效益)的名称和计算单位，国家统计局制订了《新增生产能力(或工程效益)目录及代码》。各固定资产投资单位在统计新增生产能力(或工程效益)时，必须按目录中规定的名称、计量单位和代码填报。

房屋建筑面积 指房屋建筑物勒脚以上外墙外围的水平截面面积，包括房屋建筑物的有效面积和结构面积。该指标是从实物形态上反映建设规模和建设成果的重要指标之一，也是检查工程形象进度、计算工程造价、分析投资效果、研究施工任务和建筑材料之间平衡情况的重要依据。

住宅建筑面积 指施工和竣工房屋建筑面积中供居住用的房屋建筑面积。

施工面积 指报告期内施工的全部房屋建筑面积。包括本期新开工的面积和上期开工跨入本期继续施工的房屋面积，以及上期已停建在本期恢复施工的房屋面积。本期竣工和本期施工后又停缓建的房屋，其建筑面积仍计入本期房屋施工面积中。

竣工面积 指在报告期内房屋建筑按照设计要求已经全部完工，达到住人和使用条件，经验收鉴定合格(或达到竣工验收标准)，正式移交使用单位的各栋房屋建筑面积的总和。

房屋建筑面积竣工率 指一定时期内房屋竣工面积占同期房屋施工面积的比率。

新增固定资产 指报告期内已经完成建造和购置过程，并已交付生产或使用单位的固定资产价值。该指标是表示固定资产投资成果的价值指标，也是反映建设进度，计算固定资产投资效果的重要指标。

项目建成投产率 指一定时期内全部建成投产项目个数与同期施工项目个数的比率。该指标是从建设单位建设速度的角度反映投资效果的指标。

固定资产交付使用率 指一定时期新增固定资产与同期完成投资额的比率。该指标是反映固定资产动用速度，衡量建设过程中宏观投资效果的综合指标。由于新增固定资产是较长时期内形成的结果，而投资额则是当年完成的，因此，该指标一般适宜于反映较长时期内固定资产的动用情况。

商品房销售面积 指报告期内出售商品房屋的合同总面积(即双方签署的正式买卖合同中所确定的建筑面积)。由现房销售建筑面积和期房销售建筑面积两部分组成。

商品房销售额 指报告期内出售商品房屋的合同总价款(即双方签署的正式买卖合同中所确定的合同总价)。该指标与商品房销售面积同口径，由现房销售额和期房销售额两部分组成。

EXPLANATORY NOTES ON MAIN STATISTICAL INDICATORS

Total Investment in Fixed Assets in the Whole Country refers to the volume of activities in construction and purchases of fixed assets of the whole country and related fees, expressed in monetary terms during the reference period. It is a comprehensive indicator which shows the size, structure and growth of the investment in fixed assets, providing a basis for observing the progress of construction projects and evaluating results of investment. Total investment in fixed assets in the whole country includes, by type of ownership, the investment by State-owned units, collective-owned units, individuals, joint ownership units, share-holding units, as well as investments by entrepreneurs from foreign countries and from Hong Kong, Macao and Taiwan, and by other units, by investment in construction projects and investment in real estate development two parts.

Investment in Construction Projects refers to construction projects involving a total planned (or required) investment of 5 million yuan and over by enterprises of various types of ownership, institutions, administrative units and individuals in urban areas.

Investment in Real Estate Development refers to investment by real estate development companies, commercialized buildings construction companies and other real estate development units of various types of ownership in the construction of buildings, such as residential buildings, factory buildings, warehouses, hotels, guesthouses, holiday villages, office buildings, and the complementary service facilities and land development projects, such as roads, water supply, water drainage, power supply, heating supply, telecommunications, land leveling and other infrastructural projects. It does not include activities in pure land transactions.

Sources of Funds for Investment in Fixed Assets are categorized as funds from the State budget, domestic loans, foreign investment, self-raised funds, and others, depending on the sources of investment.

(1) Fund from the State budget consists of budgetary appropriation and loans from the State budget. More specifically, it includes, from the budget of the central government, capital construction fund (operation fund and non-operational fund), special expenses (e.g. expenses on substituting petroleum with coal), loans from repayment, discount fund, expenses on innovation and trial production of new products, expenses on urban construction, expenses on temporary construction from business departments, development fund for less developed areas, as well as local budgetary fund transferred from the central budget.

(2) Domestic loans refer to loans of various forms borrowed by investing units from banks and non-bank financial institutions during the reference period for the purpose of investment in fixed assets, including loans issued by banks from their self-owned funds and deposit, loans appropriated by higher authorities, special loans by government, loans arranged by local government from special funds, domestic reserve loan, and working loan.

(3) Foreign investment refers to foreign funds received during the reference period for the construction and purchase of investment in fixed assets (covering equipment, materials and technology), including foreign borrowings (loans from foreign governments and international financial institutions, export credit, commercial loans from foreign banks, issue of bonds and stocks overseas), foreign direct investment and other foreign investments. Excluded from this category is capital in foreign exchanges owned by China (foreign exchanges owned by the central and local governments, foreign exchanges retained by enterprises, foreign exchanges by enterprises through the regulating mechanism, loans in foreign exchanges issued by the Bank of China with its own fund, etc.). In calculating the utilization of foreign capital, foreign currencies are converted into Chinese Renminbi applying the current exchange rate when the foreign capitals are actually used.

(4) Self-raised funds refer to extra-budgetary funds for investment in fixed assets received during the reference period by investing units from central government ministries, local governments, enterprises and institutions, including their self-raised funds.

(5) Others refer to funds for investment in fixed assets received from sources other than those listed above, including capital raised through issuing bonds by enterprises or financial institutions, funds raised from individuals and through donations, and funds transferred from other units.

Investment in Fixed Assets by Sector The classification of construction projects by sector is determined by the major products or the purpose of the projects when they are put into production or use, and by the nature of their social economic activities. In general, one project or one enterprise or institution can only be classified into one sector.

Investment in Fixed Assets by Jurisdiction of Management refers to the classification of investment by the competent authorities under which investment is made by construction units, enterprises, institutions or administrative units.

(1) Central investment refers to the investment in projects or by enterprises, institutions or administrative units which are under the direct leadership and management of the State Council and of the national commissions, ministries, agencies and State-owned large corporations. Various ministries and departments of the State Council prepare and implement plans for investment in fixed assets by those departments, and arrange and ensure the supply of materials and key equipment required for the projects.

(2) Local investment refers to the investment in projects or by enterprises, institutions or administrative units which are under the direct leadership and management of departments under the provincial, prefecture and county governments. Also included are projects by foreign-invested enterprises and enterprises without competent managing authorities.

Investment in Fixed Assets by Type of Construction Construction projects in general can be classified, by the type of construction, into new construction, expansion, reconstruction and technical transformation, moving and restoration. However, investment by type of construction is not applied to investment by real-estate development units, investment in rural areas and private investment in housing construction in urban areas and in industrial and mining areas.

(1) New construction in general refers to construction projects, which start from scratch, of enterprises, institutions, administrative agencies. Construction in existing enterprises, institutions or agencies is generally not considered as new construction. In case the size of the existing unit is quite small, and the value of newly added fixed assets is more than three times of the original value, the expansion will be considered as new construction.

(2) Expansion refers to construction of new major production workshop, branch factory or independent production line within a factory or in other locations, for the purpose of increasing the production capacity (or improving efficiency) or adding new production capacity. Newly constructed accommodation for the operation of institutions and administrative organizations (such as newly constructed buildings for teaching in schools, buildings for clinics or wards in hospitals, etc.) are also classified as expansion.

Also included in expansion are investments by existing enterprises or institutions in building major production line(s) or branch factory(ies) along with some work on innovation, for the purpose of expanding the production capacity of original products or producing new products.

(3) Reconstruction and technical transformation refers to construction projects by existing enterprises or institutions in innovation or technical transformation of the old facilities (including auxiliary production equipment and welfare facilities). Also considered as reconstruction is the construction of new workshops by the existing enterprises or institutions to change the variety of products to meet the market demand (such as the production of civil products by defence industries), or to bring the designed production capacity into full play through a more balanced production process on production lines. Technical transformation refers to replacement of old technology or equipment by new technology or equipment, in order to expand the reproduction through improvement of technology contents in production, to improve product quality, to promote new products, to save energy, to reduce consumption, to expand the production scale and to improve overall social-economic efficiency. Contents of technical transformation include: updating of machinery, equipment and tools; reforming production process by using energy or materials saving technology; construction of factory workshops and transformation of public facilities; improvement of working conditions and environment, etc.

Investment in Fixed Assets by Structure By their contents and the mode of implementation, investment activities are classified into 3 categories, i.e. construction and installation, purchase of equipment and instrument, and other expenses.

(1) Construction and installation (work volume of construction and installation) refers to the construction of houses and buildings and the installation of various kinds of equipment and instruments. They include construction of houses; equipment foundations, industrial kilns and stoves, and metal structure work; preparation works and temporary works for project construction, and clearing up works post project construction; pavement of railways and roads, drilling of mines and putting up of oil pipes; construction of water conservancy; construction of underground air-raid shelters and construction of other special projects; value of equipment for heating, sanitation, ventilation, lighting, gas, painting, etc. that are covered by the budget of housing projects; laying out of various pipelines (for steam, compressed air, petroleum, tap water and sewage) and wiring and cabling for electric power and for communications; installation of various machinery and equipment; testing operation for pre-testing the quality of installation projects, and land and other development work conducted by real estate developers for commercialized housing. The value of equipment installed is itself not included in the value of installation projects.

(2) Purchase of equipment and instruments refers to the total value of equipment, tools, and instruments purchased or self-produced which come up to the cut-off point for fixed assets by the construction units or investing enterprises or institutions. Equipment, tools and instruments purchased or self-produced for new workshops by newly established or expanded units are categorized as "purchase of equipment and instruments" no matter whether they come up to the cut-off point for fixed assets.

(3) Other expenses refer to expenses arising during the construction or purchase of fixed assets other than those mentioned above.

Projects under Construction refer to projects with construction and installation activities undertaken in the reference period. All projects that have construction activities undertaken during the reference period are reported as projects under construction irrespective of the length of construction work. The number of projects under construction can reflect the actual size of investment in fixed assets during a given period, and when compared with the number of projects completed and put into use during the same period, it demonstrates the results of investment in fixed assets from the angle of the speed of the construction. Depending on the nature of construction activities, projects under construction can also be classified into projects beginning construction in current year, winding-up projects in current year and stopped or suspended projects in previous years (with resumption of work in current year).

Projects Completed and Put into Use Industrial projects refer to the major projects and anxilliary facilities having been completed in accordance with the design documents, resulting in forming production capacity and having checked and accepted after relevant tests, while the living and welfare facilities having been completed and being capable of ensuring normal production. Non-industrial projects refer to the major projects and anxilliary facilities which have been completed in accordance with the design documents ; have been checked, accepted after relevant examination; and have been formally delivered for use.

Newly Increased Production Capacity (or Project Efficiency) refers to the increase in design capacity (or project efficiency) through investment in fixed assets, which reflects the accomplishment of investment in fixed assets in physical form and serves as an important basis for evaluating the economic efficiency of investment.

The newly increased production capacity (project efficiency) are usually expressed in one of the following forms:

(1) volume of output of products, i.e. the volume of output that the project can produce during a given period (usually a year). For instance, the capacity in coal mining is expressed in 10,000 tons/year, the capacity in producing chemical pesticides expressed in ton/year, the capacity in producing tractors in tractor/year, etc. For some chemical products where the effective contents differ significantly, the production capacity is expressed as the designed effective content equivalent, such as in the case of sulphuric acid, soda ash, caustic soda, etc;

(2) volume of raw materials processed per unit of time, i.e. the volume of raw materials that could be processed by the project per day (or per hour), such as tons of materials processed per day by a sugar refining project or edible vegetable oil project, or tons of urban sewage processed per day, etc;

(3) number or capacity of major equipment increased, such as number of cotton or silk looms increased, wool spindles increased, or capacity (in kilowatts) of power generators increased, etc;

(4) physical measures (volume, capacity, area, and length) of construction, which is typical for non-industrial projects, for instance, the length of railways put into operation, the length of highways, the capacity of reservoirs, the capacity of warehouses, the floor space of housing projects, capacity for new students in schools or beds in hospitals, areas under new irrigation project, etc.

The special features of projects may sometimes call for the combined use of two or more measurements to reflect the increase in production capacity (or project efficiency); for instance, the new capacity for the production of internal combustion engines is expressed in sets per year and kilowatts per year simultaneously.

To standardize the nomenclature and unit of measurement for newly increased production capacity (or project efficiency), the National Bureau of Statistics has developed the *Nomenclature and Codes for New Production Capacity (Project Efficiency)*. All reporting units with investment activities are required to follow these two nomenclatures in reporting statistics on new production capacity (project efficiency).

Floor Space of Buildings under Construction refers to the total floor space of the horizontal section of outer walls above the plinth of the building, including the effective area and the area occupied by the structure. This indicator is one of the important indicators in physical terms to reflect the scale and accomplishment of the construction industry and also an important basis for monitoring the progress, calculating the cost, analyzing the efficiency and studying the supply of building materials in relation to the construction projects.

Floor Space of Residential Buildings refers to the floor space of the residential buildings among the total space of buildings under construction or completed.

Floor Space under Construction refers to total floor space of all buildings under construction during the reference period, including floor space of newly started buildings during the reference period, floor space of construction extended from the previous period to the current period, and floor space of construction suspended during the previous period and resumed in the current period. Floor space of construction completed in the current period, and floor space of construction started and then suspended in the current period are also included in the floor space under construction of the current year.

Floor Space Completed refers to the floor space of all buildings completed in the reference period, which have been appraised and accepted (or come up to the designed standards) and have been transferred to owner units.

Completion Rate of Floor Space of Buildings refers to the ratio of the floor space of buildings completed in a certain period of time to the floor space of buildings under construction in the same period.

Newly Increased Fixed Assets refer to the newly increased value of fixed assets, constructed or purchased, that have been transferred to the investors. This is an indicator that demonstrates the results of investment in fixed assets in monetary terms, and an important indicator to reflect the speed of construction and to calculate the efficiency of investment.

Rate of Construction Projects Completed and Put into Use refers to the ratio of the number of construction projects completed and put into use in a certain period of time to the number of projects under construction in the same period. This reflects the investment efficiency from the perspective of the speed of projects construction.

Rate of Projects of Fixed Assets Completed and Put into Operation refers to the ratio of the newly increased fixed assets to the total investment made in the same period. This is a comprehensive indicator reflecting the speed of the employment of fixed assets and the investment efficiency at the macro-level. As the newly increase fixed assets is the result of a long period while the investment is completed in the current year, this indicator is expected to be used to reflect the employment of fixed assets over a long period of time.

Area of Commercialized Housing Sold refers to total contracted area of commercialized housing (i.e. area of floor space as designated in the formal contracts signed by both sides) during the reference time. It constitutes floor space of completed housing and floor space of future housing.

Value of Commercialized Housing Sold refers to the total contracted value (i.e. value of sales/purchase for selling/purchase of commercialized housing as designated in the contract signed by both sides) during the reference time. This indicator has the same coverage as the area of commercialized housing sold, which constitutes floor space of completed housing and floor space of housing yet to be completed.

十二、企业调查

CHAPTER 12 ENTERPRISES SURVEY

12 企业调查
ENTERPRISES SURVEY

主要统计指标
MAJOR STATISTICAL INDICATORS

2016年末苏州市总部经济企业数	Number of Suzhou Corporate Headquarters	268	个	unit
2016年苏州市总部经济营业收入	Business Income of Suzhou Corporate Headquarters	16 150.13	亿元	100 million yuan
2016年苏州市总部经济利润总额	Total Profits of Suzhou Corporate Headquarters	850.58	亿元	100 million yuan
2016年末苏州市企业集团数	Number of Suzhou Enterprises Groups	93	个	unit
2016年苏州市企业集团营业收入	Business Income of Suzhou Enterprises Groups	10 728.74	亿元	100 million yuan
2016年苏州市企业集团利润总额	Total Profits of Suzhou Enterprises Groups	426.20	亿元	100 million yuan
2016年末苏州市上市公司数	Number of Suzhou Listing Corporation	113	个	unit
2016年苏州市上市公司营业收入	Business Income of Suzhou Listing Corporation	2 864.24	亿元	100 million yuan
2016年苏州市上市公司利润总额	Total Profits of Suzhou Listing Corporation	245.80	亿元	100 million yuan
2016年末苏州市总部企业数	Number of Suzhou Corporate Headquarters	86	个	unit
2016年苏州市总部企业营业收入	Business Income of Suzhou Corporate Headquarters	7 910.43	亿元	100 million yuan
2016年苏州市总部企业利润总额	Total Profits of Suzhou Corporate Headquarters	277.37	亿元	100 million yuan

表12-1

总部经济主要经济指标 (2016年)

单位：万元

项　　目	Item	单位数 (个) Number of Units (unit)	从业人员(人) Number of Employed Persons (person)
总部经济	**Corporate Headquarters**	**268**	**834 438**
按企业类型分	**Classified by Enterprise Type**		
# 企业集团	Enterprises Groups	93	445 992
# 上市公司	Listing Corporation	113	233 995
# 总部企业	Corporate Headquarters	86	311 563
# 重点企业	Key Enterprises	22	61 321
按公司控股情况分	**Classified by Number of Shares Held by Companies**		
国有控股	Stately Majority Share Holding	41	102 206
集体控股	Collectively Majority Share Holding	19	43 864
私人控股	Privately Majority Share Holding	146	547 212
港澳台商控股	Majority Share Holding by Investors from Hong Kong, Macau and Taiwan	28	67 687
外商控股	Majority Share Holding by Foreign Investors	34	73 469
按总部经济主营行业分	**Classified by Main Field of Operation**		
工　业	Industry	161	472 116
建筑业	Construction	18	100 819
批发和零售业	Wholesale and Retail Sale Trades	33	94 305
交通运输、仓储和邮政业	Transportation, Logistics and Postal	6	14 371
住宿和餐饮业	Accommodation and Catering Services	1	11 948
信息传输、软件和信息技术服务业	Information Transmission, Software and Information Technology Services	6	28 123
金融业	Financial Industries	8	15 359
房地产业	Real Estate	5	11 961
租赁和商务服务业	Leasing and Business Services	22	78 686
科学研究和技术服务业	Scientific Research and Technical Services	6	6 399
水利、环境和公共设施管理业	Water Conservancy, Environment and Public Facilities Management	1	351
文化、体育和娱乐业	Culture, Sports and Entertainment	1	–

MAIN ECONOMIC INDICATORS ON CORPORATE HEADQUARTERS(2016)

(10 000 yuan)

# 研发人员 Research and Development Personnel	从业人员劳动报酬 Labor Reward of Employed Persons	#研发人员劳动报酬 Labor Reward of Research and Development Personnel	固定资产投资完成额 Actually Completed Investment in Fixed Assets	年末资产总计 Total Assets at the End of Year	固定资产净值 Net Value of Fixed Assets
63 382	**7 876 190**	**618 451**	**5 558 547**	**221 233 449**	**30 816 341**
29 614	3 417 793	255 843	2 847 275	105 155 573	20 118 405
25 637	3 094 097	258 976	2 126 473	72 841 629	7 643 010
29 459	2 694 899	300 135	2 722 765	103 906 063	14 627 044
3 079	550 022	41 611	199 296	8 174 001	2 254 075
6 345	1 334 928	58 169	674 204	68 250 254	5 427 762
2 031	385 362	16 461	194 421	30 698 379	1 318 074
46 756	4 855 476	459 000	3 736 803	97 673 835	19 966 212
2 296	574 337	32 013	568 526	9 994 883	1 516 906
5 954	726 087	52 808	384 593	14 616 098	2 587 387
41 063	4 377 323	379 187	3 353 084	95 527 766	21 220 669
3 927	943 274	50 835	40 842	10 508 554	492 152
4 922	816 492	33 302	1 309 230	24 475 911	3 974 946
199	136 365	2 047	56 776	1 370 184	383 849
–	35 997	–	4 546	51 246	14 550
4 868	318 546	62 317	237 879	2 738 590	1 308 631
62	394 998	2 383	195 126	60 538 319	670 771
72	79 581	650	18 945	3 650 260	348 355
6 474	658 822	70 675	280 285	20 909 804	2 006 993
1 795	106 664	17 055	47 314	963 252	300 755
–	8 128	–	14 520	499 563	94 670
–	–	–	–	–	–

表12-1 续表 1

单位：万元

项　　目	Item	累计折旧 Accumulated Depreciation	本年折旧 Depreciation Charge of the Year
总部经济	**Corporate Headquarters**	**22 367 488**	**3 164 567**
按企业类型分	**Classified by Enterprise Type**		
# 企业集团	Enterprises Groups	15 387 081	1 947 198
# 上市公司	Listing Corporation	4 049 254	891 046
# 总部企业	Corporate Headquarters	10 804 426	1 419 028
# 重点企业	Key Enterprises	2 230 941	261 679
按公司控股情况分	**Classified by Number of Shares Held by Companies**		
国有控股	Stately Majority Share Holding	4 223 104	543 953
集体控股	Collectively Majority Share Holding	1 156 386	141 582
私人控股	Privately Majority Share Holding	13 969 591	2 035 734
港澳台商控股	Majority Share Holding by Investors from Hong Kong, Macau and Taiwan	793 250	134 070
外商控股	Majority Share Holding by Foreign Investors	2 225 157	309 228
按总部经济主营行业分	**Classified by Main Field of Operation**		
工　业	Industry	16 331 269	2 275 997
建筑业	Construction	641 889	59 513
批发和零售业	Wholesale and Retail Sale Trades	1 650 402	289 314
交通运输、仓储和邮政业	Transportation, Logistics and Postal	320 139	39 508
住宿和餐饮业	Accommodation and Catering Services	18 134	2 792
信息传输、软件和信息技术服务业	Information Transmission, Software and Information Technology Services	1 619 863	235 228
金融业	Financial Industries	265 786	51 841
房地产业	Real Estate	161 349	19 434
租赁和商务服务业	Leasing and Business Services	1 207 617	157 154
科学研究和技术服务业	Scientific Research and Technical Services	100 874	24 879
水利、环境和公共设施管理业	Water Conservancy, Environment and Public Facilities Management	50 166	8 907
文化、体育和娱乐业	Culture, Sports and Entertainment	–	–

Continued 1

(10 000 yuan)

累计对外投资 Accumulated Value of Investing Abroad	# 本年对外投资 Value of Investing Abroad of the Year	存 货 Inventory	流动资产年平均余额 Annual Average Balance of Circulation Funds	年末负债合计 Total Liabilities at the End of Year	流动负债 Liquid Liabilities	年末股东(所有者)权益合计 Total Creditors Equity
10 559 942	**1 697 041**	**24 372 883**	**111 247 787**	**151 093 584**	**101 372 354**	**70 139 865**
6 341 412	702 160	12 938 787	59 257 048	69 516 439	54 581 685	35 639 134
3 751 894	1 058 455	9 092 518	37 113 726	47 141 571	31 330 066	25 700 058
3 148 423	467 738	7 900 571	49 307 520	74 036 585	46 324 156	29 869 478
141 784	10 000	818 168	4 659 200	4 232 331	3 546 449	3 941 670
3 106 118	494 512	4 517 697	32 825 241	53 466 365	28 538 460	14 783 889
1 833 187	457 644	5 159 672	9 370 278	25 512 970	12 624 858	5 185 409
5 152 548	714 269	11 636 265	53 242 818	58 287 567	47 597 697	39 386 268
138 614	17 612	1 642 083	6 839 092	6 372 721	5 658 068	3 622 162
329 475	13 004	1 417 166	8 970 358	7 453 961	6 953 271	7 162 137
5 023 096	726 905	11 763 506	50 769 831	52 579 536	44 141 176	42 948 230
123 341	67 067	1 002 488	9 093 439	7 939 213	7 705 963	2 569 341
906 097	56 580	2 670 154	16 059 593	16 463 194	13 283 817	8 012 717
144 614	7 515	10 347	500 228	635 109	469 293	735 075
–	–	1 477	9 281	23 905	22 259	27 341
57 686	14 197	5 907	309 042	1 611 040	969 801	1 127 550
1 950 141	493 064	4 497 342	18 698 462	53 887 565	21 438 689	6 650 754
507 741	31 720	1 557 533	1 422 737	2 230 472	1 569 320	1 419 788
1 646 625	287 861	2 839 791	13 898 169	15 110 616	11 282 387	5 799 188
1 942	1 321	1 653	344 344	419 332	328 392	543 920
198 659	10 811	22 685	142 661	193 602	161 257	305 961
–	–	–	–	–	–	–

表12-1 续表 2

单位：万元

项　目	Item	营业收入 Business Revenue	营业成本 Business Costs
总部经济	**Corporate Headquarters**	**161 501 283**	**140 303 791**
按企业类型分	**Classified by Enterprise Type**		
# 企业集团	Enterprises Groups	107 287 404	97 046 004
# 上市公司	Listing Corporation	28 642 448	23 526 829
# 总部企业	Corporate Headquarters	79 104 329	70 768 332
# 重点企业	Key Enterprises	9 721 365	6 823 704
按公司控股情况分	**Classified by Number of Shares Held by Companies**		
国有控股	Stately Majority Share Holding	28 404 980	24 384 031
集体控股	Collectively Majority Share Holding	4 754 599	3 786 956
私人控股	Privately Majority Share Holding	103 199 676	94 061 127
港澳台商控股	Majority Share Holding by Investors from Hong Kong, Macau and Taiwan	13 036 107	9 582 965
外商控股	Majority Share Holding by Foreign Investors	12 105 921	8 488 712
按总部经济主营行业分	**Classified by Main Field of Operation**		
工　业	Industry	95 684 561	84 523 149
建筑业	Construction	9 804 841	8 915 779
批发和零售业	Wholesale and Retail Sale Trades	35 460 958	30 255 497
交通运输、仓储和邮政业	Transportation, Logistics and Postal	609 677	500 621
住宿和餐饮业	Accommodation and Catering Services	215 998	111 694
信息传输、软件和信息技术服务业	Information Transmission, Software and Information Technology Services	3 869 809	3 175 576
金融业	Financial Industries	2 437 652	1 545 655
房地产业	Real Estate	1 127 097	796 740
租赁和商务服务业	Leasing and Business Services	11 846 343	10 189 634
科学研究和技术服务业	Scientific Research and Technical Services	347 507	217 064
水利、环境和公共设施管理业	Water Conservancy, Environment and Public Facilities Management	96 840	72 382
文化、体育和娱乐业	Culture, Sports and Entertainment	–	–

Continued 2

(10 000 yuan)

营业税金及附加 Business Tax and Surcharges	出口额 Value of Exports	利润总额 Total Profits	应交所得税 Income Taxes Payable	应交增值税 Added Value Tax Payable	研究开发费用 Expenditure for Research and Development
1 048 241	**17 257 496**	**8 505 793**	**1 623 736**	**1 856 752**	**2 240 178**
579 705	8 466 746	4 261 981	833 730	1 059 489	1 214 002
172 741	6 639 318	2 458 014	396 784	371 411	697 308
337 237	4 422 513	2 773 695	558 047	747 463	793 845
216 345	1 257 894	1 184 370	227 414	255 264	330 157
446 632	5 622 463	2 066 688	475 585	357 211	139 579
44 480	264 426	510 040	89 111	59 369	59 369
417 814	7 536 389	3 713 834	713 684	1 091 583	1 571 899
67 794	1 055 549	1 086 189	167 444	167 750	126 144
71 521	2 778 669	1 129 042	177 912	180 839	343 187
329 987	10 389 656	4 545 104	789 548	1 135 625	1 854 072
121 962	219 796	409 088	71 990	109 452	105 048
269 603	4 566 019	1 791 530	300 869	417 152	71 292
3 990	–	79 381	23 775	13 582	3 643
4 342	–	25 649	6 302	1 167	–
3 405	59 396	466 682	159 253	27 211	55 450
45 820	–	655 560	107 395	20 970	3 658
113 950	3 840	169 662	35 048	13 545	155
149 715	2 018 789	263 961	119 628	110 947	126 430
3 243	–	51 581	8 530	6 847	20 430
2 224	–	47 595	1 398	254	–
–	–	–	–	–	–

表12-2 企业集团主要经济指标（2016年）

单位：万元

项　　目	Item	单位数(个) Number of Units (unit)	从业人员(人) Number of Employed Persons (person)
企业集团	**Enterprises Groups**	**93**	**445 992**
按母公司控股情况分	**Classified by Number Shares Held by Parent Companies**		
国有控股	Stately Majority Share Holding	21	66 061
集体控股	Collectively Majority Share Holding	9	20 727
私人控股	Privately Majority Share Holding	58	347 116
港澳台商控股	Majority Share Holding by Investors from Hong Kong, Macau and Taiwan	2	3 086
外商控股	Majority Share Holding by Foreign Investors	3	9 002
按企业集团主营行业分	**Classified by Main Field of Operation**		
工　业	Industry	53	240 170
#纺织业	Textile Industry	6	20 719
化学纤维制造业	Chemical Fiber Manufacturing	7	46 112
黑色金属冶炼和压延加工业	Smelting and Pressing of Ferrous Metals	6	50 694
电气机械和器材制造业	Electric Equipment and Machinery Manufacturing	8	46 085
建筑业	Construction	12	83 533
批发和零售业	Wholesale and Retail Sale Trades	11	50 684
交通运输、仓储和邮政业	Transportation,Logistics and Postal	2	10 514
信息传输、软件和信息技术服务业	Information Transmission, Software and Information Technology Services	1	2 652
房地产业	Real Estate	4	8 092
租赁和商务服务业	Leasing and Business Services	8	49 150
金融业	Financial Industries	1	846
水利、环境和公共设施管理业	Water Conservancy, Environment and Public Facilities Management	1	351

MAIN ECONOMIC INDICATORS ON ENTERPRISES GROUPS (2016)

(10 000 yuan)

# 研发人员 Research and Development Personnel	从业人员劳动报酬 Labor Reward of Employed Persons	#研发人员劳动报酬 Labor Reward of Research and Development Personnel	固定资产投资完成额 Actually Completed Investment in Fixed Assets	年末资产总计 Total Assets at the End of Year	固定资产净值 Net Value of Fixed Assets
29 614	**3 417 793**	**255 843**	**2 847 275**	**105 155 573**	**20 118 405**
3 642	752 937	38 842	343 840	24 629 300	3 157 722
837	149 047	5 796	62 804	6 763 124	460 957
23 794	2 370 983	209 851	2 370 565	69 175 549	15 664 955
–	69 973	–	–	1 465 430	106 155
1 341	74 853	1 354	70 066	3 122 170	728 616
19 246	1 574 459	156 187	1 236 385	58 593 266	13 914 721
1 080	104 573	10 289	24 358	1 779 960	439 747
4 158	258 857	29 868	91 210	11 550 751	2 877 489
4 531	334 968	46 715	465 350	20 303 525	6 199 139
3 490	295 150	24 710	189 279	9 377 619	1 249 298
1 024	731 575	12 633	33 113	6 782 440	359 017
4 802	427 427	32 396	1 287 713	15 946 020	3 147 466
154	101 204	1 457	45 939	794 876	200 240
–	53 078	–	124 718	638 988	560 578
72	63 457	650	18 945	3 631 662	347 208
4 316	445 809	52 520	81 956	14 783 301	1 432 340
–	12 656	–	3 986	3 485 457	62 165
–	8 128	–	14 520	499 563	94 670

表12-2 续表 1

单位：万元

项　　目	Item	累计折旧 Accumulated Depreciation	本年折旧 Depreciation Charge of the Year
企业集团	**Enterprises Groups**	**15 387 081**	**1 947 198**
按母公司控股情况分	**Classified by Number Shares Held by Parent Companies**		
国有控股	Stately Majority Share Holding	2 682 354	298 133
集体控股	Collectively Majority Share Holding	419 541	49 208
私人控股	Privately Majority Share Holding	11 852 974	1 489 721
港澳台商控股	Majority Share Holding by Investors from Hong Kong, Macau and Taiwan	75 935	12 915
外商控股	Majority Share Holding by Foreign Investors	356 277	97 221
按企业集团主营行业分	**Classified by Main Field of Operation**		
工　业	Industry	11 547 701	1 415 335
#纺织业	Textile Industry	521 982	40 821
化学纤维制造业	Chemical Fiber Manufacturing	1 938 390	223 928
黑色金属冶炼和压延加工业	Smelting and Pressing of Ferrous Metals	6 866 120	797 382
电气机械和器材制造业	Electric Equipment and Machinery Manufacturing	727 304	108 553
建筑业	Construction	591 166	49 089
批发和零售业	Wholesale and Retail Sale Trades	1 097 666	219 456
交通运输、仓储和邮政业	Transportation,Logistics and Postal	235 958	26 259
信息传输、软件和信息技术服务业	Information Transmission, Software and Information Technology Services	845 250	111 539
房地产业	Real Estate	160 011	19 221
租赁和商务服务业	Leasing and Business Services	828 613	92 056
金融业	Financial Industries	30 550	5 336
水利、环境和公共设施管理业	Water Conservancy, Environment and Public Facilities Management	50 166	8 907

Continued 1

(10 000 yuan)

累计对外投资 Accumulated Value of Investing Abroad	# 本年对外投资 Value of Investing Abroad of the Year	存 货 Inventory	流动资产年平均余额 Annual Average Balance of Circulation Funds	年末负债合计 Total Liabilities at the End of Year	流动负债 Liquid Liabilities	年末股东(所有者)权益合计 Total Creditors Equity
6 341 412	**702 160**	**12 938 787**	**59 257 048**	**69 516 439**	**54 581 685**	**35 639 134**
2 309 434	366 497	3 949 561	15 832 427	17 882 150	14 010 449	6 747 150
188 597	36 267	379 862	2 369 323	5 296 069	3 072 091	1 467 055
3 815 078	298 910	8 137 943	37 835 436	43 476 103	34 933 845	25 699 446
9 507	486	242 564	1 130 064	980 566	973 727	484 864
18 796	–	228 857	2 089 798	1 881 551	1 591 573	1 240 619
3 591 280	288 345	6 908 385	30 839 104	34 921 762	29 028 734	23 671 504
269 312	15 706	337 122	949 678	854 677	732 065	925 283
221 089	49 899	1 500 285	5 745 412	7 201 203	5 531 332	4 349 548
1 776 772	108 555	2 275 525	8 971 787	13 036 854	11 127 937	7 266 671
826 474	153 325	1 189 272	5 278 665	5 506 827	4 624 541	3 870 792
107 679	57 667	801 024	5 990 959	5 635 322	5 405 534	1 147 118
550 874	50 245	1 582 822	9 993 710	11 897 446	8 874 202	4 048 574
143 366	7 515	5 651	315 613	399 638	301 825	395 238
–	–	2 645	25 059	382 863	333 473	256 125
506 996	31 570	1 557 524	1 406 354	2 224 524	1 563 372	1 407 138
1 242 248	256 007	2 058 051	9 944 382	10 642 100	7 692 536	4 141 201
310	–	–	599 206	3 219 182	1 220 752	266 275
198 659	10 811	22 685	142 661	193 602	161 257	305 961

表12-2 续表 2

单位：万元

项　目	Item	营业收入 Business Revenue	营业成本 Business Costs
企业集团	**Enterprises Groups**	**107 287 404**	**97 046 004**
按母公司控股情况分	**Classified by Number Shares Held by Parent Companies**		
国有控股	Stately Majority Share Holding	19 165 885	16 885 085
集体控股	Collectively Majority Share Holding	2 034 007	1 758 275
私人控股	Privately Majority Share Holding	82 245 936	76 081 753
港澳台商控股	Majority Share Holding by Investors from Hong Kong, Macau and Taiwan	2 340 158	1 175 045
外商控股	Majority Share Holding by Foreign Investors	1 501 418	1 145 846
按企业集团主营行业分	**Classified by Main Field of Operation**		
工　业	Industry	69 403 676	63 958 542
#纺织业	Textile Industry	3 355 950	3 193 795
化学纤维制造业	Chemical Fiber Manufacturing	17 583 920	16 908 111
黑色金属冶炼和压延加工业	Smelting and Pressing of Ferrous Metals	25 914 611	24 180 456
电气机械和器材制造业	Electric Equipment and Machinery Manufacturing	12 410 722	11 655 325
建筑业	Construction	6 909 433	6 459 779
批发和零售业	Wholesale and Retail Sale Trades	20 700 226	18 404 859
交通运输、仓储和邮政业	Transportation,Logistics and Postal	411 580	334 327
信息传输、软件和信息技术服务业	Information Transmission, Software and Information Technology Services	997 444	632 347
房地产业	Real Estate	1 077 367	761 163
租赁和商务服务业	Leasing and Business Services	7 526 477	6 291 283
金融业	Financial Industries	164 361	131 322
水利、环境和公共设施管理业	Water Conservancy, Environment and Public Facilities Management	96 840	72 382

Continued 2

(10 000 yuan)

营业税金及附加 Business Tax and Surcharges	出口额 Value of Exports	利润总额 Total Profits	应交所得税 Income Taxes Payable	应交增值税 Added Value Tax Payable	研究开发费用 Expenditure for Research and Development
579 705	**8 466 746**	**4 261 981**	**833 730**	**1 059 489**	**1 214 002**
230 252	3 318 064	897 494	241 256	165 310	91 094
21 772	50 956	130 123	27 556	32 916	16 097
297 047	4 988 076	2 811 009	519 148	828 322	1 065 390
21 617	–	342 017	32 765	25 298	–
9 017	109 650	81 338	13 005	7 643	41 421
177 833	4 922 041	2 383 899	444 816	716 996	1 012 909
6 415	276 470	63 065	15 048	27 691	23 539
35 260	472 248	288 119	45 593	107 622	164 266
43 048	2 722 874	635 312	136 904	279 822	326 187
33 190	419 124	615 646	109 996	154 597	313 604
93 321	–	134 554	28 903	62 423	21 593
56 817	2 484 936	755 599	118 692	147 879	65 663
3 228	–	51 953	16 791	11 351	3 643
1 494	–	361 781	90 807	11 835	–
112 872	3 840	165 054	33 703	12 817	155
130 107	1 055 929	328 733	95 125	93 454	110 039
1 809	–	32 813	3 495	2 480	–
2 224	–	47 595	1 398	254	–

表12-3

上市公司主要经济指标 (2016年)

单位：万元

项 目	Item	单位数(个) Number of Units (unit)	从业人员(人) Number of Employed Persons (person)
上市公司	**Listing Company**	**113**	**233 995**
按上市公司控股情况分	**Classified by Number Shares Held by Listing Companies**		
国有控股	Stately Majority Share Holding	9	16 594
集体控股	Collectively Majority Share Holding	8	17 900
私人控股	Privately Majority Share Holding	69	149 847
港澳台商控股	Majority Share Holding by Investors from Hong Kong, Macau and Taiwan	13	30 285
外商控股	Majority Share Holding by Foreign Investors	14	19 369
按上市公司主营行业分	**Classified by Main Field of Operation**		
工 业	Industry	92	189 712
#化学原料和化学制品制造业	Raw Chemical Materials and Chemical Products	10	10 226
金属制品业	Metal Products	7	20 510
电气机械和器材制造业	Electric Equipment and Machinery Manufacturing	11	38 236
计算机、通信和其他电子设备制造业	Computer Telecommunications and Other Electronic Equipment Manufacture	18	42 545
建筑业	Construction	3	15 741
批发和零售业	Wholesale and Retail Sale Trades	3	7 349
交通运输、仓储和邮政业	Transportation,Logistics and Postal	2	3 489
金融业	Financial Industries	5	9 110
#资本市场服务	Capital Market Services	1	2 663
租赁和商务服务业	Leasing and Business Services	3	4 196
科学研究和技术服务业	Scientific Research and Technical Services	4	4 398
文化、体育和娱乐业	Culture, Sports and Entertainment	1	–

MAIN ECONOMIC INDICATORS ON LISTING CORPORATION (2016)

(10 000 yuan)

# 研发人员 Research and Development Personnel	从业人员劳动报酬 Labor Reward of Employed Persons	#研发人员劳动报酬 Labor Reward of Research and Development Personnel	固定资产投资完成额 Actually Completed Investment in Fixed Assets	年末资产总计 Total Assets at the End of Year	固定资产净值 Net Value of Fixed Assets
25 637	**3 094 097**	**258 976**	**2 126 473**	**72 841 629**	**7 643 010**
1 245	302 474	10 961	54 143	13 883 481	924 154
1 194	214 109	10 665	131 617	23 837 792	842 756
19 001	2 198 940	188 895	1 351 706	28 520 461	4 375 203
2 147	216 717	27 276	533 845	4 039 241	878 188
2 050	161 857	21 179	55 162	2 560 654	622 709
21 327	2 384 829	203 312	2 039 348	34 730 979	6 624 155
922	96 915	11 534	49 191	2 372 591	637 267
1 959	956 420	15 129	208 707	2 772 041	569 986
3 894	282 278	26 897	390 467	6 739 726	1 060 304
5 827	434 171	81 038	527 498	5 735 211	1 239 509
2 815	219 779	36 511	10 890	3 117 755	114 188
120	91 296	906	207	1 596 820	149 552
45	30 648	590	–	332 224	38 195
62	268 620	2 383	18 588	30 266 966	272 024
62	138 844	2 349	5 823	8 947 670	77 313
641	37 815	4 788	28 961	2 016 947	196 721
627	61 110	10 486	28 479	779 938	248 175
–	–	–	–	–	–

表12-3 续表 1

单位：万元

项　　目	Item	累计折旧 Accumulated Depreciation	本年折旧 Depreciation Charge of the Year
上市公司	**Listing Company**	**4 049 254**	**891 046**
按上市公司控股情况分	**Classified by Number Shares Held by Listing Companies**		
国有控股	Stately Majority Share Holding	510 814	81 374
集体控股	Collectively Majority Share Holding	727 858	91 221
私人控股	Privately Majority Share Holding	2 078 663	541 674
港澳台商控股	Majority Share Holding by Investors from Hong Kong, Macau and Taiwan	336 449	61 119
外商控股	Majority Share Holding by Foreign Investors	395 470	115 658
按上市公司主营行业分	**Classified by Main Field of Operation**		
工　业	Industry	3 621 937	806 750
#化学原料和化学制品制造业	Raw Chemical Materials and Chemical Products	348 179	57 305
金属制品业	Metal Products	163 517	47 410
电气机械和器材制造业	Electric Equipment and Machinery Manufacturing	461 010	80 006
计算机、通信和其他电子设备制造业	Computer Telecommunications and Other Electronic Equipment Manufacture	767 195	288 730
建筑业	Construction	45 761	8 922
批发和零售业	Wholesale and Retail Sale Trades	59 430	14 617
交通运输、仓储和邮政业	Transportation,Logistics and Postal	18 546	3 323
金融业	Financial Industries	147 196	25 685
#资本市场服务	Capital Market Services	37 986	8 043
租赁和商务服务业	Leasing and Business Services	87 963	14 232
科学研究和技术服务业	Scientific Research and Technical Services	68 421	17 517
文化、体育和娱乐业	Culture, Sports and Entertainment	–	–

Continued 1

(10 000 yuan)

累计对外投资 Accumulated Value of Investing Abroad	# 本年对外投资 Value of Investing Abroad of the Year	存 货 Inventory	流动资产年平均余额 Annual Average Balance of Circulation Funds	年末负债合计 Total Liabilities at the End of Year	流动负债 Liquid Liabilities	年末股东(所有者)权益合计 Total Creditors Equity
3 751 894	**1 058 455**	**9 092 518**	**37 113 726**	**47 141 571**	**31 330 066**	**25 700 058**
646 264	123 458	388 289	9 784 375	9 545 366	7 242 614	4 338 115
1 643 845	421 227	4 768 672	6 942 904	20 155 015	9 495 862	3 682 777
1 375 875	493 640	2 959 629	16 334 495	13 856 275	11 732 691	14 664 186
58 001	17 126	685 418	2 312 181	2 238 362	1 642 869	1 800 879
27 909	3 004	290 510	1 739 771	1 346 553	1 216 030	1 214 101
1 488 010	502 855	4 217 111	18 918 110	16 430 754	13 519 556	18 300 225
112 494	40 842	295 775	1 209 830	1 002 306	911 009	1 370 285
82 061	35 930	307 334	1 194 210	1 225 568	978 600	1 546 473
785 189	218 925	794 237	3 844 411	3 402 941	2 621 776	3 336 785
226 498	76 373	755 913	2 784 525	2 961 817	2 549 177	2 773 394
34 463	28 201	48 584	2 482 322	1 911 490	1 908 955	1 206 265
40 532	5 635	226 827	1 248 958	948 313	930 685	648 507
1 248	–	3 360	148 423	125 854	117 690	206 370
1 800 596	489 207	4 497 342	12 789 987	26 231 461	13 861 744	4 035 505
166 547	67 980	–	6 902 978	6 898 748	5 148 759	2 048 922
385 522	31 236	97 748	1 254 469	1 166 153	742 375	850 794
1 523	1 321	1 546	271 457	327 546	249 061	452 392
–	–	–	–	–	–	–

表12-3 续表 2

单位：万元

项　目	Item	营业收入 Business Revenue	营业成本 Business Costs
上市公司	**Listing Company**	**28 642 448**	**23 526 829**
按上市公司控股情况分	**Classified by Number Shares Held by Listing Companies**		
国有控股	Stately Majority Share Holding	4 388 640	3 626 153
集体控股	Collectively Majority Share Holding	2 349 896	1 686 357
私人控股	Privately Majority Share Holding	15 740 927	12 827 338
港澳台商控股	Majority Share Holding by Investors from Hong Kong, Macau and Taiwan	3 903 742	3 349 409
外商控股	Majority Share Holding by Foreign Investors	2 259 243	2 037 572
按上市公司主营行业分	**Classified by Main Field of Operation**		
工　业	Industry	21 390 011	17 860 281
#化学原料和化学制品制造业	Raw Chemical Materials and Chemical Products	1 428 696	1 269 457
金属制品业	Metal Products	1 803 211	1 613 285
电气机械和器材制造业	Electric Equipment and Machinery Manufacturing	4 450 032	3 826 863
计算机、通信和其他电子设备制造业	Computer Telecommunications and Other Electronic Equipment Manufacture	3 324 120	2 736 614
建筑业	Construction	2 332 217	1 951 919
批发和零售业	Wholesale and Retail Sale Trades	3 092 411	2 911 876
交通运输、仓储和邮政业	Transportation,Logistics and Postal	146 796	130 493
金融业	Financial Industries	1 155 825	321 253
#资本市场服务	Capital Market Services	464 523	–
租赁和商务服务业	Leasing and Business Services	322 166	232 516
科学研究和技术服务业	Scientific Research and Technical Services	203 022	118 491
文化、体育和娱乐业	Culture, Sports and Entertainment	–	–

Continued 2

(10 000 yuan)

营业税金及附加 Business Tax and Surcharges	出口额 Value of Exports	利润总额 Total Profits	应交所得税 Income Taxes Payable	应交增值税 Added Value Tax Payable	研究开发费用 Expenditure for Research and Development
172 741	**6 639 318**	**2 458 014**	**396 784**	**371 411**	**697 308**
26 194	2 102 572	420 774	99 769	89 272	34 003
21 430	213 470	374 600	59 912	24 043	43 272
108 825	2 659 699	1 361 087	172 759	228 340	516 659
10 749	756 762	216 624	41 159	13 417	64 935
5 543	906 815	84 929	23 185	16 339	38 439
113 065	4 574 212	1 594 895	216 635	231 771	593 046
10 831	169 911	17 253	7 318	23 620	30 921
7 314	607 557	79 649	14 374	29 379	37 938
26 745	799 781	446 906	49 023	36 793	160 879
15 812	1 032 150	201 053	25 152	20 229	151 195
24 032	22 746	226 337	35 055	41 855	70 730
4 562	1 997 604	145 010	34 636	75 932	4 978
645	-	11 363	2 726	1 057	-
24 004	-	406 783	96 410	4 632	3 658
12 278	-	199 923	56 733	1 376	3 614
4 180	44 756	39 770	4 812	11 220	11 789
2 253	-	33 856	6 510	4 944	13 107
-	-	-	-	-	-

表12-4

总部企业主要经济指标 (2016年)

单位：万元

项　　目	Item	单位数(个) Number of Units (unit)	从业人员(人) Number of Employed Persons (person)
总部企业	**Corporate Headquarters**	**86**	**311 563**
按母公司控股情况分	**Classified by Number Shares Held by Parent Companies**		
国有控股	Stately Majority Share Holding	15	22 253
集体控股	Collectively Majority Share Holding	4	6 172
私人控股	Privately Majority Share Holding	44	237 510
港澳台商控股	Majority Share Holding by Investors from Hong Kong, Macau and Taiwan	11	22 752
外商控股	Majority Share Holding by Foreign Investors	12	22 876
按总部企业主营行业分	**Classified by Main Field of Operation**		
工　业	Industry	35	140 532
#纺织业	Textile Industry	2	14 643
化学纤维制造业	Chemical Fiber Manufacturing	3	36 680
黑色金属冶炼和压延加工业	Smelting and Pressing of Ferrous Metals	3	36 555
电气机械和器材制造业	Electric Equipment and Machinery Manufacturing	1	2 430
建筑业	Construction	7	28 906
批发和零售业	Wholesale and Retail Sale Trades	15	57 655
交通运输、仓储和邮政业	Transportation, Logistics and Postal	3	937
信息传输、软件和信息技术服务业	Information Transmission, Software and Information Technology Services	4	22 352
金融业	Financial Industries	3	8 066
#货币金融服务	Monetary and financial services	1	3 846
#资本市场服务	Capital Market Services	1	2 663
房地产业	Real Estate	2	6 294
租赁和商务服务业	Leasing and Business Services	13	43 845
#商务服务业	Business Services	12	43 250
科学研究和技术服务业	Scientific Research and Technical Services	3	2 625
水利、环境和公共设施管理业	Water Conservancy, Environment and Public Facilities Management	1	351

MAIN ECONOMIC INDICATORS ON CORPORATE HEADQUARTERS (2016)

(10 000 yuan)

# 研发人员 Research and Development Personnel	从业人员劳动报酬 Labor Reward of Employed Persons	#研发人员劳动报酬 Labor Reward of Research and Development Personnel	固定资产投资完成额 Actually Completed Investment in Fixed Assets	年末资产总计 Total Assets at the End of Year	固定资产净值 Net Value of Fixed Assets
29 459	**2 694 899**	**300 135**	**2 722 765**	**103 906 063**	**14 627 044**
1 318	398 040	8 760	249 697	40 250 849	1 243 927
100	32 260	920	8 727	804 297	184 321
26 305	1 803 449	283 565	1 763 025	49 178 429	11 284 727
240	166 338	1 671	471 767	4 450 685	748 710
1 496	294 812	5 219	229 549	9 221 803	1 165 359
12 119	974 056	119 186	1 059 592	38 786 324	10 440 140
1 009	72 753	9 777	10 490	1 393 003	337 695
3 255	213 361	20 901	62 749	8 881 213	2 577 115
2 631	240 433	28 054	203 970	16 101 393	4 860 664
317	13 822	2 500	13 600	535 365	82 915
3 422	330 004	42 595	12 155	4 319 737	154 739
3 352	432 009	15 742	1 186 553	13 282 913	2 230 448
–	12 557	–	10 837	375 787	164 255
4 660	211 521	60 263	57 247	1 272 703	64 717
62	252 566	2 349	178 375	35 733 566	413 895
–	85 447	–	170 654	25 192 078	333 975
62	138 844	2 349	5 823	8 947 670	77 313
–	34 222	–	–	1 403 561	127 469
4 492	388 445	50 373	184 651	7 979 561	862 343
4 492	380 654	50 373	184 651	7 778 763	843 970
1 352	51 391	9 627	18 835	252 348	74 368
–	8 128	–	14 520	499 563	94 670

表12-4 续表 1

单位：万元

项　　目	Item	累计折旧 Accumulated Depreciation	本年折旧 Depreciation Charge of the Year
总部企业	**Corporate Headquarters**	**10 804 426**	**1 419 028**
按母公司控股情况分	**Classified by Number Shares Held by Parent Companies**		
国有控股	Stately Majority Share Holding	515 865	79 029
集体控股	Collectively Majority Share Holding	79 094	7 040
私人控股	Privately Majority Share Holding	9 184 537	1 124 141
港澳台商控股	Majority Share Holding by Investors from Hong Kong, Macau and Taiwan	298 197	59 533
外商控股	Majority Share Holding by Foreign Investors	726 733	149 285
按总部企业主营行业分	**Classified by Main Field of Operation**		
工　业	Industry	8 675 318	1 071 385
#纺织业	Textile Industry	393 226	30 804
化学纤维制造业	Chemical Fiber Manufacturing	1 439 057	177 560
黑色金属冶炼和压延加工业	Smelting and Pressing of Ferrous Metals	5 801 122	630 272
电气机械和器材制造业	Electric Equipment and Machinery Manufacturing	52 871	9 858
建筑业	Construction	68 078	12 054
批发和零售业	Wholesale and Retail Sale Trades	1 067 314	175 216
交通运输、仓储和邮政业	Transportation, Logistics and Postal	72 071	10 536
信息传输、软件和信息技术服务业	Information Transmission, Software and Information Technology Services	37 820	11 405
金融业	Financial Industries	126 026	28 863
#货币金融服务	Monetary and financial services	84 212	19 331
#资本市场服务	Capital Market Services	37 986	8 043
房地产业	Real Estate	50 197	4 389
租赁和商务服务业	Leasing and Business Services	624 238	88 458
#商务服务业	Business Services	605 464	87 187
科学研究和技术服务业	Scientific Research and Technical Services	33 198	7 815
水利、环境和公共设施管理业	Water Conservancy, Environment and Public Facilities Management	50 166	8 907

Continued 1

(10 000 yuan)

累计对外投资 Accumulated Value of Investing Abroad	# 本年对外投资 Value of Investing Abroad of the Year	存货 Inventory	流动资产年平均余额 Annual Average Balance of Circulation Funds	年末负债合计 Total Liabilities at the End of Year	流动负债 Liquid Liabilities	年末股东(所有者)权益合计 Total Creditors Equity
3 148 423	**467 738**	**7 900 571**	**49 307 520**	**74 036 585**	**46 324 156**	**29 869 478**
758 327	130 294	949 591	14 154 552	34 023 637	13 483 592	6 227 212
745	150	100 321	374 898	379 126	357 533	425 171
2 097 547	337 294	5 391 229	26 069 329	31 579 190	25 528 496	17 599 239
21 442	–	622 898	2 695 594	2 923 839	2 238 561	1 526 846
270 362	–	836 532	6 013 147	5 130 793	4 715 974	4 091 010
2 036 081	305 979	4 512 263	19 049 613	23 007 970	18 547 213	15 778 354
212 194	13 906	252 395	752 465	656 302	540 539	736 701
52 514	–	1 065 414	3 883 708	5 450 634	3 927 663	3 430 579
1 263 321	88 578	1 866 200	7 182 282	10 081 679	8 438 420	6 019 714
130 971	78 809	78 750	326 536	270 538	264 300	264 827
55 539	36 925	317 646	3 583 581	2 755 817	2 666 561	1 563 920
316 279	700	1 626 089	8 575 255	9 150 400	7 142 512	4 132 513
–	–	1 336	93 606	170 785	109 894	205 002
57 686	14 197	672	231 584	599 894	583 280	672 809
315 782	71 837	–	12 212 247	31 335 670	11 504 952	4 397 896
149 235	3 857	–	4 678 476	23 208 169	6 256 320	1 983 909
166 547	67 980	–	6 902 978	6 898 748	5 148 759	2 048 922
143 762	26 671	646 320	16 383	1 011 370	561 157	392 191
24 216	618	772 037	5 294 074	5 689 754	4 946 467	2 289 807
24 216	618	729 973	5 119 927	5 560 232	4 816 945	2 218 531
419	–	1 523	108 516	121 323	100 863	131 025
198 659	10 811	22 685	142 661	193 602	161 257	305 961

表12-4 续表 2

单位：万元

项　　目	Item	营业收入 Business Revenue	营业成本 Business Costs
总部企业	**Corporate Headquarters**	**79 104 329**	**70 768 332**
按母公司控股情况分	**Classified by Number Shares Held by Parent Companies**		
国有控股	Stately Majority Share Holding	5 382 668	4 477 377
集体控股	Collectively Majority Share Holding	770 614	663 531
私人控股	Privately Majority Share Holding	59 901 222	55 993 411
港澳台商控股	Majority Share Holding by Investors from Hong Kong, Macau and Taiwan	5 836 514	4 983 586
外商控股	Majority Share Holding by Foreign Investors	7 213 311	4 650 427
按总部企业主营行业分	**Classified by Main Field of Operation**		
工　业	Industry	46 613 370	42 536 040
#纺织业	Textile Industry	2 857 749	2 726 504
化学纤维制造业	Chemical Fiber Manufacturing	14 855 252	14 255 144
黑色金属冶炼和压延加工业	Smelting and Pressing of Ferrous Metals	20 409 201	19 057 684
电气机械和器材制造业	Electric Equipment and Machinery Manufacturing	285 695	223 818
建筑业	Construction	3 245 301	2 774 324
批发和零售业	Wholesale and Retail Sale Trades	18 288 285	15 913 696
交通运输、仓储和邮政业	Transportation, Logistics and Postal	122 229	93 807
信息传输、软件和信息技术服务业	Information Transmission, Software and Information Technology Services	2 192 565	2 258 256
金融业	Financial Industries	1 581 989	1 093 080
#货币金融服务	Monetary and financial services	659 154	659 154
#资本市场服务	Capital Market Services	464 523	-
房地产业	Real Estate	355 931	249 340
租赁和商务服务业	Leasing and Business Services	6 439 270	5 671 334
#商务服务业	Business Services	6 236 775	5 486 704
科学研究和技术服务业	Scientific Research and Technical Services	168 549	106 073
水利、环境和公共设施管理业	Water Conservancy, Environment and Public Facilities Management	96 840	72 382

Continued 2

(10 000 yuan)

营业税金及附加 Business Tax and Surcharges	出口额 Value of Exports	利润总额 Total Profits	应交所得税 Income Taxes Payable	应交增值税 Added Value Tax Payable	研究开发费用 Expenditure for Research and Development
337 237	**4 422 513**	**2 773 695**	**558 047**	**747 463**	**793 845**
98 884	201 827	664 331	106 729	40 896	18 299
2 525	79 717	26 656	5 137	4 192	10 950
177 329	2 953 200	1 157 420	299 517	557 893	719 435
15 554	87 742	221 219	49 429	60 037	3 050
42 945	1 100 027	704 069	97 235	84 445	42 111
114 482	2 890 708	1 159 537	249 765	431 005	517 808
5 476	133 878	52 954	13 239	20 497	22 277
29 748	331 385	249 827	41 142	73 977	102 005
35 834	1 921 745	506 403	112 542	228 273	244 094
1 411	21 530	25 027	3 690	12 521	9 506
38 075	219 796	274 002	43 532	51 168	90 468
51 352	186 174	820 186	119 058	183 794	50 020
198	–	19 326	4 924	1 688	–
2 202	59 396	-153 628	5 135	5 077	55 450
32 285	–	415 887	64 223	15 234	3 614
19 652	–	247 506	7 490	12 187	–
12 278	–	199 923	56 733	1 376	3 614
54 964	–	47 286	12 697	728	–
40 030	1 066 439	120 856	54 893	53 601	65 640
39 593	1 066 439	119 503	54 272	51 381	65 640
1 425	–	22 648	2 422	4 914	10 845
2 224	–	47 595	1 398	254	–

表12-5

总部经济营业收入50强（2016年）
TOP 50 HEADQUARTER ECONOMY OF THE MAJOR BUSINESS REVENUE (2016)

序号 No.	企业名称 Name of Enterprises	所在地区 Location	序号 No.	企业名称 Name of Enterprises	所在地区 Location
1	江苏沙钢集团有限公司	张家港	26	苏州胜利精密制造科技股份有限公司	高新区、虎丘区
2	恒力集团有限公司	吴江区	27	阿特斯（中国）投资有限公司	高新区、虎丘区
3	盛虹控股集团有限公司	吴江区	28	中亿丰建设集团股份有限公司	相城区
4	亨通集团有限公司	吴江区	29	紫光数码（苏州）集团有限公司	相城区
5	江苏国泰国际集团有限公司	张家港	30	江苏省烟草公司苏州市公司	姑苏区
6	江苏永钢集团有限公司	张家港	31	江苏吴中集团有限公司	吴中区
7	中铁二十局集团第一工程有限公司	高新区、虎丘区	32	苏州市相城区江南化纤集团有限公司	相城区
8	通鼎集团有限公司	吴江区	33	恩斯克投资有限公司	昆　山
9	波司登股份有限公司	常　熟	34	阿特斯光伏科技（苏州）有限公司（加拿大太阳能）	常　熟
10	江苏国泰国际集团国贸股份有限公司	张家港	35	中国移动通信集团江苏有限公司苏州分公司	姑苏区
11	澳洋集团有限公司	张家港	36	金红叶纸业集团有限公司	工业园区
12	昆山润华商业有限公司	昆　山	37	中国石化销售有限公司江苏苏州石油分公司	姑苏区
13	华芳集团有限公司	张家港	38	江苏康得新复合材料股份有限公司	张家港
14	苏州创元投资发展（集团）有限公司	姑苏区	39	中石化壳牌（江苏）石油销售有限公司	姑苏区
15	永鼎集团有限公司	吴江区	40	唯品会（昆山）电子商务有限公司	昆　山
16	苏州金螳螂企业（集团）有限公司	工业园区	41	中利科技集团股份有限公司	常　熟
17	耐克体育（中国）有限公司	太　仓	42	苏州东山精密制造股份有限公司	吴中区
18	东华能源股份有限公司	张家港	43	江苏爱康实业集团有限公司	张家港
19	苏州金螳螂建筑装饰股份公司	工业园区	44	江苏骏马集团有限责任公司	张家港
20	江苏亨通光电股份有限公司	吴江区	45	苏州高新区经济发展集团总公司	高新区、虎丘区
21	同程网络科技股份有限公司	工业园区	46	江苏沙钢股份有限公司	张家港
22	通力电梯有限公司	昆　山	47	江苏隆力奇集团有限公司	常　熟
23	阿迪达斯体育（中国）有限公司	工业园区	48	香塘集团有限公司	太　仓
24	同程国际旅行社有限公司	工业园区	49	江苏华昌（集团）有限公司	张家港
25	常熟龙腾特种钢有限公司	常　熟	50	中国电信股份有限公司苏州分公司	姑苏区

表12-6

总部经济利润总额50强（2016年）
TOP 50 HEADQUARTER ECONOMY OF THE TOTAL PROFITS (2016)

序号 No.	企业名称 Name of Enterprises	所在地区 Location	序号 No.	企业名称 Name of Enterprises	所在地区 Location
1	江苏沙钢集团有限公司	张家港	26	阿特斯（中国）投资有限公司	高新区、虎丘区
2	阿迪达斯体育（中国）有限公司	工业园区	27	威富服饰（中国)有限公司	昆　山
3	通力电梯有限公司	昆　山	28	江苏吴中集团有限公司	吴中区
4	中国移动通信集团江苏有限公司苏州分公司	姑苏区	29	艾默生环境优化技术（苏州）有限公司	工业园区
5	耐克体育（中国）有限公司	太　仓	30	澳洋集团有限公司	张家港
6	波司登股份有限公司	常　熟	31	波司登国际控股有限公司	常　熟
7	中国电信股份有限公司苏州分公司	姑苏区	32	恩斯克投资有限公司	昆　山
8	通鼎集团有限公司	吴江区	33	东华能源股份有限公司	张家港
9	苏州银行股份有限公司	工业园区	34	莱克电气股份有限公司	高新区、虎丘区
10	江苏康得新复合材料股份有限公司	张家港	35	江苏沙钢股份有限公司	张家港
11	东吴证券股份公司	工业园区	36	利乐包装（昆山）有限公司	昆　山
12	苏州金螳螂建筑装饰股份公司	工业园区	37	苏州胜利精密制造科技股份有限公司	高新区、虎丘区
13	苏州金螳螂企业（集团）有限公司	工业园区	38	康力电梯股份有限公司	吴江区
14	亨通集团有限公司	吴江区	39	苏州高新区经济发展集团总公司	高新区、虎丘区
15	江苏省烟草公司苏州市公司	姑苏区	40	昆山润华商业有限公司	昆　山
16	江苏亨通光电股份有限公司	吴江区	41	江苏爱康实业集团有限公司	张家港
17	恒力集团有限公司	吴江区	42	芬欧汇川(中国)有限公司	常　熟
18	江苏国泰国际集团有限公司	张家港	43	天顺风能（苏州）股份有限公司	太　仓
19	江苏国泰国际集团国贸股份有限公司	张家港	44	金红叶纸业集团有限公司	工业园区
20	江苏常熟农村商业银行股份有限公司	常　熟	45	中新苏州工业园区市政公用发展集团有限公司	工业园区
21	江苏永钢集团有限公司	张家港	46	苏州汽车客运集团有限公司	姑苏区
22	盛虹控股集团有限公司	吴江区	47	香塘集团有限公司	太　仓
23	中新苏州工业园区开发集团股份有限公司	工业园区	48	卫材（中国）药业有限公司	工业园区
24	永鼎集团有限公司	吴江区	49	苏州工业园区建屋发展集团有限公司	工业园区
25	江苏吴江农村商业银行股份有限公司	吴江区	50	华芳集团有限公司	张家港

表12-7

总部经济资产50强（2016年）
TOP 50 HEADQUARTER ECONOMY OF THE TOTAL ASSETS (2016)

序号 No.	企业名称 Name of Enterprises	所在地区 Location	序号 No.	企业名称 Name of Enterprises	所在地区 Location
1	苏州银行股份有限公司	工业园区	26	江苏吴中集团有限公司	吴中区
2	江苏沙钢集团有限公司	张家港	27	长江润发集团有限公司	张家港
3	江苏常熟农村商业银行股份有限公司	常　熟	28	苏州胜利精密制造科技股份有限公司	高新区、虎丘区
4	东吴证券股份公司	工业园区	29	通力电梯有限公司	昆　山
5	江苏吴江农村商业银行股份有限公司	吴江区	30	永鼎集团有限公司	吴江区
6	盛虹控股集团有限公司	吴江区	31	东吴人寿保险股份有限公司	高新区、虎丘区
7	恒力集团有限公司	吴江区	32	澳洋集团有限公司	张家港
8	苏州高新区经济发展集团总公司	高新区、虎丘区	33	波司登国际控股有限公司	常　熟
9	亨通集团有限公司	吴江区	34	苏州东山精密制造股份有限公司	吴中区
10	中铁二十局集团第一工程有限公司	高新区、虎丘区	35	江苏国泰国际集团国贸股份有限公司	张家港
11	江苏太仓农村商业银行股份有限公司	太　仓	36	苏州工业园区建屋发展集团有限公司	工业园区
12	苏州金螳螂企业（集团）有限公司	工业园区	37	通鼎集团有限公司	吴江区
13	江苏永钢集团有限公司	张家港	38	耐克体育（中国）有限公司	太　仓
14	苏州金螳螂建筑装饰股份公司	工业园区	39	中利科技集团股份有限公司	常　熟
15	江苏康得新复合材料股份有限公司	张家港	40	苏州新区高新技术产业股份有限公司	高新区、虎丘区
16	波司登股份有限公司	常　熟	41	江苏华昌（集团）有限公司	张家港
17	金红叶纸业集团有限公司	工业园区	42	中国石化销售有限公司江苏苏州石油分公司	姑苏区
18	苏州创元投资发展（集团）有限公司	姑苏区	43	昆山润华商业有限公司	昆　山
19	江苏爱康实业集团有限公司	张家港	44	同程网络科技股份有限公司	工业园区
20	东华能源股份有限公司	张家港	45	华芳集团有限公司	张家港
21	阿特斯（中国）投资有限公司	高新区、虎丘区	46	苏州天沃科技股份有限公司	张家港
22	江苏亨通光电股份有限公司	吴江区	47	江苏骏马集团有限责任公司	张家港
23	中新苏州工业园区开发集团股份有限公司	工业园区	48	苏州市相城区江南化纤集团有限公司	相城区
24	阿迪达斯体育（中国）有限公司	工业园区	49	阿特斯光伏科技（苏州）有限公司（加拿大太阳能）	常　熟
25	江苏国泰国际集团有限公司	张家港	50	芬欧汇川(中国)有限公司	常　熟

表12-8

制造业采购经理指数（2016年）
THE MANUFACTURING PURCHASING MANAGERS INDEX (2016)

月　份	制造业采购经理指数 The Manufacturing Purchasing Managers Index	分项指数 Partial Index				
		生产指数 The Production Index	新订单指数 The New Orders Index	原材料库存指数 Raw Materials Inventory Index	从业人员指数 Practitioners Index	供应商配送时间指数 The Supplier Delivery Time Index
1	47.8	51.8	45.9	51.5	40.4	52.4
2	47.7	40.1	48.5	52.5	44.7	59.6
3	49.0	51.1	49.5	48.3	50.3	43.3
4	51.3	53.8	54.7	48.0	47.1	48.3
5	52.1	54.6	55.4	49.8	47.4	49.3
6	49.9	51.3	50.4	48.8	47.6	50.1
7	48.9	48.1	49.8	48.6	48.2	49.7
8	50.2	51.6	49.9	47.9	49.6	50.4
9	51.8	52.4	55.0	50.4	48.6	49.5
10	52.5	54.2	55.2	50.9	48.2	50.8
11	52.5	53.7	53.7	52.2	49.5	52.3
12	54.0	57.0	57.4	51.1	47.4	53.1

表12-9

非制造业采购经理指数（2016年）
NON THE MANUFACTURING PURCHASING MANAGERS INDEX (2016)

月　份	非制造业采购经理指数 Non Manufacturing Purchasing Managers Index	分项指数 Partial Index			
		业务总量指数 The Total Business Index	新订单指数 The New Orders Index	从业人员指数 Practitioners Index	供应商配送时间指数 The Supplier Delivery Time Index
1	48.4	48.7	50.3	44.2	49.0
2	48.3	48.8	48.9	44.6	50.5
3	50.8	52.4	51.6	49.6	47.3
4	50.6	52.1	50.4	49.3	50.0
5	52.1	56.0	51.9	49.3	48.7
6	49.2	50.8	49.9	45.8	48.9
7	50.6	52.7	50.0	49.3	49.7
8	51.1	51.7	51.6	49.6	50.7
9	51.3	53.0	51.7	49.8	49.3
10	49.6	52.6	48.6	46.6	49.8
11	48.4	49.0	46.8	49.9	49.0
12	50.5	54.8	50.0	47.8	46.7

主要统计指标解释

总部经济 包括在2016年度达到统计口径的所有企业集团，苏州市政府金融办对外公布的截止2016年末所有境内外上市公司，苏府[2013]8号文公布的首批总部企业、苏总办发[2014]5号文的第二批总部企业、苏总办发[2015]4号文的第三批总部企业，具有行业代表性和产业代表性、市场份额较高、资产和营业收入达到一定标准的重点企业。

企业集团 是指以母子公司为主体，通过投资及生产经营协作等多种方式，与众多的企事业单位共同组成的经济联合体。企业集团的统计范围包括：由国务院批准的国家试点企业集团、国家重点企业、由省政府及省级主管部门以上批准的企业集团、列入全省产业经济结构调整规划的市重点企业集团、年营业收入 20 亿元以上的其他各类企业 (集团)。

上市公司 其统计范围是 2016 年末在境内外证券交易所上市的，在苏州注册的上市企业。

总部企业 其统计范围是2016年末苏州市总部经济发展领导小组认定的总部企业。

采购经理指数（简称PMI） 是宏观经济先行监测指标，是经济景气监测的重要指标和反映经济增长和衰退的晴雨表。PMI指数体系无论对于政府部门、金融机构、投资公司，还是企业来说，在经济预测和商业分析方面都有重要的意义，是政府部门调控、金融机构与投资公司决策的重要依据，也是企业及时判断行业供应及整体走势，更好地进行决策的依据。PMI是国际上通行的宏观经济监测指标体系之一，通常以50作为经济强弱的分界点，PMI高于50时，反映经济扩张；低于50，则反映经济衰退。

EXPLANATORY NOTES ON MAIN STATISTICAL INDICATORS

Headquarters economy including all the enterprise groups up to the statistical caliber in 2016, by the end of 2016 all the overseas listed companies announced by Suzhou government finance office, the first batch of headquarter enterprises announced in the document of Suzhou government [2013] no. 8, the second batch of headquarter enterprises announced in the document of Su zong ban fa [2014] no. 5, and the third batch of headquarter enterprises announced in the document of Su zong ban fa [2015] no. 4, and the key enterprises with the representativeness of the industry, high market shares, and assets and revenues reaching a certain standard.

Enterprise Group refers to the economic union composed, with the parent-subsidiary companies as the main body, and through investment, production, operation cooperation and so on, with numerous enterprises and institutions. The statistical scope includes: the national pilot enterprise groups approved by the state council, the enterprise groups approved by the provincial government or the departments in charge at or above the provincial level, the municipal key enterprise groups included in the planning of the province industry economy structure adjustment, and other kinds of enterprises (groups) with an annual business income of above 2 billion yuan.

Public Enlisted Company the statistics include those enterprises registered in Suzhou and enlisted in domestic and overseas at the end of 2016.

Corporate headquarters the statistical range is the corporate headquarters which were recognized by Suzhou Headquarters Economic Development Leading Group at the end of 2016.

Purchasing Managers Index (PMI for short) is the first monitoring indicators of the macro-economy, an important indicator of economic monitoring and a barometer reflecting economic growth and decline. The PMI index system is of important significance both for government departments, financial institutions, investment companies, and for enterprises, in terms of economic forecasts and business analysis. It is an important basis for the regulation of government departments, and for the decision-making of financial institutions and investment companies. It is also a basis for enterprises to make timely judgment of the industry supply and the overall trend, and to make better decisions. PMI is one of the systems of macro-economic monitoring indicators internationally accepted, usually with 50 as the cut-off point of an economic strength, PMI above 50, reflecting the economic expansion; less than 50, reflecting the recession.

十三、财政 金融 保险

CHAPTER 13
FINANCE, BANKING AND INSURANCE

13 财政　金融　保险
FINANCE，BANKING AND INSURANCE

主 要 统 计 指 标
MAJOR STATISTICAL INDICATORS

2016年一般公共预算收入	General Public Budget Revenue	1 730.04	亿元	100 million yuan
比上年增长	Increase Over Last Year	10.8	%	
2016年一般公共预算支出	General Public Budget Expenditure	1 617.11	亿元	100 million yuan
比上年增长	Increase Over Last Year	5.9	%	
2016年末金融机构人民币存款余额	Deposits of National Banking System at Year-end	25 864.26	亿元	100 million yuan
比上年末增长	Increase Over Last Year	9.3	%	
2016年末住户存款余额	Deposits of Households	7 913.85	亿元	100 million yuan
比上年末增长	Increase Over Last Year	7.6	%	
2016年末金融机构人民币贷款余额	Balance of Loans of National Banking System at Year-end	21 924.44	亿元	100 million yuan
比上年末增长	Increase Over Last Year	14.2	%	

表13-1

历年财政收入
FINANCIAL REVENUE OVER THE YEARS

单位：万元 (10 000 yuan)

年 份 Year	全 市 Whole Municipality	市 区 Urban Area	# 吴江区 Wujiang District	常 熟 Changshu	张家港 Zhangjiagang	昆 山 Kunshan	太 仓 Taicang
1952	11 251	6 106	1 421	1 930	765	1 209	1 241
1957	17 138	9 966	1 636	3 104	1 027	1 367	1 674
1962	16 563	11 668	1 670	1 959	729	1 034	1 173
1965	27 813	19 879	1 854	3 399	1 404	1 636	1 495
1970	41 165	31 014	2 269	4 325	1 628	2 149	2 049
1975	65 520	49 938	3 824	6 687	3 258	2 654	2 983
1978	82 766	62 001	5 111	9 194	4 450	3 460	3 661
1980	94 589	67 815	6 442	11 557	5 789	3 556	5 872
1985	159 096	97 221	13 584	25 537	16 713	8 384	11 241
1990	214 680	126 502	18 986	36 318	24 951	13 203	13 706
1995	538 593	279 951	49 787	98 009	73 734	51 115	35 784
1996	640 757	326 326	57 334	115 312	95 003	60 160	43 956
1997	765 384	387 414	68 093	138 426	115 227	73 734	50 583
1998	876 327	440 359	73 743	159 545	130 249	86 128	60 046
1999	1 093 804	557 107	81 264	186 523	150 258	127 172	72 744
2000	1 582 711	833 883	106 646	243 622	205 188	201 301	98 717
2001	2 089 492	1 069 290	152 901	304 622	320 800	273 562	121 218
2002	2 908 234	1 490 171	223 888	410 202	430 845	415 188	161 828
2003	4 099 267	2 055 731	328 818	556 785	627 867	642 696	216 188
2004	5 851 358	2 982 783	511 746	800 228	892 464	858 288	317 595
2005	7 181 043	3 594 932	585 761	882 272	1 083 838	1 168 196	451 805
2006	9 180 988	4 671 269	827 594	1 017 168	1 368 866	1 513 797	609 888
2007	12 177 211	6 152 990	1 105 026	1 259 335	1 945 775	2 018 523	800 588
2008	14 575 825	7 290 004	1 360 000	1 449 914	2 334 586	2 472 075	1 029 246
2009	15 933 881	7 999 765	1 680 152	1 611 302	2 336 753	2 821 062	1 164 999
2010	19 506 250	9 564 134	1 988 296	2 076 075	2 665 601	3 806 191	1 394 249
2011	23 116 177	11 445 413	2 372 558	2 503 456	3 173 383	4 244 896	1 749 029
2012	25 616 731	13 130 082	2 698 828	2 651 427	3 241 958	4 636 206	1 957 058
2013	27 889 065	14 527 206	2 749 649	2 848 460	3 225 903	5 120 769	2 166 727
2014	26 888 620	13 941 040	2 488 754	2 798 119	3 088 007	4 973 826	2 087 628
2015	29 365 477	15 328 497	2 702 687	2 974 603	3 463 008	5 407 306	2 192 063
2016	31 547 850	16 683 039	2 944 951	3 233 837	3 531 233	5 769 176	2 330 565

注：1.历年财政收入中不含土地类基金。
2.从2014年起，社会保险基金收入单列反映，不计入全口径财政收入统计范围。（下同）

Note: 1.Financial revenue excluding land class funds.
2. From 2014 onwards, the social insurance funds are listed separately to show, and are not included in the full scope of the fiscal revenue statistics.(the same below)

表13-2

历年财政支出
FINANCIAL EXPENDITURE OVER THE YEARS

单位：万元 (10 000 yuan)

年份 Year	全市 Whole Municipality	市区 Urban Area	# 吴江区 Wujiang District	常熟 Changshu	张家港 Zhangjiagang	昆山 Kunshan	太仓 Taicang
1952	1 046	551	110	241	85	84	85
1957	3 716	2 436	268	597	240	206	237
1962	3 114	1 857	344	472	298	248	239
1965	4 217	2 713	337	546	349	327	282
1970	5 652	3 494	499	686	575	497	400
1975	9 145	5 609	932	1 216	817	840	663
1978	13 547	8 737	1 290	1 573	1 197	1 072	968
1980	16 735	10 819	1 353	2 107	1 384	1 178	1 247
1985	40 495	23 874	3 941	5 984	4 697	2 895	3 045
1990	79 935	46 049	6 965	13 612	7 450	7 465	5 359
1995	247 333	129 417	21 096	42 195	35 238	26 941	13 542
1996	315 448	162 435	24 415	53 210	47 272	32 506	20 025
1997	393 869	209 549	28 111	64 492	57 210	40 036	22 582
1998	463 983	250 919	34 555	75 710	63 863	44 949	28 542
1999	571 415	309 081	41 040	88 058	75 918	61 232	37 126
2000	799 092	445 210	53 973	112 178	101 957	92 028	47 719
2001	1 137 936	617 789	75 501	158 178	178 492	125 668	57 809
2002	1 585 494	858 574	119 282	222 005	224 959	196 736	83 220
2003	2 321 003	1 236 312	170 532	284 839	342 600	342 366	114 886
2004	2 948 045	1 518 476	232 270	463 078	417 782	386 915	161 794
2005	4 098 596	2 179 226	300 925	559 251	545 977	567 256	246 886
2006	4 868 722	2 599 693	392 220	562 639	650 922	747 909	307 559
2007	6 106 391	3 153 268	523 669	650 083	962 482	958 123	382 435
2008	7 732 756	4 017 169	670 001	814 542	1 088 361	1 215 399	597 286
2009	8 570 438	4 502 427	959 441	833 603	1 280 797	1 361 232	592 379
2010	10 957 462	5 306 909	1 142 832	1 246 422	1 569 294	2 113 446	721 391
2011	12 848 077	6 370 115	1 400 303	1 502 618	1 685 041	2 311 790	978 513
2012	14 795 934	7 560 218	1 614 201	1 695 190	1 841 592	2 571 453	1 127 481
2013	15 938 929	8 255 641	1 633 450	1 682 253	1 816 938	2 945 667	1 238 430
2014	13 660 121	7 193 319	1 300 390	1 502 064	1 621 483	2 312 544	1 030 711
2015	15 926 591	8 704 306	1 425 825	1 639 158	1 778 595	2 666 512	1 138 020
2016	17 006 775	9 394 437	1 653 979	1 654 067	1 913 738	2 841 092	1 203 441

注：1.历年财政支出中不含土地类基金。

2.从2014年起，社会保险基金支出单列反映，不计入全口径财政支出统计范围。（下同）

Note: 1.Financial expenditure excluding land class funds.

2.From 2014 onwards, the social insurance funds are listed separately to show, and are not included in the full scope of the fiscal expenditure statistics.（the same below）

表13-3

历年一般公共预算收入
GENERAL PUBLIC BUDGET REVENUE OVER THE YEARS

单位：万元 (10 000 yuan)

年 份 Year	全 市 Whole Municipality	市 区 Urban Area	# 吴江区 Wujiang District	常 熟 Changshu	张家港 Zhangjiagang	昆 山 Kunshan	太 仓 Taicang
1998	450 672	235 316	34 966	77 365	64 941	43 437	29 613
1999	549 832	291 332	42 259	94 065	76 646	53 144	34 645
2000	803 864	445 455	56 143	118 919	100 605	90 389	48 496
2001	1 088 083	578 465	84 198	144 216	179 545	125 967	59 890
2002	1 237 382	661 452	98 906	163 360	180 060	164 104	68 406
2003	1 704 977	904 360	148 022	223 860	246 102	241 717	88 938
2004	2 195 667	1 142 030	182 188	300 598	316 380	315 368	121 291
2005	3 167 841	1 607 909	249 298	370 725	483 838	516 168	189 201
2006	4 002 284	2 030 997	350 788	430 845	610 858	653 718	275 866
2007	5 418 177	2 739 597	480 957	600 630	839 800	865 562	372 588
2008	6 689 063	3 289 067	601 600	701 528	1 039 800	1 156 868	501 800
2009	7 451 800	3 701 670	702 000	780 778	1 050 018	1 331 331	588 003
2010	9 005 527	4 512 708	902 828	1 000 864	1 160 618	1 631 331	700 006
2011	11 008 808	5 504 360	1 128 772	1 225 011	1 423 188	2 002 188	854 061
2012	12 043 336	6 161 435	1 193 202	1 281 504	1 496 131	2 202 750	901 516
2013	13 310 254	6 946 083	1 295 133	1 385 809	1 541 828	2 435 188	1 001 346
2014	14 438 174	7 636 194	1 373 583	1 474 042	1 626 618	2 636 593	1 064 727
2015	15 607 575	8 295 463	1 473 908	1 576 969	1 742 188	2 847 589	1 145 366
2016	17 300 398	9 198 240	1 652 525	1 735 805	1 900 019	3 189 188	1 277 146

表13-4

历年一般公共预算支出
GENERAL PUBLIC BUDGET EXPENDITURE OVER THE YEARS

单位：万元 (10 000 yuan)

年份 Year	全市 Whole Municipality	市区 Urban Area	#吴江区 Wujiang District	常熟 Changshu	张家港 Zhangjiagang	昆山 Kunshan	太仓 Taicang
1998	459 927	247 165	34 257	75 706	63 863	44 667	28 526
1999	565 065	304 851	40 565	87 996	75 883	59 954	36 381
2000	781 116	438 872	53 291	102 686	101 276	91 126	47 156
2001	1 103 617	604 354	74 599	139 945	177 519	124 218	57 581
2002	1 363 942	747 019	106 271	171 273	196 867	171 093	77 690
2003	1 835 976	1 027 454	154 202	204 747	264 175	235 768	103 832
2004	2 331 312	1 252 319	191 322	272 511	337 245	329 541	139 696
2005	3 352 789	1 823 140	254 902	408 625	476 269	442 380	202 375
2006	3 861 990	2 064 381	308 308	420 980	556 075	562 293	258 261
2007	4 969 424	2 576 611	420 502	537 613	787 004	718 040	350 156
2008	6 223 668	3 197 262	530 858	643 676	942 317	968 965	471 448
2009	6 867 778	3 510 161	638 326	678 286	988 444	1 143 625	547 262
2010	8 256 650	4 116 504	840 293	953 904	1 140 706	1 387 647	657 889
2011	10 026 263	4 997 507	1 080 593	1 150 183	1 327 723	1 745 761	805 089
2012	11 134 678	5 609 766	1 088 494	1 282 681	1 429 162	1 951 473	861 596
2013	12 126 837	6 255 136	1 229 246	1 280 824	1 450 240	2 217 013	923 624
2014	13 048 293	6 933 722	1 262 843	1 380 187	1 527 799	2 229 762	976 823
2015	15 271 682	8 361 405	1 378 659	1 552 550	1 713 442	2 553 588	1 090 697
2016	16 171 070	8 887 164	1 592 870	1 587 404	1 848 059	2 690 029	1 158 414

表13-5

财 政 收 入 (2016年)

单位：万元

指　　标	Item	全　市 Whole Municipality
财政收入	**Total of Financial Revenue**	**31 547 850**
一、上划中央收入	**Revenue of Central Government**	**13 468 575**
增值税	Value-added Tax	7 462 781
消费税	Consumption Tax	288 454
企业所得税（60%）	Enterprise's Income Tax (60%)	4 142 001
个人所得税（60%）	Individual Income Tax (60%)	1 575 339
二、地方财政收入	**Local Financial Revenue**	**18 079 275**
（一）一般公共预算收入	**Public Finance Budget Revenue**	**17 300 398**
# 税收收入	Tax Revenue	15 058 176
1. 增值税	Value-added Tax	5 531 136
2. 营业税	Business Tax	1 657 913
3. 企业所得税（40%）	Enterprise's Income Tax (40%)	2 761 334
4. 个人所得税（40%）	Individual Income Tax (40%)	1 050 228
5. 资源税	Resources Tax	101
6. 城市维护建设税	Tax on Urban Construction and Maintenance	1 036 344
7 . 房产税	Tax on Real Estates	711 199
8. 印花税	Stamp Tax	208 650
9. 城镇土地使用税	Tax on Use of Urban Land	347 845
10.土地增值税	Land Value Added Tax	1 109 037
11.车船使用税和牌照税	Tax on the Use of Vehicles and Ships	106 169
12.耕地占用税	Tax on the Occupancy of Cultivated Land	39 071
13.契　税	Contract Tax	499 149
14.专项收入	Expert Project Income	1 131 073
15.行政性收费收入	Income From Administrative Fees	379 198
16.罚没收入	Penalty and Confiscatory Income	151 252
17.国有资源(资产)有偿使用收入	Revenues of Compensation for Use of State-owned Resources (Assets)	460 944
18.其他收入	Other Income	119 755
（二）政府性基金收入	**Government Fund's Income**	**404 957**
（三）国有资本经营收入	**State-owned Assets Profit**	**373 920**
附：增值税出口退税	**VAT Export Tax Drawback**	**7 627 654**
土地基金收入	**Land Fund Income**	**19 619 281**
社保基金收入	**Social Security Fund's Income**	**7 049 919**

FINANCIAL REVENUE (2016)

(10 000 yuan)

市区 Urban Area	#吴江区 Wujiang District	常熟 Changshu	张家港 Zhangjiagang	昆山 Kunshan	太仓 Taicang
16 683 039	**2 944 951**	**3 233 837**	**3 531 233**	**5 769 176**	**2 330 565**
7 023 750	**1 239 791**	**1 437 304**	**1 566 236**	**2 432 441**	**1 008 844**
3 821 698	768 294	785 593	851 428	1 425 514	578 548
170 074	4 278	91 026	3 831	13 593	9 930
2 211 816	356 364	435 499	364 420	780 758	349 508
820 162	110 855	125 186	346 557	212 576	70 858
9 659 289	**1 705 160**	**1 796 533**	**1 964 997**	**3 336 735**	**1 321 721**
9 198 240	**1 652 525**	**1 735 805**	**1 900 019**	**3 189 188**	**1 277 146**
8 055 881	1 449 936	1 455 393	1 601 071	2 840 660	1 105 171
2 811 106	557 531	591 589	641 286	1 044 300	442 855
1 009 991	169 220	116 661	134 111	314 901	82 249
1 474 544	237 576	290 333	242 947	520 505	233 005
546 775	73 904	83 458	231 038	141 718	47 239
101	–	–	–	–	–
570 779	106 999	95 319	94 390	193 844	82 012
380 906	72 680	79 753	66 872	134 200	49 468
110 331	23 771	18 536	29 582	37 306	12 895
149 008	53 429	42 168	44 440	73 551	38 678
661 460	117 122	82 612	59 204	248 579	57 182
60 765	10 520	12 839	11 714	14 746	6 105
17 343	2 344	4 927	5 235	3 996	7 570
262 772	24 840	37 198	40 252	113 014	45 913
606 189	165 047	113 925	149 847	178 559	82 553
203 208	11 694	75 534	62 299	16 318	21 839
74 539	6 960	18 053	18 560	28 600	11 500
157 851	9 149	69 652	66 042	124 464	42 935
100 572	9 739	3 248	2 200	587	13 148
135 703	**29 542**	**54 675**	**50 894**	**127 918**	**35 767**
325 346	**23 093**	**6 053**	**14 084**	**19 629**	**8 808**
3 960 149	**851 391**	**829 192**	**1 049 732**	**1 495 403**	**293 178**
15 992 976	**4 205 718**	**511 512**	**749 381**	**1 827 272**	**538 140**
3 492 230	**737 702**	**919 557**	**732 015**	**1 424 102**	**482 015**

表13-6

财 政 支 出 (2016年)

单位：万元

指 标	Item	全 市 Whole Municipality
财政支出	**Financial Expenditure**	**17 006 775**
一、一般公共预算支出	**Public Finance Budget Expenditure**	**16 171 070**
1. 一般公共服务支出	General Public Services Spending	1 461 576
2. 国防支出	Expenditure on National Defense	15 181
3. 公共安全支出	Public Safety Spending	1 161 279
4. 教育支出	Expenditure for Operating Expenses of Education	2 623 221
5. 科学技术支出	Science and Technology Spending	951 962
6. 文化体育与传媒支出	Culture, Sports and the Media	375 714
7. 社会保障与就业支出	Social Security and Employment	1 423 910
8. 医疗卫生与计划生育支出	Expenditure for Medicine and Public Health	936 290
9. 节能环保支出	Energy Saving and Environmental Protection Spending	439 664
10. 城乡社区支出	Urban and Rural Community Affairs Spending	3 540 548
11. 农林水支出	Agricultural, Forestry and Water Affairs Spending	893 553
12. 交通运输支出	Transportation Spending	616 793
13. 资源勘探信息等支出	Resource Exploring, Mining, Power, Information and Other Matters	576 102
14. 商业服务业等支出	Expenditure for Affairs of Commerce and Services	308 200
15. 金融支出	Financial Supervision Expenditures	168 891
16. 住房保障支出	Housing Security Expenditure	397 086
17. 其他支出	Other Expenditure	281 100
二、政府性基金支出	**Fund Expenditure**	**503 333**
三、国有资金经营支出	**State-owned Assets Expenditure**	**332 372**
附：土地基金支出	**Land Fund Expenditures**	**18 903 044**
社保基金支出	**Social Insurance Funds Spending**	**5 877 194**

FINANCIAL EXPENDITURE (2016)

(10 000 yuan)

市 区 Urban Area	# 吴江区 Wujiang District	常 熟 Changshu	张家港 Zhangjiagang	昆 山 Kunshan	太 仓 Taicang
9 394 437	**1 653 979**	**1 654 067**	**1 913 738**	**2 841 092**	**1 203 441**
8 887 164	**1 592 870**	**1 587 404**	**1 848 059**	**2 690 029**	**1 158 414**
807 443	170 408	159 095	167 369	233 364	94 305
8 870	15	248	5 163	704	196
671 361	111 234	120 478	110 122	184 654	74 664
1 349 039	297 235	317 994	308 908	452 211	195 069
452 826	61 300	153 273	104 941	177 026	63 896
267 322	17 131	25 020	30 192	37 839	15 341
723 696	144 016	123 535	146 264	305 328	125 087
548 636	96 416	80 151	105 553	150 949	51 001
195 792	49 987	39 078	63 178	115 835	25 781
1 982 504	290 791	258 922	476 626	556 722	265 774
358 355	127 936	125 362	139 596	183 902	86 338
400 445	50 682	58 117	69 216	72 339	16 676
381 979	41 846	59 343	13 715	65 317	55 748
177 080	52 485	26 253	26 524	71 021	7 322
153 310	986	590	12 408	1 882	701
257 833	48 768	10 675	39 509	33 572	55 497
150 673	31 634	29 270	28 775	47 364	25 018
200 794	**41 626**	**63 759**	**59 751**	**139 954**	**39 075**
306 479	**19 483**	**2 904**	**5 928**	**11 109**	**5 952**
15 567 905	**4 014 617**	**603 961**	**701 218**	**1 436 775**	**593 185**
2 803 256	**617 734**	**885 273**	**821 781**	**876 046**	**490 838**

表13-7

历年末金融机构人民币存贷款余额
RMB SAVINGS DEPOSITS AND LOANS BALANCES OF BANK OVER THE YEARS

单位：万元 (10 000 yuan)

年 份 Year	存款余额 Deposits Balance	# 非金融企业存款 Deposits of Non-financial Enterprises	# 住户存款 Deposits of Households	贷款余额 Loans Balance	# 短期贷款 Short-term Loans	# 中长期贷款 Medium-term & Long-term Loans
1949	156			42		
1952	2 628			1 129		
1957	10 086			14 829		
1962	15 282			43 349		
1970	46 648		6 594	55 652		
1975	58 822		12 166	107 202		
1978	73 712		17 650	154 512		
1980	156 817		36 420	211 885		
1985	375 702		148 233	530 070		
1990	1 321 970		733 332	1 340 967		
1995	5 666 541		2 964 938	4 240 689		
1996	7 447 982		4 082 649	5 370 165		
1997	9 115 624	3 777 846	5 337 778	6 109 437	5 222 982	704 285
1998	11 124 378	4 633 989	6 490 389	7 242 834	6 012 839	738 929
1999	12 938 251	5 425 457	7 512 794	8 116 631	6 622 337	870 493
2000	14 770 111	6 733 142	8 036 969	9 705 954	7 932 854	1 083 065
2001	17 316 246	7 946 830	9 369 416	10 598 232	7 180 674	2 092 396
2002	22 320 343	10 677 086	11 643 257	14 909 634	9 628 354	3 566 462
2003	31 497 894	16 792 849	14 705 045	23 592 819	13 182 488	7 852 521
2004	38 145 281	21 022 535	17 122 746	29 157 370	13 238 438	12 332 891
2005	47 300 532	26 705 335	20 595 197	34 783 428	14 500 920	16 102 524
2006	57 979 732	33 705 530	24 274 202	44 297 084	19 137 227	20 910 608
2007	70 688 313	44 754 186	25 934 127	53 438 723	23 500 261	27 119 966
2008	83 407 921	50 034 758	33 373 163	63 018 052	25 972 919	32 042 110
2009	109 502 460	69 961 663	39 540 797	85 053 331	29 919 426	49 617 005
2010	135 703 495	89 147 878	46 555 617	101 331 459	36 213 284	62 210 323
2011	151 807 837	93 011 695	50 785 927	118 738 914	46 491 697	68 747 120
2012	176 634 972	107 584 791	57 877 466	136 268 590	57 167 975	75 039 745
2013	200 375 764	121 140 828	64 083 214	154 952 420	64 243 243	85 633 724
2014老口径	214 281 958	131 009 027	67 534 428	172 479 352	65 043 131	99 991 516
2014新口径	217 551 680	88 486 421	70 226 320			
2015	236 590 970	96 762 241	73 580 383	192 001 015	66 332 289	114 026 353
2016	258 642 564	103 976 434	79 138 477	219 244 382	64 904 030	139 918 079

注：2014年老口径及以前年份，住户存款为城乡居民人民币储蓄存款余额口径，非金融企业存款为单位存款口径。2014年新口径及以后调整为住户存款口径和非金融企业存款。下同。

Note: 2014 year old caliber and previous years, the scope of household deposits was amount of saving deposits in urban and rural areas, the scope of non-financial enterprises deposits was the unit deposit caliber. 2014 new caliber and later adjusted to the scope of the household deposits and non-financial enterprises deposits. The same below.

表13-8

历年末分地区住户存款余额
RMB SAVINGS DEPOSITS OF URBAN HOUSEHOLDS OVER THE YEARS BY REGION

单位：万元 (10 000 yuan)

年份 Year	全市 Whole Municipality	市区 Urban Area	# 吴江区 Wujiang District	常熟 Changshu	张家港 Zhangjiagang	昆山 Kunshan	太仓 Taicang
1952				146		73	77
1957		346	346	237		243	125
1962		206	206	479		272	343
1965	6 474	3 430	253	1 393	389	517	745
1970	6 594	3 248	366	1 372	628	401	945
1975	12 166	6 483	734	2 510	1 290	594	1 289
1978	17 650	9 195	966	3 502	1 927	1 151	1 875
1980	36 420	18 145	2 394	7 302	3 859	3 238	3 876
1985	148 233	70 885	12 565	28 046	21 082	11 861	16 359
1990	733 332	347 646	59 407	145 781	105 913	63 927	70 065
1995	2 964 938	1 321 069	240 825	575 609	511 887	301 570	254 803
1996	4 082 649	1 814 960	370 600	837 401	693 996	398 843	337 449
1997	5 337 778	2 396 520	476 463	1 167 116	836 985	493 287	443 870
1998	6 490 389	2 943 064	614 061	1 412 262	1 018 310	581 477	535 276
1999	7 512 794	3 423 525	731 059	1 637 148	1 177 583	673 184	601 354
2000	8 036 969	3 679 369	779 731	1 688 509	1 280 208	764 219	624 664
2001	9 369 416	4 377 810	915 158	1 920 292	1 447 239	923 303	700 772
2002	11 643 257	5 636 011	1 131 190	2 342 284	1 719 504	1 138 562	806 896
2003	14 705 045	7 461 035	1 497 336	2 791 462	1 989 168	1 488 977	974 403
2004	17 122 746	8 672 455	1 747 441	3 187 039	2 285 995	1 827 811	1 149 446
2005	20 595 197	10 582 414	2 231 149	3 790 046	2 668 182	2 229 722	1 324 832
2006	24 274 202	12 646 581	2 715 870	4 207 394	3 162 974	2 740 382	1 516 871
2007	25 934 127	13 413 765	2 861 672	4 404 905	3 385 526	3 126 929	1 603 002
2008	33 373 163	17 243 013	3 648 183	5 545 651	4 393 591	4 148 668	2 042 241
2009	39 540 797	20 485 695	4 414 443	6 522 628	5 208 800	4 921 289	2 402 385
2010	46 555 617	23 992 753	5 155 580	7 563 039	5 970 374	6 092 794	2 936 656
2011	50 785 927	25 914 766	5 556 569	8 120 828	6 656 161	6 840 035	3 254 137
2012	57 877 466	29 695 083	6 349 442	9 071 807	7 467 598	7 871 313	3 771 664
2013	64 083 214	32 856 112	7 009 079	9 874 241	8 330 538	8 814 077	4 208 246
2014老口径	67 534 428	34 328 749	7 387 036	10 219 900	8 770 608	9 709 029	4 506 142
2014新口径	70 226 320	36 315 257	7 745 463	10 499 016	9 051 169	9 800 530	4 560 348
2015	73 580 383	37 621 561	8 079 506	11 046 000	9 587 678	10 460 263	4 864 881
2016	79 138 477	40 250 001	8 711 252	11 927 531	10 182 254	11 551 279	5 227 413

表13-9

金融机构人民币信贷收支情况（2016年末）

单位：万元

指　标	Item	全　市 Whole Municipality
年末金融机构人民币存款余额	**Deposits Balance of National Banking System by Year End**	**258 642 564**
# 住户存款	Deposits of Households	79 138 477
# 活期存款	Demand Deposits	29 887 403
定期及其他存款	Time & Other Deposits	49 251 073
非金融企业存款	Deposits of Non-financial Enterprises	103 976 434
# 活期存款	Demand Deposits	38 192 364
定期及其他存款	Time & Other Deposits	65 784 071
广义政府存款	Fiscal Deposit	60 906 196
年末金融机构人民币贷款余额	**Loans Balance of National Banking System by Year End**	**219 244 382**
境内贷款	Domestic Loans	218 847 259
住户贷款	Loans to Households	74 271 964
# 短期贷款	Short-term Loans	7 653 870
中长期贷款	Mid & Long-term Loans	66 618 094
非金融企业及机关团体贷款	Loans to Non-financial Enterprises and Government Departments & Organizations	144 575 295
# 短期贷款	Short-term Loans	57 250 160
中长期贷款	Mid & Long-term Loans	73 299 985
票据融资	Paper Financing	13 328 913
境外贷款	Overseas Loans	397 123

RMB CREDIT FUNDS BALANCE OF FINANCIAL INSTITUTIONS (END OF 2016)

(10 000 yuan)

市 区 Urban Area	# 吴江区 Wujiang District	常 熟 Changshu	张家港 Zhangjiagang	昆 山 Kunshan	太 仓 Taicang
157 054 282	**22 097 581**	**26 928 802**	**25 082 720**	**35 622 652**	**13 954 108**
40 250 001	8 711 252	11 927 531	10 182 254	11 551 279	5 227 413
16 150 702	3 488 080	4 078 595	2 869 252	4 988 087	1 800 766
24 099 298	5 223 172	7 848 935	7 313 002	6 563 192	3 426 646
66 451 395	8 357 826	9 480 957	9 729 186	12 299 806	6 015 091
24 759 782	3 208 153	3 531 721	3 085 930	5 100 237	1 714 693
41 691 612	5 149 672	5 949 235	6 643 256	7 199 569	4 300 398
37 589 103	4 804 790	5 124 218	4 667 811	10 965 147	2 559 917
139 932 501	**22 199 995**	**21 394 887**	**19 944 046**	**25 522 221**	**12 450 727**
139 643 429	22 180 665	21 390 754	19 941 806	25 424 978	12 446 292
47 776 138	6 374 665	5 600 303	3 779 776	13 786 473	3 329 273
4 467 175	750 778	1 321 495	674 793	769 701	420 706
43 308 964	5 623 887	4 278 808	3 104 983	13 016 772	2 908 567
91 867 290	15 806 000	15 790 451	16 162 031	11 638 504	9 117 019
31 151 073	9 491 450	7 492 337	9 432 858	4 817 192	4 356 700
50 006 767	5 140 408	7 366 277	5 408 559	6 199 563	4 318 819
10 118 306	1 132 229	903 859	1 275 026	617 747	413 975
289 072	19 330	4 132	2 240	97 244	4 435

表13-10 金融机构本外币信贷收支情况（2016年末）

单位：万元

指　标	Item	全　市 Whole Municipality
年末金融机构本外币存款余额	**Deposits Balance of National Banking System by Year End**	**277 275 511**
# 住户存款	Deposits of Households	80 681 999
# 活期存款	Demand Deposits	30 790 116
定期及其他存款	Time & Other Deposits	49 891 883
非金融企业存款	Deposits of Non-financial Enterprises	120 279 995
# 活期存款	Demand Deposits	44 760 890
定期及其他存款	Time & Other Deposits	75 519 104
广义政府存款	Fiscal Deposit	61 310 735
年末金融机构本外币贷款余额	**Loans Balance of National Banking System by Year End**	**227 522 207**
境内贷款	Domestic Loans	226 993 234
住户贷款	Loans to Households	74 278 945
# 短期贷款	Short-term Loans	7 660 822
中长期贷款	Mid & Long-term Loans	66 618 123
非金融企业及机关团体贷款	Loans to Non-financial Enterprises and Government Departments & Organizations	152 714 288
# 短期贷款	Short-term Loans	64 402 375
中长期贷款	Mid & Long-term Loans	74 241 650
票据融资	Paper Financing	13 328 937
境外贷款	Overseas Loans	528 974

RMB AND FOREIGN CURRENCY CREDIT FUNDS BALANCE OF FINANCIAL INSTITUTIONS (END OF 2016)

(10 000 yuan)

市 区 Urban Area	# 吴江区 Wujiang District	常 熟 Changshu	张家港 Zhangjiagang	昆 山 Kunshan	太 仓 Taicang
166 192 607	**23 914 002**	**29 136 370**	**26 320 617**	**41 229 084**	**14 396 833**
41 309 063	8 803 487	12 067 012	10 314 008	11 698 986	5 292 931
16 793 893	3 538 110	4 142 549	2 936 826	5 080 352	1 836 496
24 515 170	5 265 377	7 924 463	7 377 182	6 618 634	3 456 435
73 807 211	10 078 468	11 516 135	10 830 489	17 738 171	6 387 989
28 319 055	3 672 959	4 093 025	3 945 885	6 415 638	1 987 288
45 488 156	6 405 509	7 423 110	6 884 604	11 322 533	4 400 702
37 983 168	4 804 807	5 125 591	4 667 843	10 974 213	2 559 919
144 010 946	**23 373 013**	**22 627 152**	**20 441 911**	**27 897 047**	**12 545 151**
143 635 415	23 328 127	22 594 356	20 439 228	27 783 520	12 540 715
47 780 763	6 375 096	5 601 045	3 780 418	13 787 093	3 329 625
4 471 800	751 209	1 322 237	675 435	770 321	421 029
43 308 964	5 623 887	4 278 808	3 104 983	13 016 772	2 908 596
95 854 651	16 953 031	16 993 311	16 658 810	13 996 427	9 211 090
34 423 218	10 594 163	8 685 615	9 865 640	6 987 612	4 440 290
50 688 178	5 184 046	7 375 834	5 461 271	6 387 066	4 329 301
10 118 306	1 132 229	903 883	1 275 026	617 747	413 975
375 531	44 886	32 796	2 684	113 527	4 435

表13-11

金融机构人民币法定存款利率
OFFICIAL INTEREST RATES OF DEPOSITS OF FINANCIAL INSTITUTIONS

单位:年利率 % (% p.a.)

调整时间 Adjustment Time	活 期 Demand	定 期 Time					
		3个月 3 Months	6个月 6 Months	1年 1 Year	2年 2 Years	3年 3 Years	5年 5 Years
1990.04.15	2.88	6.30	7.74	10.08	10.98	11.88	13.68
1990.08.21	2.16	4.32	6.48	8.64	9.36	10.08	11.52
1991.04.21	1.80	3.24	5.40	7.56	7.92	8.28	9.00
1993.05.15	2.16	4.86	7.20	9.18	9.90	10.80	12.06
1993.07.11	3.15	6.66	9.00	10.98	11.70	12.24	13.86
1996.05.01	2.97	4.86	7.20	9.18	9.90	10.80	12.06
1996.08.23	1.98	3.33	5.40	7.47	7.92	8.28	9.00
1997.10.23	1.71	2.88	4.14	5.67	5.94	6.21	6.66
1998.03.25	1.71	2.88	4.14	5.22	5.58	6.21	6.66
1998.07.01	1.44	2.79	3.96	4.77	4.86	4.95	5.22
1998.12.07	1.44	2.79	3.33	3.78	3.96	4.14	4.50
1999.06.10	0.99	1.98	2.16	2.25	2.43	2.70	2.88
2002.02.21	0.72	1.71	1.89	1.98	2.25	2.52	2.79
2004.10.29	0.72	1.71	2.07	2.25	2.70	3.24	3.60
2006.08.19	0.72	1.80	2.25	2.52	3.06	3.69	4.14
2007.03.18	0.72	1.98	2.43	2.79	3.33	3.96	4.41
2007.05.19	0.72	2.07	2.61	3.06	3.69	4.41	4.95
2007.07.21	0.81	2.34	2.88	3.33	3.96	4.68	5.22
2007.08.22	0.81	2.61	3.15	3.60	4.23	4.95	5.49
2007.09.15	0.81	2.88	3.42	3.87	4.50	5.22	5.76
2007.12.21	0.72	3.33	3.78	4.14	4.68	5.40	5.85
2008.10.09	0.72	3.15	3.51	3.87	4.41	5.13	5.58
2008.10.30	0.72	2.88	3.24	3.60	4.14	4.77	5.13
2008.11.27	0.36	1.98	2.25	2.52	3.06	3.60	3.87
2008.12.23	0.36	1.71	1.98	2.25	2.79	3.33	3.60
2010.10.20	0.36	1.91	2.20	2.50	3.25	3.85	4.20
2010.12.26	0.36	2.25	2.50	2.75	3.55	4.15	4.55
2011.02.09	0.40	2.60	2.80	3.00	3.90	4.50	5.00
2011.04.06	0.50	2.85	3.05	3.25	4.15	4.75	5.25
2011.07.07	0.50	3.10	3.30	3.50	4.40	5.00	5.50
2012.06.08	0.40	2.85	3.05	3.25	4.10	4.65	5.10
2012.07.06	0.35	2.60	2.80	3.00	3.75	4.25	4.75
2014.11.22	0.35	2.35	2.55	2.75	3.35	4.00	
2015.03.01	0.35	2.10	2.30	2.50	3.10	3.75	
2015.05.11	0.35	1.85	2.05	2.25	2.85	3.50	
2015.06.28	0.35	1.60	1.80	2.00	2.60	3.25	
2015.08.26	0.35	1.35	1.55	1.75	2.35	3.00	
2015.10.24	0.35	1.10	1.30	1.50	2.10	2.75	

注：自2014年11月22日起，人民银行不再公布金融机构人民币五年期定期存款基准利率。
Note: Since November 22, 2014, People's Bank of China stoped publishing five years benchmark deposit rate on a regular basis of financial institutions.

表13-12

金融机构人民币法定贷款利率
OFFICIAL INTEREST RATES OF LOANS OF FINANCIAL INSTITUTIONS

单位:年利率 % (% p.a.)

调整时间 Adjustment Time	6个月 6 Months	1年 1 Year	1至3年(含) 1-3 Years (include 3 years)	3至5年(含) 3-5 Years (include 5 years)	5年以上 Above 5 Years
1991.04.21	8.10	8.64	9.00	9.54	9.72
1993.05.15	8.82	9.36	10.80	12.06	12.24
1993.07.11	9.00	10.98	12.24	13.86	14.04
1995.01.01	9.00	10.98	12.96	14.58	14.76
1995.07.01	10.08	12.06	13.50	15.12	15.30
1996.05.01	9.72	10.98	13.14	14.94	15.12
1996.08.23	9.18	10.08	10.98	11.70	12.42
1997.10.23	7.65	8.64	9.36	9.90	10.53
1998.03.25	7.02	7.92	9.00	9.72	10.35
1998.07.01	6.57	6.93	7.11	7.65	8.01
1998.12.07	6.12	6.39	6.66	7.20	7.56
1999.06.10	5.58	5.85	5.94	6.03	6.21
2002.02.21	5.04	5.31	5.49	5.58	5.76
2004.10.29	5.22	5.58	5.76	5.85	6.12
2006.04.28	5.40	5.85	6.03	6.12	6.39
2006.08.19	5.58	6.12	6.30	6.48	6.84
2007.03.18	5.67	6.39	6.57	6.75	7.11
2007.05.19	5.85	6.57	6.75	6.93	7.20
2007.07.21	6.03	6.84	7.02	7.20	7.38
2007.08.22	6.21	7.02	7.20	7.38	7.56
2007.09.15	6.48	7.29	7.47	7.65	7.83
2007.12.21	6.57	7.47	7.56	7.74	7.83
2008.09.16	6.21	7.20	7.29	7.56	7.74
2008.10.09	6.12	6.93	7.02	7.29	7.47
2008.10.30	6.03	6.66	6.75	7.02	7.20
2008.11.27	5.04	5.58	5.67	5.94	6.12
2008.12.23	4.86	5.31	5.40	5.76	5.94
2010.10.20	5.10	5.56	5.60	5.96	6.14
2010.12.26	5.35	5.81	5.85	6.22	6.40
2011.02.09	5.60	6.06	6.10	6.45	6.60
2011.04.06	5.85	6.31	6.40	6.65	6.80
2011.07.07	6.10	6.56	6.65	6.90	7.05
2012.06.08	5.85	6.31	6.40	6.65	6.80
2012.07.06	5.60	6.00	6.15	6.40	6.55
2014.11.22	1年(含)以内：5.60		1-5年(含)：6.00		6.15
2015.03.01	1年(含)以内：5.35		1-5年(含)：5.75		5.90
2015.05.11	1年(含)以内：5.10		1-5年(含)：5.50		5.65
2015.06.28	1年(含)以内：4.85		1-5年(含)：5.25		5.40
2015.08.26	1年(含)以内：4.60		1-5年(含)：5.00		5.15
2015.10.24	1年(含)以内：4.35		1-5年(含)：4.75		4.90

注：自2014年11月22日起，金融机构人民币贷款基准利率期限档次简并为一年以内（含一年）、一至五年（含五年）和五年以上三个档次。
Note::Since November 22, 2014, financial institutions RMB loan benchmark interest rates merge into three grades, within a year (including one year), one to five years (including five years) and more than five years .

表13-13

保险业务情况 (2016年)

单位：万元

指　　标	Item	全　市 Whole Municipality
一、财产险承保额	**Insurance Value of Property Insurance**	**1 133 673 366**
# 企业财产险	Enterprise Property Insurance	307 911 312
机动车辆险	Motor Vehicle Insurance	319 550 790
货物运输险	Freight Transport Insurance	113 315 903
家庭财产险	Family Property Insurance	21 414 768
二、保费收入	**Premiums**	**5 251 854**
1.财产险	Property Insurance	1 708 356
# 企业财产险	Enterprise Property Insurance	137 298
机动车辆险	Motor Vehicle Insurance	1 335 886
货物运输险	Freight Transport Insurance	26 132
家庭财产险	Family Property Insurance	23 237
2.人身险	Life Insurance	3 543 497
# 寿　险	Life Insurance	2 639 943
三、当年赔款和给付	**Indemnity Expenditure and Payment of the Year**	**1 563 818**
1.财产险	Property Insurance	1 013 254
# 企业财产险	Enterprise Property Insurance	86 263
机动车辆险	Motor Vehicle Insurance	812 792
货物运输险	Freight Transport Insurance	10 619
家庭财产险	Family Property Insurance	7 412
2.人身险	Life Insurance	550 565
# 寿　险	Life Insurance	413 104

CONDITIONS OF INSURANCE BUSINESS (2016)

(10 000 yuan)

市 区 Urban Area	# 吴江区 Wujiang District	常 熟 Changshu	张家港 Zhangjiagang	昆 山 Kunshan	太 仓 Taicang
854 725 962	**55 389 148**	**75 790 736**	**70 992 592**	**92 256 385**	**39 907 692**
221 087 632	16 349 146	23 736 050	27 378 847	23 895 855	11 812 928
228 061 541	18 309 596	29 424 619	24 279 119	24 536 396	13 249 116
90 639 674	5 756 502	6 650 910	7 042 011	4 589 489	4 393 819
12 477 563	1 878 870	2 755 018	923 258	3 133 337	2 125 592
3 527 684	**334 043**	**465 785**	**453 665**	**590 904**	**213 816**
1 031 926	141 884	188 049	163 491	229 330	95 560
88 847	9 486	17 447	11 916	11 769	7 320
775 151	121 470	152 964	135 552	193 463	78 757
19 772	1 315	1 682	1 768	1 775	1 135
19 235	1 390	1 437	719	1 011	835
2 495 758	192 159	277 736	290 173	361 574	118 256
1 793 003	159 013	230 120	243 919	273 072	99 829
968 028	**117 381**	**185 965**	**155 071**	**172 647**	**82 107**
617 691	84 188	109 274	105 797	127 857	52 635
62 837	4 439	6 542	7 739	6 199	2 945
482 466	73 517	91 326	87 704	107 677	43 619
8 344	1 530	195	978	804	297
4 586	396	1 399	209	833	385
350 337	33 193	76 691	49 274	44 790	29 472
252 605	24 024	65 640	39 202	31 349	24 308

表13-14

外资金融机构及代表处一览表
LIST OF FOREIGN FINANCIAL LNSTITUTIONS AND REPRESENTATIVE OFFICES

机构(代表处)名称 Name of Institutions	所属国家(地区) Representative Offices	所在地区 Location	批准日期 Date of Approval
三井住友银行(中国)有限公司苏州分行	日 本	高新区、虎丘区	1997年11月11日
汇丰银行(中国)有限公司苏州分行	中国香港	工业园区	2004年10月15日
渣打银行(中国)有限公司苏州分行	英 国	工业园区	2005年11月08日
星展银行(中国)有限公司苏州分行	新加坡	工业园区	2006年03月16日
日本池田泉州银行股份有限公司苏州代表处	日 本	吴中区	2006年07月17日
友利银行(中国)有限公司苏州分行	韩 国	工业园区	2007年07月19日
企业银行(中国)有限公司苏州分行	韩 国	工业园区	2007年11月05日
东亚银行(中国)有限公司苏州分行	中国香港	工业园区	2010年03月08日
国民银行(中国)有限公司苏州分行	韩 国	工业园区	2010年06月07日
瑞穗实业银行(中国)有限公司苏州分行	日 本	工业园区	2010年08月24日
合作金库商业银行股份有限公司苏州分行	中国台湾	工业园区	2010年12月17日
彰化商业银行股份有限公司昆山分行	中国台湾	昆山市	2010年12月17日
华一银行(中国)苏州分行	中国台湾	工业园区	2011年06月22日
摩根大通银行(中国)有限公司苏州分行	美 国	工业园区	2012年05月08日
兆丰国际商业银行股份有限公司苏州分行	中国台湾	工业园区	2012年06月13日
三菱东京日联银行(中国)有限公司苏州分行	日 本	工业园区	2014年04月25日
南洋商业银行(中国)有限公司苏州分行	中国香港	工业园区	2014年05月28日
华侨银行(中国)有限公司苏州分行	新加坡	工业园区	2014年09月26日
大华银行(中国)有限公司苏州分行	新加坡	工业园区	2015年02月06日

表13-15

外资保险公司及代表处一览表
LIST OF FOREIGN INSURANCE COMPANIES AND REPRESENTATIVE OFFICES

机构(代表处)名称 Name of Institutions	所属国家(地区) Representative Offices	所在地区 Location	批准日期 Date of Approval
史带财产保险股份有限公司苏州分公司	美　国	姑苏区	2001年09月28日
信诚人寿苏州营销服务部	英　国	吴中区	2005年04月21日
北大方正人寿苏州营销服务部	日　本	姑苏区	2006年12月19日
安盛天平财产保险股份有限公司苏州中心支公司	法　国	工业园区	2006年12月20日
陆家嘴国泰人寿江苏分公司苏州营销服务部	中国台湾	姑苏区	2007年11月09日
中德安联人寿江苏分公司苏州营销服务部	德　国	高新区、虎丘区	2007年12月26日
华泰人寿苏州中心支公司	美　国	工业园区	2008年03月28日
恒安标准人寿江苏分公司苏州中心支公司	英　国	姑苏区	2008年05月26日
友邦保险苏州中心支公司	中国香港	工业园区	2008年05月29日
三星财产(中国)苏州分公司	韩　国	工业园区	2008年07月10日
工银安盛人寿保险有限公司苏州中心支公司	法　国	姑苏区	2008年12月02日
中美联泰大都会人寿保险有限公司苏州支公司	美　国	高新区、虎丘区	2010年03月05日
日本财险(中国)江苏分公司	日　本	工业园区	2010年06月10日
长生人寿江苏分公司苏州营销服务部	日　本	高新区、虎丘区	2010年07月21日
乐爱金苏州营销服务部	韩　国	工业园区	2011年01月04日
三井住友海上火灾保险(中国)江苏分公司苏州营销服务部	日　本	工业园区	2011年05月20日
东京海上日动(中国)江苏分公司	日　本	工业园区	2011年07月19日
国泰产险江苏分公司苏州营销服务部	中国台湾	吴中区	2011年07月21日
中意人寿江苏省分公司苏州中心支公司	意大利	工业园区	2011年08月02日
中宏人寿保险有限公司江苏分公司苏州中心支公司	中国香港	姑苏区	2011年08月03日
交银康联苏州市中心支公司	澳大利亚	工业园区	2012年04月10日
瑞泰人寿苏州中心支公司	英　国	工业园区	2013年05月07日
美亚保险江苏分公司苏州营业部	美　国	工业园区	2014年10月13日
招商信诺人寿保险有限公司江苏省苏州分公司	美　国	工业园区	2016年07月28日

表13-16 分地区养老、医疗、失业、工伤、生育及居民养老保险人数 (2016年末)
NUMBER OF PEOPLE PARTICIPATING IN PENSION, MEDICAL, UNEMPLOYMENT, WORK INJURY, MATERNITY AND RESIDENT INSURANCE BY REGION(END OF 2016)

单位：人 (person)

地 区	Region	基本养老保险参保人数 Number of People Covered by Endowment Insurance	基本医疗保险参保人数 Number of People Covered by Medical Insurance		
				在职职工参保人数 Fully Employed Staff and Workers	离退休人员参保人数 Number of Retired People
全 市	**Whole Municipality**	**5 206 815**	**6 350 852**	**5 013 161**	**1 337 691**
市 区	**Urban Area**	**2 628 090**	**3 167 592**	**2 588 454**	**579 138**
本 级	The Level	768 687	1 067 264	764 862	302 402
吴中区	Wuzhong District	374 557	456 934	382 314	74 620
相城区	Xiangcheng District	209 410	238 208	209 855	28 353
工业园区	Industrial Park	724 684	757 195	729 192	28 003
吴江区	Wujiang District	550 752	647 991	502 231	145 760
县级市	**Cities at County Level**	**2 578 725**	**3 183 260**	**2 424 707**	**758 553**
常 熟	Changshu	639 446	810 479	561 013	249 466
张家港	Zhangjiagang	472 473	663 276	483 649	179 627
昆 山	Kunshan	1 167 645	1 268 149	1 079 625	188 524
太 仓	Taicang	299 161	441 356	300 420	140 936

表13-16 续表 Continued

单位：人 (person)

地 区	Region	失业保险参保人数 Number of People Covered by Unemployment Insurance	工伤保险参保人数 Number of People Covered by Work Injury Insurance	生育保险参保人数 Number of People Covered by Childbirth Insurance	居民养老保险参保人数 Rural Number of People Covered by Endowment Insurance
全 市	**Whole Municipality**	**4 466 224**	**4 393 038**	**4 507 577**	**463 709**
市 区	**Urban Area**	**2 337 338**	**2 327 761**	**2 496 700**	**229 335**
本 级	The Level	697 497	686 017	772 381	23 391
吴中区	Wuzhong District	318 505	319 180	371 277	21 266
相城区	Xiangcheng District	182 453	182 451	212 506	60 110
工业园区	Industrial Park	707 351	707 571	729 192	1 148
吴江区	Wujiang District	431 532	432 542	411 344	123 420
县级市	**Cities at County Level**	**2 128 886**	**2 065 277**	**2 010 877**	**234 374**
常 熟	Changshu	455 006	446 181	415 171	93 866
张家港	Zhangjiagang	395 395	391 750	385 833	76 059
昆 山	Kunshan	1 017 640	965 801	958 807	35 695
太 仓	Taicang	260 845	261 545	251 066	28 754

注:本级数据为姑苏区和高新区、虎丘区的合计数。
Note: The level data is the totals of Gusu District, Suzhou New District and Huqiu (Tiger Hill) District.

表13-17 分地区养老、医疗、失业、工伤、生育及居民养老保险基金收入(2016年)

FUND INCOME OF PENSION, MEDICAL, UNEMPLOYMENT, WORK INJURY, MATERNITY AND RESIDENT INSURANCE BY REGION(2016)

单位：万元 (10 000 yuan)

地区	Region	基本养老保险基金收入 Fund's Income Covered by Endowment Insurance	基本医疗保险基金收入 Fund's Income Covered by Medical Insurance	失业保险基金收入 Fund's Income Covered by Unemployment Insurance
全市	**Whole Municipality**	**4 936 857**	**1 836 308**	**284 958**
市区	**Urban Area**	**3 031 967**	**979 825**	**172 586**
本级	The Level	936 238	390 301	75 674
吴中区	Wuzhong District	354 620	130 082	21 551
相城区	Xiangcheng District	244 205	72 311	11 343
工业园区	Industrial Park	1 095 387	233 761	42 898
吴江区	Wujiang District	401 517	153 370	21 121
县级市	**Cities at County Level**	**1 904 890**	**856 483**	**112 372**
常熟	Changshu	489 140	223 170	25 278
张家港	Zhangjiagang	356 588	191 132	22 780
昆山	Kunshan	790 223	325 225	48 864
太仓	Taicang	268 939	116 956	15 450

表13-17 续表 Continued

单位：万元 (10 000 yuan)

地区	Region	工伤保险基金收入 Fund's Income Covered by Work Injury Insurance	生育保险基金收入 Fund's Income Covered by Childbirth Insurance	居民养老保险基金收入 Fund's Income Covered by Endowment Insurance
全市	**Whole Municipality**	**235 866**	**94 916**	**193 199**
市区	**Urban Area**	**96 789**	**60 262**	**77 174**
本级	The Level	22 386	20 927	7 871
吴中区	Wuzhong District	9 173	6 745	11 037
相城区	Xiangcheng District	5 779	3 704	10 641
工业园区	Industrial Park	36 275	21 745	4 822
吴江区	Wujiang District	23 176	7 141	42 803
县级市	**Cities at County Level**	**139 077**	**34 654**	**116 025**
常熟	Changshu	32 427	9 363	51 489
张家港	Zhangjiagang	34 633	6 813	23 755
昆山	Kunshan	49 994	13 943	27 953
太仓	Taicang	22 023	4 535	12 828

注:本级数据为姑苏区和高新区、虎丘区的合计数。
Note: The level data is the totals of Gusu District, Suzhou New District and Huqiu (Tiger Hill) District.

主 要 统 计 指 标 解 释

财政收入 指国家财政参与社会产品分配所取得的收入，是实现国家职能的财力保证。财政收入所包括的内容几经变化，目前主要包括：

(1)各项税收：包括增值税、营业税、消费税、土地增值税、城市维护建设税、资源税、城市土地使用税、企业所得税、个人所得税、关税、证券交易印花税、车辆购置税、农牧业税和耕地占用税等。

(2)专项收入：包括排污费收入、城市水资源费收入、矿产资源补偿费收入、教育费附加收入等。

(3)其他收入：包括利息收入、基本建设贷款归还收入、基本建设收入、捐赠收入等。

(4)国有企业亏损补贴：此项为负收入，冲减财政收入。主要包括对工业企业、商业企业、粮食企业的补贴。

财政支出 国家财政将筹集起来的资金进行分配使用，以满足经济建设和各项事业的需要，主要包括：

中央财政收入和地方财政收入 指按现行分税制财政体制划分的中央本级收入和地方本级收入。1994年实行分税制财政体制以后，属于中央财政的收入包括关税、海关代征消费税和增值税，消费税，中央企业所得税，地方银行和外资银行及非银行金融企业所得税，铁道部门、各银行总行、各保险总公司等集中缴纳的营业税、利润和城市维护建设税，车辆购置税，船舶吨税，增值税的75%部分，证券交易税(印花税)94%部分，个人所得税中的利息所得税，利息所得税之外的个人所得税中央分享的部分，海洋石油资源税。属于地方财政的收入包括营业税，地方企业所得税，利息所得税之外的个人所得税地方分享的部分，城镇土地使用税，固定资产投资方向调节税，城镇维护建设税，房产税，车船使用税，印花税，屠宰税，农牧业税，农业特产税，耕地占用税，契税，土地增值税、国有土地有偿使用收入，增值税25%部分，证券交易税(印花税)6%部分和除海洋石油资源税以外的其他资源税。

中央财政支出和地方财政支出 指根据政府在经济和社会活动中的不同职责，划分中央和地方政府的责权，按照政府的责权划分确定的支出。中央财政支出包括国防支出，武装警察部队支出，中央级行政管理费和各项事业费，重点建设支出以及中央政府调整国民经济结构、协调地区发展、实施宏观调控的支出。地方财政支出主要包括地方行政管理和各项事业费，地方统筹的基本建设、技术改造支出，支援农村生产支出，城市维护和建设经费，价格补贴支出等。

存款 指企业、机关、团体或居民根据资金必须收回的原则，把货币资金存入银行或其他信贷机构保管并取得一定利息的一种信用活动形式。根据存款对象或性质的不同可划分为住户存款、非金融企业存款、政府存款、非银行业金融机构存款等科目。它是银行信贷资金的主要来源。

贷款 指银行或其他信贷机构根据资金必须归还的原则，按一定利率，为企业、个人等提供资金的一种信用活动形式。我国银行贷款分为短期贷款、中长期贷款、融资租赁、票据融资、各项垫款、境外贷款等。

保险公司 在中国境内的、经过保险监督管理部门批准设立，并依法登记注册的各类商业保险公司。

保险金额 指保险人承担赔偿或者给付保险金责任的最高限额。

保费 指投保人为取得保险人在约定范围内所承担赔偿责任而支付给保险人的费用。

赔款 指保险人根据保险合同的规定，向被保险人支付的赔偿保险责任损失的金额。

给付 包括死伤医疗给付和满期给付。死伤医疗给付是指保险人根据人寿保险及长期健康保险合同的规定，因被保险人在保险期内发生保险责任范围内的保险事故支付给被保险人(或受益人)的金额。满期给付是指被保险人生存期满，保险人按人寿保险合同规定支付给被保险人的满期保险金额。

基本养老保险（参保）职工人数 指报告期末按照国家法律、法规和有关政策规定参加基本养老保险并在社保经办机构已建立缴费记录档案的职工人数，包括中断缴费但未终止养老保险关系的职工人数，不包括只登记未建立缴费记录档案的人数。

基本医疗保险参保人数 指报告期末按国家有关规定参加基本医疗保险的人数。包括参加保险的职工人数和退休人员人数。

失业保险参保人数 指报告期末按照国家法律、法规和有关政策规定参加了失业保险的城镇企业事业单位的职工及地方政府规定参加失业保险的其他人员的人数。

工伤保险参加保险人数 指报告期末依据国家有关规定参加工伤保险的职工人数。

生育保险参保人数 指报告期末依据有关规定参加生育保险的职工人数。

居民养老保险参保人数 指报告期末，参加城乡居民养老保险（在经办机构参保登记并已建立缴费记录以及制度实施当年已经年满60周岁并在经办机构参保登记）的总人数（不包括已经办理注销登记手续的人数）。

EXPLANATORY NOTES ON MAIN STATISTICAL INDICATORS

Government Revenue refers to income for the government finance through participating in the distribution of social products. It is the financial guarantee to ensure government functioning. The contents of government revenue have changed several times. Now it includes the following main items:

(1) Various tax revenues, including value added tax, business tax, consumption tax, land value added tax, tax on city maintenance and construction, resources tax, tax on use of urban land, enterprise income tax, personal income tax, tariff, stamp tax on security transactions, tax on purchase of motor vehicles, tax on agriculture and animal husbandry and tax on occupancy of cultivated land, etc.

(2) Special revenues, including revenues from the fee on sewage treatment, fee on urban water resources, fee for the compensation of mineral resources and extra-charges for education, etc.

(3) Other revenues, including revenue from interest, revenue from the repayment of capital construction loan, revenue from capital construction projects, and donations and grants.

(4) Subsidies for the losses of State-owned enterprises. This is an item of negative revenue, counteracting revenues and consisting of subsidies to industrial, commercial and grain purchasing and supply enterprises.

Government Expenditure refers to the distribution and use of the funds which the government finance has raised, so as to meet the needs of economic construction and various causes. It includes the following main items:

Revenue of the Central Government and Revenue of the Local Governments refer to the revenue of the Central Government and that of the local governments as defined by the decentralized taxation system starting from 1994. In accordance with this system, the revenue of the Central Government includes tariff, consumption tax and value added tax levied by the Customs, consumption tax, income tax of the enterprises subordinate to the Central Government, income taxes of local banks, foreign-funded banks and non-bank financial institutions, business tax and profits of railways, head offices of banks, head office of insurance company, which are handed over to the government in a centralized way, tax on city maintenance and construction, tax on purchasing motor vehicles, tonnage tax of ships, 75% of the value added tax, 94% of the tax on stock dealing (stamp tax), interest income tax in the personal income tax, that proportion of the personal income tax (other that interest income tax) to be shared by the Central Government, and tax on ocean petroleum resources. The revenue of the local governments includes business tax, income tax of the enterprises subordinate to the local government, that proportion of the personal income tax (other that interest income tax) to be shared by the Central Government, tax on the use of urban land, tax on the adjustment of investment in fixed assets, tax on town maintenance and construction, tax on real estates, tax on the use of vehicles and ships, stamp tax, slaughter tax, tax on agriculture and animal husbandry, tax on special agricultural products, tax on the occupancy of cultivated land, contract tax, value-added tax on land, income from charges on use of State-owned land, 25% of the value added tax, 6% of the tax on stock dealing (stamp tax) and tax on resources other than the tax on ocean petroleum resources.

Expenditure of the Central Government and Expenditure of the Local Governments according to the different functions of the Central Government and local governments in economic and social activities, the rights of affairs administration are demarcated between those of the Central Government and those of local governments; and the classification of the expenditure between the Central Government and local governments are made on the basis of the classification of the rights of affairs administration between them. The expenditure of the Central Government includes the expenditure for national defence, expenditure for armed police forces, the administrative expenses and various operating expenses at the level of Central Government, expenditure for key projects and the expenditure of the Central Government for adjusting the national economic structure; coordinating the development among different regions; and exercising macro-economic regulation and control. The expenditure of the local governments includes mainly the administrative expenses and various operating expenses at the level of local governments, the expenditure for capital construction and technological innovation with the funds raised by the local government, expenditure for supporting rural production, expenditure for city maintenance and construction and expenditure for price subsidies, etc.

Deposit is a form of credit by which enterprises, institutions, organizations or households can put money into banks and other credit institutions for safekeeping and interest earning under the principle of free withdrawal. According to different depositors, deposits are divided into household deposits, non financial enterprise deposits, government deposits, non banking financial institutions deposits. Deposits are major sources of the credit funds of banks.

Loan is a form of credit by which banks and other credit institutions provide funds at certain interest rate to enterprises and individuals in the light of the principle of unconditional repayment. Loans from Chinese banks include short-term loan, medium-term and long-term loans, financial lease, bill financing, various money advanced, foreign loans.

Insurance Companies refer to commercial insurance companies of various forms registered by law and established in China with the approval of insurance regulatory agencies.

Amount Insured refers to the maximum that the insurant will get for the claim of the case insured.

Premium is the fee paid by the insurant to the insurer to obtain the obligation of compensation from the insurance within the agreed terms.

Settled Claim is the compensation paid by the insurer to the insurant in accordance with the insurance contract.

Payment includes payment for death, injury or medical treatment and payment at maturity. Payment for death, injury or medical treatment refers to the money paid to the insurant (or the beneficiary) in accordance with the life or health insurance contract when the insurant encounters accidents within the insured period covered in the contract. Payment at maturity refers to the payment to the insurant in accordance with the life insurance contract at the end of the insured period.

Number of People Covered by Endowment Insurance refers to staff and workers participating in the basic pension insurance programme according to national laws, regulations and related policies at the end of the reference period, who have already had payment records in social security management agencies, including those who have interrupt payment without terminating the insurance programme. Those who have registered in the programme but with no payment records are not included.

Number of People Covered by Medical Insurance refers to people participating in the basic medical care insurance programme according to related regulations as at the end of reference period, including number of staff and workers and retirees participating in this insurance programme.

Number of People Covered by Unemployment Insurance refers to staff and workers in urban enterprises or institutions who have participated in the unemployment insurance programme according to relevant policies and regulations, and other people who have participated according to local government regulations, as at the end of reference period.

Number of People Covered by Labor Injury Work Injury Insurance refers to staff and workers who have participated in the work injury insurance programme according to relevant national regulations.

Number of People Covered by Insurance refers to staff and workers who have participated in the maternity insurance programme according to relevant regulation at the end of the reporting period.

Number of Residents Participating in Pension Insurance refers to the total number (not including the number of the residents who have already gone through the deregistration procedures) of the urban and rural residents participating in pension insurance (residents who have been registered to participate in pension insurance at the agency and have established payment records and in the year of the implementation of the system are 60 years of age or older and have been registered to participate in pension insurance at the agency) at the end of the reporting period.

十四、物价指数

CHAPTER 14
PRICE INDICES

14 物价指数 PRICE INDICES

主 要 统 计 指 标
MAJOR STATISTICAL INDICATORS

(以上年价格为100 The Price of Preceding Year is Taken as 100)

2016年市区居民消费价格总指数	General Consumer Price Index of Urban Residents	102.7
食品烟酒类价格指数	General Price Index of Food, Cigarette and Wine in Urban Area	104.3
衣着类价格指数	General Price Index of Clothing in Urban Area	102.0
居住类价格指数	General Price Index of Residence in Urban Area	101.7
生活用品及服务价格指数	General Price Index of Life Articles and Service in Urban Area	102.0
交通和通信类价格指数	General Price Index of Transportation and Communication in Urban Area	97.7
教育文化和娱乐价格指数	General Price Index of Education, Cultural and Recreation in Urban Area	101.4
医疗保健价格指数	General Price Index of Medical Service in Urban Area	114.0
其他用品和服务价格指数	General Price Index of Other Articles and Service in Urban Area	102.8
2016年市区商品零售价格总指数	General Retail Price Index in Urban Area	100.5

表14-1

市区居民消费价格指数及商品零售价格指数
RESIDENTS CONSUMER PRICE INDICES AND RETAIL PRICE INDICES OF COMMODITIES

(2016年以下列各年价格为100 The Price of Following Years is Taken as 100 in 2016)

年 份 Year	居民消费价格总指数 General Residents Consumer Price Index	# 食 品 Food	# 衣 着 Clothing	# 居 住 Inhabitation	# 服务项目 Services	商品零售价格总指数 General Retail Price Index
1978	–	–	–	–	–	527.3
1979	–	–	–	–	–	516.5
1980	–	–	–	–	–	495.6
1981	–	–	–	–	–	490.3
1982	–	–	–	–	–	485.4
1983	–	–	–	–	–	476.9
1984	676.2	1 258.9	499.1	–	1 276.1	460.3
1985	604.3	1 072.4	489.8	–	1 162.2	410.6
1986	567.3	986.6	473.8	–	1 081.1	385.8
1987	510.2	849.0	433.4	–	1 046.6	345.1
1988	415.8	667.5	338.0	–	969.9	278.6
1989	356.0	593.9	278.6	–	773.4	239.9
1990	342.6	574.3	260.8	–	690.0	232.4
1991	316.2	508.2	241.8	–	654.1	213.8
1992	286.8	455.7	228.8	–	503.5	197.6
1993	233.2	368.1	199.2	414.5	360.1	162.8
1994	189.0	279.8	158.4	378.2	302.1	132.8
1995	160.1	228.8	131.8	300.9	254.8	117.2
1996	144.3	209.1	122.9	216.3	223.9	110.4
1997	143.4	213.3	121.0	194.1	191.5	112.2
1998	144.9	220.6	129.3	175.2	180.0	115.7
1999	146.1	231.3	131.9	164.0	159.8	119.9
2000	146.2	234.9	132.5	154.9	151.6	121.8
2001	147.0	242.0	135.9	150.0	139.5	124.1
2002	146.3	238.4	139.4	150.5	134.4	124.7
2003	145.1	231.1	137.2	149.1	131.0	125.3
2004	138.2	207.2	133.8	140.5	124.2	123.3
2005	135.0	198.2	132.2	132.6	120.0	122.0
2006	132.9	191.6	130.5	126.1	118.7	120.9
2007	127.5	173.1	127.5	119.2	117.5	117.8
2008	121.1	150.7	125.0	116.3	116.7	112.4
2009	121.4	147.3	119.5	119.4	117.4	114.4
2010	117.4	138.9	121.7	115.1	113.9	110.9
2011	111.7	121.2	117.1	111.7	113.3	105.9
2012	108.7	115.4	112.2	108.8	111.5	104.0
2013	106.5	110.7	110.7	106.4	109.8	102.7
2014	104.4	108.0	105.4	103.8	107.3	101.0
2015	102.7	105.5	102.0	101.7	104.1	100.5

注：本章市区数据不包含吴江区。

Note: The data of urban area in this chapter does not include Wujiang District.

表14-2

市区居民消费价格指数及商品零售价格指数
RESIDENTS CONSUMER PRICE INDICES AND RETAIL PRICE INDICES OF COMMODITIES

(各年以上年价格为100 The Price of Preceding Year is Taken as 100)

年 份 Year	居民消费价格总指数 General Residents Consumer Price Index	# 食 品 Food	# 衣 着 Clothing	# 居 住 Inhabitation	# 服务项目 Services	商品零售价格总指数 General Retail Price Index
1979	-	-	-	-	-	102.1
1980	-	-	-	-	-	104.2
1981	-	-	-	-	-	101.1
1982	-	-	-	-	-	101.0
1983	-	-	-	-	-	101.8
1984	-	-	-	-	-	103.6
1985	111.9	117.4	101.9	-	109.8	112.1
1986	106.5	108.7	103.4	-	107.5	106.4
1987	111.2	116.2	109.3	-	103.3	111.8
1988	122.7	127.2	128.2	-	107.9	123.9
1989	116.8	112.4	121.3	-	125.4	116.1
1990	103.9	103.4	106.9	-	112.1	103.2
1991	108.4	113.0	107.8	-	105.5	108.7
1992	110.2	111.5	105.7	-	129.9	108.2
1993	123.0	123.8	114.9	-	139.8	121.4
1994	123.4	131.6	125.7	109.6	119.2	122.6
1995	118.0	122.3	120.2	125.7	118.6	113.3
1996	111.0	109.4	107.2	139.1	113.8	106.2
1997	100.6	98.0	101.6	111.4	116.9	98.4
1998	99.0	96.7	93.6	110.8	106.4	97.0
1999	99.2	95.4	97.8	106.9	112.6	96.4
2000	99.9	98.4	99.8	105.8	105.4	98.5
2001	99.5	97.1	97.5	103.3	108.7	98.1
2002	100.4	101.5	97.5	99.7	103.8	99.5
2003	100.8	103.2	101.6	100.9	102.6	99.5
2004	105.0	111.6	102.5	106.1	105.4	101.7
2005	102.4	104.5	101.2	106.0	103.6	101.1
2006	101.6	103.4	101.3	105.1	101.1	100.9
2007	104.2	110.7	102.4	105.8	101.0	102.6
2008	105.3	114.9	102.0	102.5	100.7	104.8
2009	99.8	102.3	104.6	97.4	99.4	98.3
2010	103.4	106.0	98.1	103.7	103.1	103.1
2011	105.1	114.6	104.0	103.1	100.5	104.7
2012	102.7	105.1	104.4	102.7	101.6	101.9
2013	102.1	104.2	101.3	102.2	101.5	101.2
2014	102.1	102.5	105.0	102.6	102.4	101.7
2015	101.6	102.4	103.3	102.0	103.1	100.4
2016	102.7	105.5	102.0	101.7	104.1	100.5

表14-3

市区居民消费价格指数
RESIDENTS CONSUMER PRICE INDICES

(以上年价格为100 The Price of Preceding Year is taken as 100)

项　目	Item	2016年
居民消费价格总指数	**General Residents Consumer Price Index**	**102.7**
服务项目价格指数	**Price Index of Service**	**104.1**
消费品价格指数	**Price Index of Consumer Goods**	**101.8**
一、食品烟酒	**Food, Cigarette and Wine**	**104.3**
1.食　品	Food	105.5
(1)粮　食	Grain	100.5
(2)薯　类	Tubers	114.8
(3)豆　类	Beans	100.6
(4)食用油	Edible Oil	99.8
(5)菜	Vegetables	112.3
#鲜　菜	Fresh Vegetables	113.5
(6)畜肉类	Livestock Meat	110.9
(7)禽肉类	Poultry Meat	103.1
(8)水产品	Aquatic Products	106.6
(9)蛋　类	Eggs	98.0
(10)奶　类	Dairy	99.2
(11)干鲜瓜果	Dried and Fresh Melons and Fruits	100.4
#鲜瓜果	Fresh Fruits	100.6
(12)糖果糕点类	Confectionery	99.8
#食　糖	Sugar	102.3
(13)调味品	Flavoring	101.5
(14)其他食品类	Other Food	102.4
2.茶及饮料	Tea and Beverage	99.1
3.烟　酒	Cigarette and Wine	102.0
4.在外餐饮	Foods Consumed not at Home	102.9
二、衣　着	**Clothing**	**102.0**
1.服　装	Garments	101.6
#男式服装	Man's Garments	101.7
女式服装	Women's Garments	102.4
儿童服装	Children's Garments	99.2

注：居民消费价格调查每5年为一轮基期，2016年为新基期，国家对消费价格调查八大类结构做出调整。

表14-3 续表 Continued

项　目	Item	2016年
2.服装材料	Garments Material	103.2
3.其他衣着及配件	Other Clothing and Accessories	101.7
4.衣着加工服务费	Tailoring Service	102.4
5.鞋　类	Footwear	103.5
三、居　住	**Residence**	**101.7**
1.租赁房房租	House Rent	102.7
2.住房保养维修及管理	Housing Maintenance and Management	100.1
3.水电燃料	Light, Water and Fuel	101.6
4.自有住房	Own Housing	101.9
四、生活用品及服务	**Life Articles and Service**	**102.0**
1.家具及室内装饰品	Furniture and Interior Decorations	103.0
# 家　具	Furniture	103.8
2.家用器具	Household Appliances	100.3
3.家用纺织品	Household Textiles	103.0
4.家庭日用杂品	Daily Use Household Articles	100.8
5.个人护理用品	Personal Care Products	101.3
6.家庭服务	Household Service	107.6
五、交通和通信	**Transportation and Communication**	**97.7**
1.交　通	Transportation	96.9
2.通　信	Communication	99.6
六、教育文化和娱乐	**Education Cultural and Recreation**	**101.4**
1.教　育	Education	103.9
2.文化娱乐	Cultural and Recreational Articles	98.8
七、医疗保健	**Medical Service**	**114.0**
1.药品及医疗器具	Drugs and Medical Devices	99.4
2.医疗服务	Medical Service	122.5
八、其他用品及服务	**Other Articles and Service**	**102.8**
1.其他用品类	Other Articles	103.6
2.其他服务类	Other Service	102.2

Note: The survey of consumer prices is conducted in five years as a base period, 2016 was the first year of a new base period, and the state had made adjustments to the structure of the eight major categories for consumer price surveys.

表14-4

市区商品零售价格指数

RETAIL PRICE INDICES OF COMMODITIES

(以上年价格为100 The Price of Preceding Year is taken as 100)

项　　目	Item	2016年
商品零售价格总指数	**General Retail Price Index**	**100.5**
一、食　品	**Food**	**104.8**
1.粮　食	Grain	100.5
2.薯　类	Tubers	114.8
3.豆　类	Beans	100.7
4.食用油	Edible Oil	99.8
5.菜	Vegetables	112.6
6.畜肉类	Livestock Meat	111.0
7.禽肉类	Poultry Meat	103.1
8.水产品	Aquatic Products	106.5
9.蛋　类	Eggs	98.0
10.奶　类	Dairy	99.2
11.干鲜瓜果	Dried and Fresh Melons and Fruits	100.4
12.糖果糕点类	Confectionery	99.7
13.调味品	Flavoring	101.5
14.其他食品类	Other Food	102.4
15. 在外餐饮	Foods Consumed not at Home	102.9
二、饮料、烟酒	**Beverage, Tobacco and Liquor**	**101.5**
1.茶及饮料	Tea and Beverage	98.9
2.烟　草	Cigarette	102.5
3.酒　类	Wine	101.0
三、服装、鞋帽	**Garments, Shoes and Hats**	**102.1**
1.服　装	Garments	101.7
2.鞋帽袜	Footwear and Hats	103.6
3.其他衣着配件	Other Clothing and Accessories	99.3
四、纺织品	**Textiles**	**103.2**
1.服装材料	Garments Material	103.2
2.床上用品	Bed Articles	103.2
五、家用电器及音像器材	**Household Electric Appliances and Sound-video Equipment**	**99.0**
1.家庭设备	Household Facilities and Articles	100.3
2.文娱用耐用消费品	Durable Consumer Goods for Recreational Use	96.8

表14-4 续表 Continued

项　　目	Item	2016年
3.专业音像器材	Sound-video Equipment	98.4
六、文化办公用品	**Culture and Office Articles**	**97.8**
七、日用品	**Articles for Daily Use**	**101.3**
1.日用百货	Daily Consumer Goods	101.5
2.厨具餐具茶具	Kitchenware, Tableware, Tea Set	101.0
3.清洗用品	Washing Articles	103.1
4.其他日用品	Others Articles for Daily Use	99.0
八、体育娱乐用品	**Sports and Recreational Goods**	**97.6**
1. 体育户外用品	Sports and Outdoor Goods	88.3
2. 娱乐用品	Recreational Goods	102.2
九、交通、通信用品	**Transportation and Communication**	**98.4**
1. 交通运输机械	Transportation Machines	98.0
2. 通讯器材	Communication Apparatus	100.6
十、家　具	**Furniture**	**103.8**
十一、化妆品	**Cosmetics**	**101.4**
十二、金银饰品	**Jewelry**	**106.5**
十三、中西药品及医疗保健用品	**Chinese and Western Medicines and Medical Care Articles**	**98.9**
1.医疗卫生器具	Medical Appliances	100.0
2.中　药	Traditional Chinese Medicine	100.1
3.西　药	Western Medicine	92.1
4.保健器具及用品	Health Articles	109.1
十四、书报杂志及电子出版物	**Newspapers, Magazines and Electronic Publication**	**100.5**
1.教材及参考书	Teaching Materials and Reference Books	101.2
2.书报杂志	Newspapers and Magazines	100.0
3.计算机办公软件	Office Software	99.9
十五、燃　料	**Fuels**	**97.1**
1. 煤炭及制品	Coal and Coal Products	99.6
2. 石油及制品	Petroleum and Petroleum Products	96.9
十六、建筑材料及五金电料	**Building Materials and Metal Hardware**	**100.4**
1. 建筑装璜材料	Building Decoration Materials	100.2
2. 五金水暖	Hardware Plumbing	101.0

表14-5

分月市区居民消费价格指数及商品零售价格指数

(2016年以上年同期价格为100)

项　目	Item	全　年 Annual Total	1月 Jan.	2月 Feb.	3月 Mar.
居民消费价格总指数	**Urban General Consumer Price Index**	**102.7**	**102.5**	**102.9**	**103.0**
1.食品烟酒	Food, Tobacco and Alcohol	104.3	103.7	105.9	105.9
2.衣　着	Clothing	102.0	104.1	103.3	101.7
3.居　住	Residence	101.7	101.5	101.3	101.9
4.生活用品及服务	Life Articles and Service	102.0	101.4	101.7	101.9
5.交通和通信	Transportation and Communication	97.7	96.6	97.0	96.1
6.教育文化和娱乐	Education Cultural and Recreation	101.4	102.1	100.4	101.9
7.医疗保健	Medical Service	114.0	116.0	116.1	116.1
8.其他用品及服务	Other Articles and Service	102.8	98.6	100.1	101.0
商品零售价格总指数	**Urban General Retail Price Index**	**100.5**	**99.6**	**100.3**	**100.0**
1.食　品	Food	104.8	104.0	106.6	106.8
2.饮料、烟酒	Beverages, Tobacco and Liquor	101.5	102.2	102.6	101.7
3.服装、鞋帽	Garments , Shoes and Hats	102.1	104.2	103.4	101.8
4.纺织品	Textiles	103.2	104.0	104.2	104.2
5.家用电器及音像器材	Household Electric Appliances and Sound-video Equipment	99.0	99.5	99.1	99.0
6.文化办公用品	Culture and Office Articles	97.8	98.3	98.7	99.2
7.日用品	Articles for Daily Use	101.3	100.6	100.1	100.2
8.体育娱乐用品	Sports and Recreational Goods	97.6	99.2	98.6	99.0
9.交通、通信用品	Transportation and Communication	98.4	97.7	98.1	98.3
10.家　具	Furniture	103.8	102.1	103.3	107.1
11.化妆品	Cosmetics	101.4	97.8	99.7	98.1
12.金银珠宝	Jewelry	106.5	91.3	95.0	102.7
13.中西药品及医疗保健用品	Chinese and Western Medicines and Medical Care Articles	98.9	94.5	94.6	94.6
14.书报杂志及电子出版物	Newspapers, Magazines and Electronic Publication	100.5	102.7	101.9	100.8
15.燃　料	Fuels	97.1	93.9	95.7	92.1
16.建筑材料及五金电料	Building Materials and Metal Hardware	100.4	100.1	100.2	100.1

CONSUMER PRICE INDICES AND RETAIL PRICE INDICES OF COMMODITIES BY MONTH

(The Price of 2016 Takes the Price of Preceding Year as 100)

4月 Apr.	5月 May	6月 Jun.	7月 Jul.	8月 Aug.	9月 Sept.	10月 Oct.	11月 Nov.	12月 Dec.
102.7	**102.4**	**102.9**	**103.0**	**102.4**	**102.9**	**102.9**	**102.7**	**102.0**
105.7	104.5	104.3	104.1	102.7	103.4	103.9	104.9	102.2
101.7	101.7	102.0	101.8	101.4	101.0	101.9	102.1	101.7
101.6	101.6	101.3	101.6	101.0	101.6	101.5	102.6	103.1
102.0	102.4	103.0	102.7	102.5	102.3	101.5	101.0	101.9
95.4	95.1	96.8	97.4	98.0	99.1	99.6	100.6	101.4
101.4	101.4	101.9	101.6	101.5	100.9	101.4	101.8	100.2
116.0	116.1	118.4	118.2	117.3	118.4	114.8	102.4	102.3
101.4	101.3	103.7	104.5	104.8	104.7	104.7	104.8	104.4
99.8	**99.4**	**100.4**	**100.6**	**100.3**	**100.9**	**100.8**	**102.3**	**102.1**
106.4	105.1	104.9	104.7	103.0	103.8	104.3	105.6	102.2
102.4	101.1	100.2	100.7	100.6	101.4	101.9	101.7	101.2
101.8	101.9	102.0	101.8	101.5	101.0	101.9	102.3	101.8
105.4	103.1	103.1	101.9	101.8	103.1	104.4	102.0	101.4
98.3	97.8	99.0	99.7	99.2	99.8	97.4	98.2	100.5
98.3	97.5	97.6	97.4	97.4	96.9	96.9	98.4	96.5
101.5	102.9	103.2	102.4	101.5	100.8	100.9	99.5	101.8
98.7	98.6	95.3	95.0	95.3	98.8	94.4	99.3	98.5
97.1	97.4	98.4	99.0	98.7	98.2	98.7	99.6	99.6
105.5	104.8	104.4	103.3	103.9	103.9	101.9	102.8	102.6
101.0	101.2	102.0	102.8	102.6	103.4	102.5	104.7	101.5
103.6	104.0	106.7	110.6	114.2	112.0	112.2	114.1	114.4
94.3	94.6	100.6	100.3	98.3	100.9	99.4	107.8	107.3
100.8	100.7	100.7	98.9	98.9	100.0	100.0	100.0	100.1
93.0	91.8	94.1	95.6	97.7	101.5	101.5	103.0	107.3
100.1	100.3	100.3	100.1	100.0	100.0	99.8	102.2	101.9

表14-6

主要食品年平均价格
MAJOR FOOD AVERAGE PRICE

单位：元/千克 (yuan/kg)

商品名称	Item	代表规格品	Standard and Rate	2015年	2016年
大　米	Rice	袋装东北大米	Bagged Northeast rice	6.41	6.45
面　粉	Flour	特一粉	Special class	5.62	5.59
小　米	Millet	一　级	First class	15.58	14.72
黄　豆	Soybeans	一　级	First class	8.50	8.51
绿　豆	Mung beans	一　级	First class	13.63	13.46
花生油　(元/升)	Peanut oil (yuan/L)	瓶装5升　鲁花压榨	Luhuayazha (5l. a bottle)	27.85	26.72
调和油　(元/升)	Blend oil (yuan/L)	瓶装5升　金龙鱼	Jinlongyu (5l. a bottle)	11.39	11.80
动物油	Animal oil	猪板油　一级	Lard　(first class)	19.86	22.60
猪　肉	Pork	后　腿	Hind legs	28.14	32.86
鸡	Chickens	活草母鸡	Live grass hens	29.69	30.51
蛋	Eggs	洋鸡蛋	Plant-feeding eggs	9.08	8.56
鲫　鱼	Crucian carp	尾重350克左右	About 350 grams a fish	21.54	25.71
带　鱼	Hairtail fish	尾重250克左右	About 250 grams a fish	43.63	46.50
大白菜	Chinese cabbages	一　级	First class	3.92	4.42
菠　菜	Spinach	一　级	First class	9.26	11.39
青　菜	Greens	一　级	First class	7.25	8.46
黄　瓜	Cucumbers	一　级	First class	7.86	8.05
番　茄	Tomatoes	一　级	First class	8.57	9.47
黄豆芽	Soybean sprouts	一　级	First class	5.65	6.30
生　姜	Ginger	一　级	First class	13.63	11.73
青　蒜	Garlic	一　级	First class	10.41	14.94
苹　果	Apples	红富士　一级	Red Fuji (first class)	15.17	14.40
香　蕉	Bananas	国　产　一级	Home-grown (first class)	10.85	7.71
西　瓜	Watermelons	普　通　一级	Ordinary (first class)	6.50	7.33

主 要 统 计 指 标 解 释

居民消费价格指数 是反映一定时期内城乡居民所购买的生活消费品价格和服务项目价格变动趋势和程度的相对数，是对城市居民消费价格指数和农村居民消费价格指数进行综合汇总计算的结果。该指数可以观察和分析消费品的零售价格和服务项目价格变动对城乡居民实际生活费支出的影响程度。

商品零售价格指数 是反映一定时期内城乡商品零售价格变动趋势和程度的相对数。商品零售价格的变动直接影响到城乡居民的生活支出和国家的财政收入，影响居民购买力和市场供需的平衡，影响到消费与积累的比例关系。因此，该指数可以从一个侧面对上述经济活动进行观察和分析。

代表规格品 居民消费价格指数要根据市场上的实际商品价格来计算，市场上的商品和服务项目数量繁多，在编制价格指数时不可能也没有必要把全部商品都纳入指数计算。因此，要选择一部分有代表性的商品和服务来代表全部的商品和服务，也就是从众多的不同的产地、规格、等级、牌号、花色的商品中抽选一部分，又称为规格品。

EXPLANATORY NOTES ON MAIN STATISTICAL INDICATORS

Consumer Price Indices reflect the trend and degree of changes in prices of consumer goods and services purchased by urban and rural households during a given period. They are obtained by combining the Urban Consumer Price Indices and the Rural Consumer Price Indices. The Indices enable the observation and analysis of the degree of impact of the changes in the prices of retailed goods and services on the actual living expenses of urban and rural residents.

Retail Price Indices reflect the trend and degree of change in retail prices of commodities during a given period. The change in retail prices of commodities directly affect the living expenses of urban and rural residents, government revenue, purchasing power of residents and the equilibrium of market supply and demand, and the ratio of consumption to accumulation. Therefore, the retail price indices are useful from an oblique perspective for observing and analyzing the changes of the above economic activities.

Representative specification items The consumer price index is calculated according to the actual price of the product on the market. However, there is a vast amount of goods and services on the market, and in the preparation of the price index it is neither possible nor necessary to include all the goods in the index calculation. Therefore, it is necessary to select a representative part of the goods and services to represent all the goods and services, that is, to select a part from the many commodities of different places of origin, sizes, grades, trademarks, and colors, also known as specification items.

十五、人民生活

CHAPTER 15
PEOPLE 'S LIVELIHOOD

15 人民生活 PEOPLE'S LIVELIHOOD

主要统计指标 MAJOR STATISTICAL INDICATORS

2016年全体常住居民人均可支配收入	Per Capita Disposable Income of the Resident Population	46 595	元	yuan
比上年增长	Increase Over Last Year	8.4	%	
2016年全体常住居民人均消费支出	Per Capita Consumer Spending of the Resident Population	28 983	元	yuan
比上年增长	Increase Over Last Year	8.0	%	
2016年城镇常住居民人均可支配收入	Per Capita Disposable Income of the Urban Residents	54 341	元	yuan
比上年增长	Increase Over Last Year (by the same caliber)	7.8	%	
2016年城镇常住居民人均消费支出	Per Capita Consumer Spending of the Urban Residents	33 305	元	yuan
比上年增长	Increase Over Last Year (by the same caliber)	7.0	%	
2016年农村常住居民人均可支配收入	Per Capita Disposable Income of the Rural Residents	27 691	元	yuan
比上年增长	Increase Over Last Year (by the same caliber)	8.3	%	
2016年农村常住居民人均消费支出	Per Capita Consumer Spending of the Rural Residents	18 820	元	yuan
比上年增长	Increase Over Last Year (by the same caliber)	12.3	%	

表15-1

居民家庭人均收入和消费支出(1985-2016年)
PER CAPITA DISPOSABLE INCOME AND CONSUMPTION EXPENDITURE OF THE RESIDENTS (1985-2016)

单位：元 (yuan)

年 份 Year	全体常住居民人均可支配收入 Per Capita Disposable Income of the Resident Population	全体常住居民人均消费支出 Per Capita Consumer Spending of the Resident Population	城镇常住居民人均可支配收入 Per Capita Disposable Income of the Urban Resident	城镇常住居民人均消费支出 Per Capita Consumer Spending of the Urban Residents	农村常住居民人均可支配收入 Per Capita Disposable Income of the Rural Residents	农村常住居民人均消费支出 Per Capita Consumer Spending of the Rural Residents
1985			918	787	739	661
1989			1 865	1 619	1 470	1 281
1990			2 150	1 805	1 664	1 415
1991			2 427	2 187	1 731	1 527
1992			2 788	2 199	2 001	1 722
1993			3 695	3 416	2 558	1 893
1994			4 885	4 027	3 457	2 676
1995			5 790	4 877	4 444	3 414
1996			6 591	5 264	5 088	3 804
1997			7 479	5 955	5 219	4 014
1998			7 812	6 289	5 347	3 958
1999			8 406	6 545	5 308	3 785
2000			9 274	7 027	5 462	4 073
2001			10 515	7 270	5 796	4 127
2002			10 617	7 682	6 140	4 229
2003			12 361	9 272	6 681	4 641
2004			14 451	9 783	7 503	5 436
2005			16 276	11 163	8 393	6 143
2006			18 532	12 472	9 278	6 811
2007			21 260	13 959	10 475	7 623
2008			23 867	15 183	11 785	8 443
2009			26 320	16 402	12 969	9 354
2010			29 219	17 879	14 657	10 397
2011			33 243	21 046	17 226	12 485
2012			37 531	23 092	19 396	14 381
2013			41 143	25 197	21 578	16 251
2014	39 780	24 920	46 677	28 973	23 560	15 390
2015	42 987	26 847	50 390	31 136	25 580	16 761
2016	46 595	28 983	54 341	33 305	27 691	18 820

注:2014年起公布城乡住户调查一体化改革后的新口径数据。2013年及以前，城镇居民收支为不包含吴江区的市区居民收支；农村居民人均可支配收入为全市农民人均纯收入。

Note: Starting from 2014, the new caliber data is announced by the reform of urban-and-rural integration of the household survey ; in 2013 and the previous years , the urban residents' income and expenditure did not include those of the urban residents of Wujiang District.; Per capita disposable income of the rural residents is the per capita net income of the farmers of the city.

表15-2

调查户和调查人口基本情况（2016年）
BASIC INFORMATION ON THE HOUSEHOLDS AND THE POPULATION OF THE SURVEY (2016)

指标	Item	全体常住居民 All The Residents	城镇常住居民 Urban Residents	农村常住居民 Rural Residents
一、调查户数（户）	**Number of Households of Survey (household)**	**1 684**	**1 155**	**529**
二、期末家庭常住成员基本情况	**Basic Information of Family Members**			
（一）户均常住人口（人）	Average Number of Residents Per Household (person)	3.31	3.15	3.67
（二）性别比例（%）	Sex Ratio (%)	100.0	100.0	100.0
1.男性	Male	50.2	50.7	49.2
2.女性	Female	49.8	49.3	50.8
（三）15岁及以上常住成员受教育程度比例	Proportion of Level of Education of Residents of 15 Years Old and Above	100.0	100.0	100.0
1.未上过学	Uneducated	2.8	2.2	4.0
2.小学	Primary School	20.8	17.7	26.5
3.初中	Junior Secondary School	29.3	26.7	34.0
4.高中	Senior Secondary School	19.8	21.4	17.0
5.大学专科	Junior College	15.6	17.2	12.6
6.大学本科	Undergraduate College	11.1	14.0	5.7
7.研究生	Graduate College	0.6	0.8	0.2
三、常住家庭成员就业情况	**Information on Employment of Family Members**			
（一）户均常住从业人数（人）	Number of Employees Per Household (person)	2.09	1.93	2.46
（二）就业状况比例（%）	Employment Ratio (%)	100.0	100.0	100.0
1.雇主	Employers	1.9	2.2	1.2
2.公职人员	Public Officials	1.2	1.8	0.3
3.事业单位人员	Institution Employees	6.4	8.0	3.6
4.国有企业雇员	State-owned Enterprise Employees	2.2	3.2	0.4
5.其他雇员	Other Employees	79.2	77.5	82.2
6.农业自营	Agricultural Self-employed	1.8	0.7	3.7
7.非农自营	Non-agricultural Self-employed	7.3	6.6	8.6
（三）主要从事行业比例	Ratio of Industries Mainly Engaged in	100.0	100.0	100.0
1.第一产业	Primary Industry	2.1	0.9	4.1
2.第二产业	Secondary Industry	48.7	41.8	60.4
3.第三产业	Tertiary Industry	49.2	57.3	35.5

表15-3

居民人均可支配收入(2016年)
PER CAPITA DISPOSABLE INCOME OF THE RESIDENTS (2016)

单位：元 (yuan)

指　　标	Item	全体常住居民 All The Residents	城镇常住居民 Urban Residents	农村常住居民 Rural Residents
人均可支配收入	**Per Capita Disposable Income**	**46 594.67**	**54 341.42**	**27 691.02**
一、工资性收入	**Wage Income**	**29 635.72**	**35 074.49**	**16 364.03**
(一)工　资	Wages	28 086.83	33 039.91	15 761.81
(二)实物福利	Physical Benefits	322.43	379.65	180.50
(三)其　他	Others	1 226.45	1 654.93	421.71
二、经营净收入	**Net Operating Income**	**4 841.16**	**4 676.41**	**5 243.18**
(一)第一产业净收入	Net Income of the Primary Industry	330.98	268.68	409.43
(二)第二产业净收入	Net income of the Secondary Industry	1 875.95	1 163.58	2 679.46
(三)第三产业净收入	Net Income of the Tertiary Industry	2 634.23	3 244.14	2 154.28
三、财产净收入	**Property Net Income**	**6 994.35**	**8 603.88**	**3 066.78**
# 利息净收入	Net Interest Income	138.44	132.54	120.67
红利收入	Dividend Income	1 193.74	1 228.19	904.94
出租房屋净收入	Net Income of Renting Houses	2 404.65	2 575.89	1 661.16
四、转移净收入	**Transfer Net Income**	**5 123.44**	**5 986.64**	**3 017.04**

注：转移净收入=转移性收入-转移性支出。
Note: Transfer net income = Transfer income - Transfer expenditure

表15-3 续表 Continued

单位：元 (yuan)

指　标	Item	全体常住居民 All The Residents	城镇常住居民 Urban Residents	农村常住居民 Rural Residents
(一)转移性收入	Transfer Income	7 311.42	8 771.18	4 049.80
1.养老金或离退休金	Pensions or Retirement Pensions	6 545.09	7 942.90	3 523.18
2.社会救济和补助	Social Relief and Subsidies	34.99	34.56	27.70
3.惠农补贴	Subsidies Benefiting Farmers	3.64	1.73	4.97
4.政策性生活补贴	Policy-oriented Living Allowances	112.39	132.80	64.53
5.报销医疗费	Reimbursement of Medical Expenses	400.78	408.93	302.62
6.外出从业人员寄回带回收入	Income Sent Back or Brought Back Home by Employees Working in Other Places	32.95	47.21	9.62
7.赡养收入	Maintenance Income	75.55	101.87	29.25
8.其他经常转移收入	Other Frequent Transfer Incomes	106.04	101.19	87.93
(二)转移性支出	Transfer Expenditure	2 187.99	2 784.54	1 032.77
1.个人所得税	Individual Income Tax	217.48	335.11	37.21
2.社会保障支出	The Expenditure of Social Security	1 790.61	2 186.85	948.37
3.外来从业人员寄给家人的支出	Spending Sent Home by Employees from Other Places	38.79	61.12	5.13
4.赡养支出	Maintenance Expenses	82.87	120.64	22.10
5.其他经常转移支出	Other Frequent Transfer Expenses	58.23	80.82	19.95

15-4

居民人均消费支出(2016年)
PER CAPITA CONSUMPTION EXPENDITYRE OF THE RESIDENTS (2016)

单位：元 (yuan)

指　　标	Item	全体常住居民 All The Residents	城镇常住居民 Urban Residents	农村常住居民 Rural Residents
居民生活消费支出	**Consumer Expenditure of the Residents**	**28 983.17**	**33 305.28**	**18 819.90**
一、食品烟酒	**Food, Alcoholic Drinks and Tobacco**	**7 673.78**	**8 882.37**	**4 831.85**
食　品	Food	4 861.59	5 642.16	3 040.84
烟　酒	Alcoholic Drinks and Tobacco	881.89	855.77	780.09
饮　料	Beverages	165.90	190.04	107.17
饮食服务	Catering Services	1 764.40	2 194.39	903.75
二、衣　着	**Clothing**	**1 777.67**	**2 083.64**	**1 058.19**
衣　类	Clothes	1 409.40	1 655.00	835.04
鞋　类	Footwear	368.27	428.64	223.15
三、居　住	**Residence**	**6 623.20**	**7 539.72**	**4 468.04**
# 租赁房房租	Rent for Renting Houses	121.99	156.82	55.65
住房维修及管理	Housing Maintenance and Management	1 032.95	889.53	1 122.02
水电燃料及其他	Water, Electricity, Fuel and Others	810.02	842.61	664.47
四、生活用品及服务	**Daily Necessities and Services**	**1 583.93**	**1 796.41**	**1 084.31**
家具及室内装饰品	Furniture and Interior Decoration	264.20	289.81	195.01
家用器具	Household Appliances	439.24	484.48	320.38

15-4 续表 Continued

单位：元 (yuan)

指 标	Item	全体常住居民 All The Residents	城镇常住居民 Urban Residents	农村常住居民 Rural Residents
家用纺织品	Home Textiles	135.04	156.84	87.16
家庭日用杂品	Household Sundries	400.99	459.80	267.29
个人用品	Personal Articles	271.31	307.48	186.06
家庭服务	Family Services	73.14	98.00	28.42
五、交通通信	**Transportation and Communication**	**5 191.64**	**5 917.85**	**3 483.99**
交 通	Transportation	3 901.98	4 532.78	2 491.79
通 信	Communication	1 289.66	1 385.08	992.20
六、教育文化娱乐	**Education, Culture and Entertainment**	**3 964.92**	**4 727.97**	**2 170.65**
教 育	Education	1 641.16	1 930.96	939.73
文化娱乐	Culture and Entertainment	2 323.76	2 797.00	1 230.92
七、医疗保健	**Healthcare**	**1 346.10**	**1 410.97**	**1 193.54**
医疗器具及药品	Medical Equipment and Medicines	378.95	470.15	227.35
医疗服务	Medical Services	967.14	940.83	966.19
八、其他用品及服务	**Other Supplies and Services**	**821.92**	**946.35**	**529.32**
其他用品	Other Supplies	436.08	488.20	302.91
其他服务	Other Services	385.84	458.15	226.40
附：通过互联网购买的商品和服务	**Appendix: Goods and Services Purchased Over the Internet**	**584.46**	**664.38**	**435.02**

表15-5

全体常住居民家庭基本情况(2016年)

(按收入等级分)

项　　目	Item	总平均 Average
一、家庭成员情况	**Basic Situation of Households**	
（一）调查户数　（户）	Number of Households Surveyed　(household)	1 684
（二）平均每户家庭常住人口　（人）	Average Household Size　(person)	3.31
# 从业人员	Average Number of Employees per Household	2.09
（三）平均每一从业者负担人数(包括从业者本人)	Number of Persons Supported by Each Employee (including the employee himself or herself)	1.58
二、家庭收支情况	**Family Income and Expenditure**	
（一）人均可支配收入　（元）	Per Capita Disposable Income　(yuan)	46 595
1.工资性收入	Wage Income	29 636
2.经营净收入	Net Operating Income	4 841
3.财产净收入	Property Net Income	6 994
4. 转移净收入	Transfer Net Income	5 123
（二）人均消费支出	Per Capita Annual Living Expenditure	28 983
1.食品烟酒	Food, Alcoholic Drinks and Tobacco	7 674
2.衣　着	Clothing	1 778
3.居　住	Residence	6 623
4.生活用品及服务	Household Facilities, Articles and Services	1 584
5.交通通信	Medicine and Medical Services	5 192
6.教育文化娱乐	Transport, Post and Communication Services	3 965
7.医疗保健	Education, Cultural and Recreation Services	1 346
8.其他用品和服务	Miscellaneous Commodities and Services	822

BASIC INTORMATION OF ALL RESIDENT HOUSEHOLDS (2016)
(DIVIDED BY INCOME LEVEL)

20% 低收入户 Low Income House-holds	20% 中低收入户 Lower Middle Income House-holds	20% 中等收入户 Middle Income House-holds	20% 中高收入户 Upper Middle Income House-holds	20% 高收入户 High Income House-holds
338	337	337	336	336
3.79	3.64	3.25	3.02	2.85
2.21	2.37	2.13	1.99	1.77
1.72	1.53	1.52	1.52	1.62
22 812	32 884	41 988	53 638	93 696
15 931	22 367	28 025	35 632	51 019
1 828	2 107	2 322	3 133	15 823
1 723	3 592	5 752	9 045	16 505
3 330	4 819	5 891	5 829	10 350
17 542	24 175	27 332	33 532	45 558
5 280	6 723	7 852	8 676	11 093
1 000	1 261	1 622	1 818	2 683
4 856	6 478	7 642	9 264	11 923
927	1 295	1 594	1 782	2 558
2 519	4 540	4 247	6 263	6 993
1 504	2 175	2 461	3 535	6 112
1 058	1 128	1 347	1 397	2 354
397	574	565	797	1 841

表15-6

城镇常住居民家庭基本情况(2016年)
(按收入等级分)

项　　目		Item		总平均 Average
一、家庭成员情况		**Basic Situation of Households**		
（一）调查户数	(户)	Number of Households Surveyed	(household)	1 155
（二）平均每户家庭常住人口	(人)	Average Household Size	(person)	3.15
# 从业人员		Average Number of Employees per Household		1.93
（三）平均每一从业者负担人数(包括从业者本人)		Number of Persons Supported by Each Employee (including the employee himself or herself)		1.63
二、家庭收支情况		**Family Income and Expenditure**		
（一）人均可支配收入	(元)	Per Capita Disposable Income	(yuan)	54 341
1.工资性收入		Wage Income		35 074
2.经营净收入		Net operating Income		4 676
3.财产净收入		Property net Income		8 604
4. 转移净收入		Transfer net Income		5 987
（二）人均消费支出		Per Capita Annual Living Expenditure		33 305
1.食品烟酒		Food, Alcoholic Drinks and Tobacco		8 882
2.衣　着		Clothing		2 084
3.居　住		Residence		7 540
4.生活用品及服务		Household Facilities, Articles and Services		1 796
5.交通通信		Medicine and Medical Services		5 918
6.教育文化娱乐		Transport, Post and Communication Services		4 728
7.医疗保健		Education, Cultural and Recreation Services		1 411
8.其他用品和服务		Miscellaneous Commodities and Services		946

THE BASIC SITUATION OF THE URBAN RESIDENT FAMILIES(2016)
(DIVIDED BY INCOME LEVEL)

20% 低收入户 Low Income House-holds	20% 中低收入户 Lower Middle Income House-holds	20% 中等收入户 Middle Income House-holds	20% 中高收入户 Upper Middle Income House-holds	20% 高收入户 High Income House-holds
232	231	231	231	230
3.67	3.32	3.14	2.88	2.72
2.11	2.05	1.97	1.81	1.68
1.74	1.62	1.59	1.59	1.62
28 462	39 437	49 874	63 243	103 580
19 765	26 567	32 710	41 531	62 234
2 184	1 959	2 507	2 282	10 075
3 605	5 828	8 253	11 088	19 486
2 908	5 082	6 403	8 342	11 786
20 981	28 846	32 122	39 748	52 520
6 435	8 236	9 130	9 803	12 687
1 234	1 631	1 736	2 099	3 158
5 559	8 007	8 937	11 054	13 450
1 000	1 730	1 621	1 995	3 086
3 165	4 777	5 149	8 115	7 702
2 159	2 624	3 551	4 070	7 569
953	1 186	1 390	1 644	2 485
476	656	607	968	2 384

表15-7

农村常住居民家庭基本情况(2016年)
(按收入等级分)

项　目		Item		总平均 Average
一、家庭成员情况		**Basic Situation of Households**		
（一）调查户数	(户)	Number of Households Surveyed	(household)	529
（二）平均每户家庭常住人口	(人)	Average Household Size	(person)	3.67
# 从业人员		Average Number of Employees per Household		2.46
（三）平均每一从业者负担人数(包括从业者本人)		Number of Persons Supported by Each Employee (including the employee himself or herself)		1.49
二、家庭收支情况		**Family Income and Expenditure**		
（一）人均可支配收入	(元)	Per Capita Disposable Income	(yuan)	27 691
1.工资性收入		Wage Income		16 364
2.经营净收入		Net operating Income		5 243
3.财产净收入		Property Net Income		3 067
4. 转移净收入		Transfer Net Income		3 017
（二）人均消费支出		Per Capita Annual Living Expenditure		18 820
1.食品烟酒		Food, Alcoholic Drinks and Tobacco		4 832
2.衣　着		Clothing		1 058
3.居　住		Residence		4 468
4.生活用品及服务		Household Facilities, Articles and Services		1 084
5.交通通信		Medicine and Medical Services		3 484
6.教育文化娱乐		Transport, Post and Communication Services		2 171
7.医疗保健		Education, Cultural and Recreation Services		1 194
8.其他用品和服务		Miscellaneous Commodities and Services		529

THE BASIC SITUATION OF THE RURAL RESIDENT FAMILIES(2016)
(DIVIDED BY INCOME LEVEL)

20% 低收入户 Low Income House-holds	20% 中低收入户 Lower Middle Income House-holds	20% 中等收入户 Middle Income House-holds	20% 中高收入户 Upper Middle Income House-holds	20% 高收入户 High Income House-holds
106	106	106	105	106
3.92	3.89	3.84	3.35	3.33
2.13	2.63	2.75	2.43	2.36
1.84	1.48	1.39	1.38	1.41
13 427	19 092	23 649	30 033	56 804
9 755	12 986	16 493	20 204	24 083
995	1 346	1 927	2 005	20 746
433	826	1 304	3 347	7 779
2 245	3 935	3 924	4 477	4 197
11 891	14 001	15 736	18 823	24 148
3 356	3 950	4 362	5 327	6 020
570	755	841	1 140	1 480
3 536	4 026	4 120	4 928	6 575
629	957	759	1 201	1 336
1 991	1 706	3 328	3 281	3 776
823	1 097	1 195	1 409	2 595
720	1 178	785	1 033	1 641
266	332	346	504	726

表15-8

居民家庭现住房情况(2016年末)
THE HOUSING SITUATION OF THE RESIDENT FAMILIES (END OF 2016)

指　标	Item	全体常住居民 All The Residents	城镇常住居民 Urban Residents	农村常住居民 Rural Residents
一、居民人均住房建筑面积 (平方米)	**Per Capita Housing Construction Area** (square meter)	**51.1**	**43.3**	**65.6**
二、居民家庭现住房构成 (%)	**Housing for the Residents Households** (%)			
(一)按主要建筑材料分的住房比例	Proportion of Number of Households According to Main Building Materials	100.0	100.0	100.0
# 钢筋混凝土	Reinforced Concrete	49.8	60.6	26.3
砖混材料	Brick and Concrete Material	46.5	36.2	69.0
砖瓦砖木	Brick, Tile and Timber	3.3	2.6	4.7
(二)按房屋来源分的住房比例	Proportion of Number of Households According to The Source of Housing	100.0	100.0	100.0
# 租赁住房	Rental Housing	5.2	5.6	4.4
自建住房	Self-built Housing	45.1	24.1	90.9
购买商品房	Purchased Commercial Housing	32.0	44.7	4.3
购买房改住房	Purchased Housing-reform Housing	2.7	4.0	-
购买保障性住房	Purchased Affordable Housing	-	-	-
拆迁安置房	Removal and Resettlement Housing	13.2	19.1	0.2
(三)住房外道路为硬化路面的户比例	Proportion of Number of Households with Roads of Hardened Pavement Outside Their Housing	99.6	99.5	99.8

表15-9

每百户居民家庭耐用消费品拥有量(2016年末)
THE OWNERSHIP OF DURABLE CONSUMER GOODS PER ONE-HUNDRED HOUSEHOLDS (END OF 2016)

指　　标		Item		全体常住居民 All The Residents	城镇常住居民 Urban Residents	农村常住居民 Rural Residents
家用汽车	(辆)	Home Car	(car)	72.2	74.3	67.4
摩托车		Motorcycle		17.1	8.9	34.9
电冰箱(柜)	(台)	Refrigerator	(unit)	107.6	106.0	111.2
洗衣机		Washing Machine		105.6	105.7	105.2
热水器		Water Heater		111.3	112.1	109.6
# 太阳能热水器		Solar Water Heater		42.2	32.0	64.6
空　调		Air Conditioner		262.4	272.6	240.1
彩色电视机		Color TV Set		216.4	214.2	221.3
摄像机		Video Camera		11.2	11.9	9.6
照相机		Camera		54.4	62.3	37.2
计算机		Computer		119.0	126.8	102.0
# 接入互联网的计算机		Computer Access to the Internet		108.6	116.6	91.2
中高档乐器	(架)	Middle- and High-grade Musical Instrument	(unit)	9.3	11.3	4.7
固定电话	(部)	Fixed Telephone	(unit)	78.2	76.1	82.5
移动电话		Mobile Phone		271.5	264.0	288.0
# 接入互联网的移动电话		Mobile Phone Access to the Internet		168.7	172.2	160.9

表15-10

分地区全体常住居民收支情况(2016年)

指　　标	Item	全　市 Whole Municipality
一、家庭成员情况	**Basic Situation of Households**	
（一）调查户数　(户)	Number of Households Surveyed　(household)	1 684
（二）平均每户家庭常住人口　(人)	Average Household Size　(person)	3.31
# 从业人员	Average Number of Employees per Household	2.09
（三）平均每一从业者负担人数(包括从业者本人)	Number of Persons Supported by Each Employee (including the employee himself or herself)	1.58
二、家庭收支情况	**Family Income and Expenditure**	
（一）人均可支配收入　(元)	Per Capita Disposable Income　(yuan)	46 595
1.工资性收入	Wage Income	29 636
2.经营净收入	Net operating Income	4 841
3.财产净收入	Property Net Income	6 994
4. 转移净收入	Transfer Net Income	5 123
（二）人均消费支出	Per Capita Annual Living Expenditure	28 983
1.食品烟酒	Food, Alcoholic Drinks and Tobacco	7 674
2.衣　着	Clothing	1 778
3.居　住	Residence	6 623
4.生活用品及服务	Household Facilities, Articles and Services	1 584
5.交通通信	Medicine and Medical Services	5 192
6.教育文化娱乐	Transport, Post and Communication Services	3 965
7.医疗保健	Education, Cultural and Recreation Services	1 346
8.其他用品和服务	Miscellaneous Commodities and Services	822

THE INCOME AND EXPENDITURE OF ALL THE RESIDENTS IN THE REGION (2016)

市 区 Urban Area	# 吴江区 Wujiang District	常 熟 Changshu	张家港 Zhangjiagang	昆 山 Kunshan	太 仓 Taicang
902	198	201	191	190	200
3.39	3.46	3.14	3.30	3.25	3.20
2.09	2.23	2.01	2.03	2.07	2.26
1.62	1.55	1.56	1.62	1.57	1.42
47 785	44 570	45 061	44 977	46 339	43 867
29 944	29 765	29 642	28 767	30 218	29 073
5 023	5 920	5 932	5 724	4 313	5 141
7 352	4 487	3 838	5 011	6 367	4 883
5 466	4 398	5 648	5 475	5 441	4 770
29 812	28 796	27 337	26 837	28 161	28 120
8 159	8 138	7 807	7 648	8 006	8 502
1 831	2 753	1 614	1 636	1 896	1 728
7 444	4 691	5 207	5 257	5 899	5 653
1 481	1 386	1 355	1 465	1 550	1 659
5 127	5 878	4 697	5 221	4 517	4 635
3 694	4 125	4 321	3 688	4 432	4 206
1 220	1 152	1 441	1 157	1 123	1 070
855	674	895	766	738	667

表15-11

分地区城镇常住居民收支情况(2016年)

指　　标		Item		全　市 Whole Municipality
一、家庭成员情况		**Basic Situation of Households**		
（一）调查户数	(户)	Number of Households Surveyed	(household)	1 155
（二）平均每户家庭常住人口	(人)	Average Household Size	(person)	3.15
# 从业人员		Average Number of Employees per Household		1.93
（三）平均每一从业者负担人数(包括从业者本人)		Number of Persons Supported by Each Employee (including the employee himself or herself)		1.63
二、家庭收支情况		**Family Income and Expenditure**		
（一）人均可支配收入	(元)	Per Capita Disposable Income	(yuan)	54 341
1.工资性收入		Wage Income		35 074
2.经营净收入		Net operating Income		4 676
3.财产净收入		Property Net Income		8 604
4. 转移净收入		Transfer Net Income		5 987
（二）人均消费支出		Per Capita Annual Living Expenditure		33 305
1.食品烟酒		Food, Alcoholic Drinks and Tobacco		8 882
2.衣　着		Clothing		2 084
3.居　住		Residence		7 540
4.生活用品及服务		Household Facilities, Articles and Services		1 796
5.交通通信		Medicine and Medical Services		5 918
6.教育文化娱乐		Transport, Post and Communication Services		4 728
7.医疗保健		Education, Cultural and Recreation Services		1 411
8.其他用品和服务		Miscellaneous Commodities and Services		946

THE INCOME AND EXPENDITURE OF ALL THE URBAN IN THE REGION (2016)

市 区 Urban Area	# 吴江区 Wujiang District	常 熟 Changshu	张家港 Zhangjiagang	昆 山 Kunshan	太 仓 Taicang
693	99	134	115	112	101
3.25	3.17	2.95	3.26	2.94	2.80
1.95	1.83	1.77	1.96	1.88	1.95
1.66	1.73	1.66	1.67	1.56	1.44
54 200	54 321	54 411	54 602	54 728	54 099
34 374	37 739	35 826	36 108	36 139	36 673
4 937	4 728	6 169	5 690	4 151	4 932
8 467	5 717	5 110	6 259	7 952	6 544
6 423	6 138	7 306	6 546	6 486	5 951
33 497	35 369	31 520	31 590	32 578	33 721
9 078	9 815	9 087	9 025	9 194	10 148
2 036	3 603	1 952	1 907	2 202	2 107
8 317	5 872	5 911	6 035	6 917	6 959
1 669	1 680	1 575	1 660	1 753	2 008
5 952	7 181	5 222	6 565	5 260	5 459
4 244	5 027	5 065	4 344	5 197	5 041
1 285	1 342	1 646	1 101	1 226	1 176
917	848	1 061	953	829	824

表15-12

分地区农村常住居民收支情况(2016年)

指　　标	Item	全　市 Whole Municipality
一、家庭成员情况	**Basic Situation of Households**	
（一）调查户数 (户)	Number of Households Surveyed (household)	529
（二）平均每户家庭常住人口 (人)	Average Household Size (person)	3.67
# 从业人员	Average Number of Employees per Household	2.46
（三）平均每一从业者负担人数(包括从业者本人)	Number of Persons Supported by Each Employee (including the employee himself or herself)	1.49
二、家庭收支情况	**Family Income and Expenditure**	
（一）人均可支配收入 (元)	Per Capita Disposable Income (yuan)	27 691
1.工资性收入	Wage Income	16 364
2.经营净收入	Net operating Income	5 243
3.财产净收入	Property net Income	3 067
4. 转移净收入	Transfer net Income	3 017
（二）人均消费支出	Per Capita Annual Living Expenditure	18 820
1.食品烟酒	Food, Alcoholic Drinks and Tobacco	4 832
2.衣　着	Clothing	1 058
3.居　住	Residence	4 468
4.生活用品及服务	Household Facilities, Articles and Services	1 084
5.交通通信	Medicine and Medical Services	3 484
6.教育文化娱乐	Transport, Post and Communication Services	2 171
7.医疗保健	Education, Cultural and Recreation Services	1 194
8.其他用品和服务	Miscellaneous Commodities and Services	529

THE INCOME AND EXPENDITURE OF ALL THE RURAL IN THE REGION (2016)

市 区 Urban Area	# 吴江区 Wujiang District	常 熟 Changshu	张家港 Zhangjiagang	昆 山 Kunshan	太 仓 Taicang
209	99	67	76	78	99
3.86	3.76	3.51	3.35	3.69	3.61
2.56	2.63	2.48	2.14	2.33	2.58
1.51	1.43	1.42	1.56	1.58	1.40
27 468	27 448	27 956	27 849	28 178	27 766
15 914	15 765	18 330	15 703	17 402	17 115
5 298	8 013	5 499	5 785	4 663	5 470
3 821	2 328	1 512	2 791	2 936	2 268
2 434	1 342	2 616	3 569	3 177	2 913
18 605	17 723	21 024	18 687	18 890	19 589
5 365	5 314	5 876	5 286	5 511	5 994
1 209	1 321	1 103	1 170	1 255	1 152
4 790	2 701	4 146	3 922	3 763	3 665
910	889	1 022	1 131	1 123	1 126
2 621	3 683	3 904	2 916	2 958	3 381
2 022	2 606	3 198	2 562	2 826	2 934
1 024	830	1 130	1 253	907	907
665	380	646	446	547	429

主 要 统 计 指 标 解 释

调查户 以家庭成员关系为主，居住在一个住宅内，共同分享生活开支或收入家庭成员为家庭住户。依照《中华人民共和国统计法》规定，开展住户收支与生活状况调查的住户为调查户。住户调查为中华人民共和国境内的住户，既包括城镇住户，也包括农村住户；既包括以家庭形式居住的户，也包括以集体形式居住的户。无论户口性质和户口登记地，中国公民均以住户为单位，在常住地参加本调查。

可支配收入 指调查户在调查期内获得的、可用于最终消费支出和储蓄的总和，即调查户可以用来自由支配的收入。可支配收入既包括现金收入，也包括实物收入。按照收入的来源，可支配收入包含四项，分别为：工资性收入、经营净收入、财产净收入和转移净收入。计算公式为：

可支配收入 ＝工资性收入 ＋经营净收入 ＋财产净收入 ＋ 转移净收入

工资性收入 指就业人员通过各种途径得到的全部劳动报酬和各种福利，包括受雇于单位或个人、从事各种自由职业、兼职和零星劳动得到的全部劳动报酬和福利。

经营净收入 指住户或住户成员从事生产经营活动所获得的净收入，是全部经营收入中扣除经营费用、生产性固定资产折旧和生产税之后得到的净收入。

财产净收入 指住户或住户成员将其所拥有的金融资产、住房等非金融资产和自然资源交由其他机构单位、住户或个人支配而获得的回报并扣除相关的费用之后得到的净收入。财产净收入包括利息净收入、红利收入、储蓄性保险净收益、转让承包土地经营权租金净收入、出租房屋净收入、出租其他资产净收入和自有住房折算净租金等。但转让资产所有权的溢价所得计入“非收入所得”，不包含在财产净收入中。

转移性收入 指国家、单位、社会团体对住户的各种经常性转移支付和住户之间的经常性收入转移。 包括政府、非行政事业单位、社会团体对居民转移的养老金或退休金、社会救济和补助、惠农补贴、政策性生活补贴、救灾款、经常性捐赠和赔偿以及报销医疗费等；住户之间的赡养收入、经常性捐赠和赔偿以及农村地区（村委会）在外（含国外）工作的本住户非常住成员寄回带回的收入等。转移性收入不包括住户之间的实物馈赠。

转移性支出 指调查户对国家、单位、住户或个人的经常性或义务性转移支付。包括缴纳的税款、各项社会保障支出、赡养支出、经常性捐赠和赔偿支出以及其他经常转移支出等。

转移净收入 计算公式为：转移净收入=转移性收入-转移性支出

消费支出 指调查户在调查期内用于满足家庭日常生活消费需要的全部支出，包括用于消费品的支出和用于服务性消费的支出。根据用途不同，消费支出可划分为食品烟酒、衣着、居住、生活用品及服务、交通通信、教育文化娱乐、医疗保健、其他用品及服务八大类。根据来源不同，消费支出可划分为现金消费支出、实物消费支出（含自产自用、来自单位、来自政府和其他社会组织）。

EXPLANATORY NOTES ON MAIN STATISTICAL INDICATORS

Households of the Survey The family members who are based on family membership, live in a house, and commonly share living expenses or income form a household. In accordance with the provisions of 《The Statistical Law of the People's Republic of China》, the households whose income and expenditure and living conditions are to be surveyed are households of the survey.The households of the survey are the households within the People's Republic of China, including both urban and rural households, and households living both in the form of a family and in the form of collective housing. Regardless of the nature of registered residence and the place where residence is registered, the Chinese citizens take the household as the unit, and take part in the survey.

Disposable Income It refers to the sum total of the income which is obtained by the household in the survey period, and can be used for final consumer spending and savings, namely, the income which the household can freely dispose of. Disposable income includes both cash and physical income. According to the sources of income, disposable income includes four incomes, and they are respectively wage income, net operating income, property net income and transfer net income.

Disposable income = wage income + net operating income + property net income + transfer net income.

Wage Income It refers to the total remuneration and benefits which the employed person gets through a variety of ways, including the total remuneration and benefits which the person gets by being employed to units or individuals, and engaged in vaious freelance, part-time work and sporadic labor.

Net Operating Income It refers to the net income which the household or household members get by being engaged in production and business activities, and is the net income of the total operating income after the deduction of operating expenses, the depreciation of fixed assets for production and production tax.

Property Net Income It refers to the net income which a household or household member obtains in return when they have their own financial assets, housing and other non-financial assets and natural resources administrated by other institutional units, households or individuals and after the deduction of the related expenses. Property net income includes net interest income, dividend income, savings insurance net income, rent net income from the transfer of land contracted management right, rental housing net income, rental other assets net income and converted net rent for one's own houses. However, the premium income of the transfer of property rights is included in the "non income", which is not included in the property net income.

Transfer Income It refers to the various regular transfer payments which the state, units and social groups give to households and frequent transfer of income between households. It includes pensions or retirement pensions, social benefits or subsidies, subsidies benefiting farmers, policy-oriented living allowances, relief funds, regular donations and compensations and reimbursement of medical expenses, etc. which the government, the non-administrative institutions, social groups transfer to residents; the maintenance income between residents, the regular donations and compensations, and the income sent back or brought back by the non-resident members of the household from the rural areas (village committees) working in other places (including foreign countries). The transfer income does not include the physical gifts between households.

Transfer Expenditure It refers to the payment which the household of the survey recurrently or compulsorily transfers to the state, units, households or individuals. It includes the payment of taxes, social security expenses, maintenance expenses, recurrent expenses for donations and compensations and other recurrent transfer spendings.

Transfer Net Income The formula of calculation is: transfer net income = transfer income - transfer expenditure.

Consumer spending It refers to all the expenditures which the household of the survey spends to meet all consumption needs of family life in the survey period, including spending on consumer goods and service consumption. Depending on the use, consumption expenditure can be divided into the eight categories of food, alcoholic drinks and tobacco, clothing, housing, articles for daily use and services, transportation and communications, education, culture and entertainment, healthcare, and other supplies and services. According to different sources, consumption expenditure can be divided into cash consumer spending and physical consumption expenditure (including production of one's own use, from the unit, from the government and other social organizations).

十六、科　技

CHAPTER 16
SCIENCE AND TECHNOLOGY

16 科 技 SCIENCE AND TECHNOLOGY

主要统计指标 MAJOR STATISTICAL INDICATORS

2016年高新技术企业数	Number of High & New Tech Enterprises	4 133	个	unit
2016年发明专利申请数	Invention Patent Applications	47 429	件	unit
比上年增长	Increase Over Last Year	9.7	%	
2016年发明专利授权数	Invention Patents Warrants	13 267	件	unit
比上年增长	Increase Over Last Year	26.5	%	
2016年末专业技术人员数	Number of Scientific & Technical Personnel	1 634 233	人	person
比上年增长	Increase Over Last Year	9.2	%	
2016年末高级职称专业技术人员数	Number of Scientific & Technical Personnel with Senior Professional Titles	84 236	人	person
比上年增长	Increase Over Last Year	13.1	%	

表16-1

部分年份国有事业独立科研机构和人员情况
STATE-OWNED SCIENCE & RESEARCH INSTITUTIONS AND PERSONNEL OF PARTIAL YEARS

项目	Item	2011年	2012年	2013年	2014年	2015年	2016年
机构数 (个)	**Number of Institutions** (unit)						
全市	**Whole Municipality**	**70**	**75**	**80**	**80**	**78**	**80**
市区	Urban Area	56	60	62	62	60	60
# 吴江区	Wujiang District	2	2	2	2	2	3
常熟	Changshu	5	6	7	7	6	6
张家港	Zhangjiagang	3	2	4	4	5	6
昆山	Kunshan	4	5	5	5	5	5
太仓	Taicang	2	2	2	2	2	3
职工人数 (人)	**Number of Staff & Workers** (person)						
全市	**Whole Municipality**	**6 834**	**8 897**	**9 715**	**9 687**	**9 678**	**8 876**
市区	Urban Area	6 259	7 859	8 421	8 672	8 800	8 056
#吴江区	Wujiang District	22	22	17	17	15	152
常熟	Changshu	108	164	143	133	109	127
张家港	Zhangjiagang	150	184	410	223	281	319
昆山	Kunshan	201	553	608	528	397	317
太仓	Taicang	116	137	133	131	91	57
专业技术人员数 (人)	**Number of Scientific and Technical Personnel** (person)						
全市	**Whole Municipality**	**3 856**	**5 701**	**6 265**	**6 306**	**6 100**	**7 188**
市区	Urban Area	3 359	4 767	5 100	5 438	5 301	6 496
# 吴江区	Wujiang District	18	20	14	14	13	152
常熟	Changshu	99	125	126	122	103	113
张家港	Zhangjiagang	130	171	352	197	255	263
昆山	Kunshan	191	542	592	462	368	262
太仓	Taicang	77	96	95	87	73	54

表16-2

部分年份分地区专利申请情况
PATENT APPLICATIONS EXAMINED BY REGION OF PARTIAL YEARS

单位：件 (unit)

地 区	Region	1995年	2000年	2010年	2011年	2012年	2013年	2014年	2015年	2016年
全 市	**Whole Municipality**	**773**	**2 021**	**77 194**	**102 164**	**139 965**	**141 076**	**103 249**	**98 704**	**106 700**
市 区	Urban Area	478	731	38 361	55 679	76 214	68 537	51 393	61 738	64 855
# 吴江区	Wujiang District	82	58	19 469	28 729	38 590	23 828	12 010	12 295	10 438
常 熟	Changshu	98	205	12 812	16 416	15 024	13 079	12 246	6 324	6 571
张家港	Zhangjiagang	105	221	7 147	7 351	9 196	15 735	13 232	9 964	8 889
昆 山	Kunshan	22	787	14 923	17 626	31 515	34 053	18 302	14 229	18 159
太 仓	Taicang	70	77	3 951	5 092	8 016	9 672	8 076	6 449	8 226

表16-3

部分年份分地区专利授权情况
PATENT GRANTED BY REGION OF PARTIAL YEARS

单位：件 (unit)

地 区	Region	1995年	2000年	2010年	2011年	2012年	2013年	2014年	2015年	2016年
全 市	**Whole Municipality**	**415**	**1 922**	**46 109**	**77 281**	**98 276**	**81 665**	**54 709**	**62 263**	**53 528**
市 区	Urban Area	244	599	25 466	44 860	49 566	38 966	26 418	38 387	32 823
# 吴江区	Wujiang District	35	38	14 698	30 041	30 775	17 438	6 998	11 878	5 872
常 熟	Changshu	81	159	4 242	7 980	13 366	13 070	3 990	3 267	3 078
张家港	Zhangjiagang	27	136	3 049	7 702	8 469	8 011	10 086	6 791	4 162
昆 山	Kunshan	30	972	10 750	12 742	20 495	15 439	9 867	10 947	9 833
太 仓	Taicang	33	56	2 602	3 997	6 380	6 179	4 348	2 871	3 632

表16-4

部分年份专利申请和授权分类情况
PATENT APPLICATIONS EXAMINED AND GRANTED BY TYPE OF PARTIAL YEARS

单位：件 (unit)

年份 Year	申请 Applications Examined	发明 Inventions	实用新型 Utility Models	外观 Designs	授权 Applications Granted	发明 Inventions	实用新型 Utility Models	外观 Designs
1995	773	47	405	321	415	41	252	122
2000	2 021	224	927	870	1 922	32	1 076	814
2001	2 653	175	1 205	1 273	1 749	33	807	909
2002	3 109	271	1 504	1 334	2 324	64	1 058	1 202
2003	3 780	328	1 644	1 808	2 593	126	1 317	1 150
2004	4 687	580	1 759	2 348	2 783	167	1 128	1 488
2005	6 780	988	2 349	3 443	3 315	148	1 496	1 671
2006	12 874	2 002	2 841	8 031	4 855	180	2 075	2 600
2007	33 752	4 666	4 106	24 980	9 157	292	2 948	5 917
2008	48 558	5 371	6 209	36 978	18 270	645	4 217	13 408
2009	61 336	8 281	8 972	44 083	39 288	1 030	5 585	32 673
2010	77 194	12 935	12 833	51 426	46 109	1 370	10 541	34 198
2011	102 164	21 765	19 428	60 971	77 281	2 492	14 220	60 569
2012	139 965	31 984	28 778	79 203	98 276	4 309	21 577	72 390
2013	141 076	44 477	36 235	60 364	81 665	4 413	30 082	47 170
2014	103 249	40 842	35 432	26 975	54 709	5 264	32 012	17 433
2015	98 704	43 241	42 760	12 703	62 263	10 488	35 901	15 874
2016	106 700	47 429	51 866	7 405	53 528	13 267	34 656	5 605

表16-5

分地区专利申请和授权分类情况 (2016年)
PATENT APPLICATIONS EXAMINED AND GRANTED BY TYPE AND REGION (2016)

单位：件 (unit)

地区	Region	申请 Applications Examined	发明 Inventions	实用新型 Utility Models	外观 Designs	授权 Applications Granted	发明 Inventions	实用新型 Utility Models	外观 Designs
全　市	**Whole Municipality**	**106 700**	**47 429**	**51 866**	**7 405**	**53 528**	**13 267**	**34 656**	**5 605**
市　区	Urban Area	64 855	28 843	31 237	4 775	32 823	7 923	21 444	3 456
# 吴江区	Wujiang District	10 438	3 974	5 787	677	5 872	1 354	3 893	625
常　熟	Changshu	6 571	3 105	2 976	490	3 078	810	1 830	438
张家港	Zhangjiagang	8 889	4 246	4 225	418	4 162	1 265	2 580	317
昆　山	Kunshan	18 159	6 443	10 283	1 433	9 833	2 237	6 586	1 010
太　仓	Taicang	8 226	4 792	3 145	289	3 632	1 032	2 216	384

表16-6

部分年份科技计划及科技成果获奖情况
SCIENTIFIC AND TECHNOLOGICAL PLANNING AND PRIZES WON OF PARTIAL YEARS

单位：项 (item)

年份 Year	星火计划 Spark Plan	火炬计划 Torch Plan	年末高新技术企业(个) Number of High & New Tech Enterprises at Year-end (unit)	# 当年认定 Certified In this Year	科技进步奖 Scientific and Technological Progress Prizes 苏州市 Suzhou City	江苏省 Jiangsu Province	国家 Nation
1995	19	24	102	38	137	50	–
2000	13	37	346	68	162	32	–
2001	8	39	404	64	153	26	1
2002	14	48	484	80	133	23	–
2003	15	69	555	80	130	17	–
2004	19	69	622	76	133	20	1
2005	12	51	706	103	132	8	3
2006	21	110	844	162	114	13	–
2007	19	125	1 430	599	104	11	1
2008	22	79	1 246	361	103	19	2
2009	1	3	680	319	115	15	3
2010	36	99	975	297	117	17	4
2011	62	96	1 345	430	113	16	4
2012	61	112	1 864	588	122	33	3
2013	61	108	2 416	623	127	26	3
2014	38	91	2 950	910	124	23	3
2015	29	73	3 478	712	113	21	1
2016	–	–	4 133	1 521	113	28	4

注：2008年国家实行高新技术企业新标准认定办法，原认定办法有效期二年，因此，从2009年开始是新标准企业数。
Note: From 2008 the state started to implement the measuring method for the new standards for high-tech enterprises, and the original method was valid for two years, so the number of enterprises beginning from 2009 was that of enterprises of the new standards.

表16-7

分地区科技创新载体情况 (2016年末)
CARRIER OF SCIENTIFIC AND TECHNOLOGICAL INNOVATION BY REGION (END OF 2016)

单位：个 (unit)

地区 Region	高新技术企业 Number of High & New Tech Enterprises	# 当年认定 Certified In this Year	省级以上研发机构 Research And Development Institutions at or above the Provincial Level 工程技术研究中心 Engineering Technology Centers	企业技术中心 Enterprise Technology Centers	工程中心(实验室) Engineering Centers (Laboratories)
全 市 Whole Municipality	**4 133**	**1 521**	**625**	**381**	**68**
市 区 Urban Area	2 182	811	306	206	44
# 吴江区 Wujiang District	330	130	46	57	11
常 熟 Changshu	345	119	76	46	7
张家港 Zhangjiagang	387	133	101	42	5
昆 山 Kunshan	939	345	105	63	7
太 仓 Taicang	280	113	37	24	5

表16-8 规模以上工业科技活动企业与机构数 (2016年末)

THE NUMBER OF ABOVE-SCALE ENTERPRISES AND INSTITUTIONS WITH INDUSTRIAL SCIENTIFIC AND TECHNOLOGICAL ACTIVITIES (END OF 2016)

单位：个 (unit)

项　　目	Item	企业数 Number of Enterprises	# 有R&D活动企业数 Number of Enterprises With R&D Activities	# 有科技机构企业数 The Number of Enterprises with Scientific Institutions
总　计	**Total**	**9 616**	**4 366**	**4 646**
一、按地区分	**Grouped by Region**			
市　区	**Urban Area**	**4 358**	**1 937**	**2 167**
姑苏区	Gusu District	15	6	6
吴中区	Wuzhong District	835	446	473
相城区	Xiangcheng District	742	214	240
高新区、虎丘区	New & Hi-tech Zone , Huqiu District	690	366	363
工业园区	Industrial Park	772	549	681
吴江区	Wujiang District	1 304	356	404
县级市	**Cities at County Level**	**5 258**	**2 429**	**2 479**
常熟市	Changshu	1 309	441	443
张家港市	Zhangjiagang	1 078	419	429
昆山市	Kunshan	1 851	1 251	1 262
太仓市	Taicang	1 020	318	345
二、按企业规模分	**By Size of Enterprises**			
大　型	Large	407	331	359
中　型	Medium-sized	1 529	1 283	1 355
小　型	Small	7 362	2 723	2 898
微　型	Micro	318	29	34
三、按登记注册类型分	**Grouped by Registration Status**			
内资企业	**Domestic Funded Enterprises**	**5 442**	**2 199**	**2 322**
国有企业	State-owned Enterprises	5	2	2
集体企业	Collective-owned Enterprises	10	–	–
股份合作企业	Share-holding Cooperative Enterprises	14	6	6
联营企业	Joint Ownership Enterprises	4	3	3
有限责任公司	Limited Liability Corporations	603	329	351
股份有限公司	Share-holding Corporations Ltd.	245	203	210
私营企业	Private Enterprises	4 557	1 653	1 747
其他企业	Other Enterprises	4	3	3
港、澳、台商投资企业	**Enterprises with Investment from HongKong, Macao and Taiwan**	**1 264**	**647**	**687**
外商投资企业	**Enterprises with Foreign Investment**	**2 910**	**1 520**	**1 637**
四、按国民经济行业大类分	**Grouped by Sector**			
采矿业	**Mining and Quarrying**	**1**	**1**	**1**
有色金属矿采选业	Nonferrous Metals Mining and Processing	–	–	–
非金属矿采选业	Nonmetal Minerals Mining and Dressing	1	1	1

表16-8 续表 Continued

单位：个 (unit)

项 目	Item	企业数 Number of Enterprises	# 有R&D活动企业数 Number of Enterprises With R&D Activities	# 有科技机构企业数 The Number of Enterprises with Scientific Institutions
制造业	**Manufacturing**	**9 531**	**4 337**	**4 617**
农副食品加工业	Food Processing	45	19	19
食品制造业	Food Production	55	26	31
酒、饮料和精制茶制造业	Wine, Beverage and Refined tea manufacturing	19	10	9
烟草制造业	Manufacture of Tobacco	1	–	–
纺织业	Textile Industry	1 201	241	262
纺织服装、服饰业	Garments and Apparel Industry	379	133	142
皮革、毛皮、羽毛及其制品和制鞋业	Leather, Fur, Wool and Shoes Products	55	19	16
木材加工和木、竹、藤、棕、草制品业	Wood Processing, Wood, Bamboo, Rattan and Coir Products Straw Products	43	9	9
家具制造业	Furniture Manufacturing	75	28	29
造纸和纸制品业	Papermaking and Paper Products	146	66	67
印刷和记录媒介复制业	Printing and Record Medium Reproduction	157	53	60
文教、工美、体育和娱乐用品制造业	Stationary,Educational,Industrial arts, Sports and Entertainment products	125	61	62
石油加工、炼焦和核燃料加工业	Oil Processing, Coking and Nuclear Fuel Processing	22	8	10
化学原料和化学制品制造业	Raw Chemical Materials and Chemical Products	653	301	330
医药制造业	Medical and Pharmaceutical Products	107	75	78
化学纤维制造业	Chemical Fiber	329	63	75
橡胶和塑料制品业	Rubber and Plastic Products	609	246	268
非金属矿物制品业	Nonmetal Mineral Products	318	99	108
黑色金属冶炼和压延加工业	Smelting and Pressing of Ferrous Metals	165	63	66
有色金属冶炼和压延加工业	Smelting and Pressing of Nonferrous Metals	231	83	92
金属制品业	Metal Products	650	244	263
通用设备制造业	General Equipment Manufacture	831	473	492
专用设备制造业	For Special Purposes Equipment Manufacturing	678	432	442
汽车制造业	Automobile Manufacturing	413	232	244
铁路、船舶、航空航天和其他运输设备制造业	Railway, Ship, Aerospace and other transportation equipment manufacturing	119	64	60
电气机械和器材制造业	Electric Equipment and Machinery	743	445	476
计算机、通信和其他电子设备制造业	Computer Telecommunications and Other Electronic Equipment Manufacture	1 145	719	779
仪器仪表制造业	Instruments, Meters Machinery	167	115	117
其他制造业	Other Products Manufacture	10	3	3
废弃资源综合利用业	Comprehensive Utilization of Waste Resources	40	7	8
电力、热力、燃气及水生产和供应业	**Production and Supply of Electricity, Gas and Water**	**84**	**28**	**28**
电力、热力生产和供应业	Production and Supply of Electricity and Thermal Power	38	14	13
燃气生产和供应业	Production and Supply of Gas	21	3	4
水的生产和供应业	Production and Supply of Water	25	11	11

表16-9 规模以上工业企业科技活动人员情况（2016年末）

NUMBER OF PERSONS ENGAGED IN SCIENTIFIC & TECHNOLOGICAL ACTIVTIES OF ABOVE-SCALE INDUSTRIAL ENTERPRISES (END OF 2016)

单位：人 (person)

项　目	Item	研究与试验发展人员 Research and Development Personnel	# 参加项目人员 Present Item Personnel	企业办科技机构人员 Personnel in Science & Technology Institutions Run by Enterprises
总　计	**Total**	**155 163**	**148 265**	**172 191**
一、按地区分	**Grouped by Region**			
市　区	**Urban Area**	**75 800**	**72 931**	**81 195**
姑苏区	Gusu District	141	136	191
吴中区	Wuzhong District	8 892	8 569	11 345
相城区	Xiangcheng District	7 959	7 704	8 857
高新区、虎丘区	New & Hi-tech Zone , Huqiu District	17 131	16 434	14 638
工业园区	Industrial Park	25 736	25 070	26 765
吴江区	Wujiang District	15 941	15 018	19 399
县级市	**Cities at County Level**	**79 363**	**75 334**	**90 996**
常熟市	Changshu	12 726	12 162	14 934
张家港市	Zhangjiagang	16 405	15 469	13 496
昆山市	Kunshan	41 718	39 370	53 254
太仓市	Taicang	8 514	8 333	9 312
二、按企业规模分	**By Size of Enterprises**			
大　型	Large	65 453	61 620	64 328
中　型	Medium-sized	47 659	45 855	56 168
小　型	Small	41 922	40 663	51 503
微　型	Micro	129	127	192
三、按登记注册类型分	**Grouped by Registration Status**			
内资企业	**Domestic Funded Enterprises**	**66 862**	**63 624**	**74 307**
国有企业	State-owned Enterprises	137	137	156
集体企业	Collective-owned Enterprises	-	-	-
股份合作企业	Share-holding Cooperative Enterprises	103	102	125
联营企业	Joint Ownership Enterprises	95	88	121
有限责任公司	Limited Liability Corporations	16 639	15 380	16 897
股份有限公司	Share-holding Corporations Ltd.	11 519	11 137	12 949
私营企业	Private Enterprises	38 272	36 689	43 944
其他企业	Other Enterprises	97	91	115
港、澳、台商投资企业	**Enterprises with Investment from HongKong, Macao and Taiwan**	**24 970**	**23 484**	**30 964**
外商投资企业	**Enterprises with Foreign Investment**	**63 331**	**61 157**	**66 920**
四、按国民经济行业大类分	**Grouped by Sector**			
采矿业	**Mining and Quarrying**	**35**	**35**	**70**
有色金属矿采选业	Nonferrous Metals Mining and Processing	-	-	-
非金属矿采选业	Nonmetal Minerals Mining and Dressing	35	35	70

表16-9 续表 Continued

单位：人 (person)

项 目	Item	研究与试验发展人员 Research and Development Personnel	# 参加项目人员 Present Item Personnel	企业办科技机构人员 Personnel in Science & Technology Institutions Run by Enterprises
制造业	**Manufacturing**	**154 474**	**147 594**	**171 528**
农副食品加工业	Food Processing	223	220	379
食品制造业	Food Production	537	513	679
酒、饮料和精制茶制造业	Wine, Beverage and Refined tea manufacturing	121	119	148
烟草制造业	Manufacture of Tobacco	–	–	–
纺织业	Textile Industry	5 094	4 631	5 345
纺织服装、服饰业	Garments and Apparel Industry	2 732	2 643	2 595
皮革、毛皮、羽毛及其制品和制鞋业	Leather, Fur, Wool and Shoes Products	280	271	311
木材加工和木、竹、藤、棕、草制品业	Wood Processing, Wood, Bamboo, Rattan and Coir Products Straw Products	254	250	315
家具制造业	Furniture Manufacturing	432	426	461
造纸和纸制品业	Papermaking and Paper Products	3 045	2 966	2 230
印刷和记录媒介复制业	Printing and Record Medium Reproduction	1 140	1 063	1 354
文教、工美、体育和娱乐用品制造业	Stationary,Educational,Industrial arts, Sports and Entertainment products	2 072	1 883	2 194
石油加工、炼焦和核燃料加工业	Oil Processing, Coking and Nuclear Fuel Processing	115	110	158
化学原料和化学制品制造业	Raw Chemical Materials and Chemical Products	7 519	7 018	9 171
医药制造业	Medical and Pharmaceutical Products	1 922	1 878	2 136
化学纤维制造业	Chemical Fiber	5 036	4 886	3 589
橡胶和塑料制品业	Rubber and Plastic Products	6 010	5 790	7 974
非金属矿物制品业	Nonmetal Mineral Products	2 306	2 246	2 905
黑色金属冶炼和压延加工业	Smelting and Pressing of Ferrous Metals	3 278	3 162	2 724
有色金属冶炼和压延加工业	Smelting and Pressing of Nonferrous Metals	1 838	1 795	2 093
金属制品业	Metal Products	5 718	5 533	7 039
通用设备制造业	General Equipment Manufacture	13 273	12 372	17 063
专用设备制造业	For Special Purposes Equipment Manufacturing	12 930	12 473	15 431
汽车制造业	Automobile Manufacturing	8 158	7 787	10 601
铁路、船舶、航空航天和其他运输设备制造业	Railway, Ship, Aerospace and other transportation equipment manufacturing	1 744	1 699	2 117
电气机械和器材制造业	Electric Equipment and Machinery	17 618	16 931	20 163
计算机、通信和其他电子设备制造业	Computer Telecommunications and Other Electronic Equipment Manufacture	47 317	45 349	47 993
仪器仪表制造业	Instruments, Meters Machinery	3 691	3 514	4 237
其他制造业	Other Products Manufacture	8	8	9
废弃资源综合利用业	Comprehensive Utilization of Waste Resources	63	58	114
电力、热力、燃气及水生产和供应业	**Production and Supply of Electricity, Gas and Water**	**654**	**636**	**593**
电力、热力生产和供应业	Production and Supply of Electricity and Thermal Power	397	381	240
燃气生产和供应业	Production and Supply of Gas	44	44	62
水的生产和供应业	Production and Supply of Water	213	211	291

表16-10 规模以上工业企业科技活动经费支出情况（2016年）

THE EXPENDITURE OF SCIENTIFIC AND TECHNOLOGICAL ACTIVITIES OF ABOVE-SCALE INDUSTRIAL ENTERPRISES (2016)

单位：万元 (10 000 yuan)

项　目	Item	R&D经费内部支出合计 Internal Expenditures on Research and Development	# 政府资金 Government Funds	# 企业资金 Enterprises Funds	# 境外资金 Abroad Funds
总　计	**Total**	**3 615 017**	**38 038**	**3 503 187**	**44 023**
一、按地区分	**Grouped by Region**				
市　区	**Urban Area**	**1 539 086**	**19 180**	**1 458 916**	**39 182**
姑苏区	Gusu District	1 015	30	985	–
吴中区	Wuzhong District	167 024	1 913	163 964	130
相城区	Xiangcheng District	134 753	2 402	130 099	198
高新区、虎丘区	New & Hi-tech Zone , Huqiu District	358 482	5 075	348 274	4 241
工业园区	Industrial Park	575 902	6 780	520 276	34 208
吴江区	Wujiang District	301 910	2 981	295 318	405
县级市	**Cities at County Level**	**2 075 931**	**18 857**	**2 044 271**	**4 841**
常熟市	Changshu	460 588	4 201	454 460	447
张家港市	Zhangjiagang	614 129	3 711	608 493	1 154
昆山市	Kunshan	750 215	9 299	734 576	2 851
太仓市	Taicang	251 000	1 646	246 742	390
二、按企业规模分	**By Size of Enterprises**				
大　型	Large	1 762 503	10 083	1 726 353	20 985
中　型	Medium-sized	1 020 476	16 540	968 691	17 824
小　型	Small	829 967	11 381	806 117	5 215
微　型	Micro	2 072	34	2 027	–
三、按登记注册类型分	**Grouped by Registration Status**				
内资企业	**Domestic Funded Enterprises**	**1 634 222**	**29 012**	**1 594 668**	**1 290**
国有企业	State-owned Enterprises	8 429	–	8 429	–
集体企业	Collective-owned Enterprises	–	–	–	–
股份合作企业	Share-holding Cooperative Enterprises	961	–	961	–
联营企业	Joint Ownership Enterprises	1 449	45	1 404	–
有限责任公司	Limited Liability Corporations	601 650	10 020	588 902	961
股份有限公司	Share-holding Corporations Ltd.	274 196	7 427	266 136	–
私营企业	Private Enterprises	746 063	11 521	727 362	329
其他企业	Other Enterprises	1 474	–	1 474	–
港、澳、台商投资企业	**Enterprises with Investment from HongKong, Macao and Taiwan**	**542 765**	**4 329**	**530 415**	**6 029**
外商投资企业	**Enterprises with Foreign Investment**	**1 438 030**	**4 696**	**1 378 104**	**36 705**
四、按国民经济行业大类分	**Grouped by Sector**				
采矿业	**Mining and Quarrying**	**373**	**–**	**373**	**–**
有色金属矿采选业	Nonferrous Metals Mining and Processing	–	–	–	–
非金属矿采选业	Nonmetal Minerals Mining and Dressing	373	–	373	–

表16-10 续表 Continued

单位：万元 (10 000 yuan)

项目	Item	R&D经费内部支出合计 Internal Expenditures on Research and Development	# 政府资金 Government Funds	# 企业资金 Enterprises Funds	# 境外资金 Abroad Funds
制造业	**Manufacturing**	**3 593 918**	**38 018**	**3 482 335**	**44 023**
农副食品加工业	Food Processing	13 917	–	13 917	–
食品制造业	Food Production	17 429	–	16 902	176
酒、饮料和精制茶制造业	Wine, Beverage and Refined tea manufacturing	2 078	124	1 954	–
烟草制造业	Manufacture of Tobacco	–	–	–	–
纺织业	Textile Industry	97 682	1 295	95 813	34
纺织服装、服饰业	Garments and Apparel Industry	55 215	328	54 517	–
皮革、毛皮、羽毛及其制品和制鞋业	Leather, Fur, Wool and Shoes Products	3 480	–	3 352	–
木材加工和木、竹、藤、棕、草制品业	Wood Processing, Wood, Bamboo, Rattan and Coir Products Straw Products	5 805	–	5 218	–
家具制造业	Furniture Manufacturing	7 395	3	7 121	269
造纸和纸制品业	Papermaking and Paper Products	90 677	1 246	89 431	–
印刷和记录媒介复制业	Printing and Record Medium Reproduction	14 522	103	13 841	–
文教、工美、体育和娱乐用品制造业	Stationary,Educational,Industrial arts, Sports and Entertainment products	25 285	1 355	23 919	–
石油加工、炼焦和核燃料加工业	Oil Processing, Coking and Nuclear Fuel Processing	2 890	72	2 818	–
化学原料和化学制品制造业	Raw Chemical Materials and Chemical Products	241 036	3 287	228 527	4 562
医药制造业	Medical and Pharmaceutical Products	78 263	997	76 740	515
化学纤维制造业	Chemical Fiber	153 234	699	152 455	–
橡胶和塑料制品业	Rubber and Plastic Products	123 845	291	122 232	43
非金属矿物制品业	Nonmetal Mineral Products	47 600	323	46 894	328
黑色金属冶炼和压延加工业	Smelting and Pressing of Ferrous Metals	264 596	1 308	262 503	–
有色金属冶炼和压延加工业	Smelting and Pressing of Nonferrous Metals	49 984	645	47 844	–
金属制品业	Metal Products	104 477	893	102 659	816
通用设备制造业	General Equipment Manufacture	281 585	3 564	276 687	571
专用设备制造业	For Special Purposes Equipment Manufacturing	230 294	4 666	218 975	4 212
汽车制造业	Automobile Manufacturing	205 995	1 624	201 694	1 845
铁路、船舶、航空航天和其他运输设备制造业	Railway, Ship, Aerospace and other transportation equipment manufacturing	46 459	284	42 518	3 080
电气机械和器材制造业	Electric Equipment and Machinery	465 031	5 698	447 971	7 048
计算机、通信和其他电子设备制造业	Computer Telecommunications and Other Electronic Equipment Manufacture	894 979	6 643	860 389	18 994
仪器仪表制造业	Instruments, Meters Machinery	69 238	2 572	64 553	1 531
其他制造业	Other Products Manufacture	95	–	95	–
废弃资源综合利用业	Comprehensive Utilization of Waste Resources	833	–	796	–
电力、热力、燃气及水生产和供应业	**Production and Supply of Electricity, Gas and Water**	**20 726**	**20**	**20 480**	–
电力、热力生产和供应业	Production and Supply of Electricity and Thermal Power	12 494	–	12 355	–
燃气生产和供应业	Production and Supply of Gas	2 020	–	2 020	–
水的生产和供应业	Production and Supply of Water	6 211	20	6 104	–

表16-11

规模以上工业企业自主知识产权情况（2016年）
THE INDEPENDENT INTELLECTUAL PROPERTY RIGHTS OF ABOVE-SCALE INDUSTRIAL ENTERPRISES (2016)

单位：件 (unit)

项目	Item	专利申请数 Patents Submitted for Examination	# 发明专利 Invention	年末拥有发明专利数 Owning Inventive Patent by Year End
总计	**Total**	**30 277**	**11 680**	**39 553**
一、按地区分	**Grouped by Region**			
市区	**Urban Area**	**15 604**	**5 856**	**22 105**
姑苏区	Gusu District	12	4	36
吴中区	Wuzhong District	3 037	797	2 789
相城区	Xiangcheng District	2 754	617	3 167
高新区、虎丘区	New & Hi-tech Zone , Huqiu District	3 991	1 983	3 913
工业园区	Industrial Park	2 471	1 067	6 744
吴江区	Wujiang District	3 339	1 388	5 456
县级市	**Cities at County Level**	**14 673**	**5 824**	**17 448**
常熟市	Changshu	1 991	823	2 561
张家港市	Zhangjiagang	2 593	1 224	3 223
昆山市	Kunshan	7 935	3 028	9 133
太仓市	Taicang	2 154	749	2 531
二、按企业规模分	**By Size of Enterprises**			
大型	Large	8 806	3 991	10 402
中型	Medium-sized	7 353	2 705	11 986
小型	Small	14 034	4 934	17 085
微型	Micro	84	50	80
三、按登记注册类型分	**Grouped by Registration Status**			
内资企业	**Domestic Funded Enterprises**	**17 930**	**7 180**	**21 275**
国有企业	State-owned Enterprises	17	6	–
集体企业	Collective-owned Enterprises	–	–	–
股份合作企业	Share-holding Cooperative Enterprises	41	12	38
联营企业	Joint Ownership Enterprises	31	27	28
有限责任公司	Limited Liability Corporations	3 642	1 743	3 913
股份有限公司	Share-holding Corporations Ltd.	3 287	1 260	4 304
私营企业	Private Enterprises	10 907	4 128	12 977
其他企业	Other Enterprises	5	4	15
港、澳、台商投资企业	**Enterprises with Investment from HongKong, Macao and Taiwan**	**4 480**	**1 622**	**6 227**
外商投资企业	**Enterprises with Foreign Investment**	**7 867**	**2 878**	**12 051**
四、按国民经济行业大类分	**Grouped by Sector**			
采矿业	**Mining and Quarrying**	**9**	**3**	**16**
有色金属矿采选业	Nonferrous Metals Mining and Processing	–	–	–
非金属矿采选业	Nonmetal Minerals Mining and Dressing	9	3	16

表16-11 续表　Continued

单位：件　(unit)

项　目	Item	专利申请数 Patents Submitted for Examination	# 发明专利 Invention	年末拥有发明专利数 Owning Inventive Patent by Year End
制造业	**Manufacturing**	**30 149**	**11 654**	**39 407**
农副食品加工业	Food Processing	39	18	84
食品制造业	Food Production	55	37	147
酒、饮料和精制茶制造业	Wine, Beverage and Refined tea manufacturing	7	3	10
烟草制造业	Manufacture of Tobacco	–	–	–
纺织业	Textile Industry	620	207	630
纺织服装、服饰业	Garments and Apparel Industry	108	39	175
皮革、毛皮、羽毛及其制品和制鞋业	Leather, Fur, Wool and Shoes Products	14	–	10
木材加工和木、竹、藤、棕、草制品业	Wood Processing, Wood, Bamboo, Rattan and Coir Products Straw Products	18	6	49
家具制造业	Furniture Manufacturing	323	85	374
造纸和纸制品业	Papermaking and Paper Products	474	196	576
印刷和记录媒介复制业	Printing and Record Medium Reproduction	113	36	122
文教、工美、体育和娱乐用品制造业	Stationary,Educational,Industrial arts, Sports and Entertainment products	802	110	788
石油加工、炼焦和核燃料加工业	Oil Processing, Coking and Nuclear Fuel Processing	51	27	46
化学原料和化学制品制造业	Raw Chemical Materials and Chemical Products	1 427	928	2 334
医药制造业	Medical and Pharmaceutical Products	399	296	890
化学纤维制造业	Chemical Fiber	621	189	479
橡胶和塑料制品业	Rubber and Plastic Products	1 298	529	1 565
非金属矿物制品业	Nonmetal Mineral Products	658	206	798
黑色金属冶炼和压延加工业	Smelting and Pressing of Ferrous Metals	431	208	592
有色金属冶炼和压延加工业	Smelting and Pressing of Nonferrous Metals	224	69	428
金属制品业	Metal Products	1 647	567	1 712
通用设备制造业	General Equipment Manufacture	3 782	1 381	5 583
专用设备制造业	For Special Purposes Equipment Manufacturing	3 730	1 449	5 269
汽车制造业	Automobile Manufacturing	1 221	437	1 690
铁路、船舶、航空航天和其他运输设备制造业	Railway, Ship, Aerospace and other transportation equipment manufacturing	230	71	441
电气机械和器材制造业	Electric Equipment and Machinery	4 445	1 431	4 816
计算机、通信和其他电子设备制造业	Computer Telecommunications and Other Electronic Equipment Manufacture	6 278	2 771	8 491
仪器仪表制造业	Instruments, Meters Machinery	1 102	352	1 260
其他制造业	Other Products Manufacture	4	3	3
废弃资源综合利用业	Comprehensive Utilization of Waste Resources	28	3	45
电力、热力、燃气及水生产和供应业	**Production and Supply of Electricity, Gas and Water**	**119**	**23**	**130**
电力、热力生产和供应业	Production and Supply of Electricity and Thermal Power	51	9	39
燃气生产和供应业	Production and Supply of Gas	15	6	–
水的生产和供应业	Production and Supply of Water	53	8	91

表16-12

大中型工业科技活动企业与机构数 (2016年末)

NUMBER OF ENTERPRISES AND INSITITUTIONS OF LARGE & MEDIUM-SIZED INDUSTRIAL ENTERPRISES ON SCIENTIFIC AND TECHNOLOGICAL ACTIVITIES (END OF 2016)

单位：个 (unit)

项　目	Item	企业数 Number of Enterprises	# 有R&D活动企业数 Number of Enterprises With R&D Activities	# 有科技机构企业数 The Number of Enterprises with Scientific Institutions
总　计	**Total**	**1 936**	**1 614**	**1 714**
一、按地区分	**Grouped by Region**			
市　区	**Urban Area**	**932**	**726**	**813**
姑苏区	Gusu District	3	3	3
吴中区	Wuzhong District	124	109	122
相城区	Xiangcheng District	121	93	109
高新区、虎丘区	New & Hi-tech Zone , Huqiu District	158	125	134
工业园区	Industrial Park	268	236	255
吴江区	Wujiang District	258	160	190
县级市	**Cities at County Level**	**1 004**	**888**	**901**
常熟市	Changshu	213	175	178
张家港市	Zhangjiagang	158	148	149
昆山市	Kunshan	496	458	460
太仓市	Taicang	137	107	114
二、按企业规模分	**By Size of Enterprises**			
大　型	Large	407	331	359
中　型	Medium-sized	1 529	1 283	1 355
三、按登记注册类型分	**Grouped by Registration Status**			
内资企业	**Domestic Funded Enterprises**	**715**	**628**	**665**
国有企业	State-owned Enterprises	2	2	2
集体企业	Collective-owned Enterprises	–	–	–
股份合作企业	Share-holding Cooperative Enterprises	3	3	3
联营企业	Joint Ownership Enterprises	–	–	–
有限责任公司	Limited Liability Corporations	154	138	146
股份有限公司	Share-holding Corporations Ltd.	94	92	93
私营企业	Private Enterprises	461	392	420
其他企业	Other Enterprises	1	1	1
港、澳、台商投资企业	**Enterprises with Investment from HongKong, Macao and Taiwan**	**360**	**294**	**308**
外商投资企业	**Enterprises with Foreign Investment**	**861**	**692**	**741**
四、按国民经济行业大类分	**Grouped by Sector**			
采矿业	**Mining and Quarrying**	**1**	**1**	**1**
有色金属矿采选业	Nonferrous Metals Mining and Processing	–	–	–
非金属矿采选业	Nonmetal Minerals Mining and Dressing	1	1	1

表16-12 续表 Continued

单位：个 (unit)

项 目	Item	企业数 Number of Enterprises	# 有R&D活动企业数 Number of Enterprises With R&D Activities	# 有科技机构企业数 The Number of Enterprises with Scientific Institutions
制造业	**Manufacturing**	**1 918**	**1 599**	**1 699**
农副食品加工业	Food Processing	6	6	6
食品制造业	Food Production	19	12	15
酒、饮料和精制茶制造业	Wine, Beverage and Refined tea manufacturing	6	6	6
烟草制造业	Manufacture of Tobacco	–	–	–
纺织业	Textile Industry	129	105	113
纺织服装、服饰业	Garments and Apparel Industry	101	83	89
皮革、毛皮、羽毛及其制品和制鞋业	Leather, Fur, Wool and Shoes Products	12	9	9
木材加工和木、竹、藤、棕、草制品业	Wood Processing, Wood, Bamboo, Rattan and Coir Products Straw Products	8	6	7
家具制造业	Furniture Manufacturing	21	15	16
造纸和纸制品业	Papermaking and Paper Products	19	18	18
印刷和记录媒介复制业	Printing and Record Medium Reproduction	23	19	22
文教、工美、体育和娱乐用品制造业	Stationary,Educational,Industrial arts, Sports and Entertainment products	27	25	27
石油加工、炼焦和核燃料加工业	Oil Processing, Coking and Nuclear Fuel Processing	–	–	–
化学原料和化学制品制造业	Raw Chemical Materials and Chemical Products	72	57	63
医药制造业	Medical and Pharmaceutical Products	28	26	27
化学纤维制造业	Chemical Fiber	31	25	27
橡胶和塑料制品业	Rubber and Plastic Products	91	75	78
非金属矿物制品业	Nonmetal Mineral Products	33	29	30
黑色金属冶炼和压延加工业	Smelting and Pressing of Ferrous Metals	22	18	18
有色金属冶炼和压延加工业	Smelting and Pressing of Nonferrous Metals	27	24	25
金属制品业	Metal Products	94	77	84
通用设备制造业	General Equipment Manufacture	131	115	118
专用设备制造业	For Special Purposes Equipment Manufacturing	115	107	110
汽车制造业	Automobile Manufacturing	119	98	106
铁路、船舶、航空航天和其他运输设备制造业	Railway, Ship, Aerospace and other transportation equipment manufacturing	24	23	23
电气机械和器材制造业	Electric Equipment and Machinery	189	165	175
计算机、通信和其他电子设备制造业	Computer Telecommunications and Other Electronic Equipment Manufacture	531	423	453
仪器仪表制造业	Instruments, Meters Machinery	38	33	34
其他制造业	Other Products Manufacture	1	–	–
废弃资源综合利用业	Comprehensive Utilization of Waste Resources	1	–	–
电力、热力、燃气及水生产和供应业	**Production and Supply of Electricity, Gas and Water**	**17**	**14**	**14**
电力、热力生产和供应业	Production and Supply of Electricity and Thermal Power	8	7	6
燃气生产和供应业	Production and Supply of Gas	2	1	2
水的生产和供应业	Production and Supply of Water	7	6	6

表16-13 大中型工业企业科技活动人员情况（2016年末）

NUMBER OF PERSONS ENGAGED IN SCIENTIFIC & TECHNOLOGICAL ACTIVTIES IN LARGE AND MEDIUM-SIZED INDUSTRIAL ENTERPRISES (END OF 2016)

单位：人 (person)

项目	Item	研究与试验发展人员 Research and Development Personnel	# 参加项目人员 Present Item Personnel	企业办科技机构人员 Personnel in Science & Technology Institutions Run by Enterprises
总计	**Total**	**113 112**	**107 475**	**120 496**
一、按地区分	**Grouped by Region**			
市区	**Urban Area**	**57 219**	**54 914**	**57 027**
姑苏区	Gusu District	94	89	95
吴中区	Wuzhong District	4 527	4 293	5 653
相城区	Xiangcheng District	5 538	5 335	6 164
高新区、虎丘区	New & Hi-tech Zone , Huqiu District	13 268	12 667	9 559
工业园区	Industrial Park	20 915	20 422	20 442
吴江区	Wujiang District	12 877	12 108	15 114
县级市	**Cities at County Level**	**55 893**	**52 561**	**63 469**
常熟市	Changshu	8 829	8 384	10 150
张家港市	Zhangjiagang	11 419	10 619	8 443
昆山市	Kunshan	30 321	28 321	39 453
太仓市	Taicang	5 324	5 237	5 423
二、按企业规模分	**By Size of Enterprises**			
大型	Large	65 453	61 620	64 328
中型	Medium-sized	47 659	45 855	56 168
三、按登记注册类型分	**Grouped by Registration Status**			
内资企业	**Domestic Funded Enterprises**	**41 408**	**38 928**	**43 402**
国有企业	State-owned Enterprises	137	137	156
集体企业	Collective-owned Enterprises	-	-	-
股份合作企业	Share-holding Cooperative Enterprises	60	59	73
联营企业	Joint Ownership Enterprises	-	-	-
有限责任公司	Limited Liability Corporations	13 085	11 933	12 368
股份有限公司	Share-holding Corporations Ltd.	8 845	8 518	9 513
私营企业	Private Enterprises	19 220	18 225	21 212
其他企业	Other Enterprises	61	56	80
港、澳、台商投资企业	**Enterprises with Investment from HongKong, Macao and Taiwan**	**19 795**	**18 444**	**24 697**
外商投资企业	**Enterprises with Foreign Investment**	**51 909**	**50 103**	**52 397**
四、按国民经济行业大类分	**Grouped by Sector**			
采矿业	**Mining and Quarrying**	**35**	**35**	**70**
有色金属矿采选业	Nonferrous Metals Mining and Processing	-	-	-
非金属矿采选业	Nonmetal Minerals Mining and Dressing	35	35	70

表16-13 续表 Continued

单位：人 (person)

项 目	Item	研究与试验发展人员 Research and Development Personnel	# 参加项目人员 Present Item Personnel	企业办科技机构人员 Personnel in Science & Technology Institutions Run by Enterprises
制造业	**Manufacturing**	**112 733**	**107 105**	**120 107**
农副食品加工业	Food Processing	81	81	97
食品制造业	Food Production	383	372	477
酒、饮料和精制茶制造业	Wine, Beverage and Refined tea manufacturing	103	102	135
烟草制造业	Manufacture of Tobacco	–	–	–
纺织业	Textile Industry	3 541	3 130	3 595
纺织服装、服饰业	Garments and Apparel Industry	2 306	2 237	2 070
皮革、毛皮、羽毛及其制品和制鞋业	Leather, Fur, Wool and Shoes Products	211	202	254
木材加工和木、竹、藤、棕、草制品业	Wood Processing, Wood, Bamboo, Rattan and Coir Products Straw Products	233	229	295
家具制造业	Furniture Manufacturing	339	338	340
造纸和纸制品业	Papermaking and Paper Products	2 572	2 508	1 638
印刷和记录媒介复制业	Printing and Record Medium Reproduction	764	690	821
文教、工美、体育和娱乐用品制造业	Stationary,Educational,Industrial arts, Sports and Entertainment products	1 584	1 425	1 641
石油加工、炼焦和核燃料加工业	Oil Processing, Coking and Nuclear Fuel Processing	–	–	–
化学原料和化学制品制造业	Raw Chemical Materials and Chemical Products	3 479	3 123	4 237
医药制造业	Medical and Pharmaceutical Products	1 008	993	1 114
化学纤维制造业	Chemical Fiber	4 502	4 358	2 959
橡胶和塑料制品业	Rubber and Plastic Products	3 728	3 559	5 065
非金属矿物制品业	Nonmetal Mineral Products	1 242	1 198	1 557
黑色金属冶炼和压延加工业	Smelting and Pressing of Ferrous Metals	2 534	2 475	1 959
有色金属冶炼和压延加工业	Smelting and Pressing of Nonferrous Metals	1 142	1 129	1 071
金属制品业	Metal Products	3 238	3 126	3 983
通用设备制造业	General Equipment Manufacture	6 975	6 249	9 675
专用设备制造业	For Special Purposes Equipment Manufacturing	7 318	7 028	8 707
汽车制造业	Automobile Manufacturing	5 647	5 358	7 521
铁路、船舶、航空航天和其他运输设备制造业	Railway, Ship, Aerospace and other transportation equipment manufacturing	1 242	1 205	1 510
电气机械和器材制造业	Electric Equipment and Machinery	13 150	12 565	14 715
计算机、通信和其他电子设备制造业	Computer Telecommunications and Other Electronic Equipment Manufacture	43 050	41 214	42 180
仪器仪表制造业	Instruments, Meters Machinery	2 361	2 211	2 491
其他制造业	Other Products Manufacture	–	–	–
废弃资源综合利用业	Comprehensive Utilization of Waste Resources	–	–	–
电力、热力、燃气及水生产和供应业	**Production and Supply of Electricity, Gas and Water**	**344**	**335**	**319**
电力、热力生产和供应业	Production and Supply of Electricity and Thermal Power	196	189	96
燃气生产和供应业	Production and Supply of Gas	5	5	15
水的生产和供应业	Production and Supply of Water	143	141	208

表16-14

大中型工业企业科技活动经费支出情况（2016年）
EXPENDITURES OF SCIENTIFIC & TECHNOLOGIAL ACTIVITIES OF LARGE & MEDIUM-SIZED INDUSTRIAL ENTERPRISES (2016)

单位：万元 (10 000 yuan)

项　目	Item	R&D经费内部支出合计 Internal Expenditures on Research and Development	# 政府资金 Government Funds	# 企业资金 Enterprises Funds	# 境外资金 Abroad Funds
总　计	**Total**	**2 782 979**	**26 623**	**2 695 044**	**38 809**
一、按地区分	**Grouped by Region**				
市　区	**Urban Area**	**1 193 750**	**12 197**	**1 129 732**	**34 970**
姑苏区	Gusu District	490	30	460	–
吴中区	Wuzhong District	92 064	275	91 759	30
相城区	Xiangcheng District	94 454	1 463	90 873	85
高新区、虎丘区	New & Hi-tech Zone , Huqiu District	283 264	3 622	274 643	4 142
工业园区	Industrial Park	472 213	4 783	426 043	30 537
吴江区	Wujiang District	251 266	2 023	245 955	176
县级市	**Cities at County Level**	**1 589 228**	**14 426**	**1 565 312**	**3 839**
常熟市	Changshu	353 367	3 212	348 263	445
张家港市	Zhangjiagang	494 057	3 161	489 903	754
昆山市	Kunshan	575 830	7 632	563 278	2 453
太仓市	Taicang	165 975	421	163 868	187
二、按企业规模分	**By Size of Enterprises**				
大　型	Large	1 762 503	10 083	1 726 353	20 985
中　型	Medium-sized	1 020 476	16 540	968 691	17 824
三、按登记注册类型分	**Grouped by Registration Status**				
内资企业	**Domestic Funded Enterprises**	**1 147 695**	**20 867**	**1 118 423**	**1 194**
国有企业	State-owned Enterprises	8 429	–	8 429	–
集体企业	Collective-owned Enterprises	–	–	–	–
股份合作企业	Share-holding Cooperative Enterprises	580	–	580	–
联营企业	Joint Ownership Enterprises	–	–	–	–
有限责任公司	Limited Liability Corporations	518 107	9 041	506 555	961
股份有限公司	Share-holding Corporations Ltd.	222 712	5 086	217 281	–
私营企业	Private Enterprises	397 101	6 740	384 813	233
其他企业	Other Enterprises	765	–	765	–
港、澳、台商投资企业	**Enterprises with Investment from HongKong, Macao and Taiwan**	**443 165**	**2 762**	**433 750**	**5 075**
外商投资企业	**Enterprises with Foreign Investment**	**1 192 119**	**2 994**	**1 142 871**	**32 540**
四、按国民经济行业大类分	**Grouped by Sector**				
采矿业	**Mining and Quarrying**	**373**	–	**373**	–
有色金属矿采选业	Nonferrous Metals Mining and Processing	–	–	–	–
非金属矿采选业	Nonmetal Minerals Mining and Dressing	373	–	373	–

表16-14 续表 Continued

单位：万元 (10 000 yuan)

项 目	Item	R&D经费内部支出合计 Internal Expenditures on Research and Development	# 政府资金 Government Funds	# 企业资金 Enterprises Funds	# 境外资金 Abroad Funds
制造业	**Manufacturing**	**2 769 948**	**26 603**	**2 682 033**	**38 809**
农副食品加工业	Food Processing	2 014	–	2 014	–
食品制造业	Food Production	13 926	–	13 399	176
酒、饮料和精制茶制造业	Wine, Beverage and Refined tea manufacturing	1 869	–	1 869	–
烟草制造业	Manufacture of Tobacco	–	–	–	–
纺织业	Textile Industry	64 384	765	63 257	34
纺织服装、服饰业	Garments and Apparel Industry	46 461	305	45 803	–
皮革、毛皮、羽毛及其制品和制鞋业	Leather, Fur, Wool and Shoes Products	2 902	–	2 774	–
木材加工和木、竹、藤、棕、草制品业	Wood Processing, Wood, Bamboo, Rattan and Coir Products Straw Products	5 488	–	4 902	–
家具制造业	Furniture Manufacturing	5 666	–	5 626	40
造纸和纸制品业	Papermaking and Paper Products	81 541	1 179	80 361	–
印刷和记录媒介复制业	Printing and Record Medium Reproduction	8 474	102	7 846	–
文教、工美、体育和娱乐用品制造业	Stationary,Educational,Industrial arts, Sports and Entertainment products	20 036	1 019	19 017	–
石油加工、炼焦和核燃料加工业	Oil Processing, Coking and Nuclear Fuel Processing	–	–	–	–
化学原料和化学制品制造业	Raw Chemical Materials and Chemical Products	121 034	753	116 118	1 846
医药制造业	Medical and Pharmaceutical Products	54 221	822	53 012	388
化学纤维制造业	Chemical Fiber	143 310	691	142 619	–
橡胶和塑料制品业	Rubber and Plastic Products	83 230	7	82 254	25
非金属矿物制品业	Nonmetal Mineral Products	26 463	10	26 275	125
黑色金属冶炼和压延加工业	Smelting and Pressing of Ferrous Metals	245 195	1 292	243 903	–
有色金属冶炼和压延加工业	Smelting and Pressing of Nonferrous Metals	30 859	420	29 826	–
金属制品业	Metal Products	54 972	353	53 884	720
通用设备制造业	General Equipment Manufacture	176 377	1 398	174 424	438
专用设备制造业	For Special Purposes Equipment Manufacturing	139 413	3 197	130 055	3 870
汽车制造业	Automobile Manufacturing	154 997	1 438	151 375	1 519
铁路、船舶、航空航天和其他运输设备制造业	Railway, Ship, Aerospace and other transportation equipment manufacturing	36 228	201	32 448	3 003
电气机械和器材制造业	Electric Equipment and Machinery	377 183	5 006	362 275	6 438
计算机、通信和其他电子设备制造业	Computer Telecommunications and Other Electronic Equipment Manufacture	827 958	5 249	795 211	18 736
仪器仪表制造业	Instruments, Meters Machinery	45 748	2 398	41 488	1 452
其他制造业	Other Products Manufacture	–	–	–	–
废弃资源综合利用业	Comprehensive Utilization of Waste Resources	–	–	–	–
电力、热力、燃气及水生产和供应业	**Production and Supply of Electricity, Gas and Water**	**12 658**	**20**	**12 638**	–
电力、热力生产和供应业	Production and Supply of Electricity and Thermal Power	8 027	–	8 027	–
燃气生产和供应业	Production and Supply of Gas	76	–	76	–
水的生产和供应业	Production and Supply of Water	4 555	20	4 535	–

表16-15

大中型工业企业自主知识产权情况（2016年）
SELF-OWNED INTELLECTUAL PROPERTY RIGHTS OF SCIENTIFIC & TECHNOLOGICAL ACTIVITIES OF LARGE & MEDIUM-SIZED INDUSTRIAL ENTERPRISES (2016)

单位：件 (unit)

项 目	Item	专利申请数 Patents Submitted for Examination	# 发明专利 Invention	年末拥有发明专利数 Owning Inventive Patent by Year End
总 计	**Total**	**16 159**	**6 696**	**22 388**
一、按地区分	**Grouped by Region**			
市 区	**Urban Area**	**8 137**	**3 361**	**12 172**
姑苏区	Gusu District	–	–	6
吴中区	Wuzhong District	937	267	1 018
相城区	Xiangcheng District	1 683	415	1 550
高新区、虎丘区	New & Hi-tech Zone , Huqiu District	1 682	879	1 567
工业园区	Industrial Park	1 625	763	4 418
吴江区	Wujiang District	2 210	1 037	3 613
县级市	**Cities at County Level**	**8 022**	**3 335**	**10 216**
常熟市	Changshu	1 212	483	1 392
张家港市	Zhangjiagang	1 432	719	1 729
昆山市	Kunshan	4 718	1 912	6 087
太仓市	Taicang	660	221	1 008
二、按企业规模分	**By Size of Enterprises**			
大 型	Large	8 806	3 991	10 402
中 型	Medium-sized	7 353	2 705	11 986
三、按登记注册类型分	**Grouped by Registration Status**			
内资企业	**Domestic Funded Enterprises**	**8 114**	**3 640**	**9 967**
国有企业	State-owned Enterprises	17	6	–
集体企业	Collective-owned Enterprises	–	–	–
股份合作企业	Share-holding Cooperative Enterprises	1	1	19
联营企业	Joint Ownership Enterprises	–	–	–
有限责任公司	Limited Liability Corporations	2 358	1 291	2 500
股份有限公司	Share-holding Corporations Ltd.	2 130	726	2 417
私营企业	Private Enterprises	3 606	1 615	5 019
其他企业	Other Enterprises	2	1	12
港、澳、台商投资企业	**Enterprises with Investment from HongKong, Macao and Taiwan**	**3 025**	**1 122**	**4 165**
外商投资企业	**Enterprises with Foreign Investment**	**5 020**	**1 934**	**8 256**
四、按国民经济行业大类分	**Grouped by Sector**			
采矿业	**Mining and Quarrying**	**9**	**3**	**16**
有色金属矿采选业	Nonferrous Metals Mining and Processing	–	–	–
非金属矿采选业	Nonmetal Minerals Mining and Dressing	9	3	16

表16-15 续表 Continued

单位：件 (unit)

项 目	Item	专利申请数 Patents Submitted for Examination	# 发明专利 Invention	年末拥有发明专利数 Owning Inventive Patent by Year End
制造业	**Manufacturing**	**16 083**	**6 686**	**22 299**
农副食品加工业	Food Processing	19	1	28
食品制造业	Food Production	29	20	51
酒、饮料和精制茶制造业	Wine, Beverage and Refined tea manufacturing	6	3	7
烟草制造业	Manufacture of Tobacco	–	–	–
纺织业	Textile Industry	285	90	351
纺织服装、服饰业	Garments and Apparel Industry	97	38	153
皮革、毛皮、羽毛及其制品和制鞋业	Leather, Fur, Wool and Shoes Products	1	–	10
木材加工和木、竹、藤、棕、草制品业	Wood Processing, Wood, Bamboo, Rattan and Coir Products Straw Products	18	6	49
家具制造业	Furniture Manufacturing	111	78	256
造纸和纸制品业	Papermaking and Paper Products	237	82	378
印刷和记录媒介复制业	Printing and Record Medium Reproduction	47	14	33
文教、工美、体育和娱乐用品制造业	Stationary,Educational,Industrial arts, Sports and Entertainment products	723	86	449
石油加工、炼焦和核燃料加工业	Oil Processing, Coking and Nuclear Fuel Processing	–	–	–
化学原料和化学制品制造业	Raw Chemical Materials and Chemical Products	575	461	859
医药制造业	Medical and Pharmaceutical Products	151	126	163
化学纤维制造业	Chemical Fiber	304	140	354
橡胶和塑料制品业	Rubber and Plastic Products	446	154	627
非金属矿物制品业	Nonmetal Mineral Products	227	67	408
黑色金属冶炼和压延加工业	Smelting and Pressing of Ferrous Metals	269	138	381
有色金属冶炼和压延加工业	Smelting and Pressing of Nonferrous Metals	79	23	205
金属制品业	Metal Products	630	199	847
通用设备制造业	General Equipment Manufacture	1 387	548	2 681
专用设备制造业	For Special Purposes Equipment Manufacturing	1 759	814	2 875
汽车制造业	Automobile Manufacturing	635	272	908
铁路、船舶、航空航天和其他运输设备制造业	Railway, Ship, Aerospace and other transportation equipment manufacturing	88	30	260
电气机械和器材制造业	Electric Equipment and Machinery	2 837	923	2 618
计算机、通信和其他电子设备制造业	Computer Telecommunications and Other Electronic Equipment Manufacture	4 723	2 202	6 764
仪器仪表制造业	Instruments, Meters Machinery	400	171	584
其他制造业	Other Products Manufacture	–	–	–
废弃资源综合利用业	Comprehensive Utilization of Waste Resources	–	–	–
电力、热力、燃气及水生产和供应业	**Production and Supply of Electricity, Gas and Water**	**67**	**7**	**73**
电力、热力生产和供应业	Production and Supply of Electricity and Thermal Power	21	1	12
燃气生产和供应业	Production and Supply of Gas	–	–	–
水的生产和供应业	Production and Supply of Water	46	6	61

表16-16

部分年份专业技术人员
SCIENTIFIC AND TECHNICAL PERSONNEL OF PARTIAL YEARS

单位：人 (person)

项目	Item	2012年	2013年	2014年	2015年	2016年
总计	**Total**	**1 099 869**	**1 234 777**	**1 366 119**	**1 496 406**	**1 634 233**
# 高级职称人员	Personnel with Senior Professional Titles	46 661	55 800	65 108	74 493	84 236
中级职称人员	Personnel with Medium Professional Titles	271 384	308 325	338 951	371 186	390 474
总计中：市区	Urban Area	501 968	594 757	663 804	736 746	816 804
# 吴江区	Wujiang District	143 919	159 090	173 201	187 374	188 649
常熟	Changshu	163 603	170 717	189 601	208 754	223 184
张家港	Zhangjiagang	150 802	170 606	191 598	210 668	231 686
昆山	Kunshan	205 859	214 004	225 909	236 400	250 875
太仓	Taicang	77 637	84 693	95 207	103 838	111 684

表16-17

分经济类型专业技术人员（2016年末）
SCIENTIFIC AND TECHNICAL PERSONNEL BY SECTOR (END OF 2016)

单位：人 (person)

类型	Sector	总计 Total	按职称分 Grouped by Professional Titles		按学历分 Grouped by Educational Level		
			# 高级职称 Senior Professional Titles	#中级职称 Medium Professional Titles	#研究生 Postgraduates	#大学本科 University and College	#大学专科 Specialized Institutions of Higher Education
总计	**Total**	**1 634 233**	**84 236**	**390 474**	**94 198**	**636 796**	**670 989**
全民事业	Institutions Owned by the Whole People	120 658	21 630	55 027	10 409	87 937	17 741
国有企业	State-owned Enterprises	15 238	1 105	3 754	1 101	7 670	4 113
部省属	Province and State Council Department Owned Enterprises	40 470	6 213	7 504	6 895	22 261	8 258
外资及港澳台资企业	Enterprises with Foreign Investment or Investment from Hongkong, Macao and Taiwan	810 532	27 955	173 835	45 696	271 231	375 272
民营企业	Enterprises of Private Ownership	647 335	27 333	150 354	30 097	247 697	265 605

表16-18

分地区专业技术人员（2016年末）
NUMBER OF SCIENTIFIC AND TECHNICAL PERSONNEL BY REGION (END OF 2016)

单位：人 (person)

地 区	Region	总 计 Total	# 女 性 Female	按职称分 Grouped by Professional Titles # 高级职称人员 Personnel with Senior Professional Titles	# 中级职称人员 Personnel with Medium Professional Titles	# 初级职称人员 Personnel with Junior Professional Titles
全 市	**Whole Municipality**	**1 634 233**	**616 297**	**84 236**	**390 474**	**662 002**
市 区	Urban Area	816 804	319 826	46 573	227 627	319 381
# 吴江区	Wujiang District	188 649	90 723	6 172	20 761	31 640
常 熟	Changshu	223 184	69 035	11 286	40 194	82 788
张家港	Zhangjiagang	231 686	88 726	11 287	51 973	125 181
昆 山	Kunshan	250 875	98 573	10 646	44 642	90 754
太 仓	Taicang	111 684	40 137	4 444	26 038	43 898

表16-18 续表 Continued

单位：人 (person)

地 区	Region	按学历分 Grouped by Educational Level 研究生 Postgraduates	大学本科 University and College	大学专科 Specialized Institutions of Higher Education	中 专 Specialized Secondary School	高中以下 Senior Middle School and below
全 市	**Whole Municipality**	**94 198**	**636 796**	**670 989**	**161 857**	**70 393**
市 区	Urban Area	66 585	327 116	324 897	64 134	34 072
# 吴江区	Wujiang District	5 420	69 702	74 097	31 199	8 231
常 熟	Changshu	7 123	88 085	111 222	11 986	4 768
张家港	Zhangjiagang	8 933	81 403	87 862	41 285	12 203
昆 山	Kunshan	7 126	102 124	103 285	26 090	12 250
太 仓	Taicang	4 431	38 068	43 723	18 362	7 100

主 要 统 计 指 标 解 释

专利 是专利权的简称，是对发明人的发明创造经审查合格后，由专利局依据专利法授予发明人和设计人对该项发明创造享有的专有权。包括发明、实用新型和外观设计。反映拥有自主知识产权的科技和设计成果情况。

发明（专利） 指对产品、方法或者其改进所提出的新的技术方案。是国际通行的反映拥有自主知识产权技术的核心指标。

实用新型（专利） 指对产品的形状、构造或者其结合所提出的适于实用的新的技术方案。反映具有一定技术含量的技术成果情况。

外观设计（专利） 指对产品的形状、图案、色彩或者其结合所作出的富有美感并适于工业上应用的新设计。反映拥有自主知识产权的外观设计成果情况。

专业技术人员 指从事专业技术工作的人员以及从事专业技术管理工作且已在1983年以前评定了专业技术职称或在1984年以后聘任了专业技术职务的人员。

专业技术人员具体指工程技术人员、农业技术人员、科研人员(自然科学研究、社会科学研究及实验技术人员)、卫生技术人员、教学人员(含高等院校、中等专业学校、技工学校、中学、小学)、民用航空飞行技术人员、船舶技术人员、经济人员、会计人员、统计人员、翻译人员、图书资料、档案、文博人员、新闻、出版人员、律师、公证人员、广播电视播音人员、工艺美术人员、体育人员、艺术人员及政工人员。

专业技术管理人员具体指企业、事业单位的领导；企业、事业单位下设的职能机构、企业的生产车间和辅助车间(或附属辅助生产单位)中从事生产、技术、经济管理和政治工作人员。

按照公务员管理或参照公务员管理的人员不统计为专业技术人员。

EXPLANATORY NOTES ON MAIN STATISTICAL INDICATORS

Patent is an abbreviation for the patent right and refers to the exclusive right of ownership by the inventors or designers for the creation or inventions, given from the patent offices after due process of assessment and approval in accordance with the Patent Law. Patents are granted for inventions, utility models and designs. This indicator reflects the achievements of S&T and design with independent intellectual property.

Patented Inventions refer to new technical proposals to the products or methods or their modifications. This is universal core indicator reflecting the technologies with independent intellectual property.

Patented Utility Models refer to the practical and new technical proposals on the shape and structure of the product or the combination of both. This indicator reflects the condition of technological results with certain technical content.

Designs refer to the aesthetics and industrially applicable new designs for the shape, pattern and colour of the product, or their combinations. This indicator reflects the appearance design achievements with independent intellectual property.

Professional Personnel refers to the persons who are engaged in special professional work or in professional management who got the titles of a professional post before 1983 or who were appointed to professional positions since 1984.

Professional personnel specifically refers to engineering professionals, agricultural professionals, scientific research professionals (natural science researchers, social science researchers and laboratory technicians), health professionals, teaching professionals (including institutions of higher education, specialized secondary schools, technical schools, regular secondary schools, and primary schools), civil aviation professionals, nautical professionals, economic professionals, accounting professionals, statistical professionals, interpretation professionals, library professionals, archives professionals, professionals of culture, arts and cultural relics, newsman and publishing professionals, lawyers, notary professionals, radio and television announcers, industrial arts professionals, sports professionals, artists and political professionals.

Professional management personnel specifically refers to the managers of enterprises and institutions, the personnel engaged in the management of production, technical, economic management and political aspects in the functional departments under the enterprise and institution, production workshops and accessorial workshops (or accessorial production units) under the enterprises.

Professional personnel do not include personnel under or managed according to the system of civil servants.

十七、教育 文化

CHAPTER 17
EDUCATION AND CULTURE

17 教育 文化 EDUCATION AND CULTURE

主要统计指标 MAJOR STATISTICAL INDICATORS

2016年各类学校数	Number of Schools of Various Types	754	所	unit
普通高等学校数	Number of Institutions of Higher Education	22	所	unit
中等职业教育学校	Secondary Vocational Education Schools	27	所	unit
技工学校	Technical Schools	10	所	unit
普通中学	Regular Secondary Schools	292	所	unit
小　学	Primary Schools	391	所	unit
特殊教育学校	Special Education Schools	12	所	unit
2016年在校学生数	Number of Students Enrollment	1 310 358	人	person
普通高等学校	Institutions of Higher Education	219 347	人	person
中等职业教育学校	Secondary Vocational Education Schools	61 202	人	person
技工学校	Technical Schools	23 593	人	person
普通中学	Regular Secondary Schools	309 824	人	person
小　学	Primary Schools	693 657	人	person
特殊教育学校	Special Education Schools	2 735	人	person
2016年毕业生数	Graduates	268 560	人	person
2016年招生数	New Student Enrollment	343 549	人	person
2016年幼儿园数	Number of Kindergartens	754	所	unit
2016年在园幼儿数	Number of Enrollment in Kindergartens	324 380	人	person
2016年末艺术表演团体	Number of Art Troupes (Year-end)	15	个	unit
2016年末公共图书馆	Number of Public Libraries (Year-end)	11	个	unit
2016年末博物馆	Number of Museums (Year-end)	42	个	unit

表17-1

历年各类学校及幼儿园数
NUMBER OF SCHOOLS OF ALL TYPES AND KINDERGARTENS OVER THE YEARS

单位：所 (unit)

年 份 Year	各类学校总 计 Total	普通高等学校 Institutions of Higher Education	中等职业教育学校 Secondary Vocational Education Schools	技工学校 Technical Schools	普通中学 Regular Secondary Schools	小 学 Primary Schools	特殊教育学校 Special Education Schools	幼儿园 Kindergartens
1949	1 694	2	14		60	1 617	1	
1952	3 272	2	17		67	3 185	1	
1957	3 373	2	14		94	3 262	1	
1962	3 685	4	13	1	164	3 502	1	
1965	4 472	4	143	1	136	4 187	1	
1970	5 445	4	1	1	519	4 919	1	
1975	4 986	4	6	2	606	4 365	3	
1978	4 392	4	7	6	544	3 828	3	
1980	4 103	5	19	9	523	3 543	3	
1985	3 788	10	48	13	544	3 169	3	
1990	3 276	9	58	17	424	2 757	10	
1991	3 048	9	58	17	380	2 573	10	
1992	2 851	9	59	17	341	2 413	11	
1993	2 716	9	64	17	321	2 293	11	
1994	2 636	9	67	18	308	2 222	11	
1995	2 471	8	71	18	302	2 061	10	
1996	2 234	8	73	20	288	1 834	10	
1997	2 018	7	72	21	278	1 628	11	
1998	1 740	7	72	21	262	1 366	11	
1999	1 542	7	78	21	260	1 164	11	
2000	1 352	7	69	20	264	980	11	
2001	1 151	8	66	19	270	776	11	
2002	1 047	9	62	18	268	678	11	
2003	902	12	41	17	270	550	11	
2004	832	13	39	11	268	488	12	
2005	802	16	40	12	270	452	12	347
2006	745	17	41	13	265	397	12	357
2007	681	18	33	14	260	344	12	368
2008	677	18	34	15	261	337	12	389
2009	668	19	33	13	257	334	12	385
2010	652	20	34	12	257	317	12	411
2011	646	20	34	11	263	306	12	444
2012	632	20	33	11	261	294	13	465
2013	639	21	30	10	261	304	13	509
2014	733	21	30	10	276	383	13	555
2015	744	21	29	10	283	387	14	731
2016	754	22	27	10	292	391	12	754

注：1.1980年至2004年的学校相关资料中包含1所工读学校数据（下同）。
2.2014年起，外来工子弟学校学生学籍计入普通中小学，普通中小学相关数据包含外来工子弟学校（下同）。

Note:1.From 1980 to2004, the total number of schools including a reform school.
2.Starting from 2014, the student status of schools for the children of migrant workers is included in the students' enrollment of ordinary primary and secondary schools, and the related data of ordinary primary and secondary schools contains that of schools for the children of migrant workers. (Same below)

表17-2

历年在校学生数
STUDENT ENROLLMENT OVER THE YEARS

单位：人 (person)

年 份 Year	各类学校在校学生总计 Total	普通高等学校 Institutions of Higher Education	中等职业教育学校 Secondary Vocational Education Schools	技工学校 Technical Schools	普通中学 Regular Secondary Schools	小 学 Primary Schools	特殊教育学校 Special Education Schools	幼儿园在园幼儿数 Number of Enrollment in Kindergartens
1949	167 633	847	2 443		15 121	149 148	74	
1952	339 287	2 349	8 616		34 028	294 220	74	
1957	415 729	3 251	7 738		55 497	349 164	79	
1962	436 498	5 772	1 896	344	58 585	369 788	113	
1965	560 023	2 579	12 070	515	62 397	482 322	140	
1970	839 053	37			171 242	667 632	142	
1975	956 704	3 922	1 309	540	215 023	735 619	291	
1978	968 070	6 502	2 748	1 181	327 561	629 614	464	
1980	812 756	8 819	5 231	1 757	228 618	567 858	460	
1985	706 893	12 443	19 802	3 244	235 600	435 340	445	
1990	711 333	16 280	25 293	5 866	217 284	445 627	951	
1991	694 742	16 445	27 181	6 234	230 192	413 623	1 027	
1992	700 882	17 045	32 014	6 417	244 981	399 231	1 158	
1993	730 611	20 247	40 599	6 591	251 034	410 205	1 911	
1994	761 988	22 837	49 432	8 450	264 899	413 831	2 505	
1995	789 526	23 182	57 999	10 844	270 832	422 643	3 993	
1996	822 296	25 749	63 162	13 228	260 130	455 903	4 071	
1997	833 785	29 031	67 844	15 174	233 225	484 903	3 537	
1998	845 618	32 375	73 606	16 442	230 019	488 831	4 312	
1999	860 296	39 341	68 594	14 347	263 133	470 812	4 025	
2000	876 897	47 701	60 185	12 346	304 661	448 363	3 605	
2001	900 019	61 165	58 273	12 783	335 136	429 066	3 552	
2002	918 446	69 614	69 588	15 297	360 305	400 183	3 389	
2003	939 800	80 523	84 731	22 118	367 460	381 542	3 361	
2004	936 782	94 960	93 708	21 206	358 882	364 951	3 060	
2005	956 948	113 090	115 541	27 215	338 222	359 930	2 950	141 666
2006	941 320	130 622	102 737	28 875	324 690	351 549	2 847	149 387
2007	948 683	152 389	93 656	31 119	314 089	354 569	2 861	158 521
2008	961 934	166 828	94 661	33 018	300 886	363 807	2 734	174 886
2009	960 812	187 678	81 493	32 627	285 990	370 224	2 800	183 467
2010	958 474	187 829	74 828	32 158	272 541	388 353	2 765	197 889
2011	972 642	188 750	71 409	29 371	265 442	414 972	2 698	209 965
2012	989 146	192 206	64 706	27 244	261 788	440 400	2 802	229 746
2013	1 026 996	201 926	57 936	25 069	266 943	472 418	2 704	248 006
2014	1 179 769	209 479	57 606	24 173	279 557	606 251	2 703	273 769
2015	1 243 728	214 816	59 227	23 743	292 521	650 730	2 691	300 936
2016	1 310 358	219 347	61 202	23 593	309 824	693 657	2 735	324 380

表17-3

历年毕业生数
NUMBER OF GRADUATES OVER THE YEARS

单位：人 (person)

年 份 Year	各类学校毕业生数总计 Total	普通高等学校 Institutions of Higher Education	中等职业教育学校 Secondary Vocational Education Schools	技工学校 Technical Schools	普通中学 Regular Secondary Schools	小 学 Primary Schools	特殊教育学校 Special Education Schools
1949	12 766	126	802		3 919	7 919	
1952	21 973	140	920		4 936	15 972	5
1957	46 371	890	2 300		12 572	30 609	
1962	55 127	1 416	879	29	20 200	32 595	8
1965	50 427	1 280	401	131	15 828	32 780	7
1970	135 095	528			46 969	87 585	13
1975	180 176	501	850	368	76 247	102 189	21
1978	262 706	1 757	83	422	152 832	107 604	8
1980	184 353	1 260	614	571	90 439	91 414	55
1985	140 384	2 386	5 829	758	65 943	65 410	54
1990	141 461	4 965	8 787	1 814	55 259	70 574	57
1991	151 203	4 888	8 438	1 931	61 993	73 877	57
1992	159 976	4 913	7 684	2 127	66 181	78 991	55
1993	157 013	4 862	7 658	2 177	70 032	72 170	93
1994	185 068	5 266	9 657	1 971	85 474	82 515	167
1995	181 891	7 246	12 214	2 239	83 993	76 053	134
1996	155 056	6 817	14 666	2 730	78 902	51 737	165
1997	166 338	6 791	18 346	4 231	92 661	43 866	373
1998	189 452	6 612	21 549	4 853	91 013	65 061	312
1999	184 905	7 926	18 739	4 861	69 435	83 525	379
2000	192 596	9 094	21 331	5 818	67 780	88 191	311
2001	213 613	9 551	22 390	4 965	88 808	87 317	533
2002	223 826	11 544	16 179	3 807	103 193	88 466	591
2003	217 663	15 187	12 434	3 014	109 347	76 964	645
2004	231 199	18 756	17 295	4 302	117 878	72 349	571
2005	247 087	22 498	21 257	6 965	126 944	68 878	545
2006	235 206	23 236	22 050	5 953	115 345	68 092	530
2007	236 025	30 335	23 937	7 532	108 974	64 845	402
2008	238 243	39 717	21 950	8 104	107 089	60 936	447
2009	234 727	40 995	23 992	7 387	102 375	59 494	484
2010	241 924	54 009	22 825	8 403	98 078	58 109	500
2011	231 498	55 176	18 098	9 539	90 001	58 206	478
2012	224 189	49 652	17 726	8 651	86 898	60 769	493
2013	226 286	49 441	19 761	8 467	84 580	63 533	504
2014	229 653	53 211	19 708	6 305	83 958	65 982	489
2015	250 341	57 243	18 659	5 901	87 906	80 085	547
2016	268 560	59 274	17 681	9 031	92 143	89 873	558

表17-4

历年专任教师数
NUMBER OF FULL-TIME TEACHERS OVER THE YEARS

单位：人 (person)

年 份 Year	各类学校专任教师总计 Total	普通高等学校 Institutions of Higher Education	中等职业教育学校 Secondary Vocational Education Schools	技工学校 Technical Schools	普通中学 Regular Secondary Schools	小 学 Primary Schools	特殊教育学校 Special Education Schools	幼儿园专任教师数 Number of Full-time Teachers in Kindergartens
1949	6 285	86	321	–	780	5 090	8	
1952	10 573	270	485	–	1 280	8 530	8	
1957	12 636	513	723	–	1 876	9 516	8	
1962	17 518	797	261	51	3 194	13 201	14	
1965	19 512	880	571	46	3 289	14 706	20	
1970		789	86	48		20 823	21	
1975	35 441	886	154	98	9 820	24 434	49	
1978	40 127	1 288	264	161	15 217	23 134	63	
1980	35 978	1 375	591	167	12 570	21 209	62	
1985	36 103	2 358	1 432	435	12 833	18 962	77	
1990	40 145	2 927	2 164	656	14 584	19 609	192	
1991	40 724	2 865	2 168	762	14 995	19 717	201	
1992	39 771	2 739	2 244	817	14 708	19 041	207	
1993	40 400	2 763	2 535	828	15 170	18 871	221	
1994	41 989	2 774	2 910	1 044	15 804	19 211	229	
1995	44 140	2 793	3 367	1 220	16 585	19 896	265	
1996	45 800	2 691	3 869	1 225	17 017	20 698	273	
1997	45 824	2 775	3 847	1 365	17 026	20 543	247	
1998	46 459	2 821	4 143	1 184	17 109	20 895	285	
1999	47 072	2 877	3 881	1 179	17 644	21 232	238	
2000	47 908	3 127	3 543	824	19 023	21 122	245	
2001	49 736	3 461	3 324	957	20 548	21 181	236	
2002	51 125	3 769	3 529	806	21 870	20 893	238	
2003	53 125	4 408	3 750	655	23 366	20 671	249	
2004	54 324	5 435	3 024	552	24 220	20 821	248	
2005	56 371	6 428	4 040	545	24 268	20 851	239	4 963
2006	58 189	7 138	4 423	1 153	24 323	20 909	243	5 480
2007	59 898	7 762	4 563	1 351	24 614	21 353	255	6 045
2008	61 704	8 498	4 739	1 351	24 868	21 969	279	6 988
2009	62 881	8 787	4 626	1 237	25 270	22 668	293	7 611
2010	65 174	10 104	4 680	1 411	25 295	23 375	309	8 658
2011	66 265	9 832	4 697	1 350	25 558	24 555	273	9 702
2012	68 404	10 392	4 830	1 310	25 916	25 656	300	11 082
2013	69 739	10 704	4 988	1 310	25 792	26 619	326	11 967
2014	76 340	11 316	5 070	1 296	26 337	31 985	336	13 436
2015	79 114	11 647	5 107	1 257	26 772	33 969	362	14 800
2016	82 015	11 706	4 956	1 484	27 726	35 770	373	16 087

表17-5 分地区各类学校基本情况（2016年）

项　　目	Item	全　市 Whole Municipality
学校数　(所)	**Number of Schools**　(unit)	**754**
普通高等学校	Institutions of Higher Education	22
中等职业教育学校	Secondary Vocational Education Schools	27
技工学校	Technical Schools	10
普通中学	Regular Secondary Schools	292
# 高　中	Senior	68
小　学	Primary Schools	391
特殊教育学校	Special Education Schools	12
招生数　(人)	**New Student Enrollment**　(person)	**343 549**
普通高等学校	Institutions of Higher Education	67 413
中等职业教育学校	Secondary Vocational Education Schools	21 300
技工学校	Technical Schools	9 074
普通中学	Regular Secondary Schools	112 302
# 高　中	Senior	30 491
小　学	Primary Schools	133 006
特殊教育学校	Special Education Schools	454
在校学生数　(人)	**Student Enrollment**　(person)	**1 310 358**
普通高等学校	Institutions of Higher Education	219 347
中等职业教育学校	Secondary Vocational Education Schools	61 202
技工学校	Technical Schools	23 593
普通中学	Regular Secondary Schools	309 824
# 高　中	Senior	84 676
小　学	Primary Schools	693 657
特殊教育学校	Special Education Schools	2 735

BASIC CONDITION OF SCHOOLS BY REGION (2016)

市　区 Urban Area	# 吴江区 Wujiang District	常　熟 Changshu	张家港 Zhangjiagang	昆　山 Kunshan	太　仓 Taicang
391	**96**	**110**	**89**	**104**	**60**
15	1	1	1	4	1
14	2	3	5	4	1
8	–	1	1	–	–
146	38	44	43	40	19
39	9	8	9	8	4
200	54	60	38	55	38
8	1	1	1	1	1
195 867	**34 263**	**38 721**	**35 641**	**54 250**	**19 070**
50 176	1 937	5 229	2 591	7 546	1 871
11 506	2 088	2 955	3 079	2 570	1 190
8 596	–	100	378	–	–
55 812	13 879	15 868	15 331	17 688	7 603
15 525	3 984	4 442	4 151	4 416	1 957
69 511	16 276	14 483	14 217	26 398	8 397
266	83	86	45	48	9
727 835	**137 122**	**154 638**	**143 966**	**209 650**	**74 269**
161 166	5 013	18 672	10 284	23 926	5 299
32 413	6 048	8 415	9 327	7 471	3 576
21 094	–	851	1 648	–	–
154 418	38 943	44 459	42 275	47 615	21 057
43 480	11 637	12 422	11 506	11 734	5 534
357 485	86 902	81 542	80 146	130 243	44 241
1 259	216	699	286	395	96

表17-5 续表

项　　目		Item		全　市 Whole Municipality
毕业生数	(人)	**Graduates**	(person)	**268 560**
普通高等学校		Institutions of Higher Education		59 274
中等职业教育学校		Secondary Vocational Education Schools		17 681
技工学校		Technical Schools		9 031
普通中学		Regular Secondary Schools		92 143
# 高　中		Senior		25 633
小　学		Primary Schools		89 873
特殊教育学校		Special Education Schools		558
教职工数	(人)	**Staff and Teachers**	(person)	**95 932**
普通高等学校		Institutions of Higher Education		17 850
中等职业教育学校		Secondary Vocational Education Schools		5 676
技工学校		Technical Schools		1 795
普通中学		Regular Secondary Schools		31 864
小　学		Primary Schools		38 315
特殊教育学校		Special Education Schools		432
专任教师数	(人)	**Number of Full-time Teachers**	(person)	**82 015**
普通高等学校		Institutions of Higher Education		11 706
中等职业教育学校		Secondary Vocational Education Schools		4 956
技工学校		Technical Schools		1 484
普通中学		Regular Secondary Schools		27 726
# 高　中		Senior		9 218
小　学		Primary Schools		35 770
特殊教育学校		Special Education Schools		373

Continued

市 区 Urban Area	# 吴江区 Wujiang District	常 熟 Changshu	张家港 Zhangjiagang	昆 山 Kunshan	太 仓 Taicang
151 529	**26 683**	**34 251**	**30 783**	**36 889**	**15 108**
43 774	1 330	4 466	2 914	6 770	1 350
9 229	1 704	2 442	2 895	2 095	1 020
8 276	–	478	277	–	–
45 859	12 239	13 587	12 683	13 270	6 744
13 324	3 786	3 865	3 473	3 235	1 736
44 213	11 403	13 043	11 977	14 663	5 977
178	7	235	37	91	17
55 019	**9 101**	**12 291**	**10 475**	**13 194**	**4 953**
14 076	248	1 156	652	1 638	328
2 632	372	1 051	1 072	689	232
963	–	679	153	–	–
17 526	4 036	4 365	3 976	3 964	2 033
19 536	4 412	4 994	4 583	6 862	2 340
286	33	46	39	41	20
46 389	**8 309**	**10 588**	**9 134**	**11 370**	**4 534**
9 250	203	731	429	1 060	236
2 300	356	929	921	595	211
761	–	583	140	–	–
15 102	3 515	3 697	3 525	3 589	1 813
5 194	1 217	1 217	1 314	976	517
18 726	4 204	4 611	4 083	6 094	2 256
250	31	37	36	32	18

表17-6

普通高等学校基本情况（2016年）
CONDITIONS OF INSTITUTIONS OF HIGHER EDUCATION (2016)

单位：人 (person)

学校名称	Schools	毕业生数 Graduates	招生数 New Student Enrollment	在校学生数 Student Enrollment	专任教师数 Number of Full-time Teachers
总　计	**Total**	**59 274**	**67 413**	**219 347**	**11 706**
# 研究生	Postgraduates	3 620	4 238	12 563	–
苏州大学	Soochow University	9 090	10 112	37 283	3 183
苏州科技大学	Suzhou University of Science and Technological	4 326	4 906	17 725	1 039
常熟理工学院	Changshu Science and Engineering College	3 612	5 229	18 150	731
西交利物浦大学	Xijiao Liverpool University	2 014	3 152	10 761	687
昆山杜克大学	Duke Kunshan University	32	70	86	18
苏州工艺美术职业技术学院	Suzhou Arts and Handicrafts Technical School	1 612	1 840	4 950	289
苏州农业职业技术学院	Suzhou Agricultural Vocational College	2 569	3 132	8 322	430
苏州市职业大学	Suzhou Vocational College	2 863	3 449	9 808	415
沙洲职业工学院	Shazhou Vocational Institute of Engineering	2 838	3 249	9 073	387
苏州工业园区职业技术学院	Suzhou Industrial Park Vocational College	4 170	4 103	12 973	776
苏州市工业职业技术学院	Suzhou Industry Profession Technology Institute	2 552	2 846	7 963	350
苏州经贸职业技术学院	Suzhou Economy and Trade Technology Institute	1 366	1 021	4 489	238
苏州卫生职业技术学院	Suzhou Health College	1 350	1 871	5 299	236
健雄职业技术学院	Jianxiong Vocational College	1 758	1 825	5 143	180
硅湖职业技术学院	Silicone Lake Vocational College	1 871	1 539	5 442	202
苏州托普信息技术学院	Suzhou Tuopu Information Technology Institute	1 889	1 118	4 736	244
昆山登云科技职业学院	Kunshan Dengyun Technological College	1 332	1 465	4 472	158
港大思培科技职业技术学院	Gangda Technical College	1 593	2 428	6 957	218
苏州高博软件技术职业学院	Suzhou Global Institute of Software Technology	617	11	904	74
苏州信息职业技术学院	Suzhou Institute of Information Technology	1 278	2 049	5 595	243
苏州工业园区服务外包职业技术学院	Suzhou Industrial Park Institute of Sernces Outsourcing	1 330	1 937	5 013	203
苏州幼儿师范高等专科学校	Suzhou Early Childhood Education College	475	674	1 164	133
*江苏科技大学苏州理工学院	Suzhou Institute of Technology,Jiangsu University of Science and Technology	2 608	3 310	11 162	368
*苏州大学文正学院	Wenzheng College of Soochow University	1 924	2 465	7 675	422
*苏州大学应用技术学院	Applied Technology School of Soochow University	1 803	2 042	7 885	291
*苏州科技大学天平学院	Tianping College of Suzhou University of Science and Technology	1 548	1 570	5 795	191
*常熟理工学院虞山学院	Yushan College of Changshu Institute of Technology	854	–	522	–

注：带“*”号的五所学院为二级学院。　Note: The college With "*" is secondary colleges.

表17-7

成人高等教育基本情况（2016年）
BASIC STATISTICS OF ADULT HIGHER EDUCATION (2016)

单位：人　(person)

学校名称	Schools	毕业生数 Graduates	招生数 New Student Enrollment	在校学生数 Student Enrollment
成人高等教育	**Adult Education**	**12 288**	**13 400**	**30 647**
苏州大学	Soochow University	3 639	3 835	10 369
苏州科技大学	Suzhou University of Science and Technological	2 232	2 074	4 732
常熟理工学院	Changshu Science and Engineering College	1 627	2 258	5 574
苏州工艺美术职业技术学院	Suzhou Arts and Handicrafts Technical School	2	131	188
苏州农业职业技术学院	Suzhou Agricultural Vocational College	488	650	1 479
苏州市职业大学	Suzhou Vocational College	2 352	1 489	3 412
沙洲职业工学院	Shazhou Vocational Institute of Engineering	735	851	1 471
苏州工业园区职业技术学院	Suzhou Industrial Park Vocational College	513	499	1 012
苏州市工业职业技术学院	Suzhou Industry Profession Technology Institute	166	492	748
苏州经贸职业技术学院	Suzhou Economy and Trade Technology Institute	78	88	275
健雄职业技术学院	Jianxiong Vocational College	323	767	1 039
硅湖职业技术学院	Silicone Lake Vocational College	133	266	348

注：成人高等教育学生不含自学考试学生。　Note: Adult education students do not include the self-examination students.

表17-8

幼儿园基本情况 (2016年)
BASIC CONDITION OF KINDERGARTENS (2016)

单位：人 (person)

地　区	Region	园数 (所) Number of Kindergartens (unit)	招生数 Number of Newly Enrolled in Kindergartens	在园幼儿数 Number of Enrollment in Kindergartens	专任教师 Number of Full-time Teachers
全　市	**Whole Municipality**	**754**	**116 994**	**324 380**	**16 087**
市　区	Urban Area	441	64 840	173 196	9 581
# 吴江区	Wujiang District	99	10 994	32 457	1 266
常　熟	Changshu	85	12 431	35 554	1 594
张家港	Zhangjiagang	60	14 114	41 273	1 309
昆　山	Kunshan	128	20 129	58 869	2 911
太　仓	Taicang	40	5 480	15 488	692

表17-9

专任教师合格率 (2016年)
RATE OF QUALIFIED FULL-TIME TEACHERS (2016)

单位：% (%)

地　区	Region	专任教师合格率 Rate of Qualified Full-time Teachers in Secondary and Primary Schools				
		高　中 Senior Secondary Schools	初　中 Junior Secondary Schools	中等职业学校 Specialized Secondary Schools	小　学 Primary Schools	幼儿园 Kindergartens
全　市	**Whole Municipality**	**99.73**	**99.81**	**98.22**	**99.99**	**99.94**
市　区	Urban Area	99.75	99.82	98.30	99.97	99.91
# 吴江区	Wujiang District	99.84	99.48	99.72	99.88	99.84
常　熟	Changshu	100.00	100.00	98.71	100.00	100.00
张家港	Zhangjiagang	99.54	99.86	97.72	100.00	100.00
昆　山	Kunshan	99.59	99.62	97.48	100.00	100.00
太　仓	Taicang	99.61	99.61	99.53	100.00	100.00

表17-10

各类学校师资配备情况（2016年）
TEACHING STAFF SITUATION OF ALL TYPES OF SCHOOLS (2016)

单位：人 (person)

地 区	Region	普通中学 Regular Secondary Schools					中等职业教育 Specialized Secondary Schools	
		每一教职工负担学生数 Every staff of average number of students	高 中 Senior Secondary Schools		初 中 Junior Secondary Schools			
			每班教师数 Teachers per class	每一教师负担学生数 Every burden on Teachers' number	每班教师数 Teachers per class	每一教师负担学生数 Every burden on Teachers' number	每一教职工负担学生数 Every staff of average number of students	每一教师负担学生数 Every burden on Teachers' number
全 市	**Whole Municipality**	**9.72**	**4.33**	**9.19**	**3.59**	**12.16**	**10.78**	**12.35**
市 区	Urban Area	8.81	4.45	8.37	3.74	11.20	12.31	14.09
# 吴江区	Wujiang District	9.65	3.83	9.56	3.67	11.88	16.26	16.99
常 熟	Changshu	10.19	4.49	10.21	3.59	12.92	8.01	9.06
张家港	Zhangjiagang	10.63	4.55	8.76	3.31	13.92	8.70	10.13
昆 山	Kunshan	12.01	3.63	12.02	3.36	13.73	10.84	12.56
太 仓	Taicang	10.36	3.86	10.70	3.49	11.98	15.41	16.95

表17-10 续表 Continued

单位：人 (person)

地 区	Region	小 学 Primary Schools			幼儿园 Kindergartens		
		每一教职工负担学生数 Every staff of average number of students	每班教师数 Teachers per class	每一教师负担学生数 Every burden on Teachers' number	每一教职工负担学生数 Every staff of average number of students	每班教师数 Teachers per class	每一教师负担学生数 Every burden on Teachers' number
全 市	**Whole Municipality**	**18.10**	**2.39**	**19.39**	**12.04**	**1.77**	**20.16**
市 区	Urban Area	18.30	2.38	19.09	9.99	1.89	18.08
# 吴江区	Wujiang District	19.70	2.18	20.67	18.76	1.34	25.64
常 熟	Changshu	16.33	2.51	17.68	14.32	1.60	22.30
张家港	Zhangjiagang	17.49	2.41	19.63	24.34	1.26	31.53
昆 山	Kunshan	18.98	2.35	21.37	12.84	1.84	20.22
太 仓	Taicang	18.91	2.28	19.61	18.50	1.57	22.38

注：表中市区数据含市直属学校和代管学校。
Note:The urban data in the table contains the schools directly under the city supervision and those hosted by the city authorities.

表17-11

部分年份文化事业基本情况
BASIC STATISTICS ON CULTURAL UNDERTAKINGS OF PARTIAL YEARS

项目	Item	2012年	2013年	2014年	2015年	2016年
机构数 (个)	**Number of Institutions** (unit)					
艺术事业	Art	14	14	13	13	13
文物事业	Historical Relics	45	51	51	53	53
图书馆事业	Libraries	12	11	11	11	11
群众文化事业	Mass Cultural	111	110	109	109	109
艺术教育事业	Art Education	2	2	2	2	2
其他文化事业	Others	10	25	13	12	12
职工人数 (人)	**Number of Staff and Workers** (person)					
艺术事业	Art	557	585	368	364	427
文物事业	Historical Relics	761	845	871	869	913
图书馆事业	Libraries	520	524	526	559	667
群众文化事业	Mass Cultural	846	1 108	1 127	1 182	1 319
艺术教育事业	Art Education	73	75	58	56	55
其他文化事业	Others	70	284	98	154	158
主要文化活动	**Main Culture Activities**					
艺术表演团体演出场次 (千场次)	Number of Art Performance Troupes' Performers (1 000 show-times)	17.4	20.8	15.9	15.3	16.3
博物馆参观人数 (千人次)	Number of Visitor to Museums(1 000 person-times)	3 683	3 597	5 721	7 940	9 185
书刊文献外借人次	Person-times of Borrowers of Books, Magazines and Documents	4 712	6 948	7 607	8 240	9 067
书刊文献外借册次 (千册次)	Number of Books, Magazines and Documents Borrowed by the Readers (1 000 volume-times)	11 102	13 338	15 286	15 493	16 092

表17-12

艺术表演团体基本情况 (2016年)
BASIC STATISTICS ON ART TROUPES (2016)

地 区	Region	机构数(个) Number of Institutions (unit)	从业人员(人) Employed Persons (person)	演出场次(场次) Number of Performances (show-time)	观众人次(千人次) Number of Spectators (1 000 person-times)	公用房屋建筑面积(平方米) Floor Space of Public Buildings (sq.m)
全 市	**Whole Municipality**	**15**	**577**	**16 329**	**3 659**	**18 989**
市 区	Urban Area	9	425	8 089	1 697	7 738
# 吴江区	Wujiang District	2	9	990	102	-
常 熟	Changshu	2	76	3 090	573	2 171
张家港	Zhangjiagang	2	76	5 150	1 389	9 080
昆 山	Kunshan	2	-	-	-	-
太 仓	Taicang	-	-	-	-	-

表17-13

艺术表演场馆基本情况 (2016年)
BASIC SITUATION OF PERFORMING ARTS VENUES (2016)

地 区	Region	机构数(个) Number of Institutions (unit)	从业人员(人) Employed Persons (person)	座席数(个) Seating Capacity (set)	演(映)出场次(场次) Number of Performances (show-time)	观众人次(千人次) Number of Spectators (1 000 person-times)	公用房屋建筑面积(平方米) Floor Space of Public Buildings (sq.m)
全 市	**Whole Municipality**	**23**	**1 098**	**26 807**	**235 944**	**6 347**	**751 028**
市 区	Urban Area	12	776	15 434	153 034	4 167	632 501
# 吴江区	Wujiang District	2	41	2 316	18 070	635	9 731
常 熟	Changshu	3	64	3 498	240	157	57 931
张家港	Zhangjiagang	5	148	4 419	41 798	1 086	43 703
昆 山	Kunshan	3	110	3 456	40 872	937	16 893
太 仓	Taicang	-	-	-	-	-	-

表17-14 文化馆、文化站及文物保护基本情况 (2016年)

指　标		Item		全　市 Whole Municipality
文化馆		**Cultural Centers**		
机构数	(个)	Number of Institutions	(unit)	11
从业人员	(人)	Employed Persons	(person)	276
举办展览个数	(个)	Number of Exhibitions	(unit)	154
组织文艺活动次数	(次)	Art Performances and Story-Telling Sessions	(time)	2 302
举办训练班班次		Number of Training Courses		1 117
举办训练班培训人次	(人次)	Number of People Trained in Training Courses	(person-time)	68 136
公用房屋建筑面积	(平方米)	Floor Space of Public Buildings	(sq.m)	97 555
# 业务用房		Space for Business		77 894
群众业余文艺团队	(个)	Masses' Amateur Arts Teams	(unit)	1 210
文化站		**Cultural Stations**		
机构数	(个)	Number of Institutions	(unit)	98
从业人员	(人)	Employed Persons	(person)	1 043
举办展览个数	(个)	Number of Exhibitions	(unit)	871
组织文艺活动次数	(次)	Art Performances and Story-Telling Sessions	(time)	9 849
藏　书	(册)	Collection of Books	(volume)	4 200 492
举办训练班班次	(次)	Number of Training Courses	(time)	3 059
举办训练班培训人次	(人次)	Number of People Trained in Training Courses	(person-time)	239 357
公用房屋建筑面积	(平方米)	Floor Space of Public Buildings	(sq.m)	649 408
# 文化活动用房		Space for Cultural Activities		424 768
村（社区）文化室个数	(个)	Number of Culture Rooms	(unit)	3 330
文物保护		**Historical Relics Preservation**		
机构数	(个)	Number of Institutions	(unit)	10
从业人员	(人)	Employed Persons	(person)	109
文物藏品	(件)	Number of Collections	(piece)	10 773
公用房屋建筑面积	(平方米)	Floor Space of Public Buildings	(sq.m)	6 717
# 展览用房		Space for Exhibitions		2 981

BASIC SITUATION OF CULTURAL CENTERS, CULTURAL STATIONS AND HISTORICAL RELICS PRESERVATION (2016)

市 区 Urban Area	# 吴江区 Wujiang District	常 熟 Changshu	张家港 Zhangjiagang	昆 山 Kunshan	太 仓 Taicang
7	1	1	1	1	1
112	13	60	62	22	20
118	6	17	1	16	2
1 170	369	355	270	306	201
381	45	320	217	91	108
14 836	8 600	3 800	14 500	14 000	21 000
68 383	7 600	10 000	7 600	6 726	4 846
54 529	7 600	7 800	5 000	5 719	4 846
346	–	15	100	651	98
62	8	10	9	11	6
600	80	81	71	241	50
513	73	82	96	134	46
4 080	970	1 721	973	2 613	462
1 879 056	562 198	866 593	601 784	707 018	146 041
1 839	108	221	204	621	174
93 161	7 027	15 886	48 120	65 240	16 950
363 698	139 659	57 823	110 814	93 482	23 591
185 556	36 104	48 132	105 690	68 971	16 419
1 380	347	329	706	798	117
7	3	1	1	1	–
93	5	4	4	8	–
5 407	1	–	–	5 366	–
6 421	–	–	–	296	–
2 981	–	–	–	–	–

表17-15

博物馆及公共图书馆基本情况 (2016年)

指　　标		Item		全　市 Whole Municipality
博物馆		**Museums**		
机构数	(个)	Number of Institutions	(unit)	42
从业人员	(人)	Employed Persons	(person)	790
文物藏品	(件)	Number of Collections	(piece)	162 074
# 一级品		Grade One		916
二级品		Grade Two		1 789
参观人次	(千人次)	Number of Visitors	(1000 person-times)	9 185
公用房屋建筑面积	(平方米)	Floor Space of Public Buildings	(sq.m)	172 389
# 展览用房		Space for Exhibitions		91 493
公共图书馆		**Public Libraries**		
机构数	(个)	Number of Institutions	(unit)	11
从业人员	(人)	Employed Persons	(person)	667
总藏量	(册、件)	Total Collections	(volume)	27 416 651
# 电子书		E-book		7 394 916
# 图　书		Books Published		18 721 719
# 古　籍		Ancient Books		454 697
报　刊		Newspapers and Magazines		405 620
累计发放有效借书证数	(个)	Grand Total Number of Valid Library Cards Released	(unit)	8 024 575
书刊文献外借人次	(人次)	Number of Borrowers of Books, Magazines and Documents	(person-time)	9 067 239
书刊文献外借册次	(册次)	Number of Books, Magazines and Documents Borrowed by the Readers	(volume-time)	16 092 466
为读者举办各种活动	(次)	Various Activities Held for Readers	(time)	1 351
参加人数	(人次)	Number of Visitors	(person-time)	345 454
公用房屋建筑面积	(平方米)	Floor Space of Public Buildings	(sq.m)	178 969
# 书　库		Stock Rooms		10 850
阅览室		Reading Rooms		54 654
阅览室座席数	(个)	Seating Capacity of Reading Rooms	(set)	9 210
# 少儿阅览室座席数		Seating Capacity of Children's Reading Rooms		2 122

BASIC STATISTICS ON MUSEUMS AND PUBLIC LIBRARIES (2016)

市 区 Urban Area	# 吴江区 Wujiang District	常 熟 Changshu	张家港 Zhangjiagang	昆 山 Kunshan	太 仓 Taicang
25	2	6	1	3	7
420	50	188	47	42	93
131 840	28 582	21 586	2 642	3 469	2 537
879	10	22	1	–	14
1 475	17	293	8	–	13
4 908	243	3 024	120	287	846
103 160	6 515	28 096	12 060	5 043	24 030
50 595	4 262	15 533	8 000	4 252	13 113
7	1	1	1	1	1
352	65	75	105	72	63
18 580 157	5 221 000	2 617 820	2 197 089	2 799 513	1 222 072
6 843 921	3 000 000	85 300	27 000	366 192	72 503
10 940 394	2 114 950	2 236 410	2 078 382	2 423 049	1 043 484
247 667	72 839	205 065	104	168	1 693
195 171	15 330	75 847	59 134	2 385	73 083
5 866 400	124 000	1 344 630	151 175	250 018	412 352
5 184 498	400 000	767 741	840 760	1 523 821	750 419
9 855 829	1 260 000	1 533 950	2 119 504	1 523 821	1 059 362
701	112	51	418	103	78
212 996	46 200	18 450	71 453	16 970	25 585
100 626	16 000	12 128	27 500	18 600	20 115
3 759	775	2 191	4 200	250	450
35 247	4 000	3 300	6 200	4 000	5 907
6 869	1 107	525	620	665	531
1 230	214	200	446	97	149

表17-16

广播节目播出情况 (2016年)
BROADCASTING BROADCAST SITUATION (2016)

单位：小时 (hours)

地　区	Region	全年公共广播节目播出时间合计 The Whole year's Public Radio Program Broadcast Time	# 新闻资讯类 News and Information	# 专题服务类 Feature Services	# 综艺益智类 Variety Puzzles	合计中：自制节目 In Total：Self-made Program
全　市	**Whole Municipality**	**62 134**	**9 700**	**20 401**	**18 265**	**51 684**
市　区	Urban Area	34 587	4 004	11 416	10 123	32 223
# 吴江区	Wujiang District	6 022	803	3 372	1 026	4 900
常　熟	Changshu	8 760	1 825	3 285	2 190	6 935
张家港	Zhangjiagang	6 647	2 321	2 610	1 519	4 527
昆　山	Kunshan	6 300	820	901	2 061	4 550
太　仓	Taicang	5 840	730	2 190	2 373	3 450

表17-17

电视节目播出情况(2016年)
TV BROADCAST SITUATION (2016)

单位：小时 (hours)

地　区	Region	全年公共电视节目播出时间合计 The Whole year's Public TV Program Broadcast Time	# 新闻资讯类 News and Information	# 专题服务类 Feature Services	# 影视剧类 Film and Television Drama	合计中：自制节目 In Total：Self-made Program
全　市	**Whole Municipality**	**57 239**	**9 366**	**7 979**	**27 225**	**37 702**
市　区	Urban Area	35 877	4 989	6 597	18 646	26 226
# 吴江区	Wujiang District	6 073	900	1 565	2 626	2 563
常　熟	Changshu	7 782	763	201	3 138	4 444
张家港	Zhangjiagang	4 097	1 277	585	1 162	2 842
昆　山	Kunshan	3 660	340	105	2 175	790
太　仓	Taicang	5 823	1 997	491	2 104	3 400

表17-18

广播节目制作情况(2016年)
BROADCASTING PROGRAMMING SITUATION (2016)

单位：小时 (hours)

地 区	Region	全年制作广播节目时间 Annual Production of Broadcasting Programs	# 新闻资讯类 News and Information	# 专题服务类 Feature Services	# 综艺益智类 Variety Puzzles	# 广告类 Advertisements
全 市	**Whole Municipality**	**47 038**	**6 887**	**18 442**	**12 759**	**1 618**
市 区	Urban Area	29 566	3 471	10 392	8 802	435
# 吴江区	Wujiang District	4 455	548	2 880	967	60
常 熟	Changshu	5 855	1 277	3 285	1 277	13
张家港	Zhangjiagang	3 811	1 133	2 190	365	120
昆 山	Kunshan	2 550	365	545	–	780
太 仓	Taicang	5 256	641	2 030	2 315	270

表17-19

电视节目制作情况 (2016年)
TV PROGRAMMING SITUATION (2016)

单位：小时 (hours)

地 区	Region	全年制作电视节目时间 Annual Production of TV Programs	# 新闻资讯类 News and Information	# 专题服务类 Feature Services	# 广告类 Advertisements	全年购买、交换国内电视节目时间 Purchase and Exchange of Domestic TV Time of The Whole Year
全 市	**Whole Municipality**	**18 104**	**5 341**	**4 109**	**4 270**	**17 936**
市 区	Urban Area	12 288	4 113	3 704	861	8 601
# 吴江区	Wujiang District	1 012	286	239	243	3 310
常 熟	Changshu	3 551	216	74	2 944	3 155
张家港	Zhangjiagang	762	442	173	98	1 072
昆 山	Kunshan	920	288	36	288	2 870
太 仓	Taicang	583	282	122	79	2 238

主 要 统 计 指 标 解 释

普通高等学校 指按照国家规定的设置标准和审批程序批准举办的，通过全国普通高等学校统一招生考试，招收高中毕业生为主要培养对象，实施高等教育的全日制大学、独立设置的学院和高等专科学校、高等职业学校和其他机构。

大学、独立设置的学院主要实施本科层次以上教育，高等专科学校、高等职业学校实施专科层次教育，其他机构是承担国家普通招生计划任务不计校数的机构。包括普通高等学校分校和批准筹建的普通高等学校等。

文化事业机构 指从事专业文化工作和为专业文化工作服务的独立建制的单位。不包括这些单位另外举办独立核算的其他机构和各部门的业余文化组织。该指标主要反映文化事业机构发展规模水平。

艺术表演团体 指由文化部门主办或实行行业管理（经文化行政部门审批或已申报登记并领取相关许可证），专门从事表演艺术等活动的各类专业艺术表演团体，含民间职业剧团。不包括群众业余文艺表演团体。

艺术表演观众人数(人次) 指售票、包场演出或民族地区免费演出的艺术表演观众人次数，不包括彩排审查和内部观摩演出的观看人次数。该指标主要反映全国观看专业艺术表演团体演出的效益规模。

EXPLANATORY NOTES ON MAIN STATISTICAL INDICATORS

Regular Institutions of Higher Learning refer to educational establishments set up according to the government evaluation and approval procedures, enrolling graduates from senior secondary schools and providing higher education courses and training for senior professionals. They include full-time universities, colleges, institutions of higher professional education, institutions of higher vocational education and others.

Universities and colleges primarily provide undergraduate courses; institutions of higher professional education and institutions of higher vocational education primarily provide professional trainings; and others refer to educational establishments, which are responsible for enrolling higher education students under the State Plan but not enumerated in the total number of schools, including: branch schools of universities and colleges, and universities and colleges that have been approved and under plan for construction.

Cultural Institutions refer to units which have their own organizational system and independent accounting system and specialize in cultural work or service cultural work. They do not include other establishments run by these units with separate accounting system and amateur cultural groups established by various departments. The statistics reflect the scale and level of development of institutions engaged in cultural undertakings.

Arts Performance Troupes refer to the various professional performing arts groups, which sponsored by the cultural sectors or guided by the cultural society (approved by the cultural administration authority, or registered and permitted with the relative certificate), including non-governmental troupes. The mass amateur arts performance troupes are not included.

Number of Audience at Art Performance refers to the number of spectators at commercial shows, privately organized shows or free shows given in ethnic minority areas, and does not include the number of spectators at rehearsals and internal viewings. This indicator mainly reflects the scale and effects of viewing of performances given by professional art troupes across the country.

十八、卫生 体育

CHAPTER 18
PUBLIC HEALTH AND SPORTS

18 卫生 体育 PUBLIC HEALTH AND SPORTS

主要统计指标 MAJOR STATISTICAL INDICATORS

2016年末卫生机构数	Number of Health Institutions	3 175	个	unit
2016年末卫生机构床位数	Number of Beds in Health Institutions	63 241	张	unit
2016年末卫生技术人员	Number of Medical Technical Personnel	72 166	人	person
# 医生数	Doctors	27 667	人	person
注册护士数	Professional Nurses	30 699	人	person
2016年末按常住人口计算:	Calculated by Resident Population:			
每万人拥有卫生机构床位数	Number of Beds in Health Institutions Per 10 000 Persons	59.40	张	unit
每万人拥有医院床位数	Number of Hospital Beds Per 10 000 Persons	53.25	张	unit
每万人拥有卫生技术人员	Number of Medical Technical Personnel Per 10 000 Persons	67.78	人	person
每万人拥有医生数	Number of Doctors Per 10 000 Persons	25.98	人	person
每万人拥有注册护士数	Number of Professional Nurses Per 10 000 Persons	28.83	人	person
2016年发展二级以上等级裁判员	Newly-added Number of Referees of Grade II and Above	441	人	person
2016年发展二级以上等级运动员	Newly-added Number of Sportsmen of Grade II and Above	130	人	person

表18-1

历年卫生事业基本情况
BASIC STATISTICS ON PUBLIC HEALTH OVER THE YEARS

年 份 Year	机 构 数 (所) Institutions (unit)	# 医 院、 卫生院 Hospitals	# 诊所、卫生所、医务室、社区卫生服务站 Clinics	床位数 (张) Number of Beds (unit)	人员数 (人) Number of Persons (person)	# 卫生技术人员 Medical Technical Personnel
1949	27	12	7	778	3 270	3 100
1952	238	16	163	1 372	4 908	3 256
1957	447	16	410	2 655	7 773	6 037
1962	683	155	457	6 727	9 582	7 831
1965	823	170	549	7 661	10 891	8 862
1970	675	169	496	9 001	9 338	7 593
1975	806	194	581	13 759	14 202	11 174
1978	971	204	714	14 470	16 465	12 902
1980	1 125	207	864	13 720	18 752	14 514
1985	1 544	203	1 280	15 064	24 921	19 343
1990	1 537	207	1 256	18 424	29 545	22 253
1995	1 486	210	1 197	19 535	33 076	25 326
1996	1 485	212	1 196	19 489	33 321	25 835
1997	1 433	212	1 143	19 747	32 669	25 070
1998	1 440	212	1 147	19 486	32 855	25 233
1999	1 466	209	1 175	19 293	30 303	25 550
2000	1 319	197	1 045	19 504	31 793	24 881
2001	1 254	191	986	19 791	31 559	24 706
2002	1 463	213	1 187	19 978	31 601	24 535
2003	1 450	199	1 152	20 631	33 958	27 805
2004	1 715	207	1 392	21 662	34 970	29 069
2005	1 945	197	1 582	26 185	38 736	32 049
2006	2 285	205	1 902	28 872	43 954	36 951
2007	2 314	214	1 901	31 261	46 952	38 091
2008	2 344	233	1 876	33 631	50 810	40 336
2009	2 524	234	2 041	37 235	53 869	43 232
2010	2 675	216	2 152	39 204	56 910	46 507
2011	2 858	242	2 292	42 972	63 409	50 866
2012	2 992	251	2 380	46 070	70 449	57 168
2013	3 007	263	2 363	51 663	74 661	61 051
2014	3 063	263	2 353	55 218	78 811	64 281
2015	3 121	271	2 418	59 304	83 997	68 179
2016	3 175	283	2 387	63 241	89 276	72 166

表18-2

部分年份分地区卫生事业基本情况
BASIC STATISTICS ON PUBLIC HEALTH BY REGION OF PARTIAL YEARS

项　　目	Item	2011年	2012年	2013年	2014年	2015年	2016年
机构数　(所)	**Institutions (unit)**	**2 858**	**2 992**	**3 007**	**3 063**	**3 121**	**3 175**
市　区	Urban Area	1 390	1 471	1 488	1 489	1 500	1 514
# 吴江区	Wujiang District	348	370	385	394	403	419
常　熟	Changshu	443	453	446	455	468	481
张家港	Zhangjiagang	417	410	405	418	422	429
昆　山	Kunshan	419	435	445	474	493	504
太　仓	Taicang	189	223	223	227	238	247
床位数　(张)	**Beds (unit)**	**42 972**	**46 070**	**51 663**	**55 218**	**59 304**	**63 241**
市　区	Urban Area	23 698	25 376	27 654	29 701	32 495	34 757
# 吴江区	Wujiang District	4 714	4 661	5 255	5 317	5 700	5 723
常　熟	Changshu	5 883	6 454	6 868	7 052	7 346	7 882
张家港	Zhangjiagang	5 615	6 013	7 878	8 588	9 093	9 601
昆　山	Kunshan	4 609	5 043	5 966	6 300	6 640	7 148
太　仓	Taicang	3 167	3 184	3 297	3 577	3 730	3 853
卫生技术人员　(人)	**Medical Technical Personnel (person)**	**50 866**	**57 168**	**61 051**	**64 281**	**68 179**	**72 166**
市　区	Urban Area	26 661	29 423	31 551	33 044	35 771	38 174
# 吴江区	Wujiang District	5 218	5 351	6 174	6 357	6 578	6 917
常　熟	Changshu	6 634	7 493	7 887	8 278	8 569	9 114
张家港	Zhangjiagang	6 702	7 440	7 937	8 441	8 910	9 288
昆　山	Kunshan	7 572	9 166	9 804	10 375	10 626	11 070
太　仓	Taicang	3 297	3 646	3 872	4 143	4 303	4 520
医生数　(人)	**Doctors (person)**	**19 518**	**23 194**	**24 296**	**25 352**	**26 197**	**27 667**
市　区	Urban Area	9 951	11 626	12 168	12 717	13 174	13 929
# 吴江区	Wujiang District	1 672	2 386	2 521	2 536	2 547	2 547
常　熟	Changshu	2 635	3 193	3 350	3 495	3 570	3 834
张家港	Zhangjiagang	2 712	3 062	3 278	3 331	3 599	3 814
昆　山	Kunshan	2 940	3 845	3 959	4 194	4 218	4 312
太　仓	Taicang	1 280	1 468	1 541	1 615	1 636	1 778

表18-3 分地区卫生机构、人员及床位数 (2016年末)

指 标		Item		全 市 Whole Municipality
卫生机构数	(个)	**Number of Health Institutions**	(unit)	**3 175**
医 院		Hospitals		206
社区卫生服务中心		Neighborhood Medical Service Station		83
卫生院		Rural Township Hospitals		77
门诊部		Clinics		311
急救中心（站）		First Aide Center		4
采供血机构		Blood Collection and Supply Center		7
妇幼保健院（所、站）		Hospitals for Maternity and Child Care		7
专科疾病防治院		Disease Control Center		4
疾病预防控制中心		Disease Prevention Center		11
卫生监督所		Medical Supervision Station		9
医学在职培训机构		On-the-Job Medical Training		2
健康教育所（站、中心）		Health Education Station		4
诊所、卫生所、医务室、社区卫生服务站		Clinic, Medical Station, Medical Office and Neighborhood Medical Station		2 387
其他卫生机构		Other Health Care Institutions		63
卫生机构人员数	(人)	**Number of Persons Engaged in Health Institution**	(person)	**89 276**
# 卫生技术人员		Medical Technical Personnel		72 166
医 生		Doctors		27 667
执业医师		Professional medical worker		25 201
执业助理医师		Professional assistant medical worker		2 466
注册护士		Professional nurse		30 699
药师（士）		Apothecary and Assistant Pharmacist		4 203
技师（士）		Technician		3 597
其 他		Others		6 000
# 私营卫生机构人员数		Number of Medical Staff in Privately Owned Medical Institutions		20 011
# 医 生		Doctors		5 355
卫生机构床位数	(张)	**Number of Beds in Health Institutions**	(unit)	**63 241**
医 院		Hospitals		56 697
# 综合医院		General Hospitals		33 199
中医医院		Hospitals of Chinese Medicine		4 713
专科医院		Disease Control and Prevention Station		7 042
卫生院		Rural Township Hospitals		4 150
专科疾病防治院		Disease Prevention Academy		20
其 他		Others		2 374

NUMBER OF HEALTH INSTITUTIONS, PERSONS ENGAGED AND BEDS BY REGION (END OF 2016)

市 区 Urban Area	# 吴江区 Wujiang District	常 熟 Changshu	张家港 Zhangjiagang	昆 山 Kunshan	太 仓 Taicang
1 514	**419**	**481**	**429**	**504**	**247**
100	13	24	40	32	10
49	5	8	1	21	4
28	16	20	8	4	17
98	26	43	11	120	39
1	–	1	–	1	1
2	1	2	1	1	1
3	1	1	1	1	1
4	2	–	–	–	–
7	1	1	1	1	1
5	1	1	1	1	1
1	–	–	1	–	–
1	1	1	–	1	1
1 188	340	366	355	308	170
27	12	13	9	13	1
47 468	**7 870**	**11 400**	**11 259**	**13 824**	**5 325**
38 174	6 917	9 114	9 288	11 070	4 520
13 929	2 547	3 834	3 814	4 312	1 778
12 956	2 307	3 361	3 262	4 067	1 555
973	240	473	552	245	223
16 839	2 749	3 598	3 723	4 745	1 794
2 230	420	567	509	617	280
1 800	347	432	449	638	278
3 376	854	683	793	758	390
10 319	802	1 431	3 892	3 338	1 031
2 474	306	441	1 182	973	285
34 757	**5 723**	**7 882**	**9 601**	**7 148**	**3 853**
31 669	4 923	6 491	9 262	6 547	2 728
16 380	3 353	3 736	7 151	4 533	1 399
1 343	377	850	838	982	700
4 717	320	757	648	371	549
1 392	668	1 099	339	367	953
20	–	–	–	–	–
1 676	132	292	–	234	172

表18-4

卫生机构诊疗基本情况 (2016年)

BASIC STATISTICS OF MEDICAL INSTITUTIONS ON PATIENTS TREATING (2016)

地区或类别	Region and Type	诊疗总人次 (万人次) Total Number of Patients Treated (10 000 person-times)	#门 诊 Out-patients	入院人数 (人) Hospital Admissions (person)	病床使用率 (%) Utilization Rate of Beds (%)	病床周转次数 Bed Turnover
总 计	**Total**	**9 327.60**	**8 453.29**	**1 766 268**	**85.06**	**29.39**
一、按地区分	**Grouped by Region**					
市 区	Urban Area	4 761.66	4 293.54	862 988	84.68	26.31
# 吴江区	Wujiang District	847.78	763.12	152 744	81.59	29.18
常 熟	Changshu	1 306.77	1 182.74	261 874	88.57	34.06
张家港	Zhangjiagang	1 136.58	1 061.10	311 258	86.98	33.41
昆 山	Kunshan	1 589.85	1 446.79	211 112	80.11	31.96
太 仓	Taicang	532.74	469.10	119 036	85.17	32.28
二、按类别分	**Grouped by Type of Hospital**					
1. 医 院	Hospitals	4 965.37	4 376.01	1 607 642	88.17	29.88
# 综合医院	General Hospitals	3 669.65	3 242.65	1 227 404	89.19	38.27
中医医院	Hospitals of Chinese Medicine	711.33	621.81	189 488	95.85	40.08
专科医院	Disease Control and Prevention Station	448.67	395.72	122 644	84.72	18.78
儿童医院	Children's Hospital	190.22	157.23	45 574	82.18	42.78
传染病院	Hospitals for Infectious Diseases	26.61	21.75	8 515	98.32	20.67
精神病院	Mental Hospitals	69.28	62.61	15 220	97.82	6.03
口腔医院	Stomata logical Hospitals	56.34	56.34	–	–	–
耳鼻喉科医院	Otolaryngology Hospitals	12.84	12.39	6 791	63.88	43.94
其他专科医院	Other Specialized Hospitals	93.39	85.39	46 544	71.63	19.68
2. 社区卫生服务中心	Community Medical Service Station	1 732.91	1 616.22	41 168	47.26	21.01
3. 卫生院	Rural Township Hospitals	1 275.01	1 166.05	116 798	64.35	28.56
4. 门诊部	Outpatient Department	309.07	295.75	559	–	–
5. 妇幼保健院（所、站）	Hospitals for Maternity and Child Care	34.03	33.60	–	–	–
6. 专科疾病防治院	Disease Prevention Academy	17.77	5.16	1	0.15	0.09
7. 其 他	Others	993.44	960.50	100	49.81	0.45

注:床位周转次数是指在一定时期内每张床位的病人出院人数，其公式：床位周转次数=出院人数/平均开放床位数。

Note: The bed turnover refers to the number of patients per bed discharged from hospital within a certain period of time, and the formula is: bed turnover times = number of discharged patients / average number of open beds.

表18-5

全市前十位疾病死因及比重 (2016年)
DEATH RATE OF 10 MAJOR DISEASES IN WHOLE MUNICIPALITY (2016)

位　次 NO.	死　　因	Cause of Death	占全部死因比重(%) As % of Total Deaths
	总　　计	**Total**	**93.96**
1	恶性肿瘤	Malignant Tumor	30.13
2	脑血管病	Cerebrovascular Disease	19.56
3	心脏病	Heart Trouble	11.89
4	呼吸系统疾病	Respiratory Disease	11.57
5	损伤和中毒外部原因	Trauma and Toxicosis	8.41
6	内分泌、营养和代谢的其他疾病	Endocrine, Nutrition and Metabolic Diseases	4.53
7	消化系统疾病	Digestive Disease	3.13
8	神经系统疾病	Nervous System Diseases	2.19
9	精神障碍	Mental Disease	1.30
10	泌尿生殖系统疾病	Urinary Disease	1.25

表18-6

体育系统从业人员 (2016年)
SPORTS SYSTEM EMPLOYEES (2016)

单位：人　(person)

人员分类	Category of Personnel	总　计 Total	#体育行政机关 Sports Administration	#运动项目管理部门 Sports Management	#体育运动学校 Physical Education and Sports Schools	#业余体校 Spare-time Sports Schools
总　计	**Total**	**889**	**115**	**327**	**132**	**174**
公务员	Orderly	115	115	–	–	–
教练员	Coaches	121	–	8	38	75
运动员	Athletes	117	–	117	–	–
科研人员	Scientific and Technical Personnel	9	–	–	–	–
管理人员	Administrative Staff	393	–	202	91	99
其　他	Others	134	–	–	3	–

表18-7

运动员获奖牌情况（2016年）
ATHLETES' AWARD-WINNING (2016)

单位：枚 (unit)

项　目	Item	总　计 Total	金　牌 Gold Medal	银　牌 Silver Medal	铜　牌 Bronze Medal
合　计	**Total**	**29**	**14**	**8**	**7**
世界比赛	World Competition	11	2	4	5
亚洲比赛	Asian Competition	2	1	1	–
全国比赛	National Competition	16	11	3	2
省内比赛	Province Competition	–	–	–	–

表18-8

发展等级运动员、裁判员及社会体育指导员认证人数
NUMBER OF CERTIFIED LEVEL ATHLETES, REFEREES AND COMMUNITY PHYSICAL EDUCATION INSTRUCTORS RECRUITED

单位：人 (person)

项　目	Item	2012年	2013年	2014年	2015年	2016年
年内发展二级以上等级运动员	**Newly-added Number of Sportsmen of Grade II and Above**	**153**	**245**	**169**	**115**	**130**
运动健将	Master of Sports	–	–	–	–	–
一　级	First Grade	–	–	–	–	–
二　级	Second Grade	153	245	169	115	130
年内发展二级以上等级裁判员	**Newly-added Number of Referees of Grade II and Above**	**471**	**537**	**522**	**374**	**441**
国家(际)级	National (International) Referees	–	–	–	–	–
一　级	First Grade	–	–	–	–	–
二　级	Second Grade	471	537	522	374	441
年末社会体育指导员认证总人数	**Total Number of Certified Community Physical Education Instructors by the End of the Year**	**21 002**	**24 960**	**29 829**	**32 838**	**38 773**

表18-9

体育彩票
SPORT LOTTERY

项　目	Item	2015年	2016年
体育彩票销售网点（个）	**Number of Computer Sport Lottery Sold** (unit)	**1 797**	**1 665**
体育彩票销售金额（万元）	**Circulation of Sport Lottery** (10 000 yuan)	**388 750**	**391 701**
电脑彩票	Computer Lottery	348 280	347 230
即开型彩票	Instant Lottery	40 469	44 471
体育彩票公益基金提取额	**Public Welfare Funds Drawn form Sport Lottery**	**34 398**	**34 745**
电脑彩票	Computer Lottery	31 148	30 743
即开型彩票	Instant Lottery	3 250	4 002

主要统计指标解释

卫生机构 包括医疗机构、疾病预防控制中心(防疫站)、采供血机构、卫生监督及监测(检验)机构、医学科研和在职培训机构、健康教育所等。

医疗机构 包括医院、社区卫生服务中心(站)、疗养院、卫生院、门诊部、诊所(卫生所、医务室)、妇幼保健院(所、站)、专科疾病防治院(所、站)、急救中心(站)和临床检验中心。医疗机构分为非赢利性医疗机构和赢利性医疗机构。

医院 包括综合医院、中医医院、中西医结合医院、民族医院、各类专科医院和护理院。

卫生技术人员 指卫生机构中医生、护理人员 、药剂人员、检验人员等卫生技术人员。

医生 指在医疗、预防保健机构工作且取得《执业医师证书》的执业医师和执业助理医师。

等级运动员人数 指经考核正式批准授予等级运动员称号的人数。运动员等级分为国际级运动健将、运动健将、一级运动员、二级运动员、三级运动员、少年级运动员。

等级裁判员人数 指经考核正式批准授予等级裁判员称号的人数。裁判员等级分为国际裁判、国家级裁判、一级裁判、二级裁判、三级裁判。

EXPLANATORY NOTES ON MAIN STATISTICAL INDICATORS

Health Care Institutions include: medical institutions, disease prevention and control centres (epidemic prevention stations), blood gathering and supplying institutions, health supervision and inspection (check up) institutions, medicinal scientific research and on-job training institutions, health education centres and so on.

Medical Organizations include: hospitals, health service centres (stations) in communities, sanatoria, health centres, out-patient clinics, clinics (health stations and infirmaries), maternity and child care agencies (centres and stations), special disease prevention and curing agencies (centres and stations), first aid centres (stations) and clinical inspection centres. Medical organizations are grouped by two types: profit-making and non-profit-making medical organizations.

Hospitals include: polyclinics, traditional Chinese medical hospitals, hospitals integrating traditional Chinese therapeutics and western therapeutics, ethnic hospitals, various specialist hospitals and nursing homes.

Medical Technical Personnel refers to doctors, nurses, pharmacists and laboratory technicians working in medical institutions.

Doctors refer to certified physicians and certified assistant physicians with certifications working in medical and health care and prevention agencies.

Number of Athletes in Grades refers to the number of athletes who have been given titles through examination. The titles of athletes include international masters of sports, masters of sports, first-grade, second-grade and third-grade sportsmen and young athletes.

Number of Referees in Grades refers to the number of referees who have been given titles after examination. They are classified as international referees, national referees and referees of the first, second and third grades.

十九、民政 司法

CHAPTER 19
CIVIL ADMINISTRATION, JUDICIARY

19 民政 司法 CIVIL ADMINISTRATION, JUDICIARY

主要统计指标 MAJOR STATISTICAL INDICATORS

2016年末社会福利院数	Number of Social Welfare Homes	9	个	unit
2016年末社会福利医院数	Number of Social Welfare Hospitals	2	个	unit
2016年末养老机构数	Number of Old-age Care Institutions	226	个	unit
2016年末社会福利院床位数	Number of Beds in Social Welfare Homes	4 199	张	unit
2016年末社会福利医院床位数	Number of Beds in Social Welfare Hospitals	580	张	unit
2016年末机构养老床位数	Number of Beds in Old-age Care Institutions	65 301	张	unit
2016年末律师事务所	Number of Law Offices	268	所	unit
2016年末专职律师数	Number of Full-time Lawyers	3 346	人	person
2016年末人民调解委员会数	Number of People's Mediation Committees	8 288	个	unit
2016年调解纠纷总数	Number of Disputes Mediated	116 695	起	case

表19-1

部分年份民政事业基本情况

指标		Item		1990年	1995年	2000年	2005年
社会福利院		**Social Welfare Homes**					
院数	(个)	Number of Homes	(unit)	6	6	6	10
职工人数	(人)	Number of Staff and Workers	(person)	268	331	410	817
床位数	(张)	Number of Beds	(unit)	845	970	1 315	2 964
在院人数	(人)	Number of Persons Housed	(person)	561	732	971	1 879
社会福利医院		**Social Welfare Hospitals**					
院数	(个)	Number of Hospitals	(unit)	5	4	4	2
职工人数	(人)	Number of Staff and Workers	(person)	282	302	302	192
床位数	(张)	Number of Beds	(unit)	524	554	694	560
在院人数	(人)	Number of Persons Housed	(person)	399	405	690	469
养老机构		**Old-age Care Institutions**					
院数	(个)	Number of Homes	(unit)	169	183	181	144
职工人数	(人)	Number of Staff and Workers	(person)	921	1 022	938	1 470
床位数	(张)	Number of Beds	(unit)	4 135	5 005	5 400	10 125
在院人数	(人)	Number of Persons Housed	(person)	3 133	3 326	3 391	6 716

BASIC STATISTICS ON CIVIL ADMINISTRATION OF PARTIAL YEARS

2006年	2007年	2008年	2009年	2010年	2011年	2012年	2013年	2014年	2015年	2016年
10	10	10	10	10	10	10	9	9	9	9
838	859	879	888	904	928	949	950	946	949	939
2 994	2 994	2 994	2 994	3 164	3 214	3 659	4 199	4 199	4 199	4 199
1 931	2 027	2 103	2 148	2 297	2 316	2 299	2 217	2 172	2 170	2 118
2	2	2	2	2	2	2	2	2	2	2
208	213	229	235	238	240	253	243	231	234	230
560	560	560	560	560	560	560	580	580	580	580
477	492	523	515	555	571	565	528	509	511	507
174	166	139	152	162	179	205	213	221	234	226
2 215	2 313	2 088	2 155	2 325	3 065	4 677	4 837	4 330	4 453	4 882
16 893	15 700	16 696	21 623	25 455	30 809	46 223	51 840	57 915	64 014	65 301
8 958	9 786	9 415	9 793	16 035	19 369	24 327	24 751	28 062	28 173	28 850

表19-2

分地区民政事业基本情况 (2016年末) BASIC STATISTICS ON CIVIL ADMINISTRATION BY REGION (END OF 2016)

地 区	Region	院 数 (个) Number of Homes (unit)	职工人数 (人) Number of Staff and Workers (person)	床位数 (张) Number of Beds (unit)	在院人数 (人) Number of Persons Housed (person)
社会福利院	**Social Welfare Homes**				
全 市	**Whole Municipality**	**9**	**939**	**4 199**	**2 118**
市 区	Urban Area	4	415	2 280	1 139
# 吴江区	Wujiang District	1	42	480	68
常 熟	Changshu	2	235	790	435
张家港	Zhangjiagang	1	53	135	75
昆 山	Kunshan	1	160	474	210
太 仓	Taicang	1	76	520	259
社会福利医院	**Social Welfare Hospitals**				
全 市	**Whole Municipality**	**2**	**230**	**580**	**507**
市 区	Urban Area	2	230	580	507
# 吴江区	Wujiang District	–	–	–	–
常 熟	Changshu	–	–	–	–
张家港	Zhangjiagang	–	–	–	–
昆 山	Kunshan	–	–	–	–
太 仓	Taicang	–	–	–	–
养老机构	**Old-age Care Institutions**				
全 市	**Whole Municipality**	**226**	**4 882**	**65 301**	**28 850**
市 区	Urban Area	122	2 724	30 312	14 348
# 吴江区	Wujiang District	30	294	8 803	2 937
常 熟	Changshu	22	553	12 294	5 309
张家港	Zhangjiagang	47	617	10 015	3 933
昆 山	Kunshan	17	578	6 974	2 313
太 仓	Taicang	18	410	5 706	2 947

表19-3

部分年份社会保障相关待遇标准
THE TREATMENT STANDARDS RELATED TO SOCIAL SECURITY OF PARTIAL YEARS

单位：元/月 (yuan/month)

年 份 Year	职工最低工资标准 Minimum Wage Standard for Employees	失业保险金最低标准 Minimum Standard of Unemployment Insurance Benefits	城市最低生活保障标准 Standards of Subsistence Allowances for Urban Residents	农村最低生活保障标准 Standards of Subsistence Allowances for Rural Residents	企业退休人员基本养老金最低标准 Minimum Standards of Basic Pensions for Enterprise Retirees
1995	210	120			
1996	240	144	180		
1997	280	168	180		
1998	280	168	180	100	
1999	320	220	200	100	
2000	390	220	200	100	
2001	430	220	200	100	
2002	460	220	220	100	
2003	540	260	260	120	
2004	620	260	260	130	
2005	690	300	300	180	
2006	750	300	300	180	
2007年1月	750	320	300	180	
2007年7月	850	400	320	200	
2008	850	450	350	230	
2009	850	500	380	260	
2010	960	500	420	340	
2011年1月	960	650	450	400	
2011年7月	1 140	650	500	500	
2012	1 370	741	570	570	650
2013	1 530	820	630	630	750
2014	1 680	910	700	700	800
2015	1 680	975	750	750	860
2016	1 820	1 053	810	810	910

表19-4

社会救助情况 (2016年)
SOCIAL ASSISTANCE (2016)

地　区	Region	社会救助总人数(人) Total Number of people Who Received Social Assistance (person)	城市低保 Subsistence Allowances For Urban		农村低保 Subsistence Allowances For Rural Residents	
			人数(人) Number of People (person)	资金(万元) Fund (10 000 yuan)	人数(人) Number of People (person)	资金(万元) Fund (10 000 yuan)
全　市	**Whole Municipality**	**71 589**	**12 184**	**9 380**	**16 165**	**11 179**
市　区	Urban Area	39 515	9 235	6 958	7 419	4 799
# 吴江区	Wujiang District	11 678	715	600	4 965	3 429
常　熟	Changshu	9 801	340	323	3 217	2 285
张家港	Zhangjiagang	10 584	1 104	894	3 332	2 580
昆　山	Kunshan	6 996	1 028	818	1 192	850
太　仓	Taicang	4 693	477	387	1 005	666

表19-4 续表　　Continued

地　区	Region	农村五保 Rural Residents Enjoying Five Guarantees		低保边缘 On the Margin of Subsistence Allowances		残疾人生活补贴 Living Allowances For The Disabled	
		人数(人) Number of People (person)	资金(万元) Fund (10 000 yuan)	人数(人) Number of People (person)	资金(万元) Fund (10 000 yuan)	人数(人) Number of People (person)	资金(万元) Fund (10 000 yuan)
全　市	**Whole Municipality**	**2 935**	**2 959**	**14 451**	**8 825**	**25 854**	**17 493**
市　区	Urban Area	1 142	888	9 707	5 265	12 012	8 084
# 吴江区	Wujiang District	439	462	1 276	994	4 283	2 968
常　熟	Changshu	500	633	822	650	4 922	3 178
张家港	Zhangjiagang	493	670	944	729	4 711	3 261
昆　山	Kunshan	611	531	1 819	1 193	2 346	1 674
太　仓	Taicang	189	237	1 159	988	1 863	1 295

表19-5

社会组织情况（2016年末）
SITUATION OF SOCIAL ORGANIZATIONS (END OF 2016)

单位：个 (unit)

地　区	Region	社会组织数 Number of Social Organizations	社会团体 Social Groups	民办非企业 Private Non-Enterprises	基金会 Foundation
全　市	**Whole Municipality**	**8 752**	**3 152**	**5 575**	**25**
市　区	Urban Area	4 730	1 677	3 036	17
# 吴江区	Wujiang District	1 029	313	716	–
常　熟	Changshu	1 286	353	932	1
张家港	Zhangjiagang	930	490	439	1
昆　山	Kunshan	959	413	541	5
太　仓	Taicang	847	219	627	1

表19-6

社区服务平台建设情况（2016年末）
CONSTRUCTION OF COMMUNITY SERVICE PLATFORMS (END OF 2016)

地　区	Region	社区服务平台建设 Construction of Community Service Platforms				社区工作者人数（人） Number of Community Workers (person)	
		区（市）级社区服务平台达标个数（个） Number of District-(City-) Level Community Service Platforms Up To The Standard (unit)	镇（街）级社区服务平台达标个数（个） Number of Town-(Street-) Level Community Service Platforms Up To The Standard (unit)	城市社区办公活动用房平均面积（平方米） Average Area of Urban Community Offices And Activity Rooms (sq.m)	农村社区办公活动用房平均面积（平方米） Average Area of Rural Community Offices And Activity Rooms (sq.m)	城市社区 Urban Communities	农村社区 Rural Communities
全　市	**Whole Municipality**	**9**	**108**	**1 379**	**1 584**	**9 565**	**10 322**
市　区	Urban Area	5	65	1 395	1 699	6 063	4 704
# 吴江区	Wujiang District	1	8	1 710	1 541	436	2 016
常　熟	Changshu	1	11	1 120	1 260	558	1 758
张家港	Zhangjiagang	1	10	1 515	1 950	845	2 000
昆　山	Kunshan	1	15	1 453	1 403	1 535	1 234
太　仓	Taicang	1	7	1 200	1 450	564	626

表19-7

部分年份律师、公证工作情况
STATISTICS ON LAWYERS AND NOTARIZATION OF PARTIAL YEARS

指 标	Item	2012年	2013年	2014年	2015年	2016年
律师工作情况	**Lawyers**					
律师事务所 (所)	Number of Law Offices (unit)	194	206	224	242	268
律师事务所人员 (人)	Personnel of Law Offices (person)	2 330	2 576	2 706	3 048	3 435
# 女律师	Female	492	689	748	900	1 061
# 专职律师	Full-time Lawyers	2 292	2 495	2 667	2 963	3 346
兼职律师	Part-time Lawyers	38	39	39	41	46
义务法律咨询服务件数 (件)	Agent of Voluntary Legal Advisory Services (case)	15 551	27 298	9 184	9 940	15 682
参加义务法律咨询律师人次 (人次)	Number of Lawyers Participating in Voluntary Legal Advisory Services (person-time)	1 960	1 150	1 442	2 205	2 608
担任法律顾问 (家)	Number of Units with Permanent Legal Advisors (unit)	10 426	11 800	12 713	12 445	13 976
刑事诉讼辩护及代理 (件)	Defender and Agent of Criminal Cases (case)	4 514	4 989	5 396	4 372	6 347
民事案件诉讼代理	Agent of Civil Cases	29 493	37 500	46 819	47 940	68 502
经济案件诉讼代理	Agent of Economic Cases	–	–	–	–	–
非诉讼法律事务	Agent of Non-litigious Legal Affairs	5 064	4 062	4 814	4 565	5 644
涉外及涉港澳台	Agent of Foreign-related, Hong Kong, Macao & Taiwan Legal Affairs	–	–	–	–	–
经济案件索回赔欠款 (万元)	Debt and Indemnity Claimed in Economic Cases (10 000 yuan)	–	–	–	–	–
公证工作情况	**Notarization**					
公证处 (所)	Number of Notary Offices (unit)	12	11	11	11	11
公证处人员 (人)	Notarial Personnel (person)	158	160	175	199	218
# 公证员	Notaries	67	71	71	83	82
办理公证总数 (件)	Number of Notarial Documents Issued (case)	108 892	131 041	128 556	152 252	188 224
# 国内民事和经济	Domestic Civil Relations and Economic Affairs	78 762	96 177	91 791	113 388	147 503
涉外及涉港澳台	Foreign-related, Hong Kong, Macao & Taiwan Legal Affairs	30 130	34 864	36 765	38 864	40 721

表19-8

部分年份人民调解基层司法工作情况
STATISTICS ON PEOPLE'S MEDIATION AND BASIC-LEVEL JUDICIAL WORK OF PARTIAL YEARS

指　标		Item		2012年	2013年	2014年	2015年	2016年
人民调解委员会	(个)	Number of People's Mediation Committees	(unit)	5 379	8 374	7 253	8 064	8 288
调委会人员数	(人)	Number of Mediators	(person)	24 139	29 576	29 474	26 066	28 578
调解纠纷总数	(起)	Number of Disputes Mediated	(case)	89 317	94 380	99 686	108 915	116 695
#婚姻家庭		Marriage and family		4 425	3 290	2 577	2 673	2 844
邻里纠纷		Neighbor Disputes		6 126	5 055	4 170	3 698	4 436
调解纠纷成功数		Number of Disputes Successful Mediated		89 091	94 232	99 534	108 686	116 301
防止民间纠纷引起自杀	(件)	Prevention of Suicide Due to Civil Disputes	(case)	–	–	126	1	–
	(人)		(person)	–	–	124	4	–
防止民间纠纷转化为刑事案件	(件)	Prevention of Civil Disputes from Turning into Criminal Cases	(case)	32	26	41	10	6
	(人)		(person)	89	115	175	108	71
宣讲法律	(场)	Lectures on Law	(time)	6 613	5 018	4 600	4 556	4 185
受教育人数	(万人次)	Number of Persons Receiving Law Education	(10 000 person-times)	101	115	94	92	101
为基层政府提供司法建议	(条)	Providing Legal Advice for Local Governments	(piece)	101	71	30	94	129
协助基层政府处理社会矛盾纠纷	(件)	Helping Local Government on Social Conflicts	(case)	1 018	1 096	1 063	1 232	1 312
代理诉讼事务		Service as legal representative		8 469	8 261	8 687	7 753	6 593
代理非诉讼事务		Service not as legal representative		2 866	3 094	3 010	2 026	2 195
担任法律顾问	(家)	Number of Units with Legal Advisors	(unit)	1 197	1 887	2 915	1 404	1 771
避免、挽回经济损失	(万元)	Economic Loss Avoided and Reclaimed	(10 000 yuan)	47 108	48 931	51 901	50 513	61 011

表19-9

分地区律师、公证工作情况（2016年）

指　标		Item		全　市 Whole Municipality
律师工作情况		**Lawyers**		
律师事务所	(所)	Number of Law Offices	(unit)	268
律师事务所人员	(人)	Personnel of Law Offices	(person)	3 435
# 女律师		Female		1 061
# 专职律师		Full-time Lawyers		3 346
兼职律师		Part-time Lawyers		46
义务法律咨询服务件数	(件)	Agent of Voluntary Legal Advisory Services	(case)	15 682
参加义务法律咨询律师人数	(人次)	Number of Lawyers Participating in Voluntary Legal Advisory Services	(person-time)	2 608
担任法律顾问	(家)	Number of Units with Permanent Legal Advisors	(unit)	13 976
刑事诉讼辩护及代理	(件)	Defender and Agent of Criminal Cases	(case)	6 347
民事案件诉讼代理		Agent of Civil Cases		68 502
非诉讼法律事务		Agent of Non-litigious Legal Affairs		5 644
公证工作情况		**Notarization**		
公证处	(所)	Number of Notary Offices	(unit)	11
公证处人员	(人)	Notarial Personnel	(person)	218
# 公证员		Notaries		82
办理公证总数	(件)	Number of Notarial Documents Issued	(case)	188 224
# 国内民事和经济		Domestic Civil Relations and Economic Affairs		147 503
涉外及涉港澳台		Foreign-related, Hong Kong, Macao & Taiwan Legal Affairs		40 721

STATISTICS ON LAWYERS AND NOTARIZATION BY REGION (2016)

市 区 Urban Area	# 吴江区 Wujiang District	常 熟 Changshu	张家港 Zhangjiagang	昆 山 Kunshan	太 仓 Taicang
184	12	13	12	45	14
2 468	185	204	205	437	121
769	39	56	55	150	31
2 384	185	199	205	437	121
44	–	2	–	–	–
10 920	826	60	2 106	1 471	1 125
2 164	55	24	252	80	88
8 075	1 080	1 167	884	2 825	1 025
3 799	510	839	369	1 011	329
39 705	5 230	6 487	6 203	13 710	2 397
4 395	106	15	94	888	252
6	1	1	1	2	1
144	19	14	20	27	13
49	9	6	10	12	5
144 524	8 115	15 048	7 904	16 194	4 554
117 030	5 458	11 152	4 586	11 957	2 778
27 494	2 657	3 896	3 318	4 237	1 776

表19-10

分地区人民调解基层司法工作情况（2016年）

指　标		Item		全　市 Whole Municipality
人民调解委员会	（个）	Number of People's Mediation Committees	(unit)	8 288
调委会人员数	（人）	Number of Mediators	(person)	28 578
调解纠纷总数	（起）	Number of Disputes Mediated	(case)	116 695
# 婚姻家庭		Marriage and family		2 844
邻里纠纷		Neighbor Disputes		4 436
调解纠纷成功数		Number of Disputes Successful Mediated		116 301
防止民间纠纷引起自杀	（件）	Prevention of Suicide Due to Civil Disputes	(case)	-
	（人）		(person)	-
防止民间纠纷转化为刑事案件	（件）	Prevention of Civil Disputes from Turning into Criminal Cases	(case)	6
	（人）		(person)	71
宣讲法律	（场）	Lectures on Law	(time)	4 185
受教育人数	（万人次）	Number of Persons Receiving Law Education	(10 000 person-times)	101
为基层政府提供司法建议	（条）	Providing Legal Advice for Local Governments	(piece)	129
协助基层政府处理社会矛盾纠纷	（件）	Helping Local Government on Social Conflicts	(case)	1 312
代理诉讼事务		Service as legal representative		6 593
代理非诉讼事务		Service not as legal representative		2 195
担任法律顾问	（家）	Number of Units with Legal Advisors	(unit)	1 771
避免、挽回经济损失	（万元）	Economic Loss Avoided and Reclaimed	(10 000 yuan)	61 011

STATISTICS ON PEOPLE'S MEDIATION AND BASIC-LEVEL JUDICIAL WORK BY REGION (2016)

市 区 Urban Area	# 吴江区 Wujiang District	常 熟 Changshu	张家港 Zhangjiagang	昆 山 Kunshan	太 仓 Taicang
4 539	610	758	1 764	955	272
13 945	2 052	2 954	6 335	4 434	910
70 431	9 114	13 135	11 070	14 691	7 368
1 314	259	239	810	393	88
2 308	159	611	800	614	103
70 110	8 968	13 134	11 063	14 626	7 368
–	–	–	–	–	–
–	–	–	–	–	–
6	–	–	–	–	–
71	–	–	–	–	–
1 970	101	463	945	489	318
11	5	12	41	33	4
58	11	42	15	12	2
770	148	140	151	139	112
905	1 393	911	2 735	1 123	919
1 418	129	122	456	32	167
513	257	217	583	159	299
10 914	18 305	3 267	23 823	14 026	8 981

表19-11

道路、船舶交通事故及火灾情况（2016年）
STATISTICS ON HIGHWAY，WATERWAY TRAFFIC ACCIDENTS AND FIRES (2016)

地　区	Region	事故数（起） Number of Traffic Accidents (case)	死亡（人） Number of Deaths (person)	伤人（人） Number of Injuries (person)	损失折款(万元) Losses Converted into Cash (10 000 yuan)
道路交通事故	**Road Accidents**				
全　市	**Whole Municipality**	**2 977**	**595**	**2 825**	**2 414**
市　区	Urban Area	1 161	251	1 113	1 390
# 吴江区	Wujiang District	656	89	634	220
常　熟	Changshu	663	123	622	586
张家港	Zhangjiagang	602	85	557	232
昆　山	Kunshan	209	76	176	69
太　仓	Taicang	342	60	357	137
船舶交通事故	**Waterway Accidents**				
全　市	**Whole Municipality**	**14**	**6**	**1**	**111**
市　区	Urban Area	9	4	1	42
# 吴江区	Wujiang District	2	2	–	1
常　熟	Changshu	–	–	–	–
张家港	Zhangjiagang	–	–	–	–
昆　山	Kunshan	2	2	–	51
太　仓	Taicang	3	–	–	18
火　灾	**Fires**				
全　市	**Whole Municipality**	**2 727**	**16**	**36**	**10 610**
市　区	Urban Area	954	9	17	2 446
# 吴江区	Wujiang District	163	1	14	1 082
常　熟	Changshu	541	4	8	2 468
张家港	Zhangjiagang	372	2	–	2 174
昆　山	Kunshan	551	–	9	2 962
太　仓	Taicang	309	1	2	560

主 要 统 计 指 标 解 释

社会福利事业单位 指集中收养社会孤老、残、幼的机构，包括由民政部门管理的社会福利院、儿童福利院、精神病人福利院和城镇集体举办的福利院及农村集体举办的敬老院以及优抚医院和具有收养能力的社区服务中心等。该指标主要反映我国社会福利性单位的投入水平。

社会福利事业单位收养人数 包括民政部门管理和城镇、农村集体举办的社会福利事业单位中收养的老人、少年儿童、缺乏生活自理能力的残疾人员和精神病人。该指标主要反映收养性社会福利单位的收养能力。

城市居民最低生活保障人数 指在报告期末共同生活的家庭成员人均收入低于当地最低生活保障标准，且家庭财产状况符合相关规定的城镇居民，并已发放补助经费的人数。

农村居民最低生活保障人数 指报告期末共同生活的家庭成员人均收入低于当地最低生活保障标准，得到当地政府给予最低生活保障待遇的农业人口家庭人数。

五保户 指无劳动能力、无生活来源、又无法定赡养、抚养、扶养义务人，或者其法定赡养、抚养、扶养义务人无赡养、抚养、扶养能力的老年、残疾或者未满16岁的村民。

律师 指依法取得律师执业证书，担任法律顾问，民事(刑事、行政)案件代理人、刑事案件辩护人、办理非诉讼业务，解答法律询问，代写法律事务文书等，为社会提供法律服务的人员。

公证人员 指在公证处工作的人员总称，包括公证处主任、副主任、公证员、公证员助理(助理公证员)和其他从事辅助性工作的人员。

公证文书 指公证处根据当事人申请，依照事实和法律，按照法定程序制作的，具有法律效力的司法证明文书。根据公证书用途和使用地，公证书分为国内公证书、国内经济公证书、涉外民事公证书、涉外经济公证书四类。

调解员 指在人民调解委员会担负调解民间纠纷工作的人员，包括调解委员会的委员和调解小组的调解员。该指标主要反映从事人民调解工作的人员数量。

调解民间纠纷 指调解委员会按照法律规定，根据自愿原则，用说服教育的方法调解民间发生的有关民事权利和义务争执的件数，包括调解成功数和调解未成功数。该指标主要反映人民调解委员会的工作量。

EXPLANATORY NOTES ON MAIN STATISTICAL INDICATORS

Social Welfare Institutions refer to institutions taking care of old people without children, handicapped people and orphans. They include social welfare institutions run by civil affairs departments, children welfare institutions, social welfare institutions for mental patients, collective-owned old people's homes in rural areas, convalescent homes and community service centers with the capacity of receiving those people. This indicator reflects the input in social welfare institutions.

Number of People Accommodated by Social Welfare Institutions refers to the number of old people, children, totally dependent handicapped people and mental patients Accommodated by social welfare institutions run by civil affairs departments and those run by collective units in urban and rural areas. This indicator reflects the capacity of social welfare institutions.

Number of Urban Residents Entitled to Minimum Living Allowances refers to the number of those urban residents whose average family income is below a minimum local standard, and status of family property meets the relevant regulation, and have received subsidies by the end of the reporting period.

Number of Rural Residents Entitled to Minimum Living Allowances refers to the number of those rural residents whose average family income is below a minimum local standard, and receiving the minimum living allowances from the local government by the end of the reporting period.

Households Enjoying Five Guarantees refers to the elderly, disabled or under the age of 16 villagers, without working capacity, without the source of life, and without legal supporter, upbringing persons, brought up persons, or legal supporter, upbringing persons, brought up persons can not support, upbringing, bring up.

Lawyers are certified legal workers according to law, and who are employed by legal counselling firms to act as legal advisers; agents in criminal or civil lawsuits; and defenders in criminal lawsuits; or to handle non-litigious legal affairs, to advise on matters of law or to write legal papers for others and provide service to the public.

Notary Personnel refers to people working for notary offices including: directors, deputy directors, notaries, assistant notaries and other people providing assistance.

Notary Documents refer to the judicial notary documents drawn up at the request of the interested party and are in accordance with facts and the law and following certain legal proceedings. According to usage and locality, notary documents are divided into the following 4 types: domestic notary documents, domestic economic notary documents, foreign-related civil notary documents and foreign-related economic notary documents.

Mediators refer to workers on people's mediation committees responsible for mediating in civil disputes and cases of slight infraction of the law. They include members of the mediation committees and mediators of mediation groups. This indicator reflects the number of people engaged in mediation.

Mediation of Civil Disputes refers to number of cases made by mediation committees in mediating in civil disputes concerning civil rights and duties through persuasion and education in accordance with the provisions of law on a voluntary basis, so as to solve disputes by helping the parties involved come to an agreement and understanding, including those unsuccessful ones. This indicator reflects the workload of the mediation committees.

二十、城市建设 环境保护

CHAPTER 20
URBAN CONSTRUCTION AND ENVIRONMENTAL PROTECTION

20 城市建设 环境保护
URBAN CONSTRUCTION AND ENVIRONMENTAL PROTECTION

主要统计指标
MAJOR STATISTICAL INDICATORS

2016年市区建成区面积	Build up Area of Urban District	461.65	平方公里	sq.km
2016年市区人均城市道路面积	Per Capita Roads Area of Urban District	34.21	平方米	sq.m
2016年市区人均公园绿地面积	Per Capita Park Green Space of Urban District	14.71	平方米	sq.m
2016年市区建成区绿化覆盖率	Coverage Rate of Green Areas in Developed Areas of Urban District	41.99	%	
2016年市区污水处理率	Treatment Rate of Urban District	95.16	%	
2016年市区供水总量	Total Water Supply of Urban District	78 279	万立方米	10 000 cu.m
2016年市区天然气供气总量	Total Natural Gas Supply of Urban District	117 130	万立方米	10 000 cu.m
2016年市区公共汽车客运量	Number of Passengers Carried by Bus of Urban District	61 917	万人次	10 000 person-times
2016年市区轨道交通客运量	Number of Passengers Carried by Urban Rail Transit	15 057	万人次	10 000 person-times

表20-1

分地区城市设施水平 (2016年)
URBAN FACILITY CONDITION BY REGION (2016)

地 区	Region	人均日生活用水量(升) Per Capita Daily Consumption of Tap Water for Residential Use (liter)	人均城市道路面积(平方米) Per Capita Area of Roads (sq.m)	人均公园绿地面积(平方米) Per Capita Park Green Areas (sq.m)	建成区绿化覆盖率(%) Coverage Rate of Green Areas in Developed Areas (%)	污水处理率(%) Treatment Rate of Sewage (%)
全 市	**Whole Municipality**	**279.90**	**32.77**	**15.01**	**42.66**	**95.18**
市 区	Urban Area	297.72	34.21	14.71	41.99	95.16
#吴江区	Wujiang District	158.33	29.99	11.74	41.19	91.97
常 熟	Changshu	214.68	31.61	19.78	45.78	94.89
张家港	Zhangjiagang	234.31	27.44	14.58	40.38	95.02
昆 山	Kunshan	299.88	27.28	13.51	43.89	95.42
太 仓	Taicang	196.09	34.89	14.09	43.33	95.12

表20-2

分地区城市市政设施情况 (2016年末)
URBAN CIVIL FACILITIES BY REGION (END OF 2016)

地 区	Region	实有道路长度(公里) Length of Roads (km)	实有道路面积(万平方米) Area of Roads (10 000 sq.m)	路灯数(盏) Number of Street Lights (unit)	桥梁数(座) Number of Bridges (unit)	排水管道长度(公里) Length of Drainage Pipelines (km)
全 市	**Whole Municipality**	**9 373**	**15 113**	**590 139**	**3 771**	**13 212**
市 区	Urban Area	7 166	10 681	430 675	2 802	8 678
#吴江区	Wujiang District	739	1 888	62 390	434	2 181
常 熟	Changshu	681	1 325	49 358	339	1 814
张家港	Zhangjiagang	435	1 044	26 616	119	933
昆 山	Kunshan	729	1 232	42 517	191	955
太 仓	Taicang	363	832	40 973	320	833

表20-3

分地区城市建设用地 (2016年末)
LAND USE OF URBAN CONSTRUCTION BY REGION (END OF 2016)

单位：平方公里 (sq.km)

地 区	Region	建成区面积 Build up Area	城市建设用地面积 Urban Construction Areas	居住用地 Residential	公共管理与服务用地 Public Administration and Service Land	商业服务业设施用地 Land to be used for Business Services Facilities
全 市	**Whole Municipality**	**733.39**	**702.44**	**217.91**	**43.74**	**52.30**
市 区	Urban Area	461.65	458.06	130.97	30.25	29.70
#吴江区	Wujiang District	95.66	93.07	25.14	8.71	1.00
常 熟	Changshu	98.00	84.18	34.95	3.15	13.60
张家港	Zhangjiagang	51.20	42.02	16.49	3.82	3.25
昆 山	Kunshan	72.00	67.64	21.61	5.00	2.24
太 仓	Taicang	50.54	50.54	13.89	1.52	3.51

表20-3 续 表 Continued

单位：平方公里 (sq.km)

地 区	Region	工业用地 Industrial	物流仓储用地 The land to be used for logistics warehouses	道路与交通设施用地 Land to be used for Road and Traffic Facilities	公用设施用地 Public Administration Land	绿地与广场用地 Land to be Used for Green and Squares
全 市	**Whole Municipality**	**175.20**	**12.25**	**89.45**	**17.39**	**94.20**
市 区	Urban Area	128.62	7.72	64.59	9.70	56.51
#吴江区	Wujiang District	36.79	0.70	10.51	1.85	8.37
常 熟	Changshu	15.50	1.13	8.25	1.70	5.90
张家港	Zhangjiagang	2.00	0.17	2.73	0.48	13.08
昆 山	Kunshan	16.27	1.83	7.79	4.10	8.80
太 仓	Taicang	12.81	1.40	6.09	1.41	9.91

表20-4

分地区城市供水情况 (2016年)
URBAN WATER SUPPLY BY REGION (2016)

地　区	Region	综合生产能力 (万立方米/日) General Production Capacity (10 000 cu.m/day)	全年供水总量 (万立方米) Total Annual Volume of Water Supply (10 000 cu.m)	#生产运营用水量 For Productive Use	#居民家庭用水量 For Residential Use	供水管道长度 (公里) Length of Water Supply Pipelines (km)
全　市	**Whole Municipality**	**790.98**	**112 829**	**51 929**	**34 165**	**13 095**
市　区	Urban Area	417.65	78 279	36 527	24 245	8 727
#吴江区	Wujiang District	134.87	16 297	11 703	3 003	1 403
常　熟	Changshu	87.50	8 179	4 004	2 434	1 757
张家港	Zhangjiagang	65.00	5 299	964	2 106	940
昆　山	Kunshan	150.00	15 970	7 648	3 921	1 021
太　仓	Taicang	70.83	5 102	2 786	1 459	650

表20-5

分地区城市天然气供气情况 (2016年)
URBAN NATURAL GAS SUPPLY BY REGION (2016)

地　区	Region	供气总量 (万立方米) Total Gas Supply (10 000 cu.m)	# 家庭用量 Consumption for Residential Use	用气户数(户) Total Number of Residents with Access to Gas (household)	# 家庭用户 Residential Households	供气管道长度 (公里) Total Length of Gas Pipelines (km)
全　市	**Whole Municipality**	**279 408**	**46 409**	**2 076 648**	**2 066 357**	**15 727**
市　区	Urban Area	117 130	24 185	1 223 703	1 216 281	7 675
#吴江区	Wujiang District	29 273	2 270	98 008	97 468	681
常　熟	Changshu	34 299	1 513	211 350	210 394	1 951
张家港	Zhangjiagang	38 774	3 058	141 934	141 028	1 486
昆　山	Kunshan	68 047	15 539	429 104	428 647	3 462
太　仓	Taicang	21 157	2 115	70 557	70 007	1 152

表20-6

分地区城市液化石油气供气情况 (2016年)
URBAN LIQUEFIED PETROLEUM GAS SUPPLY BY REGION (2016)

地 区	Region	供气总量(吨) Total Gas Supply (ton)	# 家庭用量 Consumption for Residential Use	用气户数(户) Total Number of Residents with Access to Gas (household)	# 家庭用户 Residential Households	供气管道长度(公里) Total Length of Gas Pipelines (km)
全 市	**Whole Municipality**	**138 552**	**70 775**	**280 650**	**249 861**	**–**
市 区	Urban Area	35 905	14 117	55 050	54 550	–
#吴江区	Wujiang District	11 005	10 810	45 050	45 050	–
常 熟	Changshu	12 527	11 296	54 293	52 361	–
张家港	Zhangjiagang	35 563	20 530	73 250	72 310	–
昆 山	Kunshan	37 187	18 762	74 231	50 079	–
太 仓	Taicang	17 370	6 070	23 826	20 561	–

表20-7

分地区城市园林绿化情况 (2016年末)
URBAN PARKS, GARDENS & GREEN AREAS BY REGION (END OF 2016)

单位：公顷 (hectare)

地 区	Region	绿化覆盖面积 Coverage Space of Green Areas	# 建成区 Build up Area	绿地面积 Total Area of Green Areas	# 建成区 Build up Area	公园绿地面积 Total Area of Park Green Areas
全 市	**Whole Municipality**	**41 685**	**31 289**	**34 803**	**28 550**	**6 922**
市 区	Urban Area	27 380	19 385	22 184	17 514	4 592
#吴江区	Wujiang District	10 044	3 940	6 782	3 826	739
常 熟	Changshu	4 848	4 487	4 545	4 177	829
张家港	Zhangjiagang	2 070	2 068	1 905	1 903	555
昆 山	Kunshan	3 785	3 160	3 433	2 908	610
太 仓	Taicang	3 602	2 190	2 737	2 049	336

表20-8

分地区城市清洁卫生情况（2016年）
URBAN ENVIRONMENT SANITATION BY REGION (2016)

地 区	Region	生活垃圾清运量（万吨）Volume of Residential Garbage Disposed (10 000 tons)	生活垃圾无害化处理量（万吨）Volume of No Harm Disposal of Garbage (10 000 tons)	粪便清运量（万吨）Volume of Excrement and Urine Disposal (10 000 tons)	公共厕所(座) Number of Public Lavatories (unit)
全 市	**Whole Municipality**	**427.41**	**427.41**	**8.17**	**1 981**
市 区	Urban Area	246.18	246.18	1.62	1 016
#吴江区	Wujiang District	41.79	41.79	–	125
常 熟	Changshu	29.26	29.26	3.39	593
张家港	Zhangjiagang	48.77	48.77	1.26	150
昆 山	Kunshan	73.86	73.86	0.97	115
太 仓	Taicang	29.34	29.34	0.93	107

表20-9

分地区城市污水处理情况（2016年）
URBAN SEWAGE TREATMENT BY REGION (2016)

地 区	Region	污水处理厂（座）Sewage Treatment Plants (spots)	污水处理厂处理能力（万立方米/日）Treatment Capacity of Sewage Treatment Plants (10 000 cubic meters / day)	污水处理总量（万立方米）Total Volume of Sewage Treatment (10 000 cubic meters)	#污水处理厂处理量 Disposal Capacity of Sewage Treatment Plants
全 市	**Whole Municipality**	**47**	**269.6**	**90 158**	**79 122**
市 区	Urban Area	30	186.8	61 429	54 611
#吴江区	Wujiang District	9	40.8	12 058	11 402
常 熟	Changshu	4	22.0	6 216	5 369
张家港	Zhangjiagang	4	13.5	3 953	3 328
昆 山	Kunshan	4	30.3	14 313	11 567
太 仓	Taicang	5	17.0	4 247	4 247

表20-10

分地区保障性安居工程建设情况（2016年）
THE CONSTRUCTION SITUATION OF LOW-INCOME HOUSING PROJECTS BY REGIONS (2016)

单位：套 (set)

地　区	Region	全　市 Whole Municipality	市　区 Urban Area	# 吴江区 Wujiang District	常　熟 Changshu	张家港 Zhang-jiagang	昆　山 Kunshan	太　仓 Taicang
一、开工情况	**Work Situation**	**42 255**	**18 537**	**4 047**	**4 245**	**3 002**	**10 793**	**5 678**
公共租赁住房（含廉租住房）	Public Rental Housing (Including Low-rent Housing)	–	–	–	–	–	–	–
经济适用住房	Economically Applicable Housing	–	–	–	–	–	–	–
限价商品住房	Commercial Housing at Limited Prices	–	–	–	–	–	–	–
棚户区改造	The Transformation of Shanty Towns	42 255	18 537	4 047	4 245	3 002	10 793	5 678
二、基本建成情况	**Basic Completion Situation**	**53 812**	**20 586**	**4 047**	**3 180**	**4 855**	**21 663**	**3 528**
公共租赁住房（含廉租住房）	Public Rental Housing (Including Low-rent Housing)	3 892	–	–	1 600	2 292	–	–
经济适用住房	Economically Applicable Housing	–	–	–	–	–	–	–
限价商品住房	Commercial Housing at Limited Prices	–	–	–	–	–	–	–
棚户区改造	The Transformation of Shanty Towns	49 920	20 586	4 047	1 580	2 563	21 663	3 528

表20-11

市区轨道交通情况（2016年）
URBAN RAIL TRANSIT (2016)

指　标	Item	地　铁 Metro	有轨电车 Tram
运营车辆（辆）	The Number of Operating Vehicles (coach)	320	90
运营线路（条）	Number of Routes (line)	2	1
营运线路总长度（公里）	Total Length of Light Rail Transit Operating Routes (km)	67.9	17.8
客运量（万人次）	Number of Passengers Carried by Light Rail (10 000 person-times)	14 851	206
运营里程（万列公里）	Operating Mileage (10 000 km/ train)	722	143
年末从业人员（人）	Year-end Number of Staff and Workers (person)	5 563	253
# 驾驶员	Light Rail Driver	382	79
运营收入（万元）	Operation Revenues (10 000 yuan)	29 869	358

表20-12

分地区城市公共交通情况(2016年)

指　标		Item		全　市 Whole Municipality
公共汽车		**Bus Routes**		
运营车辆	(辆)	Operating Bus	(coach)	7 710
运营线路条数	(条)	Number of Routes	(line)	739
营运线路总长度	(公里)	Length of Bus Routes	(km)	13 002
客运量	(万人次)	Number of Passengers Carried by Bus	(10 000 person-times)	87 698
# 使用IC卡的客运量		The passenger traffic using the IC card		54 953
运营里程	(万公里)	Length of Bus Operating	(10 000 kms)	49 111
年末从业人员	(人)	Year-end Number of Staff and Workers	(person)	16 725
# 驾驶员		Bus Driver		12 580
出租车		**Taxis**		
运营车辆	(辆)	Operating Vehicles	(coach)	9 018
载客车次	(万车次)	Number of Carryings	(10 000 times)	11 617
客运量	(万人次)	Number of Passengers Carried by Taxi	(10 000 person-times)	19 256
运营里程	(万公里)	Length of Bus Operating	(10 000 kms)	124 343
# 载客里程		Transport Lengths of Passengers		63 352
年末从业人员	(人)	Year-end Number of Staff and Workers	(person)	18 719
# 驾驶员		Taxi Driver		18 208
公共自行车		**Public Bicycle**		
租赁点	(个)	Public Bicycle Rental Point	(unit)	3 691
累计投入车辆	(辆)	A Total Investment of Public Bicycle	(coach)	89 686

THE PUBLIC TRANSPORTATINN IN CITIES BY REGION (2016)

市 区 Urban Area	# 吴江区 Wujiang District	常 熟 Changshu	张家港 Zhangjiagang	昆 山 Kunshan	太 仓 Taicang
5 321	545	622	167	1 478	122
415	51	44	17	230	33
8 058	768	790	262	3 405	488
61 917	5 639	6 336	1 201	16 204	2 040
41 993	2 932	3 408	128	8 182	1 242
34 377	3 725	3 611	882	9 551	690
11 352	1 397	1 107	330	3 416	520
8 845	1 175	760	251	2 286	438
5 638	835	759	557	1 606	458
7 520	1 219	978	777	1 958	384
11 683	2 336	2 078	1 781	2 936	778
82 311	13 000	9 367	7 789	20 971	3 905
40 676	6 890	4 309	3 983	12 353	2 031
11 870	1 555	1 622	1 452	2 951	824
11 556	1 555	1 561	1 405	2 890	796
1 936	399	447	197	959	152
46 236	10 090	11 950	4 000	25 500	2 000

表20-13

分地区环境保护情况（2016年）

指　　标		Item		全　市 Whole Municipality
工业废水排放量	（万吨）	Volume of Industrial Wastewater Discharged	(10 000 tons)	46 067
工业废水处理量		Volume of Treated Industrial Wastewater		44 439
工业废气排放总量	（亿立方米）	Total Volume of Industrial Waste Gas Emission	(100 million cu.m)	12 291
工业二氧化硫产生量	（吨）	Volume of Sulphur Dioxide Produced	(ton)	583 725
工业二氧化硫排放量		Volume of Sulphur Dioxide Emission		108 706
工业化学需氧量产生量		Industrial Volume of COD Produced		380 729
工业化学需氧量排放量		Industrial Volume of COD Emission		31 005
工业氨氮产生量		Industrial Volume of Ammonia Nitrogen Produced		10 642
工业氨氮排放量		Industrial Volume of Ammonia Nitrogen Emission		2 115
工业氮氧化物产生量		Industrial Volume of Nitrogen Oxides Produced		264 572
工业氮氧化物排放量		Industrial Volume of Nitrogen Oxides Emission		118 802
工业烟（粉）尘产生量		Volume of Industrial Smoke (Powder) Dust Produced		7 364 969
工业烟（粉）尘排放量		Volume of Industrial Smoke (Powder) Dust Emission		61 923
工业固体废物产生量	（万吨）	Volume of Industrial Solid Wastes Produced	(10 000 tons)	2 577
工业固体废物处置量		Volume of Industrial Solid Wastes Treated		102
工业固体废物综合利用量		Volume of Industrial Solid Wastes Utilized in a Comprehensive Way		2 424
环境污染治理本年投资总额	（万元）	Investment For Environmental Pollution Abatement in 2016	(10 000 yuan)	3 089 502
环境噪声达标区总面积	（平方公里）	The Total Area of the Areas Reaching the Eenvironmental Noise Standards	(sq km)	466
空气质量良好以上（AQI）天数	（天）	The number of days reaching the air quality standards (AQI)	(day)	279
工业锅炉	（台）	Industrial Boilers	(unit)	1 279
	（蒸吨）		(ton vapor)	53 705
工业炉窑	（台）	Industrial Furnaces & Kilns	(unit)	478

注：空气质量良好以上（AQI）天数，市区中不含吴江区。数据为有效天数监测口径。AQI均值在0～50空气质量为优，51～100为良，101以上为污染。

ENVIRONMENTAL PROTECTION BY REGION (2016)

市 区 Urban Area	# 吴江区 Wujiang District	常 熟 Changshu	张家港 Zhangjiagang	昆 山 Kunshan	太 仓 Taicang
24 939	11 510	6 271	6 218	4 162	4 476
23 524	10 337	5 580	5 750	4 447	5 138
3 603	538	1 637	4 339	1 385	1 327
147 510	52 890	164 983	117 173	17 818	136 242
31 876	19 893	24 012	34 336	3 660	14 821
141 771	72 197	93 293	33 222	24 402	88 040
16 580	7 941	5 009	3 406	2 651	3 360
4 796	1 254	1 153	1 215	1 641	1 838
1 098	406	357	193	194	273
86 118	27 006	55 719	55 275	14 787	52 672
38 625	16 761	26 302	30 994	7 312	15 569
1 430 890	321 273	1 631 663	3 006 636	222 191	1 073 588
9 649	5 823	17 538	27 579	2 311	4 846
317	74	431	1 532	61	237
34	10	24	10	30	4
287	63	407	1 468	31	233
1 480 271	411 134	417 866	337 084	620 179	234 102
246	16	80	31	87	22
252	268	267	246	289	278
701	237	207	73	209	89
15 819	4 009	15 528	3 084	2 249	17 026
149	3	117	73	125	14

Note: About the number of days above good air quality (AQI), the urban areas did not include Wujiang district. The data was the monitoring caliber for the number of effective days. The means of AQI 0~50 is excellent air quality, 51~100 good, and above 101 pollution.

主 要 统 计 指 标 解 释

供水综合生产能力 指按供水设施取水、净化、送水、出厂输水干管等环节设计能力计算的综合生产能力。包括在原设计能力的基础上，经挖、革、改增加的生产能力。计算时，以四个环节中最薄弱的环节为主确定能力。

年末供水管道长度 指从送水泵至用户水表之间所有管道的长度。不包括新安装尚未使用、水厂内以及用户建筑物内的管道。

全年供水总量 指报告期供水企业(单位)供出的全部水量。包括有效供水量和漏损水量。

生活用水量 包括公共服务用水和居民家庭用水。公共服务用水指为城市社会公共生活服务的用水。包括行政事业单位、部队营区和公共设施服务、社会服务业、批发零售贸易业、旅馆饮食业以及其他公共服务业等单位的用水。居民家庭用水指城市范围内所有居民家庭的日常生活用水。包括城市居民、农民家庭、公共供水站用水。

用水普及率 指城市用水人口数与城市人口总数的比率。计算公式：

$$\text{用水普及率}=\frac{\text{城市用水人口数}}{\text{城市人口总数}}\times 100\%$$

供气管道长度 指报告期末从气源厂压缩机的出口或门站出口至各类用户引入管之间的全部已经通气投入使用的管道长度。不包括煤气生产厂、输配站、液化气储存站、灌瓶站、储配站、气化站、混气站、供应站等厂(站)内的管道。

全年供气总量 指全年燃气企业(单位)向用户供应的燃气数量。包括销售量和损失量。

燃气普及率 指报告期末使用燃气的城市人口数与城市人口总数的比率。计算公式为：

$$\text{燃气普及率}=\frac{\text{城市用气人口数}}{\text{城市人口总数}}\times 100\%$$

年末道路长度 指年末道路长度和与道路相通的桥梁、隧道的长度，按车行道中心线计算。在统计时只统计路面宽度在3.5米(含3.5米)以上的各种铺装道路，包括开放型工业区和住宅区道路在内。

城市桥梁 指为跨越天然或人工障碍物而修建的构筑物。包括跨河桥、立交桥、人行天桥以及人行地下通道等。按使用年限分为永久性桥和半永久性桥。

城市排水管道长度 指所有排水总管、干管、支管、检查井及连接井进出口等长度之和。

城市污水日处理能力 指污水处理厂(或污水处理装置)每昼夜处理污水量的设计能力。

年末运营车数 指年末城市用于公共交通运营业务的全部车辆数。新购、新制和调入的运营车辆，自投入之日起开始计算；调出、报废和调作他用的运营车辆，自上级主管机关批准之日起不再计入。

园林绿地面积 指报告期末用作园林和绿化的各种绿地面积。包括公园绿地、生产绿地、防护绿地、单位附属绿地、防护绿地、生产绿地、道路绿地和风景林地面积。

公园绿地 城市中向公众开放的以游憩为主要功能，有一定的游憩设施和服务设施，同时兼有健全生态、美化景观，防灾减灾等综合作用的绿化用地。包括综合公园，社区公园、专类公园、带状公园和街旁绿地。其中综合公园、专类公园和带状公园面积之和为公园面积。

工业废水排放量 指经过企业厂区所有排放口排到企业外部的工业废水量。包括生产废水、外排的直接冷却水、超标排放的矿井地下水和与工业废水混排的厂区生活污水，不包括外排的间接冷却水(清污不分流的间接冷却水应计算在内)。

工业废水排放达标量 指报告期内废水中各项污染物指标都达到国家或地方排放标准的外排工业废水量，包括未经处理外排达标的，经废水处理设施处理后达标排放的，以及经污水处理厂处理后达标排放的。

工业废水排放达标率 指工业废水排放达标量占工业废水排放量的百分率，计算公式为：

$$工业废水排放达标率=\frac{工业废水排放达标量}{工业废水排放量}\times100\%$$

生活污水排放量 指城镇居民每年排放的生活污水。用人均系数法测算。测算公式为：

$$\begin{matrix}生活污水\\排放量\end{matrix}=\begin{matrix}城镇生活污水\\排放系数\end{matrix}\times\begin{matrix}市镇非\\农业人口\end{matrix}\times365$$

工业废气排放量 指报告期内企业厂区内燃料燃烧和生产工艺过程中产生的各种排入大气的含有污染物的气体的总量，以标准状态(273K，101325Pa)计算。测算公式为：

$$\begin{matrix}工业废气\\排放量\end{matrix}=\begin{matrix}燃料燃烧过程\\中废气排放量\end{matrix}+\begin{matrix}生产工艺过程\\中废气排放量\end{matrix}$$

工业二氧化硫（SO_2）排放量 指报告期内企业在燃料燃烧和生产工艺过程中排入大气的SO_2总量，计算公式为：

$$\begin{matrix}工业SO_2\\排放量\end{matrix}=\begin{matrix}燃料燃烧过程\\中SO_2排放量\end{matrix}+\begin{matrix}生产工艺过程\\中SO_2排放量\end{matrix}$$

工业烟尘排放量 指企业厂区内燃料燃烧过程中产生的烟气中夹带的颗粒物排放量。

工业粉尘排放量 指企业在生产工艺过程中排放的能在空气中悬浮一定时间的固体颗粒物排放量。如钢铁企业的耐火材料粉尘、焦化企业的筛焦系统粉尘、烧结机的粉尘、石灰窑的粉尘、建材企业的水泥粉尘等。不包括电厂排入大气的烟尘。

工业固体废物产生量 指报告期内企业在生产过程中产生的固体状、半固体状和高浓度液体状废弃物的总量，包括危险废物、冶炼废渣、粉煤灰、炉渣、煤矸石、尾矿、放射性废物和其他废物等；不包括矿山开采的剥离废石和掘进废石(煤矸石和呈酸性或碱性的废石除外)。酸性或碱性废石指采掘的废石其流经水、雨淋水的pH值小于4或pH值大于10.5者。

工业固体废物综合利用量 指报告期内企业通过回收、加工、循环、交换等方式，从固体废物中提取或者使其转化为可以利用的资源、能源和其他原材料的固体废物量(包括当年利用往年的工业固体废物贮存量)，如用作农业肥料、生产建筑材料、筑路等。综合利用量由原产生固体废物的单位统计。

工业固体废物综合利用率 指工业固体废物综合利用量占工业固体废物产生量(包括综合利用往年贮存量)的百分率。计算公式为：

$$\begin{matrix}工业固体废物\\综合利用率\end{matrix}=\frac{\begin{matrix}工业固体废物\\综合利用率\end{matrix}}{\begin{matrix}工业固体废物产生量+\\综合利用往年贮存量\end{matrix}}\times100\%$$

工业固体废物处置量 指报告期内企业将固体废物焚烧或者最终置于符合环境保护规定要求的场所，并不再回取的工业固体废物量(包括当年处置往年的工业固体废物贮存量)。处置方式有填埋(其中危险废物应安全填埋)、焚烧、专业贮存场(库)封场处理、深层灌注、回填矿井及海洋处置(经海洋管理部门同意投海处置)等。

工业固体废物排放量 指报告期内企业将所产生的固体废物排到固体废物污染防治设施、场所以外的数量，不包括矿山开采的剥离废石和掘进废石(煤矸石和呈酸性或碱性的废石除外)。

空气质量良好以上（API）天数 API即空气污染指数，是Air Pollution Index的英文缩写，就是将常规监测的几种空气污染物浓度简化成为单一的概念性指数值形式，并分级表征空气污染程度和空气质量状况，适合于表示城市的短期空气质量状况和变化趋势。API分级计算参考的标准是老的环境空气质量标准（GB3095-1996），评价的污染物仅为SO_2、NO_2和PM_{10}等三项。

空气质量良好以上（AQI）天数 AQI是定量描述空气质量状况的无量纲指数，是Air Quality Index的英文缩写。AQI分级计算参考的标准是新的环境空气质量标准（GB3095-2012），参与评价的污染物为SO_2、NO_2、PM_{10}、$PM_{2.5}$、O_3、CO等六项 。

EXPLANATORY NOTES ON MAIN STATISTICAL INDICATORS

Production Capacity of Water Supply refers to the designed overall production capacity of water facilities, covering the four segments of water collection, purification, conveyance, and outflow through trunk pipelines. Increased capacity through transformation and innovation projects is included as well. The capacity is determined mainly on the weakest of the above-mentioned four segments.

Length of Water Supply Pipelines at the Year-end refers to the total length of all the pipelines between the water pumps and the user water meters, excluding pipelines newly installed but not used yet, pipeline in the water factory,and pipeline in the user's buildings.

Annual Volume of Water Supply refers to the total volume of water supplied by water-works (units) during the reference period, including both the effective water supply and loss during the water supply.

Consumption of Water for Residential Use refers to water consumption of households for daily life and water consumption of public service facilities. The latter refers to water consumption for urban public services, including the consumption of government agencies and public institutions, military barracks, public facilities, wholesale and retail outlets, restaurants, hotels, and other units providing public services. Household water consumption refers to consumption of water for daily life of all households within the boundary of cities, including households of urban residents and farmers, and public water supply stations.

Coverage Rate of Urban Population with Access to Tap Water refers to the ratio of the urban population with access to tap water to the total urban population. The formula is:

$$\text{Coverage of urban population with access to tap water} = \frac{\text{Urban population with access to tap water}}{\text{Urban population}} \times 100\%$$

Length of Gas Pipelines refers to the total length of pipelines in use between the outlet of the compressor of gas-work or outlet of gas stations and the leading pipe of users, excluding pipelines within gasworks, delivery stations, LPG storage stations, refilling stations, gas-mixing stations and supply stations.

Volume of Gas Supply refers to the total volume of gas provided to users by gas-producing enterprises (units) in a year, including the volume sold and the volume lost.

Coverage Rate of Urban Population with Access to Gas refers to the ratio of the urban population with access to gas to the total urban population at the end of the reference period. The formula is:

$$\text{Coverage rate of urban population with access to gas} = \frac{\text{Urban population with access to gas}}{\text{Urban population}} \times 100\%$$

Length of Paved Roads at Year-end refers to the length of roads with paved surface including bridges and tunnels connected with roads by the end of the year. Length of the roads is measured by the central lines for vehicles for paved roads with a width of 3.5 meters and over, including roads in open-ended factory compounds and residential quarters.

Urban Bridges refer to bridges built to cross over natural or man-made barriers, including bridges over rivers, overpasses for traffic and for pedestrians, underpasses for pedestrians, etc. Both permanent and semi-permanent bridges are included.

Length of Urban Sewage Pipes refers to the total length of general drainage, trunks, branch and inspection wells, connection wells, inlets and outlets, etc.

Daily Disposal Capacity of Urban Sewage refers to the designed 24-hour capacity of sewage disposal by the sewage treatment works or facilities.

Number of Vehicles under Operation at Year-end refers to the total number of vehicles under operation by public transport enterprises (units) at the end of the year, based on the records of operational vehicles by the enterprises (units).

Area of Gardens and Green Areas refers to the total area occupied for green projects at the end of the reference period, including park green land, residential area green land, subsidiary green land of the units, protection green land, production green land, roadside green land and scenic forest land.

Park Green Area refers to green areas open to the public for amusement and rest with the facilities of amusement, rest and services. Its function includes perfecting ecology, beautifying landscape, and preventing and reducing disaster. Park green areas include comprehensive park, community park, topic park, belt-shaped park and green area nearby street. Total areas of comprehensive park, topic park and belt-shaped is the area of park.

Waste Water Discharged by Industry refers to the volume of waste water discharged by industrial enterprises through all their outlets, including waste water from production process, directly cooled water, groundwater from mining wells which does not meet discharge standards and sewage from households mixed with waste water produced by industrial activities, but excluding indirectly cooled water discharged (It should be included if the discharge is not separated from waste water).

Industrial Waste Water Meeting Discharge Standards refers to volume of industrial waste water discharge which, with or without treatment, reaches national or local standards with regard to all pollutants.

Ratio of Industrial Waste Water Meeting Discharge Standards refers to percentage of industrial waste water meeting discharge standards over total industrial waste water discharge. It is calculated as:

$$\text{Ratio of industrial waste water meeting discharge standards} = \frac{\text{industrial waste water meeting discharge standards}}{\text{total industrial waste water discharge}}$$

Urban Non-industrial Waste Water Discharge refers to annual discharge of non-industrial waste water by urban households. It is estimated by per capita coefficient using the formula:

$$\text{Urban non-industrial waste water discharge} = \text{urban non-industrial waste water discharge coefficient} \times \text{urban non-agricultural population} \times 365$$

Industrial Waste Air Emission refers to the discharge into atmosphere of waste air containing pollutants generated from fuel burning and production processes in enterprises within a given period of time. It is calculated at standard status (273K, 101325Pa) as:

$$\text{Industrial waste air emission} = \text{emission through fuel burning} + \text{emission through production process}$$

SO_2 Emission through Industrial Activities refers to volume of sulphur dioxide emission from fuel burning and production process by enterprises during a given period of time. It is calculated as:

$$SO_2 \text{ emission through industrial activities} = SO_2 \text{ emission from fuel burning} + SO_2 \text{ emission from production process}$$

Industrial Soot Emission refers to the volume of soot in smoke emitted in the process of fuel burning in the premises of enterprises.

Industrial Dust Emission refers to volume of dust emitted by production process of enterprises and suspended in the air for a given period of time, including dust from refractory material of iron and steel works, dust from coke-screening systems and sintering machines of coke plants, dust from lime kilns and dust from cement production in building material enterprises, but excluding soot and dust emitted from power plants.

Industrial Solid Wastes Produced refers to total volume of solid, semi-solid and high concentration liquid residues produced by industrial enterprises from production process in a given period of time, including hazardous wastes, slag, coal ash, gangue, tailings, radioactive residues and other wastes, but excluding stones stripped or dug out in mining - gangue and acid or alkaline stones not included (a stone is acid or alkaline according to the pH value of the water being below 4 or above 10.5 when the stone is in, or soaked by water).

Industrial Solid Wastes Utilized refers to volume of solid wastes from which useful materials can be extracted or which can be converted into usable resources, energy or other materials by means of reclamation, processing, recycling and exchange (including utilizing in the year the stocks of industrial solid wastes of the previous year). Examples of such utilizations include fertilizers, building materials and road materials. The information shall be collected by the producing units of the wastes.

Rate of Utilization of Industrial Solid Wastes refers to the percentage of industrial solid wastes utilized over industrial solid wastes produced (including stocks of the previous years). It is calculated as:

$$\text{Rate of utilization of industrial solid wastes} = \frac{\text{volume of industrial solid wastes utilized}}{\text{industrial solid wastes produced + stock of previous years}} \times 100\%$$

Industrial Solid Wastes Disposed refers to the quantity of industrial solid wastes which are burnt or placed ultimately in the sites meeting the requirements for environmental protection and not salvaged or recycled (including disposition in the year of those wastes of previous years). The disposition includes landfill (Safe landfills should be conducted for hazardous wastes), incineration, containment spaces, deep underground disposal, backfill in mining pits and disposal at sea.

Industrial Solid Wastes Discharged refers to the volume of industrial solid wastes discharged by producing enterprises to disposal facilities or to other sites. The wastes exclude stones stripped or dug from mining (gangue and acid or alkaline waste stones not included).

The Above-good Air Quality (API) Days API, i.e. the air pollution index, is the abbreviation of Air Pollution Index. API is to simplify the several air pollutant concentrations routinely monitored into a single form of conceptual index value, and to classify and characterize air pollution and air quality, suitable for representing the short-term air quality status and trends of the city. The standard to which the calculation of API grade refers is (GB3095-1996), and the pollutants to be evaluated are only the three -- SO_2, NO_2 and PM_{10}.

The Above-good Air Quality (AQI) Days AQI is the dimensionless index of a quantitative description of the air quality status and is the abbreviation of Air Quality Index. The standard to which the calculation of AQI grade refers is the new ambient air quality standard (GB3095-2012), and the pollutants to be evaluated are only the six -- SO_2, NO_2, PM_{10}, $PM_{2.5}$, O_3 and CO.

二十一、城市比较

CHAPTER 21
CITIES COMPARE

21 城市比较 CITIES COMPARE

全国副省级城市
CITIES UNDER PROVINCIAL LEVELS

哈尔滨	长春	沈阳	大连	青岛	西安	成都	济南
Haerbin	Changchun	Shenyang	Dalian	Qingdao	Xi'an	Chengdu	Jinan
南京	武汉	杭州	宁波	厦门	广州	深圳	
Nanjing	Wuhan	Hangzhou	Ningbo	Xiamen	Guangzhou	Shenzhen	

全国首批沿海开放城市
FIRST BATCH OF OPEN COASTAL CITIES

大连	秦皇岛	天津	烟台	青岛	连云港	南通
Dalian	Qinhuangdao	Tianjin	Yantai	Qingdao	Lianyungang	Nantong
上海	宁波	温州	福州	广州	湛江	北海
Shanghai	Ningbo	Wenzhou	Fuzhou	Guangzhou	Zhanjiang	Beihai

全国首批历史文化名城
FIRST BATCH OF HISTORICAL AND CULTURAL CITIES

北京	承德	大同	南京	苏州	扬州
Beijing	Chengde	Datong	Nanjing	Suzhou	Yangzhou
杭州	绍兴	泉州	景德镇	曲阜	洛阳
Hangzhou	Shaoxing	Quanzhou	Jingdezhen	Qufu	Luoyang
开封	江陵	长沙	广州	桂林	成都
Kaifeng	Jiangling	Changsha	Guangzhou	Guilin	Chengdu
遵义	昆明	大理	拉萨	西安	延安
Zunyi	Kunming	Dali	Lasa	Xi'an	Yanan

表21-1

全国部分大中城市主要经济指标 (2016年)

单位：亿元

城　市	City	土地面积 (平方公里) Area of Land (sq.km)	年末常住总人口 (万人) Year-end Resident Population (10 000 persons)	地区生产总　值 Gross Domestic Product	第一产业 Primary Industry	第二产业 Secondary Industry	第三产业 Tertiary Industry	按常住人口人均地区生产总值(元) Resident Population Per-capita GDP (yuan)
苏　州	Suzhou	8 657	1 064.74	15 475.09	221.81	7 277.46	7 975.82	145 556
南　京	Nanjing	6 587	827.00	10 503.02	252.54	4 117.32	6 133.16	127 264
无　锡	Wuxi	4 627	652.90	9 210.02	135.19	4 346.78	4 728.05	141 258
常　州	Changzhou	4 373	470.83	5 773.86	152.67	2 682.46	2 938.73	122 721
上　海	Shanghai	6 341	2 419.70	27 466.15	109.47	7 994.34	19 362.34	113 615
北　京	Beijing	16 411	2 172.90	24 899.30	129.60	4 774.40	19 995.30	114 590
天　津	Tianjin	11 917	1 562.12	17 885.39	220.22	8 003.87	9 661.30	115 053
重　庆	Chongqing	82 374	3 048.43	17 558.76	1 303.24	7 755.16	8 500.36	57 902
杭　州	Hangzhou	16 596	918.80	11 050.49	304.84	3 977.39	6 768.26	121 394
宁　波	Ningbo	9 816	787.50	8 541.10	304.60	4 239.60	3 996.90	108 804
温　州	Wenzhou	12 065	917.50	5 045.40	138.81	2 112.68	2 793.91	55 165
嘉　兴	Jiaxing	4 223	461.40	3 760.12	143.85	1 911.57	1 704.70	81 751
湖　州	Huzhou	5 820	297.50	2 243.10	127.80	1 058.10	1 057.20	75 715
福　州	Fuzhou	12 251	757.00	6 197.77	492.65	2 598.31	3 106.81	82 253
厦　门	Xiamen	1 699	392.00	3 784.25	23.45	1 558.62	2 202.18	97 282
广　州	Guangzhou	7 434	1 404.35	19 610.94	240.04	5 925.87	13 445.03	142 394
深　圳	Shenzhen	1 997	1 190.84	19 492.60	6.29	7 700.43	11 785.88	163 688
珠　海	Zhuhai	1 732	167.53	2 226.37	48.21	1 059.77	1 118.39	134 546
汕　头	Shantou	2 064	557.92	2 080.54	107.57	1 051.59	921.38	37 382
海　口	Haikou	2 289	224.36	1 257.67	67.68	233.56	956.43	56 284
济　南	Jinan	7 998	723.31	6 536.10	317.30	2 368.90	3 849.90	90 999
青　岛	Qingdao	11 282	920.40	10 011.29	371.01	4 160.67	5 479.61	109 407
威　海	Weihai	5 798	281.93	3 212.20	229.34	1 463.35	1 519.51	114 220
秦皇岛	Qinhuangdao	7 802	309.46	1 339.54	195.94	461.62	681.98	43 437
烟　台	Yantai	13 852	706.40	6 925.66	467.51	3 461.66	2 996.49	98 389
沈　阳	Shenyang	12 860	829.20	5 460.00	266.40	2 135.60	3 058.00	65 850
大　连	Dalian	12 574	698.70	6 730.30	462.80	2 793.70	3 473.90	96 326
长　春	Changchun	20 594	753.40	5 928.50	323.50	2 926.20	2 678.80	78 667
吉　林	Jilin	27 120	422.46	2 531.30	240.30	1 136.00	1 155.00	58 364
武　汉	Wuhan	8 569	1 076.62	11 912.61	390.62	5 227.05	6 294.94	111 469
成　都	Chengdu	14 335	1 591.80	12 170.20	474.90	5 232.00	6 463.30	76 960
西　安	Xi'an	10 097	883.21	6 257.18	232.01	2 197.81	3 827.36	71 357
哈尔滨	Haerbin	53 100	962.00	6 101.60	691.20	1 896.70	3 513.80	63 445

MAJOR ECONOMIC INDICATORS OF MAIN LARGE AND MEDIUM-SIZED CITIES (2016)

(100 million yuan)

农林牧渔业总产值 Gross Output Value of Farming, Forestry, Animal Husbandry and Fishery	规模以上工业企业 Industry Enterprises Above Designated Size				全社会用电量（亿千瓦时） Electricity Consumption of the Whole Society (100 million kwh)	
	总产值 Gross Output Value	主营业务收入 Major Business Revenue	利税总额 Total Tax and Profits	# 利润总额 Total Profits		# 工业 Industry
424.67	30 713.99	30 380.18	2 388.24	1 772.74	1 382.58	1 116.30
451.16	12 945.02	12 442.36	1 850.00	959.35	524.79	310.81
249.98	14 352.96	14 120.24		968.02	638.67	493.73
283.97	12 096.82	12 435.86		725.27	429.93	334.78
286.27	31 082.72	34 292.43	4 852.71	2 898.52	1 486.02	798.18
338.10	18 087.27	19 746.96	2 521.58	1 608.26	1 020.30	313.00
494.44	29 443.00	27 835.81	3 159.62	1 984.87	807.93	542.34
1 968.28	24 051.56	23 213.08	2 652.01	1 584.97	918.78	549.34
468.11	12 611.92	12 760.15	1 610.31	927.94	678.29	401.55
480.30	14 440.20	13 205.20	1 746.90	993.80	646.50	476.70
223.11	5 333.86	4 594.24	468.07	272.51	378.32	226.81
243.69	7 882.94	7 589.37	789.55	510.59	453.09	368.50
223.10	4 612.19	4 217.40	427.90	282.80	222.20	165.73
866.25	8 419.65	8 036.91	680.14	433.95	409.33	236.72
43.70	5 254.71	4 725.41	416.86	272.79	229.96	117.82
436.65	21 125.06	18 256.71	2 128.18	1 231.64	823.57	416.46
16.73	26 870.53	25 900.57		1 734.32	851.08	483.37
91.32	4 356.46	4 213.59	565.93	420.58	152.90	90.50
197.56	3 325.16	3 210.38		265.29	190.93	120.20
103.83	503.56	493.53	77.02	36.03	70.34	16.85
559.76	5 486.56	5 722.60	727.60	368.60	279.92	147.08
674.30	18 280.00	15 962.97	1 615.60	934.70	367.26	212.56
466.99	7 141.29	6 970.71	570.24	390.78	108.68	66.44
351.99	1 437.68	1 484.89		34.08	137.94	90.72
871.83	16 434.66	16 148.24	1 515.90	1 169.61	463.12	368.23
534.00	5 012.40	5 164.20	530.50	270.80	325.60	160.30
954.50		5 803.50	674.10	273.00	321.07	202.20
631.60	9 278.00	9 486.20	1 337.50	737.80	209.70	110.70
466.00	3 223.90	3 089.40	330.20	118.30	144.39	107.20
669.65		11 952.00	1 622.50	672.80	491.32	252.25
841.30	12 295.60	11 864.26	1 593.52	845.01	556.28	265.27
365.02	5 266.25	4 207.80	373.00	248.90	312.06	106.22
1 296.50	3 850.00	3 994.10	384.20	175.20	215.30	92.40

表21-1 续表

单位：亿元

城　市	City	进出口总额 (亿美元) Total Imports and Exports (USD 100 million)	# 出口总额 Total Exports	实际使用外资 (亿美元) Amount of Foreign Capital Actually Used (USD 100 million)	全社会固定资产投资额 Total Investment in Fixed Assets	# 房地产开发 Real Estate Development	社会消费品零售总额 Total Retail Sales of Consumer Goods
苏　州	Suzhou	2 737.58	1 639.41	60.03	5 648.49	2 163.24	4 936.79
南　京	Nanjing	502.14	295.94	34.79	5 533.56	1 845.60	5 088.20
无　锡	Wuxi	698.05	429.10	34.13	4 793.69	1 033.62	3 119.56
常　州	Changzhou	275.84	208.60	25.00	3 605.08	446.70	2 202.83
上　海	Shanghai	4 338.05	1 834.67	185.14	6 755.88	3 709.03	10 946.57
北　京	Beijing	2 819.96	518.38	130.30	8 461.69	4 045.40	11 005.10
天　津	Tianjin	1 026.51	442.86	101.00	14 629.22	2 300.01	5 635.81
重　庆	Chongqing	627.71	406.94	26.26	17 361.12	3 725.95	7 271.35
杭　州	Hangzhou	679.00	501.66	72.09	5 842.42	2 606.41	5 176.20
宁　波	Ningbo	948.70	660.90	45.10	4 961.40	1 270.30	3 667.60
温　州	Wenzhou	180.81	160.77	2.43	3 905.74	902.01	3 006.90
嘉　兴	Jiaxing	313.48	235.07	26.92	2 790.16	478.40	1 638.49
湖　州	Huzhou	102.22	90.16	10.00	1 592.20	274.20	1 068.90
福　州	Fuzhou	313.47	211.79	18.14	5 184.36	1 679.44	3 763.14
厦　门	Xiamen	771.77	469.43	22.24	2 159.81	765.80	1 283.46
广　州	Guangzhou	1 293.09	781.77	57.01	5 703.59	2 540.85	8 706.49
深　圳	Shenzhen	3 984.39	2 375.47	67.32	4 078.16	1 756.52	5 512.76
珠　海	Zhuhai	399.00	255.06	22.95	1 389.75	641.03	1 016.13
汕　头	Shantou	85.27	64.26	0.90	1 579.53	306.38	1 515.19
海　口	Haikou	39.18	7.93	0.36	1 271.73	551.09	653.89
济　南	Jinan	108.49	73.44	16.91	3 974.30	1 163.90	3 764.80
青　岛	Qingdao	655.84	424.67	70.02	7 454.70	1 369.10	4 104.90
威　海	Weihai	179.23	118.35	12.03	2 879.35	215.07	1 456.73
秦皇岛	Qinhuangdao	43.93	29.58	9.04	892.50	251.69	699.80
烟　台	Yantai	439.57	248.84	20.62	5 297.22	551.02	2 976.07
沈　阳	Shenyang	113.30	42.50	8.20	1 631.60	709.70	3 985.90
大　连	Dalian	514.70	244.10	30.02	1 436.36	535.17	3 410.10
长　春	Changchun	141.60	19.20	12.90	4 710.60	596.60	2 650.30
吉　林	Jilin	7.80	4.50	11.54	2 829.40	131.80	1 446.50
武　汉	Wuhan	237.81	137.23	85.23	7 093.17	2 517.44	5 610.59
成　都	Chengdu	410.10	219.30	86.20	8 370.50	2 638.90	5 647.40
西　安	Xi'an	275.28	132.74	45.05	5 191.36	1 955.82	3 730.70
哈尔滨	Haerbin	39.70	16.80	32.10	5 040.10	512.10	3 744.20

Continued

(100 million yuan)

一般公共预算收入 General Public Budget Revenue	一般公共预算支出 General Public Budget Expenditure	住户存款余额 Deposits of Households	市区居民消费价格总指数(%) General Consumer Price Index (%)	城镇非私营在岗职工平均工资(元) Average Wages of Employees of Non-private Units (yuan)	城镇居民人均可支配收入(元) Per Capita Disposable Income of Town Residents (yuan)	农村居民人均可支配收入(元) Per Capita Net Income of Rural Residents (yuan)
1 730.04	1 617.11	7 913.85	102.7	79 870	54 341	27 691
1 142.60	1 173.84	5 894.47	102.7	90 191	49 997	21 156
875.00	867.36	4 867.43	102.3	78 145	48 628	26 158
480.29	508.11	3 366.85	102.5	75 946	46 058	23 780
6 406.13	6 918.94	25 785.74	103.2		57 692	25 520
5 081.30	6 406.70	28 012.00	101.4	122 749	57 275	22 310
2 723.46	3 700.68	9 125.38	102.1	87 806	37 110	20 076
2 227.90	4 001.80	13 399.44	101.8	67 386	29 610	11 549
1 402.38	1 404.31	8 313.13	102.6	87 153	52 185	27 908
1 114.50	1 289.30	5 689.40	102.1	83 656	51 560	28 572
439.87	666.75	5 135.75	101.4	70 069	47 785	22 985
387.93	442.19	3 245.59	101.8	72 250	48 926	28 997
211.18	288.62	1 744.80	101.6	65 051	45 794	26 508
598.91	831.24	3 871.26	102.3	67 630	37 833	16 346
647.94	758.64	2 032.86	101.7	69 218	46 254	18 885
1 393.64	1 943.75	13 995.79	102.7	89 096	50 941	21 449
3 136.42	4 178.04	10 391.14	102.4	89 757	48 695	–
292.27	418.16	1 424.21	101.9	74 931	42 537	22 889
137.08	297.92	2 068.70	102.1	55 867	25 121	13 663
115.51	200.30	1 445.49	103.0	62 030	30 775	12 679
641.20	741.00	4 279.90	102.7	63 996	43 052	15 346
1 100.00	1 352.80	5 326.30	102.5	76 616	43 598	17 969
260.50	338.60	1 663.69	101.8	57 812	39 363	17 573
116.01	245.64	1 741.14	101.3	59 905	30 348	11 621
577.11	679.26	3 977.12	101.8	64 219	38 744	16 721
620.90	829.40	6 145.50	101.7	67 444	39 135	14 445
611.90	870.30	5 277.66	101.9	73 764	38 050	15 664
415.50	770.60	4 218.10	101.4	66 948	31 069	12 576
321.60	380.20	1 722.30	101.8	53 028	25 520	12 285
1 322.10		6 464.88	102.4	71 963	39 737	19 152
1 175.40	1 597.20	10 807.56	102.2	77 093	35 902	18 605
641.07	942.52	7 035.81	100.9	69 611	35 630	15 191
376.20	876.30	4 671.90	101.8	62 583	33 190	14 439

表21-2

全省各设区市主要经济指标 (2016年)

城　市	City	土地面积 (平方公里) Area of Land (sq.km)	年末户籍人口 (万人) Year-end Household Population (10 000 persons)	年末常住人口 (万人) Year-end Resident Population (10 000 persons)	地区生产总值 (亿元) Gross Domestic Product (100 million yuan)	第一产业 Primary Industry	第二产业 Secondary Industry
江苏省	**Jiangsu Province**	**107 217**	**7 775.66**	**7 998.60**	**76 086.17**	**4 077.18**	**33 550.54**
南京市	Nanjing City	6 587	662.79	827.00	10 503.02	252.54	4 117.32
无锡市	Wuxi City	4 627	486.20	652.90	9 210.02	135.19	4 346.78
徐州市	Xuzhou City	11 765	1 042.40	871.00	5 808.52	542.88	2 513.85
常州市	Changzhou City	4 373	374.90	470.83	5 773.86	152.67	2 682.46
苏州市	**Suzhou City**	**8 657**	**678.20**	**1 064.74**	**15 475.09**	**221.81**	**7 277.46**
南通市	Nantong City	10 549	766.66	730.20	6 768.20	366.66	3 170.30
连云港市	Lianyungang City	7 615	533.99	449.64	2 376.48	301.56	1 049.90
淮安市	Huaian City	10 030	567.56	489.00	3 048.00	324.61	1 268.15
盐城市	Yancheng City	16 931	830.53	723.50	4 576.08	533.91	2 050.02
扬州市	Yangzhou City	6 591	461.67	449.14	4 449.38	251.39	2 197.63
镇江市	Zhenjiang City	3 840	271.98	318.13	3 833.84	137.78	1 870.40
泰州市	Taizhou City	5 787	508.21	464.58	4 101.78	240.00	1 933.89
宿迁市	Suqian City	8 524	591.60	487.94	2 351.12	275.23	1 139.97

MAJOR ECONOMIC INDICATORS OF THE MUNICIPALITY OF JIANGSU PROVINCE (2016)

第三产业 Tertiary Industry	按常住人口人均地区生产总值(元) Resident Population Per-capita GDP (yuan)	农林牧渔业总产值(亿元) Gross Output Value of Farming,Forestry,Animal Husbandry and Fishery (100 million yuan)	粮食产量 (万吨) Total of Grain (10 000 tons)	油料产量 (万吨) Total of Oil-bearing Crops (10 000 tons)	牛奶产量 (万吨) Total of Cow Milk (10 000 tons)	肉类产量 (万吨) Total of Meat (10 000 tons)
38 458.45	**95 257**	**7 235.06**	**3 466.01**	**131.93**	**59.01**	**355.63**
6 133.16	127 264	451.16	108.04	7.43	7.47	9.81
4 728.05	141 258	249.98	59.16	0.81	2.63	7.35
2 751.79	66 845	1 046.76	469.16	13.45	16.53	90.77
2 938.73	122 721	283.97	93.74	3.41	1.66	13.52
7 975.82	**145 556**	**424.67**	**97.68**	**1.34**	**10.30**	**9.75**
3 231.24	92 702	691.55	325.20	35.82	2.42	45.73
1 025.02	52 987	589.42	360.80	11.40	2.08	29.50
1 455.24	62 446	602.72	458.55	8.80	3.75	30.39
1 992.15	63 278	1 104.93	687.31	24.30	10.68	81.40
2 000.36	99 151	477.95	300.30	6.87	1.27	18.01
1 825.66	120 603	240.71	118.74	5.83	1.80	7.95
1 927.89	88 330	415.96	313.03	12.20	4.21	26.65
935.92	48 311	517.24	384.54	4.65	3.41	32.86

表21-2 续表 1

城 市	City	水产品产量(万吨) Total of Aquatic Products(10 000 tons)	规模以上工业企业(亿元) Industrial Enterprises Above Designated Size (100 million yuan)			
			总产值 Total Output Value	主营业务收入 Major Business Revenue	主营业务成本 Major Business Cost	利润总额 Total Profits
江苏省	**Jiangsu Province**	**523.15**	**157 640.23**	**156 591.04**	**135 424.65**	**10 574.40**
南京市	Nanjing City	22.31	12 945.02	12 442.36	10 182.08	959.35
无锡市	Wuxi City	12.67	14 352.96	14 120.24	12 097.75	968.02
徐州市	Xuzhou City	18.88	13 644.36	13 947.04	11 725.51	1 108.89
常州市	Changzhou City	16.64	12 096.82	12 435.86	10 880.58	725.27
苏州市	**Suzhou City**	**25.49**	**30 713.99**	**30 380.18**	**26 169.61**	**1 772.74**
南通市	Nantong City	89.03	14 525.72	14 650.80	12 761.31	1 118.27
连云港市	Lianyungang City	75.30	5 974.81	5 946.41	5 040.36	496.53
淮安市	Huaian City	26.10	6 951.32	7 014.24	6 079.35	404.81
盐城市	Yancheng City	119.43	9 180.84	8 870.47	7 701.31	475.83
扬州市	Yangzhou City	40.12	9 661.65	9 502.36	8 336.30	593.15
镇江市	Zhenjiang City	9.85	8 722.84	8 632.13	7 419.44	582.17
泰州市	Taizhou City	39.64	12 170.80	12 139.45	10 133.65	938.67
宿迁市	Suqian City	27.11	4 096.70	3 896.33	3 278.80	391.93

Continued 1

固定资产投资(亿元) Fixed Assets Investment above Designated Size (100 million yuan)	#房地产开发投资 Value of Investment in Real Estate Development	全社会用电量(亿千瓦时) Electricity Consumption of the Whole Society (100 million kwh)	# 工 业 Industry	社会消费品零售总额(亿元) Total Retail Sales of Consumer Goods (100 million yuan)	进出口总额(亿美元) Total Imports and Exports (USD 100 million)	# 出 口 Exports	实际使用外资(亿美元) Foreign Capital Actually Utilized (USD 100 million)
49 663.21	**8 956.37**	**5 458.95**	**4 081.42**	**28 707.12**	**5 096.12**	**3 193.44**	**245.43**
5 533.56	1 845.60	524.79	310.81	5 088.20	502.14	295.94	34.79
4 793.69	1 033.62	638.67	493.73	3 119.56	698.05	429.10	34.13
4 797.33	549.13	353.91	250.22	2 659.39	62.42	52.48	15.06
3 605.08	446.70	429.93	334.78	2 202.83	275.84	208.60	25.00
5 648.49	**2 163.24**	**1 382.58**	**1 116.30**	**4 936.79**	**2 737.58**	**1 639.41**	**60.03**
4 811.95	584.14	374.79	265.65	2 632.87	308.59	230.11	23.87
2 385.16	235.41	166.15	110.00	933.31	70.40	36.84	5.50
2 535.19	321.41	163.20	106.70	1 083.83	35.04	26.98	11.61
3 882.83	358.57	289.29	201.37	1 630.88	79.51	47.38	7.07
3 288.68	410.18	225.37	156.60	1 358.80	96.25	72.59	12.04
2 873.43	448.64	232.41	173.77	1 236.78	103.17	69.52	13.51
3 155.87	249.96	239.55	176.20	1 118.34	103.81	66.74	13.44
2 059.58	309.76	168.83	115.81	705.54	24.22	18.71	4.50

表21-2 续表 2

城 市	City	一般公共预算收入(亿元) General Public Budget Revenue (100 million yuan)	一般公共预算支出(亿元) General Public Budget Expenditure (100 million yuan)	金融机构人民币存款余额(亿元) RMB Deposits Balance of National Banking System (100 million yuan)	# 住户存款 Deposits of Households	金融机构人民币贷款余额(亿元) RMB Loans Balance of National Banking System (100 million yuan)
江苏省	**Jiangsu Province**	**8 121.23**	**9 981.96**	**121 106.58**	**43 900.50**	**91 107.60**
南京市	Nanjing City	1 142.60	1 173.84	27 633.55	5 894.47	21 681.28
无锡市	Wuxi City	875.00	867.36	14 101.40	4 867.43	10 382.93
徐州市	Xuzhou City	516.06	797.99	5 495.31	3 090.21	3 620.21
常州市	Changzhou City	480.29	508.11	8 540.82	3 366.85	6 043.16
苏州市	**Suzhou City**	**1 730.04**	**1 617.11**	**25 864.26**	**7 913.85**	**21 924.44**
南通市	Nantong City	590.18	749.22	11 097.74	5 554.89	6 835.46
连云港市	Lianyungang City	211.47	373.12	2 501.84	1 168.71	2 046.93
淮安市	Huaian City	315.51	483.47	3 066.00	1 360.51	2 304.22
盐城市	Yancheng City	415.18	730.33	5 255.06	2 682.46	3 699.32
扬州市	Yangzhou City	345.30	478.97	5 361.55	2 560.98	3 508.13
镇江市	Zhenjiang City	293.01	362.94	4 705.99	1 879.10	3 444.36
泰州市	Taizhou City	321.18	448.93	5 275.62	2 474.71	3 656.79
宿迁市	Suqian City	238.08	424.57	2 207.43	1 086.33	1 960.37

Continued 2

全体常住居民人均可支配收入(元) Per Capita Disposable Income of the Resident Population (yuan)	全体常住居民人均消费支出(元) Per Capita Living Expenditure for Consumption of the Resident Population (yuan)	城镇常住居民人均可支配收入(元) Per Capita Disposable Income of Town Residents (yuan)	城镇常住居民人均消费支出(元) Per Capita Living Expenditure for Consumption of Town Residents (yuan)	农村常住居民人均可支配收入(元) Per Capita Net Income of Rural (yuan)	农村常住居民人均消费支出(元) Per Capital Living Expenditure of Rural (yuan)	市区居民消费价格总指数(%) General Consumer Price Index(%)
32 070	**22 130**	**40 152**	**26 433**	**17 606**	**14 428**	**102.3**
44 009	26 802	49 997	29 772	21 156	15 773	102.7
42 757	27 932	48 628	31 438	26 158	18 463	102.3
22 348	14 321	28 421	17 255	15 274	11 059	102.3
38 435	23 980	46 058	27 080	23 780	16 567	102.5
46 595	**28 983**	**54 341**	**33 305**	**27 691**	**18 820**	**102.7**
30 084	19 827	39 247	25 217	18 741	13 440	102.3
21 230	14 333	27 853	18 344	13 932	10 113	102.1
22 762	13 381	30 335	16 912	14 319	9 633	102.2
24 463	15 503	30 496	17 546	17 172	13 145	102.1
28 633	18 054	35 659	21 064	18 057	13 722	102.4
34 064	21 167	41 794	24 388	20 922	15 925	102.2
28 259	18 218	36 828	22 480	17 861	13 250	102.1
18 957	12 315	24 086	15 521	13 929	9 395	102.0

表21-3

全省分县(市)主要经济指标(2016年)

市县名称	City and County	年末户籍人口(万人) Year-end Household Population (10 000 persons)	地区生产总值(亿元) Gross Domestic Product (100 million yuan)			
				第一产业 Primary Industry	第二产业 Secondary Industry	第三产业 Tertiary Industry
无锡市	**Wuxi**					
江阴市	Jiangyin City	124.80	3 083.26	44.31	1 680.99	1 357.93
宜兴市	Yixing City	108.34	1 377.74	48.74	709.51	619.49
徐州市	**Xuzhou**					
丰　县	Feng County	121.43	405.19	74.81	171.60	158.78
沛　县	Pei County	124.93	665.03	91.29	305.05	268.69
睢宁县	Suining County	144.16	497.38	84.09	207.65	205.64
新沂市	Xinyi City	113.56	562.06	64.91	232.17	264.98
邳州市	Pizhou City	193.87	804.14	111.92	347.27	344.95
常州市	**Changzhou**					
溧阳市	Liyang City	79.95	801.26	48.29	392.29	360.68
苏州市	**Suzhou**					
常熟市	Changshu City	106.87	2 112.39	42.76	1 082.43	987.20
张家港市	Zhangjiagang City	92.66	2 317.24	31.34	1 214.70	1 071.20
昆山市	Kunshan City	82.35	3 160.29	30.07	1 708.82	1 421.40
太仓市	Taicang City	48.30	1 155.13	36.76	583.87	534.50
南通市	**Nantong**					
海安县	Haian County	93.83	755.29	55.97	354.15	345.17

MAIN ECONOMIC INDICATORS OF COUNTRIES (CITIES) OF THE PROVINCE (2016)

粮食产量(万吨) Total of Grain (10 000 tons)	一般公共预算收入(亿元) General Public Budget Revenue (100 million yuan)	社会消费品零售总额(亿元) Total Retail Sales of Consumer Goods (100 million yuan)	工业用电量(亿千瓦时) Electricity Consumption of Industry (100 million kwh)	出口总额(亿美元) Total Exports (USD 100 million)	实际使用外资(亿美元) Foreign Capital Actually Utilized (USD 100 million)	农村常住居民人均可支配收入(元) Per Capita Net Income of Rural (yuan)
14.49	229.91	776.05	214.41	119.22	10.55	28 181
37.05	108.65	556.37	70.35	30.17	1.58	23 709
52.54	35.00	151.04	12.31	1.26	0.41	14 026
60.27	57.68	245.59	25.85	2.94	1.30	15 791
92.78	42.52	179.58	14.61	6.35	1.11	13 822
66.06	49.91	174.56	30.97	2.98	1.00	14 526
80.75	62.40	253.41	15.88	9.16	1.83	15 321
48.66	59.00	303.03	60.36	7.46	3.36	21 899
27.76	173.58	740.78	144.18	133.56	6.30	27 956
22.17	190.00	535.16	264.91	142.02	6.04	27 849
10.13	318.92	815.04	171.12	463.21	8.96	28 178
16.53	127.71	287.31	81.30	54.30	5.61	27 766
60.12	57.58	273.74	36.31	14.05	2.96	17 978

表21-3 续表 1

市县名称	City and County	年末户籍人口(万人) Year-end Household Population (10 000 persons)	地区生产总值(亿元) Gross Domestic Product (100 million yuan)	第一产业 Primary Industry	第二产业 Secondary Industry	第三产业 Tertiary Industry
如东县	Rudong County	103.53	746.69	67.87	340.57	338.25
启东市	Qidong City	111.95	881.85	66.58	422.85	392.42
如皋市	Rugao City	143.68	904.27	62.99	434.36	406.92
海门市	Haimen City	100.10	1 005.06	53.28	504.53	447.25
连云港市	**LianyunGang**					
东海县	Donghai County	123.45	433.43	67.28	186.57	179.58
灌云县	Guanyun County	105.21	328.66	64.10	143.12	121.44
灌南县	Guannan County	82.64	306.80	51.51	144.78	110.51
淮安市	**Huaian**					
涟水县	Lianshui County	115.38	387.09	56.64	147.51	182.94
盱眙县	Xuyi County	80.47	356.70	54.20	140.30	162.20
金湖县	Jinhu County	35.96	241.88	33.11	90.31	118.46
盐城市	**Yancheng**					
响水县	Xiangshui County	62.49	270.64	41.42	126.77	102.45
滨海县	Binhai County	123.00	391.61	57.99	156.72	176.90
阜宁县	Funing County	112.95	394.40	54.60	169.15	170.65
射阳县	Sheyang County	96.23	441.65	81.01	155.78	204.86

Continued 1

粮食产量(万吨) Total of Grain (10 000 tons)	一般公共预算收入(亿元) General Public Budget Revenue (100 million yuan)	社会消费品零售总额(亿元) Total Retail Sales of Consumer Goods (100 million yuan)	工业用电量(亿千瓦时) Electricity Consumption of Industry (100 million kwh)	出口总额(亿美元) Total Exports (USD 100 million)	实际使用外资(亿美元) Foreign Capital Actually Utilized (USD 100 million)	农村常住居民人均可支配收入(元) Per Capita Net Income of Rural (yuan)
90.90	54.41	318.62	36.11	14.51	2.94	17 119
26.14	71.03	324.57	19.07	26.51	2.84	19 875
70.95	71.21	342.21	34.49	20.15	2.77	16 883
19.16	72.41	344.60	25.91	35.79	2.40	20 608
114.53	22.61	175.89	13.69	3.68	0.94	14 487
81.88	21.52	119.45	6.05	2.03	0.24	12 969
63.34	22.43	93.52	24.87	1.70	0.03	12 430
88.44	28.98	130.03	14.35	3.30	1.41	13 372
97.86	30.78	123.89	10.26	1.34	1.20	14 495
53.56	22.00	90.76	6.86	3.42	1.20	15 683
53.51	29.60	66.52	36.08	4.70	0.29	14 299
95.62	34.07	110.46	17.22	3.08	0.53	14 931
91.50	36.24	130.29	20.65	2.22	0.12	15 439
111.90	21.58	167.90	12.42	1.95	0.45	16 536

表21-3 续表 2

市县名称	City and County	年末户籍人口 (万人) Year-end Household Population (10 000 persons)	地区生产总值 (亿元) Gross Domestic Product (100 million yuan)	第一产业 Primary Industry	第二产业 Secondary Industry	第三产业 Tertiary Industry
建湖县	Jianhu County	80.06	466.13	46.73	197.59	221.81
东台市	Dongtai City	112.46	727.01	91.47	292.03	343.51
扬州市	**Yangzhou**					
宝应县	Baoying County	91.25	506.30	66.44	226.31	213.55
仪征市	Yizheng City	59.62	557.05	23.36	294.27	239.42
高邮市	Gaoyou City	81.48	537.50	69.59	237.86	230.05
镇江市	**Zhenjiang**					
丹阳市	Danyang City	81.15	1 136.04	52.31	567.57	516.16
扬中市	Yangzhong City	28.20	504.73	12.96	261.44	230.33
句容市	Jurong City	59.21	493.20	43.11	231.90	218.19
泰州市	**Taizhou**					
兴化市	Xinghua City	158.25	748.85	102.59	289.85	356.41
靖江市	Jingjiang City	66.67	801.75	22.51	391.95	387.29
泰兴市	Taixing City	119.31	832.91	53.95	388.52	390.44
宿迁市	**Suqian**					
沭阳县	Shuyang County	197.05	697.31	91.27	317.95	288.09
泗阳县	Siyang County	107.34	402.75	57.85	199.21	145.69
泗洪县	Sihong County	111.06	401.14	61.13	168.93	171.08

Continued 2

粮食产量 (万吨) Total of Grain (10 000 tons)	一般公共预算收入(亿元) General Public Budget Revenue (100 million yuan)	社会消费品零售总额 (亿元) Total Retail Sales of Consumer Goods (100 million yuan)	工业用电量 (亿千瓦时) Electricity Consumption of Industry (100 million kwh)	出口总额 (亿美元) Total Exports (USD 100 million)	实际使用外资 (亿美元) Foreign Capital Actually Utilized (USD 100 million)	农村常住居民人均可支配收入(元) Per Capita Net Income of Rural (yuan)
72.86	35.01	171.98	14.32	2.92	0.55	17 083
97.28	60.26	253.53	30.12	7.07	0.62	19 727
90.04	30.81	150.34	11.40	8.43	0.50	16 856
31.14	44.74	109.75	34.40	4.64	1.29	17 516
85.98	34.12	170.10	22.38	4.33	0.50	16 952
49.33	65.55	315.61	55.67	21.40	3.22	21 706
9.19	32.50	140.92	12.96	4.54	1.18	23 855
33.18	40.48	142.02	15.93	4.71	2.21	18 893
137.91	37.06	171.24	50.46	4.90	1.83	16 915
30.98	58.93	176.24	26.43	19.36	0.23	19 605
68.47	57.20	213.95	42.46	12.33	3.53	17 842
127.49	71.75	197.68	32.62	5.12	0.80	14 107
60.37	33.34	100.47	15.30	3.43	0.51	13 952
105.55	31.75	105.40	8.82	1.34	0.33	13 625

最新图书简目

以实际出版为准）

市(县)级综合统计年鉴系列

滨海新区 石家庄 唐山 邯郸 保定 沧州 邢台 廊坊 承德 衡水 秦皇岛 张家口 太原 大同 阳泉
长治 晋城 朔州 晋中 运城 忻州 临汾 吕梁 呼和浩特 呼和浩特新区 鄂尔多斯 包头 沈阳 大连 长春
吉林 延吉 四平 通化 松原 哈尔滨 齐齐哈尔 黑龙江垦区 上海浦东新区 南京 无锡 徐州 常州 苏州 南通
连云港 淮安 盐城 扬州 镇江 泰州 宿迁 江阴 丹阳 海门 杭州 宁波 温州 嘉兴 湖州 绍兴 金华 衢州
舟山 台州 丽水 合肥 安庆 马鞍山 福州 厦门 宁德 漳州 龙岩 南昌 九江 上饶 新余 抚州 萍乡 赣州
吉安 景德镇 济南 青岛 潍坊 枣庄 日照 滕州 郑州 洛阳 平顶山 三门峡 商丘 信阳 济源 汝州 武汉 十堰
荆州 宜昌 荆门 咸宁 长沙 广州 深圳 惠州 东莞 汕尾 南宁 柳州 桂林 来宾 河池 防城港 海口 三亚 成都
贵阳 黔南 毕节 昆明 西安 咸阳 延安 宝鸡 安康 铜川 汉中 榆林 兰州 庆阳 银川 乌鲁木齐 兵团一师 兵团十师

调查年鉴系列

天津 山西 内蒙古 辽宁 吉林 上海 福建 江西 河南 湖北 湖南 广西 重庆 四川 云南 甘肃 宁夏 新疆

统计方法应用/实用手册

实用SAS统计分析教程 马克威统计分析与数据挖掘应用案例 统计公文知识问答

乡镇统计人员岗位知识培训系列教材： 辅助调查员岗位基础知识 乡镇统计人员岗位基础知识

县级统计人员岗位知识培训系列教材： EXCEL在统计工作中的应用 简明统计分析

地市级统计人员岗位知识培训系列教材： 统计报告与演示 EXCEL在统计工作中的应用

统计通俗读物/统计科普图书

国家统计局核心统计指标变迁 货架上的统计 账本里的统计

重点图书

砥砺奋进的五年——从十八大到十九大 新编英汉汉英统计大词典 中华医学统计百科全书

新常态下的中国服务业：理论与实践 新动能新产业发展报告—2017

挑大学选专业2018—考研择校指南 挑大学选专业2018—高考志愿填报指南